Law, Governance and Technology Series

Volume 71

The *Law, Governance and Technology Series* is intended to attract manuscripts arising from an interdisciplinary approach in law, artificial intelligence and information technologies. The idea is to bridge the gap between research in IT law and IT-applications for lawyers developing a unifying techno-legal perspective. The series will welcome proposals that have a fairly specific focus on problems or projects that will lead to innovative research charting the course for new interdisciplinary developments in law, legal theory, and law and society research as well as in computer technologies, artificial intelligence and cognitive sciences. In broad strokes, manuscripts for this series may be mainly located in the fields of the Internet law (data protection, intellectual property, Internet rights, etc.), Computational models of the legal contents and legal reasoning, Legal Information Retrieval, Electronic Data Discovery, Collaborative Tools (e.g. Online Dispute Resolution platforms), Metadata and XML Technologies (for Semantic Web Services), Technologies in Courtrooms and Judicial Offices (E-Court), Technologies for Governments and Administrations (E-Government), Legal Multimedia, and Legal Electronic Institutions (Multi-Agent Systems and Artificial Societies).

Carmen Pastor Sempere
Editor

Governance and Control of Data and Digital Economy in the European Single Market

Legal Framework for New Digital Assets, Identities and Data Spaces

Springer

Editor
Carmen Pastor Sempere
Faculty of Law
University of Alicante
San Vicente del Raspeig, Alicante, Spain

ISSN 2352-1902 ISSN 2352-1910 (electronic)
Law, Governance and Technology Series
ISBN 978-3-031-74891-2 ISBN 978-3-031-74889-9 (eBook)
https://doi.org/10.1007/978-3-031-74889-9

This work was supported by Conselleria de Innovación, Universidades, Ciencia y Sociedad Digital, Generalitat Valenciana (Proyecto Prometeo CIPROM/2022/26).

This Springer imprint is published by the registered company Springer Nature Switzerland AG
The registered company address is: Gewerbestrasse 11, 6330 Cham, Switzerland

Contents

Part I
Recent Technological and Legal Developments

The Legal Framework for New Digital Assets, Identities, and Data Spaces. Introduction

Carmen Pastor Sempere

Abstract The Internet has significantly transformed society, fostering technological literacy and reshaping business transactions through advancements like blockchain and distributed ledger technologies (DLT). Traditional business concepts are evolving as users increasingly engage with digital identities and smart contracts. This introductory chapter outlines the legal frameworks for emerging digital assets, identities, and the Internet of Value, with a focus on the European context, particularly Spain. Despite the rise of Big Tech, which centralises data, there are persistent trends towards decentralisation, exemplified by peer-to-peer networks and blockchain. These developments raise concerns about the monopolisation of digital infrastructure and the potential need for a "new social contract" regarding digital identity and ownership. Regulatory frameworks must adapt to address the unique legal and security challenges posed by cryptocurrencies and digital assets. As Europe navigates this transformation, initiatives like the Markets in Crypto-assets Regulation (MiCA) and the Digital Euro Package aim to create coherent legal structures. This work emphasises the importance of securing trust in the digital economy while considering the implications of emerging technologies and the evolving landscape of digital finance.

This paper expands and updates the text of the speech delivered at the III International Congress entitled "Present and future of crypto-assets regulation in the European Union," held at the University of Alicante (Spain) on December 13, 14, and 15, 2023.
This work is funded within the framework of: Proyecto CIPROM/2022/26 "Presente y futuro de la regulación de los Criptoactivos en la UE [Legalcripto]". Proyecto Prometeo CIPROM/2022/26, grupos de investigación de excelencia, de la Generalitat Valenciana (P.I. Carmen Pastor).

C. Pastor Sempere (✉)
Faculty of Law, University of Alicante, San Vicente del Raspeig, Alicante, Spain
e-mail: carmen.pastor@ua.es

C. Pastor Sempere (ed.), *Governance and Control of Data and Digital Economy in the European Single Market*, Law, Governance and Technology Series 71,
https://doi.org/10.1007/978-3-031-74889-9_1

1 The Objective of the Work

The Internet has infiltrated every corner of our lives, creating a society with vast technological literacy. In just a couple of generations, most people have learned to use ICT technologies, without which everyday life in modern society is no longer conceivable. In the same way that today, everyone knows what a username and password are, many people already handle certificates and asymmetric cryptography, and a few are even familiar with distributed ledger technologies (DLT) or blockchain in general terms.

These technologies are changing the way business transactions are conducted. Moreover, it is not just a question of how this is happening; it amounts to a conceptual revolution: all the elements in a business relationship have found alternatives to transforming traditional concepts. Smart contracts are not just a digital version of paper contracts; they are entirely different. The objects of commerce have been extended to encompass new and abstract digital assets such as crypto assets; the signing parties identify themselves differently; the conditions guaranteeing the security of the transaction are different.

All these developments are moving from mere technological possibilities to daily realities, as recognised by legislators' activity. This work describes the emerging legal framework for new digital assets, identities, and spaces in and for the Internet of Value. Therefore, this first introductory chapter outlines a necessary context for understanding the rapidly evolving and changing technological reality whose various stages are still in place, simultaneously and to different degrees, in many parts of the world. The book will focus on the European legal framework, although specific details of the Spanish case will be provided.

Several achievements have been necessary to reach this point, the extraordinary nature of which is only masked by their electrifying pace. The web was initially an exciting source of information but very soon evolved into a social platform where users shared content and consumed newly created services.

As online businesses flourished, Big Tech giants emerged and expanded, re-centralizing a web initially intended to be the epitome of decentralisation. Today, large online platforms continue to dominate the internet landscape. Despite this trend, there have been persistent instances of decentralisation, such as peer-to-peer (P2P) file-sharing networks, federated microblogging systems (Mastodon) and blockchain technologies. One of the greatest developments, which arrived largely inadvertently, was the Semantic Web development, aiming to imbue the web with meaning beyond raw data. Through adherence to W3C standards (World Wide Web Consortium –W3C-), which promoted interoperability between computer systems, the Semantic Web facilitated the exchange of structured data in a machine-readable format. This development paved the way for the integration of AI into the web ecosystem. AI technologies are gradually becoming more prevalent and infiltrating various web applications, empowering intelligent agents to gather, analyse, and interpret information autonomously. These intelligent agents, guided by algorithms and machine learning models, operate behind the scenes, facilitating tasks such as personalised recommendations, natural language processing, and predictive analytics.

Blockchain technologies have supported the decentralisation pattern. In other words, while Web 2.0 developed a technology that enabled many people to share, collaborate, co-create, and communicate, in its next evolution, web 3.0 became more decentralised; data was distributed across networks, and no single entity owned the information. The goal was to extend the Internet to more people, use it, apply it, and give it human meaning and impact for social and environmental benefit.

The Internet was disruptive because it was configured as an open-world market, where everyone had access just by connecting to a server. Therefore, the new Web 3.0 has emerged as a subsystem—immersed in a larger data space—that incorporates and rethinks trading and contracts, exchange of goods, payment, financing, clearing and settlement of transactions, registration of property, and deposit of securities.

However, centralised data platforms will probably need third parties to provide and give trust in the identification of users—and their digital twins—and in electronic payments. Traditional digital scenarios were threatened by the lack of trust between peers who do not know each other. To overcome it, citizens have tended to choose platforms (intermediaries) to arbitrate these commercial relationships—think of eBay. Bitcoins are mostly exchanged for fiat money in the so-called exchanges, and P2P platforms such as Hodlhodl had limited success. The scope of purely digital and peer-to-peer (P2P) models is minimal; in this new evolution, many individuals will have to choose a 'data community' to belong to.

This may bring about a negative social change, as it could concentrate value on a few operators, who will be the rulers of centralised infrastructures, heirs of the old social networks, the fruit of Web 2.0. These changes will affect not only the information managed and shared online but also its value, which will drastically increase with Web 3.0 and the use of the enabling technologies of financial decentralisation. These technologies have emerged to give trust and transparency to all those operations where there is an exchange of value between two strangers who need a guarantor. However, these technologies are not exempt from centralisation either, in the context of *data colonialism*, as demonstrated by the Diem (Libra) attempt, Meta's cryptocurrency project, or the recent *WorldCoin* project promoted by Sam Altman, in which the economy works with tokens and whose government promises a more egalitarian financial environment under the promise of a possible universal basic income. The project issues a digital identity called World ID. The ID is not the user's biometric data—the retina scan—but an identifier created by a cryptographic method called *zero-knowledge proof*.

However, without clear legal limits, Big Tech could end up imposing its rules of use, displacing competition law and fundamental rights, and taking over the main sovereign attributes of States: minting currency, charging for the use of digital infrastructures, and granting identities to their citizens. The evolution of the centralised web by Big Tech calls for a 'new social contract', new concepts of digital identity, business, private property, and cooperative digital markets that are more evolved, secure, and reliable, from which large flows of investors and trade would emerge. These investors may not even have bank accounts to support their transactions.

At this point, positive social change necessitates a space of evolution of the decentralisation of the web; in the words of Borges, "forking paths". Understanding the technological evolution of the web implies taking the path in which Web 3.0 appeals to the semantic or contextual web, Web 4.0 to the web of intelligent agents, and Web 5.0, its final stage, would involve the implementation of ethical values and legal norms in applications and platforms. At the same time, the other path that leads us to what is happening in the crypto world must be taken, i.e., Web 3.0 or Web 5.0, proposed by Jack Dorsey for the decentralised open-source economy. Another new possibility is the Bank for International Settlements (BIS) centralised approach called *Finternet*.

In support of the decentralisation of the web, it is noteworthy that cybersecurity frameworks, which respond to the intensification of cyber threats, cyber incidents and new attack vectors developed in cyberspace, or the technical specifications published by the World Wide Web Consortium (W3C), have always supported a decentralised and cooperative model of information sharing.

The main problem is that these regulations and standardisations, for the time being, only regulate the issues of Web 2.0. In the current analysis and regulatory treatment of cryptographic platforms, they either avoid or fail to delve into the technology itself, which takes the financial user experience to a much higher level without intermediaries. Following a classical methodology, the European regulator has stopped at the threshold of the transformation of the backend of the platforms. One could say, metaphorically, "Whatever the path, the evolution of the web, which was born blind and without an identity layer, should lead us to it in a visible and bounded way". The incursion into Web 3 (the so-called crypto world) by the Law must be approached with precision in setting clear limits (in the words of Professor Joaquín Garrigues Díaz-Cañabate), "the art of drawing limits and the limit does not exist when it is not clear".

Adopting the various use cases offered by distributed-ledger technology (DLT) is growing. Crypto assets undoubtedly stand out as the most evident and most widespread exponent of the potential of this technology. Despite the immense popularity of cryptocurrencies such as bitcoin, other crypto assets have a different legal nature and economic function. Since blockchain networks enabled the generation of tokens (crypto assets), various uses and applications of a vastly different legal nature have been developed. Thus, the existence of digital property assets allows them to be transferred *inter vivos* and *mortis causa*, as well as to digitise the powers inherent to the right of ownership, especially concerning the power of disposal and the power of exclusion.

However, technological reality again shows the inadequacy of traditional legal concepts and the need for new legal categories to address the legal treatment of new social realities, such as the right to own digital assets and other related rights. It should not be forgotten that technological reality may soon surpass the platform concept. In a world of cyber-physical systems, the Metaverse may even replace or include the familiar Internet, usually identified with web applications or search engines such as Google. In the Metaverse, there are new realities around non-financial fungible tokens—or unregulated tokens, because they do not reach a public offering—and tokens that do not function as means of payment—non-fungible tokens (NFTs) and *utility tokens*—which, although already enjoy a certain social typicity, in this context they diverge in many aspects from European regulations or are not included in their scope of application. This should be re-examined because, in addition to the financial risks already discussed, there are others that the traditional financial sector, with normally prominent levels of compliance, has been avoiding.

Indeed, this new crypto-sector must mitigate systematic security, money laundering and user protection risks of cryptographic platforms—characterised by a complete break between the banking world and DLT technology—as it may place investors and users of these platforms in a new situation of vulnerability, mainly because DLT technology does not operate with bank accounts, nor with its traditional specific file formats, but through its wallet system.

In the context of cryptocurrencies, digital identity plays an essential role, as it ensures that the parties involved are who they claim to be, which helps prevent fraud and theft. In addition, some financial services regulations require strong user authentication, a primary concern for the payments industry, where payment authentication is critical. Conformity assessment of qualified trust services is usually based on standards, typically published by ETSI, CEN/CENELEC or other international standardisation bodies, to elaborate on the requirements in the regulations. Furthermore, the provisionally established requirements for the Digital Euro and their similarities with the requirements for the EU Digital Identity (EUDI) wallet make the eIDAS2 framework a good development and conformance guide for this central bank digital currency (CBDC).

The impending market creation (Markets in Crypto-assets Regulation, hereafter referred to as MiCA) following the new crypto-assets in terms of the use of digital tools and processes should be coordinated with the EUDI wallet for citizens and businesses, as proposed in eIDAS2, as well as with payments (wholesale/retail) and e-procurement, recently regulated by the DMA (Digital Market Act) and the DSA (Digital Service Act). In other words, they must be in the same digital identity system (wallet); otherwise, the functioning of markets, financial or otherwise, could be disrupted, and traditional payment services could be displaced, as well as the coherence and mechanisms for control, supervision and prevention of fraud and money laundering (Transfer of Funds Regulation or TFR), which incorporates the cryptographic travel rule into Europe.

Therefore, in addition to the MiCA and TFR Regulations, the Digital Finance Package also includes the Market Infrastructure Pilot Regulation, a Digital Operational Resilience Regulation and a Directive to clarify or amend specific rules related to financial services in the European Union (hereafter the EU). The scope of the regulation should now be clear to the reader, as well as the impact that the technology may have on different facets of the emerging market and the crucial role that DLT or, more generally, blockchain, may have for the future social and economic development of Europe.

Regulated decentralised exchanges and the EUDI wallet system for citizens and businesses in eIDAS2 could give structure to new crypto-asset markets, far removed from the current confusing crypto-currency trading platforms (exchanges), in a way that can make data and asset portability effective in the Single Digital Market for crypto-assets, in which almost all tokens are regulated and have their scope, function and market. Thus, the crypto asset is the object traded and entails how transactions are settled. This is due to its intrinsic plasticity, which allows it to cover everything from financial instruments to digitising (tokenising) any real asset and using it as a representation and backing for financial assets, intellectual property rights, and other illiquid (non-market) assets.

It remains to be decided whether the next step is the addition at the heart of the system of the central bank's digital currencies (digital euro, CBDC, publicly issued money) and whether the technology can enable the instantaneous transfer of digital cash without the need to go through any clearing mechanism. Parts II and III of this work explore how operators and legislators should thoroughly analyse the legal interpretations, carefully weigh the proposed amendments, and consider the project's evolution when creating regulatory proposals on the Digital Euro Package. This project must be approached to establish a suitable technical and business model, balance public and private interests, ensure the sovereignty of the financial and monetary system, and manage its security. At present, technological and social laboratory is unfolding at an incredibly rapid pace. However, this new market will need professionals and new methods to regulate the digital economy.

The contributions to this work explore the correlation between blockchain and distributed-ledger technologies and the applied technologies known under the acronym 'Fintech' and review the state of the legal professions and how they have adapted to the challenges posed by the web of data and the emergence of Artificial Intelligence. Moreover, the work reports on the regulatory framework in Europe, which is particularly complex as several legal instruments have been adopted and others are in the process of adoption—such as the Digital Finance Package, the Digital Euro Package, the Digital Services Act Package (including the Digital Markets Act) or the Digital Operational Resilience Act (DORA), many of which are closely related to the European Citizen Identity Management Model to be developed under the new eIDAS2 regulation. Finally, some use cases are identified where different regulations manage citizens' identities and financial implications.

The work also deals with new digital spaces in which the principle of party autonomy emerges in an identified manner, the limit of which resides in fungibility, which is addressed in Part III. In other words, it covers the assets that are not regulated because they are unique (Non-Fungible Tokens), which, unlike cryptocurrencies, are not traded or exchanged in equivalence, a characteristic that, a priori, seemed to exclude them from any financial operation and functionally destine them to the registration of ownership of unique assets, suitable, for example, for digital works of art to which they give a singularity and value and opportunity to automate markets and resale royalties for secondary sales fully. Specific markets already use DLT technology to authenticate luxury goods. However, the plasticity mentioned above of DLT technology means that a token issued as an NFT, despite having a unique identifier, can be split and divided as aliquots, which raises serious concerns about the impossibility of it becoming a financial instrument or a fungible with attribution of payment by the parties (commodity money), including a tool for money laundering and tax evasion. In this respect, the European Securities and Markets Authority (ESMA) will soon provide guidelines.

In summary, Parts I–IV of this work, comprising twenty-two chapters, examine the possibility and limitations of the present and proposed new legal framework for the exchange of financial data and assets, which seeks to keep the EU financial sector in tune with the digital transformation while ensuring the security and trust of citizens. It also examines the implementation of this legal regime and its coordination with the crypto-assets regime in the Markets in Crypto-Assets Regulation (MiCA), the Framework for Financial Data Access Regulation Proposal (FiDA), and the Second Electronic Identification, Authentication, and Trust Services Regulation eIDAS 2), as well as the third version of the existing Payment Services Directive (PSD3) and the Digital Euro Package draft.

2 Contents of the Work

2.1 PART I. Recent Technological and Legal Developments

As pointed out, this technological evolution shaped the last fifty years, during which two significant implosions have occurred. The first comes from globalisation and the transformation of law firms into legal companies, many transnational ones. The second is the impact of technology. Web services are being developed in the legal world, and they will very likely change the structure of law that was prevalent in the nineteenth and twentieth centuries.[1]

This Part explores the proposed instruments. A general framework will be drawn to include hard and soft law, policies, and ethics within the space and the new scenarios fostered by Web and Industry 3.0, 4.0, and 5.0.

The European Commission is making a significant effort to regulate and harmonise the digital single market regarding data processing, data flows, interoperability, exchanges, and the role, responsibility and eventual liability of service owners, designers, and providers. Thus, the work addresses these issues from the internal point of view of legal governance, regulatory models, and instruments in building legal ecosystems. In principle, fourteen European common data spaces are linked in real-time and are to be regulated. Technologically supporting Web 3.0, Next Generation Internet (NGI) emerges as an initiative of the European Commission, aimed at shaping the development and evolution of the Internet towards an Internet of human beings, an Internet that responds to the fundamental needs of the people, comprising trust, security and inclusion, while reflecting the values and norms enjoyed by all citizens in Europe; a European 'Gold Standard' for the world.

This work explores the instruments, both technological and regulatory, that have been proposed. The regulation and construction of platforms in the so-called

[1] Casanovas (2022), pp. 83–114; Casanovas (2024).

platform-driven economy, and even more so in the banking and financial sector, is not only a matter of hetero-, co- and self-regulation but of intra-technological and computational regulation. And, if this is so, the perspective, the approach of the regulation itself, must necessarily be completed by a formal inside-outside point of view stemming from intelligent information systems. A general framework will be drawn to include hard and soft law, policies, and ethics within the space and the new scenarios fostered by Web and Industry 3.0, 4.0 and 5.0.

Part I presents the technologies that support centralised and decentralised identity on the web. Technical specifications published by the World Wide Web Consortium (W3C) have always supported a decentralised model for sharing information, whose advantages are first presented. The Semantic Web endeavour is then described, which paves the way for an interoperable web of data where machines can interact. The latest W3C specifications, Decentralised Identifiers (DIDs) and Verifiable Credentials (VCs) are described, including their architecture, data models and representation. Finally, an example of contract representation is given, where contracts on media rights are represented using Semantic Web standards, and they are transformed into DLT-based smart contracts using ISO/IEC standards and web technologies for decentralised identity. Part I also explores how interoperable digital identity is changing the management of personal data, offering users enhanced control and security by accessing multiple platforms with a single profile. It also analyses the crucial role of European citizens' data control, particularly in the finance sector, which is rich in value-generating data. Mastering AI technologies now depends on the quantity and quality of accessible financial data. However, providing financial data also has high barriers, such as the lack of access to high-quality private data. In particular, two high-risk use cases for the financial sector are defined as follows: AI systems used to evaluate a person's creditworthiness and risk assessment and pricing for life and health insurance, regulated on July 12, 2024, EU Regulation No. 1689/2024. The regulation lays down harmonised rules on Artificial Intelligence (AI Act), and it was finally published in the EU's Official Journal, entering into force on August 1, 2024. At the same time, the European Commission is planning to gather input from financial services stakeholders to establish an overview of how and for which purposes AI applications are used in the financial sector. Moreover, the regulation delves into new European Data Spaces that could drive widespread behavioural change in the financial markets and contribute to realising a genuinely democratic and sustainable data economy.

A horizontal legal framework, interconnected with the vertical one, will be vital to addressing the challenges posed by the data economy and the societal changes it will trigger, as well as helping address environmental and privacy concerns and transform the management of platforms. European legislation could radically change how data, assets and labour resources are valued and traded, empowering and incentivising individuals, businesses, and governments to cooperate in unlocking the social value of data. This would define essential provisions for the future of finance and payments. An Open Finance Framework that can introduce new sectoral data-sharing provisions, the proposed Regulation on Access to Financial Data (FiDA), as well as the revision of PSD2, could lead to regulatory changes in the projected PSD3, including the mechanisms through which payment data is accessed and shared, and how Europeans pay for goods and services online easily and securely, as well as the implementation of the Transfer of Funds Regulation (TFR).

An overview of the primary and most recent soft law instruments and reports of the ELI, UNIDROIT and the UK Law Commission on new digital assets is provided in Part I. Their different approaches deserve to be examined, given that the ELI and the UK Law Commission are committed to the patrimoniality of digital assets, unlike UNIDROIT. In this regard, the UK Law Commission's report and its proposal to create a third category of assets for digital assets is particularly noteworthy. Moreover, it encompasses the reference frameworks that represent a cultural change, a new way of understanding cybersecurity to prevent and counter the threat, which has taken the form of an evolution of the legal framework, the updating of terminology (minimal privilege), the introduction of new concepts (continuous vigilance), and the extension of the scope of application of the regulatory frameworks. In its preamble, Spain's National Security Scheme (ENS) mentions the evolution of threats, new attack vectors, the development of modern response mechanisms and the need to maintain compliance and alignment with European and national regulations. This requires adapting security measures to this new reality, in the knowledge that strengthening cybersecurity requires economic, human and technological resources that must be sized by the principle of proportionality and the necessary level of security, following adequate planning and with the participation of the agents involved, in line with a dynamic of continuous adaptive improvement.

In summary, Part I offers a vision of the need for legal adaptations to incorporate these technologies, ensuring more inclusive and protected e-commerce, to provide the necessary context for Part II, which is dedicated to the analysis of European Hard Law, mainly that approved in the first half of 2023: the MiCA regulation, which, after a lengthy legislative process, was finally published, along with the other provisions that make up the so-called Digital Finance Package, to ensure that the EU embraces the digital revolution and drives it forward with innovative European companies at the forefront, making the benefits of digital finance available to individuals and businesses. In parallel, the recent Roadmap to the Digital Decade, with concrete goals and targets for 2030, includes the European Digital Identity provided for in the recently approved eIDAS2 Regulation. Part IV of this work addresses its compatibility with the European Digital Identity—the EU Digital Identity Wallet, EUDI—which will enable the mutual recognition of electronic identification systems in different EU countries and allow European citizens themselves to identify and verify their personal information online, without having to use commercial providers, regardless of where they are in the EU. This ensures that every EU citizen and EU resident can use a personal digital wallet.

2.2 Part II. New Assets: Assets Regulated in MICA

Within the Digital Finance Package, fungible financial tokens are regulated by MiFID II. DLT financial instruments should be crypto assets that qualify as financial instruments and are issued, transferred and stored on a distributed ledger. Indeed, the Pilot Regime only provides a trading or record of DLT financial instruments on a distributed ledger.

In response, the Spanish Law 6/2023 of 17 March on Securities Markets and Investment Services "amends the definition of 'financial instrument' in that Directive to clarify, beyond any legal doubt, that such instruments may be issued using distributed-ledger technology" (Preamble, II. P. 4°).

The space covered by the work—and by MiCA—in this new market is that of means of payment, in which, instead of bank current accounts, two types of wallets and fungible crypto-assets for payment (privately issued money) are used: asset-referenced tokens (ARTs), which aim to stabilise their value by referencing another value or right, or combination thereof, including one or several official currencies; and electronic money tokens (EMTs), a type of crypto-asset that purports to maintain a stable value by referencing the value of one official currency. Finally, MiCA deals with utility tokens, which provide digital access to a good or service available in DLT technology and are accepted only by their issuer. MiCA also establishes issuance requirements and activity reservations for cryptocurrency service providers.

The provisions of the MiCA Regulation, which constitute the legal regime for the different crypto assets covered, clearly show that the legislator relied on the challenges and problems posed by previous experience to offer solutions to these situations, arranging these figures logically and coherently. The maturity of the crypto-asset industry and the accumulated prior experiences demanded a legal instrument that would lay the foundations for the solid growth and development of the single digital market.

Part II explores stablecoins and the main aspects of their legal regime in the MiCA Regulation. It analyses how stablecoins fit the MiCA taxonomy and the established categories. It studies the two subcategories included in the category of stable crypto assets, asset-backed tokens, and e-money tokens. It examines their main characteristics, such as their stability objective and, in turn, the differences between the two subcategories.

MiCA regulates stablecoins for the first time in the EU, establishing specific rules for asset-referenced and e-money tokens. Both are crypto assets, i.e., digital representations of a value or right that can be transferred and stored electronically using distributed-ledger technology or similar technology. Both also aim to manage a stable value by referencing the value of another security or right, which may be a specific asset, pool, or basket of assets. Finally, neither is covered by current EU financial services legislation.

Part II describes the key features of these crypto assets resulting from the MiCA Regulation, which aims to provide legal certainty for issuers of stablecoins in the EU—by imposing a standard set of provisions applicable to all issuers about their authorisation and governance requirements, among others.—. MiCA also aims to provide adequate protection for holders of such crypto assets by regulating their rights vis-à-vis issuers, establishing the rules applicable to crypto-asset white papers or marketing communications, or addressing potential risks to financial stability and monetary policy that could arise from their use as a means of exchange, by controlling and restricting their issue. These rules will undoubtedly lay the foundations for a new crypto-asset market in the EU in the coming years.

The legal regime applicable to electronic money represented by digital tokens, starting from the general regime for electronic money established by the Electronic Money Directive (EMD) and the specific regime established by the MiCA Regulation, is analysed in Part II. Particular attention is paid to the differentiation or specific elements arising from the crypto-asset status of electronic money tokens. This type of electronic money, it is concluded, is conceived as a payment instrument and can also be traded and used as an investment instrument. It, therefore, has an ambivalent or hybrid nature as a crypto-asset and exchange-traded instrument.

The MiCA Regulation typifies most crypto assets that are not financial instruments, providing a legal regime through specific regulation. Developing a single digital market requires a solid legal basis to give the participants the security to develop distributed ledger technology projects by issuing and trading crypto assets. Utility tokens can be issued without prior authorisation if the projects comply with the crypto-asset white paper's requirements for drawing up, notification, and publication. The European passport reinforces the harmonised framework inherent in the authorisation of providers by facilitating the cross-border provision of services for crypto assets based on the same rules.

In the crypto-asset market, consumers are exposed to significant risks attracted by bullish periods, lack of information about losses, asset volatility, and poor regulation. Therefore, sufficient information should be available to facilitate recourse and access to digital financial services and the crypto-asset market for the public. The crypto-asset white paper is a disclosure and transparency tool for trading crypto assets in the market. It is an obligation to promote certain crypto assets. MiCA establishes shared content and unique content for each type of crypto asset.

MiCA configures different regimes for service providers' access to the crypto-assets market, corresponding to the characteristics of each type of provider (i.e., on-demand provider, European law provider and national law provider). Multiple regimes of exemption from authorisation—both definitive and only temporary—encourage the creation of fast lanes with different paces for the access of providers to the market, to such an extent that elements of fragmentation appear in a regulatory framework, which was instead supposed to ensure a level playing field among providers.

The transition process to MiCA thus becomes uneven and varied due to transitional measures dedicated to national law providers—already operating in the domestic market—which are left to the discretion of Member States in the absence of unambiguous decision criteria. These measures include the provision of a grandfathering clause that will allow national law providers to continue to provide services for crypto-assets based on national regulation for 18 months after the MiCA application date (i.e., from 30th December 2024 to 1st July 2026).

The varied spectrum of options under the transitional measures, which has already been the subject of ESMA's attention, risks, on the one hand, introducing forced coexistence between national regimes and the European MICA regime and, on the other hand, encouraging forms of an unlevel playing field among service providers. Some providers, subject to different disciplines, could thus benefit from favourable regulatory treatment that would enable them to consolidate their position in the market at the expense of other providers. ESMA's intervention will not be decisive without specific powers in this regard. However, the definition of best practices or guidelines to be observed in the above cases could encourage greater convergence of national authorities in the transition process to MiCA.

Finally, Part II closes with an analysis of the regulatory framework applicable to disclosure and transparency tools used in promoting crypto assets with the adoption of the MiCA Regulation. Focus is given to the information in crypto-asset white papers and all relevant information on marketing communications, such as advertising messages and marketing material. Regarding marketing communications, the examination focuses on other applicable European legislation, the content of crypto-asset advertising published by professional social media profiles and how authorities are working to prevent the publication of false, misleading, or incomplete information on these issues. Advertising and providing information are the two most essential elements of marketing a product, especially in the financial markets.

2.3 Part III. New Assets: Subjects and Assets Not Regulated in MICA

Part III aims to compare the status and the development of initiatives to regulate tokens excluded from the target scope of MiCA, as well as to analyse NFTs as digital carriers of works of visual art, distinguishing between the right over the medium (corpus mechanicum) and the copyright over the tokenised work (corpus mysticum). It also examines the possibilities these new media offer for the digital exploitation of works of art and the creation of a digital art market, assessing the main legal problems that may arise. These include the rights involved in tokenisation and the authorisation to tokenise, the marketing formula, the licences for the use, sale and purchase of digital media, or the possible exhaustion of intellectual property rights to guarantee successive transfers of the token outside the will of the copyright holder and thus beyond the terms of the smart contract that serves for the first commercialisation of the NFT.

Moreover, regarding industrial design protection, Blockchain technology—particularly non-fungible tokens or NFTs—facilitates the transposition of the physical objects surrounding us to the digital environment. Although industrial design has traditionally been associated with physical industrial or artisanal products, the virtual and technological dimensions of the scope of design protection have been emphasised in recent years. Creators and right holders of industrial design works have a clear interest in exploiting the possibilities of Web 3 by tokenising their designs, as demonstrated by the tokenisation of industrial designs in various industries, such as fashion or furniture.

The analysis covers other subject matter excluded from the scope of MiCA, such as the Central Bank Digital Currencies (CBDC), which are expected to be issued by the leading central banks. This examination covers their regulation and implications, both for monetary policy and their integration and distribution in the national and international payment network, as well as for users and recipients, both in retail (retail CBDC) and, where appropriate, wholesale (wholesale CBDC) form.

Its potential interoperability with other public or private money forms is also analysed. Attention is also paid to the various projects underway by the Innovation Hub of the Bank for International Settlements (BIS), whose progress in this area will mark the final adoption of CBDC models and standards at a global level in the coming years and their interoperability and cross-border settlement, central aspects that will affect the delicate balances existing between the central powers within the international monetary and financial order.

In this context, the proposals in the Digital Euro Package provide an opportunity to analyse whether and how the concept of legal tender and the role of payment services providers (PSPs) could evolve. The drafts proposed by the EU Commission are not a mere formality to establish the legal status of the digital euro. They also aim to create a better legal framework to address its impact on individual and economic rights.

The projects underline the critical role played by the PSPs in the distribution of the digital euro. The PSPs facilitate various activities, such as the registration and deregistration of users, as well as liquidity management through cascade and inverse cascade processes. An analysis of the debate on implementing a fraud detection and prevention mechanism in the proposed digital euro legislation will be presented. This analysis is based on the interpretations made by the ECB, the EBA Clearing, and the European Data Protection Board (EDPB) in conjunction with the European Data Protection Supervisor (EDPS).

In addition, key concepts, such as the category of funds subject to the payment services regime, will be explored, and potential collisions between payment services providers and the MiCA Regulation will be analysed.

In this regard, a double regulatory proposal has already been announced that will entail the modification or at least the regulatory relocation of the substantive legal regime for electronic money, which will affect, at least formally, the MiCA Regulation. These are the proposals for new EU payment services legislation, the Proposal for a third Payment Services Directive (PSD3) and the Proposal of a Directive on payment services and electronic money services in the Internal Market, Recital 5 which states that the specific regime for the issuance, distribution and redemption of electronic money should be managed. Therefore, the relationship between the two sets of rules (MiCA and PSD2) is analysed, focusing on how the existing and planned rules (PSD3 and Payment Services Regulation) can be applied to, or somehow cover, electronic money tokens and asset-referenced tokens. The issue is now of particular interest due to the ongoing revision process that will lead to adopting the PSD3 Directive and the new Payment Services Regulation. Specific attention will be paid to e-money tokens as they are the ones that, due to their characteristics, can most successfully perform the function of a means of payment and are, therefore, likely to be widely adopted by users.

Finally, as a relevant subject excluded from MiCA, Part III closes with a chapter dedicated to the Spanish tax system. This system clings to a traditional economy linked to pre-digital criteria, such as territoriality, and attempts to update itself by introducing elements that alleviate this situation without resolving it. The lack of tax regulation leads to a problem that is difficult to resolve within the scope of administrative resolutions, such as those of the Spanish General Directorate of Taxation.

MiCA demonstrates the obsolescence of the tax system in a broad European sense. The lack of provision for the qualification of new economic products for tax purposes atomises their treatment, leads to tax conflicts and creates legal uncertainty. This contrasts with the enormous deployment of mechanisms to control compliance with tax obligations. These include, among others, the effective automatic exchange of tax information, joint audit procedures and the unscrupulous application of artificial intelligence to all types of available personal and non-personal data. The rules applicable to the taxation of crypto-assets and their necessary update are the subject matter of this examination, which focuses on the losses incurred in the income of individuals and legal entities.

2.4 Part IV. New Digital Spaces and Identities

Part IV delves into identifying individuals through the Internet as it is essential to ensure safe and trustworthy online activities, where digital identities emerge as critical parts of current societies and global markets. However, they also represent one of the main challenges of the Internet age. The regulatory framework has been unable to address some of the main risks and challenges posed by identification services and the new data spaces.

Part IV gives the reader an overview of the evolving digital identity landscape from a regulatory perspective, focusing on the forthcoming EU Digital Identity Wallet (EUDI) and its envisaged use cases. Secondly, a critical perspective is adopted to understand the implications of these legal requirements and contextualise them in the current state of the payments industry to identify the crucial factors in the EU Digital Identity Wallet's success in this sector and beyond.

Many of the recently adopted and forthcoming legal instruments will include use cases that can be deployed with the EUDI digital wallet, some of which will be described in Part IV. The eIDAS Regulation comes at a pivotal moment to enable the much-needed transformation of the digital identity ecosystem with the EU Digital Identity Wallet at its core, which is expected to be accepted by a wide range of public and private services. Mandatory acceptance in private services includes those requiring strong user authentication, a crucial payment sector element.

In this context, integrating Human Digital Twins with blockchain technology represents an effort to address contemporary digital identity and privacy challenges. The integration of two significant technological developments will be examined: the 'Human Digital Twins' (HDT) and blockchain technology, focusing on their applications and implications for digital identity and privacy management. This combination underscores the existing potential for the secure handling of personal data in the digital space. It seeks to explore how this emerging technology could offer alternative authentication and privacy management methods, potentially leading to online interaction that gives users greater control over their personal information.

Personal and financial data must be considered, as well as those originating from other space systems like the so-called 'U-space concept', a set of systems, services and procedures to enable safe and efficient airspace access for many drone operations. Part I also addresses the main aspects of implementing U-Space in Europe according to its regulatory framework. The reasons for the delay in its roadmap and the open challenges still need to be resolved. The importance of addressing data interconnectivity and information exchange and aspects related to cybersecurity and resilience in the field of U-Space are discussed. The doctrine does not analyse these issues. The applicability of the AI Act to U-Space as a critical digital infrastructure is examined, and whether some of its services could somehow fit within the "high-risk AI systems" intended to be used as security components in their management and operation, with the important consequences that such qualification entails.

3 Conclusions

In the new Internet era, where the real and virtual economies will be interconnected, problems carried over from Web 2.0 and the current market economy must be solved. This technological revolution is accompanied by a new awareness of the market, known as the revolution of producers and consumers, where both parties demand the right to participate, fair and sustainable prices, certification of the origin—the authenticity of proximity trade and composition—of products and services and their producers and intermediaries, sovereignty over data, and a fair distribution of the profits generated with the transfer of the use of their privacy, as well as protection for their non-transfer of those obtained in the interactions they develop in the electronic medium.

In a cooperative, fair, and transparent online ecosystem where companies act responsibly, consumers must also be informed about the well-being of the ecosystem. The key will be to empower users, businesses, and the digital marketplace itself—The web. 3.0, cooperatives—making it safer and more trustworthy, where large flows of investors and commerce that do not even have access to bank accounts would emerge. The European legislator has now decided that the Data Protection Law and transparency obligations for online platforms must be respected in any competitive or non-competitive market situation. However, this also requires the recently approved eIDAS2 Regulation to be implemented effectively, extending its benefits to the private sector and promoting trusted digital identities for all Europeans. In this way, digital identities will become one of the cornerstones of the new Digital Single Market.

Blockchain will provide transparency to Web 3.0 platforms and allow individuals to control their digital property, i.e., data and assets. Let us not forget that Blockchain technology ultimately makes it possible to differentiate between identity datasets per se and the information used to verify information about the subject itself, which opens infinite possibilities, as well as combinations with AI; it could, for example, automate credit ratings, or facilitate the portability of know-your-customer (hereafter KYC) attributes through the use of a centralised architecture. The GDPR would also apply in this context, where subjects have more control over their data. Blockchain may contribute by making data and asset portability effective in the Digital Single Market and also in new spaces such as the Metaverse, based on the possibilities afforded by the new Digital Identity System to provide data—truthful information about their solvency and sustainability to the market—, combined with an efficient new means of the payment system—legal tender digital money, such as the digital EURO issued by the ECB—.

This contrasts with the maturity of the crypto-asset markets, which has led to the decline of some businesses and the emergence of others, resulting in significant capital losses and new investments in products such as Bitcoin Exchange Traded Funds approved by the US Securities and Exchange Commission. The analysis of this type of new product allows us to affirm that legislators' inactivity in the face of the crypto economy has given way to a phase of intervention in the face of its transformation and growth. Thus, EU rules for financial services must comply with the principles of technological neutrality, i.e., "same activity, same risks, same rules", and apply these to crypto assets.

In this respect, the MiCA Regulation typifies these subcategories of crypto assets by providing them with specific rules. The Regulation provides a transparent legal regime for utility, asset-referenced, and e-money tokens. For utility tokens, the MiCA Regulation establishes a system that does not require prior authorisation but simply compliance with the requirements in the crypto-asset white paper to issue crypto-assets across the EU or to apply for admission to trading platforms for crypto-assets, subject to ex-post supervision.

Marketing communications must comply with MiCA requirements. The most used channel to promote crypto assets has been social media platforms. Commercial strategies focus on this type of platform because of the possibility of reaching a large audience. The format used means it is not always possible to detect crypto-asset advertising; often, they can be confused with investment recommendations. This situation highlights the importance of ensuring that communications are identifiable and that the content is fair, transparent, and not misleading. Therefore, the crypto-asset white paper is the central document by which investors and users make informed decisions to purchase crypto-assets. The MiCA Regulation provides clear rules on the information and responsibilities arising from the statements in that document. ESMA and the EBA are currently working on draft technical standards to regulate the format of these documents. It is essential that these technical standards do not contain free fields but that the file includes structured fields.

As concluded, the regulation of crypto markets by the MiCA follows a principle of minimal intervention for fear of stifling a burgeoning market. Compared to its financial market counterpart, the European legislator has opted for a simplified regime for abuse and governance control of crypto operators. However, that raises the question of what the limit of the analogical application of the simplified regulation is and what role other supervisory rules, such as Competition Law, will play. Overall, the legislation discussed in the work should be seen positively, as it finally brings much-needed legal certainty to foster the development of a digital single market.

However, neither PSD2 nor the future PSD3 would apply to ARTs (asset-referenced tokens) or other crypto-assets that fulfil payment functions. They would only apply to EMTs (e-money tokens). Future payment services regulation needs to consider the specificities of EMTs, which is not a priority at this stage. The MICA Regulation is aware of the possible collision of certain crypto-asset services with payment services involving e-money tokens. Still, it only solves the institutional problems—authorisation as PSPs—but leaves the material ones—substantive rules applicable—unresolved.

The strict legal interpretation of the eIDAS2 is that accepting the EU Digital Identity Wallet only concerns cross-border scenarios. However, in practice, the objective of the Proposal goes beyond cross-border use cases and is aimed at affecting the entire digital ecosystem. This is also evident in integrating two legal regimes: electronic identification and trust services, specifically, the new trust service for issuing electronic attestation of attributes. The needs of financial services, mainly payment services, differ significantly from those of public services. This poses significant challenges in defining the requirements for the service provision and the type of entity responsible for the provision of the EU Digital Identity (EUDI). Still, even these conclusions could also include some updated information, if available, on how the EU Digital Identity Wallet is expected to facilitate the fulfilment of the vital customer authentication requirement. Therefore, the following steps should adequately systematise existing regulations on old and new crypto-economy operations to safeguard the convenient and effective reporting of possible losses. Tax fraud and money laundering operations could be countered with the digital euro. Still, to do so, legislators must conduct a thorough analysis of legal interpretations, carefully weigh the proposed amendments, and consider the project's evolution when creating regulatory proposals on the Digital Euro Package.

Data spaces and citizen control mechanisms could be great allies for these purposes. Still, deploying these spaces will only be possible thanks to a high Artificial Intelligence (AI/ML) component supported by fully digital communications, the use of Cloud technologies and others for the scalability of the services involved in thousands of simultaneous operations. The *ad hoc* EU regulation, consisting of several regulations that have already entered into force, only solves some of the problems of deploying this new phenomenon that is about to sweep the common European area.

Furthermore, for a fair application of taxes, the EU must promote compliance control and provide European citizens with unified, effective, and enforceable protocols for dealing with tax administrations in other Member States. If they exist, the rules on the taxation of crypto assets should comply with a minimum common standard based on the treatment the tax system grants to transactions conducted with similar assets. In other words, where tax rules do not apply, the tax legislator and the tax administration should clarify the qualification and quantification of transactions. Should this not occur, the doctrine must systematically analyse the application of the tax system to the latest generation of money laundering operations in the crypto economy, to which the new artistic space is added, in which the world of art and design has much to gain by entering the Metaverse.

While considerable research and case law are needed to answer the questions surrounding the protection of works of genius in new digital spaces, our current legal framework is proving sufficiently flexible to accommodate the rapid technological changes already transforming the industry. The European legislator has rightly envisaged, for example, a technological shift in European design law. While these reforms were intended to address 3D printing, a technological breakthrough directly affecting the design world, NFTs represent a new embodiment of design works, a way to achieve greater reach, dissemination, and commercialisation for design, and indeed an exciting business and research opportunity. Design regulation must adapt to the needs of the industry about new non-physical or digital designs, such as crypto designs. On a less positive note, NFTs complicate tax fraud and laundering operations.

In conclusion, the crucial question is whether the current level of EU integration is sufficient for this purpose or should it be increased. Conformity and compliance assessment of trust services and the EUDI wallet are complex, and similar complexity can be expected from implementing the digital euro. In this respect, there may be more appropriate models for a service requiring continuous monitoring and assistance than the public sector. As stated clearly in the eIDAS2, the EU Digital Identity Wallet will be voluntary, and its success in the payments sector will be strongly conditioned by the added value it can bring. Therefore, it is worth exploring what possibilities the EU Digital Identity Wallet can offer in the payments sector, especially to develop methods that can compete with current payment methods, convince the industry of the need and value of this investment, and ultimately convince the consumer.

References

Casanovas P (2022) Inteligencia Artificial y Derecho: la doble implosión de las profesiones y servicios jurídicos en la era digital. In: Serrano M, Velarde O (eds) Mirando hacia el futuro. Cambios sociohistóricos vinculados a la virtualización. Centro de Investigaciones Sociológicas (CIS), Madrid, pp 83–114

Casanovas P (2024) La doble implosión en las profesiones jurídicas y un nuevo espacio de regulación. La clave de BAES, 17th January, 2024, https://www.baeslegalcripto.eu/legalcripto/en/the-double-implosion-in-the-legal-professions-and-a-new-integrated-data-regulation-space-by-pompeu-casanovas/

A Regulatory Framework for Legal Ecosystems in the Context of Emerging Web-Based Systems and the European AI Value Chain Regulations

Pompeu Casanovas

Abstract The European Commission is making significant efforts to regulate and harmonise the digital single market, covering areas such as data processing, data flows, interoperability, exchanges, and the roles, responsibilities, and potential liabilities of owners, designers, and service providers. This Chapter takes an internal perspective of legal governance, exploring the regulatory models and instruments crucial to constructing legal ecosystems. Initially, there were nine European common data spaces to be regulated in real-time, with an additional tenth space related to the European Open Science Cloud (EOSC). Four more spaces (including human heritage and tourism) have been recently added. This Chapter delves into the proposed instruments for regulation. The central argument is that the regulation and development of platforms within the platform-driven economy, particularly in the banking and financial sectors, go beyond traditional frameworks of hetero, co-, and self-regulation. Instead, these processes involve intra-technological and computational regulation. Therefore, regulatory approaches must incorporate a formal inside-outside and a middle-out/inside-out approach derived from intelligent information systems. A comprehensive framework will be outlined to encompass hard and soft law, policies, and ethics within the context of emerging scenarios fostered by Web 3.0, Industries 4.0 and 5.0. This Chapter will delve into the common and

This paper expands and updates the text of the speech delivered at the III International Congress entitled "Present and future of crypto-assets regulation in the European Union," held at the University of Alicante (Spain) on December 13, 14, and 15, 2023.
This work is funded within the framework of: Proyecto CIPROM/2022/26 "Presente y futuro de la regulación de los Criptoactivos en la UE [Legalcripto]". Proyecto Prometeo CIPROM/2022/26, grupos de investigación de excelencia, de la Generalitat Valenciana (P.I. Carmen Pastor).

P. Casanovas (✉)
Artificial Intelligence Research Institute of the Spanish National Research Council (IIIA-CSIC), Barcelona, Spain

LawTech La Trobe Research Group, LaTrobe University, Bundoora, VIC, Australia

UAB Institute of Law and Technology (UAB-IDT), Bellaterra, Barcelona, Spain
e-mail: pompeu.casanovas@iiia.csic.es

C. Pastor Sempere (ed.), *Governance and Control of Data and Digital Economy in the European Single Market*, Law, Governance and Technology Series 71,
https://doi.org/10.1007/978-3-031-74889-9_2

specific regulatory instruments and mechanisms proposed for these data spaces, thoroughly examining the technical and legal frameworks required to incept and flesh out these digital ecosystems.

1 Introduction

I am grateful to Carmen Pastor for her kind invitation to contribute to this book on regulating crypto assets in the European Union, organised by LegalCripto and the BAES Research Group of the University of Alicante. I am particularly honoured to have been invited to follow her introduction with my chapter. I aim to reciprocate by establishing a general framework for Fintech, LawTech, and RegTech in the context of emerging web-based legal services.

This book highlights the significant contributions of Spanish researchers in this field. This is not merely an impression but a well-established fact; they hold a prominent position in the international landscape of blockchain and financial studies. Recent bibliometric analyses place Spain among the top ten most active countries in the world in these areas.[1] Additionally, it is crucial to consider the correlation between blockchain research, distributed ledger technologies (DLT), and applied technologies, collectively known as 'Fintech.' These technologies are often described as 'disruptive,' though I prefer to characterise them as 'disturbing.'

My contribution will lie at the intersection of law and computing, specifically Law and Artificial Intelligence. This work will build upon the research conducted by scholars from IIIA-CSIC, IDT-UAB, and the La Trobe LawTech Research Group. I aim to provide a broader perspective on these technologies, situating them within the context of innovation in regulatory models.

The Chapter's title reflects technology's impact on the evolution of legal instruments and professions. I will delve into this topic in the final section, as it invites an open interpretation. This new landscape transforms the social space's legal framework, distinct from the nineteenth and twentieth centuries. Specifically, it is (i) structured through the representations of (linked) data; (ii) articulated and managed through Artificial Intelligence techniques; (iii) positioned at the intersection of the horizontal and vertical dimensions of law; and (iv) shaped by the tension between civic self-organisation, institutional construction, and the influence of political and financial elites.[2]

I will address the topic from the internal point of view of legal governance regulation models and instruments typical of legal ecosystems. The remainder of this Chapter will be structured as follows. Section 2 offers several definitions that will be useful to facilitate the reading. Section 3 delves into the European Common Data spaces, listing and aligning them with the European social data ecosystem and

[1] Aysan and Nanaeva (2022); Dosso and Aysan (2022).

[2] Casanovas (2022).

reporting some new EU regulatory tools. The main thesis of the Chapter is summarised in 3.4. Section 4 develops the thesis on designing and imbuing ethics and law into digital environments through artificial intelligence (AI) to build smart legal ecosystems (SLE) and will elicit on this through the collaborative development of the EU project OPTIMAI. The concept of the 'AI value chain' introduced by the recent Artificial Intelligence Act (2024) will also be discussed. Section 5 offers the rationale for the development of the thesis on SLE. It includes the description of social, legal and technological (semantic) dimensions of AI governance and a historical explanation of how legal professions evolved until the emergence of the RegTech market. I call it the double implosion of web legal services acting in a platform-driven economy. Finally, Sect. 6 will close the Chapter with some open questions.

2 Definitions

I will first provide a roster of concepts, clarifying their specific meanings in this chapter. These concepts can be exemplified through the operational system of OPTIMAI, an EU platform for zero-defect manufacturing. Most of these terms have already been defined in our previous work.[3]

According to a comprehensive IBM definition, the *Internet of Things* (IoT) refers to "a network of physical devices, vehicles, appliances, and other physical objects that are embedded with sensors, software, and network connectivity, allowing them to collect and share data, monitoring environmental conditions in farms, managing traffic patterns with smart cars and other smart automotive devices, controlling machines and processes in factories, tracking inventory and shipments in warehouses."[4]

Industry 4.0 (I4.0) is a term coined by the German industry in 2011[5] which is synonymous with *smart manufacturing*, i.e., "the realisation of the digital transformation of the field, delivering real-time decision making, enhanced productivity, flexibility and agility to revolutionise the way companies manufacture, improve and distribute their products".[6] *Industry 5.0* (I5.0) entails embedding legal and ethical values into cyber-physical systems and smart manufacturing (including a focus on customer experience, human-robotic interaction (HRI), and responsive and

[3]The reader can find a more complete explanation in Casanovas et al. (2022); and especially in Casanovas et al. (2024b).

[4]https://www.ibm.com/topics/internet-of-things#.

[5]The term was proposed and adopted by the German government as part of the "High-Tech Strategy 2020 Action Plan", cf. "Recommendations for implementing the strategic initiative INDUSTRIE 4.0", April 2013. Available at: http://www.acatech.de/fileadmin/user_upload/Baumstruktur_nach_Website/Acatech/root/de/Material_fuer_Sonderseiten/Industrie_4.0/Final_report__Industrie_4.0_accessible.pdf.

[6]https://www.ibm.com/topics/industry-4-0#.

distributed supply chain).[7] "It is the concept of a forward-looking enhancement to frame how industry and emerging societal trends and needs can co-exist".[8]

RegTech, SupTech, LawTech, FinTech, and GovTech are broad, ostensive concepts recently introduced into technology practice and regulatory instruments with no standardised meaning or consistent usage. For instance, in Europe, according to many recent provisions and working documents of the EU Commission about the building of the European Digital Market (EDM) and Common Data Spaces (CDSs), *GovTech* refers to technology at the service of Public Administration; *RegTech* to technology at the service of regulation and compliance; and *LegalTech* or *LawTech* to technology at the service of law (or the legal profession) (EU Strategy for Data, 2020).

FinTech has been broadly used both in technology, insurance and banking sectors, and legal studies as "a link between the financial industry, information technology (IT), and innovation",[9] or "the fusion of finance and technology".[10] According to the survey carried out by Giglio (2021), six FinTech business models have been identified: payment, wealth management, crowdfunding, loan, capital market, and insurance services. From a more technological approach, Gai, Qiu, and Sun (2018) have singled out five technical aspects involved: security and privacy, data techniques, hardware and infrastructure, applications and management, and service models.[11]

The term *Legal Web-Services* has been used from 2008 onwards to name engineering and law-firms offering legal services on the web of data in the platform-driven economy.[12] Until then, researchers in Artificial Intelligence and Law used to separate the domain of IT and Law into two different domains: (i) *IT law* (data protection, copyright, security, domain names, etc.) and (ii) ad *IT for lawyers* (e-government, e-court, Online Dispute Resolution, Multi-Agent Systems, etc.). The former covers regulations and protocols related to IT, whereas the latter refers to all languages, tools, and software supporting legal activities at the workplace. Developments in semantic technologies, NLP, ontologies, information retrieval (IR), and Web 2.0 and 3.0 contributed to the convergence of the two approaches into a single techno-legal one. Various words have also been used to denote the emergence

---

[7]Cf. Zhan et al. (2023); Murphy et al. (2022).

[8]Cf. Möller et al. (2022).

[9]F Giglio (2021, p. 601). "The term 'Fin-Tech' derives from the union of the words finance and technology and represents the acronym, including the development of technology and innovation to support banking and financial skills with the latest technologies. Fin-Tech also describes the relationship between technologies such as cloud computing and mobile internet, with financial services businesses such as loans, payments, money transfer and other banking".

[10]Goldstein et al. (2019), p. 262.

[11]"(...) this FinTech revolution is unique in that much of the change is happening outside the financial industry, as young start-up firms and big established technology firms are attempting to disrupt the incumbents, introducing new products and technologies and providing a significant new dose of competition." Cf. Gai et al. (2018), p. 1648.

[12]Casanovas (2008); Casanovas and Poblet (2008).

of law as a service: *legal services*, *law-tech services*, *techno-law companies*, and more recently, *AI legal services* and *Data Analytics legal services*.

Legal governance refers to processes that generate a sustainable regulatory ecosystem reflecting fundamental legal concepts in modern democracies.[13]

A *legal ecosystem* can be defined as a complex and dynamic system that includes multiple levels of governance, ranging from local to national and international, and involving a wide range of actors, including lawmakers, judges, lawyers, law enforcement officials, civil society organisations, companies, corporations, and ordinary consumers and citizens. Legal platform-driven developers have recently used the term as well.[14]

A *smart legal ecosystem* (SLE) refers to a regulatory (or legal) ecosystem embedded in cyber-physical systems (CPSs) that function in an intelligent environment encompassing the features of the Internet of Things and Industry 4.0 to achieve legal compliance in real time.[15]

Compliance, from a computational approach, can be understood as fulfilling or aligning with normative constraints. From a regulatory perspective, we should differentiate between *business compliance*, *legal compliance* and *conformance*.

Business compliance points to a previously selected set of requirements for industry and business and industry processes, as set, for instance, by ISO/IEC 2700, the international gold standard for information security management, among many others.[16] In this sense, it refers to the behaviour of a human or artificial agent in *conformity* or *conformance* (in the case of human behaviour) or *alignment* (in the case of artificial agents) with a set of provisions, norms, rules, or principles (including values). Still, it may not necessarily be codified or systematised in a code, regulatory model, or normative system.

Legal compliance refers to the whole process of conforming to the requirements set out in traditional legal instruments (mainly hard law, i.e., the laws adopted by Parliaments and judgements of Courts) and other kinds of instruments that have a regulatory effect without being binding in law (soft law, such as standards, codes of conduct, regulatory and industry guidelines, and codes of ethics).

According to the new EU vocabulary setting a comprehensive framework for developing the digital financial market, "a *crypto-asset* is a digital representation of value or a right that can be transferred or stored electronically using distributed ledger technology or similar technology".

> Crypto-assets are a digital innovation that can streamline capital-raising processes, enhance competition, and create an innovative and inclusive way of financing for consumers and Small and Medium Enterprises (SMEs). Crypto-assets can also be used as a means of

---

[13] Poblet et al. (2019).

[14] See the German *Liquid Legal Institute* (LLI created in 2018. Cf. Wagner (2020).

[15] Casanovas (2024).

[16] According to ISO/IEC 27002: "The organization must identify and document its obligations to external authorities and other third parties in relation to information security, including intellectual property, [business] records, privacy/personally identifiable information and cryptography".

> payment. By limiting intermediaries, they can present opportunities for cheaper, faster, and more efficient payments, particularly on a cross-border basis.[17]

Finally, according to the standard view, *blockchain technologies* refer to a distributed database or ledger shared among a computer network's nodes, i.e. a distributed ledger with growing lists of records (blocks) that are securely linked together via cryptographic hashes, each block containing a cryptographic hash of the previous block, a timestamp, and transaction data.[18]

These concepts are relevant to defining the scope and the new spaces the new regulatory approach opens to understanding the European data economy.

3 The Common European Data Spaces

3.1 A Social Data Economy Ecosystem

The European Union has undertaken significant legislative initiatives to regulate the impact of technology on markets, safeguard individuals' privacy, construct a cohesive European digital market, and update the tools available for these purposes. The Commission has introduced new regulations and legal instruments to address these issues. Regarding Finances, the main purpose is to create a regulated European data space to allow businesses to build on the scale of the single market. The strategy sets out four main priorities: removing fragmentation in the Digital Single Market, adapting the EU regulatory framework to facilitate digital innovation, promoting data-driven finance and addressing the challenges and risks associated with digital transformation, including enhancing the digital operational resilience of the financial system.[19]

Hence, common European rules and efficient enforcement mechanisms should ensure that (i) data can flow within the EU and across sectors; (ii) European rules and values, in particular personal data protection, consumer protection legislation and competition law, are fully respected; (iii) and fair, practical, and clear rules for access to and use of data, with clear and trustworthy data governance mechanisms, are in place.

Accordingly, four priorities were set by the EU Financial Strategy to guide EU actions and promote digital transformation up to 2024: (i) to tackle fragmentation in the Digital Single Market for financial services, thereby enabling European consumers to access cross-border services and help European financial firms scale up their digital operations; (ii) to ensure that the EU regulatory framework facilitates digital innovation in the interest of consumers and market efficiency; (iii) to create a European financial data space to promote data-driven innovation, building on the European data strategy, including enhanced access to data and data sharing within

[17] https://finance.ec.europa.eu/digital-finance/crypto-assets_en.

[18] https://en.wikipedia.org/wiki/Blockchain.

[19] https://finance.ec.europa.eu/publications/digital-finance-package_en#digital.

the financial sector; (iv) to address new challenges and risks associated with digital transformation.[20]

Carmen Pastor has recently highlighted that the idea fosters the emergence of social ecosystems to generate what she calls the *social data economy ecosystem*. In this sense, "it is essential to clarify the cooperative governance of this new Data economy, its agents, and the construction of this new digital social economy supported by the new Next Generation Internet (NGI) and European data spaces."[21]

3.2 *Common EU Data Spaces to Foster the EU Digital Market*

Initially, there were nine common data spaces to be regulated, as "data spaces should foster *an ecosystem (of companies, civil society and individuals)* creating new products and services based on more accessible data [*my emphasis*]."[22] I reproduce them in the same way they were presented (with the addition of EOSC):

(i) a *Common European industrial (manufacturing) data space*, estimated at € 1.5 trillion by 2027;
(ii) a *Common European Green Deal data space* encompassing climate change, circular economy, zero-pollution, biodiversity, deforestation and compliance assurance;
(iii) a *Common European mobility data space* to facilitate access, pooling and sharing of data from existing and future transport and mobility databases;
(iv) a *Common European health data space* for preventing, detecting and curing diseases as well as for informed, evidence-based decisions to improve the accessibility, effectiveness and sustainability of the healthcare systems;
(v) a *Common European financial data space* to stimulate through enhanced data sharing, innovation, market transparency, sustainable finance, as well as access to finance for European businesses and a more integrated market;
(vi) a *Common European energy data space* to promote availability and cross-sector sharing of data in a customer-centric, secure and trustworthy manner;
(vii) a *Common European agriculture data space* to enhance the sustainability performance and competitiveness of the agricultural sector through the processing and analysis of production and other data;
(viii) a *Common European data space for public administration* to improve transparency and accountability of public spending and spending quality, fighting corruption, both at the EU and national level, and address law enforcement

[20] Brussels, 24.9.2020 *COM(2020) 591 final Communication from The Commission to the European Parliament, The Council, the European Economic and Social Committee and The Committee to The Regions on a Digital Finance Strategy for the EU*.

[21] Pastor-Sempere (2022, p. 1).

[22] Brussels, 24.9.2020 *COM(2020) 591 Final Communication, op. cit.* p 5.

needs and support the effective application of EU law and enable innovative 'gov tech', 'reg tech' and 'legal tech' applications supporting practitioners as well as other services of public interest

(ix) a Common European skills data space is needed to reduce the skills mismatches between the education and training systems and labour market needs.[23]

(x) a *European Open Science Cloud* (EOSC), a trusted open data environment that allows reliable reuse of research data by bringing together institutional, national, and European stakeholders. The aim is to develop an inclusive research data and services ecosystem in Europe.

A comprehensive framework will be outlined later to encompass hard law, soft law, policies, and ethics within the context of emerging scenarios fostered by Web 3.0 and Industries 4.0 and 5.0. It is worth noting that these spaces have been created along what is defined as the "new legislative framework" in opposition to the old one based on more traditional legal instruments, such as Directives.[24] From 2008 onwards, the "new" legislative framework aimed to improve the internal market for goods, strengthen market surveillance, and boost the quality of *conformity assessments*. It also promotes *CE marking* and creates a *toolbox of measures* for use in product legislation. As we will detail in Section 2.4.3 (about the so-called *AI value chain*), four more spaces were recently added to the initial ones in January 2024. In the last 10 years, many Regulations have been laid down to meet these objectives while protecting consumers, enacting human rights, and sustaining the so-called "European values". In this sense, the MiCA Regulation (2023)[25] should be read and interpreted bearing in mind, among many others, the General Data Protection Regulation (2016),[26] the Digital Services Act (2022),[27] the European Data Act (2023),[28] and especially the Artificial Intelligence Act

[23] *Communication from the Commission to the European Parliament, the Council, the European Economic and Social Committee and The Committee of The Regions. A European Strategy for Data*. COM/2020/66 final.

[24] Cf. *The New Legislative Framework for EU product legislation* consisted of Decision No 768/2008/EC and Regulation (EC) No 765/2008.

[25] *Regulation (EU) 2023/1114 of the European Parliament and of the Council of 31 May 2023 on markets in crypto-assets, and amending Regulations* (EU) No 1093/2010 and (EU) No 1095/2010 and Directives 2013/36/EU and (EU) 2019/1937 (Text with EEA relevance). PE/54/2022/REV/1.

[26] *Regulation (EU) 2016/679 of the European Parliament and of the Council of 27 April 2016 on the protection of natural persons with regard to the processing of personal data and on the free movement of such data*, and repealing Directive 95/46/EC (General Data Protection Regulation) (Text with EEA relevance).

[27] *Regulation (EU) 2022/2065 of the European Parliament and of the Council of 19 October 2022 on a Single Market For Digital Services* and amending Directive 2000/31/EC (Digital Services Act) (Text with EEA relevance) PE/30/2022/REV/1.

[28] *Regulation (EU) 2023/2854 of the European Parliament and of the Council of 13 December 2023* on harmonised rules on fair access to and use of data and amending Regulation (EU) 2017/2394 and Directive (EU) 2020/1828 (Data Act) E/49/2023/REV/1.

(2024), recently approved by the EU Council on May 21st, 2024, and published on June 13th.[29]

3.3 New EU Regulatory Tools

A critical question arises: How can this "ecosystem of companies, civil society and individuals" be achieved? What instruments are employed, and how can these spaces be technically established and operationalised? The documents issued by the Commission, both legal and preparatory, introduce a plethora of new concepts that require further elaboration and development. Common to all data spaces are principles such as *privacy*, *data protection by design* and *by default*, and the division and structure of *risks* (risk analysis). In addition, certain concepts are specific to each of the fourteen fields considered. For instance, unique regulatory challenges and technical specifications arise in the context of intelligent connected vehicles (ICVs). These concepts constitute a new and complex lexical field characterised by a mixed, hybrid use of common, technical and legal terms that can be interpreted in various ways.

This occurs within the Union and is a shared phenomenon in the digital transformation space. For instance, a recent mobility project that adapted Australian regulations for people with disabilities to the new reality of Connected Automated Vehicles (CAVs) highlighted how common terms like "driver" have become problematic.[30] While the term "driver" was universally understood a decade ago, its specific regulatory use and implementation now vary significantly. Who is the "driver" of a driverless vehicle, i.e., a train, a bus, or a car, relying on the infrastructure of a platform-driven information process? According to the Department of Transportation's regulations and performance standards, the "driver" was responsible for assisting people with disabilities. However, what "driver" means in this digital context needs to be redefined, and the driver's duties and responsibilities should be reallocated.

To focus only on Europe and on a single Regulation (e.g. the Digital Services Act), what exactly do "online ecosystem" (Recital 28), "provider of intermediary services" (Recital 16), or "reliable alert" (Recital 61) mean? Not to mention political concepts such as European "technological sovereignty", "data" or "information". There is a whole network of new concepts in data regulation that are not easily compatible with the notions of data protection already in place since the enactment

[29] *Regulation (eu) 2024/1689 of the European Parliament and of the Council of 13 June 2024* laying down harmonised rules on artificial intelligence and amending Regulations (EC) No 300/2008, (EU) No 167/2013, (EU) No 168/2013, (EU) 2018/858, (EU) 2018/1139 and (EU) 2019/2144 and Directives 2014/90/EU, (EU) 2016/797 and (EU) 2020/1828 (Artificial Intelligence Act).

[30] *Australia's Disability Standards for Accessible Public Transport and Connected and Automated Vehicles*. Project n. 3-014. CRC iMOVE, 2021.

of GDPR provisions.[31] In addition, legal definitions refer to conditions of use of the introduced term, but they do not yet constitute usable requirements for a computational system.

The new edition of the *Better Regulation Toolbox*,[32] significantly more extensive than its predecessor, includes various new legal governance instruments. Among these are *codes of good practices, protocols, standards, ethical commissions and audits, regulation test banks (sandboxes), algorithmic governance mechanisms, impact evaluations, aptitude tests, monitoring systems, and mechanisms for consultation and citizen participation in regulation.*

However, a paradox emerges: While the text references, mentions, and lists a comprehensive array of instruments, and it acknowledges and values these instruments—many of which have already been developed by the industry—it fails to detail their construction, implementation, and coordination, particularly concerning traditional legal regulation mechanisms. These mechanisms include institutional designs such as laws, regulations, directives, rulings, recommendations, and decisions at the European level, as well as laws, regulations, and rulings at the national level. The text also describes an action program and a specific platform called REFIT, yet it does so without precisely indicating its internal articulation.[33] An effort has certainly been made to identify the possible impacts on different areas and possible scenarios. For instance, concerning resilience, technological sovereignty, open strategic autonomy, and supply security, the following questions have been raised: Does the option affect the EU's resilience in the relevant policy area? Does the option improve or hinder the EU's technological sovereignty regarding critical technologies? Does the option reduce or exacerbate existing dependencies on third countries as regards critical technologies and value chains? Does the option

[31] Cf. *EDPB-EDPS Joint Opinion 03/2021 on the Proposal for a regulation of the European Parliament and of the Council on European data governance* (Data Governance Act), p. 9: "(. . .) the EDPB and the EDPS consider that the Proposal raises significant inconsistencies with the GDPR, as well as with other Union law10, in particular as regards the following five aspects: (a) Subject matter and scope of the Proposal (b) Definitions/terminology used in the Proposal; (c) Legal basis for the processing of personal data; (d) Blurring of the distinction between (processing of) personal and non-personal data (and unclear relationship of the Proposal with the Regulation on free flows of non-personal data); (e) Governance/tasks and powers of competent bodies and authorities to be designated in accordance with the Proposal, having regard to the tasks and powers of data protection authorities responsible for the protection of the fundamental rights and freedoms of natural persons in relation to the processing of personal data as well as for facilitating the free flow of personal data within the Union."

[32] EU Commission. *Better Regulations Guidelines. Brussels*, 3.11.2021, SWD (2021) 305 final. *EU Commission. Better Regulations Toolbox*. July 2023, complementing the better regulation guidelines presented in SWD(2021) 305 final.

[33] "REFIT is the Commission's regulatory fitness and performance programme established in 2012 to ensure that EU law is 'fit for purpose'. It is a process under which existing legislation and measures are analysed to make sure that the benefits of EU law are reached at least cost for stakeholders, citizens and public administrations and that regulatory costs are reduced, whenever possible, without affecting the policy objectives pursued by the initiative in question." p. 9.

affect the Union's essential security interests, particularly regarding critical technologies, infrastructure, and value chains?[34]

The Better Regulations Toolbox embraces a holistic and life-cycle approach, with particular attention to the combination of quantitative and qualitative methods to calculate impacts and the costs of compliance:

> Which economic operators should be considered? All economic agents, producers and consumers, firms and households, should be considered. Producing firms also consume intermediate goods and services (such as raw materials, components or business services). EU firms increasingly rely on the global economy for diversified supplies of goods and services and sustained demand for their output. The impact analysis should, therefore, not restrict itself to the direct effects of the options on the specific sector concerned but should also consider the sectors and firms along the value chain.[35]

> Sustainability dimensions (environmental, social and economic) should be considered in an integrated and holistic manner. By adopting life cycle thinking, impacts can be assessed: (i) embracing all steps of value chains, namely of production and consumption systems (e.g. from extraction of raw materials to end-of-life/waste management); (ii) fostering comprehensiveness, e.g. entailing different kind of impacts; (iii) unveiling trade-offs and avoiding shift of burdens from one life cycle stage to another (e.g. from extraction to processing or processing to consumption phase); or across impact categories (e.g. improving on climate change while worsening in water use); or in terms of spatial and temporal resolution (e.g. shifting impacts from within the EU to other world regions or from current generations to future ones).[36]

The assumption is that laws and regulations can restrict competition in the marketplace, and this should be avoided to reduce the cost of goods and services throughout the economy, eliminating unnecessary barriers. The impact on upstream and downstream markets is also considered.[37] Along with the OECD Competition Assessment Toolkit,[38] the Better Regulations Toolbox suggests less restrictive measures that can be used to minimise negative impacts on competition: (i) Tailored transition periods or provisions when adopting new legislation; (ii) using economic incentives rather than regulation to deal with externalities; (iii) ensuring adequate consumer information rather than mandatory product characteristics; (iv) voluntary rather than mandatory product specifications; (v) reliance on enforcement under competition rules in addition to sector-specific regulation to deal with inappropriate competitive behaviour (e.g. patent settlement agreements in the pharmaceutical sector).[39]

This is valuable, but it also reflects the tension between enhancing and protecting rights and fostering the development of digital markets. Implementing better regulations instruments (including ethics) has a cost. I would like to emphasise that

---

[34] *Ibid.*, p. 146.

[35] *Ibid.*, pp. 224–225.

[36] *Ibid.* p. 571.

[37] Upstream markets of a given firm are all the markets of its suppliers, downstream markets are the markets of the firm's clients (that can be both consumers and other firms along the value chain). *Ibid.* p. 200.

[38] http://www.oecd.org/competition/assessment-toolkit.htm.

[39] *Better Regulations Toolbox.* p. 200.

regulating and constructing platforms in the so-called platform-driven economy, particularly in the banking and financial sectors, involves more than just *hetero-, co-, or self-regulation*. It also entails technological and *computational intra-regulation*.[40] Given this, the regulatory approach should adopt a *middle-out, inside-outside* perspective, encompassing internal and external aspects.[41] This is crucial for the iterative, cyclical and circular legal construction of adequacy, aligning technology itself with the requirements or conditions necessary to effectively fulfil the rights of citizens, consumers, companies, and corporations.

It is not only a top-down or bottom-up normative approach but a middle-out and inside-out design program that simultaneously satisfies the functional requirements of modular design and ethical and legal requirements. I believe that this approach allows us to change the perspective with which regulatory models have been understood until now, giving rise to conflicting and incompatible expressions, such as the unambiguous statement that the law must replace self-regulation—*dura lex, sed lex digitalis*—,[42] or that the EU organs behave with "regulatory brutality" regarding the national states.[43] I contend that complexity requires dealing with problems on a scale and from another angle. Considering this situation, exploring imaginative solutions, even if they have not been proven, should be recommended.[44]

Finally, it is worth mentioning here the different perspectives on technology regulations held by the EU and US governments. Even if it fosters the better regulation toolkit and the "new legislation" perspective, the former is mainly based on the general binding Regulations mentioned in the present Chapter. In contrast, the latter is standard-based, the result of a soft law closer and longer-term collaboration with the private sector.[45] We must realise that an international

[40]Cf. de Koker et al. (2022), and de Koker and Casanovas (2024).

[41]Cf. Pagallo et al. (2019); Casanovas et al. (2022).

[42]"Self-regulation needs to be replaced by the law; the sooner, the better. *Dura lex, sed lex digitalis* is why the EU is at the forefront in the debate on digital governance." Floridi (2021).

[43]Papakonstantinou and de Hert (2022).

[44]For instance, Marta Poblet (2022), inspired by Nassim Taleb's latest work on algorithmic governance, has noted the possible fractal structure of blockchain models. Cf. Taleb (2021), p. 5, "The idea is to (re)build political and economic systems based on axiomatic and derived principles that accommodate uncertainty and fragility".

[45]See The White House, *United States Government National Standards Strategy for Critical And Emerging Technology*, Washington, May 2023, p 3: "From computers and smartphones to cars and lightbulbs, societies rely on technology standards for everyday life. In the broadest sense, standards are the common and repeated use of rules, conditions, guidelines, or characteristics for products or related processes, practices, and production methods. They enable technology that is safe, universal, and interoperable. Standards define the requirements that make it possible for mobile phones sold in different countries to communicate across the world, for bank cards issued in one country to be recognized at ATMs in another, and for cars to run on fuel purchased from any gas station. Standards also help manage risk, security, safety, privacy, and quality in the development of new innovations. In short, good standards are good for business, good for consumers, and good for society. [. . .] Six principles govern the international standards development process: transparency,

competition is underway, if not an open confrontation, to lead the field. It is also considered a strategic issue that affects national security.[46]

I will show later that the governance dimensions presented in Section 2.5.1 (Fig. 2) can, from a more abstract perspective, cover both regulatory trends.

3.4 *Thesis*

Following a classical exposition scheme, I could summarise what I would like to convey: (i) *Research*: To design and imbue ethics and law into digital environments through AI and IT systems. (ii) *Main idea*: Regulatory models are 'hybrid', 'symbiotic', including both human beings and automated information processing in real-time, capable of generating intelligent and sustainable legal ecosystems through implementing the principles of Compliance *through* Design (CtD), Privacy *through* Design (PtD), Security *through* Design (StD), etc., i.e. *smart legal ecosystems* (SLE).

We have been developing this in computing, law, semantics and artificial intelligence studies for some time now, with a flexible and tentative battery of concepts, methodologies and specific techniques. Some, such as legal ontologies to facilitate portability and interoperability, have a long history. Others, such as generative artificial intelligence applications, are still in a preliminary and exploratory phase. We are not at all "stochastic parrots", to use the expression of Sam Altman, the CEO of OpenAI and creator of ChatGPT.[47] It would be worth indicating that the acquired

---

openness, impartiality and consensus, effectiveness and relevance, coherence, and a commitment to participation by low- and middle-income countries. The private sector has led U.S. engagement with Standards Developing Organizations SDOs for more than 100 years. [...]. This private sector leadership has come with significant assistance from government and academia. In 1901, the Congress established the National Bureau of Standards—which has since become the National Institute of Standards and Technology (NIST)—as the authoritative domestic measurement science research and standards laboratory." This Strategy has been recently developed by *the U.-S. Government National Standards Strategy For Critical And Emerging Technologies (Usg Nsscet): Implementation Roadmap*, July 2024. Cf. as well, Office of Management and Budget, Executive Office of the President, *OMB Circular A-119: Federal Participation in the Development and Use of Voluntary Consensus Standards and in Conformity Assessment Activities*, January 27, 2016.

[46]Ibid. US *National Standards Strategy* (2023), *op. cit.* p 1: "Strength in standards development has been instrumental to the United States' global technological leadership. Standards development underpins economic prosperity across the country and fortifies U.S. leadership in the industries of the future at the same time. Bolstering U.S. engagement in standards for critical and emerging technology (CET) spaces will strengthen U.S. economic and national security".

[47]See the insightful cartoon by A Wang (2023) in *The New Yorker* (15/11/2023). 'Stochastic parrots' was coined in a well-known paper by Bender et al. (2021) on the limitations and dangers of large language models. Sam Altman referred ironically to the expression when he twitted "i am a stochastic parrot and so r u." Wang (2023) compares her toddler's language-acquisition process with the learning process of large language models. The cartoon is just wonderful.

experience matters. It is prudent to understand artificial intelligence programs for what they are—designs of processes and information systems suitable for developing Web 3.0, Industry 4.0 and 5.0. This is precisely the challenge: incorporating ethical and legal principles in the regulatory models partially imbued into cyber-physical systems.

4 Development

4.1 Cyber-Physical Systems and Blockchain

I will now go to cyber-physical systems and the new role that technologies based on blockchain and distributed data ledgers (DDL) have acquired in them. The North American agency GARTNER, one of the most followed by the industry and finances, has recently paid much attention to the so-called *metaverse* (a commercial term) and its relationship with the blockchain. It has drawn an infographic map of the applications, stating: "The metaverse provides new capabilities for carrying out transactions by providing an economic foundation through the use of Web 3 technologies such as cryptocurrencies, non-fungible tokens (NFT) and blockchain."[48]

The *Hype Cycle for Blockchain and Web3*, 2023, published 2 August 2023,[49] includes some interesting hints:

- By 2027, more than 50% of metaverse users will use hybrid NFT (non-fungible token) identities (identity wallets with both verifiable claims and NFT identities) for their online personas.
- The progress in blockchain technologies maturity indicates that it is no longer mere hype but a valuable tool that can bring transformative changes to various industries.
- However, organisations must plan their blockchain architectures to allow for future upgrades and the integration of better solutions as they become available. Blockchain's use has extended beyond its early applications in finance and cryptocurrencies, and it is now being leveraged across sectors such as supply chain management, healthcare, logistics, and more.

These are not reliable statistical projections but observable trends. Nevertheless, the contention that technologies to provide transaction security have spread to other data domains is true. As we will see in the next section, using robots with built-in sensors monitored in real-time is already a reality in medical applications and intelligent industrial processes.

[48] GARTNER-ID G00761111 (2022); GARTNER-ID G00775451 (2022).

[49] GARTNER-ID G00790911 (2023).

4.2 OPTIMAI

The impact of AI in manufacturing is an important topic. Heterogeneity tests carried out by Liu et al. (2024) using transnational panel data from 61 nations and regions from 2000 to 2019 have shown that there are three primary ways by which AI contributes to improving the Global Value Chain (GVC) position of the manufacturing industry: by improving both production efficiency and technological innovation capacity, and by reducing trade costs. Below, I will use OPTIMAI,[50] a European project aimed at developing a next-generation industrial management platform, as an example.

OPTIMAI integrates various AI technologies to develop a comprehensive service-oriented functional architecture to achieve Zero-Defect Manufacturing (ZDM). These technologies include (i) multi-sensory data acquisition, (ii) distributed ledger technologies, (iii) context-aware Augmented Reality (AR), and (iv) Delta Time-enabled production optimisation inference (simulations). Consequently, OPTIMAI can create a smart ecosystem where technologies like blockchain (augmented reality) simulations and expert end-user monitoring are integrated and coordinated to elicit customer responses through established routines. Figure 1 depicts the lifecycle of the OPTIMAI smart ecosystem in a non-technical way.

As it has been described many times in the literature,[51] a "smart factory" embodies the vertical integration of diverse components to establish a flexible and reconfigurable manufacturing system. This framework incorporates a self-organising multi-agent system (MAS) enhanced by big data-driven feedback and coordination. The model includes an intelligent negotiation mechanism that enables agents to collaborate effectively. The organisation of these components across various layers and their relationship with the operating mechanism of the closed double-loop system is key. Specifically, (i) the first loop involves elements that participate in the coordination and feedback provided at the Cloud level, which facilitate the reconfiguration of assets located in the Physical Resources Layer ("Coordinator"); and (ii) the second loop pertains to the visualisation and manipulation of data occurring between the Cloud components involved in statistical analysis ("Statistical") and terminal supervisory applications. Cloud-based big data storage enables detection and action and controls and manipulates processes within the smart factory framework.

Implementing blockchain and lightweight Deep Residual Networks (DRNs) ensures that all transactions on the platform are transparently traced and recorded in real-time sequences. The underlying blockchain technology leverages the power of peer-to-peer (P2P) networks in providing a shared and trustable model that can be

---

[50] OPTIMAI. *A Decision Support Framework for quality control in produced industrial parts.* Quality control in smart manufacturing H2020-(IA) DT-FOF-11-2020. Grant agreement ID: 958264. https://optimai.eu/#about . For a general description, see Margetis et al. (2022).

[51] Cf. Wang et al. (2016); Margetis et al. (2022). I summarised this process in Casanovas (2024).

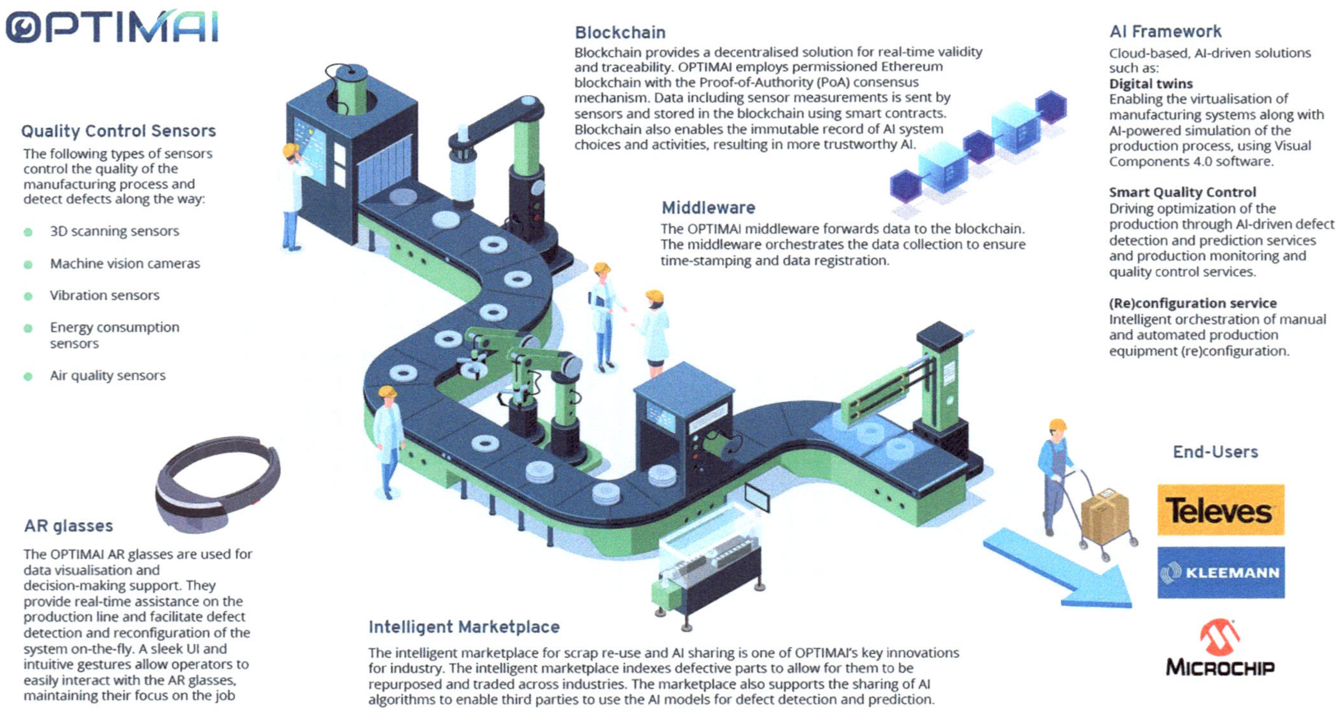

Fig. 1 OPTIMAI smart ecosystem (intuitive overview). Source: Linda Henriksson, https://optimai.eu/

used to ensure the validity of transactions and achieve trust and security among different peers. As a distributed ledger technology, all participating nodes must agree on any transaction being added to the blockchain with an immutable timestamped digital block indicating the identities of both the senders and receivers and information linking it to a previous block. To gain consensus, OPTIMAI uses Proof of Authority in a private Ethereum. OPTIMAI contributions are (i) a lightweight defect detection method that is developed to meet the very low inference latency but high-performance requirements in industrial cases; (ii) A feature learning strategy based on the Deep Residual Networks architecture to keep minimal network size while lowering the impact on the performance, (iii) A blockchain component to store AI results in an immutable and verifiable manner, following the Proof-of-Authority consensus mechanism.[52] OPTIMAI uses blockchain to verify the authenticity of firmware updates according to several technical steps in smart contracts. Namely, (i) generation of hashes; (ii) authorisation of firmware updates; (iii) secure hash storage; (iv) verification during firmware update; (v) transparent hash comparison; (vi) blockchain queries (to retrieve the hash of the firmware stored in the blockchain).[53]

Our position here is that to generate an intelligent legal ecosystem, relying solely on the validity produced in transactions and proof of authority as a consensus mechanism is not enough. *Legal validity* requires *validation*, i.e. an additional *Compliance through Design* (CtD) mechanism that represents *a legal and ethical third loop* or processing cycle independent of the middleware or intermediary software that organises, stores and manages the data provided to the blockchain.[54] Moreover, smart contracts are not yet legal contracts.[55] From a private law perspective, the third loop's legal components include end-user license agreements (EULAs), the four types of smart contracts suggested by the European Legal Institute and, broadly, the UNIDROIT Principles on digital assets and private law.[56] Smart Legal Ecosystems (SLE) require some more normative conditions to be met, fostering what has been recently called the *AI value chain* by EU legal provisions.

[52]Cf. Leontaris et al. (2023).

[53]Cf. Mitsiaki et al. (2023).

[54]Cf. Casanovas et al. (2024a, b).

[55]Cf. de Filippi and Wright (2018).

[56]Principle II of the European Legal Institute (2023): "Various types of SMART CONTRACTS can be distinguished. A SMART CONTRACT can be: mere CODE; o legal agreement exists (the situation is a mere TRANSACTION in the technical sense of the word); a tool to execute a legal agreement; the legal agreement exists OFF-CHAIN; a legally binding declaration of will, such as an offer or acceptance or constitute a legal agreement itself; or merged with the legal agreement and therefore exist simultaneously both ONCHAIN and OFF-CHAIN." It is interesting that Principles 2.1 and 2.2. of UNIDROIT (2023) higlight the properties of retrievalability and control in its definitions: "'Electronic record' means information which is (i) stored in an electronic medium and (ii) capable of being retrieved. (2) 'Digital asset' means an electronic record which is capable of being subject to control."

4.3 *Artificial Intelligence Value Chain*

V Rodriguez-Doncel (2024), in Chapter 5 of this volume, describes the technologies that support decentralised identity on the Web, according to the specifications of WWW3, advocating for decentralised models for sharing information (e.g. Decentralised Identifier, DID, and a Verifiable Credential, VC.) without the intervention of authorities.[57] Identification, authentication, validation and trust are related issues whose social and political assumptions should be clarified and have no easy solution.[58] They are crucial for global banking services, money laundering prevention, and financial inclusion policies.[59] However, the role of national and mainly EU authorities has been strengthened and potentiated in the Digital Identity Regulation and the AI Act.[60] The concepts of *legal harmonisation* (according to the well-known EU principle of subsidiarity) and the *AI value chain* constitute the backbones of the Regulation. What the AI value chain consists of has not yet been thoroughly defined. Still, to put in place legal responsibilities and liabilities, all provisions are aligned with this chain, meaning that AI systems are designed, tested and put into the market by a set of operators with different tasks and functions (providers, deployers, importers, distributors and product manufacturers) adding value to the final product. Thus, the value chain can be described as a process and system of outputs that are related among them and with human and artificial agency. Risks, loosely defined in a classical way, are "the combination of the probability of an occurrence of harm and the severity of that harm" (Art.3.2). The value chain appears to link all levels of risk along the AI system lifecycle. For instance, Recital 65 reads:

> (. . .) 'systemic risk' means a risk that is specific to the high-impact capabilities of general-purpose AI models, having a significant impact on the Union market due to their reach or due to actual or reasonably foreseeable negative effects on public health, safety, public security,

[57] Likewise, in this volume, Julián Inza and Ainhoa Inza-Blasco analyse digital identity systems and the European Digital Wallet included into the *Digital Identity Regulation* that entered into force in May 2024. *Regulation (EU) 2024/1183 of the European Parliament and of the Council of 11 April 2024* amending Regulation (EU) No 910/2014 as regards establishing the European Digital Identity Framework PE/68/2023/REV/1. Art, 2.1 reads: "This Regulation applies to electronic identification schemes notified by a Member State, to European Digital Identity Wallets provided by a Member State and to trust service providers established in the Union".

[58] Cf. *NIST Special Publication 800-162. Guide to Attribute Based Access Control (ABAC) Definition and Considerations*, January 2014; *NIST Special Publication 800-63C. Digital Identity Guidelines Federation and Assertions*, June 2017; *NIST Special Publication 800-53, Revision 5 Security and Privacy Controls for Information Systems and Organizations*, September 2020.

[59] Cf. De Koker (2014); De Koker et al. (2019); De Koker and Goldbarsht (2022).

[60] This is clear when considering the main role of official authorities to certify the AI systems compliance with legal requirements in *regulatory sandboxes* (AI Act, Art. 53 and ff). Originally, sandboxes were a financial and banking instrument to experiment with the potential regulatory effects of new standards and guidelines. Cf. L de Koker, Sandboxes have acquired a more authoritative meaning in the Act.

> fundamental rights, or the society as a whole, *that can be propagated at scale across the value chain*;[61]

Value chains have also been considered a central issue in MiCA, but with a slightly different meaning, enhancing the incentives and possibility of change as a useful innovation. Hence, the *MiCA Impact Assessment* considered it in a positive way regarding the impact of blockchain in the financial sector:

> *Crypto-assets and the underlying DLTs also hold great potential for efficiency gains in the 'traditional' financial sector.* This potential stems mainly from two features of the technology: (i) the ability to record information in a safe and immutable format and (ii) the capability to make this information accessible transparently to all market participants in the DLT network. The tokenisation of securities (shares or bonds) is an example of growth potential shortly. This can lead to increased company financing through securities token offerings (STOs) and *efficiency gains throughout the value chain by reducing the need for intermediaries and automation, resulting in faster, cheaper and frictionless transactions.*[62]

Although this term has not been retained in the Regulation, it is implicitly mentioned when considering its benefits for the financial market and SMEs.[63] The regulation covers three crypto-asset types: *asset-referenced tokens* (ART), *electronic money tokens* (EMT), and *other crypto-assets not covered by existing EU law.* The legislation regulates the issuance and trading of crypto assets and 'significant' ART and EMT. Securing liquidity and redemption (for investors) are a main concern, but it does not hold with the value chain affecting risks. This issue should be addressed in the future because it shows the tension between fostering innovation and economic

[61] Article 25 distributes responsibilities along the AI value chain. Recital 88 specifies that along the AI value chain, multiple parties often supply AI systems, tools, and services, as well as components or processes that the provider incorporates into the AI system. Recital 89 relates the value chain with promoting trustworthy AI systems in the Union. And Recital 101 reads: "Providers of general-purpose AI models have a particular role and responsibility along the AI value chain, as the models they provide may form the basis for a range of downstream systems, often provided by downstream providers that necessitate a good understanding of the models and their capabilities, both to enable the integration of such models into their products and to fulfil their obligations under this or other regulations."

[62] Brussels, 24.9.2020 SWD(2020) 380 *Final Commission Staff Working Document Impact Assessment Accompanying the document Proposal for a Regulation of the European Parliament and of the Council on Markets in Crypto-assets and amending Directive* (EU) 2019/1937), p. 9.

[63] Recital 2 reads: "Crypto-assets are one of the main applications of distributed ledger technology. Crypto assets are digital representations of value or of rights that have the potential to bring significant benefits to market participants, including retail holders of crypto assets. Representations of value include external, non-intrinsic value attributed to a crypto-asset by the parties concerned or by market participants, meaning the value is subjective and based only on the interest of the purchaser of the crypto-asset. By streamlining capital-raising processes and enhancing competition, offers of crypto-assets could allow for an innovative and inclusive way of financing, including for small and medium-sized enterprises (SMEs). When used as a means of payment, crypto-assets can present opportunities for cheaper, faster and more efficient payments, particularly on a cross-border basis, by limiting the number of intermediaries."

development and enhancing rights simultaneously.[64] Legal provisions issued only four years ago, such as the EU Data Act, seemed more focused on leveraging opportunities to develop the EU digital market, showing less concern about risks.[65] The new turn of encompassing innovation and risks in a single AI value chain should be clarified and better defined because the chain of responsibilities (and legal liabilities) has a deontic flavour[66] that was not present in the economic notion of value chain used in previous EU documents (e.g. in the Better Regulations Toolbox).[67]

More specifically, aligning the AI value chain with (i) obligations, (ii) according to a typology of risks and mitigation measures, and (iii) AI governance models seems to be the next step.[68] This should be compatible with the control of supply chains and the so-called "chain of activities of the companies", specifically regulated by the recent Directive (EU) 2024/1760 on corporate sustainability due diligence (laid down on June 13th as well).[69] This Directive has raised some concerns about its

---

[64] Supply Chain Finance (SCF) refers to the optimization of the financial flows in the supply chain and its working capital. Ronchini et al. (2024) have recently analysed the role of AI SCF innovation processes to assess the buyer's creditworthiness, to detect fraud, and to propose the right SCF solutions.

[65] See, e.g., Recital 2 of the EU Digital Act: "Barriers to data sharing prevent an optimal allocation of data for the benefit of society. Those barriers include a lack of incentives for data holders to enter voluntarily into data sharing agreements, uncertainty about rights and obligations in relation to data, the costs of contracting and implementing technical interfaces, the high level of fragmentation of information in data silos, poor metadata management, the absence of standards for semantic and technical interoperability, bottlenecks impeding data access, a lack of common data sharing practices and the abuse of contractual imbalances with regard to data access and use."

[66] See, among many other examples, Recital 85 of the AI Act: "Recital 85. General-purpose AI systems may be used as high-risk AI systems by themselves or be components of other high-risk AI systems. Therefore, due to their particular nature and in order to ensure a fair sharing of responsibilities along the AI value chain, the providers of such systems should, irrespective of whether they may be used as high-risk AI systems as such by other providers or as components of high-risk AI systems and unless provided otherwise under this Regulation, closely cooperate with the providers of the relevant high-risk AI systems to enable their compliance with the relevant obligations under this Regulation and with the competent authorities established under this Regulation."

[67] There have been some attempts of defining value chains in digital economy, adapting its classic meaning to digital innovations. E.g. "Digital Economy Value Chain is the innovation of the value chain driven by digital elements (data, digital technology, digital mode, etc.) and the integration of the digital economy and value chain." (Miao 2021). Oosthuizen et al. (2021) have identified four key roles for AI solutions in the retail value chain: knowledge and insight management, inventory management, operations optimization, and customer engagement.

[68] For instance, referring to Value Engineering as a fundamental tool to address the type of risk that is intrinsic of AI, we could differentiate inertial, disruptive and intrinsic risk. Cf. Noriega and Casanovas (2024).

[69] *Directive (EU) 2024/1760 of the European Parliament and of the Council of 13 June 2024 on corporate sustainability due diligence and amending Directive (EU) 2019/1937 and Regulation (EU) 2023/2859*. See Recital 15: "The European Parliament, in its resolution of 10 March 2021 with recommendations to the Commission on corporate due diligence and corporate accountability, calls upon the Commission to propose Union-level rules for comprehensive corporate due diligence obligations, with consequences including civil liability for those companies that cause or jointly

implementation, for the compliance costs of social and environmental regulations may be privatised in complex supply networks, particularly in third countries with weak enforcement mechanisms.[70] Other related problems arise from the fragmented nature of EU legislation. Global Value Chains (GVC) do not receive consistent and homogeneous legal treatment.[71] Besides, applying AI in supply chain management constitutes a set of related but different issues.[72]

Coming back to OPTIMAI, value chains for smart industries have been explicitly considered in the second *Commission Staff Working Document on Common European Data Spaces* (CEDS) issued in January 2024 and extending the CEDS to fourteen: agriculture, cultural heritage, energy, finance, green deal, health, industry (manufacturing), language, media, mobility, public administrations, research and innovation, skills, and tourism. Industry (smart manufacturing) is deemed a strategic sector for European development. Thus, the economic sense of what a value chain consists of prevails:

6.7 The common European industrial (manufacturing) data space will help the European manufacturing industry, characterised by the complexity of its processes and value chains, get more value out of industrial data, create more flexible and resilient supply chains, and further develop data-driven business models that fully take advantage of advanced digital innovations.

> The initiative will pave the way for secure, fair, sovereign, responsible and cost-effective data sharing in dynamic asset management, predictive maintenance and agile supply chain management in the European manufacturing sector and beyond. The data space will contribute to achieving the objectives of the New Industrial Strategy for Europe by creating new business models, allowing the industry to be more productive, providing workers with new skills and supporting the decarbonisation of the EU economy at large.[73]

---

cause harm by failing to carry out due diligence. The Council Conclusions of 1 December 2020 on Human Rights and Decent Work in Global Supply Chains called upon the Commission to table a proposal for a Union legal framework on sustainable corporate governance, including cross-sector corporate due diligence obligations along global supply chains. The European Parliament also calls for clarifying directors' duties in its own initiative report of 2 December 2020 on sustainable corporate governance. In their Joint Declaration on EU Legislative Priorities for 2022 of 21 December 2021, the European Parliament, the Council of the European Union and the Commission have committed, to deliver on an economy that works for people, and to improve the regulatory framework on sustainable corporate governance."

[70] See Felbermayr et al. (2024). The authors suggest excluding countries with sufficient regulatory systems and focusing only on supplier-buyer relationships instead of the entire network.

[71] See Beckers (2023). The contribution proposes understanding the evolving EU law on Global Value Chains (GVC) as a process of institutionalisation leading to at least three different legal forms not always compatible, according to EU company law, consumer law and trade law.

[72] Nandi et al. (2024) use the supply chain operations reference (SCOR) framework to analyse the contribution of seven AI techniques: artificial neural networks, expert systems, machine learning, genetic algorithms, agent-based systems, fuzzy logic, and rough set theory.

[73] Brussels, 24.1.2024 SWD(2024) 21 final *Commission Staff Working Document on Common European Data Spaces*, p. 29.

This is directly pointing to OPTIMAI, showing the extension of the contradiction. While it is highly valued for its use of last-generation AI information processing systems, it can be qualified as high-risk AI in the AI Act pyramid *for the same reason*. By the same token, risks and benefits are equalised in the AI value chain. A way of cutting this Gordian knot is reducing the complexity of the problem, specifying the components of its smart legal ecosystem (SLE), i.e. identifying the human-in-the-loop decisions at every level of its open triple-loop (processes, monitoring and legal and ethical layer). Its AI value chain should be decomposed to understand and reconstruct its dynamic flow.[74]

5 Rationale

5.1 Social, Legal and Technological Dimensions of AI Governance

To understand how SLE can be generated, we can consider the complex social space in which intelligent agents operate. *Hybrid Online Social Systems* (HOSS) are a hybrid online social system that supports collective activities involving human or artificial agents who can reason about social aspects and act within a regulated space holding constraints and affordances. The generated triadic space (WIT) comprises (i) the institutional system (I), (ii) the technological artefacts that implement it (T), and the real environment where the system operates (W). Thus, WIT includes three dimensions for the design of electronic institutions: (i) *legal*, (ii) *technological*, and (iii) *social*.[75]

In parallel and independently of the cognitive socio-technical systems, we have converged on the design of these three dimensions to develop regulatory models for Web 3.0 and 4.0, I4.0 and I5.0. This is relevant to the discussion because to model cyber-physical institutions or legal systems in accordance with the conditions of the rule of law, it is required to single out and link all components capable of expressing the complexity of digital environments. At least (i) two axes (vertical: binding power; horizontal: social dialogue); (iii) three dimensions (social, legal, and

[74] A more granular analysis should include at least the classic AI systems components to create, deploy and maintain them: (i) Data Collection and Generation (Dta Acquisition), (ii) Data storage and management (e.g. warehousing and data lakes), (iii) Data processing and preparation (cleaning, transformation and feature engineering), (iv) Model development (algorithm selection, training and validation); (v) Model deployment and integration, (v) Model monitoring and maintenance (performance and retraining), (vi) Error handling and debugging, (vii) Application and decision making (predictive and prescriptive analytics, automated decision), (viii) User interaction and feedback (interface and feedback loop), (ix) Governance and ethics (regulatory, legal compliance and ethical considerations), (x) Innovation and research (developing new techniques and use cases).

[75] Cf. Noriega et al. (2016), and for a development based on the so-called *Value Alignment Problem* (VAP) between AI Systems and social values, Noriega et al. (2023).

computational); (iii) four sets concerning sources (clusters: hard law, soft law, public or private policies, and ethics); (iv) and four angles or nodes to drive the implementation of regulatory systems (stakeholders governance, anchoring institutions, the trust/security binomial, and institutional strengthening). We have already drawn it in previous works.[76]

We have plotted it in Fig. 2, showing how the different components of the regulatory space can be aligned and linked in the IoT. Regulation (*Hetero, co-, self*) can be distributed within a three-dimensional space, able to contain the four legal sources that have been identified. This is the space for *legal governance* (as we have defined it above in Sect. 2.2).

It is worth mentioning that in Fig. 2, data flows in cyber-physical systems (with sensors and actuators) are not represented. *Computational intra-regulation,* as occurs in the OPTIMAI closed double-loop system, operates across this three-dimensional space. We have used it as a scheme, template or pattern to build the third legal and ethical loop of the OPTIMAI Regulatory Model (ORM) at the implementation level (see Sect. 2.3.4).

In I4.0, Web 3.0 (Web of Liked Data) and Web 4.0 (Muti-Agent Systems), legal validity can be predicated when the requirements established in the four previously defined regulatory clusters are met. But in I5.0, legal validity, i.e., the property of being 'legal', requires semi-automation, allowing compliance procedures to be executed in real-time. That is, a validation of the predicated legality is needed, which should be practised from the verification that a regulatory system has effectively been generated that can serve as a stable legal ecosystem, executed by intelligent agents and monitored by both agents and the humans who must ensure that information processes occur correctly. System autonomy and scalability are a matter of degree. We therefore distinguish *ecological validity* (i.e. the 'legality of legal ecosystems') from legal validity (the 'legality of regulatory systems').

5.2 The Double Implosion of Legal Professions and the Emergence of Web Legal Services

To broaden our perspective and understand the impact of technology on traditional professions and legal instruments, it is essential to consider recent historical developments. While this analysis involves interpretation, a future vision necessitates understanding recent history. Over the past fifty years, the legal field has experienced two significant transformations. First, globalisation has catalysed the evolution of law firms into legal corporations, many of which operate on a transnational scale. Second, technological advancements have profoundly impacted the legal industry. It is crucial to clarify these transformations to comprehend their full implications.[77]

[76] Cf. Casanovas et al. (2022, 2024a).

[77] I had the opportunity to develop this topic in Casanovas (2022).

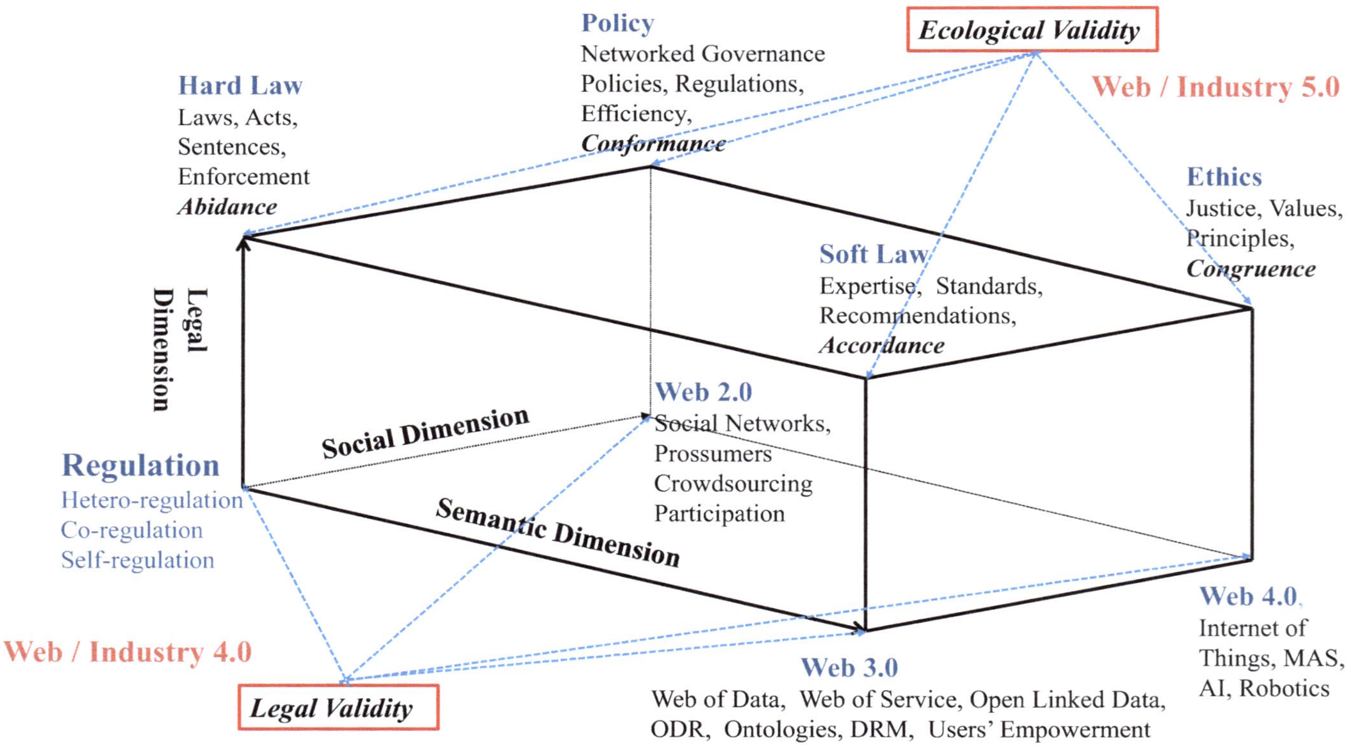

Fig. 2 AI legal governance dimensions for implementing the rule of law in IoT, Web 3.0 and 4.0, and Industry 4.0. Ecological legal validity should be reached in I5.0, i.e. encompassing and aligning ethical and legal values into cyber-physical systems in a semi-automated way, fostering the emergence of smart legal ecosystems

The economic and cultural globalisation that occurred from the mid-1980s to the end of the twentieth century followed what is referred to as the "big bang" of legal professions, which took place between 1960 and 1980 in the United States and European countries, after a long period of stagnation since the beginning of the 19th c.[78] Researchers in the field of *Law & Society* described this shift as a move from a centralised vision of the state and law to a normative decentralisation distributed among businesses, corporations, and political and social organisations.

The implosion of traditional legal forms happened because service providers aimed not only to control the supply but also to stimulate demand in line with the rapid expansion of a global economy. The primary consumers of legal services were no longer individual citizens but corporations, financial institutions, and the administrations of national states. This rapid legal expansion, along with the corresponding increase in litigation, also resulted from changes in regulation in the financial and stock markets.[79]

The second significant transformation occurred due to two major events. First, the collapse of large law firms, which had been transformed into multidisciplinary consultancies by the end of the century (e.g., Arthur Andersen), and the enactment of legislation such as the Sarbanes–Oxley Act in the United States in 2002. Second, the financial crisis of 2008-2012. Both events led to the expansion of a legal services market with characteristics distinct from traditional legal services.

This emerging market for legal services is increasingly being "Uberized" and becoming more accessible to professionals with minimal legal background but specialised technical expertise. These professionals include knowledge engineers, project managers, financial experts, client advisors, product process specialists, documentarians, risk prevention experts, data protection by design experts, compliance (automated compliance) specialists, and AI programmers.

5.3 The RegTech Market

The emergence of GPT-3.5, GPT-4, and ChatGPT following the pandemic has intensified a trend already taking shape. Since at least 2012, AI has been on the agendas of law firms. The Governance, Risk Management, and Compliance (GRC) market, which includes RegTech, LawTech, and FinTech, has seen exponential

[78] Cf. Abel and Lewis (1988); Abel (2020).

[79] CF J Flood (2005, p. 143): "The drive to Big Bang was fuelled partly by the release of currency exchange rates from direct state control in 1979. This release prompted the development of futures and options markets in financial instruments and currencies. Releasing the London Stock Exchange from the cartel arrangements that had ruled it, Big Bang - more of an implosion that an explosion - sucked in potential market-makers from the US, Japan and elsewhere. It delivered the large American banks, especially, from the restrictions of the Glass-Steagall Act and made London an attractive site for investment."

growth since then. Data tracked by Raymond Blijd through *LegalComplex* and *LegalPioneer*, covering approximately 30,000 companies and 20,000 contracts from 1984 to 2020, indicates that investment in legal technology reached $12.3 billion.[80] When potential risk, compliance, and management markets are considered, this figure rises to $3 trillion.[81] As of December 2023, the estimated total investment is 51,654 contracts and $4.3 trillion.

In summary: (i) There is the widespread use of the "platform-driven economy"; (ii) There has been an integration of traditional ICT law (e.g., intellectual and industrial property, patents, data protection) with IT solutions for lawyers, including advancements in e-discovery, semantic web technologies, search tools, and document management systems, as well as Online Dispute Resolution (ODR); (iii) A polarisation exists between large legal corporations and 'uberized' individual lawyers; (iv) Web-based legal services (LawTech) have emerged, either integrated into large law firms or operating independently online.

The development of semantics, Natural Language Processing (NLP), ontologies, and information storage and retrieval techniques, alongside Machine Learning (ML) and Deep Learning (DL), has facilitated the convergence of two approaches into a single field of techno-regulation (LawTech, also encompassing FinTech, RegTech, and more recently SupTech). The primary functions of this field include the supervision, monitoring, and automatic compliance of regulatory systems, incorporating elements such as smart contracts, cryptocurrencies, and Online Dispute Resolution (ODR).

According to the latest survey by the International Legal Technology Association (ILTA 2023), the legal profession has undergone significant modernisation. Two-thirds of law firms provide laptops to nearly 90% of their lawyers, and almost half extend this provision to 90% of their employees. Additionally, 74% of firms are transitioning their management accounts to the cloud. Nearly all firms are utilising generative artificial intelligence, notably Harvey.ai, for various purposes, including brainstorming, drafting presentations, and creating initial drafts of legal documents. Furthermore, major legal publishers offer their clients search assistants powered by generative artificial intelligence, such as CoCounsel Core by Westlaw (Thomson Reuters).

---

[80] https://www.legalcomplex.com/spark-max/.

[81] Cf. Blijd (2021) has taken into account for the estimation Docusign, Legalzoll, Disco S-1, Intapp S-1, Docusign S-1, NUIX Prospectus, Law Society SEC filing (U.S. Securities and Exchange Commision).

6 Some Open Questions

In conclusion, drawing definitive conclusions from the European Union's new legislative strategy to shape the digital market is premature. As already shown, numerous regulations and legal instruments have been introduced since the inception of the General Data Protection Regulation (GDPR). These will require harmonisation to be effective, including the redefinition of concepts in legal texts and the procedural rules for the implementation and protection of rights. Harmonisation—encompassing interpretation, consistency, and resolving normative contradictions or tensions—is a fundamental pillar under the principle of subsidiarity. However, challenges may arise due to the dual objectives of legal provisions in this domain: (i) incentivising and fostering competition and innovation in digital markets and (ii) protecting citizens' and consumers' rights. Balancing these two objectives proportionately can be challenging in certain circumstances, raising several pertinent questions:

- How will the construction of this professional legal space be compatible with the institutional construction of the new public space?
- How will "platform-driven law" be compatible with the emergence of legal ecosystems with executable components?
- How can values be imbued and modelled in information systems, platforms and digital infrastructures?
- How can the digital identity system of the various European provisions be systematised to generate a harmonised digital identity framework?
- And how can they be reconciled with the various existing national and international standards on identity and, more specifically, with the building of legal ecosystems?

Some more questions on governance:

- How could citizens, consumers, disabled people and vulnerable communities be better supported and protected?
- What roles should different types of (AI) technologies play in this ever-changing and globalised society? For example,
  - What roles can Blockchain and FinTech technologies play in the overall picture?
  - What is the role of crypto-assets and cryptocurrencies going to be?
  - What are the components of FinTech and RegTech governance that Carmen Pastor was talking about to achieve the social economy ecosystem?
- What should the role of governments and binding authorities be in such a decentralised economy?
- How to resolve the tension between smart contract federated identity management and third-party authentication services?

And even more questions addressed to commercial, financial, banking and technology lawyers:

- How value can be monetised in the new crypto-assets field?
- What does 'value chain' mean in AI and the digital financial market, i.e. 'AI value chain'?
- How should the 'value chain' be interpreted in MiCA, the Digital Act, and the AI Act?
- What connects the different interpretations?
- How could such an AI value chain be metricised and aligned with a typology of risks and mitigation tools?
- What is the difference between the economic value chain in manufacturing and the supply market?

I'm sure the authors of the chapters in this book can provide some answers to these questions, or at least, because definitive answers are elusive in this field, they will be able to offer elements to rephrase them in a more manageable and practical manner.

Acknowledgements The Chapter has benefited from several useful comments by Víctor Rodriguez-Doncel, Pablo Noriega, Ho-Pun Lam, Mustafa Hashmi, and Carmen Pastor-Sempere. I also thank Tania Martin for her excellent editing work. This research has been partially funded by the EU Project OPTIMAI. *Optimizing Manufacturing Processes through Artificial Intelligence and Virtualization.* Grant agreement ID: 958264 (2021-2024); and by the national project SGR-506 (AQU, Research Group of Excellence at UAB, SGR 00532 2022-24)

References

Abel RL, Lewis PSC (eds) (1988) Lawyers in society, vol 3. University of California Press, Berkeley

Abel. (2020) Comparative sociology of lawyers, 1988-2018: The professional project. In: Abel RL, Hammerslev O, Sommerlad H, Schultz U (eds) Lawyers in 21st-century societies. Hart, Oxford, pp 879–916

Aysan AF, Nanaeva Z (2022). Fintech as a financial disruptor: a bibliometric analysis. FinTech 1, 412–433. https://doi.org/10.3390/fintech1040031, Accessed 19 June 2024

Beckers A (2023) Global value chains in EU law. Yearb Eur Law 42:322–346

Bender EM, Gebru T, McMillan-Major A Shmitchell S (2021) On the dangers of stochastic parrots: can language models be too big?. In Proceedings of the 2021 ACM conference on fairness, accountability, and transparency. ACM, pp 610–623

Blijd R (2021) How big is the addressable market for the legal industry? Legalcomplex: Daily Archives, 21 July. Available at: https://www.legalcomplex.com/2021/07/19/how-big-is-the-addressable-marketfor-the-legal-industry. Accessed 19 June 2024

Casanovas P (2008) The future of law: relational justice and next generation of web services. Eur J Legal Stud 2:119–136

Casanovas P (2022) Inteligencia Artificial y Derecho: la doble implosión de las profesiones y servicios jurídicos en la era digital. In: Serrano M, Velarde (eds) Mirando hacia el futuro. Cambios sociohistóricos vinculados a la virtualización. Centro de Investigaciones Sociológicas (CIS), Madrid, pp 83–114

Casanovas P (2024) Building a smart legal ecosystem for industry 5.0. In: Barfield W, Weng Y-H, Pagallo U (eds) Cambridge handbook on law, policy, and regulations for human-Robot interaction. Cambridge University Press, Cambridge, pp 145–168

Casanovas P, Poblet M (2008). adding semantics to the legal domain. In: Proceedings of the 2nd Annual European Semantics Technology Conference ESTC-08, Vienna, 24th-26th September 2008. Available at SSRN: https://ssrn.com/abstract=3542084 or https://doi.org/10.2139/ssrn.3542084. Accessed 19 June 2024

Casanovas P, de Koker L, Hashmi M (2022) Law, socio-legal governance, the internet of things, and industry 4.0: a middle-out/inside-out approach. Multidiscip Sci J MDPI 5(1):64–91

Casanovas P, Hashmi M, de Koker L, Lam H-P (2024a) A three steps methodological approach to legal governance validation. In: Palmirani M, Casanovas P., Pagallo U, Sartor G et al. (2024) AI approaches to the complexity of legal systems, AICOL XIII-XIV, LNAI. Springer, Cham (preprint).

Casanovas P, Hashmi M, de Koker L, Lam H-P (2024b). Compliance, Regtech, and smart legal ecosystems: a methodology for legal governance validation. In: Barfield W, Pagallo U (eds) Research handbook on the law of artificial intelligence, vol. II. Edward Elgar Publ., Cheltenham (UK), Northampton (MA)

De Filippi P, Wright A (2018) Blockchain and the law. Harvard University Press

De Koker L (2014) The FATF's customer identification framework: fit for purpose? J Money Launder Contr 17(3):281–295

De Koker L, Casanovas P (2024) De-risking' denials of bank services: an over-compliance Dilemma? In: de Koker L, Goldbarsht D (eds) Financial crime, law and governance. Navigating challenges in different contexts. Springer International Publishing, Cham, pp 45–70. https://doi.org/10.1007/978-3-031-59547-9_3

De Koker L, Goldbarsht D (2022) Financial technologies and financial crime: key developments and areas for future research. In: de Koker L, Goldbarsht D (eds) Financial technology and the law: combating financial crime. Springer International Publishing, Cham, pp 303–320

De Koker L, Morris N, Jaffer S (2019) Regulating financial services in an era of technological disruption. Law Context 36(2):90–112

De Koker L, Ocal T, Casanovas P (2022) Where's Wally? FATF, virtual asset service providers, and the regulatory jurisdictional challenge. In: de Koker L, Goldbarsht D (eds) Financial technology and the law: combating financial crime. Springer International Publishing, Cham, pp 151–183

Dosso M, Aysan FA (2022) The technological impact in finance: A bibliometric study of Fintech research. In: Eurasian business and economics perspectives: Proceedings of the 35th Eurasia business and economics society conference. Springer International Publishing, Cham, pp 193–209

European Legal Institute (2023) ELI principles on blockchain technology, Smart Contracts and Consumer Protection. Report of the European Law Institute

Felbermayr G, Friesenbichler K, Gerschberger M, Klimek P, Meyer B (2024) Designing EU supply chain regulation. Intereconomics 59(1):28–34

Flood J (2005) The cultures of globalization: professional restructuring for the international market. In: Professional competition and professional power. Routledge, London, pp 139–169

Floridi L (2021) The end of an era: from self-regulation to hard law for the digital industry. Philos Technol 34(4):619–622

Gai K, Qiu M, Sun X (2018) A survey on FinTech. J Netw Comput Appl 103:262–273

GARTNER-ID G00761111 (2022) M. Resnick et al. Infographic: Impact Map of the Metaverse. Published 8 August

GARTNER-ID G00775451 (2022) M. Resnick et al. Building a Digital Future: The Metaverse. Published 23 June

GARTNER-ID G00790911 (2023) A. Leow et al. Hype Cycle for Blockchain and Web3, Published 2 August 2023

Giglio F (2021) Fintech: a literature review. Eur Res Stud J XXIV(2B):600–627

Goldstein I, Jiang W, Karolyi GA (2019) To FinTech and beyond. Rev Financ Stud 32(5): 1647–1661
ILTA (2023) International Legal Technology Association Technology Survey. https://www.iltanet.org/home. Accessed 17 June 2024
Leontaris L, Mitsiaki A, Charalampous P, Dimitriou N, Leivaditou E, Karamanidis A, Margetis et al (2023) A blockchain-enabled deep residual architecture for accountable, in-situ quality control in industry 4.0 with minimal latency. Comput Ind 149:103919
Liu J, Jiang X, Shi M, Yang Y (2024) Impact of artificial intelligence on manufacturing industry global value chain position. Sustainability 16(3):1341
Margetis G, Apostolakis K C, Dimitriou N, Tzovaras D, Stephanidis C (2022). Aligning emerging technologies onto I4. 0 principles: towards a novel architecture for zero-defect manufacturing”. In: 2022 IEEE 27th International Conference on Emerging Technologies and Factory Automation (ETFA), pp 1–8
Miao Z (2021) Digital economy value chain: concept, model structure, and mechanism. Appl Econ 53(37):4342–4357
Mitsiaki A, Konstantinos V, Margetis G, Dimitrios T (2023). Enhancing defect traceability and data integrity in industry 4.0 using Blockchain technology. In: Saravanos DA, Benjeddou A, Chrysochoidis N, Theodosiou T (eds) X ECCOMAS Thematic Conference on Smart Structures and Materials. SMART 2023, pp 1173–1184
Möller DPF, Vakilzadian H, Haas RE (2022) From Industry 4.0 towards Industry 5.0. In: 2022 IEEE International Conference on Electro Information Technology (eIT). IEEE, pp 61–68
Murphy C, Carew PJ, Stapleton L (2022) Ethical personalisation and control systems for smart human-centred industry 5.0 applications. IFAC-PapersOnLine 55(39):24–29
Nandi ML, Nandi S, Dave D (2024) Applying artificial intelligence in the supply chain. In: Sarkis J (ed) The Palgrave handbook of supply chain management. Springer International Publishing, Cham, pp 1241–1273
Noriega P, Casanovas P (2024) From Pascal’s wager to value engineering: a glance at AI risks and how to address them. WP, Value Engineering In AI (VALE 2024), affiliated with the 27th European Conference on Artificial Intelligence (ECAI 2024), Santiago de Compostela
Noriega P, Verhagen H, Padget J, d’Inverno M (2016) A manifesto for conscientious design of hybrid online social systems. In: Coordination, organizations, institutions, and norms in agent systems XII. Springer, Cham, pp 60–78
Noriega P, Verhagen H, Padget J, d’Inverno M (2023) Addressing the value alignment problem through online institutions. In: International workshop on coordination, organizations, institutions, norms, and ethics for governance of multi-agent systems. Springer Nature, Cham, pp 77–94
Oosthuizen K, Botha E, Robertson J, Montecchi M (2021) Artificial intelligence in retail: the AI-enabled value chain. Aust Market J 29(3):264–273
Pagallo U, Casanovas P, Madelin R (2019) The middle-out approach: assessing models of legal governance in data protection, artificial intelligence, and the Web of Data. Theory Pract Legisl 7(1):1–25
Papakonstantinou V, de Hert P (2022) The regulation of digital technologies in the EU: the law-making phenomena of “act-ification”, “GDPR mimesis” and “EU law brutality”. Technol Regul 2022:48–60. https://techreg.org/article/view/11459. Accessed 19 June 2024
Pastor-Sempere C (2022) La nueva Economía Social del Dato (ESD). CIRIEC-España, Revista Jurídica de Economía Social y Cooperativa 41:13–44. https://doi.org/10.7203/CIRIEC
Poblet M (2022) Blockchain and fractal governance: towards a decentralisation roadmap, presented at AIGEL, IDT-UAB / IIIA-CSIC, UAB, December 19th
Poblet M, Casanovas P, Rodríguez-Doncel V (2019) Linked Democracy. Foun-dations, Methodologies and Applications, Cham: Springer Nature, Law Briefs 750. Available at: https://www.springer.com/gp/book/9783030133627. Accessed 19 June 2024
Rodriguez-Doncel V (2024) Chapter 5. Web Technologies For Decentralised Identity, in this volume

Ronchini A, Guida M, Moretto A, Caniato F (2024) The role of artificial intelligence in the supply chain finance innovation process. Operat Manage Res 20:1–31
Taleb N (2021) Principia Politica. Politics & Ethics under Scaling and Uncertainty, STEM (2019). In: 2021 the title was updated: Scala Politica. Politics and Governance Under Scaling and Uncertainty
UNIDROIT (2023) Digital Assets and Private Law Principle 2(2). International Institute for the Unification of Private Law 2023, https://www.unidroit.org/work-in-progress/digital-assets-and-private-law/
Wagner J (2020) Foreword: en route to a common legal platform. In: Jacob K, Schindler D, Strathausen R (eds) Liquid law. Towards a common legal platform. Springer, Cham
Wang A (2023) Is My Toddler a Stochastic Parrot? The New Yorker, 15 November
Wang S, Wan J, Zhang D, Di L, Zhang C (2016) Towards smart factory for industry 4.0: a self-organized multi-agent system with big data based feedback and coordination. Comput Netw 10: 158–168
Zhan C, Wang Z, Zhou G, Chang F, Ma D, Jing Y, Cheng W, Ding K, Zhao D (2023) Towards new-generation human-centric smart manufacturing in Industry 5.0: a systematic review. Adv Eng Infor 57:102121

Towards Proprietary Digital Assets Under European Soft Law

Cristina Argelich-Comelles

Abstract This research provides for the legal treatment of digital assets regarding proprietary rights, possession, transfer of ownership, succession, extinction, enforcement, and applicable law, as provided for in the ELI Principles on the Use of Digital Assets as Security, the UK Law Commission Digital Assets: Final report, and the UNIDROIT Principles on Digital Assets and Private Law.

1 Proprietary Digital Assets as Smart Property

There is no European regulation on digital assets; however, the soft law was developed by the European Law Institute (ELI), the International Institute for the Unification of Private Law (UNIDROIT), and the UK Law Commission to propose legal amendments. The evolution of the legal nature of smart property from tokenisation to digital assets will be discussed, given their patrimonial value. European soft law on proprietary digital assets will be assessed, provided for in the ELI Principles on the Use of Digital Assets as Security,[1] (ELI Principles), and in the UK Law Commission Digital Assets: Final report.[2] The UNIDROIT Principles

This paper expands and updates the text of a lecture delivered at the III International Congress entitled "Present and future of crypto-assets regulation in the European Union", held at the University of Alicante (Spain) on 13, 14 and 15 December, 2023.
This work is funded within the framework of: Proyecto CIPROM/2022/26 "Presente y futuro de la regulación de los Criptoactivos en la UE [Legalcripto]". Proyecto Prometeo CIPROM/2022/26, grupos de investigación de excelencia, de la Generalitat Valenciana (P.I. Carmen Pastor).
This work has been undertaken as part of a research stay at the Sapienza University of Rome from February to April 2024.

[1]European Law Institute (2022).
[2]UK Law Commission (2023).

C. Argelich-Comelles (✉)
Law Faculty, Autonomous University of Madrid, Madrid, Spain
e-mail: cristina.argelich@uam.es

C. Pastor Sempere (ed.), *Governance and Control of Data and Digital Economy in the European Single Market*, Law, Governance and Technology Series 71,
https://doi.org/10.1007/978-3-031-74889-9_3

on Digital Assets and Private Law[3] (UNIDROIT Principles) focus on a broad concept of digital assets, considering a file hosted on a platform in Illustration 5 without patrimonial value or intellectual property rights. In contrast, non-proprietary digital assets are data regarding Private Law.

Szabo defined smart property as "software or physical devices with the desired characteristics of ownership embedded into them" and configured it as "embedding smart contracts in physical objects.[4]" Various methods for implementing smart property were described, such as Operation Necessary Data or engrained immobilising. Reinterpreting this concept, smart property is implementing blockchain technology into an object to control it remotely.

The legal fit of smart property will depend on the acquisition methods of the rights in rem: by occupation, the asset must be tokenised; in terms of smart contract transmission, the subject matter of the contract must be tokenised. Consequently, tokenisation is the pinnacle of smart property, either directly or indirectly; therefore, the functions of tokens and the tokenisation of the transfer of possession should be subsequently addressed.

Digital assets in this context are the evolution of smart property due to their digital ownership, possession, extinction, enforcement, and applicable law. Smart property nowadays refers to the tokenisation of physical assets and digital assets. In the following sections, this research focuses on the legal nature of proprietary digital assets and legal treatment concerning the transfer of ownership, digital possession, digital assets as security, digital extinction, enforcement, applicable law, and liability of online platforms for deprogramming digital assets.

The subcategory of crypto assets applies to any security or medium of exchange whose metadata is stored in an electronic registry, preferably using blockchain technology due to its traceability and immutability, and which is used to invest, pay, or create a currency to finance a project. In the European Union, crypto assets are regulated by Regulation 2023/1114 of the European Parliament and of the Council of 31 May 2023 on crypto-asset markets and amending Regulations 1093/2010 and 1095/2010. Directives 2013/36/EU and 2019/1937, known as the MiCA regulation, establish obligations for issuers and providers of crypto-asset services, and the regulation established for financial markets and instruments is in the MiFID II Directive and MiFIR Regulation. Several types of crypto assets are mentioned, such as cryptocurrencies, stablecoins and digital currencies controlled by a Central Bank or CBDCs, non-fungible tokens, and security tokens, linked to financial investments or the tokenisation of assets, either tangible or digital, examined concerning the creation of securities in digital assets.

Cryptocurrencies are payment instruments without a physical medium based on an algorithm and the electronic registry in which they are stored. Stablecoins avoid variations in exchange rates as the value of the digital asset is pegged to a reference asset, such as fiat money, an exchange-traded commodity or another cryptocurrency,

---

[3] UNIDROIT (2023).

[4] Szabo (1996, 1998).

and their operability facilitates payments and exchanges abroad. The Central Bank Digital Currencies refer to a digital currency that represents the currency controlled and issued by a Central Bank, such as the digital Euro or EURM, which is currently in the testing phase.

Non-fungible tokens or NFTs represent ownership of a unique and individualised digital asset, which is therefore not fungible and whose transfer is subject to the legal regime of specific obligations by means of a certificate to the token-holder as the owner. The token in NFTs can also be used to prove the identity of the token-holder, to tokenise the transfer of ownership with traceability of the transaction, as well as to prove ownership of virtual items in video games and online platforms, such as tokenised avatars, virtual land, or in-game digital assets. Security tokens are used for financial investments, such as stocks or bonds, as well as art and for tokenising tangible or digital assets.

Given the above, the programming in both NFTs and security tokens is as follows: the graphical representation is online, and the programming of their metadata is on-chain. Therefore, digital assets do not have a real asset linked to them, which affects their legal treatment concerning real estate tokenisation. Consequently, due to the online and on-chain existence of the digital asset, the digital asset can only exist in the material reality in the form of the storage of a copy of its graphical representation as a file and whose legal nature is data.

Regarding digital assets in real-world transactions, crypto-assets can be used remotely through crypto-wallets, which act as virtual wallets. In this respect, cryptocurrencies are accepted as a payment method on various online platforms, and their available balance can even be exchanged for payment methods. NFT wallets allow storing information about the location of NFTs on the platform where the metadata is hosted and acquiring new NFTs while ensuring interoperability by pooling collectable NFTs on various platforms.

2 Legal Nature of Proprietary Digital Assets v Data

From the patrimonial value arises the transmissibility of digital assets. Therefore, proprietary digital assets are most relevant for Private Law, considering non-patrimonial digital assets as data. Both the ELI Principles and the UK Law Commission report require the patrimonial value of digital assets, unlike the broader concept of the UNIDROIT Principles, which refer to two characteristics: control in terms of possession and transfer. Principle 2 of the UNIDROIT Principles, relating to the "electronic record" definition, establishes that it could be distributed as blockchain or centralised, and refers to information stored on an electronic medium capable of being retrieved.

As regards the concept of "digital asset", Principle 2 indicates that it is a controllable electronic record. Control is relevant in private law regarding possession and access to digital assets involving the owner, the heirs, and third parties with the authorisation of the token holder. Illustration 5 in the UNIDROIT Principles considers that a file stored on a platform accessed with private keys could be a digital asset but recognises that this type of file or document is irrelevant regarding property transfers. Concerning digital assets, a file containing a creation, for example, could become a proprietary digital asset as it has patrimonial value in intellectual property rights. Otherwise, a legal problem would arise in inheritance matters.

The "Proposed 2022 Amendments to the US Uniform Commercial Code: Digital Assets" defines a "controllable electronic record" as any controllable record in electronic form. It specifies that a person has this control when they have the right to use the electronic record. First, it specifies the power to benefit from the electronic record regarding its use. Second, it refers to the power of exclusion, considering digital assets as a rivalrous resource, in contrast with data. Third, it contains the power to transfer the digital asset control to another person, identifying the owner and the token holder concerning the power of disposal. Accordingly, controllable electronic records include cryptocurrencies, NFTs, digital assets, and security tokens linked to a digital or tangible asset.

The ELI Principles state that a digital asset is a record or representation of value, considering several requirements, irrespective of the type of electronic record used. First, it is stored, accessed, and managed exclusively electronically. Second, regardless of their legal nature, digital assets can be subject to a right of control, enjoyment, or use. Lastly, it can be transferred, including contracts and succession on proprietary digital assets.

Regarding the succession of proprietary digital assets, to guarantee control and access to the heirs, the public keys of the blockchain, the user's account and the private keys should be provided in the will. Data cannot be inherited due to its legal nature and being considered a non-rivalrous resource. Nonetheless, the will can contain instructions for the heirs as a testamentary term.[5] The UK Law Commission's report confirms the legal nature of digital assets as personal property. The final recommendations of this report refer to proprietary digital assets and do not consider the general term of the digital asset provided for in the UNIDROIT Principles, which it describes as "extremely broad" regarding digital files.

The tangible or intangible nature of proprietary digital assets is crucial regarding cryptocurrencies and NFTs. Therefore, a token containing metadata individualises a digital asset as a good. Cryptocurrencies are properly a payment instrument.[6] So, the legal nature of currencies as movable and fungible assets cannot be applied to cryptocurrencies. Central Bank Digital Coins, or CBDCs, controlled by a Central Bank, are considered a currency, although they are based on an electronic registry, such as the EURM in the EU. Currencies are movable and fungible goods, so any obligation is a sale. Also, regarding CBDCs, the price would be paid in any currency. By contrast, any obligation on a cryptocurrency is a swap.

As regards the legal treatment of proprietary digital assets, the UK Law Commission report clarifies several recommendations. It proposes the creation of a third

[5]McCarthy (2015), pp. 383–412.

[6]Schuller (2022), pp. 737–769.

category of goods, contrasting things in possession and things in action. Digital assets can have property rights constrained by two limits: the law in force and the avoidance of strict limits in their regulation, such as gas emission permits or quotas. Secondly, it indicates the need to regulate digital assets applicable to crypto-tokens, blockchain, carbon credits, in-game digital assets, and digital files. In the latter case, digital assets with intellectual property rights will be considered proprietary digital assets.

3 Legal Treatment of Proprietary Digital Assets

The "Digital Assets as Personal Property: Short Consultation on Draft Clauses" of the UK Law Commission proposes a "Property (Digital Assets etc) Act 2024". In this draft, the object of personal property rights will be an asset, including those whose legal nature is digital or in an electronic record, even if it is neither a thing in possession nor a thing in action, considering the third category referred to in the final report regarding England and Wales. Based on the first hard law proposal on proprietary digital assets and soft law, the following sections will examine the transfer of ownership, digital possession, digital assets as security, digital extinction, enforcement, applicable law, and liability of online platforms.

3.1 Transfer of Ownership and Inheritance on Proprietary Digital Assets

The occupation of a digital asset will not be possible because blockchain technology, or any electronic registry, can only be applied to contracts and goods. When a digital asset is tokenised, it cannot be occupied because the owner can control its possession remotely. The transfer of ownership in declaratory systems, without mandatory registration, occurs using a smart contract, self-executed on the platform where digital assets metadata are hosted. Control and access in declaratory systems are guaranteed with the token, and its verification is done by oracles or trusted third parties.

Szabo establishes that smart property will need a Public Registry as a title database with a decentralised or distributed character. This makes it secure, under the external control of its inalterability, so neither written records are vulnerable to loss or falsification, nor do centralised electronic records suffer from vulnerability to cyberattacks. Szabo also proposed the creation of a replicated database, in which the ownership of movable and immovable assets would be controlled, and its inalterability would be ensured in any event. Blockchain technology and its application to Public Registries makes this inalterability possible, as it is a decentralised and secure registry.

A token may exist as a credit right that obliges the debtor, as it represents the right of an investor to share in the profits on the exploitation of a right in rem. Therefore, a distinction must be made between the right to a token, such as in cryptocurrencies, and the rights certified by a token, such as property rights, as this differentiates two legal relationships: that of the token owner vis-à-vis third parties and that of the token owner and the token issuer, this latter case referred to cryptocurrencies. The issuer of the asset token becomes a debtor to the token owner for the obligations certified in an online service.

The critical issues for regulating tokens, as they are a right in rem and a credit right, under their material scope of application, are as follows: loss of control over the token; possible alteration of the token by a hacker; protection against third parties, if it is a fundamental right; the type of possession of the token, which must be mediated; and, finally, the impossibility of transferring the token without the intervention of miners or third parties. The solution calls for regulation that provides the tokenised object with the same guarantees in legal transactions as non-tokenized objects. Provisions should be made for each type of contract, especially where they are effective.

Regarding constitutive systems and Directive 2018/843 of the European Parliament and of the Council of 30 May 2018, amending Directive 2015/849 on the prevention of the use of the financial system for money laundering or terrorist financing and amending Directives 2009/138/EC and 2013/36/EU, Germany and Austria established Registries of Digital Asset Securities. In Germany, the Gesetz zur Einführung von elektronischen Wertpapieren requires a written form for cryptocurrencies, allowing the electronic issuance of bearer bonds. In Austria, the Finanzmarkt-Geldwäschegesetz incorporates the regulation of cryptocurrencies as an electronic security, which involves a public registry and all types of transfers. Since November 1, 2023, the UK has been creating a Digital Asset Registry, considering its detailed regulation proposed in a report.[7] Therefore, it could be beneficial to include a section referring to digital assets within the Spanish Public Registry of Movable Property.

The last will and testament on a blockchain or any electronic registry and the automation of succession are legal facts that self-execute the programming of a will and the inheritance of proprietary digital assets. In this regard, intestate succession is inadequate for controlling and accessing digital assets. To ensure control and access to digital assets, the public keys of the blockchain, the private account, and the access keys must be expressly mentioned in the will.

In the field of proprietary digital assets, as in non-proprietary digital assets or data, it is unfeasible to classify the testamentary clause on access to digital assets as a legacy since the keys and private accounts are a means of accessing and controlling them. As regards the partition of the inheritance, blockchain technology allows the automatic calculation of the individual inheritance portion corresponding to each

[7]Digital Preservation Coalition (2023) New Digital Asset Registers Project from The National Archives (UK) and the DPC https://www.dpconline.org/news/new-digital-asset-registers-project.

heir or legatee, guaranteeing the immutability of the will regarding those elements of objective assessment, for example, the existence of an heir.

Concerning subjective elements, these difficulties regarding self-execution can only be overcome through automated decision-making through algorithms, such as algorithmic decision-making (ADM) and algorithms based on Artificial Intelligence. In this sense, a report is being developed for the European Commission on the adaptation of the EU national regulations of B2B and B2C contracts, and the ELI, in the framework of the Project on Guiding Principles and Model Rules on Algorithmic Contracts, has published a report on its application to consumer contracts.

Therefore, to control the liability of the heir or executor in the partition of the inheritance, it will be necessary to challenge the will in court using an action for petition of inheritance, as it is a liability whose control is not programmable. Finally, the testamentary clause known as the "digital will" serves to order the data contained in the online platforms, providing for the public key of the platform, as well as the private account and the private access keys.

3.2 Digital Possession of Proprietary Digital Assets

The ELI Principles provide a legal treatment for security tokens in digital assets, including third-party effectiveness, enforcement, and extinction. Out-of-court enforcement is the main advantage of smart contracts and digital assets regarding breach of contract, given the remote control of possession and the self-execution of remedies. The ELI Principles define a "digital asset" as any record or representation of value with the following criteria: it is stored, displayed, and managed electronically on a platform or database; it can be controlled, considering its administration and rights in rem; and it can be transferred, including contracts and succession. For digital assets definition, this soft law instrument expressly mentions that the platform design and the kind of electronic record are irrelevant, although the distributed ledger technology prevents its manipulation.

The UK Law Commission's report provides for a legal treatment on digital assets possession through a third category of goods regarding personal property rights, in contrast to community property. Digital assets should be regulated differently from things in possession and things in action, considering several characteristics: they must be composed of electronically represented data; they must exist independently of their owner or legal system; and they must be rivalrous or susceptible to being used or consumed, excluding third parties. By contrast, data are non-rivalrous and replicable resources. The power of exclusion in proprietary digital assets refers to control and transfers. Regarding control, factual control or remote control of possession and legal control or the legal consequences of such possession are considered.

The report advises that powers will differ depending on the asset category, considering crypto assets and NFTs. To this end, the report refers to creating an expert group of technicians regarding digital assets categories. In proprietary digital assets, it is possible to digitise the exercise of property powers, such as remote control of ownership and possession, and to prevent adverse possession. Transfers refer to extinction or creation analysis because the blockchain is updated in any transfer or persistent input analysis, considering that the same digital asset persists in case of transfer. In this sense, off-chain crypto tokens will be transferable through control. This report also refers to protecting crypto tokens for the good faith purchaser.

The electronic registries apply to contracts and property through the tokenisation of property and digital assets, but they do not apply to either occupation or usucapion of proprietary digital assets. The tokenised digital asset cannot be vacant or acquired initially by occupation, and a non-tokenised digital asset that is vacant can only be tokenised after its original acquisition. In the case of the occupation of a vacant digital asset, it only meets one of the two objective requirements for occupation, that it is appropriable, but not the requirement of being ownerless. Digital assets are not usucaptible given that it is impossible to acquire a tokenised good because tokenisation enables remote control by the holder. This prevents compliance with the requirements for usucapion, relating to public, peaceful and uninterrupted possession as an owner for the period required according to the nature of the asset. As far as the donation is concerned, if electronic registers can be applied to contracts but not to ways of acquiring ownership, this is another reason to support the contractual legal nature of the donation so that digital assets can be donated.

Both the access and control of digital assets are required, so the transfer of ownership and the inheritance should provide the public keys of the blockchain, the private account and the private keys to constitute any right in rem. Therefore, digital assets may be leased or loaned. The assignment of a digital asset in a lease is a manifestation of the power of disposal regarding property rights reserved to the owner, and such assignment of use does not correspond to a licence of use of a digital service, for example, a subscription to an online content platform. In short, it is impossible to question the ownership of a digital asset due to limited rights in rem. Finally, regarding the right in rem of usufruct on a digital asset, it is possible to constitute it, and the usufructuary can exercise acts of administration, such as the collection of incomes in the case of cryptocurrencies.

3.3 *Digital Assets as Security and Digital Assets Registry*

Various legal proposals are provided for digital assets as security in the ELI Principles. The use of digital assets as a security has as a subjective scope a private person, regardless of whether the owner or token holder in this field is a natural or a legal person, excluding public bodies. The ELI Principles do not exclude, as expressly indicated, their possible regulation of digital assets as security in other legal systems outside the EU. Regarding the material scope, the ELI Principles exclude security rights in digital assets that do not arise from an agreement between the parties, expressly those whose origin is mandatory.

By Principles 3 and 4, the contract terms must contain legal provisions and effectiveness regarding third parties concerning digital assets security, considering the security provider and the creditor. Although a proposal for the regulation on the inheritance of digital assets is currently under consideration, it would have been helpful to mention some guidance on access to digital assets after death and limits on their management by the platform provider. In this regard, legal systems with a digital assets registry publicising security rights in intangible assets will duly comply with third-party effectiveness.

On the other hand, in jurisdictions that do not have a digital assets registry, third-party effectiveness will be guaranteed when the creditor has the digital asset control to prevent the platform provider from deprogramming. Therefore, in these jurisdictions, the acceptance of the inheritance will avoid deprogramming of the digital asset. As for enforcing digital assets security for breach of contract, this will be implemented as contained in the contract and will be extinct for contract fulfilment.[8] These Principles require that the debtor act in good faith, and the breach of contract includes insolvency by the applicable bankruptcy or insolvency rules and considering the relevant law.[9]

3.4 Digital Extinction of Digital Assets

Digital assets can only be lost by deprogramming. Such digital asset deprogramming on the platform, where the metadata are stored, will consist of the platform provider obligations under Arts. 4 and 5 P2BR (2019), in the case of infringement of third-party rights and concerning the liability exemptions of Arts. 4-6 DSA, or concerning its hacking. In this area, reference should be made to the "Metabirkins" case of plagiarism in NFTs of the Hermès Birkin bag.

In the case of Hermès Int'l v Rothschild, in the judgment handed down by the New York Federal Court on 9 February 2023, the court held that these NFTs can only be sold by Hermès. This firm won the court proceedings, and the Metabirkins firm was ordered to pay $130,000 in damages. On the other hand, in the case of a hack, the platform provider should be able to reprogram the digital asset with a hard fork, as the crypto-panic cases illustrate. The hack causes a bug in the blockchain that makes it impossible to self-execute it, so the only remedy is to reprogram from the hash before this bug so that the blockchain executes the longer chain.

The digital loss of the digital asset and reprogramming directly impact contract termination, security in a digital asset, and extinction, which aligns with the ELI Principles. The existence of proprietary digital assets requires a blockchain in which their metadata are stored, is conditional on not being deprogrammed, and is not

[8]Savelyev (2018), pp. 863–869.

[9]Wendehorst (2023), pp. 101–127. Krysa (2023), pp. 157–208.

affected by the transfer of digital assets between platforms, including business succession or interoperability.

International interoperability of digital assets requires a harmonised GUI design on online platforms to guarantee digital asset control to the owner. Similarly, and in line with the ELI Principles, the security in a digital asset can only be extinguished by contract fulfilment. In the case of deprogramming, digital assets are removed from the platform. Given the above, in case of loss of the private keys, the digital asset remains because it will be possible to recover it or, after the succession, to provide the heirs with access to the deceased's private account and its private keys if not expressly stated in the will.

3.5 Enforcement of Digital Assets

Two soft law proposals are currently being developed regarding the enforcement of digital assets: by UNIDROIT, in the project "Best Practices for Effective Enforcement", whose latest results can be found in open access in the Report Study LXXVIB - W.G.6 - Doc. 7, of May 2023; and by ELI, in the project "Access to digital assets", whose results are not public.

The UNIDROIT Report Study establishes various recommendations for the legal treatment of the enforcement of digital assets. The first recommendation is harmonising enforcement with the legal nature of digital assets, analogous to other assets. The second recommendation addresses the legal treatment of contracts and rights in rem concerning enforcing digital assets. The third recommendation addresses the duty of information about digital assets that may be relevant for enforcement. The fourth recommendation concerns this duty of information to third parties. The fifth recommendation focuses on establishing measures for accessing information on digital assets regarding their identification. The sixth recommendation imposes a duty of cooperation on the debtor to transfer digital assets in the event of a breach of contract.

3.6 Applicable Law to Digital Assets

Considering applicable law to digital assets, patrimonial value is the key concept, and the ELI Principles state some considerations in this regard. The ELI Principles advise the necessary observance of the law in force, specifying that the applicable law will be that of the State where the security provider is domiciled at the time of contract conclusion, except in two cases: that the digital asset is linked to a specific jurisdiction; or that the security is linked to a tangible asset that determines the applicable law.

In matters of succession, the EU Regulation 650/2012 provides that the applicable law to the succession shall be the law of the State of the habitual residence of the deceased and provides for the possibility for the testator to determine in the will the applicable law to the succession. The creation of a valid security depends on the ability of its provider to enforce the security in terms of control and access. It cannot be linked to other rights in digital assets. Finally, the contract may provide that the digital asset is subject to fluctuations.

European law on online platforms applies where the place of conclusion of the contract is in the EU, and, in a future strict liability regime for online platforms, the most consistent solution as to the applicable law would be the law of the domicile of the security provider. On the other hand, the 2016 UNCITRAL Model Rules on Secured Transactions determine that the applicable law refers to the debtor's habitual residence.[10] Finally, Principle 5 of the UNIDROIT Principles allows for determining the applicable law. Private international law issues will be examined jointly by UNIDROIT and the Hague Conference on Private International Law in the framework of the HCCH-UNIDROIT Joint Project on Law Applicable to Cross-Border Holdings and Transfers.

Considering soft law instruments on the applicable law to digital assets, where a national law recognises proprietary digital assets, this same rule should apply to the relevant law. The applicable law to digital assets, which usually refers to the place where the contract was concluded in European rules on online platforms or to the debtor's domicile in other cases, does not correspond to the applicable law for rights in rem, which refers to the place where the asset is located.

Of the doctrinal solutions proposed, the most appropriate will be the following:[11] for constitutive systems, it should be the *lex libri siti* regarding the digital assets registry; for declaratory systems, the best option is an elective forum or elective situs, either at the place where the contract was concluded or, in the case of a strict liability regime, at the domicile of the platform service provider. Therefore, of the alternatives proposed, the domicile of the professional user and the Primary Residence of the Coder are not considered options, given that the European regulations on online platforms aim to avoid the lack of consumer protection if the professional user is domiciled outside the Union.

3.7 Digital Identity and Liability of Online Platforms for Deprogramming of Proprietary Digital Assets

The eIDAS2 Regulation approved on 29 February 2024, and the so-called Regulation of the European Parliament and of the Council amending Regulation 910/2014 regarding establishing a framework for a European Digital Identity, substitutes the current digital signature to the digital identity. As far as online platforms are concerned, digital identity will facilitate the improvement of authentication security

[10] Haentjens and Lehmann (2023), pp. 456–478.

[11] Wendehorst (2023), pp. 101–127.

on online platforms where digital assets are hosted. Moreover, digital identity facilitates linking this digital identity to the graphical representation of the user and thus binds the corresponding liability regime to it. The main legal challenge in this regard lies in the legal treatment of the automatic processing of personal data, given the liability regime for such unlawful data processing, as advised by the Court of Justice of the European Union in the framework of the cooperation obligations between authorities established in the DSA.

The EU Regulation on platform-to-business relations was adopted in the P2B Regulation. Regarding algorithms and consumer protection, online intermediary services providers and search engine providers shall not be required to disclose algorithms that may mislead consumers or cause them harm by manipulating results, according to Art. 5.6. Regarding preventing algorithmic discrimination in consumer contracts, the DSA is based on three specific objectives in Art. 1: the adequate protection of consumers and their fundamental rights on online platforms; the establishment of transparency and accountability of online platforms; and the promotion of innovation, growth, and competitiveness in the European single market. The P2B Regulation focuses on transparency and private remedies in B2B relationships. To this end, the EU Observatory on the Online Platform Economy has been set up to examine the latest trends regarding the EU Recommendation 2018/334 of 1 March 2018 on measures to effectively tackle illegal content online, also regulated in Art. 8 DSA.

3.8 The Digital Markets Act (2022)

The DMA aims to ensure that online gatekeepers act fairly in their activity, with the objective gatekeeper criteria of Arts. 1 and 3: having a solid economic position, a significant impact on the internal market, being active in several EU States, having a robust intermediary position by linking many users to many companies, and having a consolidated position in the market. The DMA ensures fairness of terms and conditions on online platforms by establishing the unfair practices of gatekeepers in Art. 5. The DMA also improves consumer offers and enables platforms to deal with new services. In case of breach of rules set out in Art. 25, Art. 26 provides for fines of up to 10% of the company's overall annual turnover, fines of up to 5% of the average daily turnover, as well as other remedies following an investigation of the platform. Finally, the legal treatment of algorithmic transparency in the DMA is its examination and liability, the role of algorithms in the digital economy and society, data governance, and the codes of conduct concerning corporate compliance and reputation mechanisms.

Finally, the report prepared for the European Parliament, entitled 'Liability of online platforms' and published on 5 February 2021, examines the leading alternatives for regulating the liability of online platforms. The report discusses issues related to maintaining state-of-the-art regulations, raising awareness of their use, promoting self-regulation, establishing co-regulatory instruments, adopting legal rules on platform liability, and modifying the liability of online platforms through exemptions and a harmonised liability regime.

The Digital Services Act 2022 (DSA) confirms the principle of limited liability of online platforms based on the asymmetric due diligence obligations of Chapter III. This due diligence is based on transparency and platform procedures, such as notification and complaint handling, ADR and ODR, reputation mechanisms and even the incorporation of Corporate Compliance. With this approach, the DSA follows the recent trend of implementing procedures for platform regulation via reputation mechanisms and P2B Regulation. In this regard, it is worth mentioning that the ELI Model Rules on Online Platforms highlight key liability issues for online platforms, such as lack of transparency, platform influence on the provider, and lack of due diligence. Finally, Art. 33 DSA establishes a new sector-specific regulation for massive online platforms for systemically essential platforms. This approach builds on financial services regulation with various compliance obligations. In the future, more reporting and auditing obligations may be required to ensure a secure, reliable, and transparent online environment, as required by the DSA.

Regarding contractual civil liability under the DSA, the DMA and the P2B Regulation (P2BR), the professional user is liable in case of breach of contract. The platform service provider will be liable if it has breached due diligence and anti-circumvention duties under the DSA and the DMA, respectively,[12] and in relation to the breach of the suspension and end-of-service duties under Art. 4 P2BR, as in the "Metabirkins" case. This liability of online platforms is insufficient in the following cases: for deprogramming of a digital asset, in the case of infringement of third-party rights; for algorithmic collusion, as malpractice concerning free competition provided for in the P2BR and the DMA; and for algorithmic discrimination, which has no specific legal treatment. Therefore, to guarantee the liability of the professional user, and taking into account that the P2BR, the DSA and the DMA will be amended, it would be advisable to reformulate this liability in terms of strict liability or semi-strict liability, as proposed in the report for the European Parliament Online Platform Liability and in line with the European academics.[13]

4 Concluding Remarks

The digital age provides an opportunity to reinvent property law as a hot topic due to the application of electronic records to property law, smart property, and digital assets. IT law relating to digital assets facilitates their transfer of ownership and

[12] Wielsch (2019), pp. 197–220. Tereszkiewicz (2018), pp. 903–920. Rodríguez de las Heras Ballell (2014), pp. 685–702. Herrero Suárez (2023), pp. 227–239.

[13] Büyüksagis (2022), pp. 64–86. Caufmann and Goanta (2021), pp. 1–17. Frosio (2017), pp. 19–46.

inheritance, and legal remedies for breach of contract need to be adapted from soft law in this area. All these issues make legal research on digital assets as crucial as research on the tokenisation of tangible assets.

References

Büyüksagis E (2022) Extension of strict liability to E-Retailers. J Eur Tort Law 13(1):64–86

Caufmann C, Goanta C (2021) A new order: the digital services act and consumer protection. Eur J Risk Regul 1(1):1–17

Digital Preservation Coalition (2023) New Digital Asset Registers Project from The National Archives (UK) and the DPC https://www.dpconline.org/news/new-digital-asset-registers-project

European Law Institute (2022) The ELI Principles on Using Digital Assets as Security. https://www.europeanlawinstitute.eu/fileadmin/user_upload/p_eli/Publications/ELI_Principles_on_the_Use_of_Digital_Assets_as_Security.pdf

Frosio G (2017) Reforming intermediary liability in the platform economy: a European digital single market strategy. Northwestern Univ Law Rev 112:19–46

Haentjens M, Lehmann M (2023) The law governing secured transactions in digital assets. In: Bonomi A, Lehmann M, Lalani S (eds) Blockchain and private international law. Brill, Leiden, pp 456–478

Herrero Suárez C (2023) Merger control in digital markets: don't trust the trusts. In: Gómez Asensio C, Ruiz Peris JI, Estevan de Quesada C (eds) Cooperación y mercados digitales. Atelier, Barcelona, pp 227–239

Krysa F (2023) Taxonomy and characterisation of crypto assets in private international law. In: Bonomi A, Lehmann M, Lalani S (eds) Blockchain and private international law. Brill, Leiden, pp 157–208

McCarthy L (2015) Digital assets and intestacy. BUJ Sci Technol Law J 21(384):383–412

Rodríguez de las Heras Ballell T (2014) Refusal to deal, abuse of right and competition law in electronic markets and digital communities. Eur Rev Priv Law 22(5):685–702

Savelyev A (2018) Some risks of tokenisation and blockchainizaition of private law. Comput Law Secur Rev 34:863–869

Schuller RR (2022) Criptoactivos. Categorización jurídica de los criptoactivos e introducción a la tecnología DLT/Blockchain. Cuadernos de Derecho Transnacional 14(2):737–769

Szabo N (1996) Smart contracts: building blocks for digital markets, Extropy: J Transhumanist Thought, 16, http://www.fon.hum.uva.nl/rob/Courses/InformationInSpeech/CDROM/Literature/LOTwinterschool2006/szabo.best.vwh.net/smart_contracts_2.html

Szabo N (1998) Secure property titles with owner authority. Satoshi Nakamoto Institute. https://nakamotoinstitute.org/secure-property-titles/

Tereszkiewicz P (2018) Digital platforms: regulation and liability in the EU law. Eur Rev Priv Law 26(6):903–920

UK Law Commission (2023) Digital assets: Final Report. https://s3-eu-west-2.amazonaws.com/lawcom-prod-storage-11jsxou24uy7q/uploads/2023/06/Final-digital-assets-report-FOR-WEBSITE-2.pdf

UNIDROIT (2023) UNIDROIT principles on digital assets and private law. https://www.unidroit.org/wp-content/uploads/2023/01/Draft-Principles-and-Commentary-Public-Consultation.pdf

Wendehorst C (2023) Proprietary rights in digital assets and the conflict of laws. In: Bonomi A, Lehmann M, Lalani S (eds) Blockchain and private international law. Brill, Leiden, pp 101–127

Wielsch D (2019) Private law regulation of digital intermediaries. Eur Rev Priv Law 27(2):197–220

Crypto Assets and Financial Data Space Regulation in the EU's Hybrid System of Hard and Soft Law

Carmen Pastor Sempere

Abstract The new data economy needs diverse financial data from many data holders, far removed from the data a traditional bank would hold. This paper outlines the new vision for the common European Financial Data Space, where multiple interconnected data ecosystems, like the internet, are designed to empower individuals by placing them at the centre. This seeks to keep the financial sector of the European Union in tune with the digital transformation while ensuring, at the same time, the security and confidence of consumers. For these reasons, the EU seeks open finance and a legal framework that underpins a new regulatory approach based on coregulation, comprising a hybrid system of hard law and soft law for the exchange of financial data. This regulatory proposal is FiDA [proposal for a Financial Data Access regulation]. The paper also examines the proposed legal regime and its coordination with the current regulation of new crypto assets and their financial data. It examines the basis for and explores the limitations of the latest legal framework for regulating access to financial data. The current regulation that will be referred to is the existing regulation on crypto-assets (Markets in Crypto-assets-MiCA, access to payment data (such as Open banking, Payment Services Directive, PSD2), and the eIDAS 2, as well as the proposal for the modernisation of the existing EU Payment Services Directive (Open Finance, PSD3 and FiDA).

This paper expands and updates the text of a lecture delivered at the III International Congress entitled "Present and future of crypto-assets regulation in the European Union", held at the University of Alicante (Spain) on 13, 14 and 15 December 2023.This work is funded within the framework of: Proyecto CIPROM/2022/26 "Presente y futuro de la regulación de los Criptoactivos en la UE [Legalcripto]". Proyecto Prometeo CIPROM/2022/26, grupos de investigación de excelencia, de la Generalitat Valenciana (P.I. Carmen Pastor).

C. Pastor Sempere (✉)
Faculty of Law, University of Alicante, San Vicente del Raspeig, Alicante, Spain
e-mail: carmen.pastor@ua.es

C. Pastor Sempere (ed.), *Governance and Control of Data and Digital Economy in the European Single Market*, Law, Governance and Technology Series 71,
https://doi.org/10.1007/978-3-031-74889-9_4

1 Introduction

Europe seeks to achieve a data market that ensures global competitiveness and data sovereignty for Europeans; the importance of this is recognised in the *European Data Strategy*,[1] which states that in recent years, digital technologies have transformed the economy and society, affecting all sectors of activity and the daily lives of all Europeans. With data at the heart of this transformation and the profound changes in the market, data has become an essential resource for economic growth, competitiveness, innovation, job creation and social progress.[2]

The resurgence of artificial neural networks, powered by new algorithms, the ever-increasing computing power, and the availability of vast data repositories have significantly increased the potential of artificial intelligence (AI). This is what should drive the new *European sustainable digital economy*, working for the benefit of people.[3] In this vein, the European Commission's White Paper on Artificial Intelligence recalled that Europe's current and future sustainable economic growth and social well-being increasingly rely on the value created by data.[4]

The finance sector is rich in value-generating data. Mastering AI technologies now depends on the quantity and quality of accessible financial data. However, providing financial data also has high barriers, such as the lack of access to high-quality private data. In particular, two high-risk use cases for the financial sector, namely AI systems used to evaluate a person's creditworthiness and risk assessment and pricing for life and health insurance, were regulated on July 12, 2024, EU Regulation No. 1689/2024. This regulation lays down harmonised rules on Artificial Intelligence (AI Act), and it was finally published in the EU Official Journal and entered into force on August 1, 2024. This milestone represents the culmination of three years of legislative debate since the EU Commission's first proposal for a comprehensive EU regulation on AI in April 2021.[5] At the same time, the European

[1] COMMUNICATION FROM THE COMMISSION TO THE EUROPEAN PARLIAMENT, THE COUNCIL, THE EUROPEAN ECONOMIC AND SOCIAL COMMITTEE AND THE COMMITTEE OF THE REGIONS A *European strategy for data.* Brussels, 19.2.2020. COM (2020) 66 final.

[2] Pastor (2020).

[3] Pastor (2020).

[4] *White Paper on Artificial Intelligence - A European approach to excellence and trust Brussels*,19.2.2020 COM (2020) 65 final.

[5] In general, the development and use of AI in the EU will be regulated by the AI Act, the world's first comprehensive AI law. The AI Act, voted by the European Parliament on 13 March 2024 and expected to enter into force in July, aims to guarantee the safety and fundamental rights of people and businesses while strengthening AI uptake, investment and innovation across the EU. To further support these objectives, the Commission adopted an AI innovation package on 24 January 2024. It contains a series of measures to support European startups and SMEs in the development of trustworthy AI that respects EU values and rules. This follows the political agreement reached in December 2023 on the AI Act. The documents linked below are the latest version of the AI Act: European Parliament 'Corrigendum' of 16th April 2024, which corrected errors in the language and numbering present in earlier drafts. See. https://artificialintelligenceact.eu/the-act/, Accessed

Commission is planning to gather input from financial services stakeholders to get an overview of how and for which purposes AI applications are used in the financial sector.[6]

However, AI comes with certain risks in this area, discussed in this paper, some relate to respecting data protection regulations. Others concern the AI system itself. The trustworthiness of an AI system can be difficult to determine if the quality of data is not sufficiently clear. A sensitive issue related to this is algorithmic bias, which can lead to discrimination. An AI model can reproduce or amplify biases and discriminatory patterns mirrored in the data used to train the model. This is also why 'explainability' is a pivotal challenge for AI systems—the ability to explain why a certain decision was taken and which parameters were used. For example, why was a person (not) granted a loan?[7]

Geopolitical risks should not be underestimated, and many stakeholders are interested in participating in the exchange of financial data beyond payment accounts. Cross-border data flows also complicate regulatory enforcement and make it difficult for authorities to act. In addition, the concentration of data infrastructures in the private sector raises concerns about their resilience in an attack.

Given these challenges, the EU is promoting the development of the so-called Common European Data Spaces—hereafter referred to as Data Spaces—in various sectors[8]—as reliable data exchange systems through four main axes: first, facilitate the re-use of certain public sector data that cannot be available as open data—for

19 July 2024. The AI Act defines an AI system as "a machine-based system designed to operate with varying levels of autonomy, that may exhibit adaptiveness after deployment and that, for explicit or implicit objectives, infers, from the input it receives, how to generate outputs such as predictions, content, recommendations, or decisions that can influence physical or virtual environments". Recital 11 further sets out the reasons for this definition, notably setting out that it is based on key characteristics that distinguish it from simpler traditional software systems of programming approaches.

[6]The consultation was published on 18.06.2024 by Directorate-General for Financial Stability, Financial Services and Capital Markets Union (https://finance.ec.europa.eu/regulation-and-supervision/consultations-0/targeted-consultation-artificial-intelligence-financial-sector_en) The targeted consultation will gather input from all financial services stakeholders including companies and consumer associations. Views are particularly welcome from financial firms that provide or deploy/use AI systems. This consultation is designed for respondents developing or planning to develop or use AI applications in financial services. For the purpose of this targeted consultation, the concept of AI corresponds to the definition of an AI system established in the AI Act, which covers "any machine-based system designed to operate with varying levels of autonomy and that may exhibit adaptiveness after deployment and that, for explicit or implicit objectives, infers, from the input it receives, how to generate outputs such as predictions, content, recommendations, or decisions that can influence physical or virtual environments". The invited to reply by 13 September 2024 at the latest to the online questionnaire available on the following webpage: https://finance.ec.europa.eu/regulation-and-supervision/consultations-0/targetedconsultation-artificial-intelligence-financial-sector_en Accessed 19 Jun 2024.

[7]Benjamin (2024).

[8]Including health, agriculture, manufacturing, energy, mobility, financial, and public administration, see: https://digital-strategy.ec.europa.eu/en/policies/data-spaces.

example, re-using health data could advance research to find cures for rare or chronic diseases—; second, ensure the functioning of data intermediaries as trusted organisers of data exchange or sharing within common European data spaces; third, make it easier for citizens and businesses to make their data available for the benefit of society;[9] and, fourth, facilitate data exchange, particularly to enable data use across sectors and borders and to find the right data for the right purpose.

Most data consumers and businesses produce are stored and processed in infrastructures held by US-dominated Big tech. By comparison, Europe is a weak player in the data-holding arena, and fewer European players hold data in a fragmented manner. Data is a raw material that must be stored and processed to extract its value. It requires technological processing, in which Europe wants to participate, harnessing the resources generated by data of the future that comes from the financial industry (especially that arising from the development of tokenisation), businesses, and the public sector. These data will be stored in federated computing devices such as European data spaces that act as systems that will involve the following functions: an infrastructure layer for the exchange of data between two or more parties (sometimes also including the exchange of algorithms, data services, etc.); ensure that data is stored and processed in infrastructures; and, assuring data exchange is reliable and secure, guaranteeing data sovereignty (through the use of data and control mechanisms). Such a data space consists of all the necessary data and infrastructure, and it supports capabilities such as data discoverability, identity management, etc., enabling the commercial exchange of closed (and confidential) data.[10]

Existing barriers in the exchange of financial data prevent businesses, particularly small and medium-sized enterprises (SMEs), from benefiting from better, more convenient, and automated financial services. The absence of personalised financial products limits the possibility of offering interested customers more choices of financial products and services. Without an efficient way of capturing and valuing this data, it will likely go unused or exploited to our disadvantage. These customers would benefit from data-driven tools that can help them make informed decisions, compare offers in a user-friendly way, and switch to more advantageous products that match their preferences based on their data. Other benefits include, for example, the duty to identify and evaluate projects diligently, verifying that they comply with legal requirements. From a business point of view, standardised (data) information and more simplified business and commercial practices represent an attractive and

[9]The EU data portal offers access to almost 90,000 datasets in the economy and finance category alone, and organisations can leverage valuable open data to drive innovation, foster entrepreneurship, and ultimately help drive EU economic growth. As stated in entries of 20 May 2024, https://data.europa.eu/en/news-events/news/nurturing-economy-all-role-smes-and-open-data Accessed 16 Jun 2024.

[10]The main implementations of this infrastructure are Gaia-X (-Gaia-X: A Federated Secure Data Infrastructure- Home https://gaia-x.eu/) and Association International Data Spaces (-IDSA,- Home https://internationaldataspaces.org) Accessed 16 Jun 2024.

innovative approach for comparing international investment opportunities, not only for the *alternative* investor but also for the *traditional* investor.[11]

Other beneficial aspects are directly linked to European policies for a sustainable and digital Europe,[12] including implementing the *European Green Deal*,[13] the *Circular Economy Action Plan, the Data Strategy*, and the *European Social Pillar*. Europe aims to drive growth, prosperity, and stability for its citizens and businesses through a new *Digital Finance Strategy*. The Commission has set out guidelines on how Europe can support the digital transformation of finance in the coming years, especially focusing on promoting data-driven finance. In this regard, the Commission's Strategy for financing the transition to a sustainable economy placed sustainable finance at the heart of the financial system as a key means to achieve the green transition of the EU economy,[14] forming part of the Green Deal, of which the *proposal for a Financial Data Access regulation* (hereafter referred to as 'FiDA') is also an expression.

The complexity of Financial Data Space is not only the technological infrastructure; perhaps it lies in the sector itself and the European legal framework, which needs to adapt to the technological reality, as we shall see with 'FiDA'. For FiDA, the holders of the data, the financial industry, which has control over these data, do not share them among the financial sector itself, remaining in what we call financial information silos, which we have discussed in previous works.[15] Moreover, the EU lacks significant financial services with market power in cloud computing, mobile payments or digital identification. It is, therefore, essential that data is shared and that access to the large volumes of financial data and the information that the market can extract from it (and transaction metadata) is not prevented or monopolised solely by non-European players, such as VISA or Mastercard. FiDA, in this respect, we can anticipate, provides novel solutions that ensure consistency between access to financial data and open banking where additional measures are needed, including permission panels, legal obligations to grant direct access to customer data, and the requirement for data holders to establish interfaces.

However, providing data for the *personalised provision of financial products and services - sustainable* - particularly in the provision of credit- also has high

[11]Pastor (2017b).

[12]Comisión Europea, https://commission.europa.eu/strategy-and-policy/priorities-2019-2024/europe-fit-digital-age/shaping-europes-digital-future_en. Accessed 16 June 2024.

[13]COMMUNICATION FROM THE COMMISSION TO THE EUROPEAN PARLIAMENT, THE EUROPEAN COUNCIL, THE COUNCIL, THE EUROPEAN ECONOMIC AND SOCIAL COMMITTEE AND THE COMMITTEE OF THE REGIONS *The European Green Deal,* 11.12.2019 [COM (2019) 640 final].

[14]COMMUNICATION FROM THE COMMISSION TO THE EUROPEAN PARLIAMENT, THE COUNCIL, THE EUROPEAN ECONOMIC AND SOCIAL COMMITTEE AND THE COMMITTEE OF THE REGIONS *Strategy for Financing the Transition to a Sustainable Economy*, 6.7.2021 [COM(2021) 390 final].

[15]Pastor (2017b, 2023).

barriers.[16] The main external obstacles to adoption are the need for new laws or regulations, the lack of access to high-quality private data, and the lack of public or private funding.[17] On the other hand, internal barriers include the cost of adoption, the lack of internal data and the cost of adapting operational processes and data protection compliance that must be respected in any data exchange situation -including financial and payment markets as analysed in this paper- Data Protection Law must be respected.[18]

Europe has very protective legislation, and the growing volume of financial data in circulation and its crossing is also a considerable challenge for it, especially from the point of view of personal data protection. Moreover, it limits AI-driven tools for creditworthiness to avoid financial exclusion without taking advantage of the fact that they play a vital role in harnessing the potential of this data and that they (these systems) can be trained without new biases or the perpetuation of existing ones. As noted, data-intensive artificial intelligence systems, such as those used for credit scoring, can make differential references: different combinations of predicted values correlate with other predictions.[19] Another layer of complexity involves the very concept of personal data and its residual sibling non-personal data; this is particularly problematic in this field of AI, as correlations and inferences from non-personal data could lead to the identification of an individual and turn such information into personal data.

The European Data Protection Supervisor (EDPS) recognises the benefits for consumers of increased competition in financial services through the innovation that FiDA will bring but warns that allowing financial institutions to access highly sensitive personal data through the data sharing, access, and use provisions of the proposal not only constitutes an interference with their fundamental rights to privacy and personal data protection, but could also entail significant risks to the rights and freedoms of individuals, such as risks of financial exclusion through price

[16] Without going into their analysis in this paper, FiDA, it states, should include sustainability-related information that enables customers to more easily access financial services that are aligned with their sustainability preferences and sustainable financing needs, in line with the Commission's strategy for financing the transition to a sustainable economy. Access to sustainability-related data that may be contained in balances or transaction details related to a mortgage, credit, loan and savings account, as well as access to sustainability-related client data held by investment firms, can help facilitate access to the necessary data, accessing sustainable finance or making investments in the green transition.

[17] COMMUNICATION FROM THE COMMISSION TO THE EUROPEAN PARLIAMENT, THE COUNCIL, THE EUROPEAN ECONOMIC AND SOCIAL COMMITTEE AND THE COMMITTEE OF THE REGIONS *A Capital Markets Union for people and businesses-new action plan*, Brussels 24.9.2020. COM (2020) 590 final.

[18] The European Data Protection Supervisor (EDPS) on the European Data Strategy on 16 June 2020, the EDPS adopted Opinion 3/2020 on the European Data Strategy. In it, the EDPS welcomed the strategy and considered that its implementation represented an opportunity to set an example for an alternative model of data economy.

[19] Chomczyk and Trigo (2023).

discrimination or refusal to provide financial products.[20] Privacy-enhancing technologies (PETs) allow information to be extracted and shared while ensuring the security and confidentiality of personal data.[21]

In short, we will analyse some aspects of the proposed FiDA regulation that may shed light on the governance of this new financial data market, its players, and the construction of this new digital economy. We aim to create a financial ecosystem where all participants benefit from cooperation, with co-regulation and a hybrid hard and soft law system. The data market space ('Creation and governance of financial data exchange systems'), Subjects participating in the Financial Data Marketplace ('ownership and control of Financial Data'), and the Financial Data ('the Commodity').

2 Co-regulation and a Hybrid System of Hard Law and Soft Law

We can point to 2023 as the year of the change in regulatory strategy, where the European data strategy is addressed sectorally, and open finance is addressed from the perspective of cooperative access to financial data (exchange, access, and use). Open finance emerging from FiDA strengthens competition by overcoming barriers in the financial sector and facilitating the horizontal integration of different financial services. This horizontal vision is adopted as a solution to a fragmented European industry.

This horizontal design endows FiDA with high adaptability to the upcoming digitalisation and dilution of the financial sectors that will emerge after a new business model called *Embedded Finance* in which the financial service may lose autonomy,[22] or rather be diluted, as they integrate financial services directly into non-financial platforms and help companies secure new revenue streams and, at the same time, improve the customer experience.[23] It is estimated that integrated

[20] EDPS, 22 August 2023 Opinion 39/2023 on the Proposal for a Regulation on payment services in the Internal Market and the Proposal for a Directive on payment services and electronic money services in the Internal Market (EDPS 39/2023).

[21] Even more, having direct control over the flow of your personal data would not only our privacy but also "data altruism", as supported by the new European Data Governance Law proposal. Zichichi et al. (2022), propose a multi-layered architecture for personal information management based on the use of distributed ledger technologies (DLT).

[22] *Revista de Derecho del Mercado Financiero*, RDMF (2024a).

[23] New functionalities with new crypto assets, thus the so-called SCaaS (Stablecoin as a Service) aimed to reduce costs and increase electronic retail payments' efficiency. It will be the next generation of Blockchain (native) peer-to-peer payments according to the legal framework set out in the Payment Services Directive (PSD2)—under MiCA (on Cryptoasset Markets) and probably (PSD3). The legal requirements will be met with a closed-loop ecosystem created by issuers, merchants, and consumers. In other words, offering a Stablecoin without requiring an Electronic

financial services will produce USD 384.8 billion in revenues by 2029, a nearly 17-fold increase over 2020. In addition, Europe is seen as fertile ground for Embedded Finance to offer a centralised solution. This is because it simplifies compliance and provides a single integration point, with embedded finance providers as a bridge between businesses and Europe's diverse financial landscape.[24] This will be coupled with implementing the 'Open Finance' strategic plan (of which 'FiDA'is a part). The 2020 Digital Finance Strategy[25] provides a legal framework for assets represented with DLT (Blockchain) technology and integrates their data into the scope of FiDA. The volume of financial data in the announced era of tokenisation, dealt with subsequently in this paper, will be massive given the expected volume of asset transfers in the so-called 'Finternet'.[26] In fact, the Financial Regulatory Forum of July 2, 2024, Joint Statement on the EU-U.S, touched on financial data sharing proposals and recent developments in both jurisdictions, notably the European Commission's proposal FiDA and CFPB's (Consumer Financial Protection Bureau) proposed rulemaking on Personal Financial Data Rights,[27] and the Forum closed with an exchange on the work related to operational resilience, crypto-assets, and payments.[28]

Additionally, the regulation of the crypto ecosystem will help the highly diversified European financial sector to develop products based on 'crypto data' and meet the demands of customers in the data economy, unlike, for example, large monitoring platforms (which have access to many different datasets), banks, insurance companies or asset managers that typically have access to more limited, albeit high quality, datasets. Being part of a secure and efficient data exchange environment will allow them to provide a broader set of data-driven services, for example, to get a complete overview of a client's wealth situation when providing financial advice. However, it will also help in the complex task of regulating this vast amount of data from different origins and different sources.[29]

Money Institution licence is currently possible. The closed loop allows Stablecoin to be used within a brand or for a specific product or service. This is discussed in this paper, Pastor (2021).

[24] Robinson (2024).

[25] Brussels, 24.9.2020 COM (2020) 591 final: https://eur-lex.europa.eu/legal-content/EN/TXT/?uri=CELEX:52020DC0591, Accessed 16 June 2024.

[26] Carstens and Nilekani (2024).

[27] Notice of Proposed Rulemaking - Required Rulemaking on Personal Financial Data Rights, https://files.consumerfinance.gov/f/documents/cfpb-1033-nprm-reg-text-with-1001_2023-10.pdf. Accessed 16 July 2024.

[28] Press releases, https://home.treasury.gov/news/press-releases/jy2443 Accessed 16 July 2024.

[29] When you create a digital asset, you generate online metadata about its origin, creation time, date, and format. It is not enough to have it to make a profit; it must also be properly named, tagged, stored and archived in a consistent language: they must be properly named, tagged, stored and archived in language consistent with other assets in the collection, proper asset management based on a methodology that allows assets to be found and distributed, allowing the maximum possible value to be extracted.

In this context, the fragmentation of the financial sector is both a strengthening and debilitating factor for Europe. When the approach to exploiting financial data is broadened in terms of data ownership and cooperation governance, and data must be shared among many operators, the challenge is then to coordinate and manage financial silos and their corresponding data silos. At the heart of this change lies the need for the positive impact of Data Spaces to materialise, but for this, it is important to ensure that the re-use of data does not lead to anti-competitive and collusive behaviour, especially given the requirement for mandatory compliance with contractual schemes, and that data holders do not exclude competitors through high fees for data access. The Commission has, therefore, announced that it will invest in a high-impact project to fund infrastructures, data-sharing tools, architectures, and governance mechanisms for thriving data-sharing and Artificial Intelligence ecosystems.[30]

In other words, Europe will invest in infrastructure and a new bottom-up, cooperative governance model. This is a relative novelty, considering that most regulatory options will involve top-down solutions as an essential ingredient of the approach. Such models may include bottom-up forms of self-regulation, such as ex-post forms of regulation or non-imposed self-regulation.[31] This aligns with the New Legislative Framework, which uses harmonised standards to reduce trade barriers and enhance product safety and quality across Member States.[32]

As can be deduced, the solution also involves a design adapted to the current legal framework and a technological infrastructure adapted to a financial data market in which its users will be able to contact the banks' customers to allow them to access their financial data through a control panel, which is intended to ensure, broadly speaking, that financial data are shared with guarantees for their fundamental rights, as we will analyse in the following sections.

Within this co-regulatory framework, the financial institutions holding the data (data holders) are responsible for establishing these APIs and facilitating their use by third-party providers in exchange for compensation, as we shall see.[33] A system for a Multistakeholder governance for the data economy[34] that we call a hybrid of hard law and soft law gives shape to a public-private partnership, which requires the financial institutions holding the data and the companies that intend to use the data to offer their services to develop common standards and APIs to enable secure sharing, including contractual liability rules. Central to this financial ecosystem are data aggregators that establish secure connections. They access and retrieve financial data in real-time via APIs (application programming interfaces) or other secure

[30] https://digital-strategy.ec.europa.eu/en/policies/strategy-data, Accessed 16 Jun 2024.

[31] Pagallo et al. (2019).

[32] See https://single-market-economy.ec.europa.eu/single-market/goods/new-legislative-framework_en Accessed 16 June 2024.

[33] *Revista de Derecho del Mercado Financiero*, RDMF (2024b).

[34] Sebhatu and Enquist (2022).

methods.[35] These aggregators are designed to handle the complexities of multiple formats, ensuring seamless integration of data from different sources. Once retrieved, the data is processed, cleansed and organised, ready to be presented in a user-friendly format.

Thus, recently, on 26 June 2023, the European Commission proposed a package of reforms to promote (and manage) data sharing in financial services, a proposal for a Regulation on a framework for access to financial data and amending Regulations (EU) No 1093/2010, (EU) No 1094/2010, (EU) No 1095/2010 and (EU) 2022/2554.[36] This proposal (proposal for a Financial Data Access regulation) is simply known as 'FiDA' (hereafter referred to as 'FiDA'). Very schematically, it builds on the open banking regime set out in Directive (EU) 2015/2366 but creates a new right of access to data or for data sets that were not previously covered by any other EU legislative framework.[37]

The 'FiDA' proposal does not entail administrative cost savings, as this new legislation does not amend previous EU rules. For the same reason, this is also not an initiative included in the Commission's Regulatory Fitness and Performance Programme (REFIT) to ensure that EU laws meet their objectives at minimum cost for the benefit of citizens and businesses. This new proposal does not build on any existing legislation. It builds on the open banking regime set out in Directive (EU) 2015/2366, but 'FiDA' creates a new right of access to data for datasets not previously covered by any other EU legislative framework. Also, for this to be possible, governance and infrastructure will be needed, thus enabling a new European Data Space specifically for the exchange of financial data. The Economic and Financial Affairs Committee (ECON) is responsible for the dossier in the European Parliament. On 19 July 2023, the ECON Committee appointed Michiel Hoogeveen MEP as rapporteur, and the Committee on Legal Affairs (JURI), the Committee on the Internal Market and Consumer Protection (IMCO) and the Committee on Civil Liberties, Justice and Home Affairs (LIBE) were proposed for an opinion. On 13 December 2023, the rapporteur published the draft report, which welcomed the proposal and suggested amendments along the following lines: 1. Improving customer confidence; 2. The JURI and IMCO committees decided not to issue an opinion.

On April 18, 2024, the ECON Committee adopted the FiDA proposal for a harmonised framework for access to financial data at the EU level with 43 votes to 1 and five abstentions. According to the ECON members, a framework should be established to access customer data processed by financial institutions across the financial sector beyond payment account data. With the data holder's permission,

---

[35] See *Guide on effective risk data aggregation and risk reporting*. EBC, May 2024, https://www.bankingsupervision.europa.eu/ecb/pub/pdf/ssm.supervisory_guides240503_riskreporting.en.pdf, Accessed 16 June 2024.

[36] https://eur-lex.europa.eu/legal-content/EN/TXT/?uri=CELEX:52023PC0360. Accessed 16 June 2024.

[37] Europe is not alone in this shift in how data is used and shared in the financial services industry. See references and literature in, Chomczyk and Trigo (2023).

their data would be available to develop and provide personalised, data-driven financial products and services. The final version of FiDA will probably go through several drafts. Given the different legislative steps on the roadmap, we expect an entry into force of the final text in early 2025 at the very earliest.[38]

Still, the legal uniqueness of FiDA deserves an interim analysis, as it would, broadly speaking, establish a new legal framework for data sharing within the financial industry. Basically, by introducing an obligation for financial institutions (data holders) to make their customers' data available to customers upon first request and to share this data with other regulated entities (data users) when authorised by customers.[39] Therefore, FiDA's main changes will focus on enabling external service providers to access customer data held by financial institutions to provide financial and information services. The progress report published On June 14th, 2024, by the Belgian Presidency of the EU states that "Member States broadly agree on the scope of customer data in the FiDA Regulation Proposal ...Some critical elements of this proposal still need to be discussed and the drafting amended to reach a compromise".[40] The main ones refer to the type of financial data (and the risks involved in guaranteeing access to high-quality private data by the IA Systems), the question of permission dashboards, or the role that gatekeepers (such as Amazon, Alphabet, Apple, Microsoft and others) could play in this new Open Finance framework. The previously mentioned points are the subject of ongoing discussions by different stakeholders, and this chapter's contribution is to explore most of them from the legal perspective.

[38]On April 30, 2024, the REPORT (including DRAFT EUROPEAN PARLIAMENT LEGISLATIVE RESOLUTION) was published on the proposal for a regulation of the European Parliament and of the Council on a framework for Financial Data Access and amending Regulations (EU) No 1093/2010, (EU) No 1094/2010, (EU) No 1095/2010 and (EU) 2022/2554, https://www.europarl.europa.eu/doceo/document/A-9-2024-0183_EN.html Accessed 16 July 2024.

[39]https://www.europarl.europa.eu/news/en/press-room/20240408IPR20274/committee-meps-want-to-enhance-customers-control-over-their-financial-data Accessed 16 June 2024.

[40]As stated in the report (https://data.consilium.europa.eu/doc/document/ST-10949-2024-INIT/en/pdf. Accessed 16 July 2024). "Many elements of the FiDA Regulation Proposal were discussed during the third Working Party (16 May 2024), including the gradual approach to phasing in customer data in scope, the functioning of the Financial Data Sharing Schemes, safeguards against Gatekeepers and the exclusion of third-country Financial Information Service Providers. Regarding the scope, a Member State presented a non-paper on "How to tackle the risk of demutualization". At the occasion of that last Working Party meeting, the Belgian Presidency also proposed a draft consolidated version of the text, incorporating all the drafting proposals made so far and covering the whole proposal.

3 Regulatory Analysis of the European Financial Data Market

The market needs transparent and accurate information (i.e., fed by reliable data), especially when algorithms are increasingly perceived as potentially affecting our fundamental rights. With open terms of use and the widespread use of data mining formats, using such information will increase. The European initiative will also promote machine-readability in the long term. This will give greater visibility, equitably and indiscriminately, to investors, analysts, intermediaries, researchers or funds of all market participants and voluntary reporters, irrespective of their size or market size. This visibility will create funding opportunities and ensure a better allocation of capital, thereby contributing to a lower cost of capital and greater resilience of the internal market.[41]

The delineation of all the functions of an efficient data market for Europe, from the point of view of its applicability, is, right now, shared, not least because all European strategies and legislative packages post-COVID-19 pandemic, including data and payments, continue to be implemented and developed focusing, among other things, as just noted, on creating a single data market that ensures global competitiveness, sustainability and European data sovereignty. The role of common European data spaces is to ensure that more data is available in the economy and society while keeping the companies and individuals who generate the data under control. Europe is working hard to achieve this, as its benefits could be felt in every aspect of our lives, from more conscious energy consumption and traceability of products, materials, food and payments to healthier lives and better medical and financial care. Financial data and access to it will be key in this endeavour.

In this respect, it is noted that the FiDA proposal,[42] at least in theory, as we shall see, should allow the necessary access to relevant information to avoid the undesired consequences of the existence of biases that could affect fundamental rights. The European legislator, aware of the risks involved in these automated decision-making practices, allows them, in the case of creditworthiness assessment, but includes a duty to inform the data controller, as we shall see. Thus, the data controller must notify the borrower automatically what decision will be taken, the logic applied to this decision, and the importance and consequences for the data subject of the processing, Art. 13.2 f), 14.2 g) RGPD, Art. 15.1 h) RGPD.[43]

---

[41] The European Commission adopted a Communication on building a European data economy on 10 January 2017, building on the conclusions of the 2014 Communication on the data-driven economy. The unlocking of the European Data Space came when the European Commission proposed a series of policy and legislative initiatives to boost the potential for the re-use of different types of data and create a common European data space, which were published in April 2018, available on: https://digital-strategy.ec.europa.eu/en/library/elements-european-data-economy-strategy-2018 Accessed 16 June 2024.

[42] Chomczyk and Trigo (2023).

[43] Collado-Rodriguez (2023).

In addition, customer data within the scope of the Regulation should include data that are part of an assessment of the creditworthiness of enterprises, including small and medium-sized enterprises, which can provide greater insight into their sustainability objectives. Including data used to assess the creditworthiness of enterprises should improve access to finance and streamline loan applications. Such data should be limited to data on enterprises and should not infringe intellectual property rights.

3.1 Horizontal Framework Applicable to the Data Market

The delineation of all the rules that come together in a general framework for the construction of an efficient data market for Europe is, as we pointed out in our functional analysis, complex and intricate right now, not least because all the European strategies and legislative packages post COVID-19 pandemic, including data and payments, are still being implemented and developed. Added to this is a technological reality, in constant transformation, and in which the legislator in financial matters, as recognised in the Explanatory Memorandum of RD. 814/2023 of 8 November, 'must take into consideration the possible effects that these technologies generate, at present and in the near future, on the markets, the various financial instruments and their management, the possible impact that Community regulation entails on the current legal regime and the need, in such a case, to adapt and comply with the provisions on AI systems that are being developed'.[44]

On the other hand, in general and global terms, the digital market is configured through a few Big Tech ('Gatekeepers'). It seems that the digitalisation of other actors will increase social inequality by liberalising, to a certain extent, sectors that until recently were monopolised by traditional intermediaries and by the more recent ones that have emerged in the heat of the so-called online platform economy, including collaborative ones. The prohibition of abusive exploitation of a dominant position in Art. 102 TFEU does not make it possible to deal with certain situations that the new instrument, the Digital Markets Act (DMA), seeks to address insofar as intermediary service providers operating as gatekeepers may not hold a dominant position in the internal market or a substantial part of it, or some of their relevant practices may not produce sufficient effects on competition in relevant markets for Art. 102 TFEU. The DMA applies without prejudice to Articles 101 and 102 TFEU, which it seeks to complement, as its objective is not strictly speaking to protect against practices that may distort competition in the specific financial market but to ensure that the markets in which gatekeepers operate are open and fair markets.[45]

---

[44] Royal Decree 814/2023 of 8 November on *financial instruments, admission to trading, registration of negotiable securities and market infrastructures*.

[45] DMA was published in the Official Journal of the EU on 12 October 2022, after which a period of 20 days was set for its entry into force and a maximum of six months for the effective application of its obligations. In other words, it was considered that the first consequences of its implementation

Crucial to this was the vote by Economic and Monetary Affairs MEPs on 18 April 2024 proposing new, innovation-friendly rules to allow customers (**based on the explicit permission)** to keep their financial data secure and use it efficiently to obtain a better financial service.[46] In doing so, MEPs also decided that large digital platforms designated as 'Gatekeepers' under the DMA should not be able to become financial information service providers (currently, the designated gatekeepers are Alphabet, Amazon, Apple, ByteDance, Meta and Microsoft). These are platforms whose dominant online position makes it virtually impossible for companies to reach end-users other than through their portals, and their exclusion is intended to ensure that they cannot circumvent the rules if they own or control data users.[47]

---

would begin to be seen in April 2023. The DSA, published on 27 October 2022, entered into force on 16 November. Most of the provisions apply from 17 February 2023.

[46]FiDA's Parliament proposal in the new whereas 10, "Access to customer data in the scope of this Regulation should be **based on the explicit permission** of the customer. Such permission should not solely be based on a "tick-the-box" approach or the use of generalising phrases. In seeking the explicit permission of the customer for the use of his or her data, data users should specify the purpose of the use of the data, subject to the customer's consent. The legal obligation on data holders to enable access to customer data should be triggered once the customer has explicitly requested their data to be made accessible to a data user. Where permission has explicitly been granted, this request can be submitted by a data user acting on behalf of the customer. This Regulation sets out rules on gatekeepers designated pursuant to Article 3 of Regulation (EU) 2022/1925. Those rules should apply to data users owned or controlled by gatekeepers to ensure that gatekeepers do not circumvent those rules. Gatekeepers should not be eligible to become financial information service providers. A data user that is owned or controlled by a gatekeeper should be subject to a special assessment by the national competent authority of its registered office to ensure its eligibility under this Regulation. Where a data user is part of a group of companies in which one or more entities in the group has been designated as a gatekeeper, customer data should be accessed only by the entity of the group that acts as a data user. The data user should therefore not grant access to customer data under this Regulation to the gatekeeper that owns or controls it. Gatekeepers should not engage in behaviour that would undermine the effectiveness of the prohibitions and obligations laid down in this Regulation. The limitation on gatekeepers would not exclude them from the market or prevent them from offering their services, as voluntary agreements between gatekeepers and the data holders remain unaffected. Where the processing of personal data is involved, a data user should rely on one of the valid lawful bases for processing under Article 6(1) (a) or (b) of Regulation (EU) 2016/679. The customers' data can be processed only for the agreed purposes in the context of the service provided. Under this Regulation, those purposes should be strictly limited to the provision of financial products, financial services or financial information services. The processing of personal data must respect the principles of personal data protection, including lawfulness, fairness and transparency, purpose limitation and data minimisation. A customer has the right to withdraw the permission given to a data user at any time. For example, when data processing is necessary for the performance of a contract, a customer should be able to withdraw permissions according to the contractual obligations to which the data subject is party. Similarly, when personal data processing is based on consent, a data subject should be able to withdraw his or her consent at any time and free of charge, as provided for in Regulation (EU) 2016/ 679. It should not be possible for the data user to transfer customer data to a third party, or even to another entity within the same group, without such explicit permission".

[47]https://www.europarl.europa.eu/news/en/press-room/20240408IPR20274/committee-meps-want-to-enhance-customers-control-over-their-financial-data Accessed 16 June 2024.

Therefore, it is a key pillar of the European data strategy, the Data Governance Act (DGA—in force on 23 June 2022 and, after a grace period of 15 months, applicable from September 2023), as it aims to increase trust in data sharing, strengthen mechanisms to improve data availability and overcome technical barriers to data reuse.[48] The DGA will also support the creation and development of common European Data Spaces in strategic areas, involving private and public actors in health, environment, energy, agriculture, mobility, finance, manufacturing, public administration and skills. Data Spaces should allow access to data, where access means 'the use of data, in accordance with specific technical, legal or organisational requirements, without necessarily involving the transmission or downloading of data' (Article 2.13 of the DGA). Access to data does not necessarily mean data dissemination and certainly does not mean uncontrolled data filtering. Data access means implementing ways of extracting information useful for a particular context from different data sources to create value.

Management, legal, and technical tools implement a data space, which must be implemented by design. Such tools include 'secure processing environments' (DGA Article 2.20), edge computing, federated processing, differential privacy, synthetic data, anonymisation, pseudonymisation, data minimisation techniques, etc. Other tools must provide control for stakeholders and, by default, implement data lifecycle management, traceability, and access control policies in the case of data dissemination.[49] Governance and policies are key elements of management tools. They should start by clearly defining roles and responsibilities among stakeholders, purposes, risk management from different perspectives, data gap management strategies, and compliance with various regulations. In this way, FiDA establishes a framework for creating and governing financial data exchange schemes. Moreover, the DGA establishes a framework to foster a new business model for data brokering services[50] that seek to establish a secure environment where companies and individuals can share data and offer services between the holders of these data and entities that want to use them (public or private), guaranteeing their security, availability, integrity and usability. It also introduces the concept of 'data altruism' and a procedure for registering as 'Data Altruism Organisations' as a form of organisation that favours horizontal transfers, such as data cooperatives that empower individuals by giving

[48] The DSA, adopted by the Parliament on 6 April 2022, aims to incentivise data sharing in the EU so that companies have more access to it and can use it to develop new products and services. Using big data is key to unlocking the potential of artificial intelligence. Regulation (EU) 2022/868 of the European Parliament and of the Council of 30 May 2022 on European data governance and amending Regulation (EU) 2018/1724 (Data Governance Regulation). OJEU No 152 of 3 June 2022.

[49] On these, Pastor (2022), Pastor and Llopis (2023).

[50] https://avancedigital.mineco.gob.es/en-us/Servicios/Servicios_intermediacion_datos_y_altruismo_Reglamento_DGA/Paginas/Prestadores_servicios_intermediacion_datos.aspx Accessed 16 June 2024.

them control over the data they share and effectively monetising the data or handing it over for research.[51]

This is joined by the Data Regulation (Regulation (EU) 2023/2854, hereafter Data Act),[52] which aims to maximise the value of data in the economy by ensuring that a wider range of stakeholders gain control of their data and that more data is available for innovative use while preserving incentives to invest in data generation. The Data Act is another key pillar and the second major initiative announced in the data strategy. It contributes to creating a cross-sectoral governance framework for data access and use by legislating on issues affecting the relationships between actors in the data economy to provide incentives for horizontal data sharing across sectors. Not surprisingly, legal uncertainty and barriers, commercial disincentives and lack of adequate infrastructure are among the main factors preventing data sharing between businesses, ensuring fairness and establishing rules regarding the use of data generated by Internet of Things (IoT) devices. On 28 June 2023, the European Parliament and the Council of the EU reached a political agreement on the Data Act. The act was finally adopted on 9 November 2023 and entered into force 20 days after publication in the Official Journal, becoming applicable after 20 months. FiDA's (Parliament) proposal in the new whereas 47 explicitly says that the "Data Act establishes a horizontal framework for access to and use of data across the Union. This Regulation complements and specifies the Regulation (EU) 2023/2854 rules. Therefore, those rules also apply to data access governed by this Regulation. This includes provisions on the conditions under which data holders make data available to data recipients, on compensation, dispute settlement bodies to facilitate agreements between data access parties, technical protection measures, international access and transfer of data, and authorised use or disclosure of data."[53]

Finally, the AI Act establishes two high-risk use cases for the financial sector: first, AI systems intended to be used to evaluate the creditworthiness of natural persons or establish their credit score, except for those AI systems used to detect financial fraud; second, AI systems intended to be used for risk assessment and pricing in relation to natural persons in the case of life and health insurance. This paper aims to identify stakeholder needs so that the Data Space can adequately assist

---

[51] This web maintains a public register of all recognised data altruism organisations offering their services in the European Union: https://digital-strategy.ec.europa.eu/en/policies/data-altruism-organisations. Accessed 16 June 2024.

[52] REGULATION OF THE EUROPEAN PARLIAMENT AND OF THE COUNCIL on harmonised rules on fair access to and use of data (Data Act) (Text with EEA relevance) {SEC (2022) 81 de final} - {SWD (2022) 34 de final} - {SWD (2022) 35 de final}. Available at https://eur-lex.europa.eu/legal-content/EN/TXT/?uri=COM%3A2022%3A68%3AFIN Following its formal adoption by the Council of the EU, the Data Act will be published in the Official Journal of the EU in the coming weeks. It will enter into force 20 days after its publication. However, it will apply from 20 months after it enters into force.

[53] DRAFT, On the proposal for a regulation of the European Parliament and of the Council on a framework for Financial Data Access and amending Regulations (EU) No 1093/2010, (EU) No 1094/2010, (EU) No 1095/2010 and (EU) 2022/2554, https://www.europarl.europa.eu/doceo/document/A-9-2024-0183_EN.html Accessed 16 July 2024.

them with appropriate guidance for implementing the upcoming AI framework in specific market areas, especially in the high-risk use cases identified (see section 3.3.3.2.1. Data as part of an assessment of the creditworthiness of consumers). Moreover, bearing in mind there will be harmonised standards for the requirements for high-risk AI (Mandates sent to CEN-CENELEC can be monitored[54]), further guidance tailored to the financial services sector on specific AI Act requirements, particularly regarding the two high-risk AI use cases, would be helpful.

3.2 *Sectoral Framework: Open Banking and MiCA*

In June 2023, as mentioned at the beginning, the European Commission proposed a package of reforms to promote (and manage) the exchange of data in financial services, a proposal for a Regulation on a framework for access to financial data and amending Regulations (EU) No 1093/2010, (EU) No 1094/2010, (EU) No 1095/2010 and (EU) 2022/2554[55] The reforms are part of a broader EU digital financial strategy, including a new framework for access to financial data and specific rules for crypto-assets, payment, and e-money services. The open finance and retail payments framework will form an integral part of the European financial data space along with data in the public disclosure of corporate information and supervisory reporting data. The advancement of the European Data Strategy has brought about a change in legislative policy. Instead of extending Open Banking to Open Finance, it is resolved to create a specific sectoral area in the European Data Strategy. This initiative was developed through the FiDA Proposal, which builds on the general data strategy under the General Data Protection Regulation (GDPR) umbrella, incorporating the lessons provided by PSD2. Thus, on the same day of FiDA's submission, 28 June 2023, the European Commission published a set of new legislative proposals, particularly a Third Payment Services Directive (PSD3) and a Payment Services Regulation (PSR). As we will see, the latter envisages changes to the fundamental framework of the European payments market and is likely to have a material impact on the actors subject to it, both from a legal and operational perspective. It proposes to merge the payment and e-money frameworks into one, even if some key specificities of e-money are preserved. It proposes to amend the Settlement Finality Directive (SFD) to allow non-banks access to payment systems. It also proposes solutions to the recurrent 'de-risking' problem faced by some payment institutions (PIs) and Electronic Money Institutions (EMIs), which should substantially improve

[54] See, https://standards.cencenelec.eu/dyn/www/f?p=205:22:0::::FSP_ORG_ID, FSP_LANG_ID:2916257,25&cs=1827B89DA69577BF3631EE2B6070F207D Accessed 19 June 2024.

[55] https://eur-lex.europa.eu/legal-content/EN/TXT/?uri=CELEX:52023PC0360.

their ability to open and maintain bank accounts.[56] It also explicitly recognises the possibility of a self-regulated market space in addition to the regulated sphere. This is a particularly important recognition of ongoing initiatives such as the SEPA Payment Account Access (SPAA) scheme, which the European Payments Council (EPC) is leading.[57]

All these proposed regulations will lead to more innovative financial products and services for users and stimulate competition in the financial sector. For example, consumers will benefit from better management and financial advice. Previously cumbersome processes, such as comparison services or switching to a new product, will become simpler and cheaper, including, for example, automated processing of mortgage applications. SMEs would also be able to access a wider range of financial services and products, such as more competitive loans, because their creditworthiness data would be more easily accessible, and fast payments with virtually no fees, as this will be complemented by the proposed Regulation that will regulate instant payments in euro for all citizens and businesses with a bank account in the EU and EEA countries.[58]

As we see, the road to FiDA is arduous and not without obstacles and related regulations, most notably, for our purposes, the open finance legal framework for third-party service providers' access to customer data, both business and consumer, with the latter's agreement. As such, it would constitute the next EU policy step concerning access to data in the financial sector following the rights of access to payment account data introduced by the second Payment Services Directive (PSD2), which is currently under review (PSD3) and which broadens the range of obliged parties.

But even decentralised crypto exchange traffic has 'de facto' been left out of FiDA, and its data is difficult to attack from 'Open Finance', as much of it is produced P2P (Peer to Peer), creating what we call 'micro-data silos'.[59] Decentralisation is one of the strongest ideas of the Blockchain ecosystem. Still, this possibility of communicating and operating directly, without any intermediation, means there is no possibility of data processing by a 'data holder' in FiDA terminology, as we will see below, or 'cryptographic service providers' in MiCA terminology.

[56]Directive 98/26/EC of the European Parliament and of the Council of 19 May on settlement finality in payment and securities settlement systems, available at: https://eur-lex.europa.eu/legal-content/ES/TXT/?uri=celex%3A31998L0026. Accessed 16 June 2024.

[57]Speech by Commissioner McGuinness at an event hosted (25 October 2023 Brussels) by MEP Ondrej Kovarik on "The Future of Payments and Open Finance in Europe: What are the Next Steps?", available at: https://ec.europa.eu/commission/presscorner/detail/en/speech_23_5316. Accessed 16 June 2024.

[58]Proposal for a REGULATION OF THE EUROPEAN PARLIAMENT AND OF THE COUNCIL amending Regulations (EU) No 260/2012 and (EU) 2021/1230 as regards instant credit transfers in euro, Brussels, 26.10.2022 COM (2022) 546 final 2022/0341 (COD). Disponible en: https://ec.europa.eu/finance/docs/law/221026-proposal-instant-payments_en.pdf Accessed 16 June 2024.

[59]Should be distinguished from that centralised through intermediaries, such as, for example, the Exchanges.

Indeed, each cryptocurrency runs on a Blockchain network governed by a protocol, i.e. the Bitcoin network depends on the Bitcoin protocol for using the Bitcoin cryptocurrency. Within Ethereum smart contracts, some protocols deal with specific network functions, with minor or more particular protocols such as ERC-20, which allows the creation of fungible tokens following certain guidelines and conditions, or ERC-721, which is similar, but for NFT (non-fungible tokens).[60] Also, the large DeFi (Decentralised Finance) utility clusters have their protocol, often referred to as 'DeFi protocols', as in the cases of AAVE, Uniswap, or Compound.[61]

3.3 Vertical Framework: The FiDA Proposal

3.3.1 The Data Market Space ('Creation and Governance of Financial Data Exchange Systems')

A financial data exchange system should consist of a collective contractual agreement between data holders and data users to promote efficiency and technical innovation in the exchange of financial data for the benefit of customers. Under EU Union competition rules, a financial data exchange system should only impose restrictions on its Member States necessary to achieve its objectives and are proportionate to those objectives. It should not allow its members to prevent, restrict, or distort competition for a substantial part of the relevant market. Data holders and users should be allowed to use existing market standards when developing common standards for mandatory data exchange. Thus, as we have seen, 'data ecosystems' will be the next evolution in the financial market and should be approached cautiously: while they promise to open the financial market to new players, they could paradoxically increase its concentration and compromise our strategic autonomy.

The governance of these data-sharing schemes is a challenge for lawyers and technologists, given that they include rules on inclusive governance and participation of data subjects, data users, and customers (to ensure a balanced representation in the schemes), transparency requirements, and an appeal and review procedure, particularly regarding decision-making.

---

[60] Pastor (2017a).

[61] Many crypto-asset activities and markets currently operate in non-compliance with applicable regulatory frameworks or are unregulated. These Recommendations (IOSCO. *Policy Recommendations for Crypto and Digital Asset Markets Final Report*, FR11/2023, 16 November 2023) recognise that some jurisdictions have existing regulatory frameworks encompassing crypto and digital assets, while some jurisdictions are developing regulatory frameworks. In addition, in some jurisdictions, the regulatory framework may allocate responsibility for regulating and overseeing crypto and digital assets to different Regulators with discrete and complementary mandates and objectives to address investor protection and market integrity risks. Each jurisdiction should implement the Recommendations, as they deem appropriate, within their existing or developing frameworks, considering each Regulator's role within those existing or developing frameworks and the outcomes achieved through the operation of the frameworks in each jurisdiction.

Financial data exchange schemes must comply with EU consumer and data protection rules, privacy, and competition regulations. FiDA aims to enforce compliance 'technologically' by introducing a compensation system for data subjects, imposing standardisation requirements, establishing financial data exchange schemes to develop coordination mechanisms within the industry, and introducing permission dashboards for customers to monitor their data permissions.

This FiDA ecosystem also requires data holders and users to become members of one or more financial data-sharing schemes and to respect the rules of these schemes when sharing data. FiDA maintains a self-regulatory approach to this but sets out stricter rules with no room for interpretation and little space and power for financial data-sharing schemes. Europe encourages participants in such systems to develop codes of conduct like those developed by controllers and processors under Article 40 of Regulation (EU) 2016/679. While such systems may build on existing market initiatives, the requirements set out in FiDA must be specific to financial data exchange systems or parts thereof for market participants to use and comply with their obligations under FiDA. Article 9 provides that data falling within the scope of the proposed FiDA Regulation should only be made available to members of a financial data exchange system. Therefore, the existence and membership of such systems are mandatory. Article 10 sets out the governance processes of such a system, including the rules on the contractual liability of its members and the mechanism for resolving out-of-court disputes.

Article 10 also provides for developing common standards for data exchange and creating technical interfaces for data sharing. Such data exchange schemes should be notified to the competent authorities, benefit from a passport for EU-wide operations or transparency purposes and be part of a register maintained by the EBA. The minimum arrangements for a financial data exchange scheme should also provide that data subjects should be entitled to compensation for making their data available to users following the terms of the scheme to which they are both parties. In any event, the compensation should be reasonable, based on a clear and transparent methodology previously agreed upon by the scheme's members. It should aim to reflect at least the costs incurred to make a technical interface for sharing the requested data available. Article 11 empowers the Commission to adopt a delegated act in case a financial data exchange system is not developed for one or more categories of customer data.

Under the current EU framework, as we have seen, a data subject's right to data portability under the GDPR is limited to personal data. It can only be invoked when it is technically feasible to transfer the data. Therefore, the exchange of financial data requires pseudonymisation and encryption, and, in general, the use of increasingly available technology allows algorithms to be incorporated into the Data. Algorithms allow valuable information to be obtained without the transmission between the parties or the unnecessary copying of the raw or structured data itself. Likewise, financial data requires the processing of the standardisation of customer data and the technical interfaces required as part of financial data exchange schemes, of which data holders and users in FiDA must become members. As we see in this paper, customer data and technical interfaces in the financial sector beyond payment accounts are not standardised, which makes data exchange more costly. In addition, financial institutions are only legally obliged (under PSD2) to make their customers' payment data available, and even we saw that as problematic.[62]

Therefore, FiDA introduces the obligation for market participants to develop common standards for customer data and interfaces regarding data subject to mandatory access as part of the *financial data sharing schemes* provided by FiDA. When sharing customer data in the context of the FiDA regulatory framework, data holders and users would have to comply with the data standards and the APIs developed by the financial data exchange programmes, which will be discussed in more detail in the following sections.

This bottom-up self-regulation will bring together data subjects, data users and consumer organisations to develop data and interface standards, establish coordination mechanisms for the operation of financial data access permission panels (as discussed throughout the chapter), as well as establish a joint standardised contractual framework governing access to specific datasets, where the main boundary will be the processing of personal data and compensation. In addition, from a legal point of view, the financial data sharing systems' governance will have to delineate rules regarding contractual liability in case of inaccurate or inadequate quality of shared data, compromised data security or misuse, and establish a dispute resolution system. It will also have to develop a methodology for determining compensation for making customer data available under the terms of the schemes. Thus, Title IV of FiDA sets out requirements for creating and governing financial data-sharing schemes that aim to bring together data subjects, data users and consumer organisations. Such schemes should develop data and interface standards, establish coordination mechanisms for the operation of financial data access permission panels, and a joint standardised contractual framework governing access to specific datasets, rules on the governance of these schemes, transparency requirements, redress, liability and dispute resolution rules.

Given the significant amount of data that would be shared due to the implementation of FiDA, there is also an obligation to provide customers with tools to effectively control their data and manage the permissions they have granted to data users. To this end, FiDA introduces an obligation for data holders to provide their customers with a financial data access permissions dashboard. Such a dashboard would, as we have seen, allow customers to monitor their data permissions by providing them with an aggregated view of their data permissions, grant new permissions and withdraw permissions when they wish to do so.

Ensuring effective customer control over data sharing contributes to innovation and customer confidence in data sharing. Effective control is essential to encourage customers to share their data. The FiDA statement, as will be expanded in the next section, emphasises the significance of standardisation. This process can simplify, translate, and automate investment data analysis, driving innovation in retail investment services by making it easier for clients to share their current investment data.

[62] See, Pastor (2017b).

Indeed, according to FiDA, the practices employed by data users to combine new and traditional customer data sources in the FiDA domain must be proportionate to ensure that they do not lead to financial exclusion risks for consumers.

The complexity of the financial data market is how FiDA would be affected by data protection regulations and, more specifically, regarding the rights of rectification and erasure of personal data. Hence, given our current legal framework, it is necessary to separate what could be fulfilled by an effective technical standard design from what will depend on the use and purpose for which the technology is intended. As just noted, a paradigmatic example of the FiDA proposal and one of the pillars underpinning the proposed framework is ensuring customers maintain 'effective control' over their financial data. As such, data users must comply with the conditions set by the customer and process the data only to provide the requested services. Further elaborating on the idea of 'effective control', its scope would be somewhat evidenced by the 'permission' referred to in Recital 10; if personal data is involved, as in our case study, this means that '(. . .) a data user must have a valid legal basis for the processing' according to the GDPR. Given the lack of further specification in the proposed text, we can look at Recital 10 itself, which indicates that the intended legal bases for this are consent or the performance of a contract.

3.3.2 Subjects Participating in the Financial Data Market ('Ownership and Control of Financial Data')

FiDA delegates to market participants the responsibility of approving, under certain requirements, the rules of a *Financial Data Exchange System*. Such a system is intended to operate in free competition, albeit under a strict regulatory and supervisory regime. It involves voluntary agreements between data holders and data users on data sharing standards and technical features of APIs, compensation to the holding bank, and contractual liability.[63]

FiDA only covers *business-to-business* (B2B) and *business-to-customer* (B2C)—including *consumer*—data access and processing at the customer's request across a wide range of financial services, and we can expect that many citizens will use these systems. There will be exponentially more financial data transactions daily. Moreover, its centralised vision would introduce a regulatory status for financial information service providers (FISPs). As is the case for TPPs under PSD2, FiDA introduces a new category of regulated third-party providers that would be allowed access to customers under the draft regulation to provide financial information services. FISPs would be subject to a licensing regime like that of account information service providers (AISPs) under PSD2 and subject to the same prudential requirements. However, FiDA provides a review clause for the Commission to assess the possibility of integrating AISPs into the regulatory status of FISPs.

[63] *Revista de Derecho del Mercado Financiero*, RDMF (2024b).

FiDA will apply to multiple categories of financial institutions when acting as *data subjects* or *data users*. Data subjects refer to entities subject to the obligation to grant access to and share customer data under FiDA. In schematic form, we highlight their obligations and how they must be exercised, as in Title II of FiDA. Thus, Article 4 indicates that the data controller must make available to customers the data falling within the scope of this Regulation upon request. Article 5 gives the customer the right to request that the data subject share this data with a data user. Where personal data is involved, the request must comply with a valid legal basis, as referred to in the GDPR, that allows the processing of personal data. This includes credit, payment and e-money institutions, investment firms, crypto-asset service providers, issuers of asset-backed tokens (such as those recently introduced by the Regulation on crypto-asset markets, known as the MiCA Regulation), alternative investment funds and UCITS (undertakings for collective investment in transferable securities), management companies, insurance and reinsurance undertakings, insurance intermediaries (both as a principal and ancillary activity), pension funds, credit rating agencies, equity finance platforms and financial information service providers. Naturally, the word holder places us in the field, and the apparent discrepancy between common and French law, on the one hand, and Germanic civil law systems, on the other, is both semantic and legal, as is the case with crypto assets.[64]

Therefore, the categories of companies classified as data holders are broad and include insurers, investment firms, crowdfunding providers, credit rating agencies, and crypto-asset service providers.[65] Under the FiDA framework, these data holders must make customer data available for access under the proposed new regime. In addition, as data users and subject to the customer's permission, these companies would also have access rights to customer data held by other data subjects. This is perhaps because one of the biggest hurdles to be overcome by this technology is that Blockchain is, for the time being, a technology that does not solve the problem of interoperability, an issue that UN/CEFACT standards have always supported. Moreover, the different Blockchains are far from equal regarding the level of trust. A permissioned ledger run by a single corporate entity or group of companies, with very or relatively few nodes, will have much less resistance against hacker attacks than a public ledger, such as Bitcoin, a permissioned ledger with thousands of nodes, or a permissioned ledger among large permissioned ledgers operated by multiple entities. In this regard, it should be highlighted that eIDAS 2,[66] defines a new trust service consisting of 'recording electronic data in an electronic ledger'. It fosters and grants full legal validity to distributed ledger technologies such as blockchain and offers highly relevant opportunities for the transformation of digital processes by

[64]Low Kelvin and Hara (2022).

[65]Paracamco (2023).

[66]Alamillo (2021), and the new Regulation (EU) 2024/1183 of the European Parliament and of the Council of 11 April 2024 amending Regulation (EU) No 910/2014 as regards establishing the European Digital Identity Framework, PE/68/2023/REV/1. OJ L, 2024/1183, 30.4.2024, ELI: http://data.europa.eu/eli/reg/2024/1183/oj. Accessed 16 June 2024.

supporting data and document processing that, until the emergence of these technologies, required third-party databases.

In contrast, data users refer to regulated entities that lawfully access customer data under FiDA, following permission from a customer; here, Article 6 imposes certain obligations on data users who receive it at customers' request. Customer data should only be accessible under Article 5, which should only be for the purposes and under the conditions agreed with the customer. Personalised customer security credentials should not be accessible to other parties, and the data should not be stored longer than necessary.

Here, it should be noted that financial customers as currently set out in the FiDA proposal, which at most gives them the right to allow selective use; hence, the EDPS opinion urges EU legislators to require data users under the proposed framework to clearly describe the specific types of customer data they seek to access each time they submit a request for access to certain data subjects. The EDPS notes that this would ensure that clients can selectively grant access to certain types of customer data, as seen below.

3.3.3 The Financial Data ('the Commodity').

3.3.3.1 Customer Data

In its second recital, FiDA states that customers of financial institutions, both consumers and businesses, should have effective control over their financial data and the opportunity to benefit from open, fair and secure data-driven innovation in the financial sector. These customers should be empowered to decide how and by whom their financial data is used and should have the option to grant companies access to their data to obtain financial and information services if they so wish. To this end, Article 1 sets out the rules for which certain categories of customer data can be accessed, shared and used in the financial sector. It also sets out the requirements for access, sharing and use of data in finance, the respective rights and obligations of data users and data subjects and the respective rights and obligations of financial information service providers concerning providing information services as a regular occupation or business activity. Article 2 sets out the scope of application of the Regulation for certain exhaustively described data sets and lists the undertakings to which the Regulation applies. Article 3 sets out the terms and definitions used for FiDA.

The question for the European Data Protection Supervisor (EDPS),[67] in its published opinion, is reasonable since *customer* financial data could fall within one of the categories of personal data that could fall within the definition of *customer data* under the proposals, considering the risks for the individuals whose personal data would be accessed and used. The EDPS described the definition of *customer*

[67] EDPS 39/2023.

data in the proposals as *particularly broad* and said it could *capture personal data of a highly sensitive nature*. This could include, for example, health-related data and other data that would constitute *special category data* under the GDPR. This regulation requires additional protections for special category data due to their potentially sensitive and privacy-intrusive nature. The EDPS also requested that data created due to profiling be explicitly excluded from the definition of customer data in the new framework. Therefore, as we will see, *standardised* financial and non-financial information in a common reporting framework with common regimes and metadata would help address the challenges related to comparability, reliability, and reusability of data under a *single file* principle.[68] The absence of such common standards is one of the main obstacles that users and society face when dealing with financial, environmental, social and governance information.

Generally, when processing personal data, a data user must have a valid legal basis for processing under GDPR. Customer data may be processed for the purposes agreed upon in the context of the service provided. The processing of personal data must respect the principles of personal data protection, including lawfulness, fairness and transparency, purpose limitation and data minimisation. A customer has the right to withdraw the permission granted to a data user. Where data processing is necessary for the performance of a contract, a customer must be able to revoke permissions under the contractual obligations to which the data subject is a party. Where the processing of personal data is based on consent, the data subject has the right to withdraw consent at any time, as provided for in the GDPR.[69]

An impact on consumers' fundamental rights, particularly Articles 7 and 8 on the right to respect private life and protect personal data, is enshrined in the EU Charter of Fundamental Rights (the EU Charter). The proposal establishes rights of access to data in the financial sector, which would contribute to increased data exchange, including personal data, at customers' request. The impact on fundamental rights will be mitigated by ensuring that, under Article 38 of the EU Charter, there is a high level of consumer protection and that the data exchange is strictly subject to the customer request.

In expressing the abovementioned views, the EDPS has highlighted some of the fundamental principles of data protection that he considers require further consideration as the reform package proposed in FiDA develops.[70] Applying those principles and the protections they afford individuals (and ensuring that individuals remain empowered) concerning the sharing and use of their financial and related personal data is at the heart of his opinion. At some level, it reminds the stakeholders in the reform package that these principles must be respected. For example, a customer may want to share savings account information with a specific data user but not data related to pensions or investments, the EDPS points out. This requirement, in

[68] EDPS 39/2023.

[69] AEPD. (2023), Aproximación a los espacios de datos desde la perspectiva de RGPD. https://www.aepd.es/guias/aproximacion-espacios-datos-rgpd.pdf, Accessed 16 June 2024.

[70] EDPS 39/2023.

addition to the transparency requirements set out in the GDPR, would help to avoid the risk of generic and broad requests for access to personal data, regardless of the eligible entities holding it or the sensitivity of specific data sets.

In compliance with Articles 7 and 8 of the EU Charter, certain provisions of FiDA, particularly those relating to financial data access permission control panels and specific guidelines in areas of higher risk of exclusion, will increase customer confidence and provide a framework for control of users sharing personal data. The dashboard will strengthen customer control, particularly where personal data are processed for the requested service based on consent or necessary for the performance of a contract. In addition, a restriction on the re-use of data beyond the requested service is introduced. Where appropriate, the permissions dashboard should consider the accessibility requirements in Directive (EU) 2019/882 of the European Parliament and the Council. When providing a permission panel, data subjects could use a notified trust and eID service, such as a European digital identity wallet issued by a Member State, as introduced by the proposal amending Regulation (EU) No 910/2014 as regards the establishment of a framework for a European digital identity. Data subjects can also use data brokering service providers under Regulation (EU) 2022/868 of the European Parliament and the Council to provide FiDA-compliant permission dashboards.

The permissions dashboard must show permissions granted by a customer, including where personal data is shared based on consent or is necessary for the performance of a contract. The permissions dashboard should standardly warn the customer about the risk of potential contractual consequences of withdrawing permission. Still, the customer should remain responsible for managing that risk. The permissions dashboard should be used to manage existing permissions. Data holders should inform data users in real time about any withdrawal of permission. The permissions dashboard should include a record of permissions that have been withdrawn or expired for up to two years to allow the customer to track their permissions in an informed and unbiased manner. Data users should inform data subjects in real time about new and reinstated permissions granted by customers, including the length of validity of the permission and a summary of the purpose of the permission. The information provided in the permissions dashboard is without prejudice to the reporting requirements in the GDPR. Thus, Title III of FiDA sets out requirements to ensure responsible use and security of data. Article 7 guides how companies should use data for particular use cases and ensures that there will be no discrimination or restriction in access to services because of the use of data. It also ensures that customers who refuse to grant permission to use sets of their data will not be denied access to financial products just because these customers declined to grant permission. Article 8 establishes the financial data access permissions panels to ensure that customers can monitor their data permissions by being able to access an overview of their data permissions, grant new ones and withdraw permissions if necessary. Given the above discussion among the relevant actors, the final FiDA text is expected to change to accommodate their recommendations. Several changes to the original version have been incorporated in the text adopted at the ECON level[71] and in the progress report published on June 14, 2024.[72] Notably concerning the types of data sets included and companies in scope (credit rating agencies and reinsurance companies are not in scope anymore, but operators of payment schemes now are). For instance, credit card accounts and technical accounts have been added to the list of data sets and non-sensitive categories of data used by data holders to meet know-your-customer (KYC) requirements for business customers. The definition of Financial Data Access Schemes (formerly Financial Data Sharing Schemes)

[71] See DRAFT on the proposal for a regulation of the European Parliament and of the Council on a framework for Financial Data Access and amending Regulations (EU) No 1093/2010, (EU) No 1094/2010, (EU) No 1095/2010 and (EU) 2022/2554 (COM(2023)0360–C9-0215/2023– 023/0205 (COD))https://www.europarl.europa.eu/doceo/document/A-9-2024-0183_EN.html Article 2. Scope. 1. This Regulation applies to the following categories of customer data, which are derived from financial services provided within the Union:

(a) mortgage credit agreements as defined in Directive 2014/17/EU, credit agreements, and accounts, including credit card accounts, except payment accounts as defined in the Payment Services Directive (EU) 2015/2366 and technical accounts, including data on balance, conditions and transactions;

(b) savings comprising term deposits, structured deposits, and savings accounts, investments in financial instruments, in accordance with Section C of Annex I to Directive 2014/65/EU and excluding derivative transactions used for risk management purposes, insurance-based investment products, crypto-assets as defined in Article 3(1), point (5), of Regulation (EU) 2023/1114 of the European Parliament and of the Council[42], real estate and other related financial assets as well as the economic benefits derived from such assets; including data collected for the purposes of carrying out an assessment of suitability and appropriateness in accordance with Article 25 of Directive 2014/65/EU of the European Parliament and of the Council[43];

(c) pension rights in occupational pension schemes, in accordance with Directive 2009/138/EC and Directive (EU) 2016/2341 of the European Parliament and of the Council[44] that are accessible for all interested consumers, with the exception of data related to sickness and health cover of a member or beneficiary;

(d) pension rights on the provision of pan-European personal pension products, in accordance with Regulation (EU) 2019/1238;

(e) non-life insurance products in accordance with Directive 2009/138/EC, with the exception of sickness and health insurance products; including data collected for the purposes of a demands and needs assessment in accordance with Article 20 of Directive (EU) 2016/97 of the European Parliament and Council[45], and data collected for the purposes of an appropriateness and suitability assessment in accordance with Article 30 of Directive (EU) 2016/97;

(f) data which forms part of a creditworthiness assessment of a firm which is collected as part of a credit agreement application process. Data collected as part of a creditworthiness assessment of consumers shall be excluded;

(fa) non-sensitive categories of data used by data holders to meet know-your-customer requirements for business customers.

[72] This report was shared to facilitate the reading of the text and as a guideline for the incoming Hungarian Presidency. The report provides more details on the progress achieved under the Belgian Presidency regarding the FiDA Regulation Proposal, focusing on the most important discussions held. It does not preclude any future decision by the Council regarding the content of the FiDA Regulation Proposal. However, important elements in the FiDA Regulation Proposal still need to be agreed upon, and many Member States have insisted that time is needed to fine-tune several key elements of the report. Comments from Member States have not yet been addressed. https://data.consilium.europa.eu/doc/document/ST-10949-2024-INIT/en/pdf Accessed 16 July 2024.

has also been modified. Moreover, the transparency obligation relating to permission dashboards has been reinforced: "The permission dashboard [. . .] shall provide the customer, at any time and in a format that is easy to understand, to the extent that the information is in the possession of the data holder, with an overview of each ongoing permission given to each data user".

3.3.3.2 Examination on a Case-By-Case Basis: Qualified Exclusions of Financial Data

3.3.3.2.1 Data That Form Part of a Consumer Creditworthiness Assessment

In previous works, we have stressed that assessing consumer solvency is a mechanism of major importance to prevent consumer and family over-indebtedness, which impacts the robustness of the financial system in general, and that technological instruments should be made available to detect good and honest debtors.[73] Banks and financial institutions often face this challenge when they are obliged to evaluate risk. For the banking sector and its internal risk committees, one of the main uses is the analysis of the borrower's creditworthiness, as this risk analysis deploys automated data processing with the application of AI systems, but without prejudice to appropriate measures being taken to safeguard the rights, freedoms and legitimate interests of the data subject. This includes the right to obtain human intervention in the decision affecting borrowers or to challenge the decision. But there is still a need, therefore, to minimise the effects of adverse selection and moral hazard that accompany insufficient information to assess the borrower's risk and discharge the traditional guarantees—both real and personal—that often accompany, indiscriminately, the granting of credit to companies and consumers.[74]

Data is the fundamental raw material for all sectors, including financial markets, based on what has been said about AI, its concept, and the specific technologies used. The proliferation of AI has occurred because of several factors, such as the massive availability of data, the possibility of collecting, processing, and storing such data, and, finally, the increase in computers' computational capacity.[75]

Particularly illustrative is the financial domain, where some of the main and emblematic consumers of financial data, such as credit scoring agencies, commonly use algorithms as a key part of their operation. Still, not all credit scoring models need them, as credit scoring was previously performed using automatic calculators.

Data-intensive artificial intelligence systems are built, but they require that a piece of data be categorised according to its context and use. In the context of FiDA, business-to-business (B2B) and *business-to-customer* (B2C) data access and processing are covered—including *consumer*—at the customer's request across a

[73] Pastor (2017b).

[74] Payo and Pérez (2016).

[75] Collado-Rodriguez (2023).

wide range of financial services (as discussed in the next section). FiDA's data use perimeter ensures consistency between its scope, excluding data that form part of an assessment of a consumer's creditworthiness and data related to a consumer's life, health and health insurance. The scope of the guidelines set out recommendations on how the types of data from other areas of the financial sector that are within the scope of FiDA can be used to provide these products and services.

As noted, data-intensive artificial intelligence systems, such as those used for credit scoring, can make differential inferences, i.e., different combinations of predicted values that correlate with other predictions.[76] Another layer of complexity involves the very concept of personal data and its residual sibling, non-personal data. This is particularly problematic in the AI field, as correlations and inferences from non-personal data could lead to the identification of an individual and turn that information into personal data. Indeed, the results provided by the latest advances in AI are not necessarily beneficial from the consumer perspective. Considering this, on 30 October 2023, the European Union adopted a new Consumer Credit Directive (CCD 2),[77] where one of the main novelties of the directive is the assessment of consumer creditworthiness using automated data processing with artificial intelligence that invests the borrowers with some rights regarding the explanation of lenders' decisions.[78] Also, the CJEU of 11 January 2024 revitalised the lender's obligation to assess the consumer's creditworthiness.[79]

Hence, the main new feature of the CCD2 is the possibility of assessing the consumer's creditworthiness based on the automated processing of personal data using artificial intelligence systems (Art. 18.8 CCD2). The CCD2 guarantees the consumer the right to request human intervention in the creditworthiness assessment process, which takes the form of three possible guarantees: the right to obtain a clear and understandable explanation, the right to express one's point of view, and the right to request a review of the creditworthiness assessment criteria and the result.[80] Another layer of complexity involves the very concept of personal data and its residual sibling, non-personal data. This is particularly problematic in this field of AI as correlations and inferences from non-personal data could lead to the reidentification of an individual and turn that information into personal data.[81] Consistently, the CCD2 in Recital 55 refers to this and provides that such information should contain, at a minimum, the consumer's income and expenditure, including appropriate consideration of the consumer's current obligations, inter alia, the

[76] Chomczyk and Trigo (2023).

[77] DIRECTIVE (EU) 2023/2225 OF THE EUROPEAN PARLIAMENT AND OF THE COUNCIL of 18 October 2023 on consumer credit agreements and repealing Directive 2008/48/EC.

[78] As a directive, the EU member states must transpose CCD2 into their domestic law by November 20, 2025, with the new measures taking effect from November 20, 2026. For credit agreements concluded on or before November 20, 2026.

[79] Cotino (2024).

[80] Izquierdo (2024).

[81] Hurley and Adebayo (2016); Hiller and Jones (2022).

consumer's current and household expenditure, as well as the consumer's financial commitments. Such information should not contain the special categories of personal data referred to in Article 9(1) of Regulation (EU) 2016/679, such as health data, including cancer data, or information obtained from social media. This mandate is contained in Art. 19.5 DCC. Moreover, it prohibits the creditworthiness assessment from being carried out by providing data referring to the special Art. Categories. 9.1 GDPR, i.e. particularly sensitive data of a subject, such as data relating to ethnic or racial origin, political opinions, religious or philosophical beliefs, trade union membership, genetic and biometric data and the sex life or sexual orientation of a natural person. Special reference is made in the CCD2 to the prohibition of using cancer data in the assessment of the creditworthiness of a natural person.[82] However, such data may be considered in insurance policies related to credit agreements (Recital 48 CCD2) for a relevant period of 15 years.[83]

The types of customer data that could be shared under the Commission's FiDA proposal are reasonably numerous. These include customer data on mortgage credit contracts, loans and accounts—including data on balances, terms and transactions—as well as on savings and investments, crypto-assets, real estate and other related financial assets, such as customer data on pension entitlements, some non-life insurance products, as well as data forming part of an assessment of a company's creditworthiness (not consumer's creditworthiness) that is collected as part of a loan application process or a credit rating application.

Data falling within the scope of the proposed FiDA Regulation must demonstrate a high added value for financial innovation and a low risk of financial exclusion for consumers. FiDA, as just noted, will, therefore, not include data collected as part of an assessment of a consumer's creditworthiness.[84] FiDA also excludes data on assessing consumers' creditworthiness and data on life and health insurance, on which we must refer to recent judicial pronouncements for completeness. On this point, it was expressly agreed in the vote of the Economic and Monetary Affairs MEPs of 18 April 2024 (mentioned above) to exclude from the scope of FiDA data related to health and sickness cover, as well as confidential business data and undisclosed know-how.[85] Despite FiDA's merits in this area, the safeguards to prevent all data from being collected to assess a consumer's creditworthiness are debatable.[86] These safeguards may have a limited and negative effect on consumers

[82] Collado-Rodriguez (2023).

[83] Izquierdo Grau (2024).

[84] Therefore, it should not cover data relating to a consumer's health and health insurance under Directive 2009/138/EC of the European Parliament and of the Council or data on a consumer's life insurance products following Directive 2009/138/EC other than life insurance contracts covered by insurance-based investment products.

[85] TITLE III. Responsible Data Use and Permission Dashboards. Article 7. Data use perimeter. 3a. "For the purpose of paragraph 3, regulatory technical standards should address how the 'right to be forgotten' of survivors of cancer or other chronic diseases and mental conditions shall be applicable in relation to non-credit related insurance policies, including life and health insurance".

[86] TITLE III. Responsible Data Use and Permission Dashboards. Article 7. Data use perimeter. 2. "In accordance with Article 16 of Regulation (EU) No 1093/2010, the European Banking

because they are particularly useful in collecting primary data to complete a retail investor's suitability assessment, which is time-consuming for clients and a significant cost factor for advisors and distributors of investment, pension, and insurance products.[87] Sharing customer data has great innovative potential. This includes developing personalised investment advice and investment management tools to make retail investment advice more efficient.[88] These management tools are already being developed in the market. They can be produced more effectively when a client shares investment-related, risk-related data from the data contained therein.

We consider the legislator's approach rather simplistic[89] because it does not discriminate between positively and negatively nuanced data and excludes all of it from credit scoring in evaluating part of a loan application process or a credit rating application.[90] It is important to note that positive credit reporting is useful for people who manage their finances well. In many countries like Spain, this development has been delayed by the lack of a sharing culture for these positive potential customer lists and by banks' reluctance to share their data with other institutions. The sharing culture is widely adopted in the United States, Germany, Italy, and Portugal, where some Spanish institutions operate. Moreover, in Spain, the credit information of citizens, natural or legal persons, was, until recently, based almost exclusively on negative elements (Central Credit Information Centre of the Bank of Spain -CIRBE-),[91] RAI, or ASNEF-EQUIFAX), i.e., on defaults and non-compliance and not on

---

Authority (EBA) shall develop guidelines on the implementation of paragraph 1 of this Article for products and services related to the credit score of the consumer, mortgage credit agreements, accounts including credit card accounts, and investment products. When doing so, EBA shall duly take into account the relevant provisions of Directive (EU) 2023/2225, including subsequent implementing legislation and guidelines".

[87]Technology itself can provide solutions to this vid. Gallego (2022).

[88]We refer to Herrero (2022) on these questions addressed by the doctrine.

[89]Economic and Monetary Affairs MEPs of 18 April 2024 (mentioned above), Article 2. Scope. 1. This Regulation applies to the following categories of customer data, which are derived from financial services provided within the Union: (f) data which forms part of a creditworthiness assessment of a firm which is collected as part of a credit agreement application process. Data collected as part of a creditworthiness assessment of consumers shall be excluded; (fa) non-sensitive categories of data used by data holders to meet know-your-customer requirements for business customers.

[90]The Opinion of Advocate General PIKAMÄE delivered on 16 March 2023 in Case C-634/21, paragraphs 47 and 49, is very relevant. The Advocate General also reproduces the considerations of the German court, which referred to the question for a preliminary ruling, in which he affirms the value of credit scoring in credit granting and establishing the terms and conditions thereof [paragraph 46]. https://curia.europa.eu/juris/document/document.jsf?text=&docid=271343&pageIndex=0&doclang=en&mode=req&dir=&occ=first&part=1, Accessed 16 June 2024.

[91]To this end, the content of the SME financial document has been designed largely based on the data collected in the monthly data returns submitted by institutions to the Banco de España's Central Credit Register (CCR) to ensure the availability and quality of the data and their processing. On the Banco de España website (http://www.bde.es/bde/es/areas/cenbal/, Accessed 16 Jun 2024) a computer template can be accessed and downloaded called "Modelo de informe sobre la posición del acreditado" (Información financiera-Pyme, file with the extension.xls).

positive elements,[92] and a different basis of legitimacy. The AEPD published a report on the lawfulness of data processing in credit information systems on 19 April 2021 (the so-called 'Code').[93] Within the framework of the analysis of the Code, the AEPD considered that the different basis of legitimacy of information relating to the fulfilment of monetary obligations—i.e. the information contained in lists of solvent clients—cannot be protected by a legitimate interest. A restrictive interpretation of the rights and interests of the holders of personal data must prevail. In this respect, the AEPD considers that obtaining information on the positively listed clients provides an economic benefit to the data controller by consulting the credit reporting company. On the other hand, concerning the negatively listed clients, the AEPD considers that the data controller's legitimate interest covers the processing if it meets the requirements set out in Article 20 of the Spanish GDPR law—LOPD-GDD.[94] By contrast, the USA's credit rating system is based on the so-called credit score of each citizen. They are obtained based on negative and positive elements or inputs, which the credit applicant can request at minimal cost from one of the existing credit reporting agencies. The loan amount, price or term will be reduced depending on the score obtained. Thus, if the debtor's credit score falls below a certain number, it is considered subprime. Positive Credit Reporting gives the lender a more well-rounded overview of an individual's credit profile rather than just focusing on credit applications, defaults and other negative events. Not only does this benefit the lender, but it also gives borrowers the power to demonstrate their creditworthiness and manage their credit profile. It can also help clients looking for a better deal on products, such as personal loans, as some lenders will provide a more favourable interest rate based on their credit score.[95]

3.3.3.2.2 Financial Data from Wallets

The new market paradigm requires moving from bank payment account data to wallet financial data to make a vast amount of transparent, unbiased, reliable, standardised, and comparable data available to operators (regardless of whether

---

[92] Spanish Supreme Court Judgment No. 280/2024 of 27 February, ECLI:ES:TS:2024:954, stated that inclusion in a debtors' file does not infringe the right to honour. Likewise, the High Court reiterated what was stated in judgment no. 34/2024, of 11 January, ECLI:ES:TS:2024:64, and no. 53/2024, of 16 January, ECLI:ES:TS:2024:140, underlines the importance of the payment request, as it allows debtors to be aware of their debt and exercise their rights before being included in a debtors' file.

[93] Code of Conduct for the Information Industry on the Protection of Personal Data submitted by the Multisectoral Information Association (the "Code"). AEPD, Gabinete Jurídico N/REF:028891/2019, https://www.aepd.es/es/documento/2019-0081.pdf, Accessed 16 June 2024.

[94], known in Spanish as "LOPDGDD," was finally approved on 6 December, repealing Organic Law 15/1999, of 13 December, on protecting personal data and regulating its development.

[95] Chomczyk and Trigo (2023).

they are large or small, traditional or alternative). This enables the quantification of the risk involved in their financing, among other uses.

The FiDA proposal would, therefore, broaden the scope of financial data to be shared concerning PSD2 open banking to include the following categories: mortgage; credit and savings account balances terms and transactions; savings, investments in financial instruments; insurance-based investment products; crypto-assets; real estate; and other related financial assets and the economic benefits derived from such assets.[96]

However, data related to all crypto assets, such as non-fungible tokens (NFTs) or fungible unbacked (algorithmic, like bitcoin), are not standardised and are outside the scope of MiCA and anti-money laundering regulations.

In this data context, it is important to remember that the major exclusions are, therefore, to be found in the decentralised ecosystem and peer-to-peer (P2P) transfers, with some nuances and the need for clarification of some general concepts such as the ownership and transfer of unregulated digital assets, as well as a new theory of title and ownership of digital assets. The deregulation of recent phenomena, such as the deregulation of the NFTs, will require a new theory of title and mode and the role of centralised public registries. Even more, the deregulation of recent phenomena such as unique tokens in conjunction with web ecosystems3 and metaverses presents several problems and calls for a new MiCA Regulation (2)[97] to address social

[96] EDPS 39/2023. Article 2 of the Proposal outlines which categories of customer data fall within the scope of the Proposal. The following categories of customer data would be shared, accessed and used, among others: Mortgage credit agreements, loans and accounts, except payment accounts as defined in PSD2, including data on balance, conditions and transactions. According to the Recital of the Proposal, such customer data should also include information relating to sustainability needs and preferences, Savings, investments in financial instruments, insurance-based investment products, crypto-assets, real estate and other related financial assets and the economic benefits derived from such assets; including data collected to assess suitability and appropriateness under Article 25 of Directive 2014/65/EU34 ('Market in Financial instruments Directive - MiFiD II'). According to the Recital of the Proposal, such customer data should include information on sustainability needs and preferences. Pension rights in occupational pension schemes follow Directive 2009/138/EC35 ('Solvency II') and Directive (EU) 2016/234136 ('Institutions for Occupational Retirement Provision Directive - IORP II Directive'), or on the provision of pan-European personal pension products ('PEPP'), following Regulation (EU) 2019/123837. According to the Recital of the Proposal, this would include "data on pension rights concerns in particular accrued pension entitlements, projected levels of retirement benefits, risks and guarantees of members and beneficiaries of occupational pension schemes." The provision of non-life insurance products (e.g. insurance covering homes, vehicles and other property) under Solvency II, except for sickness and health insurance products. Recital (14) of the Proposal clarifies that such data should include insurance product information—such as details on insurance coverage—and data specific to the consumers' insured assets. This would include data collected for the purposes of demands and needs assessment and data collected for the purposes of an appropriateness and suitability assessment in accordance with (respectively) Articles 20 and 30 of Directive (EU) 2016/9739 ('IDD').

[97] The Regulation on Markets in Crypto-Assets, MiCA (1) was published in the Official Journal of the EU on 9 June 2023. The European Securities and Markets Authority (ESMA) has been empowered to develop technical standards and guidelines specifying certain provisions. At the end of March 2024, ESMA published the third (and last) consultation paper covering the remaining

realities not affected by the new rules, which will also not affect (decentralised P2P) tokens without issuers, such as Bitcoin.

Only data from decentralised tokens can be processed when traded on centralised platforms (data holders). The decentralised ecosystem of electronic payment instruments, schemes, and arrangements is outside the PISA framework, which has been updated to include digital payment tokens. In addition, no legal framework for Data Governance can support their technological infrastructure and data maintenance over time.[98] On the other hand, without mentioning some of the already known applications in the financial sector and means of payments, such as cryptocurrencies, NFTs and security tokens, it is difficult to say right now that the technology can support a single platform that can hold all the reliable data about a single shipment and related identity data. From our perspective, this issue will be resolved by eIDAS 2[99] by describing the *Electronic ledger service* (eIDAS 2 regulation).[100] In short, at the time of writing, FiDA also does not extend to financial data generated in decentralised

four mandates: prevention and detection of crypto-asset market abuse; suitability requirements applicable to the provision of advice and portfolio management services in crypto-assets and the format of the periodic statement to be provided for portfolio management services; transfer services for crypto-assets; and maintenance of systems and security access protocols. ESMA encourages stakeholders to provide feedback on the proposed framework by June 25, 2024. https://www.esma.europa.eu/document/consultation-paper-technical-standards-specifying-certain-requirements-mica-3rd-package . Accessed 16 June 2024. In the next weeks, this subject will be defined.

[98]Low et al. (2022), Dubovec (2022).

[99]Regulation (EU) 2024/1183 of the European Parliament and of the Council of 11 April 2024 amending Regulation (EU) No 910/2014 as regards establishing the European Digital Identity Framework, PE/68/2023/REV/1. OJ L, 2024/1183, 30.4.2024, ELI: http://data.europa.eu/eli/reg/2024/1183/oj. Accessed 16 June 2024.

[100]On 30 April 2024, the European Council finally approved the proposal to amend the eIDAS Regulation. After a waiting period of 20 days, the new Regulation will enter into force in all member states. This is an important step towards harmonising digital identity and trust services across the European Union. The Regulation (EU) 1183/2024 ("eIDAS 2") contains the reform provisions of Regulation (EU) 910/2014, better known as the "eIDAS Regulation". The most notable change is the introduction of the so-called "European Digital Identity Wallet" or "EUDI Wallet" and new types of trust services have been introduced, among them, *Electronic ledger service* maintains a sequence of electronic data records, ensuring the integrity and accuracy of their chronological order, and *Electronic archiving service* manages the receipt, storage, retrieval and disposal of electronic data and electronic documents to maintain durability, legibility, integrity, confidentiality and proof of origin throughout the retention period.

crypto-asset transactions; for the time being, it is not covered by the system created in the EU[101] and FATF (Financial Action Task Force).[102]

However, personal financial data processed by payment services providers, insurance undertakings, pension products providers and other financial institutions are inherently sensitive. Therefore, the EDPS welcomes that certain categories of data have been excluded from the scope of the Proposal under Article 2(1)(a), (e) and (f), as well as customer data related to payment accounts, the provision of life, sickness and health insurance products, and data which forms part of a creditworthiness assessment of natural persons.

Indeed, the exchange of customer data in data protection must be based on the customer's permission. The legal obligation of data subjects to share customer data must be triggered once the customer has requested that their data be shared with a data user. This request can be submitted by a data user acting on behalf of the customer. Customers should have effective control over their data and confidence in managing the permissions they have granted by FiDA. Therefore, data holders should be required to provide customers with common and consistent financial data access permissions dashboards. The permissions dashboard should allow the customer to manage their permissions in an informed and impartial manner and give them strong control over how their personal and non-personal data is used. It should not be designed to encourage or unduly influence the customer to grant or withdraw permissions. Where appropriate, the permissions dashboard should consider the accessibility requirements in Directive (EU) 2019/882 of the European Parliament and the Council.[103] Now, FiDA's (DRAFT, mentioned above) proposal in the new whereas 22 says explicitly that" the information provided on the permission dashboard is without prejudice to the requirements under Regulation (EU) 2016/679, in particular the information requirements. The permission dashboard may be

[101] In particular, the EU would extend the so-called travel rule, which currently applies to wire transfers managed by global banks, to require crypto asset service providers to collect and report data on the originators and beneficiaries of crypto asset transfers. In the pipeline, European Parliament legislative resolution of 24 April 2024 on the proposal for a directive of the European Parliament and of the Council on mechanisms to be put in place by Member States to prevent the use of the financial system for the purpose of money laundering or terrorist financing and repealing Directive (EU) 2015/849 (COM (2021)0423 - C9-0342/2021 - 2021/0250(COD))https://www.europarl.europa.eu/doceo/document/TA-9-2024-0364_EN.html, Accessed 16 June 2024.

[102] FATF (2021), *Updated Guidance for a Risk-Based Approach to Virtual Assets and Virtual Asset Service Providers*: https://www.fatf-gafi.org/en/publications/Fatfrecommendations/Guidance-rba-virtual-assets-2021.html Accessed 16 Jun 2024. Most recently, in the CEF-ML process - Cyber-enabled fraud ("CEF") and money laundering ("ML")—their recent report Illicit Financial Flows, from Cyber-Enabled Fraud https://www.fatf-gafi.org/content/dam/fatf-gafi/reports/Illicit-financial-flows-cyber-enabled-fraud.pdf.coredownload.inline.pdf November 2023. Accessed 16 June 2024.

[103] Proposal for a Regulation of the European Parliament and of the Council on payment services in the internal market and amending Regulation (EU) No 1093/2010 COM/2023/367 final. Available at: https://eur-lex.europa.eu/legal-content/EN/TXT/?uri=CELEX:52023PC0367 Accessed 16 June 2024.

combined with the permission dashboard established under Regulation ... [the Payment Services Regulation]".

In providing a permission panel, data subjects could use a notified trust and eID service, such as a European digital identity wallet issued by a Member State, as introduced by eIDAS 2 regarding establishing a framework for a European digital identity. Data subjects can also use data brokering service providers under Regulation (EU) 2022/868 of the European Parliament and the Council to provide FiDA-compliant permission panels. Perhaps more complex, however, is the integration between the so-called European Digital Identity Wallet or "EUDI Wallet" and the new Payment Services Directive (PSD3). In addition to securely storing their digital identity, a wallet will allow users to open bank accounts, make payments and store digital documents, such as a mobile driving licence, a medical prescription, a professional certificate or a travel ticket. The Wallet will offer a practical and user-friendly alternative to the online identification guaranteed by EU legislation. The main advantage for users is that personal data will be granulated and controlled by the users themselves. However, we consider that the Wallet should fully respect the user's choice to share or not to share personal data and offer the highest degree of security independently certified according to the same standards and the relevant parts of its code, and that it should be published in open source to exclude any possibility of misuse, illegal use, tracking, tracing or government interception. However, citizens will only trust and adopt data-driven innovations if they are confident that any exchange of financial data in the EU will be subject to full compliance with the EU's strict data protection rules. At the same time, the growing volume of financial, non-personal industrial and public data in Europe and technological changes in how data is, stored and processed will be a potential source of conflict.

At the time of writing, through the DIGITAL programme, the European Commission supports large-scale pilots of various use cases, "EUDI Wallet". The Nordic-Baltic "EUDI Wallet" (NOBID) project focuses on enabling national "EUDI Wallet" solutions in the Nordic and Baltic regions.[104] Together with other European partners, the NOBID Consortium focuses on the use case of payments for national and cross-border use. The payments use case is recognised as a key use case based on several fundamentals, one of which is the possible extension to the digital euro. The use case builds on the existing infrastructure used for bank payments, including instant SCT payments and traditional account-to-account transfers. The solution will be based on strong customer authentication via the wallet and will comply with PSD2 requirements. It is envisaged that several modalities will be

[104] EU Digital Identity Wallet Pilot implementation. More information on large-scale pilot projects testing the technical specifications for the Common Toolbox that will be the base of the EU Digital Identity Wallets can be found at: https://digital-strategy.ec.europa.eu/en/policies/eudi-wallet-implementation. Accessed 23 July 2024.

supported, starting with simple solutions such as QR codes, push notifications and deep links.[105]

The project focuses on a single use case: using the "EUDI Wallet" to authorise payments for products and services by the wallet user. It will address the issuance of e-wallets, the provision of means of payment by financial institutions and the acceptance of payment in a retail context. However, it should not be overlooked that the use case for payment may also be key for the potential future extension of the digital euro.[106] The PSD and its regulation (PSR) will allow payment services providers to share fraud-related information, increase consumer awareness, strengthen customer authentication rules, extend the reimbursement rights of fraud victims, and create a system to verify the alignment of payees. IBANs with their account names are mandatory for all credit transfers. It is expected that during the development of standards resulting from PSD3, there will be sufficient interest in providing standards referring to the European Digital Identity Wallet to justify their integration.[107]

4 Conclusions

One of the main pillars of the European financial market of the future is the proposed FiDA regulation. Although it is a very ambitious proposal, we believe it could solve a central problem—unrelated to sustainability, although it includes sustainability data in its scope in the data context. All this would result in a robust new data market, in which the increase in data traffic would be exponential and would go beyond account movements, payment orders, transfer orders, etc., and would allow for the exchange and cross-referencing of an ever-increasing volume of data, as well as an increase in the complexity of technical and legal compliance so that financial data can be exploited under European standards.

These difficulties are largely due to legal, contractual or technical obstacles, to which the FiDA proposal provides solutions. It is difficult at this stage to make an assessment of the degree of maturity achieved or possible and whether they will develop the strategies set out in 'Shaping Europe's digital future', in its mission to become a global model for financial data markets, which will also help the digitisation of developing economies and develop digital standards and drive this 'standardisation' at international level and in the financial sector in particular. It is therefore essential to clarify FiDA solutions to gauge the scale of Europe's commitment to digital innovation, which will depend on making the 'European parties'

[105] https://www.nobidconsortium.com/. Accessed 16 June 2024.

[106] https://digital-strategy.ec.europa.eu/es/news/eu-digital-identity-4-projects-launched-test-eudi-wallet, Accessed 16 June 2024.

[107] Wood (2023).

more efficient, helping to integrate European capital markets and channelling investment into sustainable activities in support of the European Green Deal.

The FiDA proposal is a regulatory paradigm shift and a challenge for lawyers, as it implies a hybrid system of hard law and soft law that regulates and self-regulates a technology-based ecosystem, in which, without assessing the technical quality of the concepts introduced by FiDA, on data ownership—a question that would be linked to the apparent discrepancy with other data spaces—there is no doubt that the framework proposed by FiDA is a major step forward and improves access to data in the market for payment services already developed under PSD2. It also clarifies access and other issues, such as contractual liability and dispute resolution. In addition to defining the different roles of the subjects involved in the data space and technology standards, the community should be involved in, for example, defining the control panel to ensure that financial services customers are in control of their data and to allow data sharing when customers so wish. This will democratise access to financial information to more and new market participants with equal opportunities. It will also extend the associated rights and obligations to a wider range of financial services companies, providing European industry-led financial data exchange schemes to regulate access to customer data.

In our view, one key element to the success of the financial data market remains unresolved, and it is unclear whether citizens perceive that they can and should benefit from the 'Financial data ecosystem'. To get there, there is a complex legal and technological road ahead, on which the mechanisms of data exchange schemes are also being considered. Therefore, the coming months will be very important for FiDA and market players.

Ultimately, in a society where individuals will generate increasing amounts of data, the way they are collected and used must put the interests of the individual first, in line with the principle of 'equal opportunities' as well as European values, fundamental rights and standards. FiDA is, in our view, a valuable piece in this big change, which pursues a common goal to build a sustainable digital market economy and a financial internet (Finternet) that works for people.

References

Alamillo I (2021) Regulating distributed ledgers as legal institutions based in trust services. Eur Rev Dig Adm Law – Erda 2(2) https://www.erdalreview.eu/free-download/97912599475291.pdf. Accessed 16 June 2024

Benjamin C (2024) AI in finance How does the uptake of Artificial Intelligence systems impact finance? Newsletter, 19 June 2024, Directorate-General for Financial Stability, Financial Services and Capital Markets Union, https://finance.ec.europa.eu/news/ai-finance-2024-06-19_en. Accessed 19 June 2024

Carstens A, Nilekani N (2024) Finternet: the financial system for the future BIS Working Papers No 1178 Finternet: the financial system for the future, April 2024. https://www.bis.org/publ/work1178.htm. Accessed 16 June 2024

Chomczyk A, Trigo P (2023) Can the European financial data space remove bias in financial AI development?" Opportunities regulatory challenges. Int J Law Inf Technol 31, https://doi.org/10.1093/ijlit/eaad020. Accessed 16 June 2024

Collado-Rodriguez N (2023) La evaluación de la solvencia mediante el uso de sistemas de IA. Creditworthiness assessment by AI. Revista CESCO De Derecho De Consumo 46, https://revista.uclm.es/index.php/cesco/article/view/3335. Accessed 16 June 2024

Cotino L (2024) La primera sentencia del Tribunal de Justicia de la Unión Europea sobre decisiones automatizadas y sus implicaciones para la protección de datos y el Reglamento de inteligencia artificial. en Diario la Ley, https://diariolaley.laleynext.es/Content/Documento.aspx?params=H4sIAAAAAAAEAMtMSbF1CTEAAmNLAwNzC7Wy1KLizPw827DM9NS8klS13MSSktQiWz9HAHEZZVgqAAAAWKE, 2024. Accessed 16 June 2024

Dinero digital y gobernanza TIC en la UE, PASTOR. C (dir.), (2022) Cizur Menor

Dubovec M (2022) Toward decentralized commercial law for digital assets. Northwestern J Technol Intell Prop 19:239. https://scholarlycommons.law.northwestern.edu/njtip/vol19/iss3/1. Accessed 16 June 2024

Gallego M (2022) La protección del cliente bancario en la evaluación de solvencia mediante inteligencia artificial. Revista de derecho bancario y bursátil 165, 2022

Guía de criptoactivos MiCA, MADRID A, PASTOR. C, (Dirs) (2021) Cizur Menor

Herrero R, (2022) Aspectos jurídicos del uso de la inteligencia artificial por los robo-advisors. Revista de derecho del mercado de valores 30, 2022

Hiller J, Jones LS (2022) Who's keeping score? Oversight of changing consumer credit infrastructure. Am Bus Law J 2022, 59(1)

Hurley M, Adebayo J (2016) Credit scoring in the era of big data. Yale J Law Technol 18

Izquierdo G (2024) Los derechos del consumidor en los procesos de evaluación de solvencia mediante el tratamiento automatizado de datos contenidos en la Directiva (UE) 2023/2225. Revista CESCO De Derecho De Consumo 49. https://doi.org/10.18239/RCDC_2024.49.3447. Accessed 16 June 2024

Low Kelvin FK, Hara M (2022) Cryptoassets and property, Sjef van Erp y Katja Zimmermann (eds) Edward Elgar Research Handbook on EU Property Law SSRN: https://ssrn.com/abstract=4103870 or https://doi.org/10.2139/ssrn.4103870. Accessed 16 June 2024

Pagallo U, Casanovas P, Madelin R (2019) The middle-out approach: assessing models of legal governance in data protection, artificial intelligence, and the Web of Data. The Theory and Practice of Legislation. https://www.tandfonline.com/doi/full/10.1080/20508840.2019.1664543. Accessed 16 June 2024

Paracamco M-T (2023) I prestattori de servizi per la cripto-attività, Tra mifidizzazione della MiCA e tokenizzazione della MiFiD, Torino. 2023

Pastor C (2017a) Criptodivisas: ¿una disrupción jurídica en la eurozona? Revista de Estudios Europeos 70, 2017. https://rua.ua.es/dspace/handle/10045/72687. Accessed 16 June 2024

Pastor C (2017b La estandarización de la información financiera de pymes y autónomos como clave de acceso a la financiación. Revista de derecho bancario y bursátil 146, 2017

Pastor C (2020) Economía digital sostenible. Cizur Menor

Pastor C (2021) Stablecoins y dinero electrónico como servicio de circuito cerrado, Revista de Derecho del Sistema Financiero: mercados, operadores y contratos 2, 2021, https://doi.org/10.32029/2695-9569.02.08.2021. Accessed 16 June 2024

Pastor C (2022) "La nueva Economía Social del Dato (ESD)" CIRIEC - España. Revista jurídica de economía social y cooperativa, vol 41, 2022 (Ejemplar dedicado a: Plan de Acción de la UE y nuevos Retos de la digitalización para la Economía Social). http://ciriec-revistajuridica.es/wp-content/uploads/comen41-01.pdf. Accessed 16 June 2024

Pastor C (2023) Open finance, Cuadernos de derecho y comercio, vol 80

Pastor C, Llopis L (2023) Cooperativas de iniciativa social en los sectores energéticos y de las telecomunicaciones. Valencia. https://doi.org/10.7203/10550/90499. Accessed 16 June 2024

Payo I, Pérez P (2016) Mejoras en la financiación bancaria de las pymes introducidas por la normativa española. en Cuadernos de Información Económica, 254, octubre 2016

Plataformas Digitales: aspectos jurídicos, MARTINEZ NADAL A (dir.), (2021) Cizur Menor
Revista de Derecho del Mercado Financiero, RDMF (2024a) FiDA y el nuevo sistema de intercambio de datos financieros, 15 Marzo, https://www.rdmf.es/2024/03/fida-nuevo-sistema-intercambio-datos-financieros/. Accessed 16 June 2024
Revista de Derecho del Mercado Financiero, RDMF (2024b). https://www.rdmf.es/2024/03/fida-nuevo-sistema-intercambio-datos-financieros/. Accessed 16 June 2024
Robinson A, (2024) Embedded Finance in Europe shaping narratives and building trust in financial innovation. Forbes, 3 June 2024, 02:41 p.m. EDT, https://www.forbes.com/sites/forbescommunicationscouncil/2024/06/03/embedded-finance-in-europe-shaping-narratives-and-building-trust-in-financial-innovation/. Accessed 16 June 2024
Sebhatu SP, Enquist B (2022) Values and multi-stakeholder dialog for business transformation in light of the UN sustainable development goals. J Bus Ethics 180:1059–1074. https://doi.org/10.1007/s10551-022-05195-x. Accessed 16 June 2024
Wood C, (2023) What will PSD3 mean for open banking? 14 February de 2023, a Blog. Nordic Apis https://nordicapis.com/what-will-psd3-mean-for-open-banking/. Accessed 16 June 2024
Zichichi M, Ferretti S, D'Angelo G, Rodríguez-Doncel V (2022) Data governance through a multi-DLT architecture in view of GDPR. Cluster Comput 25, December 2022, https://doi.org/10.1007/s10586-022-03691-3. Accessed 16 June 2024

Web Technologies for Decentralised Identity

Víctor Rodríguez-Doncel

Abstract This chapter analyses technologies that support decentralised identity on the Web. The World Wide Web Consortium, which maintains the technical specifications of the Web, has consistently advocated for decentralised models for sharing information. Some of their latest recommendations include the specification of a Decentralised Identifier (DID) and a Verifiable Credential (VC) following the Semantic Web principles. The claims contained in these credentials can be algorithmically verified without the intervention of authorities. These technologies are often associated with implementing the Self-Sovereign Identity paradigm, and this chapter evaluates whether this will happen in practice, particularly in the context of the financial sector. Whereas some privacy concerns are identified, the integrated use of DID, VC and Open Digital Rights Language ODRL will present clear benefits in at least some commercial settings.

This paper expands and updates the text of the lecture delivered at the III International Congress entitled "Present and future of crypto-assets regulation in the European Union", held at the University of Alicante (Spain) on 13,14, and 15 December, 2023. This work is funded within the framework of: Proyecto CIPROM/2022/26 "Presente y futuro de la regulación de los Criptoactivos en la UE [Legalcripto]". Proyecto Prometeo CIPROM/2022/26, grupos de investigación de excelencia, de la Generalitat Valenciana (P.I. Carmen Pastor). This work has also been supported by the Ministerio de Transformación Digital y Función Pública under the project "Infraestructura para la Investigación de Espacios de Datos distribuidos en UPM" (INESData).

V. Rodríguez-Doncel (✉)
Departamento de Inteligencia Artificial, Universidad Politécnica de Madrid (Spain), Madrid, Spain

C. Pastor Sempere (ed.), *Governance and Control of Data and Digital Economy in the European Single Market*, Law, Governance and Technology Series 71,
https://doi.org/10.1007/978-3-031-74889-9_5

1 Introduction

Having an identity is essential for being allowed to do things. For example, attending an exclusive party is possible by holding a physical invitation card, which identifies the holder as one of the invitees. Moreover, identifying others is useful for exerting control over them. Simply put, and to use an analogy, the goatherder must identify each goat with a proper name to avoid losing them. The legal recognition of a person also captures these two opposite dimensions of empowerment and control: we have rights and obligations before the law. Being recognised before the law is a very strong right: "Everyone has the right to recognition everywhere as a person before the law",—reads Article 6 of the Universal Declaration of Human Rights. And this recognition also very strongly obliges us to pay taxes. So, we are goats that can go to parties.

The novelty in the digital world is that there are so many parties. As our lives happen more and more in the digital sphere, we consume more and more online services for any practical aspect of life. Sometimes, in exchange for our money, more often in exchange for our attention (we are obliged to watch ads) or in exchange for our data (involving more or less dubious practices about our privacy). In any case, we have a *user account* in a myriad of internet services—although perhaps we should express it conversely: the service provider has an account with our money committed, our time employed, and our preferences and habits revealed. In this scenario, we have multiple digital *identities*.

By choice or by force, we disclose different aspects of our lives to these service providers. And very easily, we forget what we said to whom—we are content if we can remember the many usernames and passwords we must use daily. We may have some rights as per regulation. In Europe, the General Data Protection Regulation protects citizens' privacy. Still, in practice, there are so many data controllers and privacy policies we have not read that we cannot control the data controllers. There is a technical shortcut if we identify ourselves in this plethora of systems through large identity providers, such as Facebook Connect or Google Sign-in. Most surely, we have all seen these buttons inviting us to "Log in with Google". But then, by doing so, we are further empowering these giants who already know so much about us.

The main problems to be solved in any identity system are avoiding the repetition of identifiers and authenticating the identified entities, e.g., proving you are the one you claim to be. The easiest way to solve these problems is to keep a centralised record of identities (for example, my list of goats or the centralised database of the tax-payers national IDs). However, there is an emerging alternative to this paradigm. This alternative is the idea of *decentralised identity*, a method of identifying and authenticating users or entities online without the need for a centralised authority. The concept of "Self-Sovereign Identity", often referred to by its acronym SSI, is a refinement of the decentralised identity idea that emerged in 2016.[1,2] In a

[1] Tobin and Reed (2016).

[2] Allen (2016).

self-sovereign identity system, individuals *own* and *control* their identity without the intervention of administrative or commercial authorities. Under SSI, a person's identity "is neither dependent on nor subjected to any other power or state".[3]

SSI restores in the digital world the same freedom and capacity for trust people had in the physical world before digital services arrived. Decentralised identity systems enable decentralised Personal Information Management Systems (PIMS), systems designed so that individuals regain control of their personal data—see the work of Zichichi et al. on how decentralised systems can be used to build such a PIMS.[4]

SSI is still very young, and there is no prevailing technological implementation of the idea; different competing initiatives have been proposed. This chapter will only pay attention to one of the solutions based on Web standards. The reason for this choice is threefold: first, historically, the Web community has strived for distributed systems since the very beginning; second, this technology has received official support from different authorities; and third, solid implementations exist.

The chapter introduces in Sect. 2 the World Wide Web Consortium as the organisation standardising the Decentralised Identifier and the Verifiable Credential—these are described in Sects. 3 and 4, respectively. Sect. 5 describes the ODRL policy language and proposes its joint use with the credentials. Section 6 analyses the use of these technologies in Fintech and their real value as implementations of SSI and electronic commerce.

2 The World Wide Web

Everybody knows what the World Wide Web is: a collection of computer files hosted on distant computers that are globally accessible. These files can be retrieved across different information systems because, relying on heterogeneous data transmission technologies, computers ultimately implement a series of standards and protocols that make the transfer possible.

The famous TCP and IP are low-level protocols capable of reliably transporting data between two internet nodes, and they have been adopted as international standards by the Internet Engineering Task Force (IETF). The Internet infrastructure is the base for many other upper-level protocols and services, including Web protocols. Protocols such as HTTP or HTTPS transport documents of any kind on the Web, including hypertext documents (HTML). HTML, CSS and XML are some of the technical specifications maintained by the World Wide Web Consortium (W3C).

The W3C was founded in 1994 by Tim Berners-Lee with the mission "to lead its full potential by developing protocols and guidelines that ensure the long-term growth of the Web". The W3C organisation has an open nature itself: companies,

[3]Preukschat and Reed (2021).

[4]Zichichi (2022).

public institutions and individuals work together to draft the technical specifications. Although the W3C has conflict resolution mechanisms, voting is rarely necessary, for consensus is sought as a rule. Discussions occur transparently, and anyone can implement the resulting norms, for they must be patent-free and royalties-free. Unlike the norms from other standardisation bodies, such as ISO/IEC, W3C's recommendations are always freely accessible. New specifications are dynamically created (or abandoned) to respond to the web users' and industry's needs, and the consortium merely plays a coordinating role with a very light bureaucracy. Therefore, it is fair to say that the decentralised information system *par excellence*, the World Wide Web, is technically specified in a rather decentralised way.

Many say that the Internet was decentralised by design to be resilient and withstand the technical failures expected in global warfare scenarios. The Web was decentralised by design to spread worldwide the ability to publish and obtain instant, connected information and knowledge.[5] The importance of the Web's paradigm shift cannot be overstated. Never in human history has the ability to obtain and publish information been so universally accessible. The revolution is not just about the vast amount of information available virtually everywhere, at any time, and for anyone. It is also about the diversity of sources providing this information. Despite the re-centralisation forces at play, the web is essentially decentralised with search engines, social networks, generative AI system providers, and other walled-off information sources.

On the World Wide Web, humans and machines have always had equal access to published pages, with computer programs retrieving information automatically just as humans do. Over time, the W3C's most significant endeavour became the further development of this concept. Tim Berners-Lee named this idea the *Semantic Web*:

> I have a dream for the Web [in which computers] become capable of analysing all the data on the Web – the content, links, and transactions between people and computers. A 'Semantic Web', which should make this possible, has yet to emerge, but when it does, the day-to-day mechanisms of trade, bureaucracy and our daily lives will be handled *by machines talking to machines.*[6]

The Semantic Web transformed a network of documents accessible by humans into a network of documents and data, where machines will consume data,[7] many of them IoT devices. These humans and machines indistinctively exchange information in a non-hierarchically organised structure. Many have described this decentralised organisation as *rhizomatic*, in Deleuze and Guattari's sense[8] Rhizome is a term used in botany to describe a type of plant stem that grows horizontally underground. Unlike hierarchical root systems, rhizomes form a network of interconnected roots and shoots, embodying a non-hierarchical, decentralised structure. Deleuze and Guattari did not know the Web when they described this possible arrangement of information

[5] Berners-Lee (1999).

[6] Berners-Lee (1999).

[7] Berners-Lee (2001).

[8] Deleuze and Guattari (1987).

and knowledge, but the network structure of the Web certainly follows the pattern. Will identity systems adopt this form someday?

The early Web architects strived for simplicity, openness, and decentralisation. However, the initial design lacked a system to verify the identity of users or machines connecting to it—an identity layer of technologies. This identity layer was not a priority at first, and only with the growth of online services did new identity management systems and protocols become integral to the modern web. Kim Cameron, who was Microsoft's Chief Identity Architect for many years, put this bluntly: "The Internet was built without an identity layer." He meant that there existed no standard technology or protocol to verify and manage identities ready to be used by information systems. He described the ideal properties of such an abstract technological layer in a series of essays published in his blog in 2004 and 2005: "The Laws of Identity" (Cameron 2005). These laws of identity have enlightened the path for new identity systems.

The earliest systems adopting user-password schemas put the arduous task on users, who had to remember many credentials or, more dangerously, reuse weak passwords across multiple sites, compromising security. Consequently, these systems were soon replaced by more advanced technologies influenced by those Laws of Identity. OpenID, JWT, OAuth, and other identity management protocols introduced single sign-on (SSO), token-based authentication, and federated identity. These innovations significantly improved the user experience and security of online authentication, but the W3C did not play any significant role in their design.

3 W3C Decentralised Identifiers

The W3C's endeavours to specify a decentralised identifier only started in September 2019, when the Decentralised Identifier Working Group was formalised to specify the "W3C Decentralised Identifier" or DID. This group aimed to specify the data model and syntax of an identifier capable of enabling verifiable, decentralised digital identity. The specification was completed in July 2022 and published as a W3C Recommendation.[9] Also, in 2019, the complementary system WebAuthn was specified by the W3C to authenticate users using public-key cryptography.[10]

The DID is simply a URI (similar to a web address) that associates a DID subject (the identified entity) with a DID document (data describing the subject), allowing trustable interactions associated with that subject. The DID identifies persons and organisations, things or other abstract entities. The so-called "DID controller" is the entity that can create or make changes to a DID document. By default, the DID subject is a controller of their own DID, but this is not always the case (as the

[9] Sporny (2022a).

[10] Balfanz (2019).

goatherder may want to create a DID for the goat to recall the previous analogy). Anybody can become a DID controller, proving control over the DID without requiring permission from any other party—the DID has been designed to operate, in principle, independently of centralised registries, identity providers, and certificate authorities.

When the identified subject has an informational nature, the DID can provide the mechanism to return the DID subject itself—and all this is possible because of the cryptographic methods that can be invoked. Each DID document can include cryptographic material, verification methods, and services that facilitate the controller in proving control over the DID. Since there are multiple technologies available to implement these requirements, various *methods* are possible. These methods define how a particular type of DID and its associated DID document are created, resolved, updated, and deactivated. The specific method is, therefore, a crucial element of information for the DID. A W3C DID, which looks like this:

```
did:methodX:123456789abcdfghi
```

The first three letters are the scheme that identifies the string as a DID, and the word "methodX" is the chosen technology (more than 140 methods have been defined). The following string of characters is the method-specific identifier. Some common methods are `did:key`, used for public key cryptography or `did:ethr`, relying on the Ethereum blockchains and possibly supporting decentralised finance applications. The DID identifier is *resolvable*; that is to say, it may lead to the actual DID document, with the different attributes given to the identified subject (date and place of birth, name, etc.). Some attributes in the document are of particular relevance: who the controller is (if not the subject) and what the public key is—this enables the controller to prove ownership. The DID document is a set of RDF triples: the RDF triple is the information unit in the Semantic Web mentioned before.

4 W3C Verifiable Credentials

The decentralised identity ecosystem of the W3C is completed with the W3C Verifiable Credential (VC)[11] specification. In this context, a credential is a digital document containing *claims* made by an *issuer* about a subject. For example, a credential issued by a university may state that I have obtained a certain degree. The university is the issuer, and I am the *holder* of the credential. As the holder, I can present this credential in a job interview when I need to demonstrate that I have such a qualification. The job interviewer may verify that claim; hence, the interviewer will be called a *verifier*. The information shown is said to be a *presentation,* that is to say, a package of one or more verifiable credentials assembled by me as a holder and

[11] Sporny (2022b).

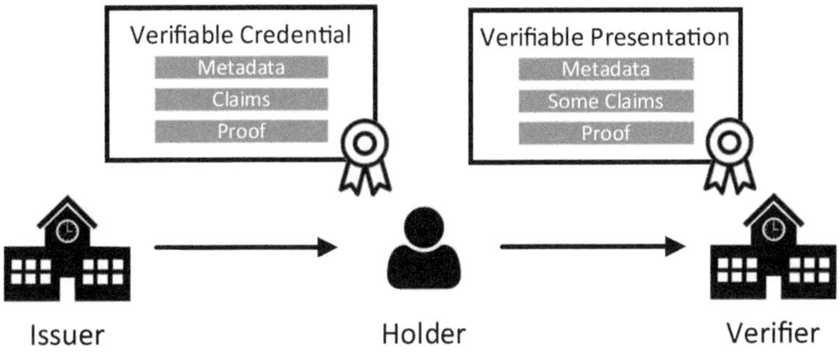

Fig. 1 The simplest use of verifiable credentials

shared with the verifier (the job interviewer). This simple schema is depicted in Fig. 1.

The beneficial property of VCs is that the presentation allows the verifier to check the validity of the credentials and the authenticity of the claims they contain. Anyone can verify the validity of a VC using the information contained within the credential itself and the referred cryptographic methods without the need for a third party; the job interviewer does not need to contact the university or check a registry. Just run an algorithm. Nowadays, university diplomas use special paper and ink to make forgery and tampering difficult; however, breaking the authenticity and integrity of cryptographically signed credentials is nearly impossible.

There is one last element missing. Additional measures may be necessary for the job interviewer to verify that the university, potentially identified with a DID, issued the VC. The university could publish its DID on a physical bulletin board, participate in a web of trust, or register with a *trust anchor*. This well-known entity would confirm the university's identity. Of course, trust anchors represent the opposite of decentralisation, as typical trust anchors are governmental bodies, accreditation organisations, or other reputable institutions. Yet, the W3C VC specification sanctions this solution with the idea of a *verifiable data registry*. A verifiable data registry is a system, decentralised or not, that serves as a trusted source of any identity-related data. Verifiable data registries are used to store and manage DIDs, DID documents, and other verifiable credentials.

In other words, a verifiable credential is a cryptographically signed message, and the W3C standard on Verifiable Credentials specifies the data structure. This data structure is simple: every credential comprises three parts: the credential metadata, the claims, and the proofs. Some metadata elements are mandatory, such as the type of claim, the claim ID, the issuer, the expiration date, or the credential subject, but adding an attribute of choice is also possible.

The specification also adheres to the Semantic Web principles described before. Thus, identifiers in a VC are URIs, strings like web addresses, many of them DIDs. Information is represented in a graph structure, possibly connected to entities out of the VC itself. This technological choice also grants that the DID and VC specification can be extended to anyone and anything, including cloud, edge, and IoT resources.

Different lifecycles for Verifiable Credentials (VCs) have been described.[12] In the archetypical case, the process begins with issuing a VC and storing the credential in a credential repository (second step). Subsequently, in the third step, one or more VCs are packaged into a verifiable presentation for verifiers. Finally, in the fourth and final step, the verifier verifies the verifiable presentation. Revocation of identifiers and credentials is also included in the specification. There are several reasons for revocations: a claim might have been made by mistake, or a private key might have been lost. A credential status property in the VC is specified to link to a status list or registry. This may be a centralised verifiable data registry or refer to information stored on a blockchain.

Credentials are, therefore, stored in credential repositories, which we usually name *digital wallets*. The role of these digital wallets is extremely important—see how the EU Digital Identity Wallet is now being introduced in Europe. Wallets must be capable of storing both VCs and the cryptographic key pairs associated with the DIDs. This capability allows users to interact with service providers without needing an internet connection, utilising Bluetooth or NFC.

5 W3C Policies

The W3C also has a specification for representing policies, the Open Digital Rights Language (ODRL). ODRL became part of the W3C standards in 2018 (Ianella and Villata 2018; Ianella et al. 2018). A policy provides information on permissions, prohibitions and duties related to an asset. The validity of the permissions can be conditioned to the satisfaction of zero or more conditions, such as a payment. Temporal or geographical constraints are also not uncommon. The language comes with vocabulary elements to represent some typical actions that are permitted (such as *play*, *publish*, etc.) and some typical constraints (payment, spatial, temporal, etc.). The language can be extended through the specification of *profiles*, which further refine the terminology used in specific domains. ODRL policies can represent policies in force (said to be of type *Set*) but can also represent *Offers* and *Agreements*. The agreement life-cycle is not described by the recommendation, though.

Policies determine the behaviour of access control systems (that selectively grant access to media content, computer files or any other information). Still, they can also be used in various scenarios —such as compliance checking[13] or contract management.[14] ODRL has been used in various domains: in digital rights management for

[12] Brunner (2020).

[13] de Vos (2019).

[14] Steyskal and Kirrane (2015).

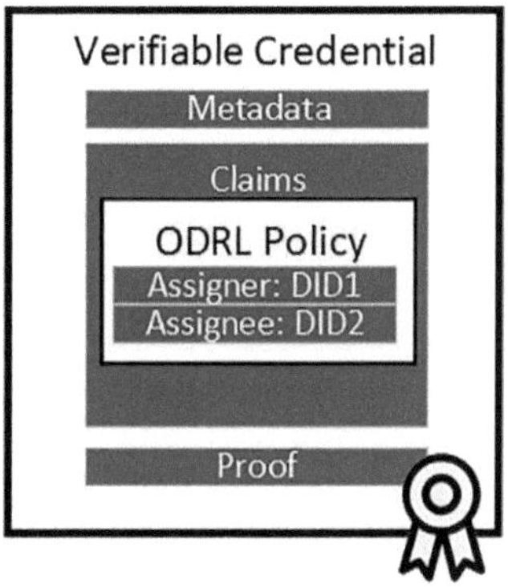

Fig. 2 ODRL Policies as a part of the Verifiable Credential

media content in mobile phones,[15] in the news sector,[16] in the language data sector,[17] and lately, in the data markets called Data Spaces[18,19] or the financial data market, where the W3C Rights Automation for Market Data Community Group has specified an ODRL profile to trade with market data.

ODRL policies are represented in RDF—the Semantic Web data format—and can be easily expanded and integrated with other W3C standards. However, no formal proposal exists to use ODRL policies with decentralised identifiers and verifiable claims. A relatively novel approach for the integration of ODRL with DID and VC would be materialised in the following manner (illustrated in Fig. 2):

- The ODRL policy, represented in RDF, could be one of the claims in a Verifiable Credential or a Verifiable Presentation. This integration would reinforce the policy's value, for its provenance would be guaranteed by an algorithm that can be run without the participation of the policy issuer or any other authority. The policy could be trusted because no forgery or tampering would be possible.
- The two parties in an ODRL policy are the policy assigner and the assignee. The assigner determines which rights, prohibitions, and obligations operate on a possible assignee. Policies with no assignee means they are intended for general consumption. There is no formal restriction on how these parties are referenced, and nothing prevents the policy from using DIDs. This integration would enable policies to be used in a decentralised environment.
- A DID may also identify the policy itself, which would be contained in a DID Document. This integration would solve the problems of policy identification, policy resolution (unspecified by ODRL) and policy encryption, which would now be possible.

[15] Torres (2008).

[16] IPTC Rights Expressions Working Group (2018).

[17] Rodríguez-Doncel and Labropoulou (2015).

[18] Steinbuß (2021).

[19] GAIA-X European Association for Data and Cloud (2022).

The joint use of these three W3C technologies (DID, VC, ODRL) is a novel idea that has only been sketched in the framework of data markets[20] but has not yet been implemented. The ability of ODRL to represent the exchange of rights and obligations present in every contract and the ability of DID and VC to grant integrity, confidentiality, availability, authenticity, and non-repudiation for these policies make their joint use an excellent choice in private commercial exchanges. It is also worth mentioning that all of this can be accomplished *without* blockchain technologies. Indeed, these policies or similar policies like those of MPEG-21 can work together with distributed ledger technologies and smart contracts.[21]—transforming policies into smart contracts has been standardised for the media content case as ISO/IEC 21000-23.

6 Analysis of Web Technologies for Decentralised Identity

The applications of decentralised identifiers and verifiable credentials are unlimited. They can be used to support a birth certificate, verify the authenticity of a legal apostille, guarantee the origin of a health certificate, or certify the authenticity of some organic food—see Mazzocca et al.[22] For an exhaustive survey. The W3C has also collected some use cases in education, retail, finance, healthcare, professional credentials, legal identity, and IoT devices.[23]

The World Economic Forum acknowledged in its 2016 report on the subject matter that the importance of digital identity for the financial sector cannot be underestimated.[24] For the financial domain, five application examples are given: (i) Reuse Know Your Customer (KYC), where the KYC obligation is satisfied by using government-supplied VCs that demonstrate the customer identity; (ii) money transfers, where the receiver and sender of the money can be identified to comply with the regulations against money laundering; (iii) closing a bank account, where the mechanisms for revoking credentials come into play; (iv) data portability among financial services, where the interoperability of wallets is crucial and (v) opening a bank account, where the use of government-supplied VCs suffices to the operation in a remote modality.

Different organisations have implemented systems based on the W3C VC specification: companies like Microsoft[25] or IBM, smaller players such as Consensys[26] (with their popular products Serto/Veramo), foundations like the Sovrin Foundation

[20] GAIA-X European Association for Data and Cloud (2022).

[21] Zichichi and Rodriguez-Doncel (2023).

[22] Mazzocca et al. (2024).

[23] McCarron (2019).

[24] McWaters (2016).

[25] https://www.microsoft.com/en-gb/security/business/identity-access/microsoft-entra-id/.

[26] https://www.uport.me/.

or the IOTA Foundation, governments (Canada, New Zealand), universities like MIT[27] or open-source projects like Hyperledger Aries[28] or the DIDKit toolkit. These efforts demonstrate the growing adoption of W3C verifiable credentials across many industries and use cases. And indeed, one of the key sectors is Fintech. However, do these technologies announce a revolution enabling decentralised financial applications?

The technical specifications of W3C Digital Identity and Verifiable Credentials embody the principles of decentralised identity and self-sovereign identity, and their joint use in various cases presents several advantages. First, they are secure, as the authenticity of the data is algorithmically guaranteed. Second, some argue they are privacy-friendly, allowing holders to disclose only the minimum necessary information to each verifier selectively. Third, they are standards-based and interoperable across different technologies. Fourth, they enable decentralisation, potentially leaving control in the hands of users rather than centralised authorities. Finally, verifiable credentials are quite efficient, as they can be easily issued, shared, and verified—unless used in connection with blockchains.

W3C Verifiable Credentials have not been free from critiques, either. The most obvious is that in practice, the two main features of self-sovereign identity, namely, that individuals own and control their identity, are not feasible. Anyone can create a decentralised identity, but this is pseudonymous information by nature—we don't know the subject's real-world identity. Without a central registry or trust schema with a root of trust (e.g., Certificate Authorities), DIDs do not provide advantages over having a pseudonymous email address.

Moreover, some have doubted that decentralisation is at the heart of the specifications.[29] In the example in this Chapter, the holder and the subject of the claim were the same. But this might not always be the case, and nothing prevents the holder from being a government database the subject has no knowledge of—verifiable data registries do not need to be decentralised at all. Suspicion has been cast on the fundamental purpose of VCs, whose specification has been generously funded[30] by the Department of US Homeland Security concerning COVID-19 passports and related restrictions—see implementations such as Consensas Information Passport,[31] BlockID[32] or those based on Solid.[33] If privacy is about unlinkability,[34] and the Semantic Web is about linkability and data integration, something is fundamentally broken with using Semantic Web postulates on identity systems. Besides, several

---

[27] https://digitalcredentials.mit.edu/.

[28] https://www.hyperledger.org/projects/aries.

[29] Halpin (2020).

[30] Department of Homeland Security Contract HSHQDC-17-C-00019 https://www.sbir.gov/sbirsearch/detail/1302459.

[31] https://github.com/Consensas/information-passport.

[32] https://www.1kosmos.com/identity-management/digital-identity-in-a-covid-world/.

[33] Eisenstadt (2020).

[34] Pfitzmann and Hansen (2010).

technical problems have been described. The standards family is incomplete, and the Verifiable Credential Data Integrity methods specification has not been finalised. The bit-serialization string of the credential is ill-defined, and software developers have identified specification gaps.[35] The resolution from a DID to the DID document differs for each method (but often on blockchains). In practice, they may resort to permissioned federations—public databases of DID documents- again against the privacy-by-default philosophy. Lack of expert review on security and lack of formal scrutiny adds to this problem.

7 Conclusion

Most of the world's population owns at least one digital identity. However, the concept of digital identity extends far beyond the authentication of human beings in online services. Identity is something more important than an invitation card. Identity is a sense of self; it is about how you perceive yourself, your values, beliefs, experiences, and relationships; it is about the internal understanding of who you are. Now, we live in the digital. Our memories are no longer disembodied, and once transformed into data, they can be processed and used by algorithms.

This chapter presents the World Wide Web Consortium and two of its latest specifications: the Decentralised Identifier and the Verifiable Credential. They promise that, as an implementation of the Self-Sovereign Identity idea, individuals will own and control their identity information. Having the technical ability to do this is already a great advance, but the chapter has also shown that, in practice, authorities will use the standards in centralised schemas.

However, the technical progress brought by these technologies is not to be disdained. The chapter also shows how to use these identifiers and credentials in conjunction with the W3C language to represent permissions, obligations, and prohibitions, known as ODRL. ODRL is already used in many sectors, and the enhanced security properties for the claims can only be a positive development.

References

Allen C (2016) The path to self-sovereign identity. Blog Posts. https://www.lifewithalacrity.com/article/the-path-to-self-soverereign-identity/. Accessed 15 June 2024

Alzahrani B (2020) An information-centric networking-based registry for decentralised identifiers and verifiable credentials. IEEE Access 8:137198–137208

Berners-Lee T (1999) Weaving the web: the original design and ultimate destiny of the World Wide Web by its inventor. Harper, San Francisco

Berners-Lee T, Hendler J, Lassila O (2001) The semantic web. Sci Am 284(5):34–43

[35] Alzahrani (2020).

Brunner C, Gallersdörfer U, Knirsch F, Engel D, Matthes F (2020) DID and VC: untangling decentralised identifiers and verifiable credentials for the web of trust. In Proceedings of the 2020 3rd Int. Conf. on Blockchain Technology and Applications, Xi'an, 14-16 Dec 2020

Cameron K (2005) The laws of identity. Kim Cameron's Identity Weblog. www.identityblog.com/?p=352. Accessed 15 June 2024

Deleuze G, Guattari F (1987) A thousand plateaus: capitalism and schizophrenia. University of Minnesota, Minneapolis

Eisenstadt M, Ramachandran M, Chowdhury N, Third A, Domingue J (2020) COVID-19 antibody test/vaccination certification: there's an app for that. IEEE Open J Eng Med Biol 1:148–155

GAIA-X European Association for Data and Cloud (2022) Gaia-X Architecture Document 22.04 Release. Gaia-X European Association for Data and Cloud AISBL

Halpin H (2020) Vision: a critique of immunity passports and W3C decentralised identifiers. In: Security Standardisation Research: 6th International Conference, Springer International Publishing, London, 30 Nov – 1 Dec 2020

Steinbuß, S. (2021) Usage control in the international data spaces. International Data Spaces Association, https://doi.org/10.5281/zenodo.5675884, Accessed 15 June 2024

IPTC Rights Expressions Working Group (2018) IPTC RightsML Standard 2.0. International Press Telecommunications Council

Mazzocca C, Acar A, Uluagac S, Montanari R, Bellavista P, Conti M (2024) A survey on decentralised identifiers and verifiable credentials. arXiv preprint arXiv:2402.02455

McCarron S et al (2019) Verifiable credentials use cases W3C Working Group Note 24 September 2019

Ianella R, Villata, S (2018) ODRL Information Model 2.2. W3C Recommendation 15 February 2018

Ianella R, Steidl M, Myles S, Rodríguez-Doncel V (2018) ODRL Vocabulary & Expression 2.2. W3C Recommendation 15 Feb 2018

Pfitzmann A, Hansen M (2010) A terminology for discussing privacy by data minimization: Anonymity, unlinkability, undetectability, unobservability, pseudonymity, and identity management. https://dud.inf.tu-dresden.de/literatur/Anon_Terminology_v0.34.pdf In TU Dresden, Accessed 15 June 2024

Preukschat A, Reed D (2021) Self-sovereign identity. Manning Publications, Shelter Island

Rodríguez-Doncel V, Labropoulou P (2015) Digital representation of rights for language resources. In Proceedings of the 4th Workshop on Linked Data in Linguistics: Resources and Application, Association for Computational Linguistics, Beijing, 31 July 2015

Sporny M, Guy A, Sabadello M, Reed D (2022a) Decentralised Identifiers (DIDs) v1.0 Core architecture, data model, and representations. W3C Recommendation 19 July 2022

Sporny M et al (2022b) Verifiable Credentials Data Model v1.1 W3C Recommendation 03 March 2022

Steyskal S, Kirrane S (2015) If you can't enforce it, contract it: Enforceability in Policy-Driven (Linked) Data Markets. In: Semantics (posters & demos), Vienna, 16–17 September 2015

De Vos M, Kirrane S, Padget J, Satoh K (2019) ODRL policy modelling and compliance checking. In: Rules and Reasoning: Third International Joint Conference, RuleML+ RR 2019, Springer International Publishing, Bolzano, 16–19 Septembe 2019

Tobin A, Reed D (2016) The inevitable rise of self-sovereign identity. The Sovrin Foundation, 29: 18

Torres V, Serrao C, Dias J, Delgado J (2008) Open DRM and the future of media. Open DRM Fut Media 2:28–36

Balfanz D et al. (2019) Web authentication: An API for accessing Public Key Credentials Level 1. W3C Recommendation, 4 March 2019

McWaters J et al (2016) A Blueprint for Digital Identity. World Economic Forum Future of Financial Services Series. https://www3.weforum.org/docs/WEF_A_Blueprint_for_Digital_Identity.pdf. Accessed 15 June 2024

Zichichi M, Ferretti S, Rodríguez-Doncel V (2022) Decentralized personal data marketplaces: how participation in a DAO can support the production of citizen-generated data. Sensors 22(16): 6260

Zichichi M, Rodriguez-Doncel V (2023) Encoding of media value chain processes through blockchains and MPEG-21 smart contracts for media. IEEE MultiMedia 22:1–8

The National Security Framework as a Cybersecurity Reference for Information Cryptosystems

Pablo López

Abstract In today's hyper-connected world, implementing security in cyberspace has become a global strategic priority. As technology's role in society increases, cybersecurity becomes an increasingly bigger challenge. In addition, the cyber threat landscape is evolving, with the emergence of new risks and the sophistication of existing threats. Cybercriminals are increasingly targeting specific sectors, such as energy, finance, government, and healthcare, to cause maximum disruption and financial gain or loss. In Spain, the successive editions of the National Report on the State of Security (INES) and the body of CCN-STIC security guides have resulted in greater accumulated experience in its application and better knowledge of the situation. The new National Security Framework 2022 stands as a pivotal platform, addressing cybersecurity in a manner intricately linked to digital transformation. This is achieved through a robust and consolidated regulatory framework, making it the most significant development in this field. In this sense, Royal Decree 311/2022 is a guiding light for security in the digital society. Its applicability to crypto-asset systems is crucial to building a reliable foundation in the new financial paradigm. It represents a reference framework, a robust framework for assessing and improving security in systems that handle crypto assets.

This paper expands and updates the text of a lecture delivered at the III International Congress entitled "Present and future of crypto-assets regulation in the European Union," held at the University of Alicante (Spain) on December 13, 14, and 15, 2023.This work is funded within the framework of: Proyecto CIPROM/2022/26 "Presente y futuro de la regulación de los Criptoactivos en la UE [Legalcripto]". Proyecto Prometeo CIPROM/2022/26, grupos de investigación de excelencia, de la Generalitat Valenciana (P.I. Carmen Pastor).

P. López (✉)
National Cryptologic Centre (National Intelligence Centre), Madrid, Spain

Ministry of Defence, Madrid, Spain
e-mail: pablol88@i3point.com

C. Pastor Sempere (ed.), *Governance and Control of Data and Digital Economy in the European Single Market*, Law, Governance and Technology Series 71,
https://doi.org/10.1007/978-3-031-74889-9_6

1 Cybersecurity in the 21st Century

In the twenty-first century, the security of information processed and services provided electronically has transcended from a mere concern to a fundamental aspect of our society. The pervasive use of electronic systems for communication, transactions, and access to public and private services has necessitated the establishment of robust regulatory frameworks to ensure data protection and trust in these systems.

The so-called *digital transformation* has revolutionised the way we interact with technology. Our daily lives are intertwined with technology, and this is impacting public administrations—which use electronic systems to manage all kinds of procedures, files, taxes and services to citizens—and private companies—which rely on information systems to support their productive, financial, commercial or human resources operations—, as well as citizens—whose daily activity relies on these systems for banking transactions, virtual healthcare, entertainment or management and use of cryptocurrencies—. However, this dependence also exposes us to countless risks, such as cyber-attacks, the loss of essential data for our privacy and economy or the existence of vulnerabilities in our security.

Before proceeding, it is important to clarify some essential concepts discussed in the following pages.

First and foremost, the concept of an information system is defined in Annex IV-Glossary of Royal Decree 311/2022 of 3 May—which regulates the National Security Framework (ENS)—and the terms can be understood as:

> Any of the following:
>
> 1. The electronic communications networks used by the entity within the scope of application of this Royal Decree over which it has management capacity.
> 2. Any device or group of interconnected or related devices in which one or more automatically processes digital data through a program.
> 3. Digital data stored, processed, retrieved or transmitted using the elements referred to in numbers 1 and 2 above, including those necessary for the operation, use, protection and maintenance of the mentioned elements.

The same should be done with the term *cybersecurity*, which is also included in the aforementioned RD:

> (information systems security): the ability of network and information systems to withstand, at a specified level of dependability, any action that compromises the availability, authenticity, integrity or confidentiality of stored, transmitted or processed data or the related services offered by or accessible through such network and information systems.

This last definition also coincides with that contained in article 3 b) of Royal Decree-Law 12/2018a, issued under the exclusive powers of the State in matters of telecommunications and the general communications system (art. 149.1.21 CE) and public security (art. 149.1.29 CE), which defines the security of information networks and systems in the same way.

As it has been stated, the concept of an *information system* includes any physical (hardware) or logical (software) element involved in the processing of data, whatever these may be, knowing, moreover, that *cybersecurity* does not seek to guarantee always and in any situation the absolute immunity of the information systems concerned against threats -a situation that is impossible to achieve-, rather, the aim is to build a security model based on resistance measures -those that reasonably prevent the penetration of the attack and, in general, the progress of the cyber-incident-, and on resilience measures -those aimed at recovering the full functionality of an information system once the cyber-incident is over.

Aligned with the above, the National Cybersecurity Strategy 2019 (Order PCI/487/2019 of 26 April), approved by the National Security Council, establishes the general objective of guaranteeing the secure and reliable use of cyberspace, protecting the rights and freedoms of citizens and promoting socio-economic progress. Based on this general objective, it sets a series of specific objectives, including the security and resilience of public sector information and communications networks and systems and essential services; the secure and reliable use of cyberspace against illicit or malicious use; the protection of the business and social ecosystem; and the enhancement of human and technological capabilities. To this end, the Strategy includes implementing security measures focused on improving incident prevention, detection, and response capabilities through developing new solutions and reinforcing coordination and adaptation of the legal system.

We must not forget, however, that we are not alone in this endeavour. Indeed, the institutions of the European Union have clearly perceived the importance of ensuring the cybersecurity of the information systems used by public and private organisations, professionals, and European citizens, especially those systems on which our normal functioning as a society is based. Thus, since 2016, the year of entry into force of the first NIS Directive (Directive (EU) 2016/1148),[1] considerable progress has been made in increasing the level of cyber resilience of the Union, showing that this legislative initiative has served as a catalyst for the institutional and regulatory approach to cybersecurity in the EU, paving the way for a significant change in mentality. It has led to the generalisation of the need for national network and information systems security frameworks through defining national network and information systems security strategies, establishing national capabilities and implementing regulatory measures covering entities and critical infrastructures determined by each Member State.

The Directive has also encouraged cooperation between EU countries by establishing the Cooperation Group—of which the author of this paper is a member—and the network of computer security incident response teams.

[1] Its development was based on Article 114 of the Treaty on the Functioning of the European Union (TFEU), which aims to establish the internal market by strengthening measures for the approximation of national rules.

However, at the European level, the review of this Directive revealed major differences in its implementation by the Member States, particularly its scope, the delimitation of which was left largely to the discretion of the Member States.

This reality encouraged the European institutions to address the drafting of a new regulation that would adapt protection measures to the reality of a new decade, a desire that finally materialised with the publication of Directive (EU) 2022/2555 of the European Parliament and of the Council, of 14 December 2022 on measures to ensure a high common level of cybersecurity throughout the Union, amending the Regulation (EU) No 910/2014 and the Directive (EU) 2018/1972 and repealing the Directive (EU) 2016/1148 (and referred to as the NIS2 Directive).

Returning to Spanish regulations, specifically the National Security Framework, its preamble mentions the evolution of threats, new attack vectors, the development of modern response mechanisms and the need to maintain compliance and alignment with European and national regulations. This requires adapting security measures to this new reality, in the knowledge that strengthening cybersecurity requires economic, human and technological resources that must be sized in accordance with the principle of proportionality and the necessary level of security, in accordance with adequate planning and with the participation of the agents involved, in line with a dynamic of continuous adaptive improvement.

In today's hyper-connected world, implementing security in cyberspace has become a global strategic priority. The risk in this environment is too big for the public sector or businesses to address alone. Both have a shared interest in and responsibility for addressing this challenge. As the role of technology in society increases, cybersecurity becomes an increasingly bigger challenge.

2 The Origins of Public Cybersecurity in Spain: The ENS of 2010

In 2010, as an unprecedented milestone in our law, the Official State Gazette published Royal Decree 3/2010 of 8 January, which regulated the National Security Framework in the field of e-Government (ENS, hereinafter). This RD aimed to determine the security policy for using electronic media, formulating the basic principles and minimum requirements to guarantee the security of the information processed and the services provided by public administration entities.

That first ENS, whose scope of application included all public sector entities, sought to establish confidence that information systems provide their services properly and safeguard information without interruptions or uncontrolled modifications—all this without allowing information to reach unauthorised persons. It established measures to guarantee the security of systems, data, communications, and electronic services to facilitate citizens and Public Administrations to exercise their rights and fulfil their obligations electronically.

Since that first regulation, there have been significant changes in Spain and the European Union, including the progressive digital transformation of our society and the realisation that information systems are increasingly exposed to the materialisation of threats. There has been a considerable increase in cyber-attacks, both in volume, frequency, sophistication and in the attackers' greater technical and operational capabilities. These threats occur in the context of our society's high dependence on information and communication technologies and high interconnection between them.

All of this significantly affects an increasing number of public and private entities, their supply chains, citizens and, therefore, national cybersecurity, which compromises the normal social and economic development of the country and the exercise of citizens' rights and freedoms, as recognised in the aforementioned National Cybersecurity Strategy of 2019.

Moreover, as we pointed out, the European and Spanish regulatory frameworks have been modified since 2010. This change has affected national security, administrative procedures, the legal regime of the public sector, personal data protection, and the security of networks and information systems. At the same time, the strategic framework for cybersecurity has evolved.

3 Cybersecurity in the National Security System

Article 10 of Law 36/2015a, of 28 September, on National Security, considers cybersecurity an area of particular interest and requires specific attention, as it is essential for preserving citizens' rights, freedoms and welfare and guaranteeing the provision of basic services and resources.

Similarly, Law 8/2011, of 28 April, on measures for the Protection of Critical Infrastructures[2] (issued under the competence attributed to the State under Article 149.1.29 of the Spanish Constitution) refers to cybersecurity. Its Article 2 defines strategic infrastructures as "*the physical and information technology facilities, networks, systems and equipment on which the functioning of essential services is based*", understanding that such services are those necessary for the maintenance of basic social functions, health, security, social and economic well-being of citizens or the efficient functioning of State institutions and public administrations.

Furthermore, maintaining cybersecurity is one of the functions of the National Intelligence Centre (CNI), as established in article 4 b) of Law 11/2002, of 6 May, which regulates it.

In this regard, we cannot fail to mention Royal Decree-Law 12/2018, of 7 September, on the security of networks and information systems, which transposes

---

[2]Defined in the aforementioned Law as those strategic infrastructures "*whose operation is indispensable and does not allow for alternative solutions, so that their disruption or destruction would have a serious impact on essential services*".

into Spanish law Directive (EU) 2016/1148 of the European Parliament and of the Council, of 6 July 2016, on measures to ensure a high common level of security of networks and information systems in the Union. The purpose of this regulation is to regulate the security of networks and information systems used for the provision of essential services and digital services, and to establish an incident notification system, as well as an institutional framework for its application and coordination between competent authorities and with the relevant cooperation bodies at EU level. As is well known, this Royal Decree-Law applies to essential services dependent on information networks and systems included in the strategic sectors defined in the annexe to Law 8/2011, as well as to information society services within the meaning of the letter a) of the annexe to Law 34/2002, of 11 July, on information society services and electronic commerce.

The Constitutional Court ruled on these issues in its judgement 142/2018, of 20 December 2018, concerning the appeal of unconstitutionality 5284-2017 filed by the President of the Government regarding Law 15/2017, of 25 July, on the Cybersecurity Agency of Catalonia, on competences in the areas of telecommunications, defence and public security.

Several conclusions can be drawn from this judgment. Firstly, cybersecurity, as a synonym for network security, is an activity that is integrated into public security and telecommunications. From its conceptualisation as a set of mechanisms aimed at protecting computer infrastructures and the digital information they host, it is easy to infer that, as it is dedicated to the security of information technologies, it has a protective component that is specifically projected onto the specific area of protection of networks and information systems used by citizens, companies and public administrations.

Secondly, cybersecurity is included in matters of state competence insofar as it affects public security and defence, infrastructures, networks and systems, and the general telecommunications regime by referring to the necessary actions of prevention, detection, and response to cyber threats.

All this has been consolidated in Royal Decree 1150/2021 of 28 December, approving the National Security Strategy 2021, in which public cybersecurity is configured as an integral part of National Security. Cyberspace is included among the material objects of security required of global common spaces, and the cybersecurity governance model is integrated into the framework of the National Security System.

Indeed, the 2021 Strategy describes cyberspace as a connected space characterised by its functional openness, lack of physical borders, and easy accessibility. It adds that in the global commons, it is difficult to attribute any irregular or criminal action, given its extent, weak regulation, and absence of sovereignty.

On this basis, the so-called National Security System has been developed. A set of bodies, agencies, resources, and procedures that enable the competent actors in National Security to carry out their functions. The fundamental components are integrated into the System following the liaison and coordination mechanisms determined by the National Security Council, acting under their structures and procedures. Depending on the needs, tasks may be assigned to other public or private bodies and entities.

The National Security System is responsible for assessing the factors and situations that may affect National Security, gathering and analysing the information that allows the necessary decisions to be taken to direct and coordinate the response to the crises contemplated in the National Security Act, detecting needs and proposing measures on planning and coordination with the public administrations as a whole, to guarantee the availability and correct functioning of the System's resources.

The National Security System is headed by the President of the Government, who the National Security Council assists.

On the other hand, the National Security Council's support bodies, under the name of Specialised Committees or such other name as may be determined, carry out the functions assigned by the National Security Council in the areas of action provided for in the National Security Strategy, or when the circumstances of crisis management so require.

The regulation of the coordination and support bodies of the Department of National Security and the mechanisms for permanent liaison and coordination with the bodies of all the State Administrations are necessary for the National Security System to exercise its functions and fulfil its objectives. They shall be the subject of regulatory development in coordination with the affected public Administrations.

Information systems handling crypto assets are no strangers to these security requirements. Table 1 gives an overview of the most important elements to be considered.

4 Cybersecurity in the Public Sector

As is well known, Law 40/2015c, of 1 October, on the Legal Regime of the Public Sector, extended the scope of application of that first ENS of 2010 to the entire public sector. Article 3, which regulates the general principles, establishes the need for public administrations to relate to each other and their bodies, public bodies and related or dependent entities through electronic means, which guarantee the interoperability and security of the systems and solutions adopted by each of them and the protection of personal data, and facilitate the provision of services to data subjects preferably by such means. In this regard, Article 156 identifies the ENS as a fundamental instrument for achieving these objectives.

In the same sense, Law 39/2015b, of 1 October, on the Common Administrative Procedure of Public Administrations, among the rights of individuals in their relations with the Administration, provided for in Article 13, includes the right to the protection of personal data and, in particular, the right to the security of the data contained in the files, systems and applications of the Administrations themselves.

As a development of the aforementioned administrative legislation, Royal Decree 203/2021 of 30 March, which approves the Regulation on the action and operation of the public sector by electronic means, specifies in different precepts the obligation to

Table 1 Cybersecurity and crypto assets. Key considerations

Integrity and authenticity of crypto assets	• Cybersecurity ensures that crypto assets (such as cryptocurrencies) are not tampered with or counterfeited. • Information systems should implement robust cryptographic mechanisms to verify the authenticity of transactions and protect the integrity of crypto-asset records.
Private key protection	• Private keys are essential for accessing and transferring crypto assets. Cybersecurity must ensure that these keys are confidential and not stolen or compromised. • Information systems must implement secure key storage and management practices.
Security of exchange platforms (*Exchanges*)	• Cryptocurrency exchange platforms are critical information systems. They must be protected against cyber-attacks, such as hacks or fund theft. • *Exchange* cybersecurity includes measures such as security audits, two-factor authentication and continuous monitoring.
Preventing harmful attacks	• Information systems that handle crypto assets are very attractive targets for cybercriminals. Therefore, measures must be implemented to prevent phishing, ransomware or malware attacks. • Cybersecurity should include firewalls, intrusion detection and regular software updates.
Transparency and audit	• While the theoretical concept of DLT or blockchain mechanisms calls for transparent behaviour, cybersecurity must ensure that records are accurate and complete. • Information systems should allow for audits and monitoring of transactions to detect suspicious activity.
Regulatory compliance	• Cybersecurity must ensure that information systems comply with crypto-asset regulations and standards, including prevention of money laundering (AML) and tax and fiscal compliance.

comply with the security measures set out in the ENS, such as those referring to electronic data exchange in closed communication environments, the agreed password systems and other systems for identifying the persons concerned, the single electronic file or internet portals, among others.

Driven by the EU's regulatory modernisation in technological matters and coinciding with the approval of the three (3) laws mentioned above, the ENS was updated through the Royal Decree 951/2015 of 23 October, which amended RD 3/2010 of 8 January. This update took place in light of the experience and knowledge of its application, the current cybersecurity situation, and the evolution of the legal framework to adapt to the provisions of Regulation (EU) No 910/2014 of the European Parliament and of the Council of 23 July 2014 on electronic identification and trust services for electronic transactions in the internal market and repealing the Directive 1999/93/EC.

Having thus established the essential framework, the Spanish legislator continued integrating and rationalising the security measures applicable to different processing and systems. Organic Law 3/2018b of 5 December on the Protection of Personal Data and the guarantee of digital rights ordered in its first additional provision that the security measures provided for in the ENS be implemented in the event of processing of personal data to prevent their loss, alteration, or unauthorised access. This brought the criteria for determining risk in data processing into line with the provisions of Article 32 of Regulation (EU) 2016/679 of the European Parliament and of the Council of 27 April 2016 on the protection of individuals concerning the processing of personal data and on the free movement of such data and repealing Directive 95/46/EC (General Data Protection Regulation).

Moreover, the first additional provision also determines the implementation of the security measures of the ENS for public sector entities and private sector entities that collaborate with them in the provision of public services that involve processing personal data. Finally, and in the same vein, the Organic Law 7/2021 of 26 May, on the protection of personal data processed for the prevention, detection, investigation and prosecution of criminal offences and the execution of criminal penalties, establishes in Article 37 the obligation to apply the ENS measures to the processing of personal data by the competent public authorities.

5 National Cybersecurity Strategies

From all the above, it is clear that it is essential to have regulations, procedures, mechanisms and tools capable of providing a sufficient degree of security to our relationship with electronic media to the extent that the risks we face make it advisable. This was established in the 2017 National Security Strategy, which states that Spain needs to guarantee a secure and responsible use of information and communications networks and systems by strengthening capacities to prevent, detect and respond to cyber-attacks, promoting and adopting specific measures to contribute to the promotion of a secure and reliable cyberspace.

Therefore, on 12 April 2019, the National Security Council approved the aforementioned National Cybersecurity Strategy 2019 to set general guidelines for cybersecurity and achieve the objectives set out in the National Security Strategy 2017.

Thus, the National Cybersecurity Strategy 2019 includes a general and five specific objectives, proposes seven lines of action to achieve them, and integrates 65 measures.

Indeed, recalling the first of these objectives is precisely the security and resilience of public sector information and communications networks and systems and essential services, developed through 2 lines of action and 24 specific measures, including ensuring the full implementation of the National Security Framework.

Figure 1 shows the most significant regulatory itinerary in recent years in eGovernment, cybersecurity and related legislation.

Fig. 1 Source: Infographics ENS (National Cryptologic Centre) https://ens.ccn.cni.es/es/que-es-el-ens/infografias

6 The National Security Framework 2022

At the same time as the scenario described in the preceding sections has been consolidating, the implementation of the ENS has been spreading. Thanks to the successive editions of the National Report on the State of Security (INES) and the body of CCN-STIC security guides, this has resulted in greater accumulated experience in its application and better knowledge of the situation.[3]

For the above reasons, it was necessary to update the ENS to meet three (3) main objectives:

(i) Align it with the existing regulatory framework and strategic context to ensure security in eGovernment.

(ii) Introduce the ability to adjust the ENS's requirements and ensure its adaptation to the reality of certain groups or types of systems where its implementation was very complicated.

This was in response to the similarity of an assortment of entities or services in terms of the risks to which their information systems and services are exposed, which made it advisable to include in the Framework the concept of a "Specific Compliance Profile", which, approved and published by the National Cryptologic Centre, allows for a more effective and efficient adaptation of the ENS, rationalising the resources required without detriment to the protection pursued and enforceable.

(iii) Review basic principles, minimum requirements, and security measures to facilitate a better response to cybersecurity trends, reduce vulnerabilities, and promote continuous surveillance.

All this is caused by the elements summarised in Fig. 2.

The new National Security Framework 2022 stands as a pivotal platform, addressing cybersecurity in a manner intricately linked to digital transformation. This is achieved through a robust and consolidated regulatory framework, making it the most significant development in this field. The impact of the framework is far-reaching, affecting both the public sector and its private sector suppliers. It encompasses all necessary elements, including governance, organisational, operational, and technological measures, compliance certification frameworks, and mechanisms for adaptation or continuous monitoring and surveillance. Importantly, this framework is deeply embedded in our legal system, as illustrated in Fig. 3, which charts the evolution of the National Security Framework.

The current ENS, implemented by 2022/2022 of 3 May, now extends its scope of application to all public sector entities. Chapter I outlines that this significant expansion includes the systems that process classified information.

One particularly novel aspect of the ENS is the extension of its requirements to the information systems of private sector entities. This extension applies when these

[3]Reference documents and guides of the National Cryptologic Centre.

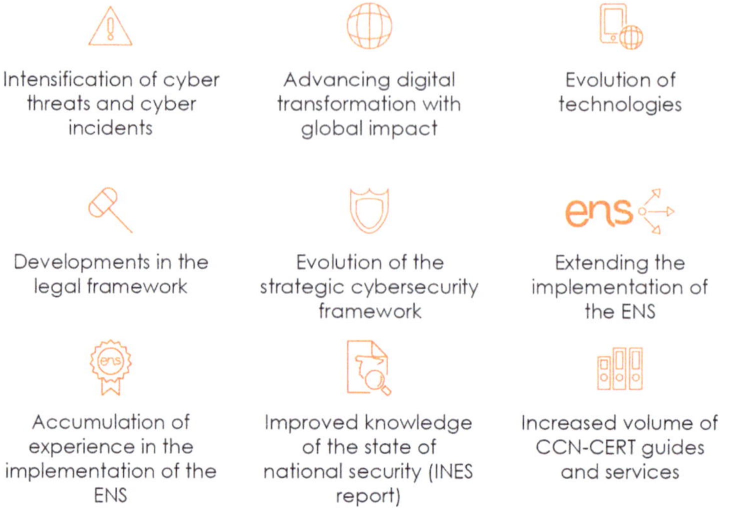

Fig. 2 Source: Infographics ENS (National Cryptologic Centre) https://ens.ccn.cni.es/es/que-es-el-ens/infografias

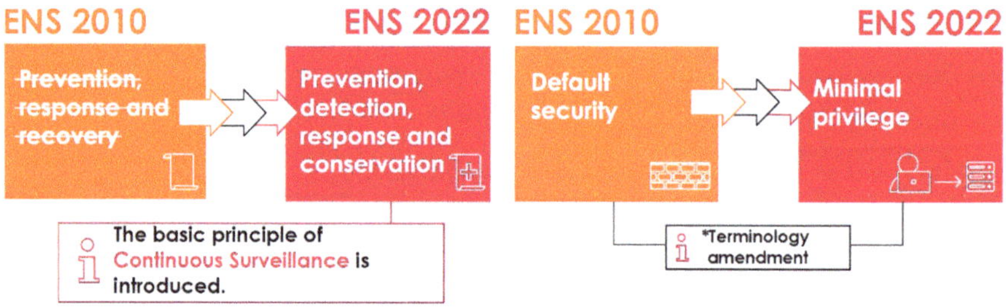

Fig. 3 Source: Infographics ENS (National Cryptologic Centre) https://ens.ccn.cni.es/es/que-es-el-ens/infografias

entities, under the relevant regulations and through a contractual relationship, provide services to public sector entities to exercise their competences and administrative powers.

In terms of content, the ENS is made up of the basic principles and minimum requirements necessary —see Table 2—for adequate protection of the information processed and the services provided by the entities within its scope of application to ensure access, confidentiality, integrity, availability, authenticity, accountability and preservation of the data, information and services used by electronic means that they manage in the exercise of their competences.

Table 2 ENS. Basic principles and minimum requirements

Basic Principles	Minimum Requirements
• Security as an integral process. • Risk-based security management. • Prevention, detection, response and protection. • Existence of lines of defence. • Continuous surveillance. • Periodic reassessment. • Differentiation of responsibilities.	• Organisation and implementation of the security process. • Risk analysis and risk management. • Personnel management. • Professionalism. • Authorisation and control of access. • Protection of installations. • Procurement of security products and contracting of security services. • Minimal privilege. • System integrity and upgradability. • Protection of information in storage and transit. • Prevention against other interconnected information systems. • Activity logging and detection of malicious code. • Security incidents. • Business continuity. • Continuous improvement of the security process.

Since digital transformation has increased the risks associated with the information systems that support public services and the private sector is also immersed in this transformation of its business processes, both types of information systems are exposed to the same threats and risks.

Therefore, due to the high degree of overlap between the two, private sector operators that provide services to public sector entities must guarantee the same level of security applied to systems and information in the sphere of the Administration. All this is in accordance, moreover, with the special requirements established both in Organic Law 3/2018, of 5 December, on the Protection of Personal Data and guarantee of digital rights, as well as in Organic Law 7/2021, of 26 May, on the protection of personal data processed for prevention, detection, investigation and prosecution of criminal offences and the execution of criminal sanctions.

Figure 4 summarises the set of measures included in the ENS.

The Royal Decree was approved in the exercise of the powers provided for in Articles 149.1.18, 149.1.21, and 149.1.29 of the Spanish Constitution, which gives the State exclusive competence over the bases of the legal system for public administration, telecommunications, and public security, respectively.

In the same line of work, as mentioned above, Directive (EU) 2022/2555, which replaces Directive (EU) 2016/1148, entered into force on 16 January 2023, bringing with it several changes, in particular regarding the measures to be taken by essential entities regarding risk management in the security of their networks and information systems.

Thus, Articles 20 (Governance) and 21 (Cybersecurity risk management measures) are the most relevant concerning these measures. However, references can be found in other articles, such as the use of European cybersecurity systems (Art. 24),

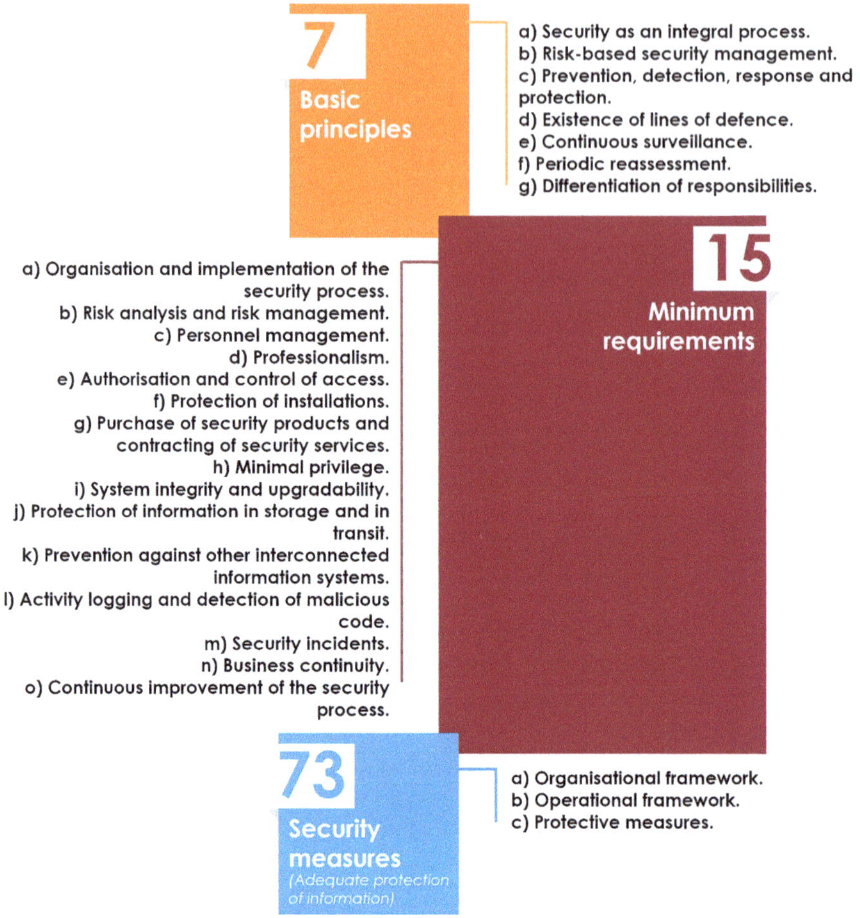

Fig. 4 Measures included in ENS

oversight and application to critical (Art. 32) and important entities (Art. 33). Similarly, the preambles, e.g. 15 (supervision), 21 (proportionality), 22/23 (sector-specific implementing acts) and 30 (interaction with the ERC) of the Directive also relate to this management.

Cybersecurity risk management measures are key obligations for both critical and important institutions. The NIS2 calls on Member States to "*ensure that critical and important entities take appropriate and proportionate technical, operational and organisational measures to manage the risks posed to the security of the networks and information systems they use for their operations or for the provision of their services, and to prevent or minimise the impact of incidents on the recipients of their services and on other services*".

The EU NIS Cooperation Group has recently adopted a document to provide non-binding technical guidance for national competent authorities on cybersecurity risk management measures laid down by Article 21 of Directive (EU) 2022/2555 (known as NIS2), a reference document on security measures for important & essential entities (Draft, v.8.1, TLP: Amber, March 2024).

This "reference document" was developed under the framework of the "Work Stream on Cybersecurity Risk and Vulnerability Management" of the NIS Cooperation Group (NIS CG or the Group) Work Programme 2023–2025 and provides a summary of the main findings of the Group. The document was completed in collaboration with other expert groups interested in the subject, such as the NIS CG Work Stream on Digital Service Providers, the NIS CG Work Stream on Digital Infrastructures, the European Competent Authorities on Secure Electronic Communications (ECASEC) and the European Competent Authorities on Trusted Services Expert Group (ECATS).

The paper addresses the changes introduced by the NIS2 on "cybersecurity risk management measures" as well as the challenges posed by the current cyber threat landscape, including:

- A set of measures applicable to all categories of entities in the scope of the directive (both essential and important entities).
- A longer list of measures (10 measures) in the NIS2 Directive than for digital service providers (5 measures) in the NIS1 Directive.
- The scope of application of the NIS2 Directive is broadened as it covers more sectors and types of entities than the NIS1 Directive.
- The broadening of the scope of application of the NIS2, as it applies to "network and information systems that such entities use for their operations or the provision of their services", as opposed to NIS1, which focuses on Critical Information Systems (CIS).

In addition, the cyber threat landscape is evolving, with the emergence of new risks and the sophistication of existing threats. Key developments in recent years include:

- The increasing sophistication of cyber-attacks, with cybercriminals becoming more ingenious and developing new and complex methods to infiltrate networks and information systems. This includes using advanced persistent threats (APTs), ransomware and supply chain attacks.
- State-sponsored attacks have increased dramatically since 2022. These attacks can be highly sophisticated and well-funded, making them difficult to defend against.
- The interconnection of systems and the convergence of information technology (IT) and operational technology (OT). As more IT and OT systems become interconnected, the potential impact of a cyber-attack on one system can quickly spread to others.

- Cybercriminals are increasingly targeting specific sectors, such as energy, finance, government, and healthcare, to cause maximum disruption and financial gain or loss.
- The growing number of IoT devices in critical infrastructure systems has opened up new vulnerabilities that cyber attackers can exploit.
- Insider threats, whether intentional or accidental, remain a significant risk to network and information systems.
- A growing need to ensure that cloud infrastructure and applications are properly secured as more organisations move their data and systems to the cloud.

The NIS Cooperation Group's recommendations align with the Spanish National Security Framework.

On the other hand, and to show public conformity, the ENS foresees two (2) possibilities: a Self-Assessment, only applicable to information systems of the BASIC security category, or a Formal Audit, applicable to information systems of any category (BASIC, MEDIUM or HIGH), developed by an ENS Certification Entity previously accredited by the National Accreditation Entity (ENAC). This is provided for in the Resolution of 27 March 2018 of the Secretary of State for Public Administration, which approves the Technical Security Instruction on Information Systems Security Audit and the Resolution of 13 October 2016 of the Secretary of State for Public Administrations, which approves the Technical Security Instruction under the National Security Framework.

In this regard, it should be noted that the purpose of the ENS Security Audit is to determine, among other issues, the following: that the Information Security Policy defines the roles and functions of those responsible for the information, services, assets and security of the information system; that there are procedures for resolving conflicts between those responsible; that persons have been designated for these roles in the light of the principle of "separation of functions"; that risk analysis has been carried out, with annual review and approval; that the protection recommendations on security measures are complied with, depending on the conditions of application in each case; and, that there is a documented information security management system with a regular process of approval by management.

In summary, the ENS Security Audit is a systematic, independent, and documented process for obtaining evidence and objectively evaluating it to determine the degree of compliance with the ENS of the audited information system. It should enable those responsible to take the appropriate measures to remedy the deficiencies, address the observations or recommendations that may have been identified by the audit team, and, where applicable, obtain the corresponding ENS Compliance Certification.

Naturally, it is very important to determine in advance what the scope of the audit will be, identifying precisely the information systems concerned and the services provided by such systems. Both the one (the information systems) and the other (the services supported by such systems) must be explicitly mentioned in the Certificate of Conformity with the ENS that, where appropriate, is issued and which will comply with the provisions of the Resolution of 13 October 2016 of the Secretary of State for Public Administrations, approving the Technical Security Instruction on Conformity with the National Security Framework.

The proper performance of ENS Security Audits also requires that the auditing entity—especially when it is accredited to issue Certifications of Conformity with the ENS, which is called the Certification Entity—has certain characteristics and capabilities.

To facilitate security audits, the ENS states that the National Cryptologic Centre, in the exercise of its powers, will draw up and disseminate the corresponding information and communications technology security guides to improve compliance with the provisions of the ENS and the CCN-STIC Guides, which should be considered "Best Practices" or *soft law*.[4] Therefore, compliance with them is not obligatory, as they are not exactly mandatory rules. However, failure to comply with them, in the event of any incident that could jeopardise the security of the information systems concerned, could result in liability.

It is common to express conformity with a given standard or regulation by using procedures that indicate the requirements to be eligible for such recognition and its subsequent public display, which, as in the case of the ENS, have been formally regulated.

The aforementioned ITS (Security Technical Instruction) of Conformity with the ENS sets out the requirements to which the so-called Declarations and Certifications of Conformity with the ENS shall be subject, namely as set out in Table 3:

Particularly important in the case of ENS Compliance Certifications is the role played by the so-called Certification Entities, which are responsible for auditing and certifying, where appropriate, the information systems subject to assessment.

Certification Entities must be accredited by the National Accreditation Body (ENAC) to certify systems within the scope of application of the National Security Framework under standard UNE-EN ISO/IEC 17065:2012 Conformity assessment Requirements for bodies certifying products, processes and services.

Accreditation is a tool established internationally to generate confidence in the correct execution of certain activities. It is called Conformity Assessment Activities. These activities include testing, calibration, inspection, certification, or verification. Generally, any activity that aims to assess whether a product, service, system, facility, etc., conforms to certain requirements may be subject to accreditation. These requirements may be established by law and, therefore, have a regulatory character or may be contained in standards, specifications, or other voluntary documents.

Finally, the ENS confers on the General Secretariat for Digital Administration (of the Secretary of State for Digitalisation and Artificial Intelligence of the Ministry for Digital Transformation and Public Administration) and the National Cryptologic

[4]The Pan-Hispanic dictionary of legal Spanish, of the Royal Spanish Academy, defines this as the set of rules or regulations not in force that can be considered by legal operators in matters of a preferably dispositive nature and which include recommendations, principles, etc., which could influence legislative development, and which can also be used as specific references in judicial or arbitration proceedings.

Table 3 Declarations and Certifications of Conformity with ENS

	Scope and content	Publication
Declaration of Conformity with the ENS	The Declaration of Conformity with the ENS, applicable exclusively to BASIC category information systems, may be issued by the entity under whose responsibility these systems are located after having passed a self-assessment and shall be displayed using a Declaration of Conformity Certificate, the use of which shall be conditional upon the prior issue of the aforementioned Declaration of Conformity.	To publish the Declaration of Conformity with the ENS, it will be sufficient to display the Declaration of Conformity Certificate on the electronic site (public sector entities) or website (private sector entities). The Certificate will include a link to the corresponding Declaration of Conformity document, which will also remain accessible through said electronic site or website.
ENS Compliance Certification	The ENS Conformity Certification, applicable to information systems of any category, may only be issued by a Certification Entity after having passed a Certification Audit and shall be displayed through a Conformity Certification Certificate, the use of which shall be conditional upon the prior issue of the aforementioned Conformity Certification.	The ENS Conformity Certification and its Conformity Mark shall be expressed in electronic documents in a non-editable format.

Centre (attached to the National Intelligence Centre of the Ministry of Defence), within their respective competences, the responsibility to ensure the proper implementation, development and monitoring of the ENS in the entities within its scope of application.

7 Conclusions

As shown in the preceding pages, 2022/2022 of 3 May, which regulates the National Security Framework (ENS) in Spain, goes beyond being a simple regulation. It represents a reference framework, a commitment to security in the digital era, and offers significant advantages for society's general information systems, including those dealing with crypto assets.

Table 4 summarises the benefits of using the ENS as a reference framework and model for cybersecurity assessment and certification and its specific applicability to crypto assets.

In short, 2022/2022 is a guiding light for security in the digital society, and its applicability to crypto-asset systems is crucial to building a reliable foundation in the new financial paradigm.

Table 4 Benefits of using ENS

Advantages and benefits	
Integral Protection	– The ENS covers public sector entities' systems and technology providers collaborating with the administration. This ensures comprehensive protection of information systems. – For systems dealing with crypto assets, this coverage is essential. Security must extend beyond organisational boundaries and consider all actors involved.
Risk Management and Service Continuity:	– ENS focuses on risk assessment and mitigation. This is crucial for systems handling crypto assets, as they face constant threats, such as cybercriminal attacks and emerging vulnerabilities. – Continuity of services is also essential. Crypto-asset systems must be available at all times to ensure secure transactions.
Transparency and Audit:	– The ENS promotes transparency in security management. Transaction and event logs must be accurate and accessible for audits. – For crypto-asset systems, this is essential to detect suspicious activity, such as money laundering or fraud.
Regulatory Compliance and Public Trust	– The ENS ensures that systems comply with regulations and laws. This is especially relevant for crypto assets, where public trust is crucial. – Trust in crypto-asset systems is a determining factor for their mass adoption.
Applicability to the Security of Crypto-asset Systems:	
The ENS provides a robust framework for assessing and improving security in systems that handle crypto assets, enhancing: – Private Key Protection: Secure management of private keys is essential to prevent theft and compromise. – Prevention of cyber-attacks: Security measures should include intrusion detection, firewalls and regular updates. – Compliance with money laundering and tax legislation: The ENS helps to comply with these regulations.	

References

Gobierno de España. Ministerio de la Presidencia, Justicia y Relaciones con las Cortes. Agencia Estatal Boletín Oficial del Estado (2002) Ley 11/2002, de 6 de mayo, reguladora del Centro Nacional de Inteligencia. https://www.boe.es/buscar/act.php?id=BOE-A-2002-8628

Gobierno de España. Ministerio de la Presidencia, Justicia y Relaciones con las Cortes. Agencia Estatal Boletín Oficial del Estado (2011) Ley 8/2011, de 28 de abril, por la que se establecen medidas para la protección de las infraestructuras críticas. https://www.boe.es/buscar/act.php?id=BOE-A-2011-7630

Gobierno de España. Ministerio de la Presidencia, Justicia y Relaciones con las Cortes. Agencia Estatal Boletín Oficial del Estado (2015a) Ley 36/2015, de 28 de septiembre, de Seguridad Nacional. https://www.boe.es/diario_boe/txt.php?id=BOE-A-2015-10389

Gobierno de España. Ministerio de la Presidencia, Justicia y Relaciones con las Cortes. Agencia Estatal Boletín Oficial del Estado (2015b) Ley 39/2015, de 1 de octubre, del Procedimiento Administrativo Común de las Administraciones Públicas. https://www.boe.es/buscar/act.php?id=BOE-A-2015-10565

Gobierno de España. Ministerio de la Presidencia, Justicia y Relaciones con las Cortes. Agencia Estatal Boletín Oficial del Estado (2015c) Ley 40/2015, de 1 de octubre, de Régimen Jurídico del Sector Público. https://www.boe.es/buscar/act.php?id=BOE-A-2015-10566

Gobierno de España. Ministerio de la Presidencia, Justicia y Relaciones con las Cortes. Agencia Estatal Boletín Oficial del Estado (2018a) Real Decreto-ley 12/2018, de 7 de septiembre, de seguridad de las redes y sistemas de información. https://www.boe.es/buscar/act.php?id=BOE-A-2018-12257

Gobierno de España. Ministerio de la Presidencia, Justicia y Relaciones con las Cortes. Agencia Estatal Boletín Oficial del Estado (2018b) Ley Orgánica 3/2018, de 5 de diciembre, de Protección de Datos Personales y garantía de los derechos digitales. https://www.boe.es/buscar/act.php?id=BOE-A-2018-16673

Gobierno de España. Presidencia del Gobierno (2019) National Cybersecurity Strategy:2019. https://www.dsn.gob.es/es/file/2989/download?token=EuVy2lNr

Gobierno de España. Ministerio de la Presidencia, Justicia y Relaciones con las Cortes. Agencia Estatal Boletín Oficial del Estado (2021) Real Decreto 1150/2021, de 28 de diciembre, por el que se aprueba la Estrategia de Seguridad Nacional 2021. https://www.boe.es/diario_boe/txt.php?id=BOE-A-2021-21884

Gobierno de España. Ministerio de Asuntos Económicos y Transformación Digital (2022) Royal Decree 311/2022, of 3 May, regulating the National Security Framework. https://administracionelectronica.gob.es/dam/jcr:eb23ff83-ebdb-487e-abd2-8654f837794f/RD_311-2022_of-3_May_ENS.pdf

Part II
New Assets: Assets Regulated in MiCA

Regulating Stablecoins in the European Union. Asset-Referenced Tokens and E-Money Tokens

José García Alcorta

Abstract Stablecoins are regulated in the European Union under Regulation (EU) 2023/1114 on Markets in Crypto-assets. That Regulation establishes a bespoke legislative regime for 'asset-referenced tokens' and 'electronic money tokens'. Both are crypto assets, i.e., digital representations of a value or a right that can be transferred and stored electronically using distributed ledger technology or similar technology. Both aim to maintain a stable value by referencing another value or right, a specified asset, pool, or basket of assets. Finally, existing EU financial services legislation covers none of them.

This work describes the main features of those crypto assets. Current rules seek to provide legal certainty for issuers of stablecoins in the UE (by imposing a common set of provisions applicable to all of them regarding their authorisation, governance requirements, etc.), give appropriate protection for holders of those crypto assets (by regulating their rights against issuers, the rules applicable to crypto-asset white papers or the marketing communications), or address potential financial stability and monetary policy risks that could arise from their use as a means of exchange (by monitoring or restricting the issuance).

This paper expands and updates the text of a lecture delivered at the III International Congress entitled "Present and future of crypto-assets regulation in the European Union", held at the University of Alicante (Spain) on 13, 14, and 15 December, 2023. This work is funded within the framework of: Proyecto CIPROM/2022/26 "Presente y futuro de la regulación de los Criptoactivos en la UE [Legalcripto]". Proyecto Prometeo CIPROM/2022/26, grupos de investigación de excelencia, de la Generalitat Valenciana (P.I. Carmen Pastor).
The contents of this work are solely the views and opinions of its author and do neither constitute legal or professional advice on any subject matter nor necessarily reflect the views of the Banco de España.

J. G. Alcorta (✉)
Banco de España, Department of Regulation, Madrid, Spain

C. Pastor Sempere (ed.), *Governance and Control of Data and Digital Economy in the European Single Market*, Law, Governance and Technology Series 71,
https://doi.org/10.1007/978-3-031-74889-9_7

1 Introduction

In the international fora, stablecoins are defined as crypto assets that aim to maintain a stable value relative to a specified asset, pool, or basket of assets.[1] As it has been rightly pointed out,[2] this broad definition implies that stablecoins could be backed by a monetary unit of account such as the dollar or euro, a commodity such as gold, or a currency basket. The value of a stablecoin, expressed against the asset to which it is pegged, would need to be stable if it is to be redeemed at par, in cash immediately, and at all times. Much hinges on how effective the stabilisation mechanisms are and whether a stablecoin issuer has the means to honour a redemption request. Some stablecoins may be far from stable.

With that in mind, this work explores the main characteristics of stablecoins, which are regulated in Regulation (EU) 2023/1114 of the European Parliament and of the Council of 31 May 2023 on Markets in Crypto-assets (MiCA). MiCA provides a set of rules on crypto assets not covered by existing European Union (EU) financial services legislation. The laws concerning stablecoins are based on a bespoke legislative regime addressing the risks posed by stablecoins and global stablecoins and the rules governing e-money under the Electronic Money Directive.[3]

MiCA classifies crypto assets into three types: electronic money tokens (EMTs), asset-referenced tokens (ARTs), and all other crypto assets that differ from EMTs and ARTs and are not excluded from MiCA. The Commission's legislative proposal labels EMTs and ARTs as 'stablecoins'.[4] MiCA does not lead to any different conclusion (see Recital (41)).

The following sections explore the features of EMTs and ARTs and the MiCA rules that apply to them.

2 EMT

2.1 Definition

An EMT is a type of crypto asset that purports to maintain a stable value by referencing the value of one official currency. Some important features can be highlighted from this definition:

- EMTs are crypto assets, i.e., digital representations of a value or right that can be transferred and stored electronically using distributed ledger technology (DLT) or similar technology.

[1] See Financial Stability Board (2023), p. 19.
[2] See Bains et al. (2022), p. 10.
[3] See European Commission (2020), p. 8.
[4] See European Commission (2020), p. 10.

- EMTs purport to maintain a stable value by referencing the value of one official currency. In our view, EMTs are designed to have a stable value against the value of one official currency. The mechanism for maintaining a stable value applied by the issuer of EMT is not relevant to the definition of EMT, as crypto assets that aim to maintain a stable value in relation to an official currency via protocols that provide for the increase or decrease in the supply of such crypto assets in response to changes in demand (algorithmic 'stablecoins') are included in the definition of EMT.
- The value referenced by the EMT is the value of one official currency, irrespective of whether it is an EU official currency. MiCA only stipulates that it must be only one, not multiple official currencies, and must have the status of legal tender, i.e. a means of payment that cannot generally be refused in settlement of a debt denominated in the same currency unit, at its full-face value, and without surcharges for the payer, with the effect of discharging the debt.[5]

According to MiCA, all EMTs must be deemed to be 'electronic money' under the Directive 2009/110/EC of the European Parliament and of the Council of 16 September 2009 on the taking up, pursuit and prudential supervision of the business of electronic money institutions (EMD). Thus, EMTs are not only crypto assets but also e-money, i.e. electronic surrogates for coins and banknotes and likely to be used for making payments (see Recital (18) of MiCA). That does not mean that e-money under EMD must be deemed an EMT as long as e-money cannot be transferred and stored electronically using DLT or similar technology.

In line with the above, MiCA establishes that Titles II (requirements for the taking up, pursuit and prudential supervision of the business of electronic money institutions) and III (issuance and redeemability of e-money) of EMD apply concerning EMTs unless otherwise stated in the specific regulations of MiCA regarding EMTs. Those regulations are explained below. According to Recital (19) of MiCA, EMTs are subject to that particular set of rules because they are crypto assets and can raise new challenges for protecting retail holders and market integrity specific to crypto assets.

2.2 *Issuers*

According to MiCA, no person shall make an offer to the public or seek admission to trading an EMT within the EU unless that person is the issuer of such EMT and is authorised as a credit institution or as an electronic money institution and has notified a crypto-asset white paper to the competent authority and has published it. MiCA also adds that an EMT that references an official currency of an EU Member State shall be deemed to be offered to the public in the EU.

---

[5] See Judgement of 26 January 2021 in Joined Cases C-422/19 and C-423/19, *Hessischer Rundfunk*, EU:C:2021:63, point 46.

It follows from those provisions that:

- Issuers of EMTs that reference a non-EU currency and are issued outside the EU are not required to be credit institutions or electronic money institutions as long as they do not offer to the public or seek admission to trading those EMTs within the EU. Otherwise, they must apply for authorisation to be a credit or electronic money institution.
- Issuers of EMTs that reference an EU currency and are issued outside the EU are required to be credit institutions or electronic money institutions, as EMTs are deemed to be offered to the public in the EU.

Those requirements for the offer to the public or admission to trading of EMTs do not apply to 'small issuers', i.e., issuers whose total business activities generate an average outstanding EMT that does not exceed a limit of EUR 5,000,000 and none of the natural persons responsible for the management or operation of the business has been convicted of offences relating to money laundering or terrorist financing or other financial crimes.

In any case, all previous issuers must notify their competent authority of that intention at least 40 working days before the date on which they intend to offer to the public those EMTs or seek their admission to trading.

The provisions of MiCA on EMTs do not apply in respect of EMTs ('exempted issuers') that:

- can only be used to acquire goods or services on the premises of the issuer or within a limited network of service providers under a direct commercial agreement with a professional issuer;
- can only be used to acquire a very limited range of goods or services;
- are valid only in a single Member State provided at the request of an undertaking or a public sector entity and regulated by a national or regional public authority for specific social or tax purposes to acquire specific goods or services from suppliers having a commercial agreement with the issuer; or,
- are used to make payment transactions by a provider of electronic communications networks or services in addition to electronic communications services for a subscriber to the network or service (i) for purchase of digital content and voiced-based services, regardless of the device used for the purchase or consumption of the digital content and charged to the related bill, or (ii) performed from or via an electronic device and charged to the related bill within the framework of charitable activity or for the purchase of tickets, provided that the value of any single payment transaction referred to in points (i) and (ii) does not exceed EUR 50 and other quantitative limits stipulated in Article 3(l) of Directive (EU) 2015/2366 of the European Parliament and of the Council of 25 November 2015 on payment services in the internal market.

2.3 *Issuance and Redeemability of EMTs*

Issuers of EMTs must issue EMTs at par value and on the receipt of funds. They must not grant interest in relation to EMTs and must redeem it, at any time and at par value, by paying in funds, other than e-money, the monetary value of the EMT held to the holder of the EMT. Without prejudice to the provisions of the recovery plan (see Sect. 2.10), the redemption is not subject to a fee. Finally, holders of EMTs shall have a claim against the issuers of those EMTs.

2.4 *Crypto-Asset White Paper for EMTs*

As stated before, issuers of EMTs, including 'small issuers' and 'exempted issuers', have to draw up, notify and publish a crypto-asset white paper containing fair, clear and not misleading information about the issuer, the EMT, the offer to the public of the EMT or its admission to trading, the rights and obligations attached to the EMT, the underlying technology, the risks and the principal adverse impacts on the climate and other environment-related adverse implications of the consensus mechanism used to issue the EMT.

The crypto-asset white paper must also contain the following statement on the first page: 'The crypto-asset white paper has not been approved by any competent authority in any Member State of the EU. The issuer of the crypto-asset is solely responsible for the content of this crypto-asset white paper'.

Additionally, the crypto-asset white paper must contain the following information:

- A clear warning that the EMT is not covered by the investor compensation schemes under Directive 97/9/EC of the European Parliament and of the Council of 3 March 1997 on investor-compensation schemes and by the deposit guarantee schemes under Directive 2014/49/EU of the European Parliament and of the Council of 16 April 2014 on deposit guarantee schemes.
- A statement from the management body of the issuer that confirms that the crypto-asset white paper complies with Title IV of MiCA and that, to the best of the knowledge of the management body, the information presented in the white paper is complete, fair and not misleading and that the white paper makes no omission likely to affect its import.
- A summary providing key information about the offer to the public of the EMT or the intended admission to trading of such EMT, appropriate information about the characteristics of the crypto-asset concerned to help prospective holders of the crypto assets to make an informed decision, and a warning that:

- it should be read as an introduction to the crypto-asset white paper;
- the prospective holder should base any decision to purchase the EMT on the content of the crypto-asset white paper as a whole and not on the summary alone;
- the offer to the public of the EMT does not constitute an offer or solicitation to purchase financial instruments, and any such offer or solicitation can be made only using a prospectus or other offer documents pursuant to the applicable national law;
- the crypto-asset white paper does not constitute a prospectus as referred to in Regulation (EU) 2017/1129 of the European Parliament and of the Council of 14 June 2017 on the prospectus to be published when securities are offered to the public or admitted to trading on a regulated market.

The summary must state that holders of the EMT have a right of redemption at any time and at par value, as well as the conditions for redemption.

- The date of its notification and a table of contents.

Issuers of EMTs must notify their competent authority of their crypto-asset white paper at least 20 working days before the date of their publication. Competent authorities shall not require prior approval of the crypto-asset white paper before publication.

Where an issuer has infringed the above provisions by providing in its crypto-asset white paper information that is not complete, fair or clear or that is misleading, that issuer and the members of its administrative, management or supervisory body shall be liable to a holder of such EMT for any loss incurred due to that infringement. Any contractual exclusion or limitation of civil liability shall be deprived of legal effect. Furthermore, MiCA does not exclude any other civil liability under national law.

The issuer and the members of its administrative, management or supervisory bodies shall not be liable for loss suffered due to reliance on the information provided in the summary of the white paper, except where the summary is misleading, inaccurate or inconsistent when read together with the other parts of the crypto-asset white paper, or does not provide when read together with the other parts of the crypto-asset white paper, key information to aid prospective holders when considering whether to purchase such EMT.

2.5 Marketing Communications

Marketing communications relating to an offer to the public of an EMT or the admission to trading of such an EMT must comply with all the following requirements:

- The marketing communications are clearly identifiable as such.
- The information in the marketing communications is fair, clear and not misleading.
- The information in the marketing communications is consistent with that in the crypto-asset white paper.
- The marketing communications clearly state that a crypto-asset white paper has been published and indicates the address of the website of the issuer of the EMT, as well as the telephone number and email address to contact the issuer.

Marketing communications must clearly state that the holders of the EMT have a right of redemption against the issuer at any time and at par value.

Marketing communications do not have to be approved by the competent authorities but must be published on the issuer's website, and the competent authorities must be notified upon request.

2.6 Investment of Funds Received by Electronic Money Institutions in Exchange for EMT

Funds received by electronic money institutions in exchange for EMTs issued must be safeguarded in accordance with Article 7(1) of EMD and comply with the following:

- At least 30 per cent of the funds received are always deposited in separate accounts in credit institutions.
- The remaining funds received are invested in secure, low-risk assets that qualify as highly liquid financial instruments with minimal market risk, credit risk, and concentration risk. They are denominated in the same official currency as the one referenced by the EMT.

2.7 Specific Additional Requirements for Electronic Money Institutions Where Necessary to Address Certain Risks

MiCA entitles competent authorities of the home Member States to require electronic money institutions that issue EMTs to comply with a set of rules where necessary to address the risks that those rules aim to address. That set of rules is applicable instead of rules of own funds and safeguarding requirements set out in the EMD for electronic money institutions. They may be described as follows.

2.7.1 Own Funds Requirements

Where required by competent authorities, electronic money institutions issuing EMTs must, at all times, have their own funds equal to an amount of at least the highest of the following:

- EUR 350,000;
- three per cent of the average amount of the reserve assets at the end of each calendar day and calculated over the preceding 6 months; and
- a quarter of the fixed overheads of the preceding year.

Where required by competent authorities, the own funds of electronic money institutions that issue EMTs must consist of the Common Equity Tier 1 (CET1) items and instruments referred to in Articles 26 to 30 of Regulation (EU) No 575/2013 of the European Parliament and of the Council of 26 June 2013 on prudential requirements for credit institutions and investment firms (CRR), after the deductions in full under Article 36 of that Regulation, without the application of the threshold exemptions referred to in Articles 46(4) and 48 of that Regulation.

Competent authorities may also require electronic money institutions issuing EMTs to hold an amount of their own funds which is up to 20 per cent higher than three per cent of the average amount of the reserve assets at the end of each calendar day and calculated over the preceding six months, where an assessment of any of the following indicates a higher degree of risk:

- Evaluation of the risk-management processes and internal control mechanisms of the issuer.
- Quality and volatility of the reserve of assets (where applicable) as described below (see Sect. 2.7.2).
- Types of rights granted by the issuer to holders.
- Where the reserve of assets (where applicable, see Sect. 2.7.2) includes investments, the risk posed by the investment policy on the reserve of assets.
- Aggregated value and number of transactions settled in the EMTs.
- Importance of the markets on which the EMT is offered and marketed.
- Where applicable, the market capitalisation of the EMT.

Additionally, electronic money institutions must regularly conduct stress testing considering severe but plausible financial stress scenarios, such as interest rate shocks, and non-financial stress scenarios, such as operational risk. Based on the outcome of such stress testing, the competent authority of the home Member State shall require the electronic money institution to hold an amount of its own funds that is between 20 per cent and 40 per cent higher than three per cent of the average amount of the reserve assets at the end of each calendar day and calculated over the preceding six months, in certain circumstances having regard to the risk outlook and stress testing results.

2.7.2 Reserve of Assets. Composition, Management, Custody and Investment

Where required by competent authorities, electronic money institutions that issue EMTs must constitute and at all times maintain a reserve of assets. The reserve of assets is the basket of reserve assets securing the claim against the issuer. It must be composed and managed so that the risks associated with the assets referenced by the EMTs are covered, and the liquidity risks associated with the permanent rights of redemption of the holders are addressed.

MiCA establishes that a minimum amount in the official currency referenced by the EMT must be held as deposits in credit institutions. That amount cannot be lower than 30 per cent of the amount referenced in the official currency.

The reserve of assets must be legally segregated from the electronic money institutions' estate, as well as from the reserve of assets of other EMTs, in the interest of the holders of EMTs in accordance with applicable law so that creditors of the issuer have no recourse to the reserve of assets, in particular in the event of insolvency.

Electronic money institutions that offer two or more EMTs to the public must operate and maintain segregated pools of reserves of assets for each EMT. Each of those pools of reserves of assets must be managed separately.

The management bodies of electronic money institutions that issue EMTs must ensure the effective and prudent management of the reserve of assets and ensure that a corresponding increase or decrease in the reserve of assets always matches the issuance and redemption of EMTs.

Electronic money institutions that issue EMTs must determine the aggregate value of the reserve of assets by using market prices. Its aggregate value must be at least equal to the aggregate value of the claims against the issuer from the holders of the EMTs in circulation. The valuation at market prices must be made by using mark-to-market, as defined in the Regulation (EU) 2017/1131 of the European Parliament and of the Council of 14 June 2017 on money market funds (Regulation (EU) 2017/1131). Where mark-to-market is not possible, or the market data lacks sufficiently good quality, the reserve asset must be valued conservatively using mark-to-model, as defined in Regulation (EU) 2017/1131.

Electronic money institutions that issue EMTs must have a clear and detailed policy describing the stabilisation mechanism of such tokens. That policy must address the following:

- Identify the official currency referenced by the EMT.
- Describe the type of assets and the precise allocation of assets included in the reserve of assets.
- Contain a detailed assessment of risks, including credit risk, market risk, concentration risk and liquidity risk resulting from the reserve of assets.
- Describe the procedure by which EMTs are issued and redeemed and the procedure by which such issuance and redemption will result in a corresponding increase and decrease in the reserve of assets.

- Mention whether a part of the reserve of assets is invested as detailed below.
- Where issuers of EMTs invest a part of the reserve assets as detailed below, describe the investment policy and contain an assessment of how that investment policy can affect the value of the reserve of assets;
- Describe the procedure for purchasing EMTs and redeeming such tokens against the reserve of assets and list the persons or categories of persons entitled to do so.

Electronic money institutions that issue EMTs must establish, maintain and implement custody policies, procedures and contractual arrangements that ensure at all times that:

- the reserve assets are not encumbered nor pledged as a financial collateral arrangement as defined in the Directive 2002/47/EC of the European Parliament and of the Council of 6 June 2002 on financial collateral arrangements;
- the reserve assets are held in custody following the rules described below;
- electronic money institutions that issue EMTs have prompt access to reserve assets to meet any requests for redemption from EMT holders;
- concentrations of the custodians of reserve assets are avoided; and,
- risk of concentration of reserve assets is avoided.

Electronic money institutions that issue two or more EMTs in the EU must have a custody policy in place for each pool of reserve of assets. Different issuers of EMTs that have issued the same EMT must operate and maintain a single custody policy.

The reserve assets must be held in custody by no later than five working days after the date of issuance of the EMT by a crypto-asset service provider (CASP) (where the reserve assets take the form of crypto assets), a credit institution (for all type of reserve assets) or an investment firm (where the reserve assets take the form of financial instruments). Electronic money institutions that issue EMTs must exercise all due skill, care, and diligence in the selection, appointment, and review of CASP, as well as credit institutions and investment firms appointed as custodians of the reserve assets. The custodian must be a legal person and not the electronic money institution that issues EMTs. The contractual arrangements between the electronic money institutions that issue EMTs and the custodians must ensure that the reserve assets held in custody are protected against claims of the custodians' creditors.

Custodians must ensure that the custody of the reserve assets is carried out in the following manner:

- Credit institutions must hold in custody funds in an account opened in the credit institutions' books. Funds must be registered on a segregated account in accordance with the provisions of national law transposing Article 16 of Commission Directive 2006/73/EC of 10 August 2006 implementing Directive 2004/39/EC of the European Parliament and of the Council, as regards organisational requirements and operating conditions for investment firms and the defined terms for that Directive (Commission Directive 2006/73/EC). That account must be opened in the name of the electronic money institution that issues EMTs to manage each EMT's reserve assets so that the funds held in custody can be identified as belonging to each reserve of assets.

- For financial instruments that can be held in custody, credit institutions or investment firms must hold in custody all financial instruments that can be registered in a financial instruments account opened in the credit institutions' or investment firms' books and all financial instruments that can be physically delivered to such credit institutions or investment firms. All financial instruments that can be registered in a financial instruments account opened in those books must be registered on a segregated account under the provisions of national law transposing Article 16 of Commission Directive 2006/73/EC. That account must be opened in the name of the electronic money institutions that issue EMTs to manage each EMT's reserve assets so that the financial instruments held in custody can be identified as belonging to each reserve of assets.
- For crypto assets that can be held in custody, CASPs must hold the crypto assets included in the reserve assets or the means of access to such crypto assets, where applicable, in the form of private cryptographic keys. CASPs must open a register of positions in the name of the electronic money institutions that issue EMTs to manage each EMT's reserve assets so that the crypto assets held in custody can be identified as belonging to each reserve of assets.
- For other assets, the credit institutions must verify the ownership of the electronic money institutions that issue EMTs and maintain a record of those reserve assets for which they are satisfied that the electronic money institutions that issue EMTs own those reserve assets. The assessment of whether those issuers own the reserve assets must be based on information or documents provided by the issuers and, where available, on external evidence.

Custodians must act honestly, fairly, professionally, independently and in the interest of the electronic money institutions that issue EMTs and the holders of such EMTs. They must not carry out activities with the electronic money institutions that issue EMTs as these may create conflicts of interest between those issuers, the holders of the EMTs and themselves unless all the following conditions are met:

- CASPs, credit institutions or investment firms have functionally and hierarchically separated the performance of their custody tasks from their potentially conflicting tasks;
- the potential conflicts of interest have been properly identified, monitored, managed and disclosed by the electronic money institutions that issue the EMTs to the holders of the EMTs.

In the case of a loss of a financial instrument or a crypto-asset held in custody, the CASP, credit institution or investment firm that lost that financial instrument or crypto-asset must compensate or make restitution to the electronic money institutions that issue EMTs with a financial instrument or a crypto-asset of an identical type or the corresponding value without undue delay. The CASP, credit institution or investment firm concerned shall not be liable for compensation or restitution where it can prove that the loss has occurred due to an external event beyond its reasonable control, the consequences of which were unavoidable despite all reasonable efforts to the contrary.

Electronic money institutions that issue EMTs may invest a part of the reserve of assets but only in highly liquid financial instruments with minimal market risk, credit risk and concentration risk. The investment must be capable of being liquidated rapidly with minimal adverse price effect. All profits or losses, including fluctuations in the value of the financial instruments and any counterparty or operational risks that result from the investment of the reserve of assets, must be borne by the issuer.

Finally, electronic money institutions that issue EMTs must mandate an independent audit of the reserve of assets every six months to assess compliance with the abovementioned rules. The electronic money institution must notify the competent authority of the audit results without delay and, at the latest, within six weeks of the valuation reference date. The electronic money institution must publish the audit's outcome within two weeks of the date of notification to the competent authority unless otherwise instructed by the competent authority in some events.

2.7.3 Remuneration Policy and Custody of EMTs

Where competent authorities require, electronic money institutions that issue EMTs must adopt, implement and maintain a remuneration policy that promotes the sound and effective risk management of such issuers and does not create incentives to relax risk standards.

Electronic money institutions that issue EMTs must also ensure that EMTs can be held in custody by different CASPs, including those that do not belong to the same group, on a fair, reasonable, and non-discriminatory basis.

2.7.4 Liquidity Requirements

Where required by competent authorities, electronic money institutions that issue EMTs must assess and monitor the liquidity needs to meet requests for redemption of EMTs by their holders. Electronic money institutions must establish, maintain and implement a liquidity management policy and procedures for that purpose. That policy and those procedures must ensure that the reserve assets (where applicable) have a resilient liquidity profile that enables electronic money institutions to continue operating normally, including under liquidity stress scenarios.

Electronic money institutions that issue EMTs must also regularly conduct liquidity stress testing. Where electronic money institutions offer two or more EMTs or provide crypto-asset services, those stress tests must comprehensively and holistically cover all those activities. Depending on the outcome of such tests, the European Banking Authority (EBA) may decide to strengthen the liquidity requirements of the electronic money institutions issuing EMTs, including by specifying the minimum amount of deposits to be held in credit institutions in the official currency referenced, which cannot be lower than 60 per cent of the amount referenced in the official currency.

2.8 Restrictions on the Issuance of an EMT Denominated in a Currency That Is Not an Official Currency of a Member State

MiCA contains a set of provisions on the monitoring and restriction of the issuance of EMTs denominated in a currency that is not an official currency of an EU Member State. To allow competent authorities to monitor the use of EMTs, MiCA requires the issuer of an EMT with an issue value that is higher than EUR 100,000,000 to report every quarter to the competent authority:

- the number of holders;
- the value of the EMT issued and the size of the reserve of assets (where applicable);
- the average number and average aggregate value of transactions per day during the relevant quarter;
- an estimate of the average number and average aggregate value of daily transactions during the relevant quarter associated with its uses as a means of exchange within a single currency area.

CASPs that provide services related to EMTs must provide the issuer of the EMT with the information necessary to prepare the report, including by reporting transactions outside the distributed ledger.

Additionally, MiCA also stipulates that where, for an EMT, the estimated quarterly average number and average aggregate value of transactions per day associated with its uses as a means of exchange within a single currency area is higher than one million transactions and EUR 200,000,000, respectively, the issuer must stop issuing the EMT and, within 40 working days of reaching that threshold, submit a plan to the competent authority to ensure that the estimated quarterly average number and average aggregate value of those transactions per day is kept below one million transactions and EUR 200,000,000 respectively. The issuer must submit the plan for approval to the competent authority. The competent authority shall require modifications, such as imposing a minimum denomination amount where necessary.

The competent authority must only allow the issuer to issue the EMT again when it has evidence that the estimated quarterly average number and average aggregated value of transactions per day associated with its use as a means of exchange within a single currency area are lower than one million transactions and EUR 200,000,000, respectively.

Finally, competent authorities must also limit the amount of an EMT to be issued or impose a minimum denomination amount in respect of the EMT when the European Central Bank (ECB) or the central bank of the Member State whose official currency is not the euro and where the issuer is established or whose official currency is not the euro and it is the official currency which the EMT references, issues an opinion that the EMT poses a serious threat to the smooth operation of payment systems, monetary policy transmission or monetary sovereignty.

Competent authorities must specify those cases' applicable limit or minimum denomination amount.

2.9 Significant EMTs

EBA must classify EMTs as significant EMTs if they meet at least three of the following criteria during a given period:

- The number of holders of the EMT is larger than ten million.
- The value of the EMT issued its market capitalisation, or the size of the reserve of assets (where applicable) of the issuer of the EMT, is higher than EUR 5,000,000,000.
- The average number and average aggregate value of transactions in that EMT per day during the relevant period is higher than 2.5 million transactions and EUR 500,000,000, respectively.
- The issuer of the EMT is a provider of core platform services designated as a gatekeeper under Regulation (EU) 2022/1925 of the European Parliament and of the Council of 14 September 2022 on contestable and fair markets in the digital sector.
- The significance of the activities of the issuer of the EMT on an international scale, including the use of the EMT for payments and remittances.
- The interconnectedness of the EMT or its issuers with the financial system.
- The fact that the same issuer issues at least one additional EMT or ART and provides at least one crypto-asset service.

Where several issuers issue the same EMT, the fulfilment of those criteria must be assessed after aggregating the data from those issuers.

Where an EMT is classified as significant pursuant to a decision of the EBA, several supervisory responsibilities concerning the issuer of that EMT are transferred from the competent authority of the issuer's home Member State to the EBA.

EBA must annually reassess the classification of significant EMTs based on the available information. Where EBA concludes that certain EMTs no longer meet the criteria, it adopts a decision by means of which the EMT is no longer classified as significant and the supervisory responsibilities concerning the issuer of that EMT are transferred from EBA to the competent authority of the issuer's home Member State.

An issuer of an EMT may also indicate that it wishes for its EMT to be classified as a significant EMT. The issuer must demonstrate, through a detailed program of operations, that it is likely to meet at least three of the criteria already described. As mentioned above, the EBA adopts a final decision on the classification of EMTs.

Where issuers of significant EMTs are electronic money institutions, the additional requirements described in Sect. 2.7 applies to them.

2.10 Recovery and Redemption

Issuers of EMTs must draw up and maintain a recovery plan that provides for the following:

- Measures to be taken by the issuer to restore compliance with the requirements applicable to the reserve of assets (where applicable) in cases where the issuer fails to comply with those requirements.
- Preservation of the issuer's services related to the EMT, the timely recovery of operations and the fulfilment of the issuer's obligations in the case of events that pose a significant risk of disrupting operations.
- Appropriate conditions and procedures to ensure the timely implementation of recovery actions and a wide range of recovery options, including liquidity fees on redemptions, limits on the amount of the EMT that can be redeemed on any working day, and suspension of redemptions.

The issuer of the EMT must notify the recovery plan to the competent authority within six months of the date of the offer to the public or admission to trading of the EMT. The competent authority shall require amendments to the recovery plan, where necessary, to ensure its proper implementation.

Where the issuer of EMTs fails to comply with the requirements applicable to the reserve of assets (where applicable) or, due to rapidly deteriorating financial conditions, is likely in the near future to not comply with those requirements, the competent authority, to ensure compliance with the applicable requirements, has the power to require the issuer to implement one or more of the arrangements or measures set out in the recovery plan and to suspend the redemption of the EMTs temporarily, provided that the suspension is justified having regard to the interests of the holders of EMTs and financial stability.

Issuers of EMTs must also draw up and maintain an operational plan to support the orderly redemption of each EMT, which is to be implemented upon a decision by the competent authority that the issuer is unable or likely to be unable to fulfil its obligations, including in the case of insolvency or, where applicable, resolution or in the case of withdrawal of authorisation of the issuer.

The redemption plan must comply with the following requirements:

- Demonstrate the ability of the issuer of EMTs to carry out the redemption of the outstanding EMT issued without causing undue economic harm to its holders or to the stability of the markets of the reserve assets (where applicable).
- Include contractual arrangements, procedures and systems, including the designation of a temporary administrator following applicable law, to ensure the equitable treatment of all holders of EMTs and to ensure that holders of EMTs are paid promptly with the proceeds from the sale of the remaining reserve assets (where applicable).
- Ensure the continuity of any critical activities necessary for orderly redemption performed by issuers or any third-party entity.

The issuer of the EMT must notify the competent authority of the redemption plan within six months of the date of the offer to the public or admission to trading. The competent authority shall require amendments to the redemption plan where necessary to ensure its proper implementation.

Where applicable, the competent authority must notify the redemption plan to the issuer's resolution authority and the prudential supervisory authority. The resolution authority may examine the redemption plan to identify any actions that might adversely impact the issuer's resolvability and may make recommendations to the competent authority with respect to thereof.

3 ART

3.1 Definition

An ART is a type of crypto asset that is not an EMT and purports to maintain a stable value by referencing another value or right or a combination thereof, including one or more official currencies. The following features can be highlighted from this definition:

- ARTs are crypto assets, i.e., digital representations of a value or right that can be transferred and stored electronically using DLT or similar technology.
- ARTs purport to maintain a stable value by referencing another value, right, or combination thereof, including one or more official currencies. ARTs are designed to have a stable value against any other value or right. The mechanism for maintaining a stable value applied by the issuer of ARTs is not relevant to the definition of ART, as crypto assets that aim to maintain a stable value in relation to any other value or right via protocols that provide for the increase or decrease in the supply of such crypto assets in response to changes in demand (algorithmic 'stablecoins') are included in the definition of ART.
- The value referenced by the ART is not the value of only one official currency but any other value or right, thus including official currencies and different types of assets or crypto assets.

As stated by Recital (40) of MiCA, ARTs could be widely adopted by holders to transfer value or as a means of exchange and thus pose increased risks in terms of protecting holders of crypto assets, in particular retail holders, and in terms of market integrity compared to other crypto assets. Issuers of ART should, therefore, be subject to more stringent requirements than issuers of other crypto assets. Those requirements are described below.

3.2 *Issuers*

According to MiCA, offers to the public of ARTs in the EU or seeking admission to trading of such crypto assets are not permitted unless the person making that offer is the issuer of that ART and is:

- a legal person or other undertaking (provided that their legal form ensures a level of protection for third parties' interests equivalent to that afforded by legal persons and if they are subject to equivalent prudential supervision appropriate to their legal form) established in the EU and authorised by the competent authority of its home Member State; or
- a credit institution that complies with the requirements described in Sect. 3.4.

Those requirements for the offer to the public or admission to trading of ARTs do not apply where:

- over 12 months, calculated at the end of each calendar day, the average outstanding value of the ART issued by an issuer never exceeds EUR 5,000,000 or the equivalent amount in another official currency, and the issuer is not linked to a network of other exempt issuers; or
- the offer to the public of the ART is addressed solely to qualified investors, and the ART can only be held by such qualified investors.

In those cases, ART issuers must prepare a crypto-asset white paper and notify that crypto-asset white paper and, upon request, any marketing communications to the competent authority of their home Member State.

3.3 *Authorization of Issuers of ARTs That Are Not Credit Institutions*

To be authorised as issuers of ARTs, legal persons or other undertakings must submit their application for authorisation to the competent authority of their home Member State and provide certain information, including:

- A programme of operations, setting out the business model that the applicant issuer intends to follow.
- A legal opinion that the ART does not qualify as a crypto asset excluded from the scope of MiCA or an EMT.
- A description of the applicant issuer's governance arrangements, its policies and procedures, its contractual arrangements with third-party entities, its business continuity policy, its internal control mechanisms and risk management procedures and its systems and procedures in place to safeguard the availability, authenticity, integrity and confidentiality of data.

- Where cooperation arrangements with specific CASPs exist, a description of their internal control mechanisms and procedures to ensure compliance with the obligations on the prevention of money laundering and terrorist financing under Directive (EU) 2015/849 of the European Parliament and the Council of 20 May 2015 on the prevention of the use of the financial system for money laundering or terrorist financing (Directive (EU) 2015/849).
- The identity of the management body members and proof that they are of sufficiently good repute and possess the appropriate knowledge, skills, and experience to manage the applicant issuer.
- Proof that any shareholder or member, whether direct or indirect, with a qualifying holding in the applicant issuer is of sufficiently good repute.
- A crypto-asset white paper containing the same information mentioned above in Sect. 2.4 regarding the crypto-asset white paper for EMTs.
- A description of the applicant issuer's complaints-handling procedures.
- Where applicable, a list of host Member States where the applicant issuer intends to offer the ART to the public or to seek admission to trading of the ART.

Issuers that have already been authorised in respect of one ART are not required to submit, for authorisation in respect of another ART, any information that they previously submitted to the competent authority, where such information would be identical.

As a part of the assessment of the application for authorisation, the ECB or, where applicable, the central bank of the Member State whose official currency is not the euro and the applicant issuer is established or whose official currency is not the euro and it is an official currency which is referenced by the ART, shall issue an opinion as regards its evaluation of the risks that issuing that ART might pose to financial stability, the smooth operation of payment systems, monetary policy transmission and monetary sovereignty.

The authorisation granted by the competent authority is valid for the entire EU. It allows an issuer to offer to the public, throughout the EU, the ART for which it has been authorised or to seek admission to trading such ART. Where the issuer is authorised, its crypto-asset white paper is deemed to be approved.

Competent authorities must refuse authorisation where there are objective and demonstrable grounds that:

- The management body of the applicant issuer might pose a threat to its effective, sound, and prudent management and business continuity, as well as to the adequate consideration of the interests of its clients and the integrity of the market.
- Members of the management body are not of sufficiently good repute or do not possess the appropriate knowledge, skills and experience, both individually and collectively, to perform their duties, or they have been convicted of offences relating to money laundering or terrorist financing or of any other offences that would affect their good reputation, or they cannot demonstrate that they are capable of committing sufficient time to perform their duties effectively.

- Shareholders and members, whether direct or indirect, that have qualifying holdings are not of sufficiently good repute and, in particular, have been convicted of offences relating to money laundering or terrorist financing or any other crimes that would affect their good reputation.
- The applicant issuer fails to meet or is likely to fail to meet any requirements applicable to ARTs in Title III of MiCA.
- The applicant issuer's business model might seriously threaten market integrity, financial stability, and the smooth operation of payment systems or expose the issuer or the sector to serious risks of money laundering and terrorist financing.

Competent authorities must also refuse authorisation if the ECB or, where applicable, the central bank of the Member State whose official currency is not the euro and the applicant issuer is established or whose official currency is not the euro and it is an official currency which is referenced by the ART, gives a negative opinion on the grounds of a risk posed to the smooth operation of payment systems, monetary policy transmission, or monetary sovereignty.

Additionally, competent authorities must withdraw their authorisation to the issuer of ARTs in any of the following situations that apply to the issuer:

- Ceased to engage in business for six consecutive months or has not used its authorisation for 12 consecutive months.
- Obtained authorisation by irregular means, such as by making false statements in the application for authorisation or in any modified crypto-asset white paper.
- No longer meets the conditions under which the authorisation was granted.
- Serious infringement of the provisions applicable to ARTs contained in Title III of MiCA.
- Subject to a redemption plan.
- Expressly renounced its authorisation or has decided to cease operations.
- Activity poses a serious threat to market integrity, financial stability, and the smooth operation of payment systems or exposes the issuer or the sector to serious risks of money laundering and terrorist financing.

Competent authorities must also withdraw the authorisation of an issuer of an ART when the ECB or, where applicable, the central bank of the Member State whose official currency is not the euro and the applicant issuer is established or whose official currency is not the euro and it is an official currency which is referenced by the ART, issues an opinion that the ART poses a serious threat to the smooth operation of payment systems, monetary policy transmission or monetary sovereignty.

Competent authorities must limit the amount of an ART to be issued or impose a minimum denomination amount in respect of the ART when the ECB or, where applicable, the central bank of the Member State whose official currency is not the euro and the applicant issuer is established or whose official currency is not the euro and it is an official currency which is referenced by the ART, issues an opinion that the ART poses a threat to the smooth operation of payment systems, monetary policy transmission or monetary sovereignty, and specify the applicable limit or minimum denomination amount.

The relevant competent authorities must notify the competent authority of an issuer of an ART, without delay, of the following situations:

- A third-party entity in charge of operating the reserve of assets, the investment of the reserve assets, the custody of the reserve of assets or the distribution of the ARTs to the public has lost its authorisation as a credit institution as a CASP, as a payment institution, or as an electronic money institution.
- The members of the issuer's management body or shareholders or members, whether direct or indirect, that have qualifying holdings in the issuer have infringed the provisions of national law transposing Directive (EU) 2015/849.

Competent authorities must withdraw the authorisation of an issuer of ARTs where they are of the opinion that the situations mentioned above affect the good reputation of the members of the management body of that issuer or the good reputation of any shareholders or members, whether direct or indirect, that have qualifying holdings in the issuer, or if there is an indication of a failure of the governance arrangements or internal control mechanisms.

When the authorisation is withdrawn, the issuer of ARTs must implement its redemption plan.

3.4 Approval of the Crypto-Asset White Paper of Issuers of ARTs That Are Credit Institutions

An ART issued by a credit institution may be offered to the public or admitted to trading if the credit institution:

- Draws up a crypto-asset white paper for the ART containing essentially the same information mentioned in Sect. 2.4 regarding the crypto-asset white paper for EMTs, submits that crypto-asset white paper for approval by the competent authority of its home Member State and has it approved by that competent authority.
- Notifies the respective competent authority, at least 90 working days before issuing the ART for the first time, by providing it with the following information:
  - A programme of operations, setting out the business model that the credit institution intends to follow.
  - A legal opinion that the ART does not qualify as a crypto asset excluded from the scope of MiCA or an EMT.
  - A description of the governance arrangements, its policies and procedures, contractual arrangements with third-party entities, business continuity policy, internal control mechanisms and risk management procedures, and its systems

and procedures in place to safeguard data availability, authenticity, integrity and confidentiality.

A credit institution that has previously notified the competent authority as per the rules mentioned above when issuing another ART is not required to submit any information previously submitted by it to the competent authority where such information would be identical.

The competent authority must communicate to the ECB without delay the complete information received and, where the credit institution is established in a Member State whose official currency is not the euro or where an official currency of a Member State that is not the euro is referenced by the ART, also to the central bank of that Member State. The ECB and, where applicable, the central bank of the Member State must issue an opinion on that information and transmit that opinion to the competent authority.

The competent authority must require the credit institution not to offer to the public or seek admission to trading of the ART in cases where the ECB or, where applicable, the central bank of the Member State gives a negative opinion on the grounds of a risk posed to the smooth operation of payment systems, monetary policy transmission or monetary sovereignty.

The approval granted by the competent authority of the crypto-asset white paper shall be valid for the entire EU.

3.5 Requirements for All Issuers of ARTs

MiCA sets out several requirements that all issuers of ARTs, whether they are credit institutions or not, must comply with. Where those provisions apply to credit institutions, they may overlap with those of Directive 2013/36/EU of the European Parliament and of the Council of 26 June 2013 on access to the activity of credit institutions and the prudential supervision of credit institutions and investment firms. In those cases, Recital (44) of MiCA states that credit institutions must comply with the more specific or stricter requirements, ensuring compliance with both sets of rules.

3.5.1 General Requirements

All issuers of ARTs must comply with the following requirements:

- The rules on the reserve of assets described in Sect. 2.7.2 apply to all issuers of ARTs, with some specificities that are worth mentioning:
  - A minimum amount in each official currency the ART references must be held as deposits in credit institutions. That amount cannot be lower than 30 per cent of the amount referenced in each official currency.

  - Issuers of ARTs must have a clear and detailed policy describing the stabilisation mechanism of such tokens. That policy must list the assets referenced by the ART and the composition of those assets.

- The rules on the monitoring and restriction on the issuance of EMTs described in Sect. 2.8, and on the recovery and redemption plans described in Sect. 2.10 are also applicable to all issuers of ARTs. Regarding those plans, the issuer of an ART must notify the competent authority within six months of the approval of the crypto-asset white paper (in the case of credit institutions) or the date of authorisation of the applicant issuer of ART.
- Issuers of ARTs must notify the competent authority of their home Member State of any intended change of their business model likely to significantly influence the purchase decision of any holders or prospective holders of ARTs. In those cases, the issuer of an ART must draw up a draft modified crypto-asset white paper and notify the competent authority of the home Member State.

Where the competent authority considers that the modifications to the crypto-asset white paper are potentially relevant for the smooth operation of payment systems, monetary policy transmission and monetary sovereignty, it must consult the ECB and, where applicable, the central bank of the Member State whose official currency is not the euro and the issuer is established or whose official currency is not the euro and it is an official currency which is referenced by the ART.

The competent authority must approve or refuse to approve the draft modified crypto-asset white paper. Where the competent authority approves it, it may require the issuer of the ART:

- to put in place mechanisms to ensure the protection of holders of the ART when a potential modification of the issuer's operations can have a material effect on the value, stability, or risks of the ART or the reserve assets;
- to take appropriate corrective measures to address concerns related to market integrity, financial stability or the smooth operation of payment systems.

The competent authority must require the issuer of the ART to take any appropriate corrective measures to address concerns related to the smooth operation of payment systems, monetary policy transmission, or monetary sovereignty if such measures are proposed by the ECB or, where applicable, the central bank of the Member State whose official currency is not the euro and the issuer is established or whose official currency is not the euro and it is an official currency which is referenced by the ART.

- Where an issuer of ARTs has infringed the provisions regarding the crypto-asset white paper by providing in its crypto-asset white paper information that is not complete, fair or clear or that is misleading, that issuer and the members of its administrative, management or supervisory body shall be liable to a holder of such ART for any loss incurred due to that infringement. Any contractual exclusion or limitation of civil liability shall be deprived of legal effect. Furthermore, MiCA does not exclude any other civil liability under national law.

The issuer and the members of its administrative, management or supervisory bodies shall not be liable for loss suffered due to reliance on the information provided in the summary of the white paper, except where the summary is misleading, inaccurate or inconsistent when read together with the other parts of the crypto-asset white paper, or does not provide when read together with the other parts of the crypto-asset white paper, key information to aid prospective holders when considering whether to purchase the ART.

- Issuers of ARTs must act honestly, fairly and professionally and communicate with the holders and prospective holders of ARTs in a fair, clear and not misleading manner. Issuers must also act in the best interests of the holders of such tokens. They must treat them equally unless any preferential treatment is disclosed in the crypto-asset white paper and, where applicable, the marketing communications.
- Issuers of ARTs must publish the approved crypto-asset white paper on their website, which must also be publicly accessible.
- Any marketing communications relating to an offer to the public of an ART or the admission to trading of such ART must be clearly identifiable as such. Its information must be fair, clear and not misleading, must be consistent with the information in the crypto-asset white paper, must clearly state that the crypto-asset white paper has been published and indicate the address of the website of the issuer, as well as a telephone number and an email address to contact the issuer. Marketing communications must be notified to competent authorities and published on the issuer's website upon request. No marketing communications must be disseminated before the publication of the crypto-asset white paper.
- Issuers of ARTs must disclose the number of ARTs in circulation and the value and composition of the reserve of assets in a clear, accurate, transparent manner and in a publicly and easily accessible place on their website. Such information must be updated at least monthly. Issuers must also publish a brief, clear, accurate, and transparent summary of the audit report and the full and unredacted audit report concerning the reserve of assets as soon as possible. Finally, issuers of ART must disclose as quickly as possible any event that has significantly affected, or is likely to significantly affect, the value of the ARTs or the reserve of assets in a clear, accurate and transparent manner, in a publicly and easily accessible place, on their website.
- Issuers of ARTs must establish and maintain effective and transparent procedures for the prompt, fair and consistent handling of complaints received from holders of ARTs and other interested parties, including consumer associations representing holders of ARTs, and must publish descriptions of those procedures.
- Issuers of ARTs must implement and maintain effective policies and procedures to identify, prevent, manage and disclose conflicts of interest between themselves and their shareholders or members; any shareholder or member, whether direct or indirect, that has a qualifying holding in the issuers; the members of their management body; their employees; the holders of ARTs; or any third party in

charge of operating the reserve of assets, the investment of the reserve assets, the custody of the reserve of assets or the distribution of the ARTs to the public.

Issuers of ARTs must take all appropriate steps to identify, prevent, manage and disclose conflicts of interest arising from the management and investment of the reserve of assets. They must also disclose to the holders of their ARTs, in a prominent place on their website, the general nature and sources of conflicts of interest and the steps taken to mitigate them.

- Issuers of ARTs must immediately notify their competent authority of any changes to their management body. They must provide their competent authority with all the necessary information to assess compliance with the requirements described in the third paragraph of Sect. 3.5.2.
- Holders of ARTs have a right of redemption at all times against the issuers of the ARTs and in respect of the reserve assets when the issuers cannot meet their obligations as referred to in the provisions of MiCA regarding the recovery and redemption plans. Without prejudice to the provisions of the recovery plan (see Sect. 2.10), the redemption of ARTs is not subject to a fee.

Upon request by a holder of an ART, an issuer of such token must redeem either by paying an amount in funds, other than e-money, equivalent to the market value of the assets referenced by the ART held or by delivering the assets referenced by the token. Issuers must establish a policy on such permanent right of redemption setting out:

- the conditions, including thresholds, periods and timeframes, for holders of ARTs to exercise such right of redemption;
- the mechanisms and procedures to ensure the redemption of the ARTs, including in stressed market circumstances, as well as in the context of the implementation of the recovery plan or the case of an orderly redemption of ARTs;
- the valuation, or the principles of valuation, of the ARTs and of the reserve assets when the holder of ARTs exercises the right of redemption;
- the conditions for settlement of the redemption; and,
- measures that the issuers take to manage increases or decreases adequately in the reserve of assets to avoid any adverse impacts on the market of the reserve assets.

Where issuers, when selling an ART, accept a payment in funds other than e-money, denominated in an official currency, they must always provide an option to redeem the token in funds other than e-money, denominated in the same official currency.

- Finally, issuers of ARTs must not grant interest in relation to ART. Any remuneration or other benefit related to the length of time during which a holder of ARTs holds such ART shall be treated as interest.

3.5.2 Requirements Regarding Governance Arrangements

In addition to the preceding, MiCA sets out specific requirements regarding governance arrangements applicable to all issuers of ARTs, as follows:

- Issuers of ARTs must have robust governance arrangements, including a clear organisational structure with well-defined, transparent, and consistent lines of responsibility, effective processes to identify, manage, monitor, and report the risks to which they are or might be exposed, and adequate internal control mechanisms, including sound administrative and accounting procedures.
- Members of the management body of issuers of ARTs must be of sufficiently good repute and possess the appropriate knowledge, skills and experience, both individually and collectively, to perform their duties. In particular, they must not have been convicted of offences relating to money laundering or terrorist financing or of any other offences that would affect their good reputation. They must demonstrate that they can commit sufficient time to perform their duties effectively.
- The management body of issuers of ARTs must assess and periodically review the effectiveness of the policy arrangements and procedures put in place to comply with the requirements applicable to issuers of ARTs and take appropriate measures to address any deficiencies.
- Shareholders or members, whether direct or indirect, that have qualifying holdings in issuers of ARTs must be of sufficiently good repute and, in particular, must not have been convicted of offences relating to money laundering or terrorist financing or of any other offences that would affect their good reputation.
- Issuers of ARTs must adopt policies and procedures that are sufficiently effective to ensure compliance with MiCA and must establish, maintain and implement, in particular, policies and procedures on several requirements applicable to them, such as the reserve of assets, the rights granted to holders, the protocols for validating transactions, the mechanisms to ensure the liquidity of ART, the complaints-handling, the conflicts of interest, the arrangements with third-party entities for operating the reserve of assets, and for the investment of the reserve assets, the custody of the reserve assets and, where applicable, the distribution of the ARTs to the public, etc.

Where issuers of ARTs enter into the arrangements mentioned above, those arrangements must be set out in a contract with the third-party entities, establishing the roles, responsibilities, rights, and obligations of both the issuers of ARTs and the third-party entities.

- Unless they have initiated a redemption plan, issuers of ARTs must employ appropriate and proportionate systems, resources and procedures to ensure the continued and regular performance of their services and activities.
- If the issuer of an ART decides to discontinue the provision of its services and activities, including by discontinuing the issue of that ART, it must submit a plan to the competent authority to approve such discontinuation.

- Issuers of ARTs must identify sources of operational risk and minimise those risks by developing appropriate systems, controls and procedures.
- Issuers of ARTs must establish a business continuity policy and plans to ensure, in the case of an interruption of their information and communication technology (ICT) systems and procedures, the preservation of essential data and functions and the maintenance of their activities or where that is not possible, the timely recovery of such data and functions and the timely resumption of their activities.
- Issuers of ARTs must have in place internal control mechanisms and effective procedures for risk management, including effective control and safeguard arrangements for managing ICT systems as required by Regulation (EU) 2022/2554 of the European Parliament and of the Council of 14 December 2022 on digital operational resilience for the financial sector (Regulation (EU) 2022/2554). Issuers must also regularly monitor and evaluate the adequacy and effectiveness of the internal control mechanisms and procedures for risk assessment and take appropriate measures to address deficiencies.
- Issuers of ARTs must have systems and procedures in place that are adequate to safeguard the availability, authenticity, integrity and confidentiality of data as required by Regulation (EU) 2022/2554 and in line with Regulation (EU) 2016/679 of the European Parliament and of the Council of 27 April 2016 on the protection of natural persons with regard to the processing of personal data and on the free movement of such data. Those systems must record and safeguard relevant data and information collected and produced during the issuers' activities.
- Finally, issuers of ARTs must ensure that independent auditors regularly audit them. The results of those audits must be communicated to the issuer's management body and made available to the competent authority.

3.6 Additional Requirements for Issuers of ARTS That Are Not Credit Institutions

3.6.1 Own Funds Requirements

Issuers of ARTs that are not credit institutions must, at all times, have their funds equal to an amount of at least the highest of the following:

- EUR 350,000;
- two per cent of the average amount of the reserve assets at the end of each calendar day and calculated over the preceding six months; and,
- a quarter of the fixed overheads of the preceding year.

The own funds must consist of the CET1 items and instruments referred to in Articles 26 to 30 of the CRR, after the deductions in full pursuant to Article 36 of that Regulation, without the application of the threshold exemptions referred to in Articles 46(4) and 48 of that Regulation.

Competent authorities may also require issuers to hold their own funds that amount to up to 20 per cent higher than two per cent of the average amount of the reserve assets at the end of each calendar day and calculated over the preceding six months, where an assessment of any of the indicators mentioned in Sect. 2.7.1 shows a higher degree of risk.

Additionally, issuers of ARTs must regularly conduct stress testing that considers severe but plausible financial stress scenarios, such as interest rate shocks, and non-financial stress scenarios, such as operational risk. Based on the outcome of such stress testing, the competent authority of the home Member State must require the issuer to hold an amount of own funds that is between 20 per cent and 40 per cent higher than two per cent of the average amount of the reserve assets at the end of each calendar day and calculated over the preceding six months, in certain circumstances having regard to the risk outlook and stress testing results.

3.6.2 Acquisition of Issuers of ARTs

Any natural or legal persons or such persons acting in concert who intend to acquire, directly or indirectly, a qualifying holding in an issuer of an ART that is not a credit institution or to increase, directly or indirectly, such a qualifying holding so that the proportion of the voting rights or the capital held would reach or exceed 20 per cent, 30 per cent or 50 per cent, or so that the issuer of the ART would become its subsidiary, must notify the competent authority of that issuer thereof in writing, indicating the size of the intended holding.

The competent authority must assess the proposed acquisition. When performing that assessment, it must appraise the suitability of the proposed acquirer and the financial soundness of the proposed acquisition against all of the following criteria:

- The reputation of the proposed acquirer.
- The reputation, knowledge, skills and experience of any person who will direct the business of the issuer of the ART as a result of the proposed acquisition.
- The financial soundness of the proposed acquirer, in particular in relation to the type of business envisaged and pursued with respect to the issuer of the ART in which the acquisition is proposed.
- Whether the issuer of the ART will be able to comply and continue to comply with the provisions applicable to ARTs contained in Title III of MiCA.
- Whether there are reasonable grounds to suspect that, in connection with the proposed acquisition, money laundering or terrorist financing is being or has been committed or attempted, or that the proposed acquisition could increase the risk thereof.

The competent authority may oppose the proposed acquisition only where there are reasonable grounds for doing so based on the criteria mentioned above or where the information provided is incomplete or false. In that case, it must notify the proposed acquirer of its decision.

Where the competent authority does not oppose the proposed acquisition, it shall be deemed to be approved.

Any natural or legal person who has decided to dispose, directly or indirectly, of a qualifying holding in an ART issuer must notify the competent authority of its decision in writing and indicate the size of such holding before disposing of that holding. That person must also notify the competent authority where it has decided to reduce a qualifying holding so that the proportion of the voting rights or the capital held would fall below 10 per cent, 20 per cent, 30 per cent, 50 per cent, or so that the issuer of the ART would cease to be that person's subsidiary.

3.6.3 Requirements Where Necessary to Address Certain Risks

MiCA entitles competent authorities of the home Member States to require issuers of ARTs to comply with an additional set of rules where necessary to address the higher degree of risks identified in accordance with the indicators mentioned in Sect. 2.7.1, or any other risks the following requirements aim to address, such as liquidity risks. Specifically:

- Issuers of ARTs must comply with the requirements mentioned in Sect. 2.7.3 and 2.7.4.
- Issuers of ARTs must, at all times, keep their funds equal to an amount of at least the highest of the following:
  - EUR 350,000;
  - three per cent of the average amount of the reserve assets at the end of each calendar day and calculated over the preceding six months; and
  - a quarter of the fixed overheads of the preceding year.
- Where several issuers of ARTs offer the same ART, or where an issuer of ARTs offers two or more ARTs in the EU and at least one of those ARTs is classified as significant, the rules contained in the preceding paragraphs apply to each issuer.

3.7 Significant ARTs

EBA must classify ARTs as significant ARTs where they meet at least three of the criteria described in Sect. 2.9 during a given period. Where several issuers issue the same ART, the fulfilment of those criteria must be assessed after aggregating the data from those issuers.

Where an ART is classified as significant pursuant to a decision of EBA, several supervisory responsibilities concerning the issuer of that ART are transferred from the competent authority of the issuer's home Member State to EBA.

EBA must annually reassess the classification of significant ARTs based on the available information. Where EBA concludes that certain ARTs no longer meet the criteria, it adopts a decision by means of which the ART is no longer classified as significant and the supervisory responsibilities concerning the issuer of that ART are transferred from EBA to the competent authority of the issuer's home Member State.

An issuer of an ART may also indicate that it wishes for its ART to be classified as a significant ART. The issuer must demonstrate, through a detailed program of operations, that it is likely to meet at least three of the criteria already described. As above, EBA adopts a final decision on the classification of the ART.

Issuers of significant ARTs, whether they are credit institutions or not, must comply with the requirements mentioned in Sect. 2.7.3 and 2.7.4. Additionally, issuers of significant ARTs that are not credit institutions must also, at all times, keep their own funds equal to an amount of at least the highest of the following:

- EUR 350,000;
- three per cent of the average amount of the reserve assets at the end of each calendar day and calculated over the preceding six months; and,
- a quarter of the fixed overheads of the preceding year.

Where several issuers of ARTs offer the same ART, or where an issuer of ARTs offers two or more ARTs in the EU and at least one of those ARTs is classified as significant, those rules shall apply to each issuer.

References

Bains P, Ismail A, Melo F, Sugimoto N (2022) Regulating the crypto-ecosystem: the case of Stablecoins and arrangements. IMF Fintech Note 2022/008, International Monetary Fund, Washington, DC. https://www.imf.org/-/media/Files/Publications/FTN063/2022/English/FTNEA2022008.ashx. Accessed 14 June 2024

European Commission (2020) Proposal for a Regulation of the European Parliament and of the Council on Markets in Crypto-Assets, and amending Directive (EU) 2019/1937. Brussels, COM (2020) 593 final. https://eur-lex.europa.eu/resource.html?uri=cellar:f69f89bb-fe54-11ea-b44f-01aa75ed71a1.0001.02/DOC_1&format=PDF. Accessed 14 June 2024

Financial Stability Board (2023) High-level Recommendations for the Regulation, Supervision and Oversight of Global Stablecoin Arrangements. Final Report. https://www.fsb.org/wp-content/uploads/P170723-3.pdf. Accessed 14 June 2024

Judgement of 26 January 2021 in Joined Cases C-422/19 and C-423/19, Hessischer Rundfunk, EU:C:2021:63

Stablecoins in the MiCA Regulation

Apol·lònia Martínez Nadal

Abstract This work offers a legal analysis of stablecoins, a novel form of cryptocurrency that has emerged as a distinctive alternative to previous cryptocurrencies, which are characterised by their oscillating and highly volatile value, making them unsuitable for use as a payment instrument or functional legal tender equivalent. The pivotal legal framework for stablecoins is the Markets in Crypto-Assets Regulation (MiCA), which addresses the conceptual aspects of stablecoins. Despite its presence in MiCA, stablecoins lack a specific legal definition therein. The Regulation's classification is based on whether crypto assets aim to stabilise their value relative to other assets. This chapter, therefore, focuses on the in-depth examination of the two subcategories of the Regulation that fall under the umbrella of stable crypto assets: asset-referenced tokens and electronic money tokens. We delve into their unique characteristics, including their vocation for stability and, in turn, the intriguing differences between the two subcategories.

1 Introduction: A General Approach to the Stablecoin Market

Crypto assets, a new breed of technology-based economic instruments, have captivated the market with their potential for spectacular revaluations. However, they also pose risks and drawbacks, often stemming from their volatility, speculative nature, or lack of liquidity. A novel category has emerged to address these issues, forming our study's focus: stablecoins. These are crypto assets that, unlike their volatile

This work is funded within the framework of: Proyecto CIPROM/2022/26 "Presente y futuro de la regulación de los Criptoactivos en la UE [Legalcripto]". Proyecto Prometeo CIPROM/2022/26, grupos de investigación de excelencia, de la Generalitat Valenciana (P.I. Carmen Pastor).

A. Martínez Nadal (✉)
University of the Balearic Islands, Department of Private Law, Palma, Spain
e-mail: apollonia.martinez@uib.es

C. Pastor Sempere (ed.), *Governance and Control of Data and Digital Economy in the European Single Market*, Law, Governance and Technology Series 71,
https://doi.org/10.1007/978-3-031-74889-9_8

counterparts, are designed with a stability mandate, linking their value to legal tender or other assets.

In the large and diverse market of crypto assets, the category or, rather, the denomination of "stablecoins" refers to crypto assets that aim to stabilise their value by referring to one or more legal tender currencies (usually the dollar, such as USD Coin, USDC); one or more commodities, precious metals or industrial metals, such as Digix Gold Tokens (DGX); one or more crypto assets; or, a basket of these assets.[1] Depending on the type of backing, different categories of stablecoins exist as follows:

(a) Stablecoins backed by legal tender: these are issued to have parity with legal tender so that one token is equivalent to one unit of the reference currency. The companies that issue these stablecoins commit to holding reserves equivalent to the number of tokens in circulation. Examples of stablecoins based on this model and with the highest market use are Tether (USDT) and USD Coin (USDC).
(b) Stablecoins are backed by assets other than legal tender. They are based on tangible goods such as gold or oil and are based on the idea that these goods maintain their value over time. This category includes gold-backed Digix (DGX) and oil-based Petro (PTR).
(c) Cryptocurrency-backed stablecoins: in this case, cryptocurrencies are based on other cryptocurrencies. For example, the DAI (DAI) cryptocurrency is backed by Ether (ETH), the native cryptocurrency of the Ethereum network. DAI's system uses smart contracts to maintain a peg to the U.S. dollar.
(d) Algorithmic stablecoins: they are not backed by legal tender or physical assets, but their value is automatically adjusted according to market supply and demand according to an algorithm. So if, for example, the demand for the currency increases, more coins will be issued to keep its value stable. An example of this category is Ampleforth (AMPL).

This vocation for stabilisation that inspires cryptocurrencies can turn them into an interesting and powerful "monetary" instrument (they are sometimes described as "private currencies") with functions similar to legal tender (and which, precisely, for this reason, raises doubts about their coexistence with the so-called central bank digital currencies).[2] The regulatory challenges they cause are even greater in the case

[1] For a more detailed view of this broad and extensive market of the so-called "stablecoins", cf., Pastor Sempere (2021), pp. 157–188, which significantly points out that "There are as many variants as there are stablecoins in the market with this denomination".

[2] At the same time, there are open questions about whether central bank currencies (CBDCs) and other initiatives could fulfil these functions even more effectively than privately developed stablecoins. CBDCs would enjoy central bank backing and not be subject to the same conflicts of interest around the asset backing and stabilisation mechanism. Their value could be fixed by design to the currency they refer to (particularly in systems where the CBDC is the digital representation of the currency), thus eliminating fluctuations in value. The question is how a CBDC could be designed to offer robust interoperability with decentralised finance solutions. Cf., Arner et al. (2020), p. 39.

of so-called “global stablecoins”, which, like Facebook’s Libra proposal presented in 2019, are those that can take advantage of existing large cross-border user bases to develop rapidly and reach a substantial volume (global, or significant, according to the MiCA Regulation). For this reason, these stablecoins cause concern among the financial authorities of different countries. Hence, it is considered that they would need stricter specific regulation, as in the case of the MiCA Regulation, which subjects the so-called “significant” referenced tokens and electronic money tokens to additional requirements.

Stablecoins emerged and experienced a meteoric rise from the ashes of the great speculative bubble that affected cryptocurrencies in 2018. Indeed, stablecoins were born because of the shortcomings of previous cryptocurrencies (such as the emblematic Bitcoin*),* which, due to their oscillating and highly volatile value, are not suitable for use as a payment instrument nor, in general, as a functional equivalent of legal tender, or as a store of value and unit of account.

Therefore, after the emergence of Bitcoin in 2009, from 2014 onwards, and in the absence of a digital version of legal tender currencies, the stable crypto assets era began (which aims to stabilise their value by linking them to legal tender or other assets). This stage starts with presenting different “stablecoin” projects (Dai, HUSD, Paxos Standard, Tether, TrueUSD and USD Coin). It culminates with the announcement of the Libra project by Facebook as a global stablecoin that, as we have pointed out, sets off the alarm bells of the authorities due to its financial and monetary implications.[3]

Therefore, the characteristic of “stablecoins” is their vocation for stability, which, as we have seen, is achieved through at least two broad categories of mechanisms. Typically, stablecoin issuers aim to back stablecoins with legal tender, assets, or other cryptocurrencies; these are called asset-linked stablecoins. On the other hand, algorithm-based stablecoins also seek to use these automated procedures to increase or decrease the supply of stablecoins in response to changes in demand. Despite this vocation for stability, in practice, there is a certain price volatility, i.e. a fluctuation in relation to reference assets that, in any case, would be lower than that of other non-stable crypto assets.[4]

[3] Cfr., Arner et al. (2020), p. 39.

[4] Cfr., Arner et al. (2020), p. 39, who also notes that, during 2020, the market capitalisation of existing stablecoins (e.g. Tether, USD Coin, Dai and Paxos) has grown from a low level. The market value of these coins reached $14 billion in August, dominated by Tether. It is a small amount in relation to the global financial system and even with regard to the crypto-asset market. Still, the truth is that the market capitalisation of stablecoins is increasing and has more than doubled since the beginning of the COVID-19 pandemic, a period in which there has been a large increase in digital payments in general and related services such as e-commerce.

Despite the vocation of stability, these authors point out that the value of stablecoins can fluctuate more than existing digital instruments such as electronic money. It is true that by nature, they will be less susceptible to speculative bubbles of the kind that affect Bitcoin and other cryptocurrencies; however, their market capitalization can rise and fall quickly with purchases and redemptions by investors and may even be subject to significant price discounts, especially when backed by high-risk or opaque assets and in times of market turmoil.

Therefore, the term "stablecoin" does not necessarily imply that the value is stable in practice, even though it is the term commonly used by market participants. As has been pointed out doctrinally, the alternative expression "private asset-linked tokens" more accurately characterises the technical nature of these instruments, and we will see how the authorities of the European Union use a similar expression in the MiCA Regulation: "asset referenced tokens". This is probably the technical reason why the authorities of the European Union do not include the category of stablecoins as such in the articulated text in which they do include, on the contrary, the referenced tokens, together with the electronic money tokens, which are, as we will see, the two categories of stablecoins included in the MiCA Regulation.[5]

In short, following the terminological precision made by the FATF (*Financial Action Task Force*), the term "stablecoin" does not correspond to a clear legal or technical category but is a commercial term used by the promoters of such coins.[6] Beyond terminological precision and entering the conceptual level, institutions such as the European Central Bank question both the condition of currency and the stability of these products.[7]

Given their importance, we focus this work on stablecoins. After a previous reference to regulatory initiatives, we focus on their regulation in the MiCA Regulation and the two categories of stablecoins contemplated: asset-referenced tokens and electronic money tokens.

2 Regulatory Approach to Stablecoins

Recently, authorities in numerous countries have been working to regulate crypto assets, especially stablecoins. Indeed, because they are susceptible to greater and more widespread uses than those of other more volatile crypto assets and because of their enormous potential for use, there is a consensus that their regulation should be stricter. At the international level, some different groups and institutions have addressed the study of crypto assets in general and stablecoins in particular.[8]

The authorities of the European Union have also shown their concern about the enormous potential of using stablecoins and their possible implications. That is why,

[5] Cf., Arner et al. (2020), p. 39.

[6] Financial Action Task Force (FATF) (2021) Updated Guidance for a risk-based approach: Virtual assets and virtual asset service providers, note 3. Hence, it refers to them as "so-called stablecoins" and with the caveat that the use of the usual term does not in any way imply approval of the claims that may be deduced from it.

[7] European Central Bank (2020), pp. 3–10.

[8] Indeed, there are different international organizations that, in recent times, have focused their efforts on crypto assets in general and stablecoins in particular: among others, G20, G7, FSB, IOSCO, BCBS, FATF: European Central Bank Crypto-Assets Task Force (2021); European Securities and Markets Authority (2019); G7 Working Group on Stablecoins (2019); International Organization of Securities Commissions (IOSCO) (2020).

despite the formal taxonomy of the MiCA Regulation (which includes three subcategories), we can distinguish two large classes of crypto assets from a material point of view. On the one hand, the large category of stable crypto assets, which would include asset-referenced tokens and electronic money tokens, and to which a large part of the Regulation is dedicated, establishing greater and more demanding requirements for this type of cryptocurrency, whose legal regime is regulated in Titles III and IV and which will be analysed in greater detail in later sections. On the other hand, the residual category of tokens other than the above (which includes, but is not limited to, utility tokens, a type of crypto asset used solely to provide access to a good or service provided by its issuer) is regulated in Title II.

Finally, it should be mentioned that for the regulation of stablecoins, it is necessary to differentiate between stablecoins in general and those known as "global stablecoins" or, according to the MiCA Regulation, "significant stablecoins". Due to their systemic nature, this subtype of stablecoins poses additional risks to financial stability, monetary policy, and monetary sovereignty that would not exist when they have a more limited scope. For this reason, it is considered that they should be subject to additional requirements that are not necessary in the case of non-significant stablecoins, and this is the case in the Markets in Crypto-Assets Regulation.

After these introductory and approximate sections on stablecoins, we will now focus, in the following sections and subsections, on the specific analysis of the two categories of stablecoins regulated in the MiCA Regulation: asset-referenced tokens and electronic money tokens,[9] with the preliminary issue of including the "stablecoin" concept in this Regulation.

3 Regulation of Stablecoin Crypto Assets in MiCA

3.1 The Non-Existent but Present Notion of "Stablecoin" in the MiCA Regulation. Its Two Subcategories

The so-called stablecoins are a formally non-existent notion, but we consider that they are materially present in the MiCA Regulation. Indeed, there is no legal definition in the Regulation: the notion of "stablecoins" does not appear in the definitions section of the MiCA Regulation (nor in the proposal), despite the traditional legislative technique in this regard in the regulatory instruments of the European Union, which includes, in this case, up to a total of 51 definitions in the final version (28 in the proposal).

However, despite not being legally defined, the term "stablecoins" did appear frequently in the proposed MiCA Regulation; specifically, we find it on 44 occasions,

[9] As a reference bibliography on these two novel categories, it is worth mentioning Pastor Sempere (2021), pp. 157–188; Madrid Parra (2020), pp. 219–244 and Martínez Nadal (2021), pp. 41–62.

notably in the Explanatory Memorandum of the proposal for a Regulation presented on 24 September 2020. In these references, the Commission highlights the great potential of stablecoins, pointing out the possibility of widespread adoption by users to transfer value or as a means of payment. Curiously, in the definitively approved version of the Regulation, these numerous references in the proposal disappear, being reduced to only 5, basically in Recital 18, accompanied, of course, by at least nine references to the idea of stability and the stabilisation mechanisms that characterise stablecoins.

Therefore, we would face a term used in commercial and technical practice and even doctrinal works. However, that does not necessarily correspond to a legal category or definition, at least expressly, in the MiCA Regulation.[10] However, this category is well present in the Regulation, and we would even say that it constitutes its backbone, as evidenced in Recital 18, which states that: "This Regulation classifies crypto-assets into three types, which should be distinguished from each other and subject to different requirements depending on the risks involved. The ranking is based on whether crypto assets seek to stabilise their value relative to other assets." Therefore, the classification criterion is based on this idea of a vocation for stabilising crypto assets.

Based on this classificatory premise, the different categories are listed in the Recital above (a) "The first type consists of crypto assets whose objective is to stabilise their value by referring to a single official currency. Its function is like that of electronic money, as defined in Directive 2009/110/EC. Like electronic money, these crypto assets are an electronic substitute for coins and banknotes and are typically used to make payments. Those crypto assets need to be defined… as 'electronic money tokens'". (b) "The second type of crypto-asset refers to 'asset-referenced tokens', the purpose of which is to stabilise their value by referring to another security or right, or a combination thereof, including one or more official currencies. This second type covers all other crypto-assets, other than electronic money tokens, the value of which is backed by assets, to prevent circumvention of this Regulation and to make it forward-looking." (c) "Finally, the third type is crypto-assets, which are neither 'asset-referenced tokens' nor 'electronic money tokens', and covers a wide variety of crypto-assets, including consumer tokens".

It is thus clear, firstly, that this not-legally defined notion of stable crypto-assets would include in the MiCA Regulation two of its three sub-categories of crypto-assets: asset-referenced tokens and electronic money tokens. Secondly, it is revealed that, according to the authorities of the European Union, these stablecoins are more likely to expand rapidly and could, therefore, pose greater risks to investors, counterparties, and the financial system. For this reason, the Regulation focuses its

[10]Cf., in this regard, Financial Stability Board (2020) Addressing the regulatory, supervisory and oversight challenges raised by "global stablecoin" arrangements. Basilea, p. 11, where it is also indicated that the terms "stablecoin" do not necessarily imply a distinct legal or regulatory classification.

attention on them, dedicating Titles III and IV to them. At the same time, Title II is residually devoted to the rest of the tokens (including utility tokens).

In the absence of a legal definition and even a generally accepted concept of a stablecoin, given what has been explained in the introductory section, two elements characterise it: its vocation for stability (and the existence, therefore, of a stabilisation mechanism) and its functional versatility, in the sense that it is particularly suitable as a stable payment instrument, and precisely for this reason it can also be used as a store of value. Both elements are explained next in greater detail:

(a) Vocation for stability: their main characteristic is their claim and purpose of maintaining a stable value, for which they are referenced concerning the value of different goods (or a legal tender, in the case of electronic money). Therefore, as stated in the opinion of the European Economic and Social Committee (EESC) in section 2.2.7, "These instruments are crypto-assets that, among other aspects, unlike the famous Bitcoin, have a relatively stable price, as they are linked to an equally stable medium of exchange (i.e. an institutional currency), and shortly could, therefore, become very widespread payment and investment systems."[11] To these considerations, it is necessary to make the qualification related to the link to an equally stable environment since, as we will see, this stability will not necessarily always exist.

Since the main characteristic of stable cryptocurrencies is their vocation for stability, there must be a stabilisation mechanism that, in principle, can be of two main kinds: asset or algorithmic, to which we will refer in greater detail in the following sections.

(b) Functional versatility: in practice, so-called stablecoins can be used for different purposes. Some stablecoin initiatives pursue the function of facilitating payments, especially cross-border retail payments, which are still relatively slow and expensive. However, stablecoins can also be used to store value. All this without prejudice to the fact that the use of stablecoins could also evolve so that a stablecoin initially intended to be used as a means of payment could also end up being used as a store of value.[12]

We now analyse the two categories of crypto assets of the MiCA Regulation that are included in the concept of stable crypto assets: asset-referenced tokens and electronic money tokens. The Regulation focuses on them, dedicating Titles III and IV to them, respectively.

[11] Opinion of the European Economic and Social Committee on: Proposal for a regulation of the European Parliament and of the Council on markets in crypto-assets and amending Directive (EU) 2019/1937 (COM(2020) 593 final — 2020/0265 (COD)) — Proposal for a Regulation of the European Parliament and of the Council on a pilot scheme for market infrastructures based on distributed ledger technology (COM(2020) 594 final — 2020/0267 (COD)).

[12] Financial Stability Board (2020), p. 11.

3.2 Asset-Referenced Tokens as the First Category of Stable Crypto Assets

3.2.1 Concept, Characteristics, and Functions

In the initial version of the proposed Regulation, this subcategory is defined as a type of crypto asset which, to maintain a stable value, refers to the value of several legal tender fiat currencies, one or more commodities, one or more crypto assets, or a combination of such assets (art. 3.1.3). The definition undergoes a variation in the version definitively approved: "asset-referenced token": a type of crypto-asset that is not an electronic money token, and that aims to maintain a stable value referenced to another security or right, or to a combination of both, including one or more official currencies (art. 3.1.6).

As a subcategory of the so-called stablecoins, their main characteristic, shared with electronic money tokens, is their claim and purpose of maintaining a stable value, for which they are referenced concerning the value of different goods. Their specificity differentiates them from electronic money tokens because they are referenced concerning the value of different possible goods to achieve this stability. In contrast, electronic money tokens, as we will see, are necessarily referenced with respect to a single legal tender.

Although the definition in the proposal does not refer to the function or uses of these referenced tokens, the objective often pursued in stabilising the value is that the holders of the asset-referenced tokens use them as a means of payment (in the broad sense) for the purchase of goods and services or even as a store of value (a function considered main by the European Central Bank) but avoiding the speculative investments of volatile crypto assets.[13] Indeed, cryptocurrencies with large fluctuations in value become risky investments and are unsuitable as payment instruments. Stablecoins, such as referenced tokens, closely follow the value of the underlying legal tender or asset to which they are referenced, so they have a vocation for stability, as has already been shown when characterising stable cryptocurrencies. This can even turn them into safe havens in volatile markets.

The truth is that real stability will depend, as we have been saying, on the asset or assets to which these tokens are referenced (the so-called "basket of assets")), and may be higher (but not absolute) in the case of commodities (e.g., precious metals, oil) but lower in the case of referencing to other crypto assets which, in turn, can be more or less volatile. Therefore, under Article 36.8 of the Regulation, issuers of asset-referenced tokens shall adopt a clear and detailed policy describing the stabilisation mechanism for such assets; in particular, they shall list the reference

[13] Doctrinally, they are attributed the condition, and the effects, of privately issued money. Cf., in this regard, Pastor Sempere (2021), pp. 163–164.

assets to stabilise the value of the asset-referenced tokens and their composition and a detailed assessment of the risks arising from the reserve assets.[14]

For all these reasons, we consider appropriate the evolution in the definition of this category of crypto asset from the initial proposal, which established its purpose was "to maintain a stable value", to the definitively approved text, which states that "*it aims to* maintain a stable value referenced to another security or right".[15]

As we have pointed out on several occasions in the Explanatory Memorandum preceding the proposal for a MiCA Regulation, the Commission highlights the great potential of stablecoins (including asset-referenced tokens) that seek to stabilise their value and could, therefore, be widely adopted by users to transfer value or as a means of payment. Precisely because of this, they pose greater risks than other crypto assets regarding consumer protection and market integrity. Hence, greater and more demanding requirements are established for this type of cryptocurrency, whose legal regime is regulated in detail in Title III of the Regulation (articles 16 to 47) and whose main aspects we will briefly reference below.

At the outset, it should be noted that, in fact, in work leading up to the proposal, the Commission assessed several options specific to so-called 'stablecoins': the first option was to establish a specific legislative regime aimed at addressing the risks posed by 'stablecoins' and 'global stablecoins'; the second option was the regulation of "stablecoins" under the e-money directive and the third option would have been to ban the issuance of these currencies in the European Union. The Commission's decision combined the first and second options, effectively establishing a specific regulation of the tokens referenced to assets. Still, the regulation of electronic money tokens is based on the Electronic Money Directive, but there are important differences, as will be seen later.

Finally, the proposal refers to so-called algorithmic "stablecoins", which seek to maintain a stable value through protocols that foresee the increase or decrease in the supply of such crypto assets in response to changes in demand and to adjust their value. According to the proposal, they should not be considered asset-referenced tokens, provided that, to stabilise their value, they do not refer to one or more different assets.[16] According to the final text of the Regulation, in the case of

[14]More specifically, as per Article 36.8, issuers of asset-referenced tokens shall adopt a clear and detailed policy describing the stabilisation mechanism for such tokens. In particular, that policy shall: (a) list the assets referenced by the asset-referenced tokens and the composition of those assets; (b) describe the type and precise allocation of assets in the asset reserve; (c) contain a detailed assessment of the risks, including credit risk, market risk, concentration risk and liquidity risk, arising from the asset reserve; (d) describe the procedure for the issuance and redemption of asset-referenced tokens, as well as the procedure for such issuance and redemption to result in a corresponding increase or reduction in the asset reserve; (e) indicate whether part of the asset reserve is invested in accordance with Article 38; (f) where issuers of asset-referenced tokens invest a portion of the asset reserve in accordance with Article 38, it shall describe in detail the investment policy and include an assessment of the potential impact of the investment policy on the value of the asset reserve; (g) describe the procedure for the purchase of asset-referenced tokens and their redemption from the asset reserve, and list the persons or categories of persons entitled to do so.

[15]Italics are ours.

[16]Recital 26 of the Proposal for a MiCA Regulation.

algorithmic crypto assets that do not seek to stabilise the value of crypto assets by referring to one or more assets, bidders or persons requesting admission to trading of this type of crypto-asset must, in any case, comply with the provisions of Title II of the Regulation (Recital 41).

3.2.2 Legal Regime

As we have pointed out, among the various regulatory options that the Commission assessed for regulating cryptocurrencies, the Commission chose to establish a specific regulation for asset-referenced tokens. For this reason, they are regulated ex novo in Title III of the Regulation (Articles 16 to 47), which subjects them to greater and stricter requirements due to their potentially greater risk.

3.2.2.1 General Obligations of Issuers of Asset-Referenced Tokens

Once the specific regulation route is chosen, due to its potentially greater risk, as we have already anticipated, this category of crypto assets consisting of asset-referenced tokens is subject to greater and stricter requirements. Recital (40) noted that "holders can widely adopt asset-referenced tokens to transfer value or as a medium of exchange, and therefore pose greater risks than other crypto assets in terms of protecting crypto-asset holders, particularly retail holders, and market integrity. Therefore, issuers of asset-referenced tokens must be subject to stricter requirements than issuers of other crypto-assets."

Thus, issuers of asset-referenced tokens that offer them to the public or intend to apply for admission to trading on a crypto-asset trading platform must meet the following requirements:

(a) Be a legal person or undertaking established in the EU or a credit institution complying with Article 17 (Art. 16(1)). This requirement aims to ensure the proper supervision and monitoring of public offerings of asset-referenced tokens, for which the relevant issuers must have their registered office in the Union (Recital 27).
(b) Be authorised by their EU home Member State or be a credit institution producing a crypto-asset white paper approved by the national competent authority (Art. 16(1)). In addition to the requirement of a registered office in the European Union, public offerings of asset-referenced tokens in the Union or the application for admission to trading on a crypto-asset trading platform should only be allowed where the national competent authority has authorised the issuer in question (single authorisation to operate throughout the territory of the European Union, Art. 16.3) and, in addition, has approved the corresponding White Paper on crypto assets (Art. 16.4). However, the authorisation requirement does not apply where asset-referenced tokens are offered only to qualified investors or where the public offering does not exceed a certain threshold (Art. 16.2).

Competent authorities should refuse an authorisation where the business model of the future issuer of asset-referenced tokens could pose a serious threat to financial stability.

(c) Redeem its asset-referenced tokens at any time at the request of the holders at the market value of the referenced assets or by surrendering them. Holders of asset-referenced tokens must have a permanent right to reimbursement. The issuer of asset-referenced tokens must redeem the tokens either by paying in funds other than electronic money, an amount equivalent to the market value of the assets referenced by those tokens, or by surrendering the assets referenced by the tokens. The issuer of asset-referenced tokens must always provide the holder with the option to redeem the asset-referenced tokens in funds other than electronic money denominated in the same official currency that the issuer accepted when selling the tokens (art. 39).

(d) Issuers of asset-referenced tokens and crypto-asset service providers, when providing crypto-asset services related to asset-referenced tokens, should not grant asset-referenced token holders interest based on the length of time for which they hold asset-referenced tokens to reduce the risk of asset-referenced tokens being used as a store of value (Art. 40).

(e) Publish a crypto-asset white paper and any commercial communication on its website and be liable for damages caused by incorrect information in the white paper. To protect retail holders, issuers of asset-referenced tokens must provide their holders with complete, unbiased, clear, and non-misleading information. Crypto-asset white papers on asset-referenced tokens should include information on the stabilisation mechanism, the investment policy for reserve assets, the arrangements for custody of reserve assets and the rights granted to holders. In addition, issuers of asset-referenced tokens must provide information on an ongoing basis to the holders of those tokens. In particular, they must publish on their website the number of tokens referenced to assets in circulation and the value and composition of reserve assets (Art. 28).

(f) Act honestly, fairly and professionally to ensure the protection of retail operators and to establish and maintain effective and transparent procedures for the prompt, fair and consistent handling of complaints (Art. 27);

(g) Identify, prevent, manage and disclose all potential conflicts of interest (art. 32);

(h) Always maintain a reserve of assets to cover its liability vis-à-vis the holders of asset-referenced tokens, corresponding to the risks arising from that liability (art. 36). The asset reserve is to be used for the benefit of holders of asset-referenced tokens when the issuer is unable to meet its obligations to holders, for example in the event of insolvency. The asset reserve should be composed and managed in such a way as to hedge market and exchange rate risks. Issuers of asset-referenced tokens should ensure the prudent management of the asset reserve so that the value of the reserve is at least the corresponding value of the tokens in circulation and that changes in the reserve are properly managed to avoid adverse effects on the reserve asset markets. For this reason, issuers of asset-referenced tokens are required to have clear and detailed policies that outline, inter alia, the composition of the asset reserve, a comprehensive assessment of the risks associated with the reserve assets, and the procedure for the issuance and redemption of asset-referenced tokens.

(i) Own funds must be at least equal to the greater of EUR 350,000, 2% of the average amount of reserve assets, one-quarter of the fixed overheads of the previous year (Article 35);

(j) Establish recovery and reimbursement plans if they fail to meet their obligations (arts. 46 and 47).

3.2.2.2 Obligations Concerning the Reserve of Assets

The reserve of assets is the basket of reserve assets that guarantees the right of credit against the issuer (art. 3.1.32). Reserve assets are thus the basket of legal tender, commodities, or crypto assets that support the value of an asset-referenced token or the investment of such assets.

Chapter III of Title III is specifically dedicated to the establishment of rules on the reserve of assets that support asset-referenced tokens, basically regulating the following issues:

(1) Obligation to dispose of reserve assets and composition and management of the reserve of assets. Issuers are required to have a reserve of assets from the outset; specifically, article 36.1 provides that issuers of asset-referenced tokens shall constitute and maintain an asset reserve; this is a mandatory reserve for issuers to preserve the value of the referenced tokens issued.

Its composition and management are also regulated: the asset reserve must be composed and managed in such a way that (a) the risks associated with the assets referenced by the asset-referenced tokens are covered and (b) the liquidity risks associated with the holders' permanent redemption rights are addressed (art. 36.1). In addition, the asset reserve will be legally separated from the issuer's equity, as well as from the asset reserves of other asset-referenced tokens, in the interest of the holders of asset-referenced tokens, so that the issuers' creditors cannot claim the asset reserve, in particular in the event of insolvency (Art. 36.2). In addition, EBA (European Banking Authority), in close cooperation with ESMA (European Securities and Markets Authority) and the ESCB (European System of Central Banks), will develop draft regulatory technical standards to specify liquidity requirements further, taking into account the size, complexity and nature of the asset reserve and the statement referenced to the assets concerned (Article 36(4)).

Management bodies shall ensure the effective and prudent management of reserve assets, in particular by ensuring that the creation or destruction of asset-referenced tokens is always accompanied by a corresponding increase or decrease in the asset reserve (art. 36.6). A clear policy describing the stabilisation mechanism for tokens is needed (art. 36.8): in particular, reference assets to stabilise the value of tokens, their composition, derivative risks and, where appropriate, investment policies (in highly liquid and minimal risk financial instruments) should be listed with an assessment of the possible impact on the value of reserve assets; and finally, an independent audit of reserve assets must be carried out every six months (art. 36.9).

(2) Requirements relating to the custody of reserve assets. Pursuant to Article 37.1, issuers of asset-referenced tokens shall establish, maintain and apply custody policies, procedures and contractual arrangements that ensure at all times that reserve assets are kept separate from the issuer's own assets, are unencumbered and readily accessible to issuers to accommodate redemption requests from token holders.

Concerning the custody procedure (Article 37(3), the reserve assets received in exchange for the asset-referenced tokens shall be taken into custody, no later than five working days after the issuance of the asset-referenced tokens, by (a) a crypto-asset service provider authorised where the reserve assets take the form of crypto assets; (b) one credit institution for all other types of reserve assets.

Issuers of asset-referenced tokens shall exercise due competence, care and diligence in selecting, designating and reviewing credit institutions and crypto-asset service providers acting as custodians of reserve assets. Contractual agreements between issuers of asset-referenced tokens and custodians, which must be documented in writing (Art. 37.7), will ensure that the reserve assets in custody are protected against any claims by the custodians' creditors (Art. 37.4). Credit institutions and crypto-asset service providers' designated custodians shall act honestly, impartially, professionally and independently, and in the interests of the issuer of asset-referenced tokens and the holders of the tokens (Art. 33(8)) and shall not carry out activities with respect to issuers of asset-referenced tokens that may give rise to conflicts of interest (Art. 37(9)).

In the event of the loss of a financial instrument or crypto-asset held in custody, the credit institution or crypto-asset service provider that has lost that financial instrument or crypto-asset shall, without undue delay, return to the issuer of the asset-referenced tokens a financial instrument or crypto-asset of the same type or the corresponding value; unless they can demonstrate that the loss has occurred as a result of an external event beyond their reasonable control and the consequences of which would have been unavoidable despite all reasonable efforts to avoid them (Art. 37.10).

3) Investment of reserve assets. Article 38.1 provides that an issuer should only invest reserve assets in safe, low-risk assets: issuers of asset-referenced tokens that invest a portion of the reserve assets shall do so only in highly liquid financial instruments that present minimal credit and market risk. Investments must be able to be liquidated quickly and with minimal negative impact on prices. The financial instruments in which the reserve assets are invested shall be held in custody under the provisions referred to in Article 37 (Article 38.3).

Concerning the risks arising from the investment, the issuer of the asset-referenced tokens shall bear any gain or loss, including fluctuations in the value of the financial instruments and any counterparty or operational risk arising from the investment of the reserve assets (art. 38.4).

The European Banking Authority (EBA), after consulting the European Securities and Markets Authority (ESMA) and the European System of Central Banks, will develop draft regulatory technical standards to specify the financial instruments that can be considered to be highly liquid and with minimal credit and market risk, taking into account, inter alia, the conditions for the recognition of high-quality liquid assets under Article 412 of Regulation (EU) No 575/2013 and the Commission Delegated Regulation (EU) 2015/61.[17]

(4) Redemption rights on issuers of asset-referenced tokens or reserve assets. Article 39 enshrines a right of redemption in favour of holders of asset-referenced tokens. Unlike the proposal, in which the recognition of this right was optional, in the version definitively approved, the right is mandatory: holders of asset-referenced tokens shall always have a right of redemption against the issuers of the tokens and in respect of reserve assets when issuers are unable to meet their obligations referred to in Chapter 6 of Title III. (Article 39.1). To this end, issuers shall establish, maintain, and implement clear and detailed policies and procedures for such permanent right of redemption.

Concerning the operation of such a right, under Article 39(2), at the request of the holder of an asset-referenced token, the issuer of such a token must make the redemption either by paying in funds other than electronic money an amount equivalent to the market value of the assets referenced by said asset-referenced token or by handing over the assets referenced by the token.

To clarify the exercise of that right, issuers shall establish a policy on such permanent right of redemption, provided as follows (Art. 39(2): (a) the conditions, including thresholds, periods and deadlines, for the exercise of such right of redemption by holders of asset-referenced tokens; (b) the mechanisms and procedures to ensure the redemption of asset-referenced tokens, including in situations of market stress, as well as in the context of the implementation of the recovery plan under Article 46, or in the event of the orderly redemption of asset-referenced tokens pursuant to Article 47; (c) the valuation, or valuation principles, of asset-referenced tokens and reserve assets where the holder of asset-referenced tokens exercises the right of redemption; (d) the conditions for the settlement of redemption;

If issuers, when selling asset-referenced tokens, accept payment in funds other than electronic money, denominated in a certain official currency, they shall, in any case, provide the option of obtaining redemption of the tokens in funds, other than electronic money, denominated in the same official currency.

Finally, it is established that the redemption of asset-referenced tokens shall not be subject to a commission without prejudice to the provisions of Article 46 (Article 39.3).

(5) Prohibition of granting interest. Article 40 prohibits issuers of asset-referenced tokens and crypto-asset service providers from granting interest to holders of asset-referenced tokens: "... shall not provide for the accrual of interest or any other benefit related to the length of time for which a holder of asset-referenced tokens holds his or her tokens."

The reason is found in recital 46: to ensure that asset-referenced tokens are used primarily as a medium of exchange and not as a store of value, it is necessary to

[17]Commission Delegated Regulation (EU) 2015/61 of 10 October 2014 supplementing Regulation (EU) No 575/2013 of the European Parliament and the Council as regards the liquidity coverage requirement for credit institutions (OJ L 011, 17.1.2015, p. 1).

prevent issuers of electronic money tokens and crypto-asset service providers from granting holders of such tokens interest based on the length of time for which they hold them.

For this reason, such interest is expressly prohibited for asset-referenced tokens (art. 40) and electronic money tokens (art. 50); a similar provision exists in Article 12 of Directive 2009/110/EC on electronic money.

4 E-Money Tokens

4.1 Concept, Characteristics and Function

E-money tokens are the second class of "stablecoin" found in the MiCA Regulation. This second category of crypto-asset was defined, in the proposed Regulation, as "a type of crypto-asset whose main purpose is to be used as a medium of exchange and which, to maintain a stable value, refers to the value of a fiat currency of legal tender" (art. 3.1.5). The final version of the MiCA Regulation defines the "electronic money token" as "a type of crypto-asset that, to maintain a stable value, is referred to the value of an official currency" (art. 3.1.7). Therefore, in the final definition, any reference to the purpose of these electronic money tokens is removed. The initial reference to fiat currencies is also replaced by official currencies, with the definition of "official currency" being "an official currency of a country that is issued by a central bank or other monetary authority" (art. 3.1.8).

According to the initial definition of the proposal presented by the Commission, its main function is to be an instrument of exchange. It aims to maintain value by being denominated in units of a fiat currency, which would be a stable cryptocurrency, like asset-referenced tokens (although with the weak difference that while these can be referenced to several currencies, electronic money refers to the value of a single official currency.) In the text definitively approved, as we have seen in article 3.1.7, the express reference to its main purpose as a medium of exchange disappears. In any case, this reference to a single fiduciary currency gives it a clear function as a payment instrument (principal but not exclusive), which, as we shall see, determines its legal regime.[18] According to Recital 18, its objective is to "stabilise its value by referring to a single official currency." Its function is "very

[18] As pointed out by Madrid Parra (2020) Fichas de dinero electrónico, cit., pp. 223–224, the expression "means of payment" has not been used, probably to avoid the complication of entering the complex field of regulations on means of payment. However, he points out that the terminology is used in a broad and all-encompassing sense: it can be understood that a means of payment is a means of exchange and, therefore, would fall within this concept. Finally, this author points out that this exchange function, initially also attributed to tokens referenced to assets, has finally disappeared in the proposal's text so that they can be exchanged but are not legally considered as an instrument of exchange.

similar to that of electronic money, as defined in Directive 2009/110/EC," an issue we will return to below.

4.2 *Legal Regime*

4.2.1 Preliminary Question: Regulatory Options

If, as we have pointed out above, the Commission's approach to the European regulation of crypto assets is to regulate only those not regulated by the regulation of financial instruments, it turns out that, in this case, we have a prior regulation of a concept that is at least terminologically equivalent.

Directive 2009/110/EC on electronic money lays down the rules on commercial practices and supervision of electronic money institutions. It defines electronic money as the monetary value stored by electronic or magnetic means, representing a credit to the issuer. It is issued upon receipt of funds to carry out payment operations and accepted by a natural or legal person other than the electronic money issuer.

One of the regulatory options that the Commission was considering before presenting the proposal for a regulation was to apply the e-money directive to stablecoins. However, this option was discarded as such in a pure form, although it was decided to combine the option of establishing specific legislation with the partial and nuanced application of the Directive. In this sense, art. Article 48 of the MiCA Regulation provides that 'electronic money tokens' are to be considered as electronic money (within the meaning of Article 2(2) of Directive 2009/110/EC, as specified in the proposal), thus establishing a hybrid and dual nature that determines an equally dual legal regime. Moreover,

(a) On the one hand, Article 48.3 provides for the application of Titles II and III of Directive 2009/110/EC to electronic money tokens, unless otherwise provided for in Title IV of the same MiCA Regulation (a contrary provision which, as we shall see, affects issues such as repayment or the accrual of interest).
(b) and, on the other hand, Article 48(4) provides that paragraph 1 of this provision (relating to authorisation) shall not apply to issuers of electronic money tokens exempted under Article 9(1) of Directive 2009/110/EC, and art. 48(5) provides that the title relating to electronic money tokens (except Articles 48(7) and (51) shall not apply in respect of electronic money tokens exempted under Articles 1(4) and (5) of Directive 2009/110/EC. In both cases, where these paragraphs 4 or 5 apply, issuers of electronic money tokens shall draw up a white paper on crypto assets and notify the competent authority thereof (Art. 48.7).

In short, despite the pre-existence of the e-Money Directive, this dual regime is given by the fact that e-money tokens are also crypto assets and may pose new challenges, specific to crypto assets, regarding consumer protection and market integrity.

Therefore, it is necessary that they also be subject to the rules established in the MiCA Regulation to face these challenges, which would not be covered by the existing regulations (the Electronic Money Directive), which are applicable in the terms established in the MiCA regulations, as a special law.

Thus, the legal regime of electronic money tokens is regulated in Title IV of the Regulation, which we analyse very briefly below, as it is the subject of specific study in another chapter of this collective work.

4.2.2 Main Aspects of Its Regulation

Title IV of the MiCA Regulation establishes the specific regulation of electronic money tokens, with the following content, of which we highlight the most relevant aspects:

(1) Authorisation regime. Chapter 1 sets out the requirements to be met by all issuers of electronic money tokens. Article 48 states that, to publicly offer an electronic money token in the European Union or for it to be admitted to trading on a crypto-asset trading platform in the Union, the issuer (a) must be authorised as a credit institution (within the meaning of Regulation (EU) No 575/2013 of the European Parliament and the Council) or as an 'electronic money institution' (within the meaning of Article 2, point 1 of Directive 2009/110/EC); and (b) it must have notified a crypto-asset white paper to the competent authority and published that crypto-asset white paper, in accordance with Article 51. Under Article 48.1, an electronic money token referenced to an official currency of a Member State of the Union shall be deemed to be offered to the public in the Union.[19]

Indeed, to avoid regulatory arbitrage related to their function as payment instruments, strict conditions must be established for issuing electronic money tokens. Therefore, tokens must be issued by a credit institution or electronic money institution authorised under Directive 2009/110/EC and comply with the relevant operational requirements of Directive 2009/EC unless otherwise specified in the MiCA Regulation (recitals 10 and 44).

In addition, issuers must publish a crypto-asset white paper that must be notified to the competent authority and published on their website once notified. The book's content is set out in Article 51, and special reference must be made, among other aspects, to the right of reimbursement, to which we will refer below.

(2) Holder's right to reimbursement. Before the approval of the MiCA Regulation, one difference between electronic money and crypto assets referenced to legal tender was the non-existence, in the latter case, of a right of reimbursement from the holder.

[19]By way of derogation from the first subparagraph, other persons may, with the written consent of the issuer, offer to the public or apply for admission to trading of the electronic money token. Such persons shall comply with the provisions of articles 50 and 53. 2.

In this regard, Recital 19 of the Regulation points out that, despite their similarities, electronic money and crypto assets referenced to an official currency differ in some important respects, including the fact that holders of electronic money, as defined in Directive 2009/110/EC, are always recognised as having a claim against the issuer of electronic money and the contractual right to obtain, at all times and by its nominal value, the monetary value of the electronic money held by them, whereas, on the other hand, some crypto assets referenced to an official currency do not recognise their holders as receivables against the issuer of such crypto assets and could fall outside the scope of Directive 2009/110/EC; or other crypto assets referenced to an official currency do not provide for a credit for their nominal value in the currency to which they are referenced or limit the repayment period. According to the European authorities, the fact that the holders of the crypto assets mentioned above are not recognised as having a claim against the issuer of those crypto assets or that the credit is not for its nominal value in the currency referenced by those crypto assets could undermine the confidence of the holders. Consequently, to avoid circumvention of the rules laid down in Directive 2009/110/EC, issuers of electronic money tokens should ensure that holders can exercise their right to refund their tokens at any time and at face value in the currency to which they are referenced.

This right to reimbursement, exhaustively set out in recital 19, is regulated in Article 49 of the Regulation, the essence of which is highlighted.

(a) Article 49 regulates the claim to the issuer to be granted to holders of electronic money tokens (Article 49(2)): electronic money tokens must be issued at par with and against receipt of funds (Article 49(3)), and, at the request of the holder of the tokens, the issuer must reimburse them at any time and at par (Recital 19), comprising a specific right that differentiates them from other categories of crypto assets.

In this sense, Recital 19 of the proposal is exhaustive: holders of electronic money tokens must be granted a claim against the corresponding issuer; Article 49, which regulates this right, is equally thorough, which, in its second paragraph, provides that "Holders of electronic money tokens shall be granted a credit against the issuer of such tokens". Even though the express indication that "any electronic money token that does not offer credit is prohibited in the final version…".

(b) Concerning the content of this right, Article 49.1 provides that, at the request of the holder of the electronic money tokens, the issuer must reimburse at any time and at the same time as the monetary value of the electronic money tokens, paying in funds other than electronic money the monetary value of the electronic money token to the holder of the electronic money token (Art. 49.3 and 4, Recital (19). Issuers of electronic money tokens shall prominently indicate the redemption conditions in the crypto-asset white paper regulated in Article 51. Concerning the payment of fees, without prejudice to the provisions of Article 46, the refund of electronic money tokens shall not be subject to a fee.

This specific right of electronic money tokens differentiates them from the other categories of crypto assets and is linked to their specific nature as a payment instrument. For cases of electronic money, there is a different regulation of the right of refund in Art. 11 of the E-Money Directive (not applicable to e-money tokens ex Art. 49 of the MiCA Regulation, which expressly provides that, by way of derogation from Article 11 of Directive 2009/110/EC, issuers of e-money tokens shall only be subject to the following requirements relating to the issuance and the reimbursability of electronic money tokens).

(3) Prohibition of accrual of interest. Article 50 prevents issuers of e-money tokens and crypto-asset service providers from granting interest to holders of e-money tokens (Art. 50.1 and 2). As we have already noted regarding a similar prohibition on asset-referenced tokens (Article 36), this prohibition aims to ensure that these products are used primarily as a medium of exchange and not as a store of value (Recital 46). For these purposes, under Article 50.3, any remuneration or other benefit related to the time a holder of an electronic money token holds such token shall be treated as interest. This includes any net compensation or discount with an effect equivalent to interest received by the holder of the electronic money token directly from the issuer or a third party, directly related to the electronic money token or for the remuneration or pricing of other products.

(4) The White Paper. Article 51 and Annex III set out the requirements relating to the crypto-asset white paper accompanying the issuance of electronic money tokens. Under Article 51(1), before offering electronic money tokens to the public in the European Union or applying for the admission of such electronic money tokens to trading on a trading platform, their issuer shall publish a white paper on crypto assets on its website. Its content is set out in detail in the second paragraph. It includes, among other things, information on the issuer of the electronic money token, the electronic money token, the rights and obligations associated with the electronic money token, the underlying technology, the risks, and the main adverse effects on climate and other adverse effects related to the environment of the consensus mechanism used to issue the electronic money token.

The issuer of electronic money tokens shall notify its crypto-asset white paper and, where applicable, the corresponding advertising communications to the competent authority at least twenty working days before its publication date. But the white paper is not approved by any competent authority of any Member State of the European Union, so the issuer of the crypto-asset is solely responsible for the content of the crypto-asset white paper (a statement that is required to be clearly and prominently stated on the first page). Article 52 regulates the liability of issuers arising from the crypto-asset white paper on electronic money tokens, whereby they are obliged to compensate the holder if they provide information that is not clear, complete, impartial, or misleading.

(5) Marketing Communications. Article 53 lays down the requirements applicable to possible advertising communications about an offer of electronic money tokens: they must be identifiable communications, with the information presented in an impartial, clear and non-misleading manner consistent with that contained in the crypto-asset white paper. In particular, marketing communications shall clearly and unequivocally indicate that all holders of electronic money tokens have the right to obtain reimbursement from the issuer at any time.

(6) Investment of funds. Article 54 regulates the investment of funds issuers receive in exchange for electronic money tokens. In particular, it provides that

such funds, safeguarded following Article 7(1) of Directive 2009/110/EC, must comply with the following conditions: (a) at least 30 % of the funds received shall always be deposited in segregated accounts with credit institutions; (b) the remainder of the funds shall be invested in safe, low-risk assets that can be considered as highly liquid financial instruments with minimal market risk, credit risk and concentration risk, under Article 38(1) of this Regulation, and which are denominated in the same official currency as that used as the reference for the electronic money token.

Seen in its essential aspects, the regulation of electronic money tokens in Title IV of the MiCA Regulation is the law applicable to them as crypto assets. However, given the complex nature of electronic money tokens (crypto-asset and electronic money), uncertainties emerge due to the coexistence of regimes. Doubts include, for example, a possible overlap between the MiCA Regulation and the pre-existing regulation of electronic money, the MiFID regulation, or the regulation on payment services. It is necessary to avoid conflicts between these regulations, as this would increase legal uncertainty, lead to compliance costs and excessive burdens for operators, and ultimately hamper innovation.

5 Conclusions

So-called stablecoins emerge as a category of crypto assets with a vocation for stability compared to other more volatile crypto assets, stability that, as we have seen, is achieved through at least two large categories of mechanisms. Typically, stablecoin issuers aim to back stablecoins with legal tender, assets, or other cryptocurrencies, called asset-pegged stablecoins. On the other hand, algorithm-based stablecoins also seek to use these automated procedures to increase or decrease the supply of stablecoins in response to changes in demand.

Despite this desire for stability, it must be admitted that in practice, there is a certain degree of price volatility, i.e. a fluctuation in relation to the reference assets, which, in any case, would be lower than that of other non-stable crypto assets. Therefore, the term "stablecoin" does not necessarily imply that the value is stable in practice, even though market participants commonly use it. As has been pointed out doctrinally, the alternative expression "private asset-linked tokens" can more accurately characterise the technical nature of these instruments; and, possibly for that reason, a similar expression is used by the authorities of the European Union in the MiCA Regulation: "asset-referenced tokens". As we have pointed out, this is probably the technical reason why the authorities of the European Union do not include the category of stable cryptocurrencies as such in the articulated text. In contrast, they adopt the term asset-referenced tokens, together with the electronic money tokens, which are, as we will see, the two categories of stable cryptocurrencies included in the MiCA Regulation.

In short, and following the terminological precision made by the FATF (*Financial Action Task Force*) on this point, the term "stablecoin" does not correspond to a clear legal or technical category but is rather a commercial term used by the promoters of such coins, beyond terminological precision and entering the conceptual level, institutions such as the European Central Bank question both the condition of currency and the stability of these products.

In any case, this vocation for stabilisation that inspires cryptocurrencies can turn them into an interesting and powerful "monetary" instrument (they are sometimes described as "private currencies") with functions like legal tender (and which, precisely, for this reason, raises doubts about their coexistence with the so-called central bank digital currencies). For this reason, due to its enormous potential for use, there is a consensus that its regulation should be stricter. At the international level, different groups and institutions have addressed the study of crypto assets in general and stablecoins in particular.

The authorities of the European Union have also shown their concern about the enormous potential of using stablecoins and their possible implications. The so-called "stablecoins" are a notion that does not formally exist but, as we have seen, is materially in the MiCA Regulation. Indeed, there is no legal definition in the Regulation: the notion of "stablecoins" does not appear in the definitions section of the MiCA Regulation (possibly, as we have pointed out, because they are not stable but have a vocation for stability). However, this category is well present in the Regulation despite not being legally defined. We would even say that it constitutes its backbone, as evidenced in Recital 18 where, after indicating that the Regulation classifies crypto assets into three types, it states, "The classification is based on whether crypto assets seek to stabilise their value in relation to other assets". Therefore, the classification criterion is based on this idea of a vocation for the stabilisation of crypto assets. It is thus clear, firstly, that this not-legally defined notion of stable crypto-assets would include in the MiCA Regulation two of its three sub-categories of crypto assets: asset-referenced tokens and electronic money tokens. Secondly, it is revealed that, according to the authorities of the European Union, these stablecoins are more likely to expand rapidly and could, therefore, pose greater risks to investors, counterparties, and the financial system. For this reason, the Regulation focuses on them, dedicating Titles III and IV to them, while Title II is residually devoted to the rest of the files (including consumer files).

References

Arner D, Auer R, Fro J (2020) Stablecoins: risks, potential and regulation. Financ Stabil Rev 39:95–123

European Banking Authority (2019) Report with advice for the European Commission on crypto-assets. Paris

European Central Bank (2020) Stablecoins – no coins, but are they stable? In Focus 3:3–10

European Central Bank (2021) Opinion of the European Central Bank of 19 February 2021 on a proposal for a regulation on Markets in Crypto-assets and amending Directive (EU) 2019/1937 (CON/2021/4). Frankfurt

European Central Bank Crypto-Assets Task Force (2021) Stablecoins: Implications for monetary policy, financial stability, market infrastructure and payments, and banking supervision in the euro area 247:1–37
European Securities and Markets Authority (2019) Advice Initial Coin Offerings and Crypto-Assets ESMA50-157-1391. Paris
Financial Action Task Force (2021) Updated Guidance for a risk-based approach: Virtual assets and virtual asset service provider. Paris
Financial Stability Board (2020) Addressing the regulatory, supervisory and oversight challenges raised by "global stablecoin" arrangements. Basilea
G7 Working Group on Stablecoins (2019) Investigating the impact of global stablecoins
International Organization of Securities Commissions (IOSCO) (2020) Global Stablecoin Initiatives, Public Report, Madrid
Madrid Parra A (2020) Fichas de dinero electrónico. Del dinero electrónico al "viejo" dinero digital. In: Pastor Sempere C (ed) Guía de criptoactivos MiCA. Thomson Reuters Aranzadi, pp 219–244
Martínez Nadal A (2021) Ámbito de aplicación y conceptos esenciales de la Propuesta de Reglamento relativo a los mercados de criptoactivos: la noción de criptoactivo y sus subcategorías (art. 2 y 3) In: Pastor Sempere C (ed) Guía de criptoactivos MiCA. Thomson Reuters Aranzadi, pp 41–62
Pastor Sempere C (2021) Fichas con referencias a activos (Stablecoin), Guía de criptoactivos MiCA" In: Pastor Sempere C (ed) Guía de criptoactivos MiCA, Thomson Reuters Aranzadi, pp 157–172

Electronic Money Tokens Under the MiCA Regulation

Agustín Madrid Parra

Abstract This paper examines the legal regime applicable to electronic money represented by digital tokens, drawing from the general regime for electronic money established by Directive 2009/110/EC of the European Parliament and of the Council of 16 September 2009 on the taking up, pursuit and prudential supervision of the business of electronic money institutions, and the specific regime established by Regulation (EU) 2023/1114 of the European Parliament and of the Council of 31 May 2011 on markets in crypto-assets, and amending Regulations (EU) No. 1093/2010 and (EU) No. 1095/2010 and Directives 2013/36/EU and (EU) 2019/1937 (MiCA Act). Particular attention is paid to the differentiating or specific elements derived from the crypto-asset status of tokens representing electronic money. It is concluded that this type of electronic money, designed as a payment instrument, can also be negotiated and used as an investment instrument. It,

This paper expands and updates the text of a lecture delivered at the III International Congress entitled "Present and future of crypto-assets regulation in the European Union," held at the University of Alicante (Spain) on December 13, 14, and 15, 2023. This work is funded within the framework of: Proyecto CIPROM/2022/26 "Presente y futuro de la regulación de los Criptoactivos en la UE [Legalcripto]". Proyecto Prometeo CIPROM/2022/26, grupos de investigación de excelencia, de la Generalitat Valenciana (P.I. Carmen Pastor).This paper revises and updates the one originally published based on the MiCA Regulatory Proposal, which was framed in the research project of the State Program for Research, Development and Innovation Oriented to the Challenges of Society RTI2018-096201-B-I00, called "Digital Law", in which the author participated as Principal Researcher. The basic ideas contained herein have also been the subject of the author's presentation "Tokens, electronic money", on November 26, 2020, in the International Congress on "The new regulatory framework of crypto-assets MiCA, under debate", organised by the DIDINET Research Group of the University of Alicante on November 26 and 27, 2020. Likewise, this updated version was presented on December 14, 2023, at the III International Congress "Present and future of crypto-assets regulation in the European Union", held at the University of Alicante from December 13 to 15, 2023.

A. Madrid Parra (✉)
"Pablo de Olavide" University, Seville, Spain
e-mail: amadrid@upo.es

C. Pastor Sempere (ed.), *Governance and Control of Data and Digital Economy in the European Single Market*, Law, Governance and Technology Series 71,
https://doi.org/10.1007/978-3-031-74889-9_9

therefore, has an ambivalent or hybrid nature as a crypto-asset and an exchange instrument.

1 Introduction

Electronic money was regulated in the European Union by Directive 2000/46/EC of the European Parliament and of the Council of 18 September 2000 on the taking up, pursuit of and prudential supervision of the business of electronic money institutions, later repealed and replaced by Directive 2009/110/EC of the European Parliament and of the Council of 16 September 2009. The current implementation of the legal regime for electronic money in Spain is contained in Law 21/2011, of July 26, on electronic money and Royal Decree 778/2012, of May 4, 2012, on the legal regime for electronic money institutions. The relevant provisions of Royal Decree-Law 19/2018, of November 23, on payment services and other urgent measures in financial matters, and of Law 41/1999, of November 12, on payment and securities settlement systems, must also be considered.

The specific regime of e-money tokens is established by Regulation (EU) 2023/1114 of the European Parliament and of the Council of 31 May 2011 on markets in crypto-assets and amending Regulations (EU) No. 1093/2010 and (EU) No. 1095/2010 and Directives 2013/36/EU and (EU) 2019/1937 (MiCA Act, hereinafter MiCA -*Markets in Crypto-assets*-).[1] Particular attention is paid to the differentiating or specific elements derived from the crypto-asset status of tokens representing electronic money. It is concluded that this type of electronic money, designed as a payment instrument, can also be negotiated and used as an investment instrument. It, therefore, has an ambivalent or hybrid nature as a crypto-asset and an exchange instrument.

In this regard, a double regulatory proposal has already been announced, which will involve the modification or at least the regulatory "transfer" of the substantive legal regime of electronic money, which will affect, at least formally, the MiCA Act. These are the proposals for new regulation of payment services in the European Union, namely the proposal for a third Payment Services Directive, which would replace and repeal Directives 2015/2366 (payment services) and 2009/110/EC (electronic money institutions),[2] and Proposal for a Regulation of the European Parliament and the Council on payment services in the internal market and amending Regulation (EU) No. 1093/2010, Brussels, 28.6.2010. 1093/2010, Brussels,

---

[1] *Official Journal of the European Union* 9.6.2023, L 150/40.

[2] Vid. Proposal for a Directive of the European Parliament and of the Council on payment services and electronic money services in the Internal Market, amending Directive 98/26/EC and repealing Directives (EU) 2015/2366 and 2009/110/EC, Brussels, 28.6.2023 COM(2023) 366 final, 2023/0209 (COD), https://ec.europa.eu/info/law/better-regulation/have-your-say/initiatives/13904-Payment-services-revision-of-EU-rules-Directive-_en accessed 26/01/2024.

28.6.2023 COM(2023) 366 final, 2023/0210 (COD)[3] Recital 5 states that the specific regime for issuing, distributing, and redeeming electronic money should be maintained.

The electronic money medium can take different formats, such as a smart card, a computer program, an application or a token (digital token). The latter "virtual" or digital currency format has been regulated as a cryptocurrency by Regulation (EU) 2023/1114 (MiCA). We will move from the general substantive legal concept of e-money to the specifics of e-money tokens contained in MiCA. We will start by examining the legal concept of e-money under Directive 2009/110/EC and Spanish Law 21/2011 of 26 July, and we will continue by looking at the specific regime of e-money tokens contained in the MiCA, pointing out coincidences and peculiarities between both regulations.[4]

From the perspective of the MiCA Regulation, the concept of electronic money is a priority given by the Directive above 2009/110/EC. For this reason, its regulation is excluded from the scope of MiCA (Art. 2.4.c). It regulates electronic money tokens but does not contain the substantive legal regime of electronic money. It refers (inter alia in Article 48) to Directive 2009/110/EC, which sets out the general legal regime for electronic money, and the MiCA Regulation contains the specific regime of "tokenised" electronic money (electronic money tokens), to which the general conceptual regime of electronic money and the specific regime of its format as a crypto-asset (based on distributed ledger technology—blockchain—or similar) must be applied. Currently, systems using asymmetric cryptography and distributed ledger technology (DLT) are the most common, although MiCA (Art. 3.1.5) leaves the door open to using other technologies.

In relation to e-money tokens, the structure and content of Title IV of the MiCA Regulation, consisting of Articles 48 to 58, will be used as the main framework.

[3] https://ec.europa.eu/info/law/better-regulation/have-your-say/initiatives/13905-Payment-services-revision-of-EU-rules-new-Regulation-_en accessed 26/01/2024.

[4] For a better understanding of the final text of MiCA, reference is sometimes made to the legislative iter that started with the Proposal for a Regulation of the European Parliament and of the Council on crypto-asset markets, and amending Directive (EU) 2019/1937, Brussels, 24.9.2020, COM(2020) 593 final, 2020/0265 (COD), https://eur-lex.europa.eu/legal-content/EN/ALL/?uri=CELEX%3A52020PC0593 accessed 23/01/2024. See a summary, selecting the basic elements in Tapia Hermida (2021) Blog http://ajtapia.com/2021/02/desafios-en-la-regulacion-y-supervision-de-las-criptomonedas-jornada-del-instituto-iberoamericano-de-mercados-de-valores-del-24-de-febrero-de-2021/ accessed 23/01/2024.

2 Legal Concept of Electronic Money

From the beginning,[5] the regulation of electronic money was based on the technical and legal format of electronic accounting (book-entry system), whether by card, mobile phone or any other device capable of double entry of debits and credits. However, it was also possible to opt for another format: that of the token (unit of data or electronic information) representing a monetary unit to be transmitted and used as a means of payment. This would have been the closest functional equivalent to electronic money, especially if such electronic means could be used (and reused) under anonymity. Such a technological possibility existed (Digi-Cash: digital money). However, the cost of implementing a continuously developing cryptographic system for an instrument (with very few users) prevented its implementation.[6]

It was the advent of blockchain technology in the second decade of the twenty-first century, combining cryptography and decentralised or distributed-leger technology,[7] which made it possible to create real tokens that could be

[5] See the above-mentioned Directive 2000/46/EC of the European Parliament and of the Council of 18 September 2000 on the taking up, pursuit of and prudential supervision of the business of electronic money institutions (Official Journal of the European Communities L 275 of 27 October 2000), repealed by Directive 2009/110/EC of the European Parliament and of the Council of 16 September 2009 on the taking up, pursuit and prudential supervision of the business of electronic money institutions, amending Directives 2005/60/EC and 2006/48/EC and repealing Directive 2000/46/EC (Official Journal L 275 of 27 October 2000). In Spanish law, see Article 21 of Law 44/2002, of November 22, 2002, on measures to reform the financial system (BOE No. 281, of November 23), later developed by Royal Decree 322/2008, of February 29, 2008, on the legal regime of electronic money institutions (BOE No. 54, of March 3). The transposition of Directive 2009/110/EC concerning the regulation of electronic money was subsequently carried out by Law 21/2011, of July 26, 2011, on electronic money (BOE No. 179, of July 27), which repealed Article 21 of Law 44/2002, of November 22, 2002, and Royal Decree 322/2008, of February 29, 2008. Now, the legal regime of electronic money and its issuing entities is contained in Law 21/2011 and in Royal Decree 778/2012, of May 4, on the Legal Regime of Electronic Money Entities (BOE No. 108, of May 5).

[6] See Madrid Parra (2009): 14, note 11, and in (2010): 21, note 12; Solvas (2018) https://www.viaempresa.cat/es/afterwork/digicash-el-bitcoin-de-los-90_54348_102.html accessed 26/01/2024. The content of Madrid Parra (2022a) is reproduced here.

[7] In terms of technology, it is important to note that although distributed registry technology (DRT) and blockchain go hand in hand, they are not identified. Tapia Frade writes that, although colloquially, DRT is usually identified with blockchain or blockchain technology, since databases based on DRT are usually implemented through a blockchain (2) whose integrity and security of the stored data are guaranteed by cryptography (3), the truth is that both technologies have differences. Thus, we can say that the DRT is a particular case of a database "of which there are several identical copies distributed among several participants, updated synchronously by consensus of the parties" (4). On the other hand, blockchain technology is a type of TRD that stores information by grouping individual transactions by blocks in sequential order, and within blockchain technology we can again distinguish two differentiated categories, depending on whether the accessibility to the database is open or restricted (5) Tapia Frade (2023), para. 3°, citing Ibáñez Jiménez and Romero Ugarte in the notes). For a brief summary, see Sales Jiménez (2023).

"transmitted"[8] electronically, anonymously or not. The return to the "old" concept of electronic money was born from the use of a specific instrument that was intended as a response to the challenge of making digital money operational: this was bitcoin,[9] which went from being a virtual currency (means of payment) to a highly speculative crypto-asset investment.

Once again, a technological and economic reality has been implemented and implanted in society, giving rise to the need to provide it with legal certainty and security. But curiously and paradoxically, in this case, it was not the market operators (issuers, suppliers of goods and services, and users or investors) who demanded regulation. The peculiarity of the technical instrument is that it emerges and evolves in a community that seeks precisely the implementation of its own decentralised system, neither regulated nor supervised by governments. It is governments that, when they become aware of the implementation, expansion and impact of the new instruments known as crypto assets, react by drawing up rules that either directly prohibit the use of some of them in their jurisdiction or subject them to their regulation and supervision.

When the States realised the economic and social relevance of the massive use of crypto-assets and their systemic impact, they realised that they are a financial instrument that remains in a legal "limbo" between securities and means of payment (currency or other). Moreover, this instrument can be used to securitise all kinds of rights, securities (including equity) and even assets (of a tangible nature). It is therefore necessary to establish regulations to avoid possible chaos with unpredictable harmful effects on the economy. Crypto-assets are certainly here to stay. They are a technological tool that can significantly contribute to social and economic progress. However, it is no less certain that the risk of possible misuse and harmful use of such instruments must be prevented and limited.

Although both nation-states and regional blocks (in our case, the European Union) are taking regulatory measures to regulate and supervise crypto-assets, the essential cross-border nature of these assets requires international coordination to make control and supervision effective. In this scenario, and following the MiCA regulation,[10] we need to rethink[11] and reflect on electronic money and its legal

[8]There is no complete similarity between the transmission of a physical currency (*tradition*) and that of an electronic token. In the former case, there is no trace of the chain of transmission; in the latter, there is: in fact, "chaining" is the basis of the technological mechanism: distributed chain encryption. The electronic token does not "surf" in isolation, anonymously or not.

[9]Madrid Parra (2020a) p. 32, note 10, and (2020b) p. 217, footnote 5. Viedma Cabrera (2021), pp. 632–636. See also Pascual Maldonado (2019) https://www.legaltoday.com/legaltech/novedades-legaltech/tokenizacion-de-activos-naturaleza-juridica-del-token-y-del-activo-2019-11-20/ (accessed 26/01/2024), who asks the following questions: "What is a token? Is it the subjective right it represents, or is it the digital token on which a property right falls?"

[10]See, on the basis of the above-mentioned Proposal for a Regulation on crypto-asset markets (MiCA), Madrid Parra, A., Pastor Sempere, Mª.C. (dir.), Blanco Sánchez, Mª.J., Cediel, A. (coord.) (2021). See also Martí Miravalls (2021a, b).

[11]See Madrid Parra (2018a, b); Pastor Sempere (2018).

regime. *De lege data*, we are faced with the need to articulate the pre-existing legislation with the new one. However, in this "regulatory assembly" process, a new regulatory announcement that affects electronic money in the proposals for a new directive and a new regulation on payment services appears on the table. We present the current regulation of electronic money and its integration with the regime contained in the MiCA regulation (tokenised electronic money), leaving the door open to the modifications that may result in the future from the passage of the general regime of electronic money to the heart of the projected new regulation of payment services and how this may affect the use or circulation of electronic money tokens (crypto-asset format).

According to Article 2.2 of Directive 2009/110/EC, "electronic money" means an "electronically, including magnetically, stored monetary value as represented by a claim on the issuer which is issued on receipt of funds to make payment transactions as defined in point 5 of Article 4 of Directive 2007/64/EC, and which is accepted by a natural or legal person other than the electronic money issuer."[12] This definition is based on its predecessor in Directive 2000/46/EC.[13] However, some changes represent technical improvements. Thus, for example, it is no longer said that electronic

[12] The reference to Directive 2007/64/EC is to be understood as made to Article 4.5 of the Directive repealing and replacing it, namely: Directive (EU) 2015/2366 of the European Parliament and of the Council of 25 November 2015 on payment services in the internal market and amending Directives 2002/65/EC, 2009/110/EC and 2013/36/EU and Regulation (EU) No 1093/2010 and repealing Directive 2007/64/EC (OJEU No. 337 of 23 December 2015, p. 35 to 127, OJEU-L-2015-82575. The proposed third Payment Services Directive also covers electronic money services. The new Directive would replace and repeal Directives 2015/2366 (payment services) and 2009/110/EC (electronic money institutions). See the already cited Proposal for a Directive of the European Parliament and of the Council on payment services and electronic money services in the internal market, amending Directive 98/26/EC and repealing Directives (EU) 2015/2366 and 2009/110/EC. See also the Proposal for a Regulation of the European Parliament and of the Council on payment services in the internal market and amending Regulation (EU) No 1093/2010, Brussels, 28.6.2023, COM(2023) 367 final, 2023/0210 (COD), https://ec.europa.eu/info/law/better-regulation/have-your-say/initiatives/13905-Payment-services-revision-of-EU-rules-new-Regulation-_en accessed 26/01/2024, Recital 5 of which states that the specific regime for issuing, distributing and redeeming electronic money is to be maintained therein.

[13] Directive 2009/110/EC contains a definition with different wording but with similar content. The note of issuance at par is not in the definition itself, but as a requirement under Article 11.1 of the Directive: "Member States shall ensure that electronic money issuers issue electronic money at par value on the receipt of funds." For its part, Directive (EU) 2015/849 of the European Parliament and of the Council of 20 May 2015 on the prevention of the use of the financial system for the purpose of money laundering or terrorist financing provides the following definition of cryptocurrencies in Article 3.18 (number added by Directive 2018/843 of 30 May), saying that "virtual currencies" are a "digital representation of value that is not issued or guaranteed by a central bank or a public authority, is not necessarily attached to a legally established currency and does not possess a legal status of currency or money, but is accepted by natural or legal persons as a means of exchange and which can be transferred, stored and traded electronically." For a comparison of the texts of the above-mentioned Directives, see Viedma Cabrera (2021), pp. 646–647. On page 645, the author states that virtual currencies or cryptocurrencies were conceived to serve as a medium of exchange and value, i.e., intended to be exchanged for goods and services, like legal tender, fiat or fiat currencies, as desired.

money is "accepted as a means of Payment by undertakings other than the issuer" (emphasis added); but "by a natural or legal person other than the issuer" (emphasis added). Hence, the development of the law is happening in parallel with the implementation of electronic money in the marketplace. Evidently, what started as a payment instrument limited to be received only by certain entrepreneurs has become a means accepted by any natural or legal person, entrepreneur or otherwise.[14]

From the MiCA perspective, the concept of electronic money is a *prius* given by the Directive above 2009/110/EC. That is precisely why its regulation is excluded from the scope of application of the Regulation (Art. 2.4.c): "This Regulation does not apply to crypto assets that qualify as one or more of the following:

. . .

(c) funds, except if they qualify as e-money tokens".

The MiCA regulates electronic money tokens but does not contain the substantive legal regime for electronic money. It refers (inter alia in Art. 48)[15] to Directive 2009/110/EC. The latter includes the general legal regime of electronic money, and the MiCA Regulation contains the specific regime of "tokenised" electronic money (e-money token), to which the general conceptual regime of electronic money and the specific regime of its format as a crypto-asset are to be applied. As indicated, Directive 2009/110/EC was transposed into Spanish law by Law 21/2011 on July 26 and Royal Decree 778/2012 on May 4. Specifically, electronic money is defined in Article 1.2 of Law 21/2011, which provides: "Electronic money is understood to be any monetary value stored by electronic or magnetic means, representing a claim on the issuer, which is issued upon receipt of funds for the execution of payment transactions, as defined in Article 2.5 of Law 16/2009, of November 13, on payment services, and which is accepted by a natural or legal person other than the issuer of electronic money." As can be seen, Law 21/2011 faithfully reproduces in this provision the content of Article 2.2 of Directive 2009/110/EC.[16]

Although it is useful to consider other concepts of electronic money, coming from economic and legal doctrine, as well as from the operators of the financial system,[17]

---

[14] I have already expressed my views on this issue, highlighting, on the one hand, the restrictive nature of the legal text by using the term "undertaking" instead of "person" (although the rule did not prohibit the acceptance of electronic money by any person), and, on the other hand, the "subjectivization" of the term undertaking from being an object of law to being a subject of rights. See Madrid Parra (2009), pp. 25–26; and in Madrid Parra (2010), pp. 31–32.

[15] See Recitals 18 and 19.

[16] The reference to Article 2.5 of Law 16/2009, of November 13, on Payment Services is to be understood in relation to Article 3.26 of Royal Decree-Law 19/2018, of November 23, on Payment Services and Other Urgent Measures in Financial Matters (BOE No. 284, of November 24), which defines a payment transaction as an action initiated by or on behalf of the payer or by the payee that consists of the deposit, transfer or withdrawal of funds, regardless of the underlying obligations between the payer and the payee. As can be seen, this provision transposes the Article 4.5 of Directive (EU) 2015/2366 of the European Parliament and of the Council of November 25, 2015, on payment services in the internal market.

[17] See my earlier works on electronic money cited above.

it is sufficient to point out here the characteristic factors of the transcribed legal concept of electronic money, namely:

(1) It has a monetary value and is configured as an instrument or means of payment representing money. This excludes other economic rights that may also be represented by electronic means, such as book entries of securities or other financial instruments but are not intended to be monetary instruments for making payments.
(2) It represents a claim against the issuer.[18] It, therefore, has no value, as might be the case with a gold or silver coin. It is also different from the last stage of paper money, although both are fiduciary money. This initially represented a value that could ultimately be paid to the issuer. It was convertible. Today, paper money has a legal value but is not convertible with the issuer. On the other hand, electronic money represents a claim required from the issuer, who must pay the electronic money holder the corresponding monetary units. In short, as clarified in Recital 13 of Directive 2009/110/EC, electronic money is conceived as an electronic substitute for coins and banknotes for use as a means of payment, stored on an electronic medium such as a smart card or computer memory and generally intended for electronic payments of limited amounts. Directive 2009/110/EC adds to the previous regime of Directive 2000/46/EC another option for the possible hosting of electronic money. This is the possibility of remote storage on a server.[19]
(3) As mentioned above, electronic money must be stored in an electronic device. The aforementioned Recital 8 of Directive 2009/110/EC shows that the legislator has in mind two types of electronic support: on the one hand, the one that refers to the instruments held by the holder of the electronic money (for example, the smart or rechargeable card or a computer program stored in the memory of a

[18] Note that the legal definition of electronic money does not reference who should be the issuer. This is an additional or ancillary question to the concept of money itself, whether electronic or not. Who can issue paper money or electronic money is a question that does not affect the legal nature of the legal concept of money. The legislator has determined who can issue legal tender paper money at different historical moments. Similarly, the criteria for deciding who can issue electronic money may change. In fact, this is one aspect where there have been changes. For legal purposes, only the electronic money issued by the entities to which the legislator has granted such authority has the legal status of money.

[19] "The definition of electronic money should cover electronic money whether it is held on a payment device in the electronic money holder's possession or stored remotely at a server and managed by the electronic money holder through a specific account for electronic money." (Recital 8 Directive 2009/110/EC). This option allows for the inclusion of "tokenised" e-money, such as crypto-assets consisting of e-money tokens. Recital 18 of the MiCA Regulation states; "The function of such crypto assets is very similar to the function of electronic money as defined in Directive 2009/110/EC. *Like* electronic money, such crypto assets are *electronic surrogates for coins and banknotes* and are likely to be used for *making payments*. Those crypto-assets should be defined in this Regulation as 'e-money tokens'." (emphasis added).

> computer of the holder or with access to it); on the other hand, the remote server managed by the holder. All these electronic payment instruments are designed to make small electronic payments. Therefore, concerning the concept of electronic money used in practice, the legislator opts for a concept that includes both digital money created in computers or stored in a server to circulate through the global network[20] and money contained in a prepaid card, which will normally be "smart" in the sense that third parties must accept it since if its acceptance is limited to the issuer itself, it will be excluded from the legal concept of electronic money (the latter requirement demanded by the legislator).[21]

The legal concept of electronic money can be considered "quite broad", but it is certainly much narrower than a functional concept according to which digital money mobilised by mobile phones is qualified as "electronic money". However, from a strictly legal point of view, only to the extent that one of the modalities of payment by mobile phone could imply that the monetary value is stored "on the mobile" or a server (as it is stored on the computer or a wallet card), could one speak of electronic money. In practice, what happens is that the mobile phone replaces the physical card and, in many cases, even the computer.[22] Smartphones are becoming a "multi-purpose" instrument equipped with adequate security mechanisms[23] for issuing transfer orders[24] and managing and using the electronic money "deposited" in and accessible through them.

[20]The existing regulations provide for the different options allowed. In practice, operators choose one or the other. In fact, there is an evolution in use. Blockchain technology represents an innovative advance in the technical configuration of the electronic support of a given economic value in general, or monetary value in particular. In the field of cryptocurrencies, a hot wallet (connected to the Internet) or a cold wallet (not connected to the Internet) can be chosen as an instrumental support, vid. Ruiz-Rico Ruiz and Ruiz-Rico Arias (2018); Pastor Sempere (2018), p. 308.

[21]Law 21/2011 expressly contemplates this exclusion in its Article 1.3.a), when it states that this law does not apply to this monetary value: a) stored in instruments that can be used for the acquisition of goods or services only in the issuer's facilities or, by virtue of a commercial agreement with the issuer, either in a limited network of service providers or for a limited set of goods or services, in accordance with the conditions to be established by regulation. Commission Recommendation 97/489/EC of 30 July 1997 concerning transactions by electronic payment instruments and, in particular, the relationship between issuers and holders of such instruments ("OJEC No. L 208 of 2 August 1997") defined (Art. 2.c) "electronic money instrument" means a reloadable payment instrument, other than a remote access payment instrument, either a card on which the relevant amounts are stored electronically or a computer memory, to which a value is electronically loaded, thereby enabling its holder to carry out transactions as referred to in Article 1.1.

[22]In the first case, the mobile phone would behave like a mobile computer ("mini laptop"). See Pastor Sempere (2023), p. 203, note 304.

[23]Public Key Infrastructure (PKI). See Ribagorda Garnacho, Arturo, "Las infraestructuras de clave pública en el comercio electrónico", Revista de la Contratación Electrónica, nº. 9, October 2000, p. 3–30.

[24]On the functioning of the mobile payment system, see Areitio Bertolin (2002); Martínez González (2007), which does not include payment by mobile phone in the section on electronic money, but in the section on card payments, stating that it is a payment formula that is beginning to be accepted by

(4) The issuance of electronic money is conceived as a "pure" operation of exchange of the support of pre-existing funds. The Directive and the Law of incorporation define the issuance "upon receipt of funds." This reference to electronic money is further clarified in the respective provisions of the Directive and the Law of incorporation. Article 11.1 of Directive 2009/110/EC states, "Member States shall ensure that electronic money issuers issue electronic money at par value on the receipt of funds." Article 17.1 of Law 21/2011 provides that electronic money issuers shall issue electronic money at par value upon receipt of funds. Therefore, there is no room for "up" or "down" issuance (at a premium or discount). It is impossible to receive funds for an amount lower or higher than the value of the issued electronic money. Both lending and discounting operations are therefore prohibited.

These banking operations can, of course, be carried out as part of the general activity of credit institutions. What the legislator prohibits is the issuance of electronic money as a means of carrying out such operations. The aim is differentiation and demarcation. Thus, the entities issuing electronic money may not carry out such banking operations in connection with the issuance of electronic money (the additional activity of granting credit in connection with payment services under the conditions established in Article 8 of Law 21/2011 is a different matter).[25] The origin of the funds against which the electronic money is issued is not considered. The only requirement is the exact correspondence between the monetary value received by the issuer for conversion into electronic money and the value of the electronic money issued. A different issue is the collection of charges for issuing electronic money that the issuer may receive under such a scheme.

Therefore, the requirement to issue electronic money at par value against the actual receipt of the corresponding funds received and converted into digital money is already included in the legal concept of electronic money.[26] However, the MiCA Regulation insists on and reiterates this requirement when regulating e-money tokens. This type of reiteration is a constant in European regulation, which is not

banking entities. The payment is made using a customer's card, which the customer has linked to a specific mobile phone number for this purpose. Since 2016–2017, systems such as Bizum articulate the payment on the basis of an electronic transfer of funds linked to the payer's mobile phone and, where appropriate, of the payee. Cf. http://bizum.es/ accessed 29/01/2024.

[25] Berrocal states, citing Romero, that on the basis of Article 5 of Directive 2000/46/EC electronic money institutions could grant credit to their customers, whether individuals or companies, by means of the payment instruments they are authorized to issue and manage (Berrocal Lanzarot 2008, p. 61). However, Romero himself, when commenting on paragraph 5 of article 1 of the Directive (now repealed), relating to the activities that electronic money institutions can perform, states that the correction to the initial text of the Directive, which would have allowed them to issue any other means of payment, such as credit cards, was a wise decision. He concludes that the text finally approved, excluding the granting of any form of credit, has been correct and is in keeping with the spirit guiding the text of the Directive to prevent the issuance of electronic money without the actual exchange of funds. (Romero Fernández 2001, p. 41).

[26] See Alvarado Herrera (2018), pp. 325–346.

limited to establishing the additional specificities of tokens and simply requiring prior compliance with the requirements of electronic money to have such status. There are such repetitions concerning the issue of par value, although the text of the Regulation does not contain this expression, which was used in the proposal,[27] but is included in Article 50, dedicated to the prohibition of the accrual of interest, to which any discount time or other compensation is assimilated.

(5) To speak in precise legal terms of electronic money, third parties must accept it.[28] Prepaid cards only accepted by the issuer or a limited network of service providers or for acquiring a limited set of goods or services (Art. 1.3.a Law 21/2011 already mentioned) are therefore excluded.[29] As indicated above, the Directive 2009/110/EC regime overcomes the previous restrictions regarding the third parties that could receive electronic money. Article 1.2 of Law 21/2011, which follows the Directive, is clear in this regard: any natural or legal person. The condition of being an entrepreneur is not required. As in the case of cash, electronic money can also circulate between private individuals.[30] The legal possibility exists. The technical implementation will depend on the objectives

[27] Thus Article 44.3 of the MiCA Proposal provided, "Issuers of such e-money tokens shall issue e-money tokens at par value and on the receipt of funds within the meaning of Article 4(25) of Directive 2015/2366." Pursuant to Article 4.25 of the aforementioned Directive (EU) 2015/2366 of the European Parliament and of the Council of 25 November 2015 on payment services in the internal market "funds" means "banknotes and coins, scriptural money or electronic money as defined in point (2) of Article 2 of Directive 2009/110/EC". Article 6.3 of Directive 2009/110/EC provides: "funds received by electronic money institutions from the electronic money holder shall be exchanged for electronic money without delay. Such funds shall not constitute either a deposit or other repayable funds received from the public within the meaning of Article 5 of Directive 2006/48/EC." This rule is transposed in Article 8.3 of Law 21/2011.

[28] Electronic money is intended to be generally accepted. Therefore, it is not considered destined to make payments only to the issuer or its group of companies. E-money is intended to be a universal payment instrument. However, the universal acceptance of electronic money is not absolute in practice: "*Considering the variety of electronic money solutions available in the market, a prior adhesion of the payee to those electronic money systems that are accepted as eligible means of payment is needed*". (Rodríguez de Las Heras Ballell 2016, p. 266). In Spain the use of digital means of payment seems to be growing, cash payments remain at around 37.1%, according to *El País*, 21 November 2023, https://elpais.com/economia/2023-11-21/la-preferencia-por-el-dinero-en-metalico-cae-mientras-que-crece-la-confianza-en-el-pago-digital.html accessed 02/03/2024.

[29] This is clearly expressed in Recital 5 of Directive 2009/110/EC when it states that this "Directive should not apply to monetary value stored on specific pre-paid instruments, designed to address precise needs that can be used only in a limited way because they allow the electronic money holder to purchase goods or services only in the premises of the electronic money issuer or within a limited network of service providers under direct commercial agreement with a professional issuer, or because they can be used only to acquire a limited range of goods or services." Recital 17 of the MiCA Regulation excludes qualification as a crypto-asset (and thus an e-money token) in the case where digital assets "are accepted only by the issuer". It gives an example of loyalty programs using points.

[30] Limitations that constitute dysfunctions are thus overcome and a situation of functional equivalence with money in material support (paper or coins) is reached. Madrid Parra (2009), pp. 26–27; and in Madrid Parra (2010), pp. 31–32.

set by the economic operators of the financial system when offering their services. Digital money has emerged in e-commerce to pay for goods and services purchased over the Internet.[31] Similarly, the use of electronic wallets or prepaid cards is, in practice, intended to pay small amounts in face-to-face commerce. As technology makes it easier for the recipient of electronic money to be an entrepreneur and any individual, it is foreseeable that the number of recipients of electronic money who are not entrepreneurs, including individuals, will increase. In this way, with the implementation of technology and trust between individuals, the circulation of electronic money will spread similarly to that of traditional paper money. Although its use as a means of payment will prevail initially, it will gradually become established as a means of transferring funds, even when the purpose of the transfer is not to make payments. All signs point to the gradual replacement of physical money by electronic money, whether in the strict legal or broader sense of electronic fund transfers. However, full substitution is a possibility that does not seem easy to implement in practice.[32]

3 Definition of Electronic Money Token

Article 3 of the MiCA Regulation, dedicated to definitions, contains in paragraph 1.7) the concept of "Electronic Money Token" (EMTs), which it defines as "*a type of crypto-asset that purports to maintain a stable value by referencing the value of one official currency*".[33]

---

[31] If the use of electronic money is to be promoted, progress must be made in facilitating its use between individuals. A chip or microprocessor installed in a card, mobile phone or similar device can do this. Some people point to PayPal as a means of payment between individuals: "*Person-to-person (P2P) systems like PayPal now make hundreds of millions of payments a year between individuals. [FN3] The most common purpose is to facilitate the purchase of items at Internet auctions, but increasingly P2P transfers are used to transfer funds overseas.*" (Mann 2004). An example in Spain is Bizum. There is no doubt about the technological progress that the existence of electronic money tokens represents. When issued by a central bank (CBDC: Central Bank Digital Currency), they will also become official currency. Technology and the legal system already allow their existence and encourage their use.

[32] See Miguel Trula, E. (2021) Suecia pensaba convertirse en el primer país sin efectivo. Ahora intenta aumentar el dinero en circulación. *magnet.xataka.com*, 5 March https://magnet.xataka.com/preguntas-no-tan-frecuentes/suecia-pensaba-convertirse-primer-pais-efectivo-ahora-intenta-aumentar-dinero-circulacion accessed 02/03/2024.

[33] Article 3.1.4 of the MiCA Proposal contained the following definition: "a type of crypto-asset the main purpose of which is to be used as a means of exchange and that purports to maintain a stable value by referring to the value of a fiat currency that is legal tender". That version of the MiCA Proposal in Spanish only contemplated the "electronic money token" denomination. The English version also included an abbreviated denomination in the following terms: *'electronic money token' or 'e-money token' means a type of crypto-asset, the main purpose of which is to be used as a means of exchange and that purports to maintain a stable value by referring to the value of a fiat currency that is legal tender;*" (art. 3.1.4). In the version before the identification of the document as COM

The characteristics of EMTs stated in the definition are:

(1) It is a type of crypto asset. The definition of this is found in Article 3.1.5), which reads: *'crypto-asset' means a digital representation of a value or of a right that is able be transferred and stored electronically using distributed ledger technology or similar technology.* As explained later, e-money tokens represent a credit right against the issuer, referenced to a legal tender fiat currency.

The medium supporting the information relating to the security or the "incorporated" right is electronic. This information that has or represents a security is "reified" in an electronic token that, like the "old" securities, allows the transfer of rights through the transfer of the token itself, strictly speaking, through the transfer of control over the token, which, depending on the technology used, may not be the subject of a real electronic transfer, but generates an electronic accounting entry in a more or less distributed electronic registry where there is a record of the transaction and of who is the new holder of the security or right. At present, the technology used is the distributed registry. However, concerning the principle of technological neutrality, the rule provides that any other existing or future technology that provides similar or higher levels of security may be used.[34]

(2) The e-money token is linked to the value of an official currency (fiat currency as legal tender in the text of the MiCA Proposal) to stabilise the value of this digital asset. Of course, such a link does not guarantee the stability of the value; what is

(2020) 593 final of 24.9.2020, the definition was somewhat different in that it stated that the "token" would be "denominated" in a fiat (fiat) currency, not referenced as the current text states; it literally read -the enumeration was made with letters, not numbers, as now-: *(d) 'electronic money token' or 'e-money token' means a type of crypto-assets whose main purpose is to be used as a means of exchange and that purports to maintain a stable value by being denominated in (units of) a fiat currency.*

[34]The MiCA Regulation makes it clear from its first Recitals 1, 2, 6 and 9 that it is committed to the application of the principle of technological neutrality; it does not enter into the regulation of any specific technology (although it starts from the distributed registry technology currently in use) and contemplates the possibility of application to new technological developments (Recital 16). For the types of crypto assets, see López Benito (2020). The MiCA Regulation establishes a specific regime for asset-backed and e-money tokens and a general regime with requirements for issuing, storing, and transferring all other crypto assets, including utility tokens. This is clarified and summarised in Recital 18 of the Regulation. This approach represents a change from the MiCA Proposal, which focused on regulating three specific types of tokens. Now, what used to be the regulation of utility tokens has become the regulation of crypto assets in general, which includes these types of tokens; and where, for example, bitcoin can have a place, whereas before it could hardly be subsumed under the so-called "utility tokens". That is why we stated regarding the MiCA draft regulation that Bitcoin is subsumable under the general concept of crypto asset. Still, it is not subsumable under any of the three categories contemplated by MiCA. Therefore, it would not fall within the scope of the said regulation (Madrid Parra (2022b), p. 79). Bitcoin would fall under the definition of a crypto-asset, but as there is no issuer, so Titles II, III and IV of the MiCA Regulation, which regulate the issuance (with public offering) and, where applicable, trading of crypto-assets in general, asset-backed tokens and e-money tokens, do not apply to it (see Recital 22).

implemented is a dependency mechanism. The electronic money token will have the volatility or stability enjoyed by the legal tender to which it is referenced or linked, as well as the result of the offer and demand of the tokens themselves in the trading centres (exchanges). It should be noted that the difference with asset-referenced tokens in this respect is that they may (but do not have to) relate to the value of several official currencies, or only one, in combination with one or more other securities or rights; what they cannot be linked to is only one fiat currency because then it would be an electronic money token. The definition of an asset-referenced token explicitly states that it is not an electronic money token (Art. 3.1.6 MiCA). This option is reserved for e-money tokens, which must be referenced to an official currency, but only to one, not more.

This, in turn, is different from the existing general regime for electronic money,[35] which is governed by Directive 2009/110/EC.[36] It is assumed that the credit represented by electronic money is denominated in legal tender. The variant introduced by the MiCA Regulation allows the issuance of electronic money tokens with a different denomination and technology but referenced to an official currency. In this case, a stricter and more controlled issuance regime applies, which is discussed below.

(3) It is a medium of exchange. This was stated in the definition of the MiCA Proposal. The term "means of payment" was not used, probably to avoid the complications that would result from delving into the turbulent field of means of payment regulation. However, the terminology used was broad and all-encompassing. It can be understood that a means of payment is a medium of exchange and would, therefore, fall under this second concept. However, while any means of payment can be considered a means of exchange, not every means of exchange is a means of payment.

There is a gender and species relationship. In a swap, there is an exchange but no payment. When money is used, there is an exchange of goods or services for money, which is a payment that legally does not exist in an exchange.

---

[35] So-called "traditional" e-money: "Significant e-money tokens could pose greater risks to financial stability than e-money tokens that are not significant and traditional electronic money." (Recital 71 of the MiCA Regulation, which reproduces the content of Recital 49 of the MiCA Proposal). In this paragraph, the three categories of e-money appear, with levels from lower to higher risk and more demanding regulation: traditional e-money, non-significant e-money tokens, and significant e-money tokens. Recital 19 of the MiCA Regulation (19 of the Proposal with some modifications) points out the differences between e-money and e-money tokens based on certain practices. In practice, these crypto assets are used without, in some cases, a credit right being recognized and, in others, the right of redemption at a par value not being granted at all times. Therefore, the MiCA Regulation opts for a definition of "electronic money tokens" that is as broad as possible to cover all types of crypto assets that are referenced to a single official currency, ensuring that "holders of such tokens can exercise their right to redeem their tokens at any time and at par value against the currency referencing those tokens."

[36] See supra the definition of e-money in Article 2.2.

In any case, the consideration of crypto-assets in general and e-money tokens in particular as payment instruments or exchange instruments under the name of virtual currencies or crypto assets has gone through tortuous and fluctuating twists and turns according to the use given in practice or the regulatory and limiting pretensions of the regulatory project. On the other hand, and in favour of the broad interpretation advocated by the MiCA Proposal to consider the electronic money token as a payment instrument included in the concept of exchange instrument, it should be noted that this function of exchange instrument, which was initially also attributed to tokens or asset-referenced tokens, disappeared from the text of the MiCA Proposal (Art. 3.1.3 MiCA Proposal).[37] Of course, like any asset, they can be exchanged or swapped, but legally, asset-referenced tokens were not considered an exchange instrument or, strictly speaking, a payment instrument. This function was reserved for e-money tokens.[38]

Perhaps due to the double difficulty of the distinction, on the one hand conceptual (between exchange instrument and means of payment) and on the other hand practical (de facto any crypto-asset can be used as a means of exchange), the text of the MiCA Regulation has chosen to delete from the definition of e-money tokens any reference to their status as means of payment. This does not mean that they are not; they are. It simply avoids the difficulty of including them in the legal definition. In short, the rule does not address the intention of use that may exist for crypto-asset holders. They have a more or less stable value and can be used as an investment instrument or as a medium of exchange or payment. This is recognised in the explanatory text of the Recitals of the MiCA Regulation,[39] irrespective of the fact that a *security token* is theoretically understood as an investment instrument and an

[37] Article 3.1.c of the draft MiCA Proposal prior to 9/24/2020 said: *"(c) 'asset-referenced tokens' means a type of crypto-assets whose main purpose is to be used as a means of exchange and . . .;"* (emphasis added). In the text of 9/24/2020 the reference to the exchange disappeared. For the evolution of the rating of cryptocurrencies by the European Central Bank, concluding that it would be more accurate to consider them as a means of exchange, not a means of payment, see Maestre (2020). "Virtual assets" are also defined as digital representations of value that can be traded or transferred digitally and used for payment or investment purposes. This term includes digital representations of value that function as a medium of exchange, unit of account, and/or store of value (Ruano Mochales 2020, p. 16). See section II,3 Naturaleza jurídica de las criptomonedas in Sanz Bayón (2020).

[38] However, when Recital 9 of the MiCA Proposal presented the difference between the three subcategories of crypto assets, it referred to a third subcategory used as a "means of payment". This was made clear when it was stated: "A third sub-category of crypto-assets are crypto-assets that are intended primarily as a means of payment aimed at stabilising their value by referencing only one fiat currency. The function of such crypto assets is very similar to electronic money, as defined in Article 2, point 2, of Directive 2009/110/EC of the European Parliament and of the Council 35. *Like electronic money, such crypto assets are electronic surrogates for coins and banknotes and are used for making payments. These crypto-assets are defined as 'electronic money tokens' or 'e-money tokens'.*" (emphasis added).

[39] Thus, from the outset, in Recital 2 of the MiCA Regulation, it is stated with regard to crypto-assets that "When *used as a means of payment*, crypto-assets can present opportunities in terms of cheaper, faster and more efficient payments, in particular on a cross-border basis, by limiting the

e-money token as a means of payment.[40] In any case, Article 48.2 of the Regulation is clear: "E-money tokens shall be deemed to be electronic money." They are, therefore, a means of payment, a unit of account and a store of value. As money, their use as a means of payment has *pro soluto* effects in the fulfilment of monetary obligations (ex Art. 1170 of the Civil Code[41]); as a store of value, it can also be used as an investment vehicle, although its specific nature is not that of an investment instrument.

4 Issuance

As mentioned above, Title IV of the MiCA Regulation is dedicated to the legal regime of e-money tokens. The title is divided into two chapters: Chapter 1, entitled "Requirements to be fulfilled by all issuers of e-money tokens", contains Articles 48 to 55; Chapter 2, entitled "Significant e-money tokens", includes Articles 56 to 58.

The first article of Title IV, Article 48, deals with the issuers and the requirements to be met for issuing electronic money tokens. Thus, said article provides in paragraph 1:

"A person shall not make an offer to the public or seek the admission to trading of an e-money token within the Union unless that person is the issuer of such e-money token and:

(a) is authorised as a credit institution or as an electronic money institution, and
(b) has notified a crypto-asset white paper to the competent authority and has published that crypto-asset white paper following Article 51.

Notwithstanding the first subparagraph, upon the written consent of the issuer, other persons may offer to the public or seek admission to trading the e-money token. Those persons shall comply with Articles 50 and 53."

The factual assumption for applying the rule is that the intention is to make a public offer of e-money tokens in the European Union or that the admission of these tokens to a crypto-asset trading platform is planned. In such a case, a prohibition is first established, whereby the issuance or the admission for trading on the platform cannot take place unless the requirements set out in the two letters of the rule are met, namely:

(a) The issuer must be a credit or electronic money institution. A "credit institution" means "an undertaking, the business of which is to take deposits or other

number of intermediaries." (emphasis added). Recital 103 mentions "the potential widespread use of significant e-money tokens as *a means of payment*" (emphasis added).

[40] The abbreviation "e-money token" is maintained in the English version of the MiCA Regulation (definition in Article 3.1.7), but not in the Spanish version of this norm.

[41] See Madrid Parra (2018a), pp. 30–35, and (2018b), pp. 245–250.

> repayable funds from the public and to grant credits for its own account",[42] obviously incorporated under its own national law. According to Article 2(1) of Directive 2009/110/EC, "electronic money institution" means "a legal person that has been granted authorisation under Title II to issue electronic money".

Therefore, only two types of financial institutions (legal entities), subject to administrative authorisation and supervision, can be issuers of e-money tokens: credit institutions and e-money institutions. These entities are the only ones that can issue electronic money in general and in its specific variant of tokens, subject to the regime of the MiCA Regulation.

Article 2.4.c) of the MiCA Regulation excludes from its scope crypto-assets that are considered "funds, except if they qualify as e-money tokens". However, this "call or advocacy" of the MiCA Regulation to include and regulate e-money tokens within its scope does not mean that the entire legal regime applicable to them is to be found in this Regulation. On the contrary, Article 48.3 of the Regulation states that the generally applicable regime is that of Directive 2009/110/EC unless otherwise provided in Title IV, which takes precedence as a special law.[43] Therefore, the full legal regime applicable to e-money tokens must be "fine-tuned" when determining the full legal regime applicable to e-money tokens. The Regulation contains the general regime for crypto assets, excluding those listed in Article 2(3) and (4). In the excluded cases, the specific regime applies, e.g., financial instruments (such as crypto-securities or "security tokens"), securitisation or insurance. There are no exceptions. The only exception is for electronic money tokens. They are included in the scope of the Regulation, but at the same time, the application of specific legislation on electronic money is maintained. It will therefore be necessary, in each particular case, to make the relevant regulatory "assembly" to determine the applicable regime, knowing that the MiCA Regulation, which acts as a special regime, will take precedence and, where appropriate, the regime of the national law transposing the Electronic Money Directive will be applied.[44]

---

[42] Art. 4.1.2) Regulation (UE) n° 575/2013 of the European Parliament and of the Council of 26 June 2013 on prudential requirements for credit institutions and investment firms and amending Regulation (EU) n° 648/2012. DOUE (L) n° 176, 27/06/2013, p. 1-337 DOUE-L-2013-81261.

[43] "Titles II and III of Directive 2009/110/EC shall apply with respect to e-money tokens unless otherwise stated in this Title." (Art. 48.3 MiCA Regulation). These titles constitute the "body" of the Directive, namely Title II—Requirements for the taking up, pursuit and prudential supervision of the business of electronic money institutions; Title III—Issuance and redeemability of electronic money.

[44] See documents already cited: Proposal for a Directive of the European Parliament and of the Council on payment services and electronic money services in the internal market, amending Directive 98/26/EC and repealing Directives (EU) 2015/2366 and 2009/110/EC, and Proposal for a Regulation of the European Parliament and of the Council on payment services in the internal market and amending Regulation (EU) No 1093/2010.

(b) The issuer must publish a white paper on crypto assets pre-notified to the competent authority under Article 51.[45] This is the main additional requirement, which does not exist in the general regime of issuing electronic money, established for the modality of electronic money tokens. While the general regime of issuing electronic money is based on the contract between the issuer and the customer as the basis of their legal relationship with effects on possible third parties, it is not possible to establish an additional requirement for the issuance of electronic money tokens.[46] The specific regime for electronic money tokens depends on issuing an information document, which defines the rights, content, and terms of the issued tokens (crypto-assets) and based on which the competent economic authority exercises its supervisory and control functions.

Article 48.2 of the MiCA Regulation clearly and unequivocally states that e-money tokens have the legal nature of electronic money ("E-money tokens shall be deemed to be electronic money") and, therefore, as already stated, are subject to the general regime derived from Directive 2009/110/EC, without prejudice to the application of the specific rules contained in the MiCA Regulation, according to the principle of speciality (Art. 48.3 above).

As mentioned above, the first paragraph of Article 48.1 sets out the situation to which it applies. This refers to a public offer of electronic money tokens made in the European Union. In this respect, the second subparagraph of paragraph 2 establishes a presumption: "An e-money token that references an official currency of a Member State shall be deemed to be offered to the public in the Union." Therefore, irrespective of the person to whom the issue is de facto addressed, who may be persons outside the European Union, the mere fact that the electronic money token is referenced to a currency that is legal tender within the Union means that it is deemed to be an offer made within the European Union and that the legal regime of the MiCA Regulation applies to it. Such presumption is understood to be *iuris et de iure* since it is nothing more than a legal fiction to keep under the control and supervision of the economic authorities of the Union all issuances of electronic money tokens linked to a currency of the European Union.[47] Another question is whether it will be possible to apply this presumption in all cases.

The MiCA Proposal envisaged a system of authorisation for issuers of both asset-referenced tokens and e-money tokens, from which issuers were exempted when:

---

[45] "Issuers of e-money tokens shall notify their crypto-asset white paper to their competent authority at least 20 working days before the date of their publication.

Competent authorities shall not require prior approval of crypto-asset white papers before their publication." (art. 51.11 MiCA Regulation).

[46] See Directive 2009/110/EC: Article 11 Issuance and redeemability.

[47] The link or reference is not limited to the Euro, which is one of the currencies of the European Union, limited to the countries of the Union that belong to the Monetary Union. Other currencies of the Union are those of countries such as Bulgaria, Czech Republic, Hungary, Poland, Romania, Sweden and Denmark. (see https://europa.eu/european-union/about-eu/euro/which-countries-use-euro_es accessed 18-03-2024).

(a) If only qualified investors could be holders of the tokens[48];
(b) €5,000,000 tokens in circulation have not been exceeded.

The MiCA Regulation maintains this criterion for asset-referenced tokens (Art. 16). Still, regarding e-money tokens, the reference to authorisation and its possible exemption has disappeared. This seems to be a correct measure of legislative technique and coherence since the specific regime of the only two types of institutions that can issue e-money tokens requires their prior authorisation and registration as credit institutions or e-money institutions.[49]

5 Redemption

"Article 49 of the MiCA Regulations provides:

1. By way of derogation from Article 11 of Directive 2009/110/EC, in respect of the issuance and redeemability of e-money tokens, only the requirements set out in this Article shall apply to issuers of e-money tokens.
2. Holders of e-money tokens shall have a claim against the issuers of those e-money tokens.
3. Issuers of e-money tokens shall issue e-money tokens at par value and on the receipt of funds.
4. Upon request by a holder of an e-money token, the issuer of that e-money token shall redeem it, at any time and par value, by paying in funds other than electronic money, the monetary value of the e-money token held to the holder of the e-money token.
5. Issuers of e-money tokens shall prominently state the conditions for redemption in the crypto-asset white paper as referred to in Article 51(1), first subparagraph, point (d).
6. Without prejudice to Article 46, the redemption of e-money tokens shall not be subject to a fee."

Despite the wording of paragraph 1, which seems to suggest that "only" some of the requirements contained in Article 11 of Directive 2009/110/EC apply, in reality, the content of both provisions is very similar, considering, as already mentioned, that the issuance contract referred to in Article 11 of Directive 2009/110/EC is replaced by the white paper in the MiCA Regulation, which is regulated in Article 51. As in the case of electronic money in the Directive, electronic money tokens are configured in the Regulation as a credit represented by such a token, issued at par value when the issuer receives the funds from the acquirer holding the token. It also regulates the right of redemption at the request of the token holder without any fee being charged for such redemption. In this respect, the Regulation has been separated from the Proposal and the general regime applicable to electronic money. If the issuer is

[48] Pursuant to Art. 3.1.20 of the MiCA Proposal, "qualified investors" means "qualified investors" as defined in Art. 2, point (e), of Regulation (EU) 2017/1129. In the published version of the MiCA Regulation, Article 3(1)(30) defines "qualified investors" by referring directly to points 1 to 4 of Section I of Annex II to Directive 2014/65/EU.

[49] This technical inconsistency has already been pointed out in Madrid Parra (2021), p. 229.

unable to meet the redemption, and the recovery plan has to be activated, liquidity commissions may be charged for the redemptions provided for in the recovery plan (Art. 46.1.a MiCA Regulation).[50]

The Regulation follows the pattern of Directive 2009/110/EC and, based on the electronic money nature of the token, establishes the recognition of a claim against the issuer that is enforceable at any time by the holder of the digital token. Therefore, the obligation to inform about the right of redemption is emphasised. It is required that, within the "information on the rights and obligations associated with the electronic money token" (Art. 51.1.d MiCA Regulation), the conditions or the procedure for carrying out the redemption are expressly and prominently stated in the white paper.[51]

6 Crypto-Asset White Paper

As mentioned above, an essential and differentiating element concerning the general regime for the issuance of electronic money is the white paper or information document that issuers of electronic money tokens must prepare and publish on their website (Art. 51.13 MiCA Regulation) and notify the competent authority (Art. 51.11 MiCA Regulation, already transcribed) before the issuance. Its regulation is found in the extensive Article 51 of the MiCA Regulation, in 15 Sections. Section 1 lists the set of elements that must constitute the content of the white paper itself. The required information is detailed in Annex III of the Regulation. *The white paper must contain information on*:

(a) the issuer of the electronic money token;
(b) the electronic money token; not only the name but also the description of *its features*[52];

---

[50] In the event of the issuer's inability to properly redeem the tokens, the MiCA Proposal placed the burden of fulfilling this obligation on the entities that had guaranteed the safekeeping of the funds received and those that had distributed the e-money tokens as intermediaries on behalf of the issuer. Therefore, the regulation configured these persons as guarantors of fulfilling the redemption obligation in accordance with the terms set out in the issuer's information document. Finally, the Regulation has opted to require the preparation and submission to the competent authority of a redemption plan to ensure the redemption of the funds received by the issuers in exchange for the e-money tokens with the investments made.

[51] Annex III, Part D provides that the white paper must include:

> "1. A detailed description of the rights and obligations, if any, that the holder of the e-money token has, including the *right of redemption* at par value as well as the *procedure and conditions* for exercising those rights . . .
>
> 5. A description of rights in the context of the implementation of the *redemption plan*" (emphasis added).

[52] See Annex III, Part B, 2 MiCA Regulation.

(c) the public offer of the electronic money token or its admission to trading; where applicable, the names of the trading platforms on which admission is sought and the applicable law and competent jurisdiction[53];
(d) the rights and obligations associated with the electronic money token, explicitly mentioning the right to redemption at par value; contact details should accompany the detailed description of the rights and obligations for the submission of complaints and a description of the complaint handling procedures, and any dispute resolution mechanism or redress procedures established by the issuer of the electronic money token[54];
(e) the underlying technology; information on the technology used, including distributed record-keeping technology, and on the protocols and technical standards used to enable the holding, storage and transfer of the e-money tokens; information on the technical requirements to be met by the acquirer to have control over the e-money token[55];
(f) the risks, namely those of the issuer, the electronic money token and the technology used[56];
(g) the main adverse climate and other environmental impacts of the consensus mechanism used to issue the e-money token.

The crypto-asset white paper shall also include the identity of the person other than the issuer who, with the issuer's consent, offers the electronic money token to the public or applies for its admission to trading (ex Art. 48, 1, para. 2) and the reason why that particular person offers such an electronic money token or applies for its admission to trading. For information purposes, the person who intends to market the token to be issued or has already issued it is equated with the issuer.

In short, the white paper must contain the economic and legal configuration of the tokens, which are nothing more than digital securities referenced to a currency, which the legal system qualifies as money, not tangible but electronic, and therefore constitutes a means of payment, as well as a unit of value and account. For this reason, it can also be a store of value and, indirectly, an investment. In any case, since electronic money tokens are legally qualified as money (art. 48.2 MiCA Regulation), as explained above, their use as a means of payment will have *pro soluto* effects in the extinction of monetary obligations.

Paragraphs 2 to 6 of Article 51 of MiCA Regulation focus on the *characteristics that the information* contained in the white paper must have, as well as on drawing the reader's attention to the fact that the issuer is solely responsible for the content of the information and on trying to ensure that the introductory summary contains the basic information in a clear, concise and easily readable form so that the reader can make a sufficiently well-informed decision.

---

[53] See Annex III, Part C, 3 and 4 MiCA Regulation.
[54] See Annex III, Part D, 1 and 6 MiCA Regulation.
[55] See Annex III, Part E, 1 and 2 MiCA Regulation.
[56] See Annex III, Part F, 1-3 MiCA Regulation.

Thus, all information is to be "fair, clear and not misleading. The crypto-asset white paper shall not contain material omissions and shall be presented in a concise and comprehensible form." (Art. 51.2). The following statement must appear clearly and prominently on the first page: "'This crypto-asset white paper has not been approved by any competent authority in any Member State of the European Union. The issuer of the crypto-asset is solely responsible for the content of this crypto-asset white paper.'" (Art. 51.3). It shall also be stated that the electronic money tokens are not covered by any deposit guarantee or investor compensation scheme (Art. 51.4). In short, the holder of the electronic money token assumes the risk of his credit against the issuer of the token, who is solely responsible for the information provided and for the correct management of the funds received in exchange for the tokens issued.

The *issuer's responsibility for the information* in the white paper is focused and channelled through its management body, which the Regulation requires to include in the white paper a statement asserting that the information is complete, impartial, clear and not misleading. A concise, non-technical *summary* must be included at the outset, explaining the right to surrender at any time and at par, as well as the surrender rules. It is striking that the use of "characters of readable size" is required (Art. 51.6). *A contrario sensu* interpretation could lead to the conclusion that the rest of the white paper could be written in illegible characters. Rather, the concern seems to be that what often happens in practice with lengthy informational documents or general terms and conditions is that the font size is reduced, which, together with the excessive length, results in the recipient not even reading the document. Given this fact of practice, the Regulation intends that at least the summary should be read and that it should be concise and in a sufficiently large font to facilitate reading.[57]

An official language of the Member State of origin or English (although a circumlocution is used to avoid using term "English").[58] The white paper must be machine-readable.[59] As mentioned above, the issuer must file the white paper with its competent authority at least twenty business days before publication. "Competent authorities shall not require prior approval of crypto-asset white papers before their publication."[60] However, these authorities may exercise the powers of supervision, investigation and control provided for in Article 94.1 of the MiCA Regulation.

On the other hand, any material new factor, material error or material inaccuracy that may affect the valuation of the e-money token shall be described in a revised crypto asset white paper prepared by the issuer, notified to the relevant competent authority and published on the issuer's website.[61]

[57] See Art. 51.6 MiCA Regulation.

[58] Art. 51.8 MiCA Regulation.

[59] Art. 51.9 MiCA Regulation.

[60] Art. 51.11 MiCA Regulation.

[61] Art. 51.12 MiCA Regulation.

Finally, with the notification of the crypto-asset white paper, the issuer shall provide the competent authority with the information referred to in Article 109.4 of the Regulation. This information shall be made public in the Register of crypto-assets and issuers' white papers maintained by the European Securities and Markets Authority (ESMA), to which the competent authority shall forward it within five working days.[62]

7 Issuer Liability

Given the importance of the information in the white paper, Article 52 of the MiCA Regulation provides that the issuer and its administrative, management or supervisory body members shall be liable if such information is incomplete, partial, misleading or unclear. If the holder of electronic money tokens suffers damage, they may bring an action for damages against the issuer. Any exclusion of such civil liability shall be null and void.

The holders of the tokens must prove that the issuer has breached Article 51 of the Regulation governing the white paper and that this information affected their decision to buy, sell or redeem the electronic money tokens. The information deficiency must relate to the information contained in the white paper. If such deficiency is alleged only concerning the information contained in the summary, Article 52.4 provides that damages may be claimed only if the summary is misleading, inaccurate or inconsistent with the other parts of the white paper or if read in conjunction with the different parts of the white paper, it does not provide material information for potential holders to decide to purchase the tokens.

This issuer liability regime is distinct from, and in addition to, the provisions of national law. Therefore, it is hereby declared that additional civil liability claims may be brought under national law.[63]

In the absence of any other provision in the Regulation, such as a presumption, it must be understood that the claimant or plaintiff holder, in addition to proving the violation of Article 51 and that this has influenced his decision, as provided for in the Regulation, must also prove two other elements of the factual situation, namely: the actual occurrence of the damage or harm and the causal relationship, not only of the decision but also of the harm (by its link to it), with the information provided in violation of the provision of the Regulation.

---

[62] Art. 51.14 MiCA Regulation.

[63] See Art. 52 MiCA Regulation.

8 Marketing Communications

As is well known, the usual practice for any public offering in a market is to launch an advertising campaign using various media. In addition to traditional static and dynamic advertising, there is now advertising through electronic media in diverse formats, ranging from the more conventional email to banners on websites or other formulas in social networks.

Regarding e-money tokens, Article 53 of the MiCA Regulation reiterates the existing requirement in e-commerce to identify commercial communications as advertising and the requirement in all advertising that the information be clear, not misleading and unbiased. It requires that the information be accompanied and consistent with the information in the white paper on e-money tokens. In addition, marketing communications must disclose that the white paper has been published, the address of the issuer's website where the white paper is available, a contact telephone number and the e-mail address of the issuer.

Similarly, they must clearly and unambiguously state that the holders of the electronic money tokens have the right to redeem them at any time and par value. This underlines the essential nature of this right as a differentiating, although not exclusive, feature of these tokens as distinct from other crypto-assets, and which highlights their status as electronic money, which the other crypto-assets regulated by the MiCA Regulation do not have; all this without prejudice to the fact that the electronic money tokens, as crypto-assets that they are, may be traded on a crypto-assets trading platform and quoted at a price higher than the equivalent of the par value corresponding to the official currency to which they are referenced.

The final text of the Regulation has added paragraphs 3 to 6 to the initial proposal, which require that the promotional communication be published on the issuer's website, that prior approval by the competent authority is not required, although it will be notified upon request, and that it may not be disseminated before the publication of the white paper.

9 Investment of Funds Received by Issuers

Article 54 of the MiCA Regulation reiterates the application of Directive 2009/110/EC to the funds received in exchange for e-money tokens. These funds must be invested in safe and low-risk assets to ensure compliance with the obligation to redeem the tokens at any time and par value. This article also requires that these assets be denominated in the same reference currency as the tokens. This provides greater security for redemption rights by eliminating foreign exchange risks.

The final text of the MiCA Regulation adds to the Proposal a measure that largely ensures liquidity to meet normal operating reimbursements. To this end, at least 30% of the funds must be held in segregated accounts with credit institutions. The remaining funds will be invested in low-risk assets under the regime set out in

Article 38.1 of the Regulation for the asset reserve investment in the issuance of asset-referenced tokens.[64]

The final text of the Regulation introduces the notion of recovery and redemption plans, which were not included in the Proposal. These plans are intended to govern the actions to be taken in the event of temporary financial imbalances that affect the equity backing of the tokens issued or the redemption of the tokens requested.[65] The regulation of such plans is contained in the regulation of asset-referenced tokens, which is extended to e-money tokens, with only two special features relating to the *dies a quo* of notification deadlines. Thus, Article 55, entitled "Recovery and redemption plans", states, "Title III, Chapter 6 shall apply *mutatis mutandis* to issuers of e-money tokens."

Chapter 6 contains Articles 46 ("Recovery Plan") and 47 ("Redemption Plan"). Article 46.1 imposes an obligation on the issuer to prepare and maintain a recovery plan to set out the measures to restore *compliance with the requirements applicable to the asset pool* if the issuer fails to comply with those requirements. While the ultimate goal is to preserve the asset reserve, the rule also provides that the plan must include the preservation of services, the avoidance of business interruption and, if necessary, the restoration of business operations. The plan must consist of the specific measures to be applied, including fees on refunds, limits on daily refundable amounts or even the suspension of redemptions. The competent authority (Art. 46.3-5) is empowered to authorise the temporary suspension of redemptions if justified to protect the interests of token holders and financial stability.[66]

The recovery plan must be notified to the competent authority within six months from the date of the public offering or the admission to trading of the electronic money tokens (Art. 55, para. 2 MiCA Regulation).

Article 47 obliges the issuer to have a redemption plan in place, which must be implemented following a decision by the competent authority if it is found that the issuer is unable or likely to be unable to meet its redemption obligations, as well as in the event of insolvency, winding-up or withdrawal of the issuer's authorisation, without prejudice to the initiation of a crisis prevention or management or resolution measures.[67] The plan must demonstrate the issuer's ability to redeem the outstanding e-money token without causing undue economic harm to the holder or the stability of the reserve asset markets. It must include measures, including the appointment of a temporary administrator, to ensure the equitable treatment of all holders of e-money

[64]See Art. 54 MiCA Regulation.

[65]This is expressed, in a generic way, in Recital 72 of the Regulation: "Issuers of e-money tokens should have in place recovery and redemption plans to ensure that the rights of the holders of the e-money tokens are protected when issuers are not able to comply with their obligations."

[66]In dealing with the recovery plan, Recital 64 of the Regulation refers to the fact that the measures, including the temporary suspension of redemption, must be aimed at protecting the interests of the token holders.

[67]As defined in Article 2(1)(101) and (102) of Directive 2014/59/EU or a resolution action as defined in Article 2(11) of Regulation (EU) 2021/23 of the European Parliament and of the Council.

tokens and the payment of token holders from the proceeds of the sale of the remaining reserve assets.

The redemption plan must be notified to the competent authority within six months from the date of the public offer or the admission to trading of the electronic money tokens (Art. 55, para. 3 MiCA Regulation).

10 Significant Electronic Money Tokens

Recital 71 of the MiCA Regulation states, "Significant e-money tokens could pose greater risks to financial stability than e-money tokens that are not significant and traditional electronic money. Issuers of significant e-money tokens that are electronic money institutions should, therefore, be subject to additional requirements."[68] Chapter 2 of Title IV of the Regulation contains the specific legal regime for significant electronic money tokens in Articles 56, 57 and 58.

10.1 Classification as a Significant E-Money Token

Article 56 of the MiCA Regulation regulates the classification of e-money tokens as significant tokens by referring to the regime set out in Article 43.1 for the classification of asset-referenced tokens as significant tokens.[69] Consequently, to be qualified or classified as significant, they must meet at least three of the following thresholds, set by the Commission in delegated acts, per the following criteria.[70]:

(a) the number of holders of the electronic money token exceeds ten million;
(b) the value of the issued token, its market capitalisation or the volume of the asset reserve of the token issuer exceeds EUR 5,000,000,000; or

---

[68] See also Recital 59: "Asset-referenced tokens and e-money tokens should be deemed significant when they meet, or are likely to meet, certain criteria, including a *large customer base*, a *high market capitalisation*, or a *large number of transactions*. As such, they could be used by a large number of holders and their use could raise specific challenges in terms of financial stability, monetary policy transmission or monetary sovereignty. Those significant asset-referenced tokens and e-money tokens should, therefore, be subject to *more stringent requirements* than asset-referenced tokens or e-money tokens that are not deemed significant." (emphasis added). See Miguel Asensio (2020), p. 11; Bourkaib and Méndez De Vigo (2020) https://blog.cuatrecasas.com/propiedad-intelectual/propuesta-reglamento-ue-mercado-criptoactivos/ accessed 5-3-2021.

[69] "EBA shall classify e-money tokens as significant e-money tokens where at least three of the criteria set out in Article 43(1) are met" (Art. 56.1 MiCA Regulation). EBA: European Banking Authority.

[70] As provided for in Article 39.6 of the MiCA Proposal, as referred to in paragraph 1 of the same provision. "Competent authorities of the issuer's home Member State shall provide the EBA with information on the criteria referred to in Article 39(1) of this Article and specified in accordance with Article 39(6) on at least a yearly basis." (Art. 50.2 MiCA Proposal).

(c) the number and average daily aggregate value of transactions conducted with that token during the reporting period exceed 2.5 million transactions or EUR 500,000,000, respectively; or
(d) the issuer of the token is a core platform service provider designated as a gatekeeper under Regulation (EU) 2022/1925 of the European Parliament and of the Council;
(e) the importance of the token issuer's activities on an international scale, including the use of the Token for payments and remittances;
(f) the interconnectedness of the token or its issuer with the financial system;
(g) the fact that the same issuer issues at least one additional asset-referenced or e-money token and provides at least one crypto-asset service.

Suppose the European Banking Authority (EBA) considers that the electronic money tokens meet the above criteria. In that case, it shall prepare a draft decision notifying the issuer of the electronic money tokens and the competent authority of the issuer's home Member State and, where relevant, the central bank of the Member State. EBA shall offer a draft decision to the issuers of such electronic money tokens and their competent authorities and, where appropriate, to the central bank of the Member State concerned.[71] The Member State's national central bank may submit written observations and comments before adopting its final decision, and the EBA shall consider such observations and comments.[72]

The EBA shall decide whether an e-money token is a significant e-money token within 60 working days of the notification for comments and shall immediately inform the issuer of such token and its competent authorities.[73]

10.2 *Voluntary Classification as a Significant E-Money Token*

Article 57 of the MiCA Regulation provides for and regulates the possibility for issuers of electronic money tokens to indicate that they wish to classify their electronic money tokens as significant electronic money tokens. In such a case, the competent authority shall promptly notify the EBA, the European Central Bank (ECB) and, where appropriate, the national central bank of the Member State of the

[71] "Where the issuer is established in a Member State whose official currency is not the euro, or where an official currency of a Member State that is not the euro is referenced by the e-money token" (Art. 56.3, para. 2° MiCA Regulation).

[72] See Art. 56.4 MiCA Regulation; see Article 119 which regulates the colleges for issuers of asset-referenced and electronic money tokens; see also Chapter 5 of Title VII (Articles 121 to 138) which regulates the "EBA's powers and competences with respect to issuers of significant asset-referenced tokens and issuers of significant e-money tokens".

[73] See Art. 56.5 MiCA Regulation.

issuer's request.[74] For e-money tokens to be considered significant, the applicant must demonstrate, through a detailed program of activities, that such tokens are likely to meet at least three of the above criteria.[75]

EBA shall prepare a draft decision containing its opinion, based on the issuer's program of operations, as to whether the electronic money token meets or is likely to meet at least three of the abovementioned criteria set out in Article 43.1 and shall communicate that draft decision to the competent authority of the issuer's home Member State, the ECB and, in the cases referred to in the second subparagraph of Article 56.3, the central bank of the Member State concerned, allowing them to submit written observations and comments before the adoption of its final decision. EBA shall take such observations and comments into account.[76]

Within 60 working days, the EBA shall adopt its final decision on classifying the e-money token as a significant e-money token and promptly notify the issuer of that e-money token and its competent authority thereof.[77]

10.3 *Specific* Additional Obligations for Issuers of Significant E-Money Tokens

The designation of tokens as significant implies the recognition that they pose a higher systemic risk to the financial system and, therefore, must be subject to a higher level of requirements and safeguards than tokens that are not designated as significant. Thus, additional obligations are imposed on top of the general regime for e-money tokens. This is the raison d'être of this classification. Moreover, a distinction is made between the two types of institutions that may issue e-money tokens. It is understood that credit institutions are subject to a solvency regime with the highest level of requirements and supervision, so there is no need to impose additional requirements. However, in the case of electronic money institutions, the regime applicable to own funds and funds received in exchange for electronic money tokens is strengthened. Instead of applying the general regime set out in Articles 5 (own funds) and 7 (safeguarding of funds received) of Directive 2009/110/EC, electronic money institutions will be subject to the more demanding regime set out in the Regulation itself for issuers of asset-referenced tokens, although not all the additional obligations of significant asset-backed tokens.[78]

---

[74] The case of the aforementioned Art. 56.3.para. 2 MiCA Regulation.

[75] See Art. 57.1 MiCA Regulation.

[76] See Art. 57.2 MiCA Regulation.

[77] See Art. 57.3 MiCA Regulation.

[78] "As those provisions of Directive 2009/110/EC do not apply to credit institutions when issuing e-money, neither should the additional requirements for significant e-money tokens under this Regulation." (Recital 71 MiCA Regulation *in fine*).

The regime is set out in Article 58 of the Regulation under the general heading "Specific additional obligations for issuers of e-money tokens". Paragraph 1 addresses only significant issuing electronic money institutions; paragraph 2 deals with non-significant electronic money tokens where certain risks are identified; and paragraph 3 covers the case of electronic money tokens not denominated in the European Union's official currency. Paragraphs 2 and 3 make no reference to the type of entity that is the issuer; however, due to the content, paragraph 2 will be more relevant with respect to electronic money institutions, while in the case of paragraph 3, it will be irrelevant what type of entity is the issuer. Under Article 58:

1. *Electronic money institutions* issuing *significant* electronic money tokens must comply with

(a) The requirements set out in Articles 36, 37, 38 and 45(1) to (4) of the Regulation instead of Article 7 of Directive 2009/110/EC. It concerns the custody regime applicable to the funds received as consideration for the tokens issued. Instead of the regime set out in Article 7 of Directive 2009/110/EC ("Safeguarding requirements"), the regime set out in Article 36 ("Obligation to have a reserve of assets and composition and management of such reserve of assets"), Article 37 ("Custody of reserve assets"), Article 38 ("Investment of the reserve of assets") and Article 45(1) to (4) ("Specific additional obligations for issuers of significant asset-referenced tokens") shall apply.

The obligation to keep the reserve assets separate from the issuer's own assets must be highlighted from the regime contained in the lengthy Article 36. Pursuant to Article 37.5, the reserve assets must, within a maximum period of five days following the issuance of the tokens, be held in the custody of the following issuer types:

(a) a crypto-asset service provider that provides custody and administration of crypto-assets on behalf of clients where the reserve assets are in the form of crypto-assets;
(b) a credit institution for all other types of reserve assets and
(c) an investment services firm providing the ancillary service of custody and administration of financial instruments on behalf of clients referred to in point 1 of Section B of Annex I to Directive 2014/65/EU, where the reserve assets are in the form of financial instruments.

Article 37.6 specifies how the ownership of the assets is to be recorded, depending on the nature of the assets or the type of custodian involved. The criterion of separate accounts opened in the name of the issuer prevails. Custodians must ensure that cash deposits, financial instruments, or crypto assets belonging to the issuer of significant e-money tokens are accounted for in separate accounts that can be identified as belonging to the asset pool. On the other hand, conflicts of interest between issuers and custodians shall be avoided (Art. 37.7–9). In any case, "The custodian shall be a legal person different from the issuer". (Art. 37.4).

In the event of the loss of a financial instrument or crypto asset held in custody, the crypto-asset service provider, credit institution and investment services firm that has lost the financial instrument or crypto-asset shall, without undue delay, return to the issuer of the significant electronic money tokens a financial instrument or crypto-asset of the same type or the corresponding security (Art. 37.10).

On the other hand, according to Article 38.1, if issuers of significant e-money tokens invest part of their reserve assets, they shall do so only in highly liquid financial instruments with minimal credit, market, and concentration risk. Such investments shall be capable of being liquidated quickly and with the minimum negative impact on prices. The financial instruments in which the reserve assets are invested must be held under Article 37 (Art. 38.3). The issuer of the tokens shall bear any profit or loss, including fluctuations in the value of the financial instruments, as well as any counterparty or operational risk arising from the investment of the reserve assets (Art. 38.4).

(b) The requirements set out in Article 35.2, 3 and 5 and Article 45.5 of the Regulation instead of Article 5 of Directive 2009/110/EC. Thus, the own funds of the issuer of significant e-money tokens shall consist of the Common Equity Tier 1 items and instruments referred to in Articles 26 to 30 of Regulation (EU) 575/2013 of the European Parliament and of the Council of 26 June 2013 on prudential requirements for credit institutions and investment firms (Art. 35.2 MiCA Regulation). However, the competent authority of the home Member State is empowered to require, in certain cases, that the issuer hold an amount of own funds up to 20% higher than the amount to which it would be entitled (Art. 35.3 MiCA Regulation). In any case, token issuers must periodically conduct stress tests considering severe but plausible financial stress scenarios, such as interest rate shocks, and non-financial stress scenarios, such as those related to operational risk. Based on the results of such stress tests, the competent authority of the home Member State shall require the issuer to hold an amount of own funds that is between 20% and 40% higher than the amount that would be required in specific circumstances, considering the risk outlook and the results of the stress tests.

Under Article 45.5 of the Regulation, issuers of significant e-money tokens must always hold their own funds equivalent to at least 3% of the average reserve assets.

By derogating from Article 36.9, issuers of significant electronic money tokens are required to conduct an independent audit every six months *from the date of the decision to designate* an electronic money token as significant under Article 56 or 57.

2. "Competent authorities of the home Member States may require electronic money institutions issuing e-money tokens that are not significant to comply with any requirement referred to in paragraph 1 where necessary to address the risks that those provisions aim to address, such as liquidity risks, operational risks, or risks arising from non-compliance with requirements for management of reserve of assets." As mentioned above, Article 58.2 empowers the competent authorities to apply to non-significant electronic money tokens the stricter

regime provided for in paragraph 1 of the provision for tokens that are considered significant based on assessing certain *risks*. Therefore, the criterion of prudential caution takes precedence over the formal qualification criterion as a significant token. Even if the formal requirements for qualification are not met, the strictest prudential prudence and guarantee regime will be applied, seeking security and guarantee in favour of the token holders if liquidity, operational or solvency risks are detected.

3. "Articles 22, 23 and 24(3) shall apply to e-money tokens denominated in a currency that is not an official currency of a Member State." (Art. 58.3 MiCA Regulation). Article 22 of the Regulation establishes a quarterly *reporting* regime by the issuer to the competent authority on the number of token holders, the volume of the asset pool, and the number and value of transactions, specifying those consisting in the use as a medium of exchange. This rule applies to electronic money tokens denominated in an *unofficial currency of a Member State* of the European Union. For this reason, special precautions are taken as there may be a relevant impact on the European monetary system.[79] Therefore, information is required that the competent authority will share with the ECB. Once certain thresholds[80] are reached using tokens as a medium of exchange, Article 23 imposes restrictions on issuing tokens and the number and value of transactions.

11 Conclusion

Since July 2013, when the first Initial Coin Offering (ICO)[81] saw the light of day, many so-called cryptocurrencies have come and gone. At the same time, governments and legislators have been working to address the impact of this new type of product or asset on financial markets. Operators, regulators and academics have

[79] Thus, the competent authorities are obliged to limit the amount of an electronic money token to be issued or to impose a minimum denomination for the token if the ECB or, as the case may be, a central bank of a Member State concerned issues an opinion concluding that the token poses a threat to the smooth operation of *payment systems*, the transmission of *monetary policy* or *monetary sovereignty*, and specifies the applicable limit or minimum denomination. See Art. 24.3 MiCA Regulation.

[80] Estimated quarterly average aggregate number and value of daily transactions using them as a medium of exchange within the same currency area exceeding one million transactions or 200,000,000 euros.

[81] Mastercoin; see https://es.cointelegraph.com/news/wsj-telegram-cancels-plans-to-launch-public-ico-due-to-abundance-of-funds-already-raised accessed 02/03/2024. Telegram's ICO, for $1700 million already raised, had to be cancelled for lack of authorization (https://www.elespanol.com/omicrono/tecnologia/20180503/telegram-cancela-criptomoneda-recaudado-millones-dolares/304470873_0.html consulta 4-3-2021.); therefore, it was considered the best example of the end of ICOs (Raúl Marcos, citado por Gonzalo (2021), https://www-newtral-es.cdn.ampproject.org/v/s/www.newtral.es/criptomonedas-como-funcionan-tributan/20210120/?amp_js_v=a6&amp_gsa=1&

debated the legal nature of these financial products: are they securities? Or are they a special type of financial product that does not "fit" into the concept of marketable securities and, therefore, requires special regulation? Governments and legislators seem to have chosen the latter. What started with cryptocurrencies and their use as payment instruments[82] has shifted to their more general consideration as crypto assets. This is reflected in the MiCA Regulation, making the existence of this type of asset subject to regulation and supervision.

Having observed the phenomenon of the application of the new technology known as "blockchain" to the creation and management of this type of asset, the European Union has decided to give it legal status and subject its use to supervision to avoid possible systemic effects on the financial system and, consequently, on the economy in general. Finally, the systems and categories of existing financial instruments, such as negotiable securities and electronic money, will be applied to the new products.

Concerning the latter, the "old" digital money, now based on the new blockchain technology, is given a "new" legal garb, transforming the traditional electronic money "token" into the new crypto asset called "electronic money token", which, in summary, is configured as follows:

- It is a crypto asset, that is:
  - an intangible digital representation (non-physical token) that can be stored and transmitted electronically; and
  - it uses blockchain (cryptography and distributed-ledger technology) or similar technology.
- It is electronic money (Art. 48.2 MiCA Regulation), the substantive legal regime outside the MiCA Regulation.
- It represents a claim on the issuer (Art. 48.2 MiCA Regulation).
- It is designed as a payment instrument and referenced to an official currency to maintain a stable value in correspondence with that currency. While its primary purpose as money is to serve as a medium of exchange, it can also be traded on a digital platform or organised marketplace.
- In addition to being reusable as electronic money, it confers a right of free redemption against the issuer.

amp&%E2%80%A6#ampshare=https%3A%2F%2Fwww.newtral.es%2Fcriptomonedas-como-funcionan-tributan%2F20210120%2F accessed 02/03/2024).

[82] In reality, "coin" was used as a synonym for "token". They were not thinking so much about "currency" as about an instrument of value, usable as a medium of exchange, in which the means of payment or payment function also fits.

References

Alvarado Herrera L (2018) La emisión y el reembolso del dinero electrónico en la Ley 21/2011, de 26 de julio, de dinero electrónico. In: Derecho Mercantil y Tecnología. Thomson Reuters Aranzadi, Navarra, pp 325–346

Areitio Bertolín J (2002) Mecanismos de pagos a través de móviles. Revista de la Contratación Electrónica 33:47–68

Berrocal Lanzarot AI (2008) Las entidades de dinero electrónico: su régimen jurídico. Revista de la Contratación Electrónica 95:61

Bourkaib Á, Méndez De Vigo P (2020) Propuesta de Reglamento de la UE para un mercado en criptoactivos. Blog Cuatrecasas, September 25. https://blog.cuatrecasas.com/propiedad-intelectual/propuesta-reglamento-ue-mercado-criptoactivos/

Gonzalo M (2021) Criptomonedas: cómo funcionan, cómo se crean y cómo tributan, Tecnología, 20 enero, https://www-newtral-es.cdn.ampproject.org/v/s/www.newtral.es/criptomonedas-como-funcionan-tributan/20210120/?amp_js_v=a6&amp_gsa=1&amp&%E2%80%A6#ampshare=https%3A%2F%2Fwww.newtral.es%2Fcriptomonedas-como-funcionan-tributan%2F20210120%2F

López Benito P (2020) MiCA, propuesta de la Unión Europea para la regulación del mercado de criptoactivos. Diario Jurídico.com, 8 octubre

Madrid Parra, A (2009) Dinero electrónico: reflexiones sobre su calificación jurídica. Revista de Derecho Bancario y Bursátil 116: 7-51

Madrid Parra A (2010) Derecho del sistema financiero y tecnología. Marcial Pons, Madrid, pp 17–60

Madrid Parra A (2018a) Dinero electrónico revisitado. In: Derecho Mercantil y Tecnología. Thomson Reuters Aranzadi, Navarra, pp 225–279

Madrid Parra A (2018b) Revista de Derecho Bancario y Bursátil 151: 9–60

Madrid Parra A (2020a) Smart Contracts-Fintech: Reflexiones para el debate jurídico. Revista Aranzadi de Derecho y Nuevas Tecnologías 52: 25–79, and Smart Contracts/Fintech: apuntes preliminares para un debate jurídico

Madrid Parra A (2020b) FODERTICS 8.0. Estudios sobre tecnologías disruptivas y justicia (dir. F. Bueno de Mata, coord. I. González Pulido). Comares, Granada, pp 213–234

Madrid Parra A (2021) Fichas de dinero electrónico. Del dinero electrónico al 'viejo' dinero digital. In: Guía de criptoactivos MiCA. Aranzadi, Navarra, pp 219–244

Madrid Parra A (2022a) Criptoactivos: De nuevo el 'viejo' dinero electrónico. In: Derecho Digital y Nuevas Tecnologías. Thomson Reuters Aranzadi, Navarra, pp 801–856

Madrid Parra A (2022b) Del valor anotado al "tokenizado". Revista de Derecho del Sistema Financiero: mercados, operadores y contratos 3:65–97

Madrid Parra A, Pastor Sempere M ª.C (dir.), Blanco Sánchez Mª.J, Cediel A. (coord.) (2021) Guía de criptoactivos MiCA. Aranzadi, Navarra

Maestre J (2020) Análisis del borrador de Reglamento de la Unión Europea sobre Mercados de Criptoactivos (MiCA) 1. Conceptos, 25 Septiembre, https://www.maestreabogados.com/reglamento-criptoactivos-mica/; https://www.maestreabogados.com/category/bitcoins-y-dinero-electronico/

Mann RJ (2004) Regulating internet payment intermediaries. Tex Law Rev 82:681–682

Martí Miravalls J (2021a) Aproximación a la propuesta de Reglamento UE relativo a los mercados de criptoactivos: Mica. In Retos del mercado financiero digital (B. Belando & R. Marimón, dir.), Aranzadi, Navarra, pp 371–389

Martí Miravalls J (2021b) La propuesta de reglamento del parlamento europeo y del consejo relativo a los mercados de criptoactivos: la propuesta mica. Revista de Derecho del Sistema Financiero: mercados, operadores y contratos 1:473–480

Martínez González M (2007) Mecanismos de seguridad en el pago electrónico. In: Los medios electrónicos de pago. Granada, Problemas jurídicos, pp 21–22

Miguel Asensio PA (2020) Propuesta de Reglamento sobre los mercados de criptoactivos en la Unión Europea. La Ley Unión Europea, 85

Pascual Maldonado J (2019) Tokenización de activos: naturaleza jurídica del token y del activo. Legal Today, 20 https://www.legaltoday.com/legaltech/novedades-legaltech/tokenizacion-de-activos-naturaleza-juridica-del-token-y-del-activo-2019-11-20/
Pastor Sempere MC (2018) Dinero electrónico y criptodivisas: Concepto, marco legal y nuevas funcionalidades. In: Derecho Mercantil y Tecnología. Thomson Reuters Aranzadi, Navarra, pp 281–324
Pastor Sempere MC (2023) Dinero electrónico. Edersa, Madrid
Ribagorda Garnacho A (2000) Las infraestructuras de clave pública en el comercio electrónico. Revista de la Contratación Electrónica 9:3–30
Rodríguez de Las Heras Ballell T (2016) Electronic Payment Services. In Derecho TIC. Derecho de las tecnologías de la información y de la comunicación (dir. A. López-Tarruella), Tirant lo Blanch, Valencia, pp 252–271
Romero Fernández JA (2001) El marco comunitario de las entidades de dinero electrónico: perfiles jurídico-privados. Revista de la Contratación Electrónica 17:41
Ruano Mochales T (2020) Monedas virtuales y la normativa sobre el blanqueo de capitales y la financiación del terrorismo. Diario La Ley, 9745, 27 de Noviembre
Ruiz-Rico Ruiz JM, Ruiz-Rico Arias R (2018) Criptomonedas: cuestiones sobre titularidad, gestión y sucesión hereditaria de las criptomonedas en Derecho español. Diario La Ley, 80, Sección Ciberderecho, 28 de Mayo
Sales Jiménez R (2023) Blockchain, Smart Contracts y su posible desarrollo en el mundo jurídico. Diario La Ley, no. 79, Sección Ciberderecho, 15 de Diciembre
Sanz Bayón P (2020) Análisis sobre la naturaleza jurídica de las criptomonedas y la regulación europea de los proveedores de servicios de cambio y de custodia de monederos electrónicos. Revista de Derecho Bancario y Bursátil 160:69–110
Solvas V (2018) DigiCash, el bitcoin de los "90". Economía Vintage, Barcelona, 13 de Junio https://www.viaempresa.cat/es/afterwork/digicash-el-bitcoin-de-los-90_54348_102.html
Tapia Frade A (2023) Las ofertas públicas de criptoactivos distintos de fichas referenciadas a activos o fichas de dinero electrónico como medio alternativo de financiación en la propuesta de Reglamento MiCa. La Ley Mercantil 99
Tapia Hermida AJ (2021) Desafíos en la regulación y supervisión de las criptomonedas. Jornada del Instituto Iberoamericano de Mercados de Valores del 24 de febrero de 2021. 25 de Febrero Blog http://ajtapia.com/2021/02/desafios-en-la-regulacion-y-supervision-de-las-criptomonedas-jornada-del-instituto-iberoamericano-de-mercados-de-valores-del-24-de-febrero-de-2021/
Viedma Cabrera P (2021) La disrupción del Blockchain en los mercados financieros y tokenización de activos. In Estudios sobre derecho digital (dir. R. Perea Ortega), Aranzadi, Navarra, pp 617–662

Utility Tokens and Their Regulation Under MiCA

Alfonso Martínez-Echevarría y García de Dueñas and Rafael del Castillo Ionov

Abstract The MiCA Regulation regulates crypto assets which are not financial instruments, providing them with a legal regimen through a specific regulation. The MiCA regulation covers the majority of crypto asset classes currently being traded. Developing a single digital market requires a solid legal base that offers its participants security in developing distribution ledger technology projects for issuing and trading crypto assets. Utility tokens may be issued without obtaining preliminary authorisation if the projects comply with the requirements regarding the preparation, notification and publication of the crypto-asset white paper.

1 Legal and Economic Background to the Regulatory Framework for Utility Tokens

The emergence of distributed ledger technology (DLT) has transformed numerous industries, with a notable impact on the financial sector. Although the technological principles behind blockchain had existed for decades, it was not until the publication of the Bitcoin white paper in 2008 that the era of crypto assets began. Blockchain extends beyond being a tool for decentralised payments; it is also used in food traceability, Industry 4.0, and many future applications that have yet to be discovered. However, its most developed use has been in the transmission of value.

This paper expands and updates the text of a lecture delivered at the III International Congress entitled "Present and future of crypto-assets regulation in the European Union," held at the University of Alicante (Spain) on December 13, 14, and 15, 2023. This work is funded within the framework of: Proyecto CIPROM/2022/26 "Presente y futuro de la regulación de los Criptoactivos en la UE [Legalcripto]". Proyecto Prometeo CIPROM/2022/26, grupos de investigación de excelencia, de la Generalitat Valenciana (P.I. Carmen Pastor).

A. Martínez-Echevarría y García de Dueñas (✉) · R. del Castillo Ionov
Universidad San Pablo-CEU, CEU Universities, Madrid, Spain
e-mail: alfonso.martinezechevarria@ceu.es; rafael.delcastillo@colaborador.ceu.es

C. Pastor Sempere (ed.), *Governance and Control of Data and Digital Economy in the European Single Market*, Law, Governance and Technology Series 71,
https://doi.org/10.1007/978-3-031-74889-9_10

The Bitcoin project emerged and gained traction during profound economic and social changes: financial crisis, loss of confidence in the system and its institutions, and general disenchantment. The projects that followed in its wake during the first turbulent decade proposed various improvements that laid the foundation for the current state of the crypto-asset landscape.

As the technology's adoption rate expanded, crypto assets moved from the fringes of illegal transactions on the deep web into the mainstream consciousness of everyday users. The shortcomings identified during several technology developments have led to new solutions and innovations.

The Ethereum project[1] introduced a blockchain that enabled the creation of tokens, a new category of crypto-assets distinct from cryptocurrencies, and their implementation in smart contracts. Although Ethereum's proposal was compelling for business-legal applications, it did not gain significant traction among entrepreneurs for two main reasons. Firstly, smart contracts had to be executed using the network's native cryptocurrency, Ether (ETH), rather than fiat currencies. Using a highly volatile cryptocurrency introduces new risk factors that are difficult to mitigate. This led to various stablecoin projects, essentially tokens backed by an asset pool or pegged to fiat currencies such as the euro, the US dollar, or the Swiss franc.

Secondly, the responsibility for safeguarding such crypto assets and the associated risks rested entirely with the crypto-asset holder. There is no way to request new keys to a wallet in case of loss or theft. Over time, the industry responded by offering professional third-party crypto-asset custody services to address these issues.

Despite these challenges, the first decade of blockchain innovation saw significant enthusiasm from entrepreneurs, resulting in many successful and interesting projects. However, it also brought substantial disappointments, including exchange bankruptcies, large-scale thefts of crypto assets, the disappearance of projects, and the funds raised. The market's growth and increasing adoption of this technology eventually prompted the first regulatory responses from securities market authorities and central banks in the form of warnings and public statements.[2]

---

[1] *Vid.* https://ethereum.org/.

[2] In Europe, several regulatory alerts and guidelines have been issued regarding crypto-assets. The European Securities and Markets Authority (ESMA) issued an alert on 13 November 2017. This was followed by a communiqué from the Comisión Nacional del Mercado de Valores (CNMV) on 8 February 2018 and a joint communiqué from the CNMV and the Bank of Spain on 20 September 2018. Additionally, the Swiss Financial Market Supervisory Authority (FINMA) released guidelines for enquiries regarding the regulatory framework for initial coin offerings (ICOs) on 16 February 2018, supplementing the content of *FINMA Guidance* 04/2017 on the regulatory treatment of ICOs dated 29 September 2017. Across the Atlantic in the United States, the Securities and Exchange Commission (SEC) has defined its position on certain types of crypto-assets by applying the Howey test and imposing sanctions. Noteworthy actions include the report on "The DAO" and settlements regarding the TON (Telegram) and EOS (Block.one) projects. See:

https://www.esma.europa.eu/sites/default/files/library/esma50-157-828_ico_statement_firms.pdf, https://www.esma.europa.eu/sites/default/files/library/esma50-157-829_ico_statement_investors.pdf, https://www.finma.ch/en/news/2018/02/20180216-mm-ico-wegleitung, https://www.sec.

These initial regulatory responses focused on the main issue surrounding crypto assets, i.e., determining their legal nature by applying the principle of technological neutrality. These responses were specifically aimed at crypto assets with the legal characteristics of financial instruments to prevent the uncontrolled issuance and trading of securities. The proposed solution was to align crypto-assets with the legal nature of financial instruments with existing regulations, which brought order to the chaotic landscape of crypto-asset issuance. However, this approach was insufficient as it did not address other types of crypto assets that did not qualify as financial instruments.

This regulatory focus also led to a shift in projects, with many seeking to avoid financial regulation by modifying their business models to transform the issuance of financial instruments into the issuance of service tokens, now commonly known as utility tokens or payment instruments, to exploit the regulatory gap. Some countries began developing their own regulatory frameworks for crypto assets, even within the European Union, aiming to eliminate legal uncertainty and respond to the challenges posed by new technologies. This was done to embrace the digital economy and attract talent and capital. However, these varied responses encouraged regulatory arbitrage without truly eliminating legal uncertainty. Structures created in jurisdictions such as Malta or Estonia failed to disseminate inherently global projects due to the absence of a unified digital market.

For years, stakeholders in the crypto-asset industry have been calling for a cohesive regulatory framework at the European level. They sought an EU response that would provide legal certainty and serve as a foundation for effectively developing a single digital market. It is in this context that Regulation (EU) 2023/1114 of the European Parliament and of the Council of 31 May 2023 on Markets in Crypto-assets (MiCA) and amending Regulations (EU) No 1093/2010 and (EU) No 1095/2010 and Directives 2013/36/EU and (EU) 2019/1937 should be assessed. The MiCA Regulation finally proposes a legal regime for most crypto assets that are not financial instruments and have not been specifically regulated.

2 Concept of Utility Tokens

The MiCA Regulation defines in Article 3.1.5 a crypto-asset as "a crypto-asset is a digital representation of value or a right that can be transferred or stored electronically using distributed ledger technology or similar technology," such as blockchain. The regulation addresses three crypto-asset subcategories: utility tokens, asset-referenced tokens, and electronic money tokens.

In this regard, the MiCA Regulation proposes a definition of a utility token in Article 3.1.9 as "a type of crypto asset which is intended to provide digital access to

gov/litigation/complaints/2019/comp-pr2019-212.pdf, https://www.sec.gov/litigation/admin/2019/33-10714.pdf,, https://www.sec.gov/litigation/complaints/2019/comp-pr2019-212.pdf.

an application, service or resource [. . .] and is accepted only by the issuer of that token." This is a relatively acceptable but insufficient definition.

We consider this definition more accurate than the one proposed in the preliminary draft, which limited the definition to exclusively digital goods or services. It excluded potential non-digital and off-chain uses where utility tokens could be used for other purposes, such as facilitating the right to use a hotel room[3] or consuming hours of legal advice.[4]

We detected a shortcoming in the draft regulation: utility tokens could be accepted "only by the issuer of the token in question."[5] This has been addressed in the final version of the regulation, which stipulates that the issuer is not the sole acceptor of the token. Instead, the person who provides access to a good or service to the token holder can accept the token. Third parties acquiring the utility token can also accept it and turn it over to the issuer to receive the good or service. Furthermore, distributed ledger technology (DLT) inherently supports a decentralised approach. Limiting the acceptance of utility tokens to the issuer would contradict the logic of decentralisation. It is common for projects to allow the same utility token to be accepted by different entities, who are not necessarily the issuer.

3 Legal Nature of Utility Tokens

When considering the legal nature of utility tokens, it is clear that they represent a legal property relationship between the entity issuing the tokens and a subscriber who provides funds intending to receive a utility token. This token enables the subscriber to access a good or service or transfer the token to a third party, who will then exercise the rights associated with the token's ownership. Notably, Article 10 of the MiCA Regulation addresses the safekeeping of funds collected by a credit institution or a provider of crypto-asset custody and administration services on behalf of customers.[6]

---

[3]One could envisage, for example, a hotel chain issuing consumption tokens entitling the use of available rooms in the chain's establishments at any time upon presentation of the digital asset.

[4]The law firm Cuatrecasas proposed in 2019 to issue *tokens* equivalent to hours of legal advice -*vid.* https://www.cuatrecasas.com/es/actualidad/0/cuatrecasas_emite_tokens_para_ofrecer_servicios_legales_a_traves_de_blockchain.html.

[5]*Vid.* Martínez-Echevarría y García de Dueñas and del Castillo Ionov (2021), pp. 85–96.

[6]The express reference to "credit institution," interpreted in the strict sense, could exclude other operators in the credit and banking market, such as electronic money institutions or payment institutions. Conversely, when referring to providers of crypto-asset custody and administration services on behalf of customers, it refers to those entities that comply with the provisions of the MiCA Regulation. Therefore, the possibility of self-custody by the issuer of the funds is directly excluded.

There may be multiple subscribers, but the legal property relationship arises between the issuing entity and each subscriber who invests in the project, either during the primary issuance or through acquisition in a secondary market.

Thus, the first question that comes to our mind is whether the economic rights arising from the legal relationship between issuer and subscriber are rights *in rem* or rights *in personam*. This classification is significant beyond theoretical interest, as it has practical implications for the legal regime of acquisition, the general legal framework, and its treatment of prescription.

Rights *in personam* grant their holder the power to demand action or omission from another person. In rem, rights are rights over things, enforceable and effective *erga omnes*, with procedural action applicable against all.

The ownership of the subscriber or acquirer of the utility tokens is determined by the tokens being registered in their favour using distributed ledger technologies (DLT) such as blockchain. The holder of the utility token can enforce their right *erga omnes*, not only against the token's issuer but also against any third party, for instance, when transferring it to a new acquirer on a crypto-asset trading platform. Thus, the ownership of utility tokens, as a registry title, constitutes a right *in rem.*[7]

Although the utility token's ownership is real, the content of the right represented by the token is obligatory. It may consist of providing a service or delivering a good (Article 3.1.9 of the MiCA Regulation).

Ownership of such a utility token grants its original subscriber or secondary acquirer the right to enjoy the services or goods indicated in the terms and conditions contained in the crypto-asset white paper. For the issuer, it represents a payment on account or advance payment from customers for goods to be delivered or services to be provided upon presentation of the corresponding utility tokens.

The relationship established is a bilateral synallagmatic contract that generates obligations for both parties. The main obligation for the subscriber is the delivery of the funds, while the issuing institution must deliver the utility tokens when they are generated. This *delivery* occurs through the registration of the utility tokens in favour of the subscriber. Once delivered to the subscribers, the issuer assumes the obligations arising from the rights contained in the terms and conditions: the responsibility to deliver a good or the obligation to provide a service.

The binding link between the utility token issuer and the subscriber arises from the crypto-asset white paper, for which the issuer is responsible.[8] The crypto-asset white paper outlines the terms of the issuer's offer. It is configured as a contract of

[7] *Vid.* Martínez-Echevarría y García de Dueñas (1997), p. 155, where some considerations are made regarding book-entry securities that can be applied analogically to utility tokens and crypto-assets.

[8] Failure to comply with the formalities, basic mentions, and other requirements set out in the MiCA Regulation shall not diminish the rights acquired by the subscriber. The scope of the rights and services offered by the issuer to the subscriber, as well as the manner of exercising them, shall be detailed in the crypto-asset white paper. Where such rights and services can be redirected to identifiable individuals, their legal regime should apply (e.g., provision of services, etc.). It is also important to consider the regime of general contracting conditions and consumer and user protection regulations -*vid.* Ibáñez Jiménez (2018), p. 135 et seq.

adhesion, given the issuer's pre-drafting of the terms and conditions, who makes a public offer. The contract is perfected by the subscriber's payment of the established amount, which serves as acceptance of the contract.

The legal nature of the token issued will be crucial. The initial inquiry involves determining whether the rights associated with it and its operation can be classified among the financial instruments defined in Article 2 of Law 6/2023 of 17 March on Securities Markets and Investment Services or whether the analysis of the so-called Howey Test could lead to the application of the legal regime applicable to negotiable securities to this crypto asset.[9]

Thus, when classifying their legal nature, we will rely on the negative classification offered by Title II of the MiCA Regulation of "crypto-assets that are not...", which regulates utility tokens. To apply this simplified regime, we must first ascertain that the legal nature is not that of a financial instrument according to local securities market regulations. Subsequently, we must confirm that it does not fall under an e-money token (EMT) or asset-backed token (ART).

4 Legal Status of Utility Tokens

The MiCA Regulation establishes the legal regime for utility tokens, which it refers to as "crypto-assets other than asset-backed tokens or e-money tokens," in Title II, Articles 4 et seq.

As mentioned in the last paragraph of the previous section, the negative classification is noteworthy. Instead of referring to utility tokens in the title, it mentions the regime applicable to "crypto-assets other than asset-backed tokens or e-money tokens." This broad definition of "crypto assets" may lead to ambiguity, especially considering that non-fungible tokens (NFTs) are excluded from the regulation. It becomes unclear what other types of crypto assets might be encompassed under this definition.[10]

The legislative technique used to address the three main types of crypto assets regulated by the MiCA Regulation is also noteworthy. Each regulated crypto asset requires drafting a crypto assets white paper, the content of which largely coincides. The legislator could have provided individualised treatment by creating a generic crypto-assets white paper for all regulated crypto assets and then introducing specific particulars for each class.

Article 4.1 begins by prohibiting the offering to the public of crypto-assets other than asset-backed tokens or e-money tokens, i.e., utility tokens and all other

---

[9]In this respect, it is still common to submit the project to securities regulators, through a consultation or the request for so-called *no-action letters*, to resolve doubts about the project.

Vid. Maume and Fromberger (2019), pp. 548–585.

[10]*Vid.* Patti (2024). https://doi.org/10.2139/ssrn.4810910.

crypto-assets that could fall under the same category, unless certain circumstances described in this article are met.

The first requirement is that the utility token issuer be a legal person and that a white paper be drafted, notified, and published following the characteristics detailed in Article 6.

A surprising contradiction arises between recital 22, which states that "*this Regulation should apply to natural and legal persons and certain other undertakings and to the crypto-asset services and activities performed, provided or controlled, directly or indirectly, by them, including when part of such activities or services is performed in a decentralised manner*," and the requirement that the issuer must be a legal person. This contradiction may pose challenges for decentralised finance projects (DeFi) operating through common law instruments of a fiduciary nature, making it difficult to fit them into continental law under the classical application of the theory of attribution of legal personality.[11]

Certain crypto assets are exempt from the obligation to prepare a white paper under Article 6.3 of the MiCA Regulation.[12] This includes crypto-assets offered for free, cryptocurrencies created by mining (proof-of-work method) or reward for network maintenance (proof-of-stake method), and utility tokens providing access to goods or services existing or in operation, or where the holder is only entitled to use it in exchange for goods and services within a limited network of traders with contractual agreements with the offeror.

Additionally, non-fungible tokens (NFTs) and projects not exceeding the economic issuance threshold of EUR 1 million, or those offered to less than 150 natural or legal persons by a Member State or exclusively to qualified investors, are exempt from publishing a white paper under Article 6.3 of the MiCA Regulation.

Despite these exemptions, the white paper remains crucial in any crypto-asset project. Since the publication of the Bitcoin project's eight-page white paper, it has served as the primary document on which subscribers, whether consumers, users, or investors, base their decisions on purchasing the issued crypto assets. As projects evolved from Initial Coin Offerings (ICOs), issuers sought to resemble issuance prospectuses in terminology and form to establish credibility. Regulation of the white paper's content in the MiCA Regulation was necessary to prevent abuses.

The standards for elaborating crypto-asset white papers appear inspired by the traditional finance regulatory practices found in Regulation (EU) 2017/1129 of the European Parliament and of the Council of 14 June 2017 on prospectuses, following a similar process.

---

[11] *Vid.* Maia and Vieira dos Santos (2021), [21 p.]. Available from: https://ssrn.com/abstract=3875355 or https://doi.org/10.2139/ssrn.3875355.

[12] These last two exclusions raise doubts regarding their practical application. It seems that all pre-existing issuances of services already in operation would be exempt from the MiCA Regulation. Similarly, any project that proposes applying a blockchain layer to its pre-existing business model by issuing a utility token for goods or services—digital or otherwise—that are already being offered could also be exempt. Examples include usage credits for a generative AI that is already operational, airline points or miles, and loyalty points for hotel chains.

Article 4 of the MiCA Regulation also establishes the obligation to prepare and publish marketing communications under Articles 7 and 9. These rules will significantly impact the dissemination and marketing of crypto-asset projects, which have traditionally been exempt from strict regulatory compliance, except in countries where specific rules regulate crypto-asset advertising.[13] The lack of previous practice or precedents regarding crypto-asset advertising and the regulatory criteria leaves many unknowns that practice will have to resolve on a case-by-case basis.

Also noteworthy are the obligations of offerors and persons applying for admission to trading of crypto-assets other than asset-referenced tokens or e-money tokens, which include the requirements of good reputation through honest, impartial, and professional conduct. This also entails fair, clear, and non-deceptive communication and detecting, preventing, managing, and communicating any conflicts of interest.

Article 13 of the MiCA Regulation grants retail subscribers of asset-referenced or e-money tokens a right of withdrawal. This right can be exercised against the offeror of such crypto-assets or a crypto-asset service provider that places the crypto-assets on behalf of the offeror. The deadline for exercising the right of withdrawal is 14 calendar days from the date of their commitment to subscribe to the crypto assets.

Article 14.3 also imposes an obligation to reimburse funds to the holders of the utility tokens within a maximum of 25 calendar days in case of project cancellation. The practical implementation of this right-obligation can be technically complicated, especially when the utility tokens have already been in circulation and no information is available on the secondary purchasers. One way to implement such a transaction would be an exchange system where the holder of the utility tokens can exchange them for fiat money, a stablecoin, a central bank digital currency (CBDC), or a cryptocurrency.

Regarding the admission to trading crypto-assets other than asset-referenced tokens or e-money tokens, Article 5 of the MiCA Regulation sets out the requirements for an applicant seeking admission to trading this type of crypto-asset.

5 Crypto-Asset White Paper

5.1 Economic Role of the Crypto-Asset White Paper

Since their emergence in the 1990s, white papers have become essential tools for dissemination and marketing aimed at detailing and showcasing products, services, or technological developments to interested subscribers. These documents often convey the project and key ideas of the issuing entity while clarifying complex aspects of its offerings. White papers are particularly prevalent in business-to-

[13] In Spain, this is dealt with in CNMV Circular 1/2022, of 10 January, on the advertising of crypto-assets presented as investment objects -*vid.* Blanco Sánchez (2022), p. 247 et seq.

business transactions, connecting manufacturers with wholesalers or wholesalers with retailers, and provide comprehensive guides full of factual data and references.

The formats and objectives of white papers can vary widely. Some focus on problem-solving, identifying an audience's challenge and presenting a remedy. Others aim to inform on a specific topic or contribute to an ongoing discourse. Some white papers are detailed reviews or promotions of certain items or services, offering in-depth technical assessments. In contrast, others provide market intelligence through up-to-date or relevant research results tailored to potential customers.

White papers on crypto-assets or blockchain technology often delve into the intricate details of their technical frameworks, financial implications, and underlying approaches. They commonly address tokenomics, consensus mechanisms, and other critical components.

Moreover, the role of white papers in the cryptocurrency industry extends beyond mere explanation: they have been pivotal in securing investments for the projects they describe. Unlike traditional white papers, which are not usually associated with fundraising, crypto-asset white papers often serve this exact purpose. In the realm of cryptocurrencies and blockchain, a white paper can be the primary resource for investors and potential users to assess the project's validity and potential for success. This makes the quality and content of a crypto-asset white paper a critical factor in gaining trust and financial backing.[14]

Traditionally, the crypto-asset industry understood white papers as promotional documents explaining crypto-assets and targeting potential investors. Under the MiCA Regulation, Recital 24 defines the crypto-asset white paper as an informative document containing mandatory disclosures, becoming regulated information with content prescribed by legislation.

Article 6 of the MiCA Regulation deals with the content and form of the crypto-asset white paper. It is to be read and interpreted in conjunction with Annex I, which details the elements of information required for the crypto-asset white paper.

The crypto-asset white paper has thus become the key document on which potential subscribers base their critical decision on whether or not to participate in a project. The information presented is paramount, as it carries the weight of potential financial commitments. Historically unregulated, the sector and practice have revealed certain inadequacies legislators seek to rectify. These shortcomings mainly concern the protection of the subscriber, emphasising the need for transparent information that accurately describes the risks and provides exhaustive details. This transformation of the white paper from a commercial advertising brochure into an instrument of investor assurance reflects a significant shift in regulatory oversight.

The stringent requirements set out in the MiCA Regulation make it very clear that the intention is to provide maximum protection to subscribers in these asset classes and to avoid the typical abuses historically perpetrated by issuers. Given that the crypto-asset white paper is often the single decisive document guiding a subscriber's

[14] *Vid.* del Castillo Ionov (2018), p. 79 et seq.

choice, its accuracy and completeness are crucial, cementing its role as the cornerstone of crypto-asset underwriting decision-making.

5.2 *Content of the Crypto-Asset White Paper*

Article 6 of the MiCA Regulation states that the crypto-asset white paper shall contain the following information:

(a) A detailed description of the issuer and a presentation of the main participants in the project's design and development.
(b) A detailed description of the issuer's project, the type of crypto asset to be offered to the public, the reasons for the public offering, and the intended use of the funds obtained from the issuance.
(c) A detailed description of the characteristics of the public offering, the number of crypto assets to be issued, the issue price, and the subscription conditions.
(d) A detailed description of the rights and obligations associated with the crypto assets and the procedures and conditions for exercising those rights.
(e) Information on the underlying technology and standards applied by the issuer of the crypto assets for their maintenance, storage, and transfer.
(f) A detailed description of the risks associated with the issuer of the crypto-assets, the crypto assets, the public offering of the crypto-assets, and the execution of the project.

In addition to this, the crypto-asset white paper must contain several important statements: that the issuer of the crypto-assets is solely responsible for its content, that the prospective purchaser must base their purchase decision on the entire white paper, that the public offering does not constitute an offer or invitation to sell financial instruments, and that the white paper does not constitute a prospectus. The MiCA Regulation also prohibits statements about the future value of crypto assets, except to highlight circumstances that could lead to the total or partial loss of their value, the possibility that they may not always be tradable, or that they may not be exchangeable for the goods or services promised in the white paper.

The document must be dated, written in at least one of the official languages of the home Member State or a language customary in international finance, and made available in a machine-readable format.

It is common in the industry that, as a project develops, some statements in the initial version of the crypto-asset white paper need modification due to the project's evolution, changes in the concept, or the need for more nuanced information. Historically, issuers would upload a new version of the white paper to their website, discarding the previous version. For the holders of the crypto assets, this was akin to a unilateral modification of the general terms and conditions without prior notice. To address this, Article 12 of the MiCA Regulation allows issuers to change the crypto-asset white paper but requires them to notify the competent authority of such changes.

Until the adoption of the MiCA Regulation, one of the main concerns of purchasers of utility tokens was the legal status of the token holder, specifically, the rights of the holder of an issued crypto asset that did not have the legal nature of a financial instrument. Most class actions brought in the United States against project issuers, aside from alleging violations related to financial instrument regulations, argued that the crypto-asset white paper was the primary document on which the decision to purchase the crypto-asset was based and should be treated as a public offer and a contract of adhesion, where the representations made in the white paper would be enforceable. Many issuers included lengthy legal disclaimers, excluding liability for any deviations or modifications that might occur. In this regard, the MiCA Regulation expressly prohibits, in Article 15, the exclusion of civil liability and subjects the issuer and its management body to liability for incomplete, misleading, or partial representations.

Empowering crypto-asset holders to claim liability and compensation from the issuer for damages suffered due to the infringements contained in the crypto-asset white paper is a significant step forward. It provides the legal certainty that was previously lacking.

The regulation also addresses the advertising communications of crypto-asset projects, drawing on the experience accumulated during the proliferation of these projects at the end of 2017 and the first half of 2018. During that time, major social networks and search engines banned advertising related to crypto-asset projects to mitigate the numerous fraud cases. Consequently, the MiCA Regulation establishes certain rules to protect consumers and users in relation to advertising. Under Article 7, marketing communications for utility token projects must be identifiable as such, provide clear and non-misleading information, contain information consistent with that in the crypto-asset white paper where required, disclose the existence of the white paper, and provide the website address of the issuer. All such marketing communications and the crypto-asset white paper must be available on the issuer's website for as long as the utility tokens are circulated.

Unlike the regime for issuing asset-backed tokens or e-money tokens, which require prior authorisation, the issuance of utility tokens will not be subject to previous authorisation. Therefore, utility token projects that exceed the thresholds set by the MiCA Regulation will only need to comply with the requirements to prepare, notify, and publish the crypto-asset white paper. In this regard, the competent authority will carry out ex-post monitoring of the projects. Consequently, once the legal entity that has prepared the white paper has notified the competent authority, it will be entitled to offer the crypto-assets throughout the European Union or to apply for admission to trading on crypto-asset platforms (Art. 11 MiCA Regulation).

As discussed earlier, the MiCA Regulation demonstrates a profound understanding of the crypto-asset ecosystem that has been developing over the past few years. The explicit inclusion of submitting projects not only when considering an issuance but also when applying for admission to trading on crypto-asset platforms aims to address the latest phenomenon of utility token issuances through Initial Coin Offerings (ICOs), known as Initial Exchange Offerings (IEOs).

IEOs represented a new twist on the different types of crypto-asset issuance. Instead of issuing to the general public, as had been the case to date, projects migrated towards issuance directly within cryptocurrency exchanges or crypto-asset trading platforms. Issuing within the crypto-asset trading platform offered users immediate liquidity, utilising the platform's infrastructure for payment management, anti-money laundering compliance, and tapping into the platform's registered clientele.

5.3 Mandatory Disclosures

To ensure maximum protection for potential subscribers and accuracy in the information provided, as well as to establish accountability for statements made in crypto-asset white papers and to prevent misunderstandings when making investment decisions, the MiCA Regulation has instituted a set of mandatory representations and disclosures.

5.3.1 Lack of Approval by the Relevant National Authority

From a regulatory standpoint, the legal text does not require ex-ante authorisation by the competent national authority for offering crypto-assets other than asset-backed tokens and e-money tokens covered by Article 4 of the MiCA Regulation.

Therefore, the legislator has deemed it appropriate for the crypto-asset white paper to commence with the following explicit statement: "This crypto-asset white paper has not been approved by any competent authority in any Member State of the European Union. The offeror of the crypto-asset is solely responsible for the content of this crypto-asset white paper." (Art. 6.3 MiCA Regulation).

Before the MiCA Regulation was enacted, many crypto assets issued outside of regulation tended to mention regulatory authorities within their white papers. This practice was prevalent in projects not involving the issuance of financial instruments, potentially leading subscribers to believe there was some level of oversight or even approval by the competent national authority.

However, given the unregulated nature of these crypto-assets, competent national authorities did not formally assess or endorse these projects. In some cases, regulatory consultations were sought, and competent national authorities clarified that these specific crypto assets did not fall within their regulatory scope due to their legal nature. Some projects exploited this ambiguity as a marketing strategy, creating an illusion of regulatory oversight and approval.

The mandatory declaration aims to prevent any potential subscriber from being misled into believing that the content of the crypto-asset white paper has been reviewed and approved by any competent national authority of a Member State.

5.3.2 Statement by the Issuer's Management Body

Regarding the declaration of the management body of the offeror, it is required that they affirm the compliance of the crypto-asset white paper with the requirements of Title II of the MiCA Regulation. To the best of their knowledge and belief, this statement should attest that the information contained therein is "fair, clear and not misleading" and that there are no "omissions likely to affect its content."

Following Article 6.6 of the MiCA Regulation, the aforementioned statement should be formulated as follows: "This crypto-asset white paper complies with Title II of Regulation (EU) 2023/1114 and, to the best knowledge of the management body, the information presented in the crypto-asset white paper is fair, clear and not misleading, and the crypto-asset white paper makes no omission likely to affect its import."

This places the responsibility on the offeror's management body to make such statements, explicitly taking responsibility for the content of the crypto-asset white paper and ensuring its compliance with legal requirements.

Any omissions, errors, inaccuracies, or non-compliance in the crypto-asset white paper will expose the offeror to liability.

The terms "fair, clear, not misleading" or "no omission likely to affect its meaning" are inherently subject to legal interpretation. Applying these terms in the context of corporate governance and management duties is not fixed but must accurately represent the position of the offering company or entity without misrepresentation. What should have been fair, clear, and not misleading to the management body when drafting and publishing the crypto-asset white paper?

The requirement for balanced disclosure in crypto-asset white papers aligns with corporate governance principles, ensuring managers fulfil their obligations to communicate honestly and accurately. The interpretation of these concepts directly influences the standards of transparency and accountability expected from the management of companies or entities in their communication with stakeholders, particularly subscribers.[15]

5.3.3 Loss of Value, Non-Tradability, Lack of Liquidity, Lack of Hedging

The offeror must include statements highlighting the potential risks associated with the crypto assets. These include the risk of loss of value, transferability issues, illiquidity, and the absence of coverage under investor compensation or deposit guarantee schemes, such as, in the case of Spain, the Investment Guarantee Fund (FOGAIN) or the Deposit Guarantee Fund (FGD).

---

[15] *Vid.* Blemus and Guegan (2019). https://ssrn.com/abstract=3350771 or https://doi.org/10.2139/ssrn.3350771. Accessed 14 June 2024.

In the case of utility tokens, the offeror must also include a statement regarding the risk of project interruption. The final wording of Article 6(5)(c) of the MiCA Regulation emphasises the inclusion of the word "crypto-asset" in reference to the project, indicating that project disruption may not solely result from insolvency proceedings but may also stem from corporate decisions made by the offeror. The MiCA Regulation does not explicitly outline the consequences of project discontinuation, as it is understood that general national law, such as national insolvency law and contract and obligations law, would apply.

The required statement can be formulated as follows (see Art. 6.5 MiCA Regulation):

> The crypto-asset may lose its value in part or in full, may not always be transferable and may not be liquid.
>
> [The following statement contained in this paragraph shall only be included where the offer to the public concerns a utility token.] The utility token may not be exchangeable against the good or service promised in the crypto-asset white paper, especially in the case of a failure or discontinuation of the crypto-asset project.
>
> The crypto-asset is not covered by the investor compensation schemes under Directive 97/9/EC of the European Parliament and the Council.
>
> The crypto-asset is not covered by the deposit guarantee schemes under Directive 2014/49/EU of the European Parliament and the Council.

5.3.4 Executive Summary *(One-Pager)*

Following the management body's statement, a concise and easily understandable overview of the crypto-asset offering or planned admission to trading should be presented. It has been customary in the industry to release crypto-asset white papers for public offerings on websites. However, certain projects opted for intricate technical terminology and ambiguous details, leading to confusion among potential subscribers who lacked a comprehensive understanding of the product they were investing in.

Article 6.7 of the MiCA Regulation mandates that this summary offers essential details about the offering in straightforward language. It must form an integral component of the crypto-asset white paper and be presented clearly and comprehensively, enabling potential holders to make well-informed decisions about the subscription opportunity without encountering unnecessary complexity.

A statement regarding the nature of the crypto-asset white paper as not constituting an offer or invitation to purchase financial instruments, and thus not qualifying as a prospectus under Regulation (EU) 2017/1129 of the European Parliament and of the Council or any other relevant Union or national law, must be included.

This statement can be formulated as follows (see Art. 6.7 MiCA Regulation):

> The summary should be read as an introduction to the crypto-asset white paper. The prospective holder should base any decision to purchase the crypto-asset on the content of the crypto-asset white paper as a whole and not on the summary alone.

The offer to the public of the crypto-asset white paper does not constitute an offer or solicitation to purchase financial instruments, and any such offer or solicitation can be made only by means of a prospectus or other offer documents pursuant to the applicable national law.

The crypto-asset white paper does not constitute a prospectus as referred to in Regulation EU 2017/1129 of the European Parliament and of the Council or any other offer document pursuant to Union or national law.

5.3.5 Risk Information[16]

Article 6(1)(i) of the MiCA Regulation stipulates the obligation to disclose potential risks associated with the project. The issuer must thoroughly assess the specific risks that could impact it, encompassing risks related to issuing crypto-assets to the public, their admission to trading, the project implementation, the underlying technology, or crypto-assets in general.

For instance, the following risks, which may apply to most utility token projects, and their potential impact, are outlined:

(A) Risk of illiquidity. The possibility that crypto assets may not be listed on any secondary market or that there may be a lack of liquidity in OTC (Over-The-Counter) markets must be reported. The issuer disclaims responsibility for any fluctuations in the crypto asset's value on any market type or for listing such assets on markets, which may entail illiquidity risks. Even if the utility token were to be listed on a third-party platform, such platforms may lack sufficient liquidity or face regulatory or compliance change risks, potentially leading to failure, crashes, or manipulation. Furthermore, if a third-party platform admits the crypto asset to trading by assigning an exchange value in cryptocurrencies or fiat money, such value may be volatile. It is essential to note that as a purchaser of this asset, the subscriber assumes all associated speculation and risks.

[16]The MiCA Regulation provides general guidelines on the types of risks to be disclosed. Although most projects might have common risks, some will hugely depend on the particularities of such project. The industry has been issuing white papers in the pre-MiCA Regulation timelapse and usually identifies the risks we are going to list. Some of the white papers which might be interesting for analysing this part might be the following:

- Reental: https://assets-global.website-files.com/64883b1804f368bf8575ed2e/65233a14897d572885798180_White%20Paper%20Reental%20VF%20-%20ESP.pdf.
- Bit2Me: https://bit2me.com/assets/downloads/b2m-token/bit2me-whitepaper.es.pdf.
- Chiliz (Socios.com): https://www.chiliz.com/docs/CHZ_whitepaper.pdf.
- Trazable: https://token.trazable.io/static/whitepaper_trz_v1.1_es-f4cd7f95b22147f72826fd8500e29c1b.pdf.
- Alvearium: https://alvearium.io/wp-content/uploads/2022/07/Alvearium_Whitepaper_ESP_24_07_2022.pdf.
- Bnext: https://bnext.es/uploads/landing/Whitepaper-Bnext_ESP.pdf.

Also, *vid.* Zetzsche et al. (2020). https://ssrn.com/abstract=3725395 or https://doi.org/10.2139/ssrn.3725395, p. 8 et seq.

(B) Regulatory risk. Blockchain technology facilitates new forms of interaction, and certain jurisdictions may apply existing regulations or introduce new rules addressing blockchain-based applications, potentially conflicting with the current configuration of smart contracts. This could lead to significant modifications to smart contracts, including their termination, and result in the loss of crypto assets for the subscriber.
(C) Forward-looking information risk. Certain information in the crypto-asset white paper, such as financial and business growth projections, is forward-looking. This information is based on the management's reasonable assumptions, but there is no guarantee that actual results will align with these projections. Future events could diverge significantly from what is anticipated.
(D) Unanticipated risks. Cryptographic assets represent a nascent technology still undergoing testing. Additional risks related to their acquisition, storage, transmission, and utilisation exist, including some that may be challenging to anticipate. These risks could materialise due to unforeseen variations or combinations of the aforementioned risks.
(E) Competitive risk. Other entities may offer services similar to those of the offeror. The bidder may find itself in competition with these entities, potentially adversely affecting the services rendered.
(F) High-risk product warning. It is imperative to elucidate that this product carries a high implicit risk. The value of crypto assets is subject to fluctuation, and a subscriber may not recoup the initially invested capital. Furthermore, changes in taxation and potential tax deductions may occur, the value of which is contingent upon the individual circumstances of each subscriber acquiring the utility tokens.
(G) Risk of project failure or abandonment. The progression of the issuer's proposed project could encounter impediments leading to its cessation, prompted by factors such as lack of market interest, inadequate funding, or insufficient commercial success or prospects (e.g., due to competition from rival projects). The issuance of crypto-assets does not assure the complete or partial realisation of the objectives outlined in the crypto-asset white paper, nor does it guarantee any benefits for the holder of the crypto-assets offered by the issuer.
(H) Software risk. The functionality of the crypto-assets hinges on the smart contract, which operates on a specific blockchain protocol. Any malfunction, crash, or abandonment of the underlying blockchain project could detrimentally impact the performance of the offered crypto assets. Moreover, technological advancements, including developments in cryptography, such as quantum computing, pose risks that could lead to the malfunctioning of the crypto assets. It is important to note that smart contracts and their underlying software are still in the early stages of development, and there is no guarantee that the issuance and subsequent trading of crypto-assets will be uninterrupted or error-free. There is an inherent risk of defects, bugs, and vulnerabilities that may result in losing funds or crypto assets. Additionally, there is a risk of hacker attacks on the technological infrastructure, potentially hindering or even permanently halting the issuer's business activities. In a Proof-of-Work consensus mechanism

scenario, a situation may arise where an entity controls over 50% of the computational power of the blockchain miners, leading to a so-called 51% attack and subsequent network takeover. Attackers inherently represent the majority by harnessing more than half of the hash power, granting them the ability to impose their version on the blockchain. This dominance can be achieved even with less than 51% of the mining power. Once control is established, attackers can manipulate or reverse-initiate transactions. Alongside the risk of hacker attacks, there exists the possibility of sabotage by the issuer's employees or third parties, posing a threat to the integrity of the issuer's hardware and software systems.

(I) Risk of custody or loss of private keys. Except for offerings conducted on the technology platforms of crypto-asset service providers, purchasing issued crypto-assets commonly involves using a digital wallet secured by a private key and password. Typically, the private key is encrypted by a password. Buyers of crypto-assets from the issuer must acknowledge, comprehend, and agree that the loss or theft of their private key or password associated with the digital wallet could lead to permanent loss of access to the crypto-asset. Furthermore, any third party accessing this private key could unlawfully appropriate the crypto-asset held in the digital wallet. Any errors or malfunctions within the digital wallet or crypto-asset storage system chosen by the buyer for receiving their utility tokens may also result in the loss of crypto-assets.

(J) Risk of theft. Smart contracts and their software platforms are susceptible to cyber-attacks or hacks by third parties, including intentionally malicious software attacks, malware, denial of service attacks, and consensus-based attacks. These attacks could lead to theft or loss of invested capital or acquired crypto-assets, potentially hindering the achievement of the objectives outlined by the issuer in the white paper.

References

Blanco Sánchez MJ (2022) La publicidad de criptoactivos. In: Pastor Sempere C (ed) Dinero Digital y Gobernanza TIC en la UE. Thomson Reuters Aranzadi, Cizur Menor, Navarra, pp 247–262

Blemus S, Guegan D (2019) Initial Crypto-Asset Offerings (ICOs), Tokenization and Corporate Governance. https://ssrn.com/abstract=3350771 or doi:https://doi.org/10.2139/ssrn.3350771. Accessed 14 eJun 2024

del Castillo Ionov R (2018) Las Initial Coin Offerings (ICOs) y la tokenización de la economía. Thomson Reuters Aranzadi, Cizur Menor, Navarra

Ibáñez Jiménez JW (2018) Derecho de Blockchain y de la tecnología de registros distribuidos. Thomson Reuters Aranzadi, Cizur Menor, Navarra

Maia G, Vieira dos Santos J (2021) MiCA and DeFi ('Proposal for a Regulation on Market in Crypto-Assets' and 'Decentralised Finance'). In: Pereira Coutinho F, Lucas Pires M, Barradas B (eds) Blockchain and the law: dynamics and dogmatism, current and future [Preprint]. [21 p.]. Available from: https://ssrn.com/abstract=3875355 or https://doi.org/10.2139/ssrn.3875355

Martínez-Echevarría y García de Dueñas A (1997) Valores mobiliarios anotados en cuenta. Concepto, naturaleza y régimen jurídico. Aranzadi, Pamplona, Navarra

Martínez-Echevarría y García de Dueñas A, del Castillo Ionov R (2021) Las Fichas de Servicio (*Utility Tokens*) en el mercado de los criptoactivos. In: Madrid Parra A, Pastor Sempere C (eds) Guía de Criptoactivos MiCA. Thomson Reuters Aranzadi, Cizur Menor, Navarra, pp 85–96

Maume P, Fromberger M (2019) Regulation of initial coin offerings: reconciling US and EU securities laws (June 15, 2018). Chicago J Int Law 19(2):548–585

Patti FP (2024) The European MiCA regulation: a new era for initial coin offerings. Georgetown J Int Law. Bocconi Legal Studies Research Paper No. 4810910. https://doi.org/10.2139/ssrn.4810910

Zetzsche DA, Annunziata F, Arner DW, Buckley RP (2020) The Markets in Crypto-Assets Regulation (MICA) and the EU Digital Finance Strategy. European Banking Institute Working Paper Series No. 2020/77. University of Luxembourg Law Working Paper Series No. 2020-018. University of Hong Kong Faculty of Law Research Paper No. 2020/059. https://ssrn.com/abstract=3725395 or https://doi.org/10.2139/ssrn.3725395

Crypto-Asset Service Providers: Harmonised Framework Vs. Risk of an Unlevel Playing Field

Maria-Teresa Paracampo

Abstract This paper highlights issues surrounding the Markets in Crypto-Assets Regulation (MiCA) that could hinder the effective and convergent application of the new harmonised framework at the European level.

The transition process to MiCA is a complex journey, largely due to the implementation of transitional measures. A significant aspect of this complexity is the inclusion of a grandfathering clause. This clause, which permits national law providers to continue offering crypto-asset services under their existing national regulations for 18 months post-MiCA implementation, adds a layer of intricacy to the transition process and its implications for the crypto-asset services sector. The diverse options available under the transitional measures introduce a significant risk. On the one hand, they could lead to a forced coexistence between national and European regulatory regimes. On the other hand, they could create an unlevel playing field among service providers. This potential risk could result in some providers operating under different regulatory disciplines gaining an unfair advantage and consolidating their market position at the expense of others. In this complex and uncertain scenario, the importance of the European Securities and Markets Authority's (ESMA) intervention in establishing best practices or guidelines becomes a crucial step towards encouraging greater convergence of national authorities in the transition process, thereby ensuring a more harmonised and effective application of MiCA.

This paper expands and updates the text of a lecture delivered at the III International Congress entitled "Present and future of crypto-assets regulation in the European Union," held at the University of Alicante (Spain) on December 13, 14, and 15, 2023. This work is funded within the framework of: Proyecto CIPROM/2022/26 "Presente y futuro de la regulación de los Criptoactivos en la UE [Legalcripto]". Proyecto Prometeo CIPROM/2022/26, grupos de investigación de excelencia, de la Generalitat Valenciana (P.I. Carmen Pastor).

M.-T. Paracampo (✉)
Department of Law, University of Bari, Bari, Italy
e-mail: mariateresa.paracampo@uniba.it

C. Pastor Sempere (ed.), *Governance and Control of Data and Digital Economy in the European Single Market*, Law, Governance and Technology Series 71,
https://doi.org/10.1007/978-3-031-74889-9_11

1 Introduction

The European regulation on markets in crypto assets (reg. EU 2023/1114 or, more simply, MiCA)[1] was published in the Official Journal of the European Union on 9 June 2023. The finally approved text results from an arduous (Madrid Parra & Pastor Sempere 2021; Ortos 2021) and prolonged regulatory process (Pastor Sempere 2022), which has seen several stages in the debate on a topic that is articulated and developing in the market but completely innovative in the traditional financial landscape (Annunziata 2023b; Lener 2023; Maume 2023; Narain & Moretti 2022; Paracampo 2023; Lehmann 2024; Zetzsche et al. 2023). It is part of the broader regulatory definition process in the financial sector and, more precisely, digital finance (European Commission 2020; Ross 2023a; Paracampo 2021a), in which it attempts to offer the first organic response on a complex topic with ever-evolving technological implications.

The objective of overcoming market fragmentations, entrusted to individual initiatives adopted by certain Member States, sometimes in the context of anti-money laundering regulations—but still with partial and inadequate approaches—does not appear secondary. In particular, the diverse nature of these initiatives has contributed to the "endorsement" of regulatory arbitrage (Demertzis 2022), with several competitive spillovers on a market considered by the legislator to be promising and likely to attract numerous players of different natures and origins (financial and otherwise).

Therefore, the need to intervene at the European level with a harmonised framework has also become self-evident considering the purposes that guided the legislator in drafting the European regulation: consumer protection, market integrity and financial stability.[2] These purposes translate into the respect of the level playing field for those players involved in the process of distribution of crypto-assets in the market, the recognition of a European passport for the cross-border provision of services based on uniform rules, and the smooth functioning of the single market in crypto-assets (Annunziata 2023a). On this front, MiCA, despite certain inherent "limitations" in the approach chosen by the legislator, marks the first regulatory exercise on crypto assets at the European, but especially international, level (Paracampo 2023).

While setting itself as a regulatory example for non-European approaches, MiCA and the European legislator itself must, however, take into account the global and inherently cross-border nature of markets in crypto-assets,[3] which are therefore exposed to further consideration in light of initiatives taken in the international arena.

---

[1] Regulation (EU) 2023/1114 of the European Parliament and the Council of 31 May 2023 on markets in crypto-assets, and amending Regulations (EU) No 1093/2010 and (EU) No 1095/2010 and Directives 2013/36/EU and (EU) 2019/1937.

[2] Recital 6.

[3] Recital 8.

2 The Transition Process to MiCA: An Uphill Road

Once the path definition of the regulatory text is concluded, another chapter opens, probably the most important one, related to the management of the transition process towards an effective and convergent application of the new European framework (ESMA 2023c). In this sense, MiCA, besides being the point of arrival, becomes the starting point for the transition from the ante-MiCA to the post-MiCA regime. To this end, the date of publication in the OJEU (i.e., 9 June 2023) serves as the *dies a quo* for the entry into force of the regulation (i.e., 29 June 2023), which is followed by its implementation, divided into two milestones:

(a) 30 June 2024 for Titles III and IV (ART and EMT);
(b) 30 December 2024 for the remaining Titles.

Given the two dates mentioned above, the process aimed at facilitating the full launch of MiCA has been activated—at a close pace—but now it looks like an uphill road, not without obstacles looming over the transition process to the new regulations.

Several regulatory "burdens" arising from MiCA itself weigh down the pathway, such as primarily the number of interventions by the European Authorities at the secondary level in fulfilling the numerous mandates received to implement regulatory provisions. To the Authorities' credit, they promptly intervened in a dense time grid, developing a roadmap for the various interventions to ferry the system to the new regulatory order. In keeping with set deadlines, the timeline has thus been cadenced into three main steps for consulting a series of drafts with the market (ESMA 2023a, 2023b, 2024a, 2024b, 2024c, 2024d, 2024e, 2024f), some of which have been translated into final reports (ESMA 2024e, 2024g).

The service providers will then have to navigate the numerous documents and the requirements needed to comply with the new European regulations. Preparations are in full swing in a race against time that, while accelerated for some players, appear decelerated or at least delayed for others. Differentiated conditions of entry and speed of departure are provided for by MiCA about service providers, which can be attributed to three types (Paracampo 2023):

(1) On-demand providers: These are newly established entities that identify the "ordinary" subjective type, for which MiCA establishes the obligation of authorisation under Article 59 to provide crypto-asset services.
(2) European law providers already with a European passport obtained under other European financial legislation and who benefit from a regime of exemption from the ordinary authorisation procedure under Article 60, based on a presumption of equivalence of MiCA services with MiFID ones (Paracampo 2023).
(3) National law providers, licensed to provide crypto-asset services based on the legislation of the Member States where they are established.

Distinctive features and subjective classification of providers imply different legal regimes of market access, some graduated and others tailored.

Some challenges emerging at the start of MiCA derive from the transitional measures, which are only provided for certain players already operating in the national markets of those Member States that have already adopted national legislation (i.e., national law providers). These could take advantage of the opportunities provided by grandfathering clauses (explicit and implicit), such as undermining—in terms that will become clear—the convergence toward applying a harmonised system. Thus, an overall framework that looks like an operational and temporal labyrinth emerges, creating more grey areas in the transition process to MiCA.

3 National Law Providers Between Transitional Measures and Grandfathering Clause: Problematic Profiles

In the context briefly described, the aforementioned transitional measures raise multiple concerns about the possible effects each option, listed in Article 143(3) and (6), could produce in the transition to MiCA, frustrating the original legislative aims. In this regard, however, it is worth remembering that adopting European legislation, whether entirely innovative or only amending an existing one, sometimes affects prior and perhaps widespread situations at the national level, which need time to comply and "socialise" with the new regulatory framework (Ross 2023b).

Every newly adopted European legislation closes with one or more final provisions intended to introduce a transitional regime reserved for entities already operating in the market, as enabled by previous regulatory frameworks adopted at the national level.

The purpose of the transitional measures is to allow these entities to take advantage of the necessary time, perhaps through a time-limited extension of the activity already performed, to adapt to the new European provisions and not leave clients with whom they have professional relationships unprotected. Therefore, the transitional measures are aimed at "transitioning" those involved (i.e., service providers and, in turn, clients) from the old to the new European-style regulatory regime. This process, however, takes on a connotation in MiCA that goes beyond the indicated need to include these subjects in the transition to the new European legislation.

The transitional measures—as far as they concern crypto-asset service providers and, in particular, national law providers—are harbingers of many, sometimes detrimental, consequences for the single market in crypto-assets. Such effects are then likely to be amplified in the light of the multiple scenarios that can be envisaged about individual national markets, corresponding as much to each of the options envisaged in the spectrum of transitional measures as to the related deadlines that interpose themselves in the roadmap toward the entry into application of MICA.

For this purpose, the date of 30 December 2024 becomes the benchmark for the following actions:

(a) Activate a range of options for each Member State to consider regarding its market.
(b) Crystallise the transitional period granted to national law providers.
(c) Inform the European Commission and the European Securities and Markets Authority (ESMA) of the decisions taken by each Member State.

Yet, apart from the different "operational windows" that the Member States may open based on the transitional provisions, there is also a grandfathering clause that spans from 30 December 2024 to 1 July 2026, during which national law providers could benefit from an 18-month extension and continue to provide crypto-asset services based on national law (i.e., the law of the Member States in which they were authorised).

The period indicated, however, coincides with the official launch of MiCA and the harmonised framework, thus creating a difficult coexistence between national regimes, where they exist, and the European regime, which may alter the competition among all categories of crypto-asset service providers. In light of this, the different options left to the discretion of Member States mainly provide for:

(1) granting the entire transitional period (from 30 December 2024 to 1 July 2026) or a reduced period, with a simultaneous extension of the activity, as regulated by national law. However, the extension does not exempt providers (under national law) from the obligation to regularise, resulting in the submission of an application for authorisation, the assessment of which may have different outcomes and consequences as follows:

    (A) The granting of the authorisation under Article 63, even before the 1 July 2026 deadline or before the end of the transitional period, marks the transition from applying the national regime to the European one.
    (B) Likewise, the refusal of the authorisation terminates the transitional period and the provider's activity in the domestic market.

(2) The decision not to apply the transitional period.
(3) The reduction of the transitional period from 18 to 12 months.

In all the cases indicated, the choice of the individual Member States should be preceded by a comparative assessment between national and European regimes, particularly regarding the provision of comparable prudential requirements, so much so that a less stringent national regulation than the European one could justify the extreme decision not to apply the transitional regime. An identical preliminary assessment should also be conducted about national law providers' organisational requirements and governance structure (Paracampo 2021b).

However, the extreme choice—positive or negative—of whether to apply the grandfathering clause may reveal a whole series of intermediate nuances symptomatic of as many situations as need to be considered case by case. Finally, the spectrum of transitional measures offers the further possibility for Member States to decide whether to opt for:

(4) The activation of a simplified authorisation procedure for national law providers, provided that:

- they are authorised before 30 December 2024 to provide crypto-asset services based on national regulations.
- they apply for authorisation from 30 December 2024 to 1 July 2026.

The common denominator of all the scenarios indicated is the discretion that characterises Member States' decisions on the future fate of national law providers in the face of the entry into application of MiCA and its harmonised framework. It is a discretion endorsed by the failure to provide uniform criteria that would guide Member States in assessing the most appropriate measure and prevent actions detrimental to healthy competition between all market players. Different effects may result from the exercise of each of the options indicated as subsequently outlined:

(a) Justifying, for a transitional period, the coexistence of national regulatory pathways with the European MiCA pathway.
(b) Concluding the path of national law providers in the domestic market once the transitional period is over.
(c) Marking the operational upgrading of providers from the national to the European market.

Yet the discretion, as mentioned earlier, which accompanies national assessments in the field, can have (detrimental) repercussions on the competition between all types of players covered by MiCA and on the proper functioning of a harmonised market in crypto-assets, so much so, as to accentuate—rather than eliminate—the risk of an unlevel playing field. This is precisely the risk that MiCA aimed instead to counter by introducing specific measures to supervise those involved in issuing and distributing crypto assets. The aim was to simultaneously fill an important regulatory gap created by financial innovation and the growing process of the tokenisation of assets.

To this end, MiCA was adopted to provide all players with equal opportunities for market access, overcoming the fragmentation resulting from individual regulatory initiatives adopted only by certain Member States. On closer look, the transitional measures—as will be clarified—risk instead producing a boomerang effect on several fronts:

- Firstly, by perpetuating—not eliminating at its root—the possibility of regulatory arbitrage because of the new patchwork.
- Secondly, it favours only certain national law providers in competition with all other competitors, specifically European law providers and other national law providers in different Member States.
- Thirdly, generating competition (even downwards) between Member States with their own—more or less established-national markets in crypto-assets, which would attract new players into the perimeter of their respective jurisdiction, thanks to the 'coverage' provided by previous national legislation.

4 National Law Providers vs Other Crypto-Asset Service Providers Between Operational Advantages and Market Access Fast Lanes

As pointed out in the introduction, one of the main objectives the legislator aims to achieve with MiCA is to provide all players with equal opportunities to access the European market based on a harmonised framework. This should make it possible to overcome market fragmentation due to individual regulatory initiatives taken by certain Member States. Yet the legislator itself could betray such a purpose by providing a series of transitional measures in Article 143(3) and (6), which instead result in an implicit extension and "regulatory legitimisation" of market fragmentation even beyond the 30 December 2024 deadline (i.e., MiCA's implementation date).

This risk, which is common to all the options included in the list of transitional measures, spills over into healthy competition between service providers—be they newly established European law providers or national law providers—for whom different market access conditions are envisaged, between fast lanes, time advantages and various operating speeds. In this regard, multiple critical issues arise regarding the grandfathering clause, which, at the discretion of Member States, introduces an 18-month transitional period, extended from 30 December 2024 to 1 July 2026. This transitional measure consists of a regime of temporary exemption from the application of European regulations, provided that national law providers obtain an authorisation based on national regulations.

On closer inspection however, in the first phase, this exemption regime does not reflect new access to the market since national law providers are already operational, albeit limited to national borders. Their previous and current operations, which are the source of their prior knowledge of the market, allow them to gain a significant time advantage over all other players.

In the present case, the transitional measure translates into an extension of the operability already in progress for this type of provider, who could thus enjoy a fast-track and preferential treatment both before and after MiCA, i.e. also after the entry into application and theoretically until the end of the transitional period.

The favourable treatment for national law providers is twofold. They are temporarily exempted from applying European regulations in a developing market context. The competitive advantage they can thus enjoy, thanks to the transitional and albeit nationally circumscribed measures, strengthens their market reputation, especially when they are large players who, before MiCA, applied for authorisation to operate in several Member States. On the strength of this reputation, national law providers can later access the European market, using the domestic market as a springboard.

As a result, time imbalances will likely alter competitive market dynamics, conditioning the market access of different players and imparting different speeds to it. Three possible scenarios are outlined next.

(A) The first issue relates to comparing national law providers and on-demand providers, i.e., newly established players who must obtain authorisation by following the ordinary procedure under MiCA.

In such a situation, any form of competition is eliminated, which is unbalanced in favour of the national law providers, who have already entered the market, as opposed to the different time scales required for application and authorisation by on-demand providers. Indeed, these providers must wait until MiCA comes into application (i.e., 30 December 2024) to activate the ordinary procedure until authorisation is granted under Article 63.

The temporal discrepancy between national law providers, who enjoy an extension of the activity already exercised at the national level, and newly established providers is wide. The latter are concomitantly penalised, as they must comply with the uniform rules of the MiCA framework. Therefore, in the first phase of MiCA's application, the ordinary procedure could become the real exception, giving way to national and European law providers.

(B) The second issue relates to European law providers being even more penalised in competition with national law providers. Article 60 selects them based on their already-in-place authorisation to provide financial services governed by other existing financial laws.

The European passport allows them to enjoy exemption from the ordinary authorisation procedure, replaced by information processing and notification to the national competent authorities of their intention to provide crypto-asset services.

Thus, European law providers will be able to access the European market in crypto assets more quickly than under the ordinary authorisation procedure but still less favourably than those granted to national law providers, who, assuming one of the transitional measures is activated, may instead benefit from an extension of the activity already underway.

Furthermore, the domestic market itself, in which even national law providers are located and where they have been pre-authorised under national law, may already be too concentrated in the hands of the sector's pioneers (Paracampo 2022b), making access difficult for all other players, whether newly established or European law providers once MiCA comes into application.

However, national law providers and European law providers, although they share an exemption regime (temporary for the former and lasting for the latter), differ respectively by:

(a) Enabling regulatory source: national legislation specific to national law providers vs. harmonised financial regulations.
(b) The territorial scope of operation is national in the former case and European in the latter.
(c) The previous type of operation was the provision of crypto-asset services based on national legislation vs. the provision of financial services with objectives different from crypto-assets and based on European financial legislation. It is also true that the presumption of equivalence of MiCA services to MiFID services (Paracampo 2022a) allows European law providers to take advantage

of the exemption regime from authorisation and provide crypto-asset services in the market that are equivalent to those included in the European passport already in place (Paracampo 2023).

(d) Time criterion: temporary for national law providers and lasting for European law providers.

(e) All providers have access to the market in crypto-assets, but with different starting conditions and timelines.

For European law providers, who are already authorised to provide other financial services, the European passport only allows them to speed up—not zero out—the time it takes to enter the crypto market. Market access is postponed once the deadline for notification to national authorities and their verification of the information required by Article 60(7) has passed.

Thus, the imbalance between the opportunities available to national law providers and those available to European law providers seems clear.

This imbalance is reinforced especially by the fact that the exemption regimes provided for national law providers are also subject to exceptions. This reveals further prospects for them as alternative forms of operating on the market and, simultaneously, regularises their position on the (in this case) European market.

An uncertain framework emerges, supported by fast lanes with differing speeds depending on the type of provider. As a result, there is an escalation of opportunities for national law providers to consolidate their position in the market. In contrast, European law providers are penalised by time constraints and operating conditions, which, although more streamlined than the ordinary procedure, keep them at a standstill for a while, awaiting the implementation date of MiCA (i.e., 30 December 2024).

Indeed, that date serves as a time limit for officially opening the game to European law providers, allowing them to notify the relevant national authority of their intention to start providing crypto-asset services. This accentuates the temporal imbalance in the competitive arena of players.

(C) Further forms of discrimination could then affect the same national law providers, who, already enjoying preferential lanes, would find themselves at the centre of a much broader competition between the Member States where they have been licensed.

In this case, different starting conditions are left to the discretion of the Member States, which have a wide range of options from the transitional measures provided by Article 143. Presumably, the choice will fall on the measure most appropriate to the domestic market and favourable to active providers. This measure will make the domestic market more attractive to new players before MiCA is fully implemented. This scenario is even more dangerous without transparency and uniform criteria that, like the previous options, can unambiguously guide each Member State's choice.

Unlike European law providers, presumptions of equivalence of services—MiCA and Mifid—do not expressly operate in this case. However, resorting to preliminary equivalence assessments between services governed by national law and MiCA may prove useful. Likewise, an equivalence assessment could affect providers' governance and prudential requirements for granting or refusing authorisation.

Thus, the framework is still opaque, a harbinger of further market fragmentation. It also highlights the need for homogeneous criteria to select options to prevent the creation of grey areas in the transition process to MiCA.

5 The Simplified Authorisation Procedure Option

Article 143(6) provides the most complex transitional measure, introducing a simplified authorisation procedure for national law providers.

This procedure is based on two elements of selection of possible beneficiaries:

(a) The authorisation to provide crypto-asset services in compliance with national law.
(b) The submission of the application for authorisation will take place in a time range from 30 December 2024 to 1 July 2026, which coincides with the extension of the grandfathering clause.

This is an alternative transitional measure to those indicated in Paragraph 3. Still, it directly grants the prescribed ex-MiCA permit through a simplified procedure in the present case.

At the same time, the activation of such an option is again left to the discretion of Member States, which could adopt different guidelines for differently located providers, given the lack of clear and uniform evaluation criteria in favour of the simplified procedure.

Concerning the grandfathering clause under Paragraph 3, which relies on a generic reference to the equivalence of strict requirements of the national framework with the European one, for the simplified procedure, it is in no way possible to understand both what the facilitation and derogating treatment concerning the articles referred to in Paragraph 6 (i.e., Articles 62 and 63) consists of and what the steps are for the implementation of the aforementioned simplified procedure.

In other words, it is unclear what the content of the 'simplification' that should characterise the procedure in question should be, which would thus be open to different interpretations in those Member States that would consider using it for providers operating in their national markets.

The only element, which is also not entirely clear, is provided by the verification—before granting the authorisation—of compliance with Chapters 2 and 3 of Title V, i.e., both general and specific requirements provided in correspondence with the provision of crypto-asset services. These requirements thus pertain to the next stage, not before authorisation.

The remaining part, which could become relevant, concerns the provider's governance and the subjective and objective requirements, the existence of which is prescribed and must be verified before granting even an authorisation through a simplified procedure. This follows from the definition of the regulatory scope susceptible to derogation, which is limited to Articles 62 and 63 relating to the ordinary authorisation procedure.

Therefore, a possible interpretative solution could perhaps be traced back to a simplification (even in the sense of reduction) of the time required to issue the authorisation if the national legislation—which has empowered providers to continue their activities—contains provisions comparable to those contained in Title V, Chapters 2 and 3. In this direction, some Member States—such as France and Germany—are heading by rapidly introducing more stringent requirements at the national level and aligning their legislation with MiCA.

In addition to the above, the Member States are left to decide every other preliminary aspect concerning the content and prerequisites for activating the simplified procedure.

The latter will be able to exercise as wide a discretion as ever, involving:

- The choice of whether to grant a simplified procedure.
- The selection of potential beneficiaries and the cases in which such procedure may apply.
- The concrete way it is carried out and the admission requirements.
- The very "meaning" to be given to the adjective "simplified," which distinguishes the procedure.

This procedure thus results in favourable treatment, which seems to reward and ensure safe conduct for all national law providers, resulting in operational and territorial upgrading. Yet this transitional measure, like the others provided in Paragraph 3, could distort competition among the same national law providers in different Member States.

Indeed, those providers, on the strength of a reputation acquired in the market, perhaps in compliance with the different frameworks approved in each Member State, could face the dilemma of conflicting national decisions. Such a situation could, however, give them faster access to the European market given the following:

- prior knowledge of the market and supported by a simplified authorisation procedure; or
- exploiting regulatory arbitrage criteria and choosing the place of operational preference of the Member States with a more favourable orientation toward issuing a simplified procedure.

Ultimately, providing a simplified procedure in the indicated terms portends a confusing framework that leaves wide margins of decision-making manoeuvre for both Member States and potential beneficiaries.

Indeed, the provision in question is flawed by a lack of transparency and risks becoming discriminatory in the European context in the absence of precise guidelines, such as to justify the concrete activation of an alternative route of access (or, more correctly, continuation of the activity) to the European market or to standardise the prerequisites of a simplified authorisation.

6 Transitional Measures Under the Lens of the European Securities and Markets Authority (ESMA)

The complexity and fluidity of the evolving scenario and the range of national initiatives made possible by the transitional measures have alerted ESMA to the issues associated with the transition process to MiCA, especially concerning national law providers. In particular, the European Authority has begun to carefully assess the possible consequences for the single market and the orderly launch of the new harmonised legislation arising from the application of the grandfathering clause.

On the one hand, the latter is considered useful because it makes the market "socialise" with the new rules (Ross 2023b). On the other hand, allowing competent national authorities to prepare to assume new responsibilities for the supervision and enforcement of MiCA actually justifies extending the fragmentation of regulatory regimes across the EU for 18 months.

This is a period that ESMA considers excessively long, such that it would encourage—rather than deter—providers from forum shopping and choice of location, even in the period before the application of MiCA, with beneficial competitive advantages that, depending on national options, could then extend throughout the transitional period, hypothetically until 1 July 2026.

However, the risk of regulatory arbitrage in this sense could be amplified in the case of large companies that are active in more than one Member State and that, ultimately, at the end of the transitional period, could choose, as their final location, that of the Member States whose national regulations have, in the meantime, allowed them to consolidate their business and reputation in the market further.

In this regard, it is worth recalling that ESMA does not have specific powers and is only the passive recipient until 30 June 2024,[4] of the information regarding the option Member States have chosen: granting national law providers a transitional period; granting less than 18 months; non-application of the transitional period. Nor is such disclosure followed by an annotation in the soon-to-be-established register of providers by ESMA (Article 109), where there are only the data of providers with a European passport, whether authorised under MiCA or other European legislation on financial services (Paracampo 2023). Therefore, taking the date of application of MiCA (i.e., 30 December 2024) as a reference point, the time differences provided by the transitional measures inevitably result in fast lanes, staggered start times and different speeds of service providers' access to the crypto-assets market.

In a still confusing transitional context, ESMA has intervened in an attempt to redress, as far as possible, the imbalances and favourable treatments in the different market access regimes, but above all, to prevent and mitigate the (detrimental) consequences arising from an opaque framework, which could, on the one hand, incentivise opportunistic behaviours and on the other hand frustrate the efforts aimed at defining a harmonised framework. Hence, in the absence of specific powers in this

---

[4] Article 143 (3).

regard, the European Authority has resorted to moral suasion using a statement addressed to national competent authorities and market participants (ESMA 2023c), published with a letter addressed to the Member States (ESMA 2023c).

The objective of both interventions is to avoid a disorderly transition to MiCA. The latter risk will be averted by fostering effective implementation of the new European framework and promoting supervisory convergence. This will prevent distorting effects related to discretionary choices by the Member States within the varied spectrum of options codified in Article 143.

Accordingly, ESMA, in its letter to the Economic and Financial Affairs Council (ECOFIN), called on Member States to act in two very specific directions:

(a) Designate the competent authorities responsible for supervision under MiCA without delay.
(b) Reduce the transitional period (from 30 December 2024 to 1 July 2026) from 18 to 12 months. Member States should exercise this option in their jurisdictions and allow an operational extension to national providers licensed based on their national regulations.

At the same time, the statement, addressed to providers already active at the national level and to national supervisory authorities, contains a series of recommendations to protect the market, but above all, investors, whose protection represents ESMA's 'compass' towards the effective implementation of MiCA.

From this point of view, providers are urged to inform customers that they will not be able to benefit from the protections provided by MiCA until 30 December 2024. It is also true, however, that in the event of the coexistence in the same Member States—throughout the transitional period—of a national regime (for national law providers) and a European regime (for European law and on-demand providers), investors may find it difficult to discern the regulatory status of a provider and, consequently, the regulatory status of an asset or service they are accessing. In such cases, the risk of an unlevel playing field among providers results in different levels of protection for investors domiciled in the same and other Member States.

To this end, ESMA has called on NCAs to align their supervisory practices with those of other authorities throughout the European Union to initiate effective supervision from day one based on close cooperation and convergence among supervisors.

It should be noted, however, that the measures indicated, while noteworthy, may not have much impact unless followed by the use of soft law tools, such as best practices and guidelines, that can offer common and unambiguous criteria for the national choice from the various options to be exercised regarding national law providers.

7 National Law Providers Inside and Outside of MiCA: The Race to the National License Ante MiCA and the Manoeuvres of Member States

In the different options provided by Article 143, the transitional measures mark the opening and legitimisation of parallel and potentially different paths from the one regulated by MiCA.

These pathways will have to coexist until the end of the transitional period. Still, they may also—in the same timeframe—take over from MiCA in those Member States where national law providers outnumber European law or on-demand providers. In this context however, the reference deadline remains the date of application of MiCA (i.e., 30 December 2024) as the last deadline for adapting to the European framework or triggering the grandfathering clause. Instead, the legislator has not taken steps to introduce an effective starting date of application to crystallise the existing framework of national law providers on the one hand, and prevent opportunistic behaviours on the part of new providers, whose opportunities to enter national markets are open until 30 December 2024. It will only be the passing of that last deadline that will end the race for a national license by potential players, who, as of today, do not have a license but (in seeking a shortcut to access the European market) could still—in the course of MiCA's implementation—apply for one at the national level to speed up the ways and times of authorisation. This would enable them to access the European market more quickly, at a later date, perhaps through a simplified authorisation procedure.

Thus, the derogatory regime resulting from the transitional measures proposes a system of access to the European market that, although it aims to encourage the "regularisation" of national law providers, does not clarify the regulatory treatment applied. Indeed, it risks violating the uniformity of rules and the recognition of equal opportunities for all crypto-asset service providers and between national law providers authorised in different Member States.

At the same time, it encourages the creation of other fast lanes and additional unlevel playing field situations caused by advantageous positions and unfair competition in the market. All, however, are endorsed by transitional measures and thus indirectly "favoured" by the European legislator itself, which has opened other doors of entry to the market in cryptoassets outside the harmonised context of MiCA.

Ultimately, a framework emerges that envisages an operational and temporal relay race, with national law providers in pole position, followed by European law providers and, finally, on-demand providers. Such a deferred order of departure could then be subject to other isolated exceptions in those Member States that took action pre-MiCA to enable all providers established in their territory to comply with the new requirements and thus be ready to formalise their presence in the market on the date of application of the European framework.

The time range—still in progress—from MiCA's entry into force until the date of application has urged Member States to enter the field with competitive manoeuvres before MiCA and in several directions that are not always convergent. The various national initiatives between Member States that have been active for some time and others that are lagging are moving forward and involve the following developments.

(a) Earlier stricter regulations of the crypto-asset sector were used to bring domestic rules in line with the requirements of European regulation.
(b) The finalisation of domestic regulation is to comply with MiCA and, in some cases, to verify the requirements for service providers so that they can immediately enter the market with the European license.
(c) Incentives for other players in their domestic markets who could take advantage of safe conduct and shortcuts to access the European market.

This is also the consequence of the wide discretion accorded to the Member States, especially the possible different solutions adopted after the entry into force of MiCA or that are still being adopted in other jurisdictions. Ultimately, the picture remains uneven due to initiatives that do not follow an unambiguous direction, which risks prolonging the problem and leading to another form of market fragmentation.

8 Conclusions. Forced Cohabitation and Fragmented Frameworks: Toward an Unlevel Playing Field?

MiCA represents the first regulatory exercise on crypto assets internationally, resulting from a major regulatory effort to uniformly regulate the sector in the European context. The importance of the goals that moved the European legislator—from the protection of retail investors to the financial stability of markets—has become the beacon of post-MiCA action, based on a stringent and proactive approach to supervision and enforcement (Ross 2023b), aimed at fostering an effective transition to the new European framework. The latter objective represents one of the most crucial challenges for regulators and supervisors as we approach the end of 2024, the date of MiCA's implementation.

Yet, many issues remain to unravel in the transition path to MiCA. These unresolved factors contribute to a fluid and rapidly changing scenario, fostered by differences in the manner and timing of market access of different players, some of which are on favoured terms and others less favoured.

Considering the above, the transitional measures, in the various options available to Member States, thus seem to temporarily enable the cohabitation of national regimes with the European regime. Such cohabitation could lead to MiCA's application solutions not always being convergent, heralding a breakdown of the system of rules between players in and out of the regulatory framework designed by MiCA.

The framework, already complex in itself, risks being further obscured, putting a strain on precisely those goals that MiCA set out to achieve, including overcoming regulatory arbitrage and consumer protection. The latter would ultimately be conditioned by the graduation and regulatory nuances—not unambiguous—offered by the different rules applicable at the national and European levels, by the regulatory options and discretion of Member States in exercising them.

Thus, as a result of the application of the grandfathering clause, the cohabitation in the same jurisdiction of national law providers with European law and on-demand providers makes more concrete the risk that the consumer remains confused about the real regulatory status of the provider and the service provided, where, however, only providers of the last two types indicated, provide crypto-asset services under MiCA, with the consumer protections offered therein.

National rules, potentially misaligned from the harmonised framework, on the one hand, and players recognised based on the grandfathering clause, on the other hand, could also result in regulatory fragmentation and an alteration of the principle of healthy competition between operators on the same territory (some pre-existing, some newly authorised). The immediate consequence is favouring the consolidation in the market of some players at the expense of new entrants and, at the same time, the strengthening of certain domestic markets over others.

The coexistence of different regulatory regimes, whether temporary or long-lasting, could give rise to a set of "cryptic rules" for accessing the European market, shifting the focus to the national regulations for all parties involved. The crypto rules may be favoured without specific oversight at the European level, especially considering that ESMA is not directly involved and remains in the dark about the rationale behind individual national choices. These could make the transition process to MiCA disorderly, entailing high risks and costs, but frustrating regulatory efforts to harmonise a complex sector such as crypto-assets.

Against this backdrop, ESMA's interventions may be only the first step in re-establishing a level playing field. Notwithstanding, the appeals contained therein should be better specified in best practices and guidelines as soon as possible so that the options available to Member States can be exercised based on common criteria at the European level.

References

Annunziata F (2023a) The licensing rules in MiCA. In: Moura D, Diogo V, Duarte P, Granadeiro C (eds) Fintech regulation and the licensing principle. Centro de Investigaçao de direito privado, Frankfurt. https://ssrn.com/abstract=. Accessed 20 May 2024

Annunziata F (2023b) An overview of the markets in crypto-assets regulation (MiCAR). EBI Working Paper Series, no. 158. https://ssrn.com/abstract=4660379. Accessed 20 May 2024

Demertzis M (2022) Is MiCA the end of the crypto wild-west?. https://www.bruegel.org/comment/MiCA-end-crypto-wild-west. Accessed 20 May 2024

ESMA (2023a) Consultation paper, Technical Standards specifying certain requirements of Markets in Crypto-assets Regulation (MiCA) - second consultation paper, 2nd package. https://www.esma.europa.eu/sites/default/files/2023a-10/ESMA75-453128700-438_MiCA_Consultation_Paper_2nd_package.pdf. Accessed 20 May 2024

ESMA (2023b) ESMA clarifies the timeline for MiCA and encourages market participants and NCAs to start preparing for the transition. https://www.esma.europa.eu/sites/default/files/2023

b-10/ESMA74-449133380-441_Statement_on_MiCA_Supervisory_Convergence.pdf. Accessed 20 May 2024

ESMA (2023c) Consultation paper. Technical Standards specifying certain requirements of the Markets in Crypto-assets Regulation (MiCA), 1st package. https://www.esma.europa.eu/sites/default/files/2023-07/ESMA74-449133380-425_MiCA_Consultation_Paper_1st_package.pdf. Accessed 20 May 2024

ESMA (2023d) Letter to MS on effective MiCA application, Effective application of the MiCA Regulation. https://www.esma.europa.eu/sites/default/files/2023c-10/ESMA75-840896669-45_Letter_to_MS_on_effective_MiCA_application.pdf. Accessed 20 May 2024

ESMA (2024a) ESMA_QA_2085, New CASPs established before (and after) 30 December 2024. https://www.esma.europa.eu/publications-data/questions-answers/2085. Accessed 20 May 2024a

ESMA (2024b) ESMA_QA_2086, Passporting rights for entities benefiting from grandfathering. https://www.esma.europa.eu/publications-data/questions-answers/2086. Accessed 20 May 2024b

ESMA (2024c) Consultation paper on the draft Guidelines on the conditions and criteria for the qualification of crypto-assets as financial instruments. https://www.esma.europa.eu/sites/default/files/2024c-01/ESMA75-453128700-52_MiCA_Consultation_Paper_-_Guidelines_on_the_qualification_of_crypto-assets_as_financial_instruments.pdf. Accessed 20 May 2024

ESMA (2024d) Consultation Paper On the draft guidelines on reverse solicitation under the Markets in Crypto-assets Regulation (MiCA). https://www.esma.europa.eu/sites/default/files/2024d-01/ESMA35-1872330276-1619_Consultation_Paper_on_the_draft_guidelines_on_reverse_solicitation_under_MiCA.pdf. Accessed 20 May 2024

ESMA (2024e) Final Report, Draft technical Standards specifying certain requirements of the Markets in Crypto-assets Regulation (MiCA) – first package. https://www.esma.europa.eu/sites/default/files/2024e-03/ESMA18-72330276-1634_Final_Report_on_certain_technical_standards_under_MiCA_First_Package.pdf. Accessed 20 May 2024

ESMA (2024f) Consultation paper. Draft technical standards and guidelines specifying certain requirements of the Markets in Crypto-assets Regulation (MiCA) on detection and prevention of market abuse, investor protection and operational resilience – third consultation paper, 3rd package. https://www.esma.europa.eu/sites/default/files/2024-03/ESMA75-453128700-1002_MiCA_Consultation_Paper_-_RTS_market_abuse_and_GLs_on_investor_protection_and_operational_resilience.pdf. Accessed 20 May 2024

ESMA (2024g) Final Report on draft technical standards specifying requirements for cooperation, exchange of information, and notification between competent authorities, ESAs, and third countries under MiCA. https://www.esma.europa.eu/sites/default/files/2024f-03/ESMA75-453128700-949_Final_Report_MiCA_cooperation_technical_standards.pdf. Accessed 20 May 2024

European Commission (2020) Digital Finance Strategy for the EU, COM(2020) 591 final. https://eur-lex.europa.eu/legal-content/EN/TXT/PDF/?uri=CELEX:52020DC0591. Accessed 20 May 2024

Lehmann M (2024) MiCAR – Gold Standard or Regulatory Poison for the Crypto Industry?, EBI Working Paper Series, no. 160. https://papers.ssrn.com/sol3/papers.cfm?abstract_id=4692743. Accessed 20 May 2024

Madrid Parra A, Pastor Sempere C (eds) (2021) Guia de Criptoactivos MICA. Thomson Reuters ARANZADI, Spain

Maume P (2023) The regulation on markets in crypto-assets (MiCAR): landmark codification, or first step of many, or both? ECFR:243–275

Narain A, Moretti M (2022) Regulating crypto. The right rules could provide a safe space for innovation. In: Finance Dev, pp 18–19

Ortos Ch (2021) The Commission's 2020 Proposal for a markets in crypto-assets regulation ('MICAR'): a brief introductory overview. https://ssrn.com/abstract=3842824. Accessed 20 May 2024

Paracampo MT (ed) (2021a) FinTech e la Strategia per il mercato unico tecnologico dei servizi finanziari, in FINTECH. Introduzione ai profili giuridici di un mercato unico tecnologico dei servizi finanziari, vol. I, 2nd edn. Giappichelli, Torino, Italy, pp 1–41

Paracampo MT (2021b) Marco normativo armonizado sobre los proveedores de servicios de criptoactivos, reglas de comportamiento destinadas a proteger al cliente y requisitos organizativos. In: Madrid Parra A, Pastor Sempere C (eds) Guia de Criptoactivos MICA. Thomson Reuters ARANZADI, Spain, pp 261–279

Paracampo MT (2022a) La consulenza su cripto-attività nella proposta di regolamento europeo MICA tra presunte equivalenze e distonie normative con Mifid 2. In: Dir. banca e merc. fin., I, pp 229–261

Paracampo MT (2022b) Los proveedores de servicios de criptoactivos entre antiguos y nuevos players. In: Pastor Sempere C (ed) Dinero Digital y Gobernanza TIC en la UE. Thomson Reuters ARANZADI, Spain, pp 149–172

Paracampo MT (2023) I prestatori di servizi per le cripto-attività. Tra mifidizzazione della MICA e tokenizzazione della Mifid, Giappichelli, Torino, Italy

Pastor Sempere C (ed) (2022) Dinero Digital y Gobernanza TIC en la UE. Thomson Reuters ARANZADI, Spain

Ross V (2023a) Digital finance and capital markets – securing the frontier. Speech at Consob Conference on "The New Frontiers of Digital Finance", Rome, 10 March 2023. https://www.esma.europa.eu/document/verena-ross-speechconsob-conference-new-frontiers-digital-finance-10-march-2023. Accessed 20 May 2024

Ross V (2023b) Innovation with protection: the next steps on the MiCA journey, Speech at Malta FSA Forum on MICA, Malta, 16 November 2023. https://www.esma.europa.eu/sites/default/files/2023-11/ESMA75-840896669-368_Verena_Ross__speech_at_Malta_FSA_Forum_MiCA.pdf. Accessed 20 May 2024

Zetzsche DA, Buckley R, Arner D, Van Ek M (2023) Remaining regulatory challenges in digital finance and crypto-assets after MiCA, committee on economic and monetary affairs (ECON), Paper No. 23-27. https://ssrn.com/abstract=4487516. Accessed 20 May 2024

Lener R (2023) Cripto-attività e criptovalute alla luce degli ultimi orientamenti comunitari. In: Giur. Comm., I, pp 376-388

Crypto-Asset White Papers and Marketing Communications Post the MiCA Regulation

María-Teresa Otero Cobos

Abstract This paper comprehensively analyses the regulatory framework applicable to disclosure and transparency tools used in promoting crypto assets, particularly in the context of the MiCA Regulation. The paper focuses on the information a crypto-asset white paper should contain and all relevant details about marketing communications, such as advertising messages and marketing material. In commercial communications, the work delves into Directive (EU) 2019/1024 and Regulation (EU) No. 596/2014 to examine the rules and guidelines related to the content of crypto-asset advertising posted by professional social media profiles. This will highlight how the authorities are working to prevent the publication of false, misleading, or incomplete information on these issues.

1 Introduction

This work undertakes a comprehensive analysis of how disclosure and transparency instruments are addressed after the adoption of MiCA. It meticulously studies the needs and problems that still need to be addressed by the competent authorities in the cryptocurrency market.

MiCA's objectives within the transmission of information and advertisement aim to protect consumers and investors and ensure transparency in the treatment of information on unregulated crypto assets. The main aim is to build confidence in

This paper expands and updates the text of a lecture delivered at the III International Congress entitled "Present and future of crypto-assets regulation in the European Union," held at the University of Alicante (Spain) on December 13, 14, and 15, 2023. This work is funded within the framework of: Proyecto CIPROM/2022/26 "Presente y futuro de la regulación de los Criptoactivos en la UE [Legalcripto]". Proyecto Prometeo CIPROM/2022/26, grupos de investigación de excelencia, de la Generalitat Valenciana (P.I. Carmen Pastor).

M.-T. O. Cobos (✉)
Universidad de Málaga, Facultad de Derecho, Málaga, Spain
e-mail: mayteotero@uma.es

C. Pastor Sempere (ed.), *Governance and Control of Data and Digital Economy in the European Single Market*, Law, Governance and Technology Series 71,
https://doi.org/10.1007/978-3-031-74889-9_12

the market and prevent the risks to which retail investors are exposed, given that investment in crypto assets is increasing. These risks are due to the lack of information on the losses this type of product may incur, their volatility, and their scarce or incipient regulation. The aim is to stop the deception, manipulation, or confusion that the information disseminated may cause among the public.

One key objective of the MiCA Regulation is to facilitate the use of and entry into digital financial services and the crypto-asset market for the public. By ensuring the market is accessible and understandable, the regulation aims to stimulate its growth and development.

With both objectives in mind, we will analyse the information and advertising requirements that MiCA establishes for crypto-asset marketing.

2 Disclosure and Transparency Tools: Whitepaper

A crypto-assets white paper, as we have already had the opportunity to analyse when we studied the MiCA Regulation proposal,[1] is the mechanism chosen to disclose the information relating to each crypto asset regulated by MiCA. In this way, a specific homogeneous and mandatory content is established for the whole of the EU. In addition, the treatment of the information in the white paper and how it is published and disseminated is also included. The scope and description of the elements that make up the information that must be included in the white paper are detailed in Annexes I to III of MiCA under the classification of each crypto asset in the standard itself.

As detailed subsequently, there is a clear distinction between common content for all categories of crypto-assets and specific content according to the characteristics and functions of each type of crypto-asset and the risks involved.

2.1 Common Content for All Crypto Assets Regulated in MiCA

One of the most important issues regarding the common content is identifying the persons responsible for preparing and publishing the white paper. The scope extends to offerors, issuers, and persons seeking admission to trading. When a different person prepares this informative document, their identity and data must be disclosed.

In addition to these data, the whitepaper must contain information on the project, the offer to the public of crypto-assets or about their admission to trading, characteristics of the crypto-asset, rights and obligations attached to it, the underlying technology used, risks involved, and a piece of information that the MiCA proposal

[1] Otero (2021), pp. 189–204.

did not contain, i.e., information on the main effects of cryptocurrency issuance on the environment.

This last requirement is imposed because of the technology's impact on the climate and environment and the mechanisms used for validating transactions in the crypto-asset market, as stated in the opening section [Whereas: (7)], related to issuing and processing crypto assets is associated with high energy consumption, which causes obvious damage to the environment.[2]

This situation has caused an intervention to motivate a shift in blockchain consensus protocols and promote energy efficiency to mitigate environmental damage. Issuers and offerors should publish the effect and harm that the issuance and trading of crypto assets can have on the environment.[3]

The risks inherent in each crypto asset mean the white paper includes certain warnings in its content. Among others, no reference may be made to the future value of the crypto-asset, and express reference must be made to the fact that investor compensation schemes or deposit guarantee schemes do not cover the crypto-asset. In addition, there must be a statement from the management body of the obliged entity that the white paper complies with the requirements and that the information is fair, clear, and not misleading, with no omissions.

The white paper should include a summary that contains sufficient information to enable the recipient to make an informed decision. It is necessary to clarify that this informed decision should not be reached by the summary alone but by reading and viewing the entire whitepaper. In addition, the regulation states that the summary should be read as an introduction, as a preliminary to reading the white paper. The summary text should constantly refer to the whitepaper and emphasise that it is neither a financial instrument nor a prospectus.

Other aspects to be considered include the date of notification to the competent authority and a table of contents. The drafting must be in one of the official languages of the Member State of origin or host Member State of the obliged person or addressees.

Concerning the formal requirements, the information must be fair, clear, and not misleading. These are the three characteristics of any communication or information about the crypto asset. In addition, the text contained in the white paper must be concise and understandable. These requirements are aimed at preventing disclosure from being a burdening business, hence the obligation to adhere exclusively to the provisions of MiCA.

The regulation states that the white paper must be available in a machine-readable format. The Law does not contain any definition of this type of format. If we pay attention to Directive (EU) 2019/1024 of the European Parliament and of the

[2]For more on this topic, v. Herrero (2023), pp. 99–102; y Mohsin (2021), pp. 1–4. https://doi.org/10.2139/ssrn.3846774.

[3]About environmental aspects of crypto, see Badea and Mungiu-Pupăzan (2021), pp. 48091–48104. https://doi.org/10.1109/ACCESS.2021.3068636; and also, Corbet and Yarovaya (2020), p. 149.

Council of 20 June 2019 on open data and the re-use of public sector information, a document should be considered to be in a machine-readable format if it is in a file format that is structured in such a way that software applications can easily identify, recognise and extract specific data from it. Documents encoded in a file format that limits automatic processing because the data cannot, or cannot easily, be extracted from them should not be considered to be in a machine-readable format (Whereas 35).

The white paper must be published on the obliged entity's website reasonably in advance and be publicly accessible, accessible to any investor, and available on the European Single Access Point (ESAP).[4]

The intention to standardise the content of the white paper has become so important that the European Securities and Markets Authority (ESMA) has until 30 June 2024 to develop standards to establish forms and templates for white papers. The aim is for the information in the white paper to be strictly as required in MiCA so that, if additional information is to be included, it must be included in a different document, which may also be considered a marketing communication. In this regard, it should be noted that the white paper may not contain any commercial information.

For this purpose, ESMA launched a second Consultation on the Technical Standards specifying certain requirements of Markets in Crypto Assets Regulation (MiCA).[5] Also, ESMA made available a Proof of Concept to illustrate the proposed format.[6] This consultation was open from October to December 2023, and we have accessed consultations with stakeholders. Among other things, it is proposed that there should be a single form for all three categories of crypto-assets, that the number of free text fields should be limited, and that there should be more structured or auto-fillable fields.

Finally, Article 109 obligates ESMA to keep a register of crypto-asset white papers relating to crypto-assets other than asset-referenced and e-money tokens. Public access shall be provided on ESMA's website, and the register shall contain all versions of the white papers with their amendments. Obsolete versions shall be in a separate and distinguishable file from those in force.

Regarding the liability regime, persons obliged to develop a white paper are liable for any omissions or deception or if the information is not complete, impartial, or clear. In these cases, the burden of proof lies with the crypto-asset holder, who must

[4]The Council has recently adopted the regulation (EU) 2023/2859 of the European Parliament and of the Council of 13 December 2023, establishing a European single access point providing centralised access to publicly available information relevant to financial services, capital markets and sustainability. The ESAP should provide the public with easy, centralised access to information about entities and their products that is made public and relevant to financial services, capital markets, sustainability and diversity, but should exclude marketing information. It is expected to be available in 2027.

[5]Second Consultation Paper is available at: https://www.esma.europa.eu/sites/default/files/2023-10/ESMA75-453128700-438_MiCA_Consultation_Paper_2nd_package.pdf.

[6]The form, formats and templates for the crypto-asset whitepaper are available at: https://www.esma.europa.eu/document/mica-white-papers-poc.

prove that the content of the white paper influenced the purchase decision. The competent authorities, however, reserve the right to require information and documentation from crypto-asset issuers or request they include additional information where necessary. In addition, a sanctioning regime is provided for when the white paper does not contain the required information (Art. 94.1 i) or has not been notified, where there is an obligation to do so (Art. 94.1 u).

2.2 *Specific Content for Each Crypto Asset Regulated in MiCA*

2.2.1 Crypto-Assets Other Than Asset-Referenced Tokens and e-Money Tokens

The obligation to draw up a white paper in this category of crypto asset is limited to those entities that meet the requirements set out in Article 4.1 of the Regulation. Due to the second paragraph of the aforementioned provision, the following will be expressly excluded from this obligation, as they are outside the scope of application of MiCA: offers to fewer than 150 natural or legal persons per Member State when over twelve months; the total consideration of the public offer of a crypto-asset in the Union does not exceed 1,000,000 euros or the equivalent amount in another official currency or crypto assets; and, lastly, when the offer of a crypto-asset addressed solely to qualified investors where the crypto-asset can only be held by such qualified investors.

Moreover, the obligation to draw up a white paper does not arise when the crypto-asset is offered for free, is automatically created as a reward for the maintenance of the distributed ledger or the validation of transactions, the offer concerns a utility token providing access to a good or service that exists or is in operation and when the holder of the crypto-asset has the right to use it only in exchange for goods and services in a limited network of merchants with contractual arrangements with the offeror.

As a result of the less strict regime for this cryptocurrency,[7] unlike the other two regulated by the standard, that the white paper is subject only to a notification regime to the competent authority.[8] For this reason, the white paper must include a disclaimer with the following statement: "This crypto-asset white paper has not been approved by any competent authority in any Member State of the European Union. The offeror of the crypto-asset is solely responsible for the content of this crypto-asset white paper". It must also include an express reference to the investor's right to withdraw from the transaction under Article 13.

[7] See Novella (2021).

[8] As point out Novella González del Castillo (2021), ibid., in such cases the authorisation is implicit in the emission itself, unless otherwise indicated by the competent authority.

Finally, the text of the white paper should expressly mention that the crypto asset may lose value, may not always be tradable and may not be liquid.[9]

2.2.2 Asset-Referenced Tokens (ART)

Asset-referenced tokens are subject to a prior authorisation regime set out in Article 18 of the Regulation. The information and documentation submitted with the application must include the white paper following the content and form regulated in Article 19, which we have already referred to when talking about the elements common to all crypto assets.

In this case, the content must include a statement of truthfulness stating that the crypto-asset white paper "complies with this Title and that, to the best of the knowledge of the management body, the information presented in the crypto-asset white paper is fair, clear and not misleading and the crypto-asset white paper makes no omission likely to affect its import".

In addition to the general information, mention should be made about the complaints-handling procedure and the rights and conditions for redemption in this case. The right of redemption is a right granted to the holder of an ART crypto-asset over the issuer of the crypto-asset. To exercise this right, the holder must know the conditions, that is, which issuer has been granted this right and what conditions, mechanisms, and procedures must be met for it to be exercised.

2.2.3 E-money Tokens (EMT)

The issuance of this category of crypto asset also requires prior notification to the competent authority.

Regarding the white paper's specific content, there is an obligation to include a liability clause with the following text: "The crypto-asset white paper has not been approved by any competent authority in any Member State of the European Union. The issuer of the crypto-asset is solely responsible for the content of this crypto-asset white paper".

In addition, the recognition of a right of redemption and the conditions for its exercise must be reflected.

[9] About crypto-assets risks, for further analysis Fernández (2021), pp. 451–466; Del Cid (2020), pp. 477–509; Tapia (2021), p. 28; Nguyen and Maine (2024). https://doi.org/10.2139/ssrn.4431079; Arsi et al. (2021), pp. 121–145.

3 Marketing Communications

The MiCA Regulation distinguishes between marketing communications and other types of information that allow the promotion of crypto assets. It pays special attention to the content of this type of promotion and establishes the obligation to notify competent authorities. MiCA imposes a prior notification regime but prohibits competent authorities from establishing a prior authorisation system.

Marketing communications must contain information consistent with the white paper and may not be disseminated before publication. They must include the reference and location of the white paper and the issuer's contact details. Of course, they must also be fair, clear, and not misleading.[10]

Finally, as with any advertising, it must be identifiable as such. This requirement is consistent with the rules on advertising and unfair commercial practices. When drafting commercial communications, the commercial purpose must be disclosed to avoid incurring a misleading omission by hiding relevant information from the investor. This warning introduced by the regulation is merely a reminder of the application in this area of Directive 2005/29/EC of the European Parliament and of the Council of 11 May 2005 concerning unfair business-to-consumer commercial practices in the internal market. Article 7 of the 2005 Directive qualifies as an unfair practice, withholding unclear, unintelligible, ambiguous information likely to influence consumer behaviour.

4 Social Media Platforms

Social media platforms have gained prominence in advertising in general and in promoting investment products such as crypto assets. Most crypto-asset business strategies focus on social media.[11] A recent ESMA study[12] reveals the influence of social media platforms on crypto assets. Social media platforms are used extensively and in a growing way by investors these days; they can share information, opinions, and views in a very large landscape in real time. One of the main takeaways from the study is that advice extracted from social media is not appropriate for retail investors to predict and plan investment strategies. The risk exists whereby investors excessively rely on information spreading virally on social media that is unrelated to

[10]Fruther information about this subject can be found at Blanco (2022), pp. 247–262.

[11]According to the English Financial Conduct Authority in the fourth quarter of 2022, 69% of the financial promotions reported or approved by authorised companies that were modified or withdrawn following their intervention were related to promotions on websites or social media.

[12]ESMA webinar: Social media influence on financial markets and crypto-assets trading, 25 April 2024, available at: https://www.esma.europa.eu/sites/default/files/2024-04/Webinar_socialmedia_crypto.pdf.

fundamentals. There is an increasing exposure to the risk of losses, especially for investors with lower financial knowledge and resources.

The consolidated text of MiCA echoed this situation, which ESMA has researched and introduced some modifications to the initial proposal. In particular, the opening section [Whereas, (24) and (96)] should be noted. The first (24) highlights, within the framework of the application of the Regulation, advertising communications, advertising messages and advertising material, including through new channels such as social media platforms. The second (96) deals with enhancing legal certainty for crypto-asset market participants. It refers to using social media as an information dissemination mechanism that may distort the proper functioning of the crypto-asset market.

Social media is just another advertising channel. It was not necessary to allude to them expressly; however, the legislator has considered it appropriate to highlight them given their relevance in recent years, their indisputable role in advertising activity, and the increased use of social media by consumers to obtain information on financial products.

There are two main advertising resources used on social media. On the one hand, the reservation of advertising space on social media through contracting advertisements. These adverts appear in user feeds according to their tastes and the activity they carry out on the network, driven by algorithmic data processing. This type of advertising does not differ from traditional advertising beyond the advantages of new technologies targeting the user profile. It is normally clearly identified as an 'advertisement' without prejudice to the fact that these practices may merit some legal reproach.[13]

On the other hand, another type of advertisement that stands out on social media platforms is the one disseminated by its users. These users must meet certain specific characteristics to be able to define the activity they carry out as advertising. We are referring to influencers, users who have become quite prominent in the crypto-asset advertising area in recent years, among other sectors. An influencer,[14] is understood as a professional social media user to be engaged in distributing online content in exchange for remuneration. The European Commission has defined the influencer as anyone who makes money through creating social media content.[15]

Many of these influencers are active on one or more social media (Facebook, Instagram, YouTube, X or Twitch, among others). Most of them focus the content

[13] About this question it is interesting the analysis carries out by De Vivero (2023), p. 76.

[14] Tato (2019), p. 2, describes them as a "opinion leaders" who, without being famous or enjoying a reputation or professional prestige in a specific field of activity, have a large number of followers on social media networks, who follow the content they generate. Another definition that we believe aptly and describes this type of user is the one used by the Advertising Standards Authority. The organism describes an influencer as anyone who has been paid by a brand to advertise a product on their own social media, because of their social media influence.

[15] You can find this information on Influencer Legal Hub runs by European Commission, available here: https://commission.europa.eu/live-work-travel-eu/consumer-rights-and-complaints/influencer-legal-hub_en.

they disseminate through these channels on a specific area, such as lifestyle, sport, cooking, etc. Within this thematic variety, some of them have specialised in the field of finance, which is why they have been called fin-fluencers. Specifically, their profiles provide information on savings and financial products, giving opinions on the stock market or making investment recommendations.

The growing popularity of these users among consumers has led to the emergence of movements to regulate influencer marketing. In particular, the European Consumer Organisation (BEUC) has brought together several recommendations,[16] ranging from amending the Unfair Commercial Practices Directive Annex (Points 11 and 28 of the UCPD) to introduce the concept of "user-generated content" to asking the European Commission to establish EU wide 'disclosure standards' to determine "how", "how much" and "when" disclosure duties should be done by influencers (unique wording to be used, momentum, in-video insert, etc.). In financial markets, the BEUC calls for a ban on influencers doing marketing campaigns about this product type. The European Consumer Organisation gives the example of the French Loi n° 2023-451 du 9 Jun 2023 visant à encadrer lìnfluencer commercial et à lutter contre les dérives des influenceurs sur les r´seaux sociaux. The French legislation prohibits promoting certain financial products and services, i.e., complex financial products and products with unknown risk or risk greater than the initial capital, crypto and non-fungible Tokens (NFT) unless approved by the competent French authorities.

MiCA is silent on this growing phenomenon, but it takes it into account. This is illustrated by the Commission's obligation to include in the report about the implementation of the Regulation, which it will submit to the European Parliament, accompanied by a legislative proposal of an assessment of fraudulent marketing communications and scams involving crypto assets occurring through social media networks (Art. 140.2 letter n).

In addition, according to Article 141, the annual report prepared by ESMA on market developments shall mention the number of complaints received by crypto-asset service providers, issuers, and competent authorities regarding false and misleading information contained in crypto-asset white papers or marketing communications, including via social media platforms.

These obligations make it clear that it is likely that a regulatory framework regulating the crypto-asset advertising content published by influencers could be adopted in the coming years. If we look at the steps being taken by financial market regulators in the Member States and other neighbouring countries, we can presage that in the short to medium term; a European regulation will be drawn up to homogenise these topics.

Spain stands out among the Member States regulating this type of advertising. Through Circular 1/2022, of 10 January 2022, of the Spanish National Securities

[16] From influence to responsibility, https://www.beuc.eu/sites/default/files/publications/BEUC-X-2023-093_From_influence_to_responsibility_Time_to_regulate_influencer-marketing.pdf.

Market Commission (NSMC) on crypto-asset advertising,[17] NSMC regulates commercial or promoted crypto-asset advertising. It applies to any natural or legal person who advertises crypto assets on its initiative or on behalf of third parties.

The obligations regulated by the Circular are set out in Annex I. Among them, as far as we are concerned, we highlight the obligation of prior notification in certain cases, specifically in the case of mass campaigns. The parameters that make it possible to identify when a campaign is massive are the number of people to whom it is addressed. In the case of social media, the number of 100,000 people is set, which must be calculated by checking the highest value between the estimated number of users of the advertising campaign and the number of followers of the accounts used.

Concerning neighbouring countries, we must highlight the case of the United Kingdom. The Financial Conduct Authority (FCA),[18] recently published the "Finalised guidance on financial promotions on social media".[19] This guide contains a specific section on influencers and social media. It defines an influencer, the responsibility of providers of financial promotions on social media, and whether any underlying commercial interest in the promotion could mean that the advertising is subject to the restrictions in section 21 of the Financial Services and Markets Act 2000. In this sense, that actuation could be punished by up to 2 years imprisonment.

However, before, the FCA published in November 2023 the "Finalised non-handbook guidance on Crypto-asset Financial Promotions."[20] This guidance, especially, sets out guidelines applicable to influencers. The main obligation is to disclose any relevant commercial relationships, such as if they have been paid or commissioned to promote a crypto-asset or crypto-asset service. It also encourages firms to ensure that promotions provide a balanced view of the benefits and risks and communicate information to help consumers make effective, well-informed decisions.[21] This regulation applies to qualifying crypto assets.[22]

The authorities have also warned about investment recommendations. Influencers' promotional activity of crypto assets is becoming even more important,

[17] For more details about the Circular, see Blanco (2022), pp. 247–262; Tapia (2022), pp. 381–392; Tato (2022), p. 324; Llopis (2022), pp. 219–240; Otero (2022), pp. 771–800.

[18] From the 8 October 2023 the Asa is not the organism responsible of the regulation of ads for 'qualifying cryptoassets': https://www.asa.org.uk/advice-online/financial-products-and-services-cryptoassets.html#Regulation%20of%20cryptoassets.

[19] You can find the complete guidance in this link: https://www.fca.org.uk/publication/finalised-guidance/fg24-1.pdf.

[20] Following this link to acceded to complete document: https://www.fca.org.uk/publication/finalised-guidance/fg23-3.pdf.

[21] It is interesting to read researches carried out by Tinworth and Spence (2023), p. 521; Jennings-Mres et al. (2022), p. 351.

[22] It means any crypto-asset which is fungible and transferable.

and it is sometimes difficult to differentiate between a promotional action and a recommendation.[23]

There are two criteria for any investment recommendation. On the one hand, subjective, the social media user who disseminates investment recommendations must be a professional, expert,[24] or at least be knowledgeable about the subject; on the other hand, they should not receive any payment for promoting such information objectively.

In recent years, professional social media users have increased the publication of this content. Some of them have tried to evade any responsibility by including a warning in their videos or space on their profile, generally not very visible, where they inform that the opinions and comments expressed should not be considered investment advice. ESMA[25] warned about the proliferation of this investment recommendation on social media, recalling that they must respect a specific legal regime.[26]

Investment recommendations are regulated by Regulation (EU) No 596/2014 of the European Parliament and of the Council of 16 April 2014 on market abuse (market abuse regulation) and repealing Directive 2003/6/EC of the European Parliament and of the Council and Commission Directives 2003/124/EC, 2003/125/EC and 2004/72/EC (MAR). The law defines recommendations as "information

[23] According to a report commissioned by the Financial Conduct Authority (FCA) in the UK, young investors are particularly likely to turn to more modern media for investment advice, tips and news. They are generally influenced by how often they hear about certain opportunities or how persuasive the influencers are in conveying the message. The paper "Understanding self-directed investors", June 2021, is available at: https://www.fca.org.uk/publication/research/understanding-self-directed-investors.pdf.

Following the report presented in November 2022 by XTB on 'How do young Spaniards invest' available at: https://es.xtb.com/hubfs/2022%20-%20Encuesta%20PR/ENCUESTA_2022_xtb.pdf?hsCtaTracking=b16efd99-66cb-4f35-8791-e6064c94ebb2%7C997df514-e2cc-40f1-b21e-4fd9ac533f9f, the product in which young people invest the most is cryptocurrencies, with at least 74 per cent of those surveyed having invested at some point. Within the information channels, social media are used by 36.4 percent, with YouTube and Instagram standing out among them. And specifically, in 27.8 per cent of cases, influencers are a source of investment ideas.

[24] According to Commission Delegates regulation (EU) 2016/958 of 9 March 2016 supplementing Regulation (EU) No 506/2014 of the European Parliament and of the Council with regard to regulatory technical standards for the technical arrangements for objective presentation of investment recommendations or other information recommending or suggesting an investment strategy and for disclosure of particular interests or indications of conflicts of interest, expert means each person who repeatedly proposes investment decisions in respect of financial instruments and who presents himself as having financial expertise or experience; or puts forward his recommendation in such a way that other persons would reasonably believe he has financial expertise or experience.

[25] ESMA Public Statement on investment recommendations made on social media, 28th October 2021, available at: https://www.esma.europa.eu/sites/default/files/library/esma70-154-2780_esmas_statement_on_investment_recommendations_on_social_media.pdf.

[26] In Spain, NSMC reported that it had supervised around fifty influencers and detected that some of them could be issuing investment recommendations outside the regulations. This information is disclosed in a press release published by the CNMV on 24 October 2022 available at: https://www.cnmv.es/webservices/verdocumento/ver?t=%7b79c763fe-1303-45ed-b0d5-7c8569c0d649%7d.

recommending or suggesting an investment strategy, explicitly or implicitly, concerning one or several financial instruments or the issuers, including any opinion as to the present or future value or price of such instruments, intended for distribution channels or for the public."[27]

This activity is implemented by Delegated Regulation (EU) 2016/958. The regulation distinguishes between the dissemination of recommendations prepared by the person disseminating them (i.e., independent analysts, investment firms, credit institutions, etc.) and persons whose main business activity is to produce recommendations. We consider that, in most cases, influencers will be part of the latter group and do not fall within the scope of the Regulation. However, those that belong to the former category must comply with the obligations in Articles 8 and 9 of the Delegated Regulation (EU) 2016/958. These include clear and visible identification of the person disseminating the recommendation, potential conflicts of interest and the date and time when the recommendation is first communicated. When a recommendation summary is circulated, it should be clear and identified, and the original recommendation and the person(s) who prepared it should be identified.

To clarify the meaning and application of the MAR to posting investment recommendations on social media, ESMA recently published a statement,[28] warning about the risks of market manipulation when posting on social media. ESMA warns of the obligations depending on the category to which an investment recommender belongs, whether professional or not. However, certain duties always apply to anyone issuing investment recommendations, regardless of their MAR category. These duties include the following: identification of the producers of the investment recommendation (name and the job title of all the natural persons involved in the production of the recommendation); date and time of the recommendation; ensuring the objective presentation of investment recommendations—facts clearly distinguished from interpretations, estimates and opinions—; ensuring that all sources of information are reliable and, where in doubt, clearly indicate so; disclosure of any conflicts of interest in a clear way and placed within the recommendation (independently of the format) so investors would reasonably take notice of it. When recommendations are voiced via different social media channels, each must include a disclosure of interests or conflicts of interest.

Finally, one of the problems faced in monitoring the investment recommendations published by fin-fluencers is that not all of them are aimed at informing on financial instruments. Therefore, the above-mentioned regulation can only be applied to crypto assets that are financial instruments. The subjective scope of application of the Market Abuse Regulation in Art. 2 concerning Art. 3.1.1) refers

[27] Art. 3.1.35 MAR.

[28] Warning For people posting Investment Recommendation on social media, ESMA74-1103241886-912, 6 Febraury 2024, available at: https://www.esma.europa.eu/sites/default/files/2024-02/ESMA74-1103241886-912_Warnings_on_Social_Media_and_Investment_Recommendations.pdf.

to Annex I Section C of Directive 2014/65/EU. The regulation is clear enough; it does not cover crypto assets that cannot be considered financial instruments.

At this point, supervisory authorities should consider—as they have done when defining the requirements for advertising activity for investment crypto assets, which are not financial instruments—the development of guidelines and standards that set out the criteria to be considered for the dissemination of investment recommendations in social media by experts.

5 Conclusions

Analysing the regulatory framework applicable to disclosure and transparency tools used in promoting crypto assets with the adoption of the MiCA Regulation can yield five conclusions.

1. Advertising and information delivery are most important for marketing a product, especially in the financial market. In the crypto-asset market, the consumer is exposed to significant risks attracted by periods of upside, lack of information about losses, volatility of assets and poor regulation. Sufficient information must, therefore, be made available to facilitate recourse and access to digital financial services and the crypto-asset market for the public.
2. The crypto-asset white paper is a disclosure and transparency tool for trading these products. As established by MiCA, it is an obligation to promote certain crypto assets. It has common content and special content for each type of crypto asset. ESMA and EBA are currently working on draft technical standards to regulate the format of these documents. These technical standards must not contain free fields but structured fields in the file.
3. Parties required to prepare the white paper shall be liable for any omissions, misleading or incomplete information, unbiased or unclear information. The onus is on the crypto-asset owner, who, in the event of a claim, would need to prove that the misleading content of the white paper influenced their purchase decision. Competent authorities reserve the right to require information and documentation from issuers of crypto-assets or for issuers to include additional information in White Papers where necessary.
4. Marketing communications must comply with MiCA's requirements. Social media platforms are the most widely used channel to promote crypto assets. Business strategies focus on this kind of platform because of the possibility of reaching many users. The format used means it is not always possible to detect that we are dealing with crypto-asset advertising. On many occasions, they can be confused with investment recommendations. This situation alerts us to ensure that communications are identifiable and the content is fair, clear and not misleading.
5. The MiCA regulation is a good foundation, but it is expected that Member State regulations will eventually need to develop rules and guidelines for dealing with crypto-asset promotion. Also, it is crucial to pay attention to investment

recommendations made by influencers on social media and the need for these recommendations to be regulated. Concerning this, it is important to be mindful that Europe only has one regulation pertaining to investment recommendations in the Market Abuse Regulation; however, it does not apply to crypto assets.

References

Arsi S, Ben Khelifa S, Ghabri Y, Mzoughi H (2021) Cryptocurrencies: key risks and challenges. In: Goutte S, Guesmi K, Saadi S (eds) Cryptofinance. A new currency for a new economy. World Scientific, pp 121–145

Badea L, Mungiu-Pupăzan MC (2021) The economic and environmental impact of Bitcoin. IEEE Access 9:48091–48104. https://doi.org/10.1109/ACCESS.2021.3068636

Blanco MJ (2022) La publicidad de criptoactivos. In: Martínez A, Pastor C (eds) Dinero digital y gobernanza TIC en la UE. Aranzadi, Cizur Menor, pp 247–262

Corbet S, Yarovaya L (2020) The environmental effects of cryptocurrencies. In: Corbet S, Urquhart A, Yarovaya L (eds) Cryptocurrency and Blockchain technology. De Gruyter, Berlin

De Vivero C (2023) Publicidad ilícita por vía electrónica como acto de competencia desleal: publicidad personalizada en Instagram. Actas de Derecho Industrial y Derechos de Autor 43: 57–80

Del Cid JM (2020) Los riesgos de fraude, blanqueo de capitales y financiación terrorista relacionados con las monedas virtuales y los criptoactivos. In: Sánchez I, Hinojosa M (eds) Blockchain: Impacto en los sistemas financieros, notarial, registral y judicial. Thomson Reuters Aranzadi, Cizur Menor, pp 477–509

Fernández J (2021) Riesgos emergentes en los criptoactivos. Revista de derecho bancario y bursátil 164:451–466

Herrero R (2023) Sostenibilidad: un reto para los criptoactivos. In: Bataller J, Boquera J et al (eds) Libro de actas del congreso Internacional Sostenibilidad y Derecho del Sistema Financiero. Revista de Derecho del Sistema Financiero, Valencia, pp 99–102

Jennings-Mres JC, Rees QCG et al (2022) Promotion of cryptoassets to UK consumers will be regulated by the UK financial conduct authority. Banking Law J 139:351

Llopis A (2022) Algunas cuestiones de interés en la nueva circular 1/2022 de publicidad sobre criptoactivos. Revista de Derecho del sistema financiero 4:219–240

Mohsin K (2021) Cryptocurrency & Its Impact on Environment. Int J Cryp Curr Res 1:1–4. https://doi.org/10.2139/ssrn.3846774

Nguyen X, Maine JA (2024) Crypto losses. Univ Ill Law Rev. https://doi.org/10.2139/ssrn.4431079

Novella E (2021) El futuro Reglamento europeo para un mercado de criptoactivos (Propuesta MiCA). In: Barrio M (ed) Criptoactivos. Retos y desafíos normativos. La Ley, Madrid

Otero MT (2021) Régimen de información y transparencia: el libro blanco de criptoactivos. In: Madrid A, Pastor C (eds) Guía de criptoactivos MiCA. Aranzadi, Cizur Menor, pp 189–204

Otero MT (2022) Algunas consideraciones acerca del nuevo régimen de la publicidad sobre criptoactivos. In: Madrid A, Alvarado L (eds) Derecho digital y nuevas tecnologías. Aranzadi, Cizur Menor, pp 771–800

Tapia AJ (2021) Desafíos en la regulación y supervisión de los criptoactivos en la Unión europea y en España. Revista de derecho del mercado de valores 28

Tapia AJ (2022) La circular 1/2022 de la CNMV sobre la publicidad de criptoactivos. Criptoactivos presentados como objeto de inversión. Revista de derecho bancario y bursátil 165:381–392

Tato A (2019) Aspectos jurídicos de la publicidad a través de líderes de opinión en redes sociales ("influencers"). Revista de Derecho mercantil 311
Tato A (2022) Régimen jurídico de la publicidad de criptoactivos presentados como objeto de inversión. Revista de derecho mercantil 324
Tinworth J, Spence J (2023) Financial promotion of crypto assets. Banking Law J 140:521

Regulating Market Abuse in Crypto Assets

Marina Echebarría Sáenz

Abstract Articles 86 to 92 of MiCA promote a simplified regime to control unlawful disclosure, insider dealing and possible manipulation or market abuses in issuing and trading crypto assets. The tendency to assimilate the regulation with the regulatory background of the ordinary financial market is hardly avoidable. However, the most coherent option is probably to use these references as an ex-post mechanism and not as ex-ante requirements when the ESMA guidelines don't declare analogous application of Market Abuse Regulations.

1 Introduction

The MiCA regulation of crypto markets, Regulation (EU) 2023/1114 of the European Parliament and of the Council of 31 May 2023 on markets in crypto assets, and amending Regulations (EU) No. 1093/2010 and (EU) No 1095/2010 and Directives 2013/36/EU and (EU) 2019/1937, lays down the regulations regarding transparency, supervision, protection of holders and clients of crypto-assets service providers and measures to prevent insider dealing, unlawful disclosure of inside information and market manipulation related to crypto assets, to assure the integrity of crypto markets (art. 1.2 R. 2023/1114). The regulation's minimal intervention

This paper expands and updates the text of a lecture delivered at the III International Congress entitled "Present and future of crypto-assets regulation in the European Union," held at the University of Alicante (Spain) on December 13, 14, and 15, 2023. This work is funded within the framework of: Proyecto CIPROM/2022/26 "Presente y futuro de la regulación de los Criptoactivos en la UE [Legalcripto]". Proyecto Prometeo CIPROM/2022/26, grupos de investigación de excelencia, de la Generalitat Valenciana (P.I. Carmen Pastor).

M. Echebarría Sáenz (✉)
Department of Commercial Law, Valladolid University (Spain), Valladolid, Spain
e-mail: Marina.echebarria@uva.es

C. Pastor Sempere (ed.), *Governance and Control of Data and Digital Economy in the European Single Market*, Law, Governance and Technology Series 71,
https://doi.org/10.1007/978-3-031-74889-9_13

approach is a response to the delicate nature of an emerging market.[1] The European legislator has opted for a simplified regime for abuse control and governance of crypto operators, compared to their counterparts in the financial market. This decision raises intriguing questions: What is the limit of the analogical application of financial regulations? What role will other supervisory regulations, such as national authorities, play in this context?

Articles 86 to 92, title VI of the MiCA regulation, apply the basic market abuse regulations to the incipient regime for issuing and trading crypto assets, which is intended to become a parallel or "side market." The rules aim to guarantee the integrity of the Union's emerging crypto-asset market and offer guarantees and security to potential investors (art. 1.2).[2]

The rule extends its mandate to any act (and persons) concerning crypto assets admitted to trading or requesting admission, regardless of whether such transaction, order or behaviour takes place in a trading platform or not, in the EU or a third country (art.86), which implies a general submission of any related natural or legal person, including custodians or depositories, technical guarantors of negotiation mechanisms, members of supervisory committees, etc.

MiCA in art. 86 to 92, largely reproduces a simplified regulation of the Market Abuse Regulation (MAR); Regulation (EU) No. 596/2014 of the European Parliament and of the Council, modified by R. 2019/2115,[3] and its ESMA Guidelines.[4] However, issuers of crypto assets and crypto-asset service providers are often SMEs, so in line with the Commission Communication of 25 June 2008 on the European Small Business Initiative Business Act and following the indications of the report on strategy for digital finance, it would probably be disproportionate to apply all the provisions of R. 596/2014 mimetically and its multiple implementing regulations. MiCA follows a system similar to the control established for Multilateral Trading Systems (MTSs), Multilateral Trading Facilities (MTFs) etc.) and organised trading

[1]Many authors have encouraged the exclusive or preponderant use of soft law systems R. Keidar-S. Blemus, Crypto-currencies and Market Abuse Risks: It's Time/or Self-Regulation, in www.ssrn.com, 2018, page. 1, pages 2 s. SEC. (July 21 2022) "SEC Charges Former Coinbase Manager, Two Others in Crypto Assets Insider Trading Action", disposable in www.sec.gov/news/press-release/2022-127.

[2]About the need for integrity, market rules and fighting abusive market practices; Baimbridge (2001). G7 WORKING GROUP (2019). EBA (2019). In Spain, Martínez Flórez (2019).

[3]Regulation (EU) No 596/2014 of the European Parliament and of the Council of 16 April 2014 on market abuse (Market Abuse Regulation) and repealing Directive 2003/6/EC of the European Parliament and of the Council, and Commission Directives 2003/124/EC, 2003/125/EC and 2004/72/EC (OJ L 173, 12.6.2014, p. 1). Modified by Regulation (EU) 2019/2115 of the European Parliament and of the Council, of November 27, 2019, in force from January 1, 2021.

[4]ESMA. Guidelines on legitimate interests of issuers to delay disclosure of inside information and situations in which the delay of disclosure is likely to mislead the public [superseded by guidelines ESMA70-159-4966) (13-07-2016) and Guidelines on delay in the disclosure of inside information and interactions with prudential supervision (5-01-2022).

systems (OTSs), including precautionary mechanisms on asset prices that depend on operations carried out in systems over-the-counter markets (OTC).[5]

The MiCA Regulation includes several Level 2 and Level 3 measures that must be developed before applying the new regime (starting June 2023) within a 12-to-18-month deadline, depending on the mandate.[6] ESMA published a first consultation package in July 2023,[7] a second in December 2023,[8] and two additional stand-alone consultation papers in January 2024.[9] However, Dispositions of Title VI, prevention and the prohibition of market abuse, will enter partially into application in **December 2024**, once ESMA has published the technical standards and guidelines specifying certain requirements of the Markets in Crypto-assets Regulation (MiCA) on the detection and prevention of market abuse, investor protection and operational resilience technical standards and Guidelines (the third package).[10] This package is undergoing a consultation process until 25 June 2024 and must be implemented before **June 2025**. The European Commission must also adopt the ESMA consultation papers within three months after publication and require later approval of the EU Parliament and Council of the EU. Recently, the first package was passed in March 2024.

The third package contains the implementation of Art. 86 to 92 and the art. 16 R. (EU) No. 1085/2010 on supervisory practices among the competent authorities to prevent market abuses (art. 92.2). According to art. 92 MiCA, the European supervisory authorities entrust the State supervisors, with whom they coordinate ex-art—93 et seq, following the ESMA regulatory technical standards. So, right now, we don't know how many of the implementing regulations of R. 596/2014, R. 2019/2115, and R. (EU) No. 1085/2010, and how many of the ESMA Guidelines on MAR[11] will finally apply to crypto-asset markets or copied

[5]Communication from the Commission to the European Parliament, the Council, the European Economic and Social Committee and the Committee of the Regions on a Digital Finance Strategy for the EU, COM(2020) 591, of 23 September 2020.

[6]A complete tracker of ESMA developments is found in www.esma.europa.eu%2Fsites%2Fdefault%2Ffiles%2Flibrary%2Fguidelines_tracker.xlsx&wdOrigin=BROWSELINK. (May 2024).

[7]ESMA. Technical Standards specifying certain requirements of the Markets in Crypto Assets Regulation (MiCA), 12 July 2023, (First Package) ESMA74-449133380-425.

[8]ESMA Consultation paper, Technical Standards specifying certain requirements of Markets in Crypto-assets Regulation (MiCA) - second consultation paper, 5 October 2023.

[9]ESMA Consultation paper on the draft Guidelines on the conditions and criteria for the qualification of crypto-assets as financial instruments, 29 January 24. ESMA75-453128700-52. Consultation paper, On the draft guidelines on reverse solicitation under the Markets in Crypto Assets Regulation (MiCA) 29 January 2024, ESMA35-1872330276-1619.

[10]ESMA Consultation paper, Draft technical standards and guidelines specifying certain requirements of the Markets in Crypto-assets Regulation (MiCA) on detection and prevention of market abuse, investor protection and operational resilience, March 25 2023 (**to June 2024**), ESMA75-453128700-1002.

[11]ESMA Guidelines on legitimate interests of issuers to delay disclosure of inside information and situations in which the delay of disclosure is likely to mislead the public [superseded by guidelines ESMA70-159-4966. 13-7-2016). Guidelines on MAR - information relating to commodity

to some extent.[12] Nevertheless, ESMA's proposal for appropriate public disclosure of inside information or for delaying public disclosure gives us a reasonable vision of the regime on this issue.

---

derivatives markets or related spot markets for the purpose of the definition of inside information on commodity derivatives.(30-9-2016). Guidelines on delay in the disclosure of inside information and interactions with prudential supervision (5-01-2022).

[12]Specifically, it remains to be defined under art. 92.2, whether it will be considered applicable for the correct compliance with this section, and to what extent, the mandates contained in the various implementing regulations of R. 596/2014, and specifically: The Implementing Regulation (EU) 2016/1055 of the Commission of 29 June 2016 laying down implementing technical rules in relation to the technical modalities for the appropriate public dissemination of inside information and the delay of the public dissemination of inside information in accordance with Regulation (EU) No. 596/2014 of the European Parliament and of the Council. Commission Implementing Regulation (EU) 2016/959 of 17 May 2016 laying down implementing technical standards in relation to market prospecting with regard to the reporting systems and templates to be used for market participants reporting information and format records in accordance with Regulation (EU) 596/2014 of the European Parliament and of the Council. Commission Delegated Regulation (EU) 2016/958 of 9 March 2016 supplementing Regulation (EU) No 596/2014 of the European Parliament and of the Council as regards technical standards for regulations relating to the technical measures applicable to the objective presentation of investment recommendations or other information in which an investment strategy is recommended or suggested and to the communication of interests or indications of conflicts of interest. Commission Delegated Regulation (EU) 2016/957 of 9 March 2016 supplementing Regulation (EU) No 596/2014 of the Parliament and of the Council regarding regulatory technical standards applicable to the appropriate mechanisms, systems and procedures, as well as reporting templates, that should be used to prevent, detect and report abusive practices or suspicious orders or operations. Commission Delegated Regulation (EU) 2016/909 of 1 March 2016, supplementing Delegated Regulation (EU) 596/2015 of the European Parliament and of the Council regarding regulatory technical standards relating to the content of notifications to be submitted to the competent authorities, and to the compilation, publication and maintenance of the list of notifications. Commission Delegated Regulation (EU) 2016/960 of 17 May 2016 supplementing Regulation (EU) No 596/2014 of the European Parliament and the Council as regards regulatory technical standards applicable to appropriate arrangements, systems and procedures for conducting market prospecting by reporting market participants. Commission Delegated Regulation (EU) 2016/908 of 26 February 2016, which complies with Regulation (EU) No 596/2014 of the European Parliament and of the Council by establishing regulatory technical standards on the criteria, procedure and requirements to establish an accepted market practice, as well as the requirements to maintain it, repeal it or modify the conditions for its acceptance. Commission Implementing Regulation (EU) 2016/378 of 11 March 2016 laying down the implementation of technical rules regarding the deadlines, format and template of notifications submitted to competent authorities in accordance with Regulation (EU) No 596/2014 of the European Parliament and of the Council. Implementing Regulation (EU) 2016/347 of 10 March 2016 laying down implementing technical standards with regard to the specific format of insider lists and the updating of those lists, in accordance with Regulation (EU) No 596/2014 of the European Parliament and of the Council. Commission Implementing Regulation (EU) 2016/523 of 10 March 2016 lays down the technical standards relating to the format and template for the notification and publication of transactions carried out by managers in accordance with the Regulation (EU No 596/2014 of the European Parliament and of the Council. Commission Implementing Directive (EU) 2015/2392 of 17 December 2015 relating to Regulation (EU) No 596/2014 of the European Parliament and of the Council regarding the communication of possible or actual infringements of said Regulation to the competent authorities. Commission Delegated Regulation (EU) 2016/522 of 17 December 2015, supplementing Regulation (EU). No 596/2014 of

MiCA is limited to prohibiting basic conduct that could undermine trust in the crypto-asset market, such as privileged operations with inside information, public disclosure of unlawful information and market manipulation. However, the scope of protection under the mandate of Art. 86 to 92 of MiCA Regulation 1114/23 is related to the same values and scope of any EU regulations on controlling inside/unlawful information and market abuse in the financial sector. What remains to be seen is the extent to which national authorities will implement the European financial regulation. However, if the state authorities asymmetrically apply these regulations' various duties of control and disclosure, this could create an internal forum shopping in response to regulatory disparities between national authorities. Some will copy the European legal model, and others will adopt a laxer approach to attract service providers. ESMA considers the similarities between the MAR financial regulation and MiCA, the differences between financial instruments and crypto assets and the type of players operating in these markets. However, ESMA has merit in aligning the regime to prevent and detect market abuses and reporting based on the experiences gained in controlling and regulating financial markets. For example, ESMA proposes using some previous tools, such as the CIR 2020/1406, for coordination procedures between competent authorities to detect and sanction cross-border market abuse situations.

According to European regulations, market abuse occurs when unjustified harm is caused to investors or to the market confidence itself due to three basic assumptions:

- The use of inside/privileged information not available to the general public
- Price distortion through market manipulation
- The dissemination of false or misleading information for one´s own benefit or that of third parties and to the detriment of market operators and users.

Two different regulatory mechanisms address market abuse:

- The regulation of operations with inside information
- The prohibition of market manipulation.

2 The Treatment of Information Under MiCA Rules

2.1 Inside Information Ex-Art 87 MiCA

Following the regulations (art. 87) and similar developments in the Securities Markets MAR regulation as a guideline, we must understand as inside information, all information of a precise nature which has not been made public, relating, directly

the European Parliament and of the Council as regards the exemption relating to certain central banks and public bodies of third countries, market manipulation indicators, disclosure thresholds, the competent authority for notifications of delays, trading authorization for limited periods and the types of notifiable transactions carried out by management.

or indirectly, to one or more issuers, offerors, or person seeking admission to trading one or more crypto assets and, if were made public would have a significant effect on the prices of these crypto assets. This definition is nearly identical to Art. 7.1 MAR excepting the instruments and operators within the scope of the regulation (art. 1).[13] Also because MiCA adds "offerors and people seeking admission to trading" to the traditional "issuers".

To judge whether the information is precise, we must appreciate its specific nature concerning the crypto asset, its non-public nature, and its relevance to influencing its admission, dealing, or market value. Decisions to buy or sell in the market are made after assessing the existing ex-ante information, and by definition, inside information is not part of the list of ex-ante information available to the general public and can influence or significantly affect the decision-making process.

We are, therefore, faced with information or decisions that are generated within the issuers of the crypto-asset or outside it, in the field of its negotiation or the field of guarantee support, that may affect its asset valuation, its prospects of development, its behaviour in the face of the economic or political situation, the stability of its supporting values, etc. But we must be careful because the provisions require each relevant subject to disclose the information regarding them directly and no other persons subjected to regulation because information from different sources about the same facts can potentially be misaligned with those provided by the relevant part and to the detriment of the market.

By information related to crypto assets admitted to trading on a platform, we must understand information relating to facts or circumstances (not always including impressions or rumours) from which an effect on the price or diffusion of the crypto assets can reasonably be expected.

For precise nature information, follow art.87.2 and art model. 7.2 R. 596/2014, we will refer to a series of circumstances that exist or that can reasonably be expected to come into existence, or to an event that has happened, is actual, or that can reasonably be expected to happen, provided that this information is sufficiently specific to allow drawing some conclusion about the effects that those circumstances or that facts could have on the crypto-asset prices. It covers the protracted processes and intermediate steps of the related inside information (art. 87.3).

By non-public information, we should understand that which is not known by the generality of investors or users of the crypto asset and which gives its holder a competitive advantage in the acquisition or negotiation of the same. Reserved information grants the possibility of use and anticipatory exploitation. However, analysis and calculations based on public data should not be considered inside information.

Therefore, determining the public nature of information is not as easy as it may seem. In the securities market environment, information is public when it is communicated as relevant information, and on many occasions, information leaked by the press but not transmitted with official value has not been considered public. In

[13] Ad example over Art. 7 R. 596/2014. Palá Laguna (2006).

the context of the MiCA, in which the information and disclosure debts are laxer than those existing in the regular asset market and their formalisation is lighter, a door is open to consider the interpretation of the public or reserved nature of the information, which would have to be the subject of a specific analysis of the particular case. But, in which the mimesis or extension of the criteria used in MAR and National Authorities criteria (ad ex. in instruments such as Circular 5/2020 of November 25, of the Bank of Spain, to payment entities and electronic money issuers), on public and confidential financial information standards, and financial statement models, is very foreseeable.

Determining whether information is likely to influence the value or diffusion and trading of a crypto asset is not a simple matter either: we are dealing with information that a reasonable investor would take as a basis for their decisions, and therefore, the effect on decision-making must be assessed by an average investor or user, without access to the source of inside information, compared to that expected by someone who has that anticipatory value of the information. It is difficult to determine precisely what type of information has an appreciable capacity to influence, but the ESMA's interpretative guidelines on asset valuations will be useful here. In the field of crypto assets, the assessment of the concept of information as inside and its manipulative use will also be complicated by the possible existence of various phases of issuance, support and negotiation of the crypto asset, as well as by the frequent international factor of bargaining. Still, ESMA criteria are clear and cover the protracted process. Even worse, due to its possible relationships with other support or reference securities, assets or crypto assets are not subject to European rules or MiCA itself (OTC operations, DEFI systems, and crypto assets such as Bitcoin outside the MiCA regulatory scope).[14] Another factor to consider will be the more-than-predictable use of robots and automated AI programs on crypto assets, which will raise doubts about the extension of the criteria used by ESMA to the Systems and controls applied by trading platforms, investment services companies and competent authorities in an automated trading environment (02/24/2012).

2.2 *The Duty to Disclose Inside Information*

Art. 88 of MiCA is a simplified reproduction of the provisions of recital no. 49 and art. 17.4 of R. 596/2014 and in the ESMA MAR Guidelines.[15] It is worth starting by

[14]Such as the Guidelines on risk factors used in the issuance of investment prospectuses (01.10.2019), the criteria used in alternative performance measures in the circular (10.2015) or the guidelines on supervision of financial reporting (28.10.2014).

[15]ESMA. Guidelines relating to the delay in disseminating inside information (20/10/2016). Guidelines on legitimate interests of issuers to delay disclosure of inside information and situations in which the delay of disclosure is likely to mislead the public [superseded by guidelines ESMA70-159-4966. 13-7-2016). Guidelines on delay in the disclosure of inside information and interactions with prudential supervision (5-01-2022).

remembering that MiCA promotes the provision of clear, impartial and non-misleading information to consumers and market operators through the white paper that accompanies each issue and that requires continuous updating of the contents through the website and communications to the supervisors (art. 6, 9, 12, 16, 19, 25...). On the other hand, issuers of significant tokens must report any fact that may significantly affect the value of the reserve assets, whether or not they have been admitted to trading on a crypto-asset trading platform and are subject to the supervision of an Advisory Board (art. 45, 51, 52, 58 and 119, 120). Art. 88 of the MiCA reproduces, in this sense, the duty to declare relevant facts existing in the securities market but in a less formalised context. In the securities market, the inside information must be communicated to the competent authorities.[16] In the crypto-asset market, the duty of disclosure responsibility weighs on issuers, offerors, and people who promote admission to trading and are committed to publishing and disseminating the inside information.

The publication mechanism to the public is the website of the obligated parties, which must maintain the publication of this inside information for 5 years. Only if the responsible parties delay the disclosure shall the competent authority be informed and provided with a written explanation that immediate disclosure is likely to prejudice legitimate interest and that delay is not likely to mislead the public. Here, Regulation copy art. 17 R. 596/2014 and ESMA MAR provide guidelines about the delay of inside information disclosure (20/10/2016). But, on this particular topic, we must point out that the disclosure debt is "as soon as possible", which is an imprecise expression that needs concretion but doesn´t encourage unjustified delays.

The Regulation is generous here, and more if we add the Member State may provide that a record of such explanations can be provided only upon the request of the competent authority (Art. 88.3). For sure, ESMA technical standards (by June 2024)[17] will determine with greater precision the appropriate public disclosure and conditions for delaying it. And it matters if we consider that Art. 111. 5 lists specific sanctions for breaches of Art. 88, including maximum administrative fines of Euro 1 M. for natural persons and 2.5 M. Euro for legal persons.

According to the ESMA proposal of the technical means for appropriate disclosure of inside information,[18] the public must be informed as soon as possible of inside information that directly concerns the obligated party and enable a publication on their website with fast, complete, correct and timely assessments. To ensure a uniform application of the R. 2023/1114, ESMA promotes analogous requirements to MAR ITS application on art. 7.1 a). in the understanding that disclosuring debt provisions on MAR would not excessively burden the relevant parties in the crypto-

[16] In ordinary financial Markets, relevant facts must be communicated to the market supervisor and published by Authorities and information issuers, in accordance with Delegated Regulation (EU) 2016/909 of the Commission and concomitant regulations.

[17] According to Art. 15 Regulation (EU) n° 1095/2010. Then, we will see to which extent ESMA follow the Delegated Regulation (EU) 2016/909 of the Commission and concomitant regulations.

[18] Guidelines on delay... 2016, Consultation paper on technical requirements ... 2023 Ap. (n° 265 et seq. and ITS on technical means 929 (pages. 298 et seq.)

asset market. It means that making accessible information through a web publication and leaving the onus on the public to retrieve it would not be sufficient to ensure access by investors.

ESMA concludes, as in the MAR regulation, that active dissemination of inside information and its publication on the website are two separate obligations related to publishing and disseminating that achieve different objectives. Active dissemination ensures a wider distribution and knowledge; nevertheless, publishing a written statement on the website enables media and analysts to pick up the inside information and spread it further. So, ESMA, in its proposal for disclosure, makes a different treatment for web publication (art. 2) and active dissemination (art. 3). In consequence, the publication must be published in a downloadable statement for further spread of information, free of charge access, and ease in identifying the relevant information. As crypto markets operate across borders, the Instrument Technical Standards (ITS) provision requires information to be disclosed in the country's customary language and a language used internationally in the customary sphere of the global crypto market, basically English. Websites should also enable investors to receive, voluntarily, push notifications or alerts on any new publications and promote fast access to such information.

Public dissemination requirements to the widest public possible must be implemented non-discriminately, free of charge, simultaneously throughout the Union and avoid any information asymmetries in the operational field. ESMA also suggests considering the sources normally used by the crypto community and adding some specific media to a dissemination list relating to crypto assets (different from MAR). This means that some social media or web platforms of regular use for crypto investors' discussions may be useful tools to disseminate inside information and could be listed. This platform contains various information such as market data, analytics, price trackers, research, news... and now possible statements on inside information. But, and this is important, this social media used for this purpose should grant non-discriminatory and free access to information (even if they work with subscription or registration lists), avoiding asymmetric accesses or selective access (i.e. only closed groups). Finally, to ensure proper dissemination, the publication should always include a link to the website of the relevant party where the original information should be disclosure, and all further publications of the statement must ensure the integrity and confidentiality of information (which I understand, do not prohibit possible summaries or synthesis of information linked to the complete statement).

In any case, the mention of the public as the recipient of the publication, and not the average investor, indicates the intention to ensure that the information has a general scope, but this is also one of the many aspects that are entrusted to those developed by the ESMA package and by the State Authorities with more precision. Art. 4 of the draft ITS of ESMA also prescribes how to store the selected information affected by delayed disclosure and how to notify the National Authorities. The chosen information must be stored to ensure accessibility, readability, maintenance, integrity and confidentiality of the content. This allows for fast transmission to the NCA electronically as determined by the National Authority. The proposal includes a list of elements, copying MAR again, which should be included and enables identifying the responsible party, the conditions allowing delayed disclosure, temporal aspects and conditions...

The second, more far-reaching problem is, once again, determining precisely what we mean by inside privileged information of a public nature and differentiating it from information about which it is legitimate to keep confidential, or at least delayed. MiCA favours an interpretation for the greatest possible transparency by limiting the confidentiality of the dissemination of information to a simple delay, indicating that, finally, all privileged information should be public, which is highly debatable concerning the reserved information that issuers and negotiators have the right to protect. This latest information, however, is limited:

- In response to the harmful effect that dissemination may generate: (Perhaps as an example: Ongoing negotiations to ensure the financial viability or stability of the crypto asset, negotiations with supervisors for the admission or modification of the registered assets, changes in custodians of supporting securities, etc.)
- Its limited impact on users' behaviour, specifically that the reservation cannot be classified as deception. (Mainly delays or strategic omissions regarding the listing of the crypto asset)
- To guarantee the confidentiality of the content of the information as a factor that makes it neutral on the behaviour of the market.

Rumours have not been addressed similarly in MAR and MiCA regulations. In Art. 17 R. 596/2014, MAR explicitly requires issuers to disclose inside information immediately whenever confidentiality is no longer ensured. In MiCA, maintaining confidentiality is relevant for the parties to delay the publication since it does not explicitly deal with rumours.

However, this absence of mention is misleading; delay is possible only when the relevant conditions (confidentiality) remain, and when it no longer exists, the exemption is no longer applicable. A rumour that expressly refers to inside information whose dissemination has been delayed or whose degree of accuracy is sufficient indicates that the confidentiality of said information is no longer guaranteed and disclosure is a must.

ESMA and state authorities will define aspects of interest, but without a statement, prudential action could be taken by mimesis of art. 17 R. 596/2014 and ESMA instruction on delay in disseminating privileged information (10/20/2016).

2.3 Prohibition of Insider Dealing

Art. 89 introduces the expected and necessary prohibitions of insider dealing. Insider dealing shall be deemed when a person, subject to the regulation, who possesses inside information, uses it by acquiring or disposing of their own account or a third-party account, directly or indirectly, crypto assets to which this information is related. The use of the information covers any kind of manoeuvre, such as cancelling or amending previous orders concerning the crypto asset after accessing the inside information and comprising, submitting, modifying or withdrawing a bid by a person for its own account or for a third party, also, by recommendations or induction to another person to engage in insider dealing.[19]

Like the ordinary financial market regime, whoever is obliged to safeguard and reserve inside information may not recommend or induce the acquisition or sale of crypto assets or seek to influence the modification or cancellation of operations on crypto assets. The duty of abstention and neutrality that weighs on the holders of inside information is therefore reproduced to guarantee a loyal operation of the market and the holder interest protection against possible conflicts of interest, which has previously been obliged to detail, as well as the guaranteed mechanisms against said potential conflicts. Art 89.4 disclosure certainly states that recommendations or inducement understand where persons using the recommendation know or ought to know this advice is based on inside information.

MiCA does not mention, however, any duty to declare the operations of directors or the need to prepare lists of insiders, who once again will be left to the discretion of the subsequent development of the regulations, although it is foreseeable that, at least in the case of significant issuers of tokens, these application duties end up being required. The regulation (art. 89.5) is limited to explaining that the prohibition applies to any person who possesses inside information as a member of the administrative management, supervisory bodies of the issuer, the offeror or the person seeking admission to trading. As holder in the capital of the same indicated, or any professional who accesses the information through the exercise of employment, profession, or duties concerning the technology or legal treatment of the crypto assets. Of course, it also covers any person being involved in criminal activities, and it encompasses the natural persons who participate in the decision-making process of the legal persons to acquire, dispose of, cancel or amend any order of the legal person concerned (Copying Art. 8 R. 596/2014).

MiCA is following here the case of R. 596/2014 No. 24, perfectly foreseeable, "When a natural or legal person who possesses privileged information acquires, transmits or assigns, or attempts to acquire, transmit or assign, on its own account or on behalf of third parties, directly or indirectly, financial instruments to which said information refers, it must be assumed that that person has used said information. This presumption is understood without prejudice to the right of defense." But, according to the crypto market's structure today, some corporate roles are combined, generating a conflict of interest. The scenario exists where financial advisors, technical experts responsible for the issue or the trading, and the management of trading platforms act as issuers and investors. This is the case for well-established companies in the crypto-asset market, such as Ethereum or some famous trading platforms with their own issuance of crypto assets. Many companies will probably need to create and evidence the existence of watertight compartments regarding

[19]Similar to the SEC in 21 July 2022 ("SEC Charges Former Coinbase Manager, Two Others in Crypto Assets Insider Trading Action") www.sec.gov/news/press-release/2022-127.

confidential information and establish differentiated operations that eliminate the risk of conflict of interest. This ultimately also means that it will be difficult not to require lists of possible data controllers, insiders and people with data access, which are already needed discreetly in the contents of the white papers to some extent.

Finally, this raises questions without a good solution, as MiCA mandates will not cover many crypto issuers and trading platforms. This is because many of these crypto assets will be traded simultaneously inside and outside MiCA or constitute part of the support of crypto assets issued under MiCA. A simple look at the effects of Bitcoin's fluctuation over other crypto assets on international trading platforms predicts a future that will be difficult to manage in the attempt to create a European security environment.

2.4 Prohibition of Communication of Privileged Information

Art. 90 establishes the duty of confidentiality and loyalty of those who are custodians of inside information or have access to or knowledge of it, due to their position in the crypto asset's issue, maintenance or distribution chain. These custodians must not communicate said information to third parties—except for the normal exercise of the disclosure duty of Art. 88 by the proper professionals in charge. And once again, any recommendation or inducement to acquire, dispose of, cancel or amend orders concerning crypto assets will be graded as unlawful when the receiver knows or ought to know this was based on inside information.

Once again, it is foreseeable that no. 35 of R. 596/2014 and its implementing regulations will be used as an interpretative criterion in the assessment of the information communicated in prospective operations,[20] that will be considered made in the normal exercise of your work, profession or functions if, at the time of communication, you obtain the consent of the person to whom the information is disclosed, and inform them that you may be receiving inside information and the provisions of art. 89 Regulation will limit your ability to deal with or act on such information. In any case, it remains to be clarified whether the obligations to declare the operations of Directors and prepare lists of insiders will be extended to the MiCA environment (in whole or in part) as in art. 18 R. 596/2014.

[20]Commission Delegated Regulation (EU) 2016/960 of 17 May 2016 supplementing Regulation (EU) No 596/2014 of the European Parliament and of the Council as regards regulatory technical standards applicable to appropriate arrangements, systems and procedures for conducting market prospecting by reporting market participants.

3 Market Abuse

Finally, art. 91 and 92 of the MiCA reproduces the basic control rules on market abuse, establishing a basic prohibition of market manipulation (art. 91) and establishing an exemplary list of forms of manipulation (Art. 92). Various precepts of MiCA establish the duty that issuers of asset-referenced tokens always act honestly, impartially and professionally and in the best interest of the token holders. The duty is specified in the prohibitions of Art. 90 and in the subsequent supervision regime (art. 93 et seq.), and its enforcement with infractions and sanctions. According to art. 92, any person professionally arranging or executing transactions in crypto assets shall have effective systems and procedures to prevent and detect market abuses. That person shall be subject to the rules of notification of the Member State where it is registered, has its head office, or is located in the corporation branch. Notifications must be sent without delay to the Authority since any well-founded suspicion regarding orders, transactions (including cancellation or modifications), or other aspects of the operative of the distributed ledger technology (as consensus mechanism) where there might exist circumstances suggesting market abuse has been committed, is being committed or is likely to be committed. At the time of writing (June 2024), ESMA is pending publication of a regulatory draft of technical standards about procedures to comply with notifications, forms or templates. No less important is the issue of the treatment of cross-border market abuse situations and coordination procedures of the competent authorities, which must be submitted to the Commission by December 2024. The guidelines must comply with Art. 16 R. Eu 1095/2010 (Coordination of Authorities) and be implemented before 30 June 2025.

3.1 Prohibition of Market Manipulation

No person, regardless of their condition, shall engage or attempt to engage in market manipulations, whose forms are innumerable ("Tipping", "pump and dump", "close the market", "stop hunting", "51% attack").[21] Any person is a suitable subject for carrying out acts of market manipulation and can be charged for such acts regardless of the greater ease and greater responsibility they acquire for managing insider information. Moreover, market manipulation can be an external speculative attack when the behaviour in the market (order, decision or conduct) exceeds legitimate use, uses fictitious mechanisms, gimmicks, or manipulates information by any means. So, the regulation distinguishes between activities and behaviours that can give false or misleading signals about crypto assets' supply or demand.

MiCA states an open list that shall comprise some activities, such as entering transactions, placing orders to trade or engaging in any order behaviours which give false or misleading signals about the supply of, demand for or price levels of the

[21] Maugeri (2023), pp. 33–55.

crypto asset. Activities that secure or are likely to secure crypto-asset prices are at an abnormal or artificial level. Also, entering transactions and placing orders to trade affects or is likely to affect the price of crypto assets while employing fictitious devices or any other form of deception or strategies. Third, information is disseminated through media, the internet, or any other means that give or risk giving false or misleading signals about the supply of, demand for, or prices at abnormal or artificial levels. This includes rumour dissemination when the person engaged knows or ought to know the information is false or misleading.

Behaviours, such as securing a dominant position over the supply or demand for a crypto asset, which has or is likely to have the effect of fixing purchase or sale prices or unfair trading conditions. Also, placing orders in trading platforms, including cancellation or modification thereof, by any means of trading, which has the effect of misleading or disrupting the normal conduct of the market and price levels by;

- disrupting or delaying the normal operation of the trading platform or that is likely to have that effect.
- making it more difficult for other persons to identify genuine orders on the trading platform or enter orders that result in destabilisation or the normal functioning of the trader.
- creating a false or misleading signal about a crypto asset's supply or demand for or price, entering orders to initiate or exacerbate a trend, or engaging in activities likely to have that effect.

The list above compendiums the most common financial market manipulation manoeuvres, and we certainly have more than enough experience with their use in crypto-asset markets. Studies of crypto assets like Bitcoin report many manipulation episodes by qualified or large investors (the so-called blue whales), using tools forbidden in the financial market and now in the crypto markets.[22] Once again, the cross-border operability of cryptos will be the principal problem for enforcement, especially when the same cryptos, directly or indirectly, are traded inside and outside the scope of the MiCA regulation.

Behaviours also included taking advantage of occasional or regular access to the traditional or electronic media by voicing an opinion about a crypto-asset and profiting from the impact of the opinion expressed on the price of that crypto asset "without having simultaneously disclosed that conflict of interest to the public properly and effectively". Recently, there was a speculative campaign against Bitcoin investors by social influencers like Elon Musk. Social media enables many users to be exposed to influencers in crypto propaganda and a growing community of

[22] MiFID II does not include a one single definition for all types of financial instruments. The concept of financial instrument is delineated through a list of instruments in Annex I Section C: (i) transferable securities, (ii) money-market instruments, (iii) units of collective investment undertakings, (iv) various derivative contracts and (v) emission allowances, and not by statement of conditions and criteria. This has resulted in Member States transposing MiFID II not defining financial instruments in a harmonised way.

"crypto bros" who are leading inexperienced investors and, possibly, acting as agents or crypto publicists.

MiCA regulation generates several doubts, however. The first relates to the criminal code's applicability without legal reform of market manipulation laws in many European criminal code contents (ad ex. 284 et seq. of the Spanish Criminal Code). Applying the criminal code to a legal scenario not expressly defined in the criminal law texts is impossible. The criminal interpretation cannot be extensive, and not all crypto assets included in MiCA could be assimilated into the concept of financial instruments. However, some would pass the Howey and ESMA Test as a qualification criterion.[23] The Securities Market Stakeholder Group (SMSG) acknowledges different approaches in individual Member States regarding what qualifies as a financial instrument and promotes a regulatory framework in the EU. ESMA's position (according to technology neutrality) to understand the qualification as a financial instrument should depend on the rights and obligations that define its legal and economic profiles. The implications of qualifying crypto assets as financial instruments are wide, such as an EU passporting system for cross-border activities, coverage by some investor compensation schemes, and protection related to the application of MiFID II. SMSG supports adopting an extensive interpretation for the re-qualification of crypto assets as financial instruments in case of doubt, as it would reinforce investor protection thanks to the application of the MiFID II. However, this pretension can only be referred to as commercial qualifications, not criminal ones that exclusively concern the financial market. Member States can replace the list of infractions and financial sanctions with criminal sanctions (art. 111.1); however, if this option is not used, I believe it should be rejected. Only the general figures of scams or price manipulation in the market should be of concern.

Outside the criminal offence, however, and regarding administrative enforcement, there is a simple view of the regulation, especially Art. 60, indicating an almost equivalent treatment of crypto assets as MAR's treatment of financial assets. There are some relevant differences, like the omission of the MAR reference to the "reasonable investor," which fortunately is not mentioned in MiCA. The crypto-asset market, comprising mostly disintermediate operatives acting as private individuals, would make the "reasonable investor" concept inapplicable or conflictive.

With the same protective intention, SMSG supports a restrictive approach to the reverse solicitation exemption of art. 61 to increase investors' protection and fair competition because otherwise, EU investors would lose the protection afforded by MiCA when using non-European Crypto-asset service providers (CASPs). Financial and Antitrust Authorities also believe it may be disadvantaged by the European providers competing with non-European providers, which aren't compliant with MiCA. In this situation, it is very foreseeable that we will witness an extensive

[23] SMSG advice to ESMA on its consultation papers on reverse solicitation and the qualification of crypto-assets as financial instruments in the context of the Markets in Crypto-assets (MiCA) Regulation, 2 May 2024. ESMA24-229244789-4738.

cross-border application of EU community law and probably an intensive use of the MAR regulation for cross-border operatives.

MiCA prohibits any act of market manipulation unless the person who has carried out a transaction, given a trading order or engaged in any other conduct demonstrates that such operation, order or conduct has been carried out *for legitimate reasons*. Specifically, the transmission of false signals regarding a crypto asset's supply, demand or price is pointed out. The realisation of this behaviour is the abnormal or artificial price fixing, which places a good part of the known and usual operations regarding contracting unregulated crypto assets in the spotlight. Suppose the analysis of recent years in the price of crypto assets, such as Bitcoin, has given us any lessons. In that case, unregulated crypto assets are susceptible to speculative intrusions by large investors or holders of capital in a market that lacks control mechanisms, suspension of the quote, or investigation of the behaviours.[24] MiCA intends to avoid this behaviour concerning crypto assets registered in the EU but generally implemented operatives in international crypto markets often mean:

- The use of smart contracts schemes or IA machines, which can generate very fast fluctuations in a context where there is not constant supervision of the regulators and in which the notification mechanisms could react too late
- And the coexistence of European and non-European traders over the same crypto assets, which means that the intervention or suspension of trading of a crypto asset in the European market could have a limited effect if the same asset continues to be active outside the scope of European supervision

It will be crucial to determine to what extent ESMA will apply the same cautions as in the financial market. Still, even then, the less formalised crypto market could limit the effects of EU regulations and supervision.

3.2 Forms of Market Manipulation

In any case, art. 90 offers a list, exemplary and open, of various forms of market manipulation as follows:[25]

---

[24]POLASIK/PIOTROWSKA/WISNIEWSKI/KOTKOWSKI/LIGHTFOOD. "Price fluctuation and the use of Bitcoin" in *International Journal of Electronic Commerce*, vol. 20, n°1, 2016, 9. Arbelaez Pérez, F. "El trino de Elon Musk sobre Bitcoin que disparó su precio", El Tiempo.com, 20-1-2021. Avalaible in Bitcóin: Elon Musk dispara precio de la criptomoneda tras mensaje en Twitter (eltiempo.com) CID, G. "¿Está Elon Musk manipulando el Bitcoin? La gran duda tras el último bombazo de Tesla." In El Confidencial.com 9-2-2021, Avalaible in ¿Está Elon Musk manipulando el bitcoin? La gran duda tras el último bombazo de Tesla (elconfidencial.com).

[25]For a complete compilation of abuse market tactics Baena Tovar, N., La regulación del abuso de Mercado en Europa y Estados Unidos, CNMV, Dirección de Estudios, Monografías, n° 1 diciembre 2002 (avalaible in www.CNMV.com). IOSCO Guide. *Investigating and prosecuting market manipulation (*2000) (Addendum 2013). For an insight into the possible impact of the use of investment algorithms and investment robots in the trading process, OECD, *Allgorithms and*

(a) Ensure a dominant position over the supply or demand of a crypto asset, which has or may have the effect of fixing, directly or indirectly, purchase or sale prices or which creates or may create other inequitable trading conditions. Here, it must be noted that holding a dominant position over a crypto asset does not automatically have to be identified as market manipulation. However, this circumstance exponentially increases its risk and requires the behaviour of reinforced loyalty or special caution for whoever holds said position. Crypto assets, like ordinary securities, have a vocation for diffusion, but this is not always a reality, and we have detected some crypto market operative failures when the crypto community is weak and becomes susceptible to a plus 51% consensus attack. The same is true when a major investor enters a limited crypto market and sets trends, rhythms, and developments in the market (Elon Musk case). This mandate makes special reference to the coordinated actions of holders of significant quotas due to the risk that they act as an investment cartel. To use a term used in negotiating unregulated crypto assets, the "hunting campaigns" or coordinated actions of the large holders of crypto assets or "whales" would be illegal under Art. 80 of the MiCA.

(b) Send orders to a crypto asset trading platform, including any cancellation or modification thereof, by any available trading means, when this has any of the effects referred to in section 1, letter a), by:

   (i) disrupt or delay the operation of the crypto asset trading platform or carry out any activity that may have that effect. Here would be the manoeuvres of saturation or blocking of orders designed to make it difficult or delay the fixing of the index or value of the crypto asset. Those which generate a false impression about the trend level of demand or block the acquisitions of third parties, and those intended to create instability in the supply or demand (Spoofing)[26]

   (ii) make it difficult for other persons to identify authentic orders on the Crypto-asset Trading Platform or carry out any activity that may have that effect, including issuing orders that destabilise the normal functioning of the Crypto-asset Trading Platform; Once again, we would be facing tasks of obstruction or saturation of the contracting and transparency mechanisms or manoeuvres aimed at causing spikes of rise or fall in the price of the crypto asset.

   (iii) create a false or misleading signal about the supply, demand or price of a crypto asset, in particular by issuing orders to initiate or exacerbate a trend or carrying out any activity that may have that effect; Conduct that is sufficiently explained by its description, and in which in the case of crypto assets, however, we may encounter the added difficulty of the incidence of

collusion. Competition Policy in the digital age. 2017. https://web-archive.oecd.org/2019-02-17/449397-Algorithms-and-colllusion-competition-policy-in-the-digital-age.pdf.

[26] IOSCO GUIDE. *Investigating and prosecuting... cit.* Addendum 2013. As *leading case* in USA, SEC. Bunge Global Markets vs SEC: Order: Bunge Global Markets, Inc. (cftc.gov).

possible bots or algorithmic contracting mechanisms in the exacerbation of trends,[27] without it being clear whether the prudential mechanisms existing in the ordinary financial market will be applied (or about the effectiveness of this mechanism in this context).

(c) take advantage of occasional or periodic access to traditional or electronic media to express an opinion on a crypto-asset after having taken positions in said crypto-asset and then benefit from the repercussions of the opinion expressed on the price of said crypto-asset, without having simultaneously communicated that conflict of interest to the public appropriately and effectively. The behaviour is clear and understandable but not unusual in crypto assets and with frequent borderline behaviours such as those described in the note above of the text. Consider, for example, the media publicity by a high-level investor like Elon Musk about his intention to invest $1.5 billion in Bitcoin and its effects on the upward volatility of the cryptocurrency or, rather, investment crypto assets. And the subsequent impact on the market when it announced the withdrawal of the admission of the crypto asset in its commercial group after it had divested.

4 Critical Conclusions

In summary, MiCA proposes a primary anti-market abuse regime aimed at monitoring, in line with the supervisory powers of Art. 93 and seq. The European regulation is widely conscious of the illicit manipulations observed in trading unregulated crypto assets and the need to protect users and investors against the demonstrated volatility of crypto assets. The proposal, however, faces a dilemma that is difficult to solve since a complete assimilation of the transparency and supervision duties existing in the extensive regulations of ordinary financial assets could have the effect of deterring foreign operators from registration or cutting off the initiatives of European SMEs in the sector. A simplified regulation such as the one proposed, on the contrary, raises doubts about the degree of assimilation to the duties of ordinary financial market operators that can finally be defended in the interpretation of articles referring to market abuse. ESMA's interpretation favours the greatest possible protection of crypto investors and favours the full extension of the financial regulations on market abuse to that of crypto assets. Specifically, will the different state supervisors promote an asymmetric development in interpreting these precepts? Some promote complete assimilation, and others perhaps lighten the regulatory burdens. All this comes with the risk of generating a shopping forum between the different States of the Union in response to the supervision burden they ultimately impose.

[27] As example in not covered cryptos as Bitcoin: Bayes Capdevilla (TFG) (2018-2019). http://diposit.ub.edu/dspace/bitstream/2445/133279/1/TFG_ECO_BAYES%20_ROGER_FEB19.pdf.

The situation of the issuers of significant tokens will be clearer, who, under the direct supervision of the EBA, and given the diffusion and amount of the assets, are candidates for a mimetic extension of a good part of the supervision regime that subjects the operators of the ordinary financial market. Perhaps it would be convenient to establish a principle of interpretation, according to which the duties of transparency not explicit in the proposed regulation, but developed in its regulatory background, can be recommended as prudential use and perhaps required within the requirements derived from an intervention, that is, ex-post, rather than as ex-ante requirements or interpretation.

However, market abuse regulations, whether concerning the financial or crypto markets, specifically aim to eradicate disloyal manoeuvres and protect investors. Therefore, there is reason for applying the rules, and the extensive application of the best criterion for protecting the weak party is defensible in case of doubt.

However, it is also necessary to carry out a critical assessment of the enforcement system designed here. The enforcement, elaborated by MiCA regulation and ESMA developments, is expected to work well for crypto assets issued in Europe and trading platforms based in Europe. It is also expected to work well with trading platforms with a European Union subsidiary branch. The extensive application of MAR rules, akin to a complete assimilation, could secure fair play for conservative investors. But, we must also consider that many investors will continue looking for deregulated crypto assets and non-European traders. We think the crypto-asset market is much more disintermediated than the financial market and that individuals with little training directly carry out a good part of the operations. Considering that the crypto asset market is more global than the traditional financial market, the enforcement structure cannot be as effective as conventional MAR regulations. Crypto assets and trading platforms not under the scope of MiCA will continue to affect crypto investors and EU traders strongly. They will continue to attract European investment outside the community shield (ex-art. 61 exceptions). Strengthening these doubts, we must also consider the intensive use of artificial intelligence in managing buy or sell orders for crypto assets and the global effects that the use of artificial intelligence algorithms by large investors outside the protective shield of the MiCA regulation can have.

The most exciting question in this matter is, without a doubt, how the foreseeable cases of extraterritorial application of European regulations to external crypto assets and operators will be resolved.

References

AA.VV. (2016) Polasik/Piotrowska/Wisniewski/Kotkowski/Lightfood. Price fluctuation and the use of Bitcoin. Int J Electr Commer 20(1):9

Arbelaez Pérez F (2024) El trino de Elon Musk sobre Bitcoin que disparó su precio. El Tiempo. com, 20-1-2021. Avalaible in Bitcóin: Elon Musk dispara precio de la criptomoneda tras mensaje en Twitter (eltiempo.com) (Last Access may 2024)

Baena Tovar N (2002) La regulación del abuso de Mercado en Europa y Estados Unidos, CNMV. Dirección de Estudios, Monografías, n° 1 Diciembre 2002
Baimbridge SM (2001) The law and economics of insider trading: a comprehensive premier, Working Paper Series. California University, Los Ángeles
Bayes Capdevilla R (TFG) (2009–2018) Estudio económico de la primera década de Bitcoin (2009-2018). Universidad de Barcelona, 2018-2019. TFG_ECO_BAYES _ROGER_FEB19.pdf (ub.edu)
CID, G (2021) ¿Está Elon Musk manipulando el Bitcoin? La gran duda tras el último bombazo de Tesla. In El Confidencial.com (9-2-2021), Avalaible in ¿Está Elon Musk manipulando el bitcoin? La gran duda tras el último bombazo de Tesla (elconfidencial.com) (last accessed May 2024)
EBA (2019) Crypto-assets, Implications for financial stability, monetary policy and payments and market infrastructures. ECB Crypto-assets task force, Occasional Papers Series, n° 223, May 2019
ESMA (2016a) Guidelines on legitimate interests of issuers to delay disclosure of inside information and situations in which the delay of disclosure is likely to mislead the public [superseded by guidelines ESMA70-159-4966) (13-07-2016)
ESMA (2016b) Guidelines on MAR - information relating to commodity derivatives markets or related spot markets for the purpose of the definition of inside information on commodity derivatives.(30-9-2016)
ESMA (2022) Guidelines on delay in the disclosure of inside information and interactions with prudential supervision (5-01-2022)
ESMA (2023a) Consultation paper, Technical Standards specifying certain requirements of Markets in Crypto-assets Regulation (MiCA) - second consultation paper, 5 October 2023
ESMA (2023b) Consultation paper, Draft technical standards and guidelines specifying certain requirements of the Markets in Crypto-assets Regulation (MiCA) on detection and prevention of market abuse, investor protection and operational resilience, March 25 2023, Third consultation paper. ESMA75-453128700-1002
ESMA (2024a) Consultation paper On the draft Guidelines on the conditions and criteria for the qualification of crypto-assets as financial instruments, 29 January 2024 ESMA75-453128700-52
ESMA (2024b) Consultation paper, On the draft guidelines on reverse solicitation under the Markets in Crypto Assets Regulation (MiCA) 29 January 2024, ESMA35-1872330276-1619
G7 Working Group (2019) Investigating the impact of Global Stablecoins. October 2019
IOSCO Guide (2000) Investigating and prosecuting market manipulation. Technical Committee of the International Organization of Securities Commissions, May 2000, **Addendum** Abril 2013. Addendum to IOSCO Report on Investigating and Prosecuting Market Manipulation
Martínez Flórez A (2019) Los fundamentos de la prohibición del abuso de mercado. Valencia, Tirant Lo Blanch
Maugeri M (2023) Cripto attivittá e abusi di mercato. Rivista di Diritto coomerciale. 1:33–55
OCDE (2017) Allgorithms and collusion. Competition Policy in the digital age. https://web-archive.oecd.org/2019-02-17/449397-Algorithms-and-colllusion-competition-policy-in-the-digital-age.pdf
Palá Laguna R (2006) Voz: Información privilegiada. Diccionario de sociedades, Alonso Ledesma, C. (Dir) Madrid, Iustel, 2006
SEC. Bunge Global Markets vs SEC: Order: Bunge Global Markets, Inc. (cftc.gov)
SEC (2022) SEC Charges Former Coinbase Manager, Two Others in Crypto Assets Insider Trading Action. (disposable in www.sec.gov/news/press-release/2022-127 (July 21-20222)

Part III
New Assets: Subjects and Assets not Regulated in MiCA

Current and Future Central Bank Digital Currency (CBDC) Projects

Pablo Sanz Bayón

Abstract Central Bank Digital Currencies (CBDCs) are monetary projects of digital public money at different stages of development, whose issuance corresponds to central banks. It is a digital representation of money with fiat currency's legal nature. Still, like cash, and unlike electronic bank money, it has the guarantee of a central bank and not a deposit guarantee fund. This means that the monetary authority is responsible for the conditions of its issuance, distribution and value, as well as the network or infrastructure that supports its operation and possible programmability, whether retail (rCBDC) or wholesale (wCBDC). Among the most important examples of CBDC projects are the Chinese digital yuan and the digital euro, the latter still undergoing the study (or preparation) phase by the European Central Bank. The objective of this paper is to carry out a conceptual and comparative study on the development of these and other CBDC projects, providing a regulatory analysis of the consequences that the implementation of this new monetary and technological reality will bring to the banking system, as well as the impact that these digital currencies have on the banking market, the protection of users and their relationship with the rest of the Fintech environment. It will also discuss some of the initiatives taking place at the international level, such as the projects within the BIS *Innovation Hub* to address different issues that will define the final configuration of CBDCs in the near future.

This paper expands and updates the text of a lecture delivered at the III International Congress entitled "Present and future of crypto-assets regulation in the European Union," held at the University of Alicante (Spain) on December 13, 14, and 15, 2023. This work is funded within the framework of: Proyecto CIPROM/2022/26 "Presente y futuro de la regulación de los Criptoactivos en la UE [Legalcripto]". Proyecto Prometeo CIPROM/2022/26, grupos de investigación de excelencia, de la Generalitat Valenciana (P.I. Carmen Pastor).

P. Sanz Bayón (✉)
Commercial Law Professor at Comillas Pontifical University, Madrid, Spain
e-mail: psbayon@comillas.edu

C. Pastor Sempere (ed.), *Governance and Control of Data and Digital Economy in the European Single Market*, Law, Governance and Technology Series 71,
https://doi.org/10.1007/978-3-031-74889-9_14

1 Introducción

Money, like any element present in society, has evolved. Among the changes, it is essential to emphasise the latest and most disruptive transformation of money, the one brought about by the digital age. While plastic money is progressively displacing cash (metal and paper), we find the appearance of Bitcoin in 2008. This milestone marked a before and after in the history of humanity, being the origin of a new *crypto* ecosystem in which thousands of cryptocurrencies have been supporting projects with different characteristics but with a common philosophy: to dispense with financial intermediaries for the sake of financial decentralisation (*DeFi*).

With the prospects of reinventing the financial system at a global level—and supported by *Distributed Ledger Technology* (DLT)—we will probably find ourselves, together with the emergence and implementation of Artificial Intelligence, facing the greatest challenge that we face as a society: designing the legal framework in which the most powerful phenomena discovered to date will operate. CBDCs arise in a context of digital transformation in which there is a relatively widespread social awareness of the idea of decentralised finance (*DeFi*), with cryptocurrencies and, especially, Bitcoin as the greatest exponent of these. Society is changing, technological development is a reality that multiplies exponentially daily, and the world of new technologies applied to the financial industry (Fintech) has revolutionised the economic system that integrates our transactions and payments.[1]

In this context, central banks have been forced to act with the aim of, on the one hand, adapting to the phenomenon of the digitalisation of the economy and, on the other, facing the threat of the loss of monetary sovereignty that they have always held historically. In response to this phenomenon and motivated by the aim of maintaining monetary sovereignty, central banks have been forced to work on developing monetary assets with the potential to be programmable and cryptographic, projects known as "Central Bank Digital Currencies" (CBDC). As the historian Theodor Mommsen said, control of the currency is a manifestation of the power struggle for political hegemony.[2]

This paper aims to make a precise delimitation of the concept of CBDCs, establishing the differentiation concerning other digital assets, as well as between the different projects of digital currencies issued by central banks. Specifically, the various situations in which some projects find themselves will be compared at a technological and economic level. Likewise, the legal framework currently regulating this phenomenon at the European Union level will be analysed, the role of monetary authorities in distributing this type of digital currency to the public and the alternatives presented to carry out this distribution.

Finally, the advantages and disadvantages of central bank digital currencies will be examined in detail, with special reference to the potential problem of user privacy loss in financial transactions. In terms of its objectives, this study aims to establish a

[1] At this point, we refer to a previous work: Sanz Bayón (2020a), pp. 69–110.

[2] Zunzunegui (2023).

broad and precise view of CBDCs' current situation, the advantages they can provide over other alternatives, and the potential risks that may arise from their adoption. Specifically, it will attempt to present an overview of where our financial system currently stands and where it is headed.

2 Conceptual Delimitation of Central Bank Digital Currencies (CBDCs)

2.1 Concept and Common Features of CBDC Projects

It is not easy to select a particular milestone as a proxy for the origin of central bank digital currencies. Surely, the first to approach the concept of what we now consider a digital currency issued by a central bank (from now on, "CBDC") was the American economist James Tobin in 1987. However, the idea behind this concept did not develop solidly until, eleven years after Bitcoin appeared in 2008, Facebook announced its future project to launch its digital currency, known as Libra, and later called Diem (a concept that will be analysed *below*). It is then that the main central banks, representing 20% of the world's population, reacted by announcing that they were working on their respective CBDC projects with the intention of a medium-term issuance.[3]

The origin of CBDCs responds to the need for central banks to preserve their monetary sovereignty that of the State. This involves an effort at the supranational level to provide a solid and coordinated response to alternative financial assets, especially decentralised crypto assets and *stablecoins*. At the end of 2019, the *Bank for International Settlements* (from now on referred to as "BIS"), based in Basel, Switzerland, surveyed 76 banks representing 75% of the world's population, including 21 banks from advanced economies and 45 from emerging economies. The results indicated a promising future for CBDC.[4]

1. 25% of the central banks in the study considered that they had the authority to issue their digital currencies or would soon have them.
2. 80% of central banks were researching their digital currency projects.
3. 60% of central banks were already considering the impact that *stablecoins* such as Facebook's Libra could have in the future.
4. Some 10% of the central banks surveyed expected the adoption of a global purpose around CBDCs in the short term (i.e., in the next three years).

However, even if this large number of central banks acknowledged that they were advancing their CBDC research, the purposes guiding their research were not the

[3]For more on this question, see Auer et al. (2020), pp. 9–19.

[4]BIS Innovation Hub (2020) BIS: A fifth of world's population soon to have central Bank digital currency.

same. While banks in emerging countries understood (and continue to understand) that CBDCs were a mechanism aimed at improving the efficiency and security of national payments and promoting financial inclusion, advanced economies were motivated by improving payment security and financial stability. Due to their situation, the former are the ones who are taking the lead in their implementation. Emerging countries typically have vulnerabilities in terms of cash control, with large social layers excluded from the financial system. Moreover, these countries tend to experience difficulties in preventing money laundering and it is a challenge for them to rapidly implement the digitisation of their financial services sector.[5]

Regardless of the Central Bank's approach to adopting CBDCs, one thing is clear: these digital currencies have to be stable and serve not only as a store of value but as a means of payment, with the same capacity as cash has. In addition to the above findings, the BIS released the charts related to the survey, which show the boom in central bank commitment to CBDCs. In turn, the knowledge that the world population was acquiring about the concept of CBDCs was *in crescendo*, as observed by the growth in the number of public conferences organised by representatives of the main central banks, as well as in the volume of searches carried out in the main Internet browser, *Google*.

Likewise, the COVID-19 pandemic brought a series of social distancing measures that caused undoubted social concern about the health risks associated with using cash in economic transactions. Medical recommendations by the authorities to reduce the number of cash transactions to contain the spread of the virus led to a large increase in electronic payments. As a result, digital assets (including CBDCs, even if they were at the project level) benefited until they reached the stage at which they are currently.[6]

According to the *Atlantic Council*, around 90 countries are considering introducing their form of digital money soon, of which forty announced they were in a research phase in 2021. There are also experiments with wholesale CBDCs, such as the Helvetia project, in which the BIS and the Swiss National Bank participate. Thus, according to the previously mentioned source, at the beginning of 2023, up to 119 countries were involved in studies with CBDC projects in different phases, and a year later, the number of countries rose to more than 130 from countries that have started some research CBDC to nations that have already issued them. These countries represent 98% of the world economy.[7]

---

[5]Generally, we refer to documents authored by: (i) BIS (2020) Central bank digital currencies: foundational principles and core features, and (ii) BIS (2021) Central bank digital currencies for cross-border payments. Report to the G20. See also Nabilou (2019).

[6]Many central banks have initiated projects to understand DLT technology for wholesale and retail purposes. The first work to be published on retail CBDCs gave rise to "e-krona" in Sweden, while in China "e-CNY" (better known as the Chinese digital yuan) has been tested in several cities for four years. In 2020, the Central Bank of the Bahamas issued what many consider the first live retail CBDC, the Sand Dollar. To delve into these key points: Arner et al. (2020a).

[7]With all this, according to *Statista*, it is estimated that by 2030, the CBDC market will go from being worth $100 trillion (in Anglo-Saxon terminology, i.e. one hundred billion dollars) to

In recent years, more voices have been raised calling for central banks to evolve and implement the possibilities that new technology, including *Distributed Ledger Technology* (DLT), provides them.[8] In particular, the Institute and Faculty of Actuaries of the United Kingdom advocates avoiding moving away from the legal tender in favour of a private electronic money issuer since this would seriously undermine the main monetary authorities, i.e., the central bank's ability to apply its policies.[9]

Once the origins of CBDCs have been exposed, it is possible to conceptualise them based on their characteristics (which will be explained *below*) and always be aware that it is a dynamic concept about which there are still many unknowns since it may present various variants, as will be explained later. They are digital currencies issued by central banks, backed by them (which would provide them, a priori, with great security and stability) and supported by DLT technology. However, the type of technology could depend on whether it is a retail or wholesale CBDC.[10]

In this regard, we must establish the appropriate differentiation between the two classes above of CBDCs. While retail CBDCs allow for widespread use and refer to all payments between individuals, consumers, and merchants, wholesale CBDCs are designed to make transactions in the interbank market, between commercial banks, and clearing houses more efficient.

As Ashley Lannquist, Head of the Blockchain and DLT Project at the World Economic Forum (WEF), says, retail CBDCs have as their main purpose, among others, to potentially increase financial inclusion and be a strategic alternative to physical money in economies where cash is reduced. They also can improve payments between individuals in the same country and from different countries, as well as know-your-customer (KYC) and *anti-money laundering* (AML) processes to curtail money laundering. Moreover, let's consider that CBDCs were born as a reactive mechanism of central banks in the face of the rise of privately developed decentralised alternative means of payment such as cryptocurrencies. We can conclude that the phenomenon the latter were enjoying would stagnate or at least slow down, especially in those countries where the use of cash is decreasing.[11]

---

representing a value of $213 trillion (in the same terminology as the previous metric). In addition, narrowing the focus even further, in 2023 the *Official Monetary and Financial Institutions Forum* (OMFIF) predicted that by the end of 2028, more than 40% of central banks would have issued their own CBDC. Having presented the factual data, the conclusion is clear: more and more central banks in different countries are developing their digital currencies with an expected medium-term issuance. As of today, we could say that, although it is difficult to generalise, the central banks of the 130 countries are led by the Central Bank of the Russian Federation and the Central Bank of the People's Republic of China, which have made substantial progress in their CBDC projects, with some of these digital currencies already in circulation (in the testing phase).

[8] Zetzsche et al. (2018) and Raskin and Yermacl (2016).

[9] Ward and Rochemont (2021).

[10] Klein (2020).

[11] World Economic Forum (2019).

2.2 *CBDC Technological Infrastructure: With Special Reference to* DLT/Blockchain

While most CBDC projects do not determine the technology that will serve their technological infrastructure, it is worth mentioning DLT technology, which underpins several CBDC projects. DLT is a decentralised ledger system that allows data management to be distributed among several participants. In such a system, data is distributed among several nodes in a network. In terms of its origin, DLT technology comes from a combination of three technologies that already existed previously, namely[12]:

1. *Peer-to-peer* (P2P) networks: Models in which each participant acts simultaneously as a client and provider of resources.
2. Asymmetric key cryptography allows the secure exchange of information between two parties. It is used to authenticate the sender, ensure that the message is complete and, through encryption, prevent third parties from accessing the information in case they could intercept it.
3. Consensual algorithms: Thanks to these, several participants, who probably don't have to know each other, can reach an agreement to add transactions to the ledger.

DLT technology is thus characterised by being secure and tamper-resistant (data is stored in several places simultaneously and verified using cryptographic algorithms).[13] In addition, to change a part of the network, validation by most participants is required before being accepted, thus minimising errors and fraud that may occur. In this sense, the technology provided by the blockchain allows greater efficiency in financial transactions and the possibility of preserving the user's privacy. The latter is one of the major concerns hovering over CBDC research projects.[14]

Finally, although CBDCs are frequently associated with DLT technology, this causal link does not necessarily exist since CBDC projects do not use this technology. Still, other more traditional technologies are deployed on telecommunications infrastructures. A good example of the latter can be found in the Jamaican CBDC (JAM-DEX), launched in July 2022.[15]

---

[12]BBVA Research (2019).

[13]It is also necessary to differentiate two concepts that are sometimes used interchangeably: Blockchain (known to be at the base of how Bitcoin works, mainly) and DLT. The second encompasses the former, a type of DLT that records transactions on blockchains. Each of these has a set of transactions and a reference to the previous block, which makes the traceability and security of transactions possible. The cryptography and consensus of the nodes that are part of the network, in some cases using algorithms such as *proof of work* or *proof of stake*, provides security to the network. DLT technology, with implementations such as IOTA or Corda, is a digital infrastructure suitable for recording transactions, and *Blockchain* is just one more manifestation of DLT.

[14]Catalini and Gans (2016).

[15]Spanish Data Protection Agency (2023).

2.3 *Typology of CBDCs*

2.3.1 Characteristics of CBDCs

Although it may seem premature to precisely delimit the different forms of CBDC that may exist or may do so, as it is an instrument in the process of design, it is possible to choose to follow the classification proposed by Fernández de Lis and Gouveia based on the characteristics of cash. This liquid and tangible asset is exchanged between peers, is universal, anonymous and does not accrue interest.

CBDCs only share the characteristic of being exchanged between peers (*peer-to-peer*), but they have variants in the rest of the characteristics, which can be:

1. Universal or restricted access to a group of users.
2. Open or closed (limited to certain financial institutions).
3. Anonymous (such as cash) or identified (such as current accounts). The former alludes to token-based CBDCs, while the latter refers to account-based CBDCs.
4. Interest-generating or not.

Along these lines, although we are aware that the possibilities of categorising the types of CBDCs could be very numerous, in this work, it has been decided to synthesise their modalities into four:

1. CBDCs that allow interbank settlements: these would be digital currencies restricted to use by banks (which in the future would improve their wholesale payments system, currently real-time gross settlement or RTGS), identified (not anonymous) and non-interest-generating.
2. CBDCs are similar to cash, aiming to replace it with one universal, anonymous, and interest-non-generating. Cash has historically been used in fraudulent activities (see the case of money laundering, for example), and changing this means of payment for a more efficient one could be a feasible alternative to end these criminal activities.
3. CBDC as a policy tool: with the same characteristics as the previous category, but with the possibility of generating interest, applying the interest rates (negative or positive) that best suit the specific economic situation.
4. CBDCs that serve as public deposits in central banks should have universal characteristics, be identified currencies (with the risk of loss of anonymity that cash allows) and be non-interest-generating. This would eliminate the risk of instability in banking crises.

2.3.2 Advantages and Disadvantages of Each Type of CBDC: In Particular, the Problem of Loss of Privacy

On the one hand, the first option of the four described *above* would increase the efficiency of wholesale payment systems since it would replace the current infrastructure of the RGTS, which gives central banks the role of guarantors of transactions. In addition, the network would be expanded (via DLT) to new participants who could compete with banks, which would reduce costs.[16] Even so, it seems unlikely that a CBDC (based on a national payment system and therefore subject to a specific jurisdiction) can compete in this aspect with decentralised cryptocurrencies (the greatest exponents of *DeFi*).

The second option, on the other hand, would allow cash to be replaced by a more efficient alternative, especially regarding payment between individuals. This is because cash production comes at a cost and can be easily lost or stolen. However, a drawback that should not be ignored is the loss of anonymity that characterises cash. Monetary authorities supporting a CBDC through a deliberate decision could only guarantee this intrinsic characteristic of cash.

The third alternative analyses the possibility of issuing a CBDC that would generate interest, which would be very positive for applying a specific monetary policy. However, the greatest doubts lie in the fact that a central bank has at its disposal a tool that can produce the impoverishment of the entire population (in nominal terms) and that is located on the border between monetary and fiscal policy. This is surely incompatible with the independence of central banks.[17]

The fourth of the alternatives is the most disruptive since it raises the possibility that the general public could open an account with a central bank. This would end the problem of banks' weakness in times of crisis (many bailouts are carried out to save many financial institutions when they have serious liquidity problems). However, like the second option, it also has the drawback of losing privacy and raises serious questions about where commercial banks would stand in the financial system. The latter is explained by the fact that customers would likely move their deposits into their central bank accounts, causing financial panic in commercial banks. In addition, as can be deduced, there is a common drawback in the last two alternatives: central banks would be given excessive power if allowed to offer deposits to the public, and this decision can be highly controversial.

Having briefly outlined the advantages and disadvantages of each of the four types of CBDCs that have been previously defined, the issue of loss of privacy is of most concern to future users of central bank digital currencies. Thus, the most controversial issue raised by the hypothetical issuance of the digital euro, and even more because of the recent entry into the preparation phase on 1 November 2023, is the possible loss of anonymity provided by cash payments. In fact, according to a public survey conducted by the European Central Bank (from now on ECB), the main feature that the digital euro should offer is to respect the privacy of its users.[18]

[16] This is in line with the aim of regulating payment services in the Proposal for a Regulation of the European Parliament and of the Council of 28 June 2023 on payment services in the internal market and amending Regulation (EU) No 1093/2010.

[17] Barrdear and Kumhof (2016).

[18] Most recent European discussion of this available at: EDPB-EDPS (2023) Joint Opinion 02/2023 on the Proposal for a Regulation of the European Parliament and of the Council on the establishment of the digital euro European Data Protection Board y ECB (2020) The role of cash.

Even before the emergence of blockchain technology, digital wallets were already an existing reality. However, they had the exclusive function of digitally representing physical goods, such as currency or other payment instruments, to facilitate online transactions. However, the ability to manage assets that do not have a physical counterpart (as an asset to back it up), including crypto assets, establishes the need to develop secure and accessible forms of custody. As Professor Barresi and Professor Zatti rightly predicted four years ago, this scenario exposed us to the new need that went beyond increasing the efficiency of payment systems linked to Web 2.0 and focused on connectivity and data.[19] Thus, in Web 3.0, which is based on consensus and peer-to-peer algorithms, digital wallets would take on a different function, with a corresponding effect on the different technical, economic and legal aspects.[20] The first to use the concept of Web 3.0 in the context of cryptocurrencies was Ethereum co-founder Gavin Wood.

The first situation where a custody system with features such as digital wallets is necessary is CBDC management. As discussed *above,* the fundamental objective of a CBDC is to use technology to improve the efficiency of the payment system. However, this must be combined with maintaining price stability and user confidence in the payment system. Together with these issues, there are other critical aspects such as universality—as a measure of financial inclusion of all agents and social groups—and the protection of user data and privacy. Universality requires that digital wallets be managed, from a legal point of view, as necessary tools with the capacity to identify the person while simultaneously capable of guaranteeing full compliance with the rules on personal data protection. This is essential to ensure a high level of privacy and a low risk of illegal use of CBDCs, complying with anti-money laundering and countering the financing of terrorism (AML) rules. On a technical level, solutions such as creating *multi-party computations* and *zero-knowledge proof,* among others,[21] have been proposed.

Although there are specific cases in which certain central bank digital currencies use traditional technologies based on telecommunications infrastructures (as is the case of JAM-DEX), most existing projects today are based on distributed ledger technologies (DLT), using blockchains of a private nature. However, one thing seems undeniable: in all these cases, the user needs a smartphone to access and use their coins. In this way, mobile applications that function as a digital wallet have access to millions of personal data that allow the identification of the customer and the application of other legal obligations (known as the *know your client* regulation, or, for its acronym in English, KYC). Certainly, mobile phones, as present and future support for digital currencies, present serious problems in safeguarding data privacy and security, which distances these currencies from one of the basic properties of cash, its anonymity.

---

[19] Zatti and Barresi (2020).

[20] Turi (2023).

[21] Zatti and Barresi (2020).

Another factor to consider is that DLT/*Blockchain* networks are not anonymous and could be monitored. Likewise, another role that must be precisely defined is that of intermediaries between the central bank and the end user since they will also have a large amount of personal data that will be subjected to the appropriate processing to ensure the tracking of transactions.

Focusing on a more specific level, we examine the case of the digital euro. So far, the latest work on the digital euro published by the ECB in October 2023 argues that it will have characteristics similar to cash but incorporating the electronic aspect. Thus, in addition to allowing maximum security in payments (both in shops and in online purchases and transfers between individuals), the European Union's digital currency will allow, in the words of the highest monetary institution at the community level, "the highest possible level of privacy". We can deduce from the words of the ECB that its purpose is to resemble as much as possible the current physical euro, adapted to the needs of the moment in which we live.

The ECB argues that electronic transactions linked to digital euro accounts opened with credit institutions will be processed only to control and combat money laundering (for this reason, the exclusion of full anonymity is avoided). This is already done today with transactions linked to physical euros. On the other hand, the ECB is strongly committed to ensuring privacy in offline digital euro payments. However, for reasons of control over money laundering, full anonymity is excluded. However, the digitisation of a currency certainly carries a traceability risk regarding where and when transactions are made. In addition, there is a possibility of access to private personal data that should be duly regulated in the future.

In short, the ECB's purpose is clear: to strike a balance between the protection of privacy and the ability to trace financial transactions to avoid the problems that can occur (in the form of criminal activities, for example). The question arises is how far this power can go in the hands of central banks and, specifically, the ECB, to exert even greater control over economic transactions. That is the most disturbing aspect of developing this and other digital currencies. Without a doubt, the user's privacy and the existence of minimal interference in personal data must be rigorously guaranteed, and all this by doing so from the original design of these digital currencies.[22] Even so, as is logical, a proportionate and justified balance must be guaranteed between protecting data privacy and other objectives, such as fighting money laundering and tax evasion. If a thorough and joint analysis of the risks to users' rights and freedoms is conducted, CBDC projects will come to fruition more quickly than expected.

---

[22] In this regard, it will be of great relevance to refer to the latest advances in the BIS *Innovation Hub* projects that I comment on in Sect. 4.1 of this work.

2.4 *Differences Between CBDCs and Other Monetary Concepts*

To achieve a precise conceptual delimitation, in the following sections, the concept of CBDC will be distinguished from both the idea of cash and electronic bank money, as well as terms such as *stablecoins* or crypto assets, to which CBDCs are opposed, and what is known as *tokenised bank money.*

2.4.1 Cash and Electronic Bank Money

As we mentioned at the beginning of Sect. 2.2, cash is a liquid and tangible asset that can be exchanged between peers, is universal, anonymous and does not accrue interest. For their part, CBDCs, even though they share (or aspire to share) characteristics of physical money, are digital currencies and, as such, can incorporate functions that are impossible for physical money. Through them, access to the central bank's liabilities is increased, giving way to the third form of central bank money, cash and reserves, called "primary issuance".

The main distinction between *tokenised* and account-based money lies in the form of verification required for its exchange. Payment systems based on the former depend essentially on the ability of the beneficiary to verify the validity of the object used for payment. In the digital ecosystem, the concern is the authenticity of the *token* (or currency) and the possibility that it has already been spent; in the case of cash, there is concern that it has not been counterfeited; by contrast, systems based on account money rely fundamentally on the ability to verify the identity of the account holder. Consequently, one of the main concerns is identity theft, which allows criminals to withdraw money from accounts without authorisation from the owner. In fact, without the corresponding identification, it is not possible to correctly relate payers and beneficiaries.

Cash does not generate interest but is available at any time and place, is anonymous and can be transferred "peer to peer (P2P)". On the other hand, electronic bank money (called "balances in reserve and settlement accounts") can generate interest. Still, it is not available at any time and place, nor is it anonymous to the Central Bank, nor can it be transferred between individuals without a monetary authority being aware of it. Finally, digital currencies issued by retail central banks would be available anytime, anywhere. They could be anonymous (hence the importance of establishing proper regulation that safeguards users' privacy), transferred between individuals, and even generate interest. However, the characteristic that establishes the greatest difference of this category concerning the others is that CBDCs are digital currencies with programming capacity, which allows the monetary authority to set limits on the availability of funds and even for these funds to "expire" over time.

2.4.2 Cryptocurrencies and Stablecoins

In addition to the above distinction, CBDCs—as digital representations of a country's fiat money or economic area, which is issued and backed by the corresponding central bank—must be demarcated from so-called *stablecoins.*[23] CBDCs are digital currencies pegged to an official currency already in progress and with the above characteristics (see Sect. 2.2). The former constitutes a form of public money, while the latter represents private money.[24] As a mixed monetary asset, stablecoins are virtual currencies with parity or peg to a *fiat* currency, such as the euro or dollar, or pegged to the value of an asset, such as gold. Thus, *stablecoins*, unlike non-intermediated cryptocurrencies, are characterised by their ability to stabilise their price since they are backed by an underlying asset (reserve). In addition, they can correct the instability of non-intermediated cryptocurrencies, thanks to the limitation of issuers where they will operate and the setting of a reference value concerning legal tender fiat money.[25]

As introduced *above*, *stablecoins* can be backed by *fiat currencies* (*fully reserved*), cryptocurrencies (such as DAI, backed by *Ethereum*), other assets (such as gold or real estate), or controlled by algorithms (referenced to an index and without any backing). In short, *stablecoins* were born to put an end to some of the main drawbacks of the original cryptocurrencies, such as the high volatility of their value and the absence of backing, while taking advantage of their benefits, including the use of technology, programmability and financial decentralisation. The main exponent of this category was *Diem* (formerly called Libra), the failed *stablecoin* of *Facebook* (now Meta).[26]

Algorithmic *stablecoins* encounter serious problems, including, on the one hand, their volatility, understood as a lack of stability as they do not have the backing of an economic regulator, and, on the other hand, the negative consequences of anonymity in transactions, such as the possibility of being used in criminal activities.

In Prof. Zatti's opinion, before allowing the creation and issuance of coins privately (without intermediaries), it is elementary to understand the potential consequences on a particular jurisdiction's values, principles and financial objectives.[27] These are the three critical elements that condition the adoption of a currency as a *legal tender.*[28] El Salvador was the first country in the world to adopt the Bitcoin cryptocurrency as an official tender in June 2021, and it has continued to be the reference country.[29] However, adoption has not been exempted from the problems

---

[23] Iberpay (2023).

[24] Dyson et al. (2016).

[25] ECB (2020) and Arner et al. (2020b).

[26] Zetzsche et al. (2019).

[27] Zatti (2023), pp. 3–13.

[28] Sono (2023), pp. 700–720.

[29] El Salvador's Royal Decree number 57 (also referred to as the "Bitcoin Law") was passed on June 9, 2021, and came into force on September 7 of the same year, ninety days after its publication.

described above and Prime Minister Nayib Bukele's criticism because, according to polls, less than 5% of Salvadorans know what Bitcoin is.[30] In this sense, Prof. Filippo Zatti understands that two critical aspects deserve to be considered in this decision: On the one hand, El Salvador's link with the IMF, since the country is looking for a way to be financially independent; on the other, Salvadorans' relationship with the "new fiat money," which connects with the still scarce use of Bitcoin by the population of El Salvador.[31]

2.4.3 Tokenized Bank Money (e-Money Token)

Tokenised traditional assets are cryptographic representations of traditional assets that use DLT (or analogous) technology in their registry, which banks can issue. Thus, the *electronic money token* (*e-money token*) is a stablecoin, a type of crypto asset that was born to be used as a medium of exchange of stable value thanks to the fact that it is referenced to the value of a fiat currency, legal tender. As opposed to tokenised bank money, CBDCs are digital currencies issued by and backed by a central bank, not *stablecoins*. Consequently, the digital euro, for example, would not be a *stablecoin* replicating the euro's value but the digital form of the same currency whose control would fall to its issuer, the ECB.[32]

In addition, tokenised bank money is regulated in Title IV of the European Union's Markets in Crypto Assets Regulation (hereinafter, "MiCA"), while the digital euro (EU CBDC project), which will be developed in the next section of this chapter, is outside the MiCA regulatory framework.[33] This subjection of the former to the Regulation means that e-money *token* providers are subject to obligations, including the supervision and regulation of a banking authority (in this case, the European one) and that issuers of tokenised bank money will be required to have a MiCA license and an e-money license (subject to the European Directive on electronic money).[34]

In this regard, it is worth paying attention to tokenised bank deposits as an expression of bank money tokens deployed in DLT networks. In mid-2023, up to 9 banks joined the Federal Reserve Bank of New York's innovation hub to develop a proof of concept of the Regulated Liability Network (with a wholesale CBDC). BNY Mellon, Citi, HSBC, PNC Bank, Mastercard, TD Bank, Truist, U.S. Bank and Wells Fargo participated in the development of the project, with a common aim: to introduce a series of improvements in the dollar, but always maintaining the currency's hegemonic position in the international macroeconomic environment. Thus, they outlined their well-known desire to create an analogue to a US CBDC. As

[30] On this point, we refer to a previous work: Sanz Bayón (2021b), pp. 5–9.

[31] Zatti (2023), pp. 3–13.

[32] ECB (2021), p. 247.

[33] Annunziata (2023a), p. 202 and Annunziata (2023b).

[34] Madrid Parra (2021), pp. 219–244.

a result of the advances in this project, it was possible to generate a theoretical infrastructure to exchange and settle commercial bank deposit tokens and central bank liabilities using DLT technology and a simulated US central bank digital currency, a CBDC.[35] Likewise, the technical and legal reports clarified that the project did not present any legal problem since the current regulations of the United States would allow the creation of a Regulated Liability Network.[36]

3 Analysis of Major CBDC Projects

3.1 Context of the Digital Euro[37]

Although the European Central Bank (ECB) published its first reports on the digital euro project in October 2020, the research phase of the digital euro officially began within the framework of the European Union in October 2021. Almost two years later, in June 2023, the European Commission published the package of legislative proposals on the digital euro and the legal tender of cash.[38] In the words of Fabio Panetta, current Governor of the Bank of Italy and former member of the ECB's Executive Board, before the European Parliament's Committee on Economic and Monetary Affairs, these proposals shared the objective of "designing an inclusive and truly European digital means of payment that can meet the needs and preferences of citizens". In addition, the aim was to achieve a conjunction between the ECB's desire to preserve its monetary sovereignty and the demand of citizens that their freedoms be guaranteed in the digital age.[39]

Even though 60% of people recently surveyed by the ECB[40] state that they would like to continue to have the option of using cash, more and more people pay digitally in their day-to-day lives. In fact, 55% of consumers in the Eurozone prefer to do so.[41] That is why the European Commission had to define the digital euro in its June 2023 proposals as a currency issued by the ECB that guarantees the continuity of cash.

The objectives of the digital euro project include the promotion of the digitalisation of the economy, the improvement of the security and efficiency of

[35] The simulated network of regulated liabilities could be a disruptive change, mainly for international dollar users, as it would allow all *anti-money laundering* (AML) and *know-your-client* (KYC) measures to be applied in international settlements.

[36] Federal Reserve Bank of New York (2023).

[37] For more detail on this epigraph, we refer to the book's next chapter, by Professors Zatti and Barresi.

[38] ECB (2024) Update on the work of the digital euro scheme's Rulebook Development Group. Bindseil et al. (2024).

[39] Borgovono et al. (2017).

[40] Parrondo (2023), pp. 4–10.

[41] ECB (2023) Study on the payment attitudes of consumers in the euro area (SPACE).

transactions, the strengthening of the international role of the euro and the stimulation of innovation in payment services. The ECB identifies two fundamental reasons why the digital euro should be implemented. On the one hand, it carries out its functions through an innovative digital solution accessible to everyone and compatible with private solutions. On the other hand, it may contribute to developing the EU's economic policies, including continuing to have the capacity to act on interest rates, offering support in the event of cyber or any other incidents, and making the financial system more efficient and greener.

Months after these legislative proposals, on 1 November 2023, the digital euro began the preparation phase once the research phase had been completed. In this new scenario, the ECB and the national monetary authorities of each of the euro area countries will continue to analyse the functionalities of the digital currency, as well as make progress in the development and experimentation of the appropriate technical solutions and operational mechanisms to, where appropriate, start issuing the digital euro in the future. In his numerous speeches on the digital euro project, Fabio Panetta assured that this digital currency issued and backed by the funds of the European Central Bank will complement cash, as it will be enshrined in legislation in the future and against the many critical voices that have been raised in recent years around the idea of the hypothetical suppression of physical money (which the digital euro would have come to replace, as already mentioned). Thus, the current role of the European regulator would be to refine the proposals set out and ensure that the future digital euro reproduces the main essential notes of cash in the digital realm, providing an electronic means of payment available to all citizens, available free of charge, anywhere and even without an internet connection while ensuring the highest possible level of privacy in digital transactions.[42]

For Fabio Panneta, there are four decisive aspects to consider to ensure access to the digital euro for all citizens:[43] Firstly, it must have legal tender status; that is, citizens must be able to access and pay with the digital euro, even from their current commercial bank. Second, privacy must be guaranteed. Along these lines, the latest draft legislation states that the digital euro would be a novel payment solution with greater privacy and data protection, minimising the risks related to money laundering and terrorist financing. In addition, EU authorities would not be able to access the personal data of users of the digital euro, and the possibility of paying without an internet connection would be very similar to how cash works today. Thirdly, the European Commission includes in its proposals the idea of seeking a balance between the pricing objectives of both the public and private sectors. Thus, end-users would be able to use basic services of the digital euro free of charge, while intermediaries would be compensated like that of private digital means of payment. Fourth, one of the biggest conundrums in developing the digital euro was where commercial banks would stand, as many customers might think about

[42]This is another of the great concerns of the citizens of the European Union, which has been addressed in point 2.3 of this paper.

[43]ECB (2023).

withdrawing their funds by looking for deposits or other more profitable financial instruments in the ECB's digital euro. In this sense, it seems necessary to maintain the balance between private money, such as the deposits of commercial banks, and central bank money. To this end, the ECB has developed numerous instruments that will avoid undesirable effects on monetary policy, the stability of the financial system and the provision of credit to the real economy.[44] Users can also link their digital euro wallet to their bank account.[45]

The ECB is actively working with the main payment service providers at the EU level and other stakeholders to ensure that the digital euro is fully compatible with existing payment tools and that it responds to the demands of the digital revolution (notably by improving the payment system) but without compromising the stability of the financial sector or user privacy.

For his part, the governor of the Bank of Spain, Pablo Hernández de Cos, oversaw reviewing and commenting on the current digital euro project in this phase of preparation it has recently entered. In this regard, at the end of 2023 at the Financial Markets Association Annual Convention he reiterated his support for the project, considering that it has the potential to offer significant advantages, even though he is aware that risks may appear. The risks need to be mitigated with a solid regulatory framework; that is, the potential issuance is always subject to an adequate regulatory framework. His speech was based on several solid arguments:[46]

(i) On the one hand, the use of digital means of payment is increasing, and the relative weight of cash use is decreasing. The use of cash in commerce experienced a drop of 13 percentage points, going from 72% of total operations in 2019 to only 59% in 2022.
(ii) On the other hand, the digital euro would have the potential to foster innovation in the European payment system as a whole in the face of an excessively fragmented retail payments scenario across euro-area countries.
(iii) Third, the EU's digital currency would allow for "strategic autonomy of the region". Although the integration of the euro system with SEPA instruments has progressed in a very good way, there is still a great dependence on foreign brands in payments at points of sale, which weakens the strategic autonomy of the euro area. In this sense, some initiatives, including the *European Payments Initiative* (EPI), are encouraging, as they aim to design a pan-European

[44] Among the instruments designed for this purpose are "holding limits".

[45] In this regard, the second version of the Electronic Identification, Authentication and Trust Services Regulation (eIDAS 2) is worth mentioning. Proposal for a Regulation of the European Parliament and of the Council amending Regulation (EU) No 910/2014 regarding establishing a Framework for a European Digital Identity. This aims that by 2030, 80% of citizens will have a new, more robust European digital identity that allows them to carry out procedures and processes between companies and with the public administration with the greatest possible security and simplicity. Thus, in 2024, EU Member States will almost certainly have to provide the European *Digital Identity Wallet* (EDIW), with which they will be able to open bank accounts in any Member State.

[46] Hernadez de Cos (2023).

interbank network with its payment system, which aspires to compete with foreign companies such as Visa or Mastercard.[47]

For his part, about the possible remuneration of the digital euro referred to *above,* Hernández de Cos advocates a balance between commercial banks and the ECB, so he understands that it has been concluded that there are no elements that sufficiently justify the introduction of such remuneration. In line with this point, the digital euro is set to culminate the effectiveness of existing instant payment systems and, more specifically, the *TARGET Instant Payment Settlement* (better known as TIPS), launched in 2018.[48] The ECB introduced TIPS to provide a settlement layer for commercial banks. If it were to enjoy mass adoption, this would allow businesses and individuals to transact with each other instantly. According to the ECB, this network is designed to settle a regular load of more than 43 million instant payment transactions per day and about 2000 transactions per second. It is still a pending matter to know if the digital euro and the TIPS will be able to coexist in the SEPA area and if their future adoption will compromise the position of the predominant players in the retail payments market in Europe, controlled by North American companies such as Visa, MasterCard and PayPal.

On the other hand, it had been considered for some time whether the digital euro project would be the precursor to a wholesale digital currency, restricted to a limited group of financial counterparties (interbank market), or whether, on the contrary, it was considering creating a retail CBDC, accessible to all types of users. As discussed *below*, the Chinese digital yuan is an example of retail and wholesale CBDCs. However, the digital euro seems intended to be issued as a retail currency.

On a legal level, the regulation that will govern the issuance of this digital currency will depend on both its design and its purpose.[49] However, despite the many unknowns that are still present, we have some certainties. To begin with, all CBDCs are outside the scope of application of MiCA but one or another precept will apply to the digital euro depending on the design it finally adopts. For example, if it were issued as a monetary policy instrument only for central bank counterparties—although it is a highly unlikely alternative—we would be within the framework of Article 127.2 TFEU. On the other hand, if its issuance were extended to retail and private company accounts through the ECB, Article 17 of the Statute of the European System of Central Banks (ESCB) would be added to the previous provision. If it is considered equivalent to physical bank money, Article 128 TFEU and Article 16 of the Statute of the ESCB would apply to it. If it were issued as a means of settlement for types of payment processed by a dedicated payment infrastructure, Article 22 of the Statute of the ESCB would apply.

---

[47] In the US, for example, the payment management service is publicly managed by the *Automated Clearing House Association* (NACHA) through the *Automated Clearing House* (ACH) system; however, the truth is that most of the operations in terms of payment processing worldwide are carried out by private companies with great experience.

[48] Sanz Bayón (2020b), pp. 58–65.

[49] Parrondo (2023), pp. 4–10.

However, the most specific regulation in this regard comes from the *Proposal for a Regulation of the European Parliament and of the Council, of 28 June 2023, on implementing the digital euro.* This proposal for a Regulation establishes the legal framework and the essential elements of the digital currency. It shifts the focus on the decision-making of the issuance of the currency solely to the ECB, which is responsible for carrying out the technical studies in this regard, relying on the reports and projects of the BIS *Innovation Hub.* as well as other monetary authorities.

In addition, on the same day that the previous proposal was approved, *the Proposal for a Regulation of the European Parliament and of the Council of 28 June 2023 on the provision of digital euro services by payment service providers incorporated in Member States whose currency is not the euro and amending Regulation (EU) 2021/1230 of the European Parliament was also presented and approved European and Council Rules.* Its mission is to safeguard the role of cash, ensure that it remains accepted as a means of payment and easily accessible to individuals and legal entities in the euro area. In this sense, this proposal was a great step forward because it stipulates that the autonomy of the will of all citizens of the euro area must be respected so that they can choose their preferred payment method, freely. It also sets out the legal obligation to safeguard the right to access cash supply services, especially guaranteeing the financial inclusion of the most vulnerable groups, such as the elderly, who depend on cash payments.[50]

In short, the digital euro is not yet a reality. Still, it may be in the coming years, so it is the duty of the highest legislative authorities at the European level to ensure that solid foundations are laid that allow, where appropriate, the development of the future digital euro, safeguarding the fundamental rights of citizens, especially their privacy. Undoubtedly, the key to development will be that all progress in this area is made from the perspective of dialogue and dialogue with all the actors involved (especially with citizens, governments, companies, and financial institutions, etc.).[51]

3.2 Comparative Analysis of Some CBDC Projects: Special Mention of the Chinese Digital Yuan, the Russian Digital Ruble and the So-Called Digital Dollar

This section briefly reflects on the CBDC projects of the major international economic powers, mainly the Chinese digital yuan, the Russian digital ruble, and the US digital dollar.

[50] Zatti and Barresi (2024), pp. 360–375.

[51] See European Parliament (2024) y European Parliament, Committee on Economic and Monetary Affairs (2024) Draft Report on the proposal for a regulation of the European Parliament and of the Council on the establishment of the digital euro (COM (2023)0369 – C9-0219/2023 – 2023/0212 (COD)).

Although the first of the central banks to be interested in creating their digital currencies was the Swedish (known as the *Riskbank*), its digital currency project (*e-krona*), started in 2017 and not yet implemented, does not enjoy the same international knowledge as the projects that will be presented below. Sweden is waiting to know how the rest of the counterpart projects evolve at a technological level and, mainly, to study how they are regulated.

3.2.1 The Digital Yuan (e-CNY): The People's Bank of China's Digital Monetary Project

The digital yuan or e-CNY is the Chinese CBDC, i.e., the centralised digital currency expected to be used primarily for retail payments in China. The Chinese central bank, the People's Bank of China (PBOC) will be the issuer of the digital yuan, which is already experimenting with this project through large-scale pilot programs in several cities over the past few years.[52] The high digitalisation of the Chinese economy experienced in the last decade has favoured the fact that the pilot tests have been carried out very quickly and with considerable efficiency in the results obtained.[53]

The PBOC began researching the launch of its digital currency in 2014 when it established a specific research team for this task. Although more than a decade has passed, and even testing with retail payments has already begun, many of the important elements of what the digital yuan or DC/EP aims to achieve and how it will work remain open and could see substantial variations. The introduction of e-CNY by the PBOC has two different but related objectives. The first, longer-term goal is to issue and consolidate a digital currency that can compete with other digital currencies, such as bitcoins, stablecoins, and other central bank digital currencies (CBDCs), while ensuring that the yuan (fiat)—Renminbi—remains legal tender in China. The second, more immediate objective is to reshape China's current payments market by providing a digital payment method like cash, i.e. one that is accessible, low-cost, with controllable anonymity and facilitates competition between payment service providers.[54]

On a broader horizon, the digital yuan represents an aspect of China's economic digitalisation objective, which figured very prominently in China's Five-Year Plan for National Informatization in 2016, from which the broad outlines of the design of the DLT/Blockchain networks that the Chinese state intends to build in the short and medium term (called *Blockchain-based Network Service* were extracted). In this

[52] In the PBOC's white paper, published a few days after the ECB made its move on the Digital Euro in July 2021, it outlines the progress of its plan for the digital yuan (e-CNY, DC/EP). For example, *JD.com*, one of the largest e-commerce platforms in China, engaged in experimentation, allowing its customers to buy products with the subscribed units of digital yuan.

[53] Yao (2018).

[54] People's Bank of China (2021).

sense, in addition to the progress of the PBOC (specifically its Departments of Technology, Payments and particularly the Department of Research in digital money, which processes industrial and intellectual property rights related to financial innovation), it is also advisable to pay attention to the work of the National Development and Reform Commission, which guides the priority lines in the field of industry and technology as well as the development of the activities of the Cyberspace Administration of China, with its "Blockchain Information Service Management Regulation" (BISRM) Program, without forgetting the participation in this matter of the China International Economic Exchange Center (CCIEE). This organisation began research on introducing a CBDC in China almost seven years ago. At the same time, the work of the main Chinese banks, manufacturers such as Huawei and Xiaomi, technology companies such as Baidu, Tencent or Alibaba, or financial companies such as Union Pay and Ant Financial, as well as telecommunications operators (China Mobile, China Telecom and China Unicom), are relevant, since they provide timely information on the development of Chinese techno-financial services.

Meanwhile, the regulatory development of distributed ledger technology in China, which will be an important infrastructure option to host the digital yuan, is based on the National Cryptography Law, approved on October 26, 2019, by the Standing Committee of the 13th National People's Congress and entering into force on January 1, 2020.[55]

3.2.2 Characteristic Elements and Functionality of the Digital Yuan

The PBOC will fully support the e-CNY but will be put into operation by payment service providers. The PBOC defined the e-CNY as cash in circulation or M0 in monetary policy language. Defining the digital yuan as M0 rather than M1 or M2 has several implications.[56] Firstly, the PBOC will be responsible for the digital yuan. This implies that M0 is a direct liability of the central bank, while M1 and M2 include certain liabilities of commercial banks. This definition means that the e-CNY will be completely risk-free. Additionally, digital wallets containing the e-CNY will not be considered bank accounts. PBOC pilots so far only require a mobile phone number to open an e-wallet that can accommodate the digital yuan. Thirdly, as we discussed earlier concerning the Digital Euro, the e-CNY does not accrue interest,

[55]The most relevant would be in Chapter 3, Article 24. The purpose of this law was to facilitate the development of business with commercial cryptography and to guarantee the security of cyberspace and information. Under this law, cryptographic codes will be classified into two groups: "basic and common codes"—which will be administered by the State—and "commercial codes"—which can be developed and applied at the business level. It will be up to the Chinese government to establish encryption standards covering state and enterprise cryptography.

[56]The M0 definition of the digital yuan will likely prevent the disintermediation of Chinese banks because by prohibiting interest payments, the PBOC will issue a limited amount of e-CNY for circulation to replace cash but not to capture bank deposits.

unlike assets on M1 or M2 (bank deposits). This is crucial because most digital currencies, including some CBDCs that other central banks are currently considering, have not ruled out interest payments. Finally, only Chinese commercial banks could convert the e-CNY to bank deposits and vice versa. In other words, the exchange operations of this CBDC correspond to those of Chinese commercial banks.

Consequently, instead of a "fractional reserve" system used in the traditional banking system, the Chinese CBDC would require financial institutions to maintain a 100% reserve ratio. As a result, the CBDC would not have any derivative deposits or money multipliers. In this way, the digital yuan would act only as an intermediary between commercial banks and the PBOC and between commercial banks, companies, and retail users. As one of its objectives is to replace physical cash, although not imminently or close to its launch, the Chinese CBDC will not be overissued and will follow the exact and necessary issuance process, which already exists with the physical cash issued by central banks and distributed by commercial banks. Therefore, the current monetary policy tools would not be questioned in any case, so the digital yuan should not generate a priori any negative impact on the policy carried out by the PBOC, which would nevertheless clearly gain a greater presence in the Chinese economy and finance.

3.2.3 Structure and Distribution of the Digital Yuan

The e-CNY adopts a two-tier structure, according to the PBOC.[57] However, from an e-CNY user's perspective, the system has more than two layers. On the one hand, the PBOC is located at the top level and plays the role of issuer and supervisor. To open an account in an e-CNY e-wallet, the user will need to go to one of the second-tier institutions. These institutions now only include the largest state-owned banks (Industrial and Commercial Bank of China, Bank of China, Agricultural Bank of China, Construction Bank of China, China Merchants Bank) and two online banks (WeBank and MYBank). Once the e-CNY wallet is set up, the user can enjoy a wide range of services provided by the issuing bank and many other banks and payment service providers. These institutions are called "2.5 tier" institutions, which cannot conduct e-CNY exchanges but can provide payments and other services to e-CNY holders. In other words, the programmability of transactions and the scalability of services in the digital yuan system will depend on this level. Finally, on the lower level are commercial establishments, companies and consumers. Commercial companies can agree with level 2 or 2.5 institutions on their infrastructure configurations to receive e-CNY payments online and offline.

Under the planned structure, the PBOC will delegate most of the responsibilities to the second-tier institutions, which will provide direct service to the customer, assume KYC obligations, and protect their privacy. In this sense, it is conceivable

[57] Yao (2018).

that the issuance of this CBDC in China will come at a cost to second-tier institutions. Still, at the same time, it will offer a new business opportunity for commercial banks in the payments sector, putting them in a more competitive position with Internet companies.

Regarding its technological infrastructure, it remains uncertain whether the second layer of the digital yuan would also be based on a DLT/Blockchain network. As the administration of the second layer would be delegated to financial institutions, the Chinese CBDC could run on multiple different networks at the same time, which could lead to transaction performance issues. Pilot tests will determine and verify the technical feasibility of these aspects since, currently, DLT/Blockchain technology does not achieve yields as high as those necessary to sustain the entire Chinese payment market. Likewise, the PBOC suggested that its CBDC could work with smart contracts but not applications that provide functionality beyond "basic monetary requirements."[58] This is due to concerns that a programmable development layer on top of the currency could add additional value to the CBDC but undermine its security or stability in exchange for usability, negatively affecting the Renminbi's internationalisation.

3.2.4 Privacy in the Digital Yuan: The Concept of "Controllable Anonymity"

Privacy is one of the most contentious issues regarding CBDCs, mainly because the system's design can allow for much more oversight than physical cash or existing digital payment methods. The digital yuan is no exception in this regard. Privacy issues can be considered on two levels: what access state authorities have to individual transaction data and what access the parties to the transaction have (e.g., merchants, banks and payment processors, digital wallets).

While the contrast between a CBDC and physical cash is often raised—under the presumption that the latter is always anonymous public money—the truth is that cash transactions in China are no longer completely anonymous because ATMs and other scanners record the serial numbers of banknotes entering and leaving the banking system. Of course, small individual transactions do remain anonymous. However, the degree of government monitoring of transactions on systems run by banks or through e-wallets that dominate online payments in China (Ant Group's Alipay and Tencent's WeChat Pay) is largely unknown. There are also no independent courts that establish protection measures for the personal data that the government can obtain.

The PBOC promotes the digital yuan to the Chinese public as a more privacy- and anonymity-preserving form of payment than the currently dominant payment tools run by private companies in China. The PBOC's motto for digital yuan privacy is

[58] The definition of "basic monetary requirements" has not yet been specified in the digital yuan regulation.

"controllable anonymity," which seems like a juxtaposition of two mutually exclusive concepts. This concept suggests that the PBOC will have access to the ledger that shows each balance and transaction in real-time, but in which the monetary authority itself or any other competent state entity is prevented from accessing the identity of each user or the entity that owns the addresses or private keys of the digital wallet through which transactions with the digital yuan are carried out.

The information available shows that the e-CNY is built with an approach based on "three centres": authentication, registration and analysis centres. The authentication centre assumes that the PBOC would implement centralised management of financial institutions and end-user identity information, which is the basic component of the system's security. The registration centre would note the identity of each CBDC unit and the corresponding users and complete the CBDC registration for the following functions: issuance, transfer, and redemption. Finally, the analytics centre would fulfil several functions, such as preventing money laundering, analysing payment behaviour analysis, monitoring real-time indicators, etc. The "three hubs" are claimed to be designed to ensure that Chinese CBDC transactions are anonymous from the user's perspective while preventing money laundering and tax evasion. The scheme proposed by the Chinese central bank would theoretically be suitable for maintaining identification and traceability records of all transactions and users. However, the only proposal is to deactivate anonymity for illegal activities such as money laundering and tax fraud. For this reason, the PBOC has described the privacy protection capabilities of e-CNY as "controllable anonymity." This means that its users will have the option to hide their identity from their counterparts while the Government reserves the ability to monitor illegal transactions.[59]

3.2.5 Implications of the Digital Yuan for Commercial Banking and the Chinese State

In light of its nascent regulation and experimentation, e-CNY will likely bring substantial changes to China's digital payments sector, improving the positioning of commercial banks in a commercial segment such as this, which large digital technology companies currently dominate. The e-CNY became massively deployed in 2022 as a catalyst for other central banks to bring forward or accelerate their CBDC projects. On the other hand, the fact that a state can follow the flow of money in its economy and monitor general monetary activity more effectively, thanks to a new tool, contributes to its decisions being more planned. As a result, it is most likely that thanks to the digital yuan, the Chinese state will considerably increase its ability to control money movements and flows more effectively. In addition, the digital yuan will undoubtedly bring an operational advantage for the Chinese economy in terms of cross-border payments and investments, which will help to improve the

[59] Sanz Bayón (2021a).

positioning of the Renminbi as an international reserve currency, possibly enhancing its competitiveness against the US dollar and the Euro.[60]

However, another reason, this time geopolitical, underlies the issuance of the Chinese CBDC. If the Beijing government formalises interoperability between the e-CNY and other CBDCs, China could do without the Society for Worldwide Interbank Financial Telecommunication (SWIFT) infrastructure.[61] This would effectively allow the Chinese economy, along with other countries, to bypass the SWIFT intermediary node, but to do so, China would need to get other countries to accept international payments with the digital yuan.[62] A situation like this would have a direct consequence in the global geopolitical context since it would mean, in practice, the deactivation of the scope and effectiveness of hypothetical US sanctions against China.

The digital yuan (e-CNY) project is putting pressure on other major economies to accelerate their national CBDC projects. For this reason, in geopolitical terms, China is trying to accompany its digital yuan project by strengthening its international cooperation plans to promote the interoperability of its CBDC with others. The monetary policy objective behind the e-CNY is not ostensibly to supplant the US dollar as the dominant global currency but to reduce the Chinese economy's dependence on the dollar by establishing a new and alternative payment system. To push this agenda forward, China can successfully leverage its global economic power to shape and foster the international, or at least multilateral, CBDC space.[63]

---

[60] PBOC's issuance of a CBDC could alter the distribution of international payments market shares if China introduces it into its bilateral investment agreements or exports it to its international payment schemes, ceasing to rely on the U.S. dollar. If examined in comparative terms, the yuan significantly underperforms the Chinese economy globally. This makes Beijing heavily dependent on the US dollar in foreign trade. On this subject, see Huang et al. (2014), p. 482.

[61] SWIFT, faced with the potential loss of access to the Chinese economy, has set up a joint venture, called *Finance Gateway Information Services*, with the PBOC, to improve cross-border transaction services in China. 3% of the joint venture is owned by the PBOC's Digital Money Research Institute, suggesting there would be more scope to promote the use of the digital yuan globally.

[62] However, in our view, the attractiveness of a CBDC will depend on economic and institutional factors, such as general macroeconomic conditions, the openness and transparency of the issuing state's financial markets, or the credibility of its socio-political institutions. These factors are currently limiting the yuan's potential international status, and if the Chinese CBDC is issued, this limitation will most likely be extended. As some analyses suggest, political and institutional factors are weighing on the yuan's potential share of global foreign exchange reserves to around 2%. However, it does seem clear that the digital yuan could strengthen the adoption of the Renminbi in cross-border payments, linking the e-CNY to various forms of economic activities through bilateral, regional, and multilateral trade agreements, especially for those countries that already participate in China-backed programs (such as the *Belt and Road* Initiative). On this point: Liang (2020), pp. 317–328.

[63] Knoerich (2021), p. 160.

3.3 The Digital Ruble

On July 11, 2023, the Russian parliament presented the project for introducing its digital currency, the digital ruble, and creating the appropriate platform for developing its currency. This project aimed to integrate the digital ruble into its financial system, regulate it properly, and establish due control for tax purposes. In mid-August 2023, the country announced that its Central Bank (BCR) would start a "large-scale" pilot program to test the operation of the digital ruble. In this way, it consolidated itself as one of the countries leading the tests with digital currencies issued and backed by central banks, a role it continues to play today.

As announced, up to 13 Russian banks (including Sberbank, VTB and Gazprombank) and several customers of these financial institutions would be involved in this pilot project, who would carry out their operations thanks to a digital wallet. Thus, in the words of the BCR's First Deputy Governor, Olga Skorobogatova, the country is in the most important stage of its CBDC project, a testing phase that anticipates the hypothetical introduction of the digital ruble into the Russian economy in 2025. The evolution of the project is subject to the outcome of the stages of this testing phase.

Presently, through the tests being carried out in this phase, Russia intends to obtain information on the "real" operation of the payment platform of its digital currency, thanks to the participation of bank customers. The number of customers participating in the pilot project has expanded throughout the last quarter of 2023. Among the basic operations that customers can currently carry out include opening and topping up digital accounts in the national CBDC, the possibility of making digital transfers between citizens (P2P), making automatic payments and paying for purchases and services using a QR code in up to thirty businesses located in eleven Russian cities. In addition, the BCR has the power to set and limit the users who have access to the platform on which the digital ruble is based, the volume of transactions undertaken and the threshold of amounts in question. Likewise, by law, the country has prohibited crediting accounts in its CBDC and the accumulation of interest.

3.4 The So-Called "Digital Dollar"

For its part, a private project for issuing a digital dollar of the United States was promoted by the former chairman of the *Commodity Futures Trading Commission* (CFTC), Christopher Giancarlo, outside the Federal Reserve. This project is embryonic, and numerous obstacles have prevented its acceptance. Two fundamental reasons can be adduced to explain the slowdown in the progress of the U.S. CBDC:

1. In the first place, it can be said that the world economy is currently dollarised since the currency of the North American country occupies the first place in commercial transactions. Globally, more than three-quarters of these are made in dollars. In addition, 60% of central banks' foreign exchange reserves are denominated in dollars, and more than two-thirds of the debt issued by these entities are denominated in dollars. Furthermore, one only has to take a brief approach to the functioning of the digital economy to appreciate the significant presence of *stablecoins* and other digital assets in the payment of goods and services. Of these *stablecoins*, up to 95% are denominated in dollars. The conclusion is unequivocal: the United States, through its economic policy, makes decisions with a macroeconomic impact at the international level, and the hegemony of the U.S. currency seems unrivalled, as much as this is the goal of the *e-yuan*.
2. Second, the role of the private sector in issuing *stablecoins* denominated in the U.S. currency also appeases interest in accelerating the process toward the creation of the digital dollar. In this sense, more than 85% of the *stablecoins* in circulation are concentrated in the hands of Bitfinex and Tether's USDT, Circle and Coinbase's USDC and Paxos and Binance's BUSD. All these companies operate in U.S. territory or with U.S. citizens through their currency. In this way, the institutions of the United States maintain the competence and jurisdiction to supervise the aforementioned actors.

In sum, the main players in the digital financial ecosystem (and, specifically, *stablecoin* issuers) are closely linked to the US administration, either voluntarily or coercively, thus participating in positioning the dollar as the main currency used in transactions in the digital economy. In general terms, it could be said that the most representative difference between the Fed and the rest of the central banks is that, while the latter considers that *stablecoins* can violate their monetary sovereignty, the former, based on a positive and complementary vision of *stablecoins* as a tool for technological innovation, has as its main objective to be transparent with its reserves and with the investments made with them.[64]

The European Union, China, India, and the UK, among others, have expressed concern for monetary sovereignty in statements by the G7 and G20 and in the work of the *Financial Stability Board* (FSB), a body whose mission is to propose international recommendations on financial matters.[65] On the one hand, many countries assume the risk of facing the dollarisation of their economy and seeing their local currency replaced by another issued by a private company. On the other hand, the North American giant, representing the other side of the coin, considers the possibility of reinforcing its monetary hegemony.[66]

[64] Wong and Maniff (2020).

[65] Financial Stability Board (2022).

[66] Meanwhile, a sector of the Republican Party has shown its deepest rejection because it considers that a CBDC issued by the Federal Reserve may constitute a threat to individual privacy and freedom. In fact, former President Donald Trump has expressed this at the beginning of 2024 in

Finally, concerning the United States moving in the direction of a CBDC, it is worth mentioning the Hamilton Project, which developed research by the Federal Reserve Bank of Boston and the Massachusetts Institute of Technology (MIT) and whose purpose focused on studying the technical aspects of a potential digital dollar. This project brought with it the publication of a white paper and open-source research software (OpenCBDC) in two versions, although only one was based on DLT technology. At the time, the researchers promised to work on "privacy, auditability, programmability, interoperability, and much more."[67]

In short, the general impression is that today, the debate about a potential digital dollar project has a large political component, and any decision can only be made if it has broad support in Congress.[68] In any case, the decision to launch a digital dollar will require a thorough prior analysis that will take at least another two or three years in an environment that seems to lead to the coexistence of this CBDC if it is finally issued with *stablecoins*.[69] The latest statements by Fed Chairman Jerome Powell made public in March 2024 make it clear that the US power does not have the issuance of the "digital dollar" on the near horizon.[70]

3.5 *Alternative CBDC Models*

As previously introduced, CBDCs are typically divided into two general categories: wholesale (used for interbank transactions) and retail (used by merchants and the general public). The digital euro is a paradigmatic example of a CBDC presented as a retail digital currency project. In contrast, the digital yuan, on the other hand, is a digital currency being tested in wholesale and retail contexts. On the one hand, a wholesale CBDC aims to improve the efficiency and reliability of the existing financial system, ensuring that high-value cross-border transactions between banks, such as interbank lending or securities settlement, are carried out quickly

---

numerous public statements, assuring that he will block the development of the US CBDC if he comes to power again. On the other hand, more recently, Congressman Tom Emmer introduced a bill that sought to ban the U.S. digital currency, and on September 20, 2023, the House Financial Services Committee and the House itself took another step in the line of preventing the issuance of this CBDC. Another congressman, A. Mooney, introduced a bill prohibiting the Federal Reserve from initiating pilot programs to test CBDC initiatives without congressional approval. This project was soon joined by an amendment to the Federal Reserve Act, which established an additional ban on Fed banks so that they could not offer certain products or services directly to an individual, along with a ban on using a CBDC for monetary policy-related purposes.

[67] Brownworth et al. (2017).

[68] The *Digital Dollar Pilot Prevention Act* prohibits the Federal Reserve from initiating pilot programs to test CBDC initiatives without congressional approval.

[69] This approach was already defended by the economist F. Hayek, who in 1976 published his work "The Denationalization of Money", in which he argued that stability of value between two currencies was only possible through competition between them.

[70] Powell (2024).

and securely. In addition, eliminating the currently required intermediaries reduces the cost and complexity of operations and enables international transactions between banks and other financial institutions. In this way, individuals and businesses continue to use existing forms of digital money through fiat currencies (such as the euro or the dollar) stored in their bank accounts. Thus, payments between individuals are still in the traditional banking system, in which accounts are debited and credited with each transaction. On the other hand, retail CBDCs are designed to offer the general public direct access to money guaranteed by a state and, therefore, risk-free (central bank money). These digital currencies are characterised by the fact that they can be used for everyday transactions (such as purchasing goods and services or transferring money between individuals). A central bank can easily inject liquidity into the market using a retail CBDC.[71]

The results of the BIS Innovation Hub study (to be presented *below* in Sect. 4.1 of this paper), which analyse a survey that collected data from more than 86 central banks in 2022, predict that by the end of the current decade, there will be at least 15 retail CBDCs and nine wholesale CBDCs in circulation.[72]

Finally, another important foreign policy issue, which should not go unnoticed, is the strong influence of the BRICS when exploring an alternative currency to the dollar as the world's reference currency. The BRICS countries share a common commitment to discuss US hegemony globally, accounting for 40% of the world's population and 25% of the planet's GDP. With de-dollarization as one of their most prominent objectives, these countries have devised a reserve system called *the Contingent Reserve Arrangement* (CRA). Thus, extrapolating this emerging situation from the geopolitical context, the key to the CBDCs of these countries will be whether they can present themselves and be used as an element that contributes to the de-dollarization of their markets.[73]

4 CBDC Projects Under the Bank for International Settlements (BIS) Innovation Hub

Founded in 1930, the Bank for International Settlements (BIS), based in Basel, Switzerland, is an international organisation whose vision is to promote monetary and financial cooperation at the global level. This body is a forum for debate on the different economic policies to be adopted around monetary and financial research projects. Its main objective is to gain an in-depth understanding of the technological innovations that affect (or potentially will affect) central banking and to harness these innovations to improve the functioning of the global financial system.

[71] Today, we find examples of this type of CBDC in Nigeria, The Bahamas, the Western Caribbean, and Jamaica.

[72] Kosse and Mattei (2023), p. 136.

[73] Wang and Gao (2021), pp. 288–306.

The BIS is the nerve centre for international financial decision-making and a supervisor and centre for economic and monetary studies. It is the main counterparty for central bank financial operations and the agent responsible for depositing collateral in international financial transactions. The BIS published a report in July 2021 that foreshadowed the risk of forming cryptocurrency monetary areas, enabling the emergence of global private stablecoins (GSC) whose scope of operations did not coincide with traditional state jurisdictions.[74] As a result, a fracture in international payments could be triggered, putting the global money market in check.[75]

The BIS has an *Innovation Hub* that carries out very important research work to help central banks evolve their digital currency projects. A strong institutional public component and a large technological component nourish this research centre. The BIS defines a CBDC as "a digital form of central bank money distinct from balances in traditional reserve or settlement accounts" but warns that any measure aimed at achieving a potential launch of a CBDC needs to be given thorough and careful consideration, especially about its possible effects on interest rates, the financial intermediation structure, stability and supervision.[76] Many open fronts today still deserve a much more detailed analysis. Among his latest and most recognised projects in CBDC research are Mariana, Polaris, mBridge, Mandala, Tourbillon, Hertha, Promissa, and Aurum 2.0.

4.1 Some Notable CBDC Projects Under the BIS Innovation Hub

4.1.1 Mariana Project

The Mariana Project aims to show how CBDCs can be the future of cross-border transactions. The project takes ideas and concepts from decentralised finance (DeFi) through interbank exchanges, where crypto assets are immediately traded and settled through automated market makers linked to smart contracts.[77] The Mariana Project builds on previous work examining the feasibility of cross-border transactions. It is a joint proof-of-concept project between the BIS Innovation Hub, the Bank of France, the Monetary Authority of Singapore, and the Swiss National Bank. The project's

[74] IOSCO (2020).

[75] Sanz Bayón (2021a).

[76] Reserve and settlement accounts are available in most jurisdictions to "money market counterparties", i.e. financial institutions directly relevant to implementing monetary policy, such as depository institutions, which already have access to deposits and lending facilities from central banks. In certain jurisdictions, account holders may fall into more categories, such as non-monetary counterparties (e.g. the Treasury, foreign central banks or other institutions such as the IMF). Thus, introducing CBDCs would further expand access to central bank digital money but not to their lending facilities. Retrieved from: BIS Innovation Hub (2018).

[77] Sanz Bayón (2019).

findings could be valuable to central banks and financial institutions considering the future of cross-border payments and FX markets.[78]

In its development, it is intended to test the functionality of the *Automated Market-Maker* (AMM), a systematised and decentralised market based on using a liquidity pool to set prices and exchange tokenised assets. The project is based on the future existence of wholesale digital currencies (wCDBCs). For the project, an architecture of domestic platforms controlled by central banks and a decentralised transnational blockchain network were established, where the AMM would be located. In both of them, wCBDCs could circulate, thanks to the interoperability of systems and protocols. However, passage between the two spaces would be restricted, with instructions under central banks' control.

The main objective was limited to creating a functional experiment of an interbank exchange market based on an AMM, in which wCBDCs coexisted and traded uninterruptedly. Second, we sought to understand the role of liquidity providers for an AMM in this type of market, in which commercial banks would participate directly and take exit or provision orders to and from the fund. In short, the Mariana Project allows wholesale CBDCs used by commercial banks and financial institutions, using AMMs to simplify interbank FX processes through high technological developments. As reflected in the Final Report of the project, the conclusions of this proof of concept could be summarised in three:

1. It is possible to balance the need for central banks to control the issuance of and access to wCBDCs with the ability for exchange intermediaries to hold, trade, and settle trades with these currencies. Thus, the transnational network would support an interbank market according to the permits and regulations of central banks and supervisors.
2. Combining wCBDCs with an automated exchange mechanism through platforms and networks simplifies the currency exchange process, making the market more efficient and reducing counterparty risks when trading against the liquidity pool.
3. Integrating an interoperable interbank foreign exchange market with cross-border infrastructure is possible, allowing actors to trade under an AMM with a foreign exchange liquidity pool.

One possibility arising from the Mariana project is the implementation of an architecture for the cross-border Forex market that complies with the principles of the Foreign Exchange Global Code.[79] Regarding risk management, the Mariana project makes it possible to mitigate the counterparty risk (by operating against the liquidity fund) and the clearing and settlement risk by contracting the steps of the operations and making them immediate in a P2P system. While the blockchain security system can bring benefits for identifying data useful for risk management, it also poses privacy challenges, which could be exposed as a multi-jurisdictional

[78] BIS (2023) Project Mariana. Cross-border exchange of wholesale CBDCs using automated market-makers. Final report.

[79] Global Foreign Exchange Committee-GFXC (2021).

changing market. This point, as observed in the analysis made by the BIS, may become a problem of greater risk due to the impact on fundamental rights and the public's trust in the financial system and its relationship with the CBDC.

4.1.2 Project Polaris

The first one we mention here has been led by the Nordic Center of the BIS *Innovation Hub*, following a survey showing that 49% of central banks consider offline payments with their retail digital currencies essential. In comparison, another 49% think it "advantageous". However, they all agree that the reasons that lead them to give their opinion are resilience, inclusion, privacy and similarity to cash. In this way, the project published on October 26, 2023, defines itself as "a manual for offline payments with CBDCs", which aims to guide central banks. The study, entrusted to expert advisors, orbits around the design of secure and resilient CBDC systems, both *online* and *offline* and aims to help central banks to:

1. understand the available technologies and security measures, as well as the main threats, risks and risk management measures;
2. be aware of privacy issues, inclusion needs, and resilience options;
3. know the design and architecture principles involved;
4. Have a perspective on hypothetical operational and change management issues.[80]

One of the most relevant conclusions is that there is no single solution. Each country has different reasons for providing offline payments with CBDCs, so the currency's design must be adjusted to local requirements. Its implementation will certainly not be without its difficulties. It will involve many technological, operational, and security considerations that must be planned for in the early phases of a CBDC project.

4.1.3 mBridge Project

The second of these latter projects is called "mBridge".[81] This project uses DLT technology to experiment with a common multi-central bank (wholesale) digital currency platform (multi-CBDC) for cross-border bank payments. Published on October 31, 2023, the study is being developed by the BIS Innovation Center of Hong Kong and the central banks of Thailand, Hong Kong, the United Arab Emirates, and the Digital Currency Institute of the People's Bank of China. Its vocation is to solve some of the inefficiencies of cross-border payments, including its high costs, speed and transparency, and the countless operational complexities.

[80] BIS Innovation Hub (2023) Project Polaris: handbook for offline payments with CBDC.

[81] BIS Innovation Hub (2023) Project mBridge: Experimenting with a multi-CBDC platform for cross-border payments.

Thus, the objective was (and still is) to design a common technical infrastructure with the potential to improve the current system and allow cross-border payments to be affordable, immediate, and universally accessible with the final settlement.

Criticism of the current international payments system for its inefficiency is increasing due to its inefficiency. The payment system that supports cross-border financial flows has not kept pace with the rapid growth of global economic integration. Meanwhile, banks are also cutting back on their networks and correspondent services, leaving many participants without access to the global financial system. Among them, emerging markets and developing economies present the most alarming situation. It was, in fact, already tested in 2022, the year in which a pilot project was carried out involving real corporate transactions on the platform between the participating central banks, several selected commercial banks and their clients in four jurisdictions. The challenge is implementing the improvements provided by technology, legal, and governance frameworks to examine possible synergies with other BIS projects and solutions the private sector proposes.

4.1.4 Mandala Project

On 15 November 2023, the BIS *Innovation Hub* published one of its most recent works, the "Mandala Project", in line with the actions carried out by the *Financial Stability Board* in 2023 to achieve the G20 objectives.[82] The project aims to improve cross-border payments by ensuring an efficient and automated legal, regulatory, and supervisory framework for this type of transaction while maintaining its security and integrity. To this end, the project has managed to monitor transactions in real-time, increasing transparency and visibility around country-specific policies.

The project has been led by the BIS Innovation Centre Singapore, the Reserve Bank of Australia (RBA), the Bank of Korea (BOK), the Central Bank of Malaysia (BNM) and the Monetary Authority of Singapore (MAS), and has benefited from several financial institutions. It has addressed the feasibility of codifying a jurisdiction's specific policy, with its regulatory requirements, into a common protocol for cross-border use cases such as payments, foreign direct investment or lending. The particular example tested has been a cross-border loan from an entity located in Singapore to a counterpart in Malaysia. A common system authorises the transaction by implementing various technological tools that allow the simultaneous detection of sanctions and checking that the capital flow management measures (during the pre-validation phase) are complied with. It then generates proof certifying compliance with the regulation, which can be attached to the settlement asset to simplify existing compliance procedures and speed up the payment process.

[82] BIS Innovation Hub (2023) Project Mandala: shaping the future of cross-border payments compliance.

4.1.5 Tourbillon Project

Meanwhile, the interesting "Project Turbillon" studies the anonymity of retail CBDC projects (such as the digital euro).[83] This Project was launched on November 29, 2023, and has been a great advance for the entire doctrine that focused its greatest concern on its ability to respect users' privacy, just as cash currently does. This is because the project allows for a new paradigm that guarantees the privacy of the payer's anonymity, protecting buyers' identities. Furthermore, according to the latest surveys conducted by the Bank of England and the European Central Bank, privacy is essential for a retail CBDC.

This project has conducted its experiments based on payer anonymity (similar to cash to payers, but not to payees). If a consumer were to pay a seller using CBDC, they would not disclose their personal information to anyone (not the merchant, commercial banks, or the central bank). However, the seller's identity would be revealed to its bank as part of the payment and kept confidential at the checkout. The purpose of this inspection is to contribute to the reduction of tax evasion or illicit payments. Finally, the central bank could see the final amount of the transaction but not details about the consumer or seller.

Regarding technical design, the project developed two prototypes based on the eCash design: an eCash 1.0 design, which resembles a digital payment instrument similar to cash, and a second design, called eCash 2.0, which provides enhanced security features against counterfeiting.

4.1.6 Hertha Project

The so-called "Hertha Project" owes its name to the British scientist and inventor Hertha Ayrton, who made important contributions to the physical sciences during her long career.[84] Hertha, a project in which the London Centre of the *BIS Innovation Hub* and the Bank of England collaborate, is one of the projects on which the greatest public attention is focused because it aims to protect payment systems against financial crimes, preserving users' privacy. This interesting mission is a complex challenge and will be decisive for the future of payments in general and CBDCs in particular. The project maps the different typologies of current and potential financial crimes in payment systems in real-time, thanks to the exploitation of lessons from instant payment systems and the analysis of digital asset networks. The project also aims to design a series of synthetic data to test how typologies could be accurately identified while reducing false positives.

---

[83] BIS Innovation Hub (2023) Project Tourbillon: exploring privacy, security and scalability for CBDCs.

[84] BIS Innovation Hub (2024) Project Hertha: identifying financial crime patterns while preserving user privacy within a real-time payment system.

4.1.7 Promissa Project

Another project developed by the BIS that we want to reflect in this research is the one carried out between the Swiss National Bank and the World Bank, called "Project Promissa,[85]" which was born within the tests to tokenise financial instruments. In addition, the International Monetary Fund also participates in the work, albeit as an observer. For several years now, much of the work of the G20 has focused on making multilateral development banks increase their financing capacity to be more effective.

Most international financial institutions are financed by debt instruments such as (paper-based) promissory notes. However, these promissory notes could be digitised and, using DLT technology, be more efficient. This is because it would simplify management by providing a single verification for all parties throughout the life cycle of debt and payment instruments. Today, two of the World Bank's largest entities, the International Bank for Reconstruction and Development (IBRD) and the International Development Association (IDA), hold many IOUs from member countries. In other words, the number of promissory notes held by all international financial institutions is very high, and this reality requires a solution that simplifies their management between international financial institutions. In summary, the project's goal is to build a proof-of-concept (PoC) of a platform for tokenised digital promissory notes, and it is scheduled to culminate in early 2025.

4.1.8 Aurum 2.0 Project

More recently, in March 2024, the Hong Kong BIS Innovation Centre launched the second phase of its Project Aurum with the support of the Hong Kong Monetary Authority (HKMA). Known as "Project Aurum 2.0," the goal of this research project is to improve the privacy of retail CBDCs, following experimentation with a tech stack that integrated a wholesale interbank system and a retail e-wallet in its initial phase.[86]

The importance of this project lies in understanding that privacy is a key consideration and concern for users when they are presented with the idea of adopting a CBDC. They have made this known to the respective central banks through the public consultations proposed in different countries. Central banks, aware of citizens' concerns, seek to implement measures that balance the purported privacy with a necessary level of transparency. As discussed *above*, other research projects focus on studying the privacy of retail CBDCs, such as the Tourbillon Project.

[85] BIS Innovation Hub (2024) BIS Innovation Hub, Swiss National Bank and World Bank launch Project Promissa to test tokenisation of financial instruments.

[86] BIS Innovation Hub (2024) Project Aurum 2.0: Improving privacy for retail CBDC payment.

The Aurum 2.0 project will draw on the expertise of collaborating universities and many privacy experts to advance the design of privacy-respecting CBDC systems. In this sense, the project aims to explain how technology can safeguard users' data in the public sector and evaluate how strengthening privacy impacts a given system's performance and compliance. Among the technologies that will be explored to improve privacy, project leaders cite pseudonymisation and zero-knowledge proof.

5 Conclusions

Once the regulatory perspectives of the different global CBDC projects and initiatives have been exposed from an exhaustive conceptual delimitation and their characteristics, a legal analysis of the main CBDC projects, as well as the role of the main monetary authorities at the international level, it is possible to draw some conclusions. Based on the premise that this matter is continuously evolving and most CBDC projects are in the experimental phase, some provisional criteria can be shed to inspire reflection on this new monetary reality and contribute to the debate on its legislative policy.

1. At a conceptual level, to understand the characteristics and typology of CBDCs, it is necessary to start by making a correct functional and regulatory differentiation between these and other concepts such as cash and electronic bank money, cryptocurrencies and stablecoins, and tokenised bank money (*e-money token*). Likewise, the differences between alternative CBDC models (retail and wholesale) should be understood, as each CBDC project can be ascribed to one of these typologies (or both), and its design and characteristics will depend on this categorisation. In this sense, this document has tried to contribute to the appropriate conceptual demarcation.
2. CBDCs, as digital currency projects issued by a central bank responsible for their distribution and the backing of their securities, with the nature of *fiat* currencies and programming capacity, were born as a reactive response by central banks to the challenges posed by decentralised cryptocurrencies and *stablecoins*, to preserve the monetary sovereignty of States. In addition, they can be considered one of the main manifestations of the monetary digitalisation to which the financial and banking system has been subjected in recent years.
3. Among all the projects under development, 4 stand out whose current situation and development, even heterogeneous among themselves, are the object of in-depth analysis in this work; these are, according to the degree of development: the Chinese digital yuan, with hundreds of millions of digital wallets issued in China in the last year; the Russian digital ruble, in the testing phase, although on a smaller scale, since 2023 and with a view to a hypothetical future issue in 2025; the digital euro, whose recent advance from the research phase to the preparation phase has energised doctrinal study and has led to the idea of a possible issuance

at the end of 2025; and the controversial attempt at a so-called US "digital dollar", which is nothing more than a proposal in a very embryonic phase, after the numerous political obstacles that are preventing it from advancing in its design and implementation.

4. Specifically, the digital euro will take as a source of inspiration and as a legal framework for its regulation both the *Proposal for a Regulation of the European Parliament and of the Council on the implementation of the digital euro* and the *Proposal for a Regulation of the European Parliament and of the Council, on the provision of services in digital euros by payment service providers incorporated in Member States whose currency is not the euro.* both of June 28, 2023. With all this, it aims, as defended by the governor of the Bank of Italy, Fabio Panetta, to achieve its mission of safeguarding the role of cash as a complement to the digital euro and that the former remains easily accessible to natural and legal persons in the euro area.
5. Faced with this scenario, multiple questions and challenges arise at the legal and economic level that can only be tackled, on the one hand, by an adequate regulatory framework that limits the control of central banks to guarantee the privacy of users adequately and, on the other hand, by a careful technical design that takes into account the aforementioned legal framework and achieves the fit of the digital currency, whether it is retail or wholesaler, in the financial system.
6. CBDCs respond to certain interests in their market, where they will operate as legal tender and even as instruments of cross-border payments. However, the development of each CBDC project by their respective central banks is influenced by a political factor of unquestionable relevance. From a geopolitical perspective, it seems there is still a long way to go, and the next few years will be decisive.
7. The set of ongoing or already developed BIS *Innovation Hub* CBDC projects represent very significant advances in the future of CBDC standardisation and interoperability globally. Each addresses an area related to the development of any evolving CBDC project, including privacy, cross-border payment network technical support, or the viability of offline payments and transactions. Considering that most central bank digital currency projects are in the research and experimentation phase, I believe that the future regulation and development of CBDCs cannot be alien to the approaches of monetary authorities, commercial banks or the concerns of users.
8. Finally, the great challenge of any CBDC project that aspires to global adoption is that it can examine the situation of commercial banks, respecting the financial stability and integrity of the banking system, and, at the same time, be aware of the need to combine improving efficiency in the payment network by incorporating DLT (or other similar technology) while respecting users' privacy.

References

Annunziata F (2023a) An overview of the markets in crypto-assets regulation (MiCAR). EBI Working Paper Series 158

Annunziata F (2023b) The licensing rules in MICA. In: Moura D, Diogo V, Duarte P, Granadeiro C (eds) Fintech regulation and the licensing principle. Centro de Investigaçao de Direito Privado, Frankfurt

Arner D et al (2020a) After Libra, Digital Yuan and COVID-19: Central Bank Digital Currencies and the New World of Money and Payment Systems. University of Hong Kong Faculty of Law Research Paper 2020:36

Arner D, Auer R, Fro J (2020b) Stablecoins: risks, potential and regulation. Financial Stability Review 39

Auer R, Cornelli G, Frost J (2020) Rise of the central bank digital currencies: drivers, approaches and technologies, BIS Working Papers 880:9–19

Barrdear J, Kumhof K (2016) The Macroeconomics of central bank issued digital currencies. Bank of England

BBVA Research (2019) Monedas digitales emitidas por bancos centrales: características, opciones, ventajas y desventajas 3

Bindseil U, Cipollone P, Schaaf J (2024) The digital euro after the investigation phase: Demystifying fears about bank disintermediation

BIS (2020a) Central Bank digital currencies: foundational principles and core features

BIS (2020b) A fifth of the world's population is soon to have central Bank digital currency

BIS (2021) Central bank digital currencies for cross-border payments. Report to the G20

BIS Innovation Hub (2023a) Project Mariana. Cross-border exchange of wholesale CBDCs using automated market-makers. Final report

BIS Innovation Hub (2023b) Project Mandala: shaping the future of cross-border payments compliance

BIS Innovation Hub (2023c) Project Tourbillon: exploring privacy, security and scalability for CBDCs

BIS Innovation Hub (2023d) Project mBridge: Experimenting with a multi-CBDC platform for cross-border payments

BIS Innovation Hub (2023e) Project Polaris: handbook for offline payments with CBDC

BIS Innovation Hub (2024a) BIS Innovation Hub, Swiss National Bank and World Bank launch Project Promissa to test tokenisation of financial instruments

BIS Innovation Hub (2024b) Project Hertha: identifying financial crime patterns while preserving user privacy within a real-time payment system

BIS Innovation Hub (2024c) Project Aurum 2.0: Improving privacy for retail CBDC payment

Borgovono E et al (2017) Beyond Bitcoin and cash: do we like a Central Bank Digital Currency? A financial and political economics approach. Bocconi: Working Paper 65

Brownworth A et al (2017) A high-performance payment processing system designed for Central Bank Digital Currencies. MIT Media Lab Digital Currency Initiative and the Federal Reserve Bank of Boston

Catalini C, Gans J (2016) Some simple economics of the Blockhain. Rotman School of Management: MIT

Dyson B, Hodgson G, Van Lerven F (2016) Sovereign money: an introduction. Positive Money

ECB (2020a) Stablecoins – no coins, but are they stable? In Focus 3

ECB (2020b) The role of cash

ECB (2021) Stablecoins: Implications for monetary policy, financial stability, market infrastructure and payments, and banking supervision in the euro area. 247

ECB (2023a) Shaping Europe's digital future: the path towards a digital euro

ECB (2023b) Study on the payment attitudes of consumers in the euro area (SPACE)

ECB (2023c) Progress on the investigation phase of a digital euro

ECB (2024) Update on the work of the digital euro scheme's Rulebook Development Group

EDPB-EDPS (2023) Joint Opinion 02/2023 on the Proposal for a Regulation of the European Parliament and of the Council on the establishment of the digital euro European Data Protection Board
European Parliament (2024) Digital Euro in 'An Economy that Works for People'
European Parliament, Committee on Economic and Monetary Affairs. Draft Report on the proposal for a regulation of the European Parliament and of the Council on the establishment of the digital euro (COM (2023)0369 – C9-0219/2023 – 2023/0212(COD))
Federal Reserve Bank of New York (2023) Research Study Examines Feasibility of Theoretical Payments System Designed to Facilitate and Settle Digital Asset Transactions
Financial Stability Board (2022) Review of the FSB High-level Recommendations of the Regulation, Supervision and Oversight of "Global Stablecoin" Arrangements
Global Foreign Exchange Committee-GFXC (2021) FX Global Code. A set of global principles of good practice in the foreign exchange market
Hernadez de Cos (2023) The digital euro project – a new milestone Speech at the Annual Convention of the Asociación de Mercados Financieros, Madrid, 20 November 2023. https://www.bis.org/review/r231121i.htm
Huang Y, Wang D, Fan G (2014) Paths to a Reserve Currency: Internationalization of the Renminbi and Its Implications. ADBI Working Papers. 482
Iberpay (2023) Dinero digital tokenizado y programable
IOSCO (2020) Global Stablecoin Initiatives
Klein M et al (2020) The Digital Euro and the Role of DLT for Central Bank Digital Currencies. Frankfurt School Blockchain Center
Knoerich J (2021) China's new digital currency: implications for yuan internationalization and the US dollar. In: Bilotta N, Botti F (eds) The (Near) future of Central Bank Digital Currencies. Risks and opportunities for the global economy and society, p 160
Kosse A, Mattei I (2023) Making headway - Results of the 2022 BIS survey on central bank digital currencies and crypto. BIS Papers 136
Liang Y (2020) RMB internationalization and financing belt-road initiative: an MMT perspective. Chinese Econ 4:317–328
Madrid Parra A (2021) Fichas de dinero electrónico. Del dinero electrónico al 'viejo' dinero digital. In: Guía de criptoactivos MiCA. Aranzadi, Navarra, pp 219–244
Nabilou H (2019) Central Bank digital currencies: preliminary legal observations. J Bank Regul
Parrondo L (2023) El Euro Digital: beneficios, riesgos y potencial diseño. Revista de Contabilidad y Dirección:4–10
People's Bank of China (PBOC) (2021) Progress of Research & Development of E-CNY in China. Working Group on E-CNY Research and Development
Powell J (2024) The Semiannual Monetary Policy Report to the Congress. Committee on Banking, Housing, and Urban Affairs
Raskin M, Yermacl D (2016) Digital currencies, decentralized ledgers, and the future of central banking. National Bureau of Economic Research
Sanz Bayón P (2019) Key legal issues surrounding smart contract applications. Korean Legisl Res Inst J Law Legisl 1
Sanz Bayón P (2020a) Análisis sobre la naturaleza jurídica de las criptomonedas y la regulación europea de los proveedores de servicios de cambio y de custodia de monederos electrónicos. Revista de Derecho Bancario y Bursátil 160:69–110
Sanz Bayón P (2020b) Euro digital: contexto y perspectivas regulatorias. Revista Alastria Legal 2: 58–65
Sanz Bayón P (2021a) Emisión y regulación de dinero público digital: el caso de las Monedas Digitales de Banco Central (CBDC). Revista de Derecho del Mercado de Valores. 29
Sanz Bayón P (2021b) El Salvador paga con bitcóin. Revista Cambio16 2281:5–9
Sono K (2023) Legal tender: a notion associated with payment, current developments in monetary and financial law. IMF eLibrary 2:700–720

Turi AN (2023) Currency under the web 3.0 economy. Technologies for modern digital entrepreneurship: understanding emerging tech at the cutting-edge of the web 3.0 economy. Springer, pp 155–186
Wang H, Gao S (2021) The future of the international financial system: the emerging CBDC network and its impact on regulation. Regul Gov 18:288–306
Ward O, Rochemont S (2021) A cashless society- benefits, risks and issues. Understanding Central Banks Digital Currencies (CBDC). Institute and Faculty of Actuaries, pp 15–28
Wong P, Maniff JL (2020) Comparing means of payment: what role for a Central Bank Digital Currency? FEDS Notes
World Economic Forum (2019) Esta nueva forma de dinero podría cambiar la manera en que vemos el dinero
Yao Q (2018) Experimental Research on the Central Bank's Digital Currency Prototype System
Zatti F (2023) The economic law of (central bank) digital currency. Law Financ Mark Rev:3–13
Zatti F, Barresi, RG (2020) The importance of where Central Bank Digital currencies are custodied: exploring the need of a universal access device. Universitá Degli Studi Firenze, pp 7–25.
Zatti F, Barresi RG (2024) Digital assets and the law. Fiat money in the era of digital currency. Routledge, pp 360–375
Zetzsche D, Buckley R, Arner D (2018) The distributed liability of distributed ledgers: legal risks of blockchain. Univ Ill Law Rev, p 101
Zetzsche D, Buckley R, Arner A (2019) Regulating Libra: the transformative potential of Facebook's cryptocurrency and possible regulatory responses. University of New South Wales Law Research Series, pp 19–47
Zunzunegui F (2023) El euro digital al rescate de la moneda única". Revista de Derecho del Mercado Financiero

The Digital Euro Package: From Legal Tender to Payment Services Providers

Filippo Zatti and Rosa Giovanna Barresi

Abstract This paper delves into the proposals for regulating the digital euro, establishing a connection between its legal standing and physical euro cash, and requiring payment services providers to offer digital euro services regardless of their location. It raises questions about the fundamental implications of treating the digital euro as legal tender. However, labelling the digital euro as a legal tender raises uncertainties about its core nature and purpose. The analysis challenges the notion that the digital euro is merely a digital version of physical cash, emphasising the evolving roles of central bank digital currencies and their legal and policy ramifications. With the digitalisation of the economy in mind, it examines how the involvement of payment services providers in distributing the digital euro could impact individual and economic rights. It underscores the importance of balancing security measures, privacy, and data protection while fostering competition. The paper aims to provide policymakers with insights into the design and regulation of the digital euro, underlining the necessity of clarifying its legal standing and reconsidering its classification as legal tender. It stresses the importance of thoroughly examining the conceptual foundations of the digital euro to ensure its successful implementation and regulation.

This paper expands and updates the text of a lecture delivered at the III International Congress entitled "Present and future of crypto-assets regulation in the European Union," held at the University of Alicante (Spain) on December 13, 14, and 15, 2023. This work is funded within the framework of: Proyecto CIPROM/2022/26 "Presente y futuro de la regulación de los Criptoactivos en la UE [Legalcripto]". Proyecto Prometeo CIPROM/2022/26, grupos de investigación de excelencia, de la Generalitat Valenciana (P.I. Carmen Pastor).

F. Zatti (✉)
Department of Economics and Management, University of Florence, Florence, Italy
e-mail: filippo.zatti@unifi.it; filippo.zatti@ebi-europa.eu

R. G. Barresi
School of Economics and Management, University of Florence, Florence, Italy

C. Pastor Sempere (ed.), *Governance and Control of Data and Digital Economy in the European Single Market*, Law, Governance and Technology Series 71,
https://doi.org/10.1007/978-3-031-74889-9_15

1 The Proposal Regulation for the Establishment of a Digital Euro

A report was published in October 2020, and the digital euro project was launched. Soon after, academics debated whether legislative intervention was required to establish the legal framework for the project. This debate was potentially resolved through the digital euro package provisions, even if the ECB Governing Council will make no decisions until the regulations have been adopted.[1] Nevertheless, ample evidence exists to begin to analyse it *de iure condendo*.

The proposal for regulating the creation of a digital euro comprises eight key sections that deal with establishing and issuing the digital euro, its legal tender status, and distribution even beyond the euro area. It also addresses its role as a store of value and medium of exchange, its technical specifications, privacy and data protection, and measures to prevent money laundering. A comparison with the proposal for the legal tender status of the physical euro currency highlights the importance of recognising legal tender within the European project and ensuring its acceptance and accessibility across various distribution channels.

1.1 The Legal Tender 'Unveiled'

The goals of the Euro area digital currency project underscore the importance of legal tender status. It is crucial to guarantee the efficiency, credibility, flexibility, inclusivity, and independence of the euro as the primary currency of the Euro area, especially considering evolving technological developments. Although legal tender is also a feature adopted by already active CBDCs, which in any case concern smaller economies so far, and thus is not a peculiarity of the euro area, there is one aspect that is nevertheless distinctive with it. In those cases, the introduction of CBDCs has been made possible by amending existing central bank laws or introducing specific regulations or guidelines under the authority of these laws. In contrast, the proposed digital euro would be introduced through a dedicated EU Regulation (the above-mentioned 'Regulation on the establishment of the digital

[1] The Regulations have been proposed for establishing the digital euro (Proposal for a Regulation of the European Parliament and of the Council establishing the digital euro, COM(2023) 369 final, 28 June 2023), deciding the legal tender status of euro banknotes and coins (Proposal for a Regulation of the European Parliament and of the Council on the legal tender of euro banknotes and coins, COM(2023) 364 final, 28 June 2023) and on the payment services in digital euros (Proposal for a Regulation of the European Parliament and of the Council on the provision of services in digital euros by payment services providers incorporated in Member States whose currency is not the euro and amending Regulation (EU) 2021/1230 of the European Parliament and of the Council, COM(2023) 368 final, 28 June 2023.) are still being reviewed by European lawmakers as of the current publication date. This article uses the term 'payment services providers' to maintain consistency with the meaning and form outlined in the draft regulation.

euro', hereafter referred to as REDE), establishing a comprehensive legal framework for the digital euro at the EU level. This reflects the unique nature of the digital euro as a CBDC that would span multiple countries and operate within the EU's complex legal and institutional setup. The proposed Regulation is based on Article 133 TFEU, which allows for measures necessary to use the euro as the single currency. This legal basis underscores the digital euro's importance for the functioning of the economic and monetary union and the euro's status as the single currency of the Euro area. However, it also comes with Article 128(1) TFEU and Articles 10 and 11 of Council Regulation (EC) No 974/98 regarding the legal tender status of euro banknotes and coins. Although it extends beyond the legal tender status by defining the legal requirements for a currency to be legal tender within the European Union, the qualification of legal tender introduced in draft[2] echoes what the Court of Justice has ruled when referring to cash.[3] It states this status brings with it (i) mandatory acceptance, (ii) at full face value and (iii) with the effect of discharging payment obligations, as set out by Point 1 of the 2010 Commission Recommendation.[4] However, the proposed regulation on the legal tender of euro banknotes and coins outlines exceptions to the principle of mandatory acceptance. Introducing exceptions to the mandatory acceptance of legal tender could conflict with the idea of universally accepted means of payment in settling debts. Additionally, overly broad or widespread application of exceptions could erode the legal tender status of euro cash. If too many transactions or situations are exempt from the obligation to accept cash, the practical significance of cash as legal tender would be diminished.

On the other hand, the inclusion of exceptions could be interpreted as a pragmatic recognition that, in certain situations, insisting on accepting cash may be impractical, inefficient, or even contrary to other vital interests. The exceptions could be viewed as necessary flexibility and adaptation of the legal framework to the realities of modern payment systems and societal needs. However, if the exceptions are too broad or invoked too frequently, they could undermine the legal tender concept.

It is also worth noting that the tension between the principle of legal tender and the need for certain exceptions is not unique to this proposed Regulation. Many countries with legal tender laws also provide for certain exceptions. The EU proposal for the digital version of the physical euro includes restating the legal tender status for the digital euro, with exceptions outlined in Articles 9 to 11 of this proposal regulation, tailored to the unique features of the digital currency. The digital nature of money offers easier transfers than physically transporting cash while overcoming limitations imposed by regulations on individual and professional transport activities. Article 8 outlines the digital euro's scope of application as legal tender within a specific geographical area. This is especially pertinent to the role of payment services

---

[2] Art. 4, Proposal for a Regulation of the European Parliament and of the Council on the legal tender of euro banknotes and coins, COM(2023) 364 final.

[3] ECJ (2021).

[4] Commission Recommendation of 22 March 2010 on the scope and effects of the legal tender of euro banknotes and coins (2010/191/EU).

providers in the realm of digital euros, which the proposal extensively covers, as described in the following sections. This includes Articles 13 and 14, as well as 18 to 21 and 25 to 33 of the proposed regulation for establishing the digital euro. However, the distinction between the two forms of currency emerges with Article 12, which concludes Chapter II of that proposal.

Their complementarity and coexistence hide the fact that cash does not need providers to be transferred, while the digital version does, even if it would have 'similarities with transactions in cash—and should be treated similarly in terms of privacy'[5] in its offline version—and acts 'as an instrument whose liquidity is similar to that of cash but without the portability limitations implicit in cash'[6] in its online version. Naturally, digital currency shares many common features with physical cash and the various forms of payment that cash can be converted into. However, when it comes to digital currency issued by a central bank, there is a notable difference in that it does not have the potential to be transformed into physical cash. While both forms of currency are considered legal tender, they serve different purposes: physical cash is used for transactions in the physical world. In contrast, digital currency is designed for transactions within the network economy. The Regulation proposal seeks to introduce the digital euro as a supplement to, rather than a substitute for, physical euro cash. This aims to ensure that the digital euro is smoothly integrated into the current Eurosystem while maintaining the importance and usefulness of physical cash. Additionally, by decoupling the mandatory acceptance of the digital euro from the acceptance of physical cash, the Regulation guarantees that the digital euro can effectively operate as a standalone payment method, especially in light of the growing digitalisation of the economy.

1.2 The Digital Euro as a (Public Digital) Means of Payment and a Medium of Exchange

The concept of 'means of payment' refers to both euro as cash and digital currency, but it is not explicitly defined in the two proposals. However, its meaning can be inferred from the context and provisions of these Regulation proposals.

In the proposed Regulation on the legal tender of euro banknotes and coins, 'means of payment' appears to refer to physical euro cash as a method for settling monetary debts.[7]

Instead, the proposed Regulation on establishing the digital euro expands the term 'means of payment' to have a broader meaning, encompassing both the digital euro and other forms of payment. For instance, Article 1 states the Regulation establishes

[5]See Recitals (75) and (82), REDE.

[6]Recital (80), REDE.

[7]This can be seen, for example, in Art. 4, which defines the legal tender of euro banknotes and coins, and in Art. 7, which requires Member States to ensure the acceptance of cash payments.

the digital euro 'with a view to adapting the euro to technological changes and ensure its use as a single currency.' This suggests the digital euro is intended to function as a payment mechanism in the context of the economy's digitalisation.

The Regulation includes several provisions that specifically mention the digital euro in the context of payments. For instance, Article 4 specifies that the digital euro will be issued 'for the purpose of retail payments.' Additionally, Article 7 defines the legal tender status of the digital euro in terms of its mandatory acceptance for payments. In contrast, Article 15 outlines principles for ensuring the effective use of the digital euro as a 'legal tender means of payment.'

At the same time, the Regulation proposal also refers to other means of payment. For example, Article 9 provides exceptions to the obligation to accept the digital euro, including where the payee accepts 'comparable digital means of payment,' defined in Article 2(25) as including 'debit card payment and instant payment at the point of interaction.'

Furthermore, Article 12, mentioned earlier, refers to the choice between the digital euro and euro banknotes and coins as alternative payment methods.

So, while the term 'means of payment' is not explicitly defined, it appears in the proposed Regulation on the digital euro to refer to any instrument or method that can be used to pay or settle a monetary debt, including the digital euro, physical euro cash, and other digital payment methods.[8]

This broad understanding of 'means of payment' reflects the Regulation's aim to integrate the digital euro into the existing payment ecosystem, while acknowledging the diversity of payment methods in the modern economy.

The European Central Bank (the ECB) has primarily used the concept of means of payment in the economic context as a medium of exchange.[9] This approach allows differentiation between monetary and financial instruments as defined by law and helps bridge the gap between money as currency and means of payment as currency. However, even from an economic perspective, a medium of exchange can be defined differently from a means of payment. The medium of exchange stands for 'what' (is paid), and the means of payment concerns 'how' (to deliver it). According to this principle, currency, checkable deposits, and stored-value cards are money; checks, debit/credit cards, or money orders are not money.[10] Technological innovation can bring the two concepts closer and closer together. This is why it is questionable, if not a simplification, to state that a digital euro is solely a means of payment. As the digital counterpart to the euro, it must serve as a medium of exchange. Depending on the chosen approach for implementing a digital euro, it has the potential to function both as a means of payment and a medium of exchange. This could entail enhancing

---

[8] 'Money refers to anything that is generally accepted as payment for goods and services or in the settlement of debt, also called the medium of exchange' (p. 14), and a good is suitable to be used as a medium of exchange when it is acceptable, of standardised quality, durable, valuable, and divisible (p. 17). See Hubbard (2005).

[9] Coeure (2012); European Central Bank (2020).

[10] Yang (2007).

existing payment systems or ushering in a more revolutionary evolution of the concept of currency.[11]

In this regard, it is crucial to carefully examine the role the draft regulation assigns payment services providers in distributing the digital euro.

2 The Digital Euro Proposal and the PSPs

The Digital Euro Package is formed apart from the proposal on the legal tender of banknotes and coins and the establishment of the digital euro, which also provides payment services in digital euros.[12]

The European Parliament and the Council have the authority to create the digital euro, while the ECB is entitled to issue it, as outlined in the Treaties. Article 133 of the TFEU establishes the groundwork for legislating on Euro area Member States, thus constraining the Commission's ability to fully control the adoption and usage of the digital euro by non-Euro area Member States. The provisions outlined in Chapter VI of the digital euro proposal empower the ECB to engage in agreements with non-Euro area Member States to outline the conditions and procedures for utilising the digital euro. For the digital euro to be used in a third country, any arrangement between the ECB and a non-euro area national central bank requires a prior international agreement between the European Union and the respective third country. The ECB has made a notable move towards the digital euro, starting a 'preparation phase' on November 1st, 2023, scheduled to continue for two years. It aims to establish the groundwork for a potential digital euro, including finalising a rulebook[13] and choosing providers to build the platform and infrastructure. This preparatory period will set the stage for possible future decisions regarding issuing a digital euro. Legislation and design of the digital euro are progressing simultaneously, with Payment Services Providers (PSPs) responsible for its distribution. Supervised intermediaries, such as banks, will serve as the primary interface for individuals, merchants, and businesses regarding all matters related to the digital euro. They will handle all end-user services, while the central bank will be responsible for them.[14] The proposed regulation on the digital euro refers to the PSPs, as

[11]Wong and Maniff (2020).

[12]Proposal for a Regulation of the European Parliament and of the Council on the provision of services in digital euros by payment services providers incorporated in Member States whose currency is not the euro and amending Regulation (EU) 2021/1230 of the European Parliament and of the Council, COM(2023) 368 final, 28 June 2023.

[13]European Central Bank (2024a).

[14]Recital (9), REDE: '(. . .) No account or other contractual relationship would be established between the digital euro user and the European Central Bank or the national central banks. Payment services providers should manage the digital euro accounts of digital euro users on their behalf and provide them with digital euro payment services. Since payment services providers are not a party to the direct liability held by digital euro users towards the European Central Bank and the national

defined in the Second Payment Services Directive (PSD2), which regulates payment services offered by PSPs and the rights and obligations of the parties of a payment transaction.[15] PSD2 was issued in response to the increasing risks associated with the rise in transaction volumes due to the widespread use of online and mobile payments, which require a modification of the regulatory framework of the previous legislation to suit new digital payment services. The goal is to balance innovation, security, and competitiveness, promoting uniformity of rules across all Member States to protect consumer information and data security ('level playing field'). PSD2 enriches the profile of traditional PSPs, such as credit institutions, electronic money institutions (EMIs), payment institutions (PIs), and post offices, with the introduction of new entities called Third-party Payment services Providers (TPPs).[16]

Despite PSD2 representing a significant step in the regulation of payment services, reducing fraud cases, enhancing security, and pushing towards open banking, the Directive has some criticisms regarding the complexity of authentication procedures, the costs of implementing new security measures, the difficult interoperability between the technical protocols used by TPPs and different banking platforms, and the lack of uniformity in technical standards. The effectiveness of PSD2 in creating a level playing field faces constraints, mainly due to the ongoing imbalance between traditional banks and non-bank PSPs, which stems from the latter's limited access to essential payment systems.

When the proposal for a digital euro was published, the issue was whether PSD2 was a sufficient legal framework to regulate the new role of PSPs distributing digital

central banks of the Member States whose currency is the euro and are acting on behalf of digital euro users, the insolvency of payment services providers would not affect digital euro users.' The European Parliament Draft of 9 February 2024 amended the Proposal and used the word 'wallets' instead of 'digital euro accounts': European Parliament (2024). No vote has been scheduled on the Draft Report before the 2024 European elections.

[15] Art 2(7), REDE: 'payment service provider' means a payment service provider as defined in Article 4, point (11) and Art. 1(1) of the Directive 2015/2366 (PSD2), Directive (EU) 2015/2366 of the European Parliament and of the Council of 25 November 2015 on payment services in the internal market, amending Directives 2002/65/EC, 2009/110/EC and 2013/36/EU and Regulation (EU) No 1093/2010, and repealing Directive 2007/64/EC namely, credit institutions, electronic money institutions, post office giro institutions, payment institutions, the ECB and national central banks when not acting as public authorities, Member States authorities when not acting as public authorities. The objective was to create legislation that reflects the evolution of new digital payment services and the Single Euro Payments Area (SEPA) project for European integration to ensure higher security standards in using electronic devices, platforms, and remote communication channels. See also the last paragraph of footnote 1 in this document.

[16] TPPs can access information or account balances of users with an online banking contract and grant their consent to provide the requested service. However, TPPs do not have custody or management of users' payment accounts. Depending on the types of services offered by TPPs, there are payment initiation services providers (PISPs), account information services providers (AISPs), and card-based payment services providers (CISPs). The possibility for new entities to access the payment systems market is also considered an opportunity to introduce innovative payments into the market without prior control over payment instruments, as with financial instruments, thus ensuring the principle of technological neutrality.

euro or whether it needed to be modified. The specific reference of the digital euro proposal to PSD2 characterises it as a reference framework. PSPs already authorised in the EU under PSD2 are not required to seek additional authorisation from their competent authorities to offer digital euro payment services. To distribute the digital euro, PSPs must establish contractual agreements with users who will not have a contractual relationship with the ECB.[17]

On the other hand, even though the Eurosystem recognised that PSPs could act under PSD2, it is evident that the evolution of PSPs' functions within the distribution of digital euros requires more specific regulations. For example, Crypto Asset Service Providers (CASP) regulated under MiCA regulation should also be permitted to distribute the digital euro.[18] The Commission proposed amendments to PSD2 by introducing changes to the current regulatory framework through two separate legislative acts: the proposed Third Payment Services Directive (PSD3), which mainly includes rules concerning the authorisation and supervision of EU Member States payment institutions, and the proposed Payment Services Regulation (PSR), which contains rules for Payment services providers, whether they offer payment services or electronic money services in the European Economic Area (EEA).[19]

Security is one of the main objectives of PSD2, especially regarding unauthorised intrusions into payment accounts related to the theft of money and personal data. However, the measures implemented under PSD2 do not adequately tackle emerging forms of fraud. On February 14, 2024, members of the European Parliament for Economic and Monetary Affairs voted for a more open and competitive payment services sector in the EU, with increased measures to combat and mitigate fraud in payments and data breaches, strengthened consumer rights, ensured equal access to payment systems for both banking and non-banking entities, broader adoption of the

[17] Arts. 13-14, Distribution, Explanatory Memorandum, REDE.

[18] Crypto Asset Services Providers (CASPs) regulated under the MiCA regulation, which are Account Servicing Payment Services Providers (ASPSPs) as per PSD2, should also be permitted to distribute the digital euro. According to PSD2, ASPSPs should be mandated to grant access to payment account data to Payment Initiation Service Providers (PISPs) and Account Information Service Providers (AISPs) via Application Programming Interfaces (APIs), enabling them to create and offer innovative supplementary services, Recital (26) of the Proposal for a regulation on the digital euro, COM(2023) 369 final, Regulation (EU) 2023/1114 of the European Parliament and of the Council of 31 May 2023 on markets in crypto-assets, and amending Regulations (EU) No 1093/2010 and (EU) No 1095/2010 and Directives 2013/36/EU and (EU) 2019/1937 (MiCAR).

[19] Proposal for a Directive of the European Parliament and of the Council on payment services and electronic money services in the internal market amending Directive 98/26/EC and repealing Directives 2015/2366/EU and 2009/110/EC (COM(2023) 366 final), 28 June 2023, (PSD3); Proposal for a Regulation of the European Parliament and of the Council on Payment Services in the internal market and amending Regulation (EU) No 1093/210 (COM(2013) 367 final) 28 June 2023,(PSR). The legislative package also includes a proposal to create a Financial Data Access (FIDA) framework: Proposal for a Regulation of the European Parliament and of the Council on a framework for Financial Data Access and amending Regulations (EU) No 1093/2010, (EU) No 1094/2010, (EU) No 1095/2010 and (EU) 2022/2554, COM/2023/360 final, 28 June 2023.

concept of open banking, improved availability of cash, especially in remote or rural areas, and harmonisation in the application of regulations.[20]

On 23 April 2024, Members of the European Parliament adopted the amended drafts of PSD3 and PSR, improving measures against fraud and increasing access to cash within payment services.[21] These rules would encompass all types of PSPs, including banks, postal giro institutions, and payment institutions. The proposed regulations aim to address security, liability, and data protection. Uniform conditions would govern the provision of payment services across the EU, including electronic money services.[22] To protect transfers, it has been proposed that the unique identifier (a combination of letters, numbers, or symbols designated by a PSP or user that does not have to be the IBAN)[23] undergoes free verification, with PSPs ensuring Strong

[20]European Parliament (2024d).

[21]European Parliament (2024b). Parliament has concluded the initial reading of these legislative pieces. Trilogue negotiations involving the Council, the European Parliament, and the European Commission will commence after the formation of the new Parliament. ECON, MEPs want to enhance fraud protection and access to cash in payment services: European Parliament (2024c).

[22]The regulatory framework, as outlined in PSD2 and EMD2, delineates different authorisations for payment services and electronic money issuance. Specifically, non-bank entities require a distinct authorisation to operate as Electronic Money Institutions (EMIs) for the latter activity. The proposed legislation consolidates e-money and payment services regulations into a unified framework while accommodating specific nuances where necessary. Recital (29) and Art. 2(ha) of the European Parliament legislative resolution of 23 April 2024 introduce a unified licensing approach: see European Parliament (2024b). This adjustment reflects the acknowledgement that issuers of 'tokenised electronic money' should be treated on par with traditional electronic money issuers, aligning with Regulation (EU) 2023/1114 ('MiCAR', Markets in Crypto-Assets Regulation). According to MiCAR, electronic money tokens are classified as electronic money, simplifying the regulatory process and ensuring uniform application across the EU. See also European Central Bank (2024c), p. 2.

[23]Recital (70), European Parliament (2024b). Under PSD2, PSPs are not required to verify the payee's name; only their unique identifier is required. Instead, Art. 1(2) of the Instant Payments Regulation, amending Regulation (EU) No 260/2012 (the SEPA Regulation), introduced Art.5c (1) that states that PSPs throughout the Single Euro Payments Area must offer the IBAN/name check (service ensuring verification) to payers by 9 October 2025, (Art.5c(9)). The Instant Payment Regulation (IPR), which took effect on 8 April 2024, allows funds to be deposited into the payee's account within ten seconds, and the instant credit transfer is available 365/24/7. The European Payments Council (EPC) established that version 1.0 of the Verification of Payee scheme rulebook, published on 10 October 2024, will enter into force on 5 October 2025: European Payments Council (2024).

In September 2023, EBA CLEARING began experimenting with a pan-European system for detecting fraud attempts and other anomalies (FPAD). The FPAD includes real-time tools for preventing and detecting fraud, such as IBAN/name verification, to bolster fraud prevention initiatives by PSPs throughout Europe: EBA Clearing (2023). On 8 April 2024, EBA CLEARING announced its plans to roll out Verification of Payee (VoP) services at a pan-European level starting from December 2024. This initiative aims to assist PSPs in providing IBAN/name matching services to their customers for SEPA transactions and adhering to the European Payments Council scheme: EBA Clearing (2024). Beginning in May 2024, supervisors in the EU can submit individuals 'identities to EuReCA, the EU's central database for combating money laundering and terrorism financing, managed by the European Banking Authority (EBA). Only information

Customer Authentication (SCA).[24] PSPs who fail to implement adequate fraud prevention mechanisms would be liable for compensating customers for losses incurred due to fraud.[25] Customers will have the right to reimbursement from PSPs for losses caused by fraud if they have not implemented adequate anti-fraud measures, as well as from Electronic Communications Service Providers[26] in the event of malfunction. Reimbursement is also provided in spoofing cases, where scammers impersonate the customer's bank or other organisations.[27] Online platforms (like Meta or Google) are held accountable for failure to remove fraudulent content on their platforms.[28] Customers must provide consent for processing their personal data, and they should have the option to opt out of data sharing or revoke access to their data.[29] Also, to ensure better access to cash in remote or rural areas, it

about significant breaches in AML/CFT regulations can be disclosed: European Banking Authority (2024a).

[24] According to Article 4, No. 30 of the Directive (EU) 2015/2366 (PSD2), SCA involves two-factor authentication for online payments based on factors known only to the customer, such as knowledge, possession, or inherence. It generates a single-use authorisation code linked to payment details to prevent reuse in case of interception or compromise.

[25] Recital (122), as amended by the European Parliament (2024b), states that Alternative Dispute Resolution procedures should be mandatory for PSPs.

[26] Art. 3(55a), European Parliament (2024b) defines 'electronic communications service provider' as 'any provider that falls within the scope of European electronic communications code (Directive (EU) 2018/1972 and Digital Service Act, Regulation (EU) 2022/2065.'

[27] Art. 59, European Parliament (2024b) and recitals (79), (80) and (81). Art. 2 (9a) states that Article 59(Impersonation fraud) shall also apply to Electronic Communications Service Providers and online platforms. Art. 59-5(b) states '(. . .) Payment, electronic communications, and digital platform service providers shall have fraud prevention and mitigation techniques to fight fraud in all its configurations, including non-authorised and authorised push payment fraud. 'Recital (79) defines social engineering fraud as 'where a fraudster manipulates a payment services user in performing a certain action, such as initiating a payment transaction or handing over the payment service user's security credentials to the fraudsters.' Furthermore, the EBA outlines measures for PSPs, including pre-transaction monitoring and potential transaction blocking. It also defines user liability, addressing gross negligence in authorised push payment fraud. This fraud involves victims being coerced into immediate payments to fraudsters, often via social engineering tactics like impersonation. Fraud types can be a manipulation of the payer, a mixed social engineering and technical scam, and an enrolment process compromise: European Banking Authority (2024a).

[28] Recital (81a), European Parliament (2024b):' Online platforms can also contribute to increasing instances of fraud. Therefore, and without prejudice to their obligations under Regulation (EU) 2022/2065 of the European Parliament and the Council (Digital Services Act), they should be held liable where fraud has arisen as a direct result of fraudsters using their platform to defraud consumers if they were informed about fraudulent content on their platform that and did not remove it.'

[29] Meta introduced the Pay or Okay model, allowing EU users to either pay a subscription and access the service ad-free or use it for free while agreeing to have their data processed for behavioural advertising, as usual. The data protection authorities in the Netherlands, Norway, and Hamburg sought the opinion of the EDPB regarding the legality of the Pay or Okay model under the EU General Data Protection Regulation. EDPB states that if the sole option is to pay with money, opting to pay with data does not equate to voluntary consent. An alternative must be available wherein users can access all features without monetary payment or data provision, as a free account

has been proposed that businesses offering cash withdrawal services without requiring a purchase (up to 100 euros) should be exempt from the rules. Similarly, automatic teller machines (ATMs) should be subject to less stringent registration procedures. In this regard, the risk of financial desertification due to the closure of bank branches and associated ATMs should be considered.

New players should be able to join the EU's payment services market, particularly in internet payments, provided they obtain authorisation. This would enable customers to make online purchases without relying on credit cards. While similar services like Sofort, iDeal, or Trustly are available in certain member states, the providers have not been regulated at the EU level.

The PSD3 could be a launching pad for the Digital Euro, considering that TIPS (TARGET Instant Payments Service managed by the Eurosystem) lacks an anti-fraud, anti-money laundering, and sanctions system.

3 The New Role of PSPs in Distributing the Digital Euro

The ECB's Governing Council will consider a decision regarding the issue of a digital euro once the legislation has been officially adopted. As previously mentioned, during the preparatory phase, the Eurosystem will develop the rulebook for the digital euro scheme and establish criteria for selecting potential service providers. PSPs will be on the front-end, exclusively leading the distribution of the digital euro, establishing public-private cooperation, maintaining customer relations, and benefiting from digital euro open standards. The foundation of the digital euro infrastructure will depend on standardised payment protocols, enabling private service providers to extend their offerings throughout Europe and reducing their dependence on non-European PSPs. The ECB aims to establish a framework for uniform digital euro payments across the euro area through collaboration between public and private sector experts in crafting the digital euro rulebook. Digital euro users will exclusively enter contractual relationships with PSPs, not with the ECB or national central banks.[30] Supervised intermediaries would have a contractual account management relationship with end users and be the direct contacts for individuals, merchants, and businesses using the digital euro. PSPs will assume responsibility for distributing the digital euro to end-users, empowering them to enhance features and introduce pioneering services to their clientele. This approach ensures the Eurosystem maintains the pivotal position of intermediaries within the established two-tier financial system.

---

without personalised advertising, wherein advertising is permitted without data processing for profiling purposes: European Data Protection Board (2024a). See also the Euro Data Protection Board, which recommends that additional safeguards should be included in PSR and FIDA legislation regarding the sharing of data for fraud prevention to ensure data protection: European Data Protection Board (2024b).

[30] Art. 13(6), REDE.

Specifically, the regulation proposal for the establishment of a digital euro rules distribution within the euro area (Arts. 13,14), outside the euro area, cross-currency payments (Arts. 18–21), and modalities of distributions (Arts. 25–33). A draft report on the digital euro amended the proposal provisions on 9 February 2024,[31] but there is no planned vote on this draft before the conclusion of the current legislative term.[32]

PSPs are permitted to offer their services to residents (natural or legal persons) of the euro area, natural and legal persons who formerly resided or were established in the euro area and opened a digital euro account at that time, visitors (natural persons travelling to and staying in the euro area, including for tourism, business, or education and training purposes), enabling them to hold and conduct transactions in the digital euro.[33] Residents can select their digital euro service provider, which could include a PSP already associated with their commercial bank account. Individuals residing in non-euro area countries may gain access to digital euro services following the initial launch of the currency. However, the availability of digital euro in non-euro area countries would always depend on agreements reached with the authorities of those countries. Businesses operating within the Euro area can accept payments in digital euros. Additionally, businesses located in the European Economic Area (EEA)[34] and those in third countries,[35] offering services to Euro area residents in euros, can accept digital euro payments through an acquiring provider within the Euro area. PSPs authorised outside the Euro area can provide these services through either establishment or the provision of services free of charge.

The proposed regulation for the digital euro aims to maintain the free movement of payment services within the EU by regulating the provision of digital euro services by PSPs located in non-euro area Member States.[36] Its goal is to establish uniform requirements and supervisory standards for PSPs throughout the EU, regardless of their location, to preserve financial stability and promote fair competition.

Only banks offering basic payment services, not all PSPs,[37] must provide all basic digital euro payment services upon request from individual clients residing or established in the euro area.[38] PSPs, other than banks that offer basic payment services, may provide basic digital euro payment services. In contrast, all PSPs

[31] European Parliament (2024).

[32] European Parliament (2024a).

[33] Art. 13 and Art. 2(22) REDE.

[34] EEA encompasses Iceland, Liechtenstein, Norway, and the 27 EU Member States.

[35] 'Third countries' refers to nations outside the euro area and the EEA that lack an agreement permitting the use of the euro.

[36] Arts. 18-21, REDE.

[37] Account Servicing Payment services providers (ASPSPs), under PSD2.

[38] Recital 28 and 30, REDE.

may provide additional digital euro payment services as conditional digital euro payments.[39]

Annex I and II of the proposal regulation establish additional and basic digital euro payment services. The latter deals with basic services for a natural person, such as access, liquidity, and transaction management.[40]

Access management encloses onboarding and offboarding digital euro end users, payment instrument management, linking digital euro holdings to a commercial bank account, and lifecycle management procedures that empower end users to interact with their digital euro account through a PSP. It encompasses the ability to digital euro portability and account information service. PSPs would be accountable for authenticating end users for all these procedures.

Supervised intermediaries would undertake all user-facing duties, including digital euro accounts/wallets,[41] and associated payment transactions. They will perform Know Your Customer (KYC) and Anti Money Laundering (AML) verifications, oversee the user credentials (Digital Euro Account Number—DEAN),[42] and a user application for digital euro payments. Users can access digital euro services through their PSP's proprietary app and online platform or a digital euro app supplied by the Eurosystem.

The digital euro will provide features for both online and offline use,[43] considering instances of restricted connectivity. Digital euro transactions, whether conducted online or offline, will be settled instantaneously.[44] In offline digital euro transactions, only the payer and the payee will have access to payment information, ensuring utmost privacy. Additionally, individuals lacking access to bank accounts or digital devices could still use the digital euro, such as a card issued by a public institution. In fact, alongside payment services providers, designated public entities would serve as intermediaries for individuals lacking a bank account.[45]

End users could terminate their contractual agreement for the digital euro with their PSPs at any time (offboarding).[46] PSPs must defund digital euro

---

[39] Conditional digital euro payments like pay-per-use or payment initiation services, Recital 30, REDE.

[40] Art. 14(1), Annex I and II, REDE; European Central Bank (2023a), p. 19 ff.; European Central Bank (2024a), p. 5 ff.

[41] The draft report substituted the wording 'digital euro accounts' of the proposal regulation on the digital euro with 'wallets': See European Parliament (2024).

[42] Art. 22(3) REDE; European Central Bank (2023a), p. 20.

[43] Art. 23, REDE.

[44] Art. 30(1), REDE.

[45] Public entities are local or regional authorities or postal offices. See Explanatory Memorandum, REDE, 3. Moreover, each Member State must appoint a specific entity to grant access to digital euro services for individuals vulnerable to digital financial exclusion. This entity will offer tailored assistance for onboarding and ongoing support in utilising digital euro services, all provided free of charge for eligible individuals. The draft report adds to PSPs 'other service providers,' Amendments 22 and 78: see European Parliament (2024).

[46] European Central Bank (2023a), p. 21.

holdings,[47] deactivate the user's data, and return the funds linked with a DEAN/ wallet to a commercial bank account chosen by the end user.

Liquidity management includes funding, defunding, waterfall and reverse waterfall. The amount of digital euros that end users could possess would be capped to prevent an excessive outflow of bank deposits. Nevertheless, they could still make purchases exceeding this limit by linking their digital euro wallet to their commercial bank account. Even if receiving a payment pushes the digital euro balance beyond the holding limit (threshold),[48] users would always accept it. The surplus amount would then be automatically transferred to the linked commercial bank account (waterfall).

Users could also establish a threshold for this automatic transfer that is lower than the holding limit.[49] The digital euro shall not bear interest.[50]

Waterfalls integrate funding/defunding and payment processing into one operation, minimising or eliminating user delays. Users are not required to pre-fund a digital euro account before making payments. In case of insufficient funds in the digital euro account, any shortfall could be promptly transferred from the associated commercial bank account (reverse waterfall). Individuals can use the waterfall, reverse waterfall, or both functions according to their preference. Funding options include either a commercial bank account or cash. Without a linked commercial bank account, or if waterfalls are not activated, users would be tasked with maintaining the digital euro account balance below the holding limit. This increases the necessity for manual funding and defunding of the account and increases the likelihood of transaction failures.[51]

Transaction management refers to the services PSPs provide to end users regarding the administration and processing of transactions. It encompasses initiating payments, verifying user identity, notifying users of confirmation or rejection, processing refunds, managing recurring payments, handling disputes, pay-per-use enabled via pre-authorisation service, payment initiation service, and optional services.

Digital euro transactions involve devices and interfaces like physical cards, mobile phones, or wearable gadgets. These devices support diverse data exchange technologies, including chips, near-field communication (NFC), quick response (QR) codes, or potentially an alias. These transactions cater to various prioritised use cases, including person-to-person (P2P) payments, which are accessible both online and offline; e-commerce payments, encompassing government-to-consumer (G2X), consumer-to-government (X2G), as well as consecutive and recurring

[47] 'Defunding' means exchanging digital euros with cash, Art. 2(12), while 'Funding' is the reverse process, Art. 2(11) REDE.

[48] The threshold has yet to be defined, even though €3.000 per resident has been proposed: see Bindseil et al. (2024), nt. 2.

[49] Recital (36) and Art. 13(2), Art. 13(3), REDE.

[50] Art. 16(8), REDE.

[51] European Central Bank (2023a), p. 15.

transactions, available exclusively online; and point-of-sale (POS) payments, covering government-to-consumer (G2X), consumer-to-government (X2G), and available both online and offline.[52]

The digital euro compensation model is designed to encourage PSPs to distribute the digital euro and ensure that private individuals can use these payments for free.[53] Additionally, it aims to incentivise PSPs to distribute the digital euro while implementing measures to prevent merchants from facing excessive service charges. PSPs will not receive compensation for providing these essential services to private users. However, PSPs can increase fees for managing traditional bank accounts, as payments in digital euros will be an extension of these accounts.[54] Merchants will be charged for these services, with a maximum fee established to encourage competition among PSPs. The ECB will determine the maximum fee, considering operational expenses and including a reasonable profit margin. However, fees should not exceed those associated with similar private digital payment methods to promote the effective use of the digital euro. The ECB should ensure that fees do not exceed the lower amount between the relevant cost of PSPs, which would cover a reasonable profit, and the charges for comparable means of payments.[55] The ECB would also bear its own costs, and no fees are foreseen for funding/defunding operations.[56]

The proposal grants the portability of the account from one PSP to another. End users can transfer their digital euro payment account to different PSPs while retaining the same account number. To initiate the transfer, the end user must request the new PSP to facilitate the account transfer. The new PSP can access the necessary data directly from the previous PSP. Additional KYC information would only be required if the end-user does not already have an existing business relationship with the new PSP.[57]

Potential services that PSPs could offer in the context of the digital euro are delivery vs. payment, automatic reimbursement of subsidies, automatised repayment for buy now pay later (BNPL) schemes, conditional payments per type of payer and underlying goods/services, pocket money for children, split payments (multiple payers).[58]

Non-bank PSPs, such as fintech companies and payment processors, will be able to integrate digital euro transactions into their offerings seamlessly. This integration has the potential to attract a more comprehensive user demographic throughout the

[52] European Central Bank (2024a), p. 17.

[53] Annex II, REDE.

[54] European Central Bank (2023a), p. 6, 30 ff.

[55] Art. 17(2), REDE. 'Comparable means of payments' are debit card payment and instant payment at the point of interaction, Art. 2(25).

[56] Art. 17, REDE.

[57] Art. 31, REDE.

[58] European Central Bank (2022). The digital euro cannot be programmable money. Still, payment transactions can be conditional so they can be 'automatically triggered by software based on predefined and agreed conditions', Recital (55), and Art. 24(2), REDE.

euro area and enable economies of scale. Moreover, the interoperability of the digital Eurosystem could stimulate collaboration between banks and non-bank PSPs, foster new business partnerships, and drive innovation in the payment industry. As a result, this could improve the efficiency of payment systems, lower costs, and catalyse additional innovation.

4 The Dispute on the Fraud Detection and Prevention Mechanism

In a digital payment transaction, information is shared between the device used by the payer to initiate the payment and the device used by the payee to accept it. To ensure that this data remains safe from unauthorised access and fraudulent activities by third parties, these exchanges must adhere to the most stringent security measures, integrating strong encryption. Therefore, securing the cyber resilience of a prospective digital euro scheme is a primary concern for the Eurosystem.

Grasping the diverse tactics employed by fraudsters and devising prompt and efficient strategies to thwart them remains a persistent challenge for PSPs. As demands increase on PSPs to deliver more efficient and advanced fraud detection and prevention solutions, ensuring fair competition by fostering comprehensive collaboration among PSPs is imperative. Considering the potential issuance of the digital euro, it becomes crucial to guarantee exceptional secure channels for the exchange of payment-related information, including the digital euro account/wallet number.[59]

PSPs are responsible for compliance checks and improving anti-fraud measures. The Eurosystem is exploring the potential of establishing a central support service for detecting and preventing fraud, which could help intermediaries manage fraudulent activities. The general Fraud Detection and Prevention Mechanism (FDPM) might encompass activities like fraud monitoring, risk assessment of transactions, statistical analysis, and information coordination.[60] This mechanism helps evaluate the risk of fraud in real-time before completing a transaction and helps PSPs detect fraud post-transaction.[61] It would aggregate data from PSPs throughout the EU but not replace their individual fraud prevention, risk management, and detection protocols.

The ECB, EBA Clearing, and the European Data Protection Board, jointly with the European Data Protection Supervisor, are disputing the interpretation of the proposed general FDPM.

In its Opinion on the Digital Euro Proposal Regulation, the ECB welcomes the creation of a centralised FDPM. This will enable a comprehensive fraud detection

[59] Art. 22(3), REDE.

[60] Recital 68 and Art. 32, REDE. See also European Central Bank (2023b), p. 8.

[61] Art. 32(3), REDE.

and prevention system for online digital euro transactions and ensure the efficient functioning of the digital euro.[62] Both the ECB and national central banks may assist in the fraud detection and prevention tasks that PSPs must carry out. The ECB suggests that securing payment information is crucial to fraud detection and prevention. Securing payment details (such as digital euro account numbers) during exchanges between payment initiation and payment acceptance devices is essential for safeguarding digital euro users from fraud and cyber-attacks. This can be achieved by, for example, replacing payment information with a surrogate value, like an alternate account number (a surrogate account).[63] Protecting against fraudulent activities will enhance the digital euro's reputation as a reliable and secure payment option and help deter other illegal activities. According to the ECB, fraud detection and prevention are essential for user protection in any payment system. People need to feel confident in the safety and security of a payment solution to adopt and continue using it. A centralised FDPM would offer higher fraud protection than a single PSP could achieve alone. The ECB believes strong fraud protection fosters trust among end users. Additionally, the infrastructure would use pseudonymised data provided by PSPs to safeguard individuals' privacy.

EBA CLEARING's interpretation contrasts with the ECB. It aims to restrict any features of the digital euro that are not already offered by existing payment methods. Consequently, it opposes granting the digital euro legal tender status and establishing any fraud prevention mechanisms managed by the ECB.[64]

According to EBA CLEARING, maintaining a regulatory-level playing field for all types of digital payments in the euro is essential. Without this, the proposal risks creating more advantageous conditions for CBDC payments than other digital euro payments, such as SCT and SCT Inst., allowing the ECB to establish and possibly operate a fraud detection and prevention mechanism for the Digital Euro, giving the ECB a privileged position. Therefore, uniform fraud prevention and detection requirements should apply to all euro digital transactions to benefit the industry and consumers.

The operation of payment systems by both the public and private sectors guarantees European payments' safety, efficiency, resilience, and robustness.[65]

The joint opinion of the European Data Protection Board (EDPB) and the European Data Protection Supervisor (EDPS) appears to compromise the positions of ECB and EBA CLEARING.[66] While they are not entirely opposed to the FDPM, they insist on clearly demonstrating the necessity for such a mechanism or proposing less intrusive alternatives.

The EDPB and the EDPS recognise that implementing FDPM could enhance the prompt detection of fraud, making it more effective. However, they state that this

---

[62] European Central Bank (2024a), §15.5.

[63] European Central Bank (2024c).

[64] EBA Clearing (2023a), p. 1 ff.

[65] EBA Clearing (2023a), p. 4.

[66] European Data Protection Board-European Data Protection Supervisor (2023).

alone does not justify the infringement of fundamental rights to privacy and data protection, as it fails to include the necessary measures to ensure that the processing aligns with the principle of proportionality. Member States must consider it when determining the severity of penalties and imposing limitations on the exercise rights and freedoms, as recognised by the Charter of Fundamental Rights.[67] If the need for FDPM is proven, specific safeguards, including appropriate storage limitations, should be implemented to prevent anti-fraud measures from excessively and disproportionately infringing upon individuals' fundamental rights and freedoms to privacy and personal data protection.

The EDPB and the EDPS advise implementing the most suitable Privacy-Enhancing Technologies (PETs), which provide the highest level of data protection while also addressing relevant utility and scalability requirements.[68]

The digital euro regulation should balance these different approaches to the amendments proposed to the text of the FDPM.

Complementary to the interpretations mentioned earlier is the position of the European Banking Authority (EBA), which welcomes the security measures delineated in the proposals for PSD3, PSR (including the 23 April 2024 ECON report on the PSD3/PSR proposals), and the Instant Payments Regulation (IPR). These measures include verifying the payee, improved transaction monitoring, facilitating the exchange of fraud-related information among PSPs, and assigning responsibility to electronic communications service providers outside the financial sector (such as telecommunications and internet providers and social media companies) for addressing payment fraud.[69] To help enhance the upcoming legislative framework under PSD3 and PSR, which will establish anti-fraud requirements for retail payments for many years to come, the EBA states that additional security measures are necessary beyond those outlined to address the evolving nature of fraud effectively.[70]

The increased incidence of fraud in instant payments may partially be due to the PSPs' limited capacity or inability to retrieve funds in case of fraudulent transactions, given that such payments are completed in under ten seconds.[71] This swift processing can heighten the appeal of instant payments to fraudsters.

For both cards and credit transfers, cross-border fraud is roughly nine times greater than domestic transactions. This is mainly due to inadequate cross-border collaboration between PSPs and other stakeholders in combating international criminal activities. Furthermore, for cross-border transactions involving non-EEA countries, the inconsistent application of SCA further exacerbates elevated levels of

---

[67] European Data Protection Board-European Data Protection Supervisor (2023), p. 21.

[68] European Data Protection Board-European Data Protection Supervisor (2023), p. 22.

[69] See above §2.

[70] European Banking Authority (2024a), p. 8.

[71] See Regulation (EU) 2024/886 of the European Parliament and of the Council of 13 March 2024 amending Regulations (EU) No 260/2012 and (EU) 2021/1230 and Directives 98/26/EC and (EU) 2015/2366 as regards instant credit transfers in euro (IPR).

fraud.[72] The EBA, in its opinion released at the end of April 2024, identifies five additional measures for consideration by the EU co-legislators and the EU Commission in the negotiation of the PSD3/PSR proposals:

(1) enhanced security requirements for PSPs that supplement the IBAN/name check and the fraud prevention measures outlined in the PSD3/PSR proposals; (2) implementation of a fraud risk management framework by PSPs in addition to the obligatory security measures; (3) revised liability rules, including clear distinctions between authorised and unauthorised transactions; (4) strengthened and standardised supervision of fraud management, utilising fraud data already collected under PSD2; (5) adequate security requirements for a unified EU-wide platform for information sharing to prevent and detect potentially fraudulent payment transactions.[73]

The Instant Payment Regulation establishes specific sanctions screening requirements within the SEPA Regulation.[74] In fact, in the case of instant credit transfers in euros, PSPs must follow a harmonised procedure for sanctions screening. This procedure is based on daily checks of their clients to verify if they are individuals or entities subject to targeted financial restrictive measures, thus eliminating the need for checks on each transaction.

While extended settlement periods allow more time for fraud detection and prevention procedures, instant transactions require these checks to be completed within seconds, significantly altering the PSPs' transaction processing systems. Real-time payment systems present unprecedented challenges to PSPs, making it essential to establish a pan-European network for exchanging fraud-related data and insights. Additionally, fraudulent cash-outs can occur minutes after a transfer, as funds are immediately available in the recipient's account with instant payments. To mitigate fraud risks and improve the accuracy of anti-financial crime measures, often plagued by false positives leading to unnecessary rejections, PSPs must continually enhance their internal systems. This includes 24/7 real-time monitoring to optimise fraud prevention capabilities.[75]

The lack of a universal classification system creates difficulties for PSPs, complicating cross-border criminal investigations and hindering collaborative efforts to combat fraud across different industries. Standardised terminology for various types of fraud is essential for effectively exchanging fraud-related data and insights among institutions.[76] To address these issues, in June 2024, the Euro Banking Association introduced version 5.0 of the Fraud Taxonomy, a pan-European method for

---

[72] European Banking Authority (2024a), p. 5.

[73] European Banking Authority (2024a), p. 8 ff.

[74] Art. 1(2), IPR, amending Regulation (EU) No 260/2012 (the SEPA Regulation), introduced Art. 5d 'Screening of PSUs by PSPs that offer instant credit transfers to verify whether a PSU is a person or entity subject to targeted financial restrictive measures.' See also European Banking Authority (2024c), p. 49.

[75] European Central Bank (2021), p. 3.

[76] Moes and Ruesing (2024), p. 66.

categorising payment fraud to enhance the fight against payment and card fraud across Europe. Its implementation offers PSPs and intelligence-sharing initiatives the opportunity to improve cross-border intelligence and data sharing, establishing a shared vocabulary for fraud types to strengthen reporting, prevention, and detection, assisting PSPs in creating effective fraud prevention campaigns for their customers.[77]

5 Conclusions

The Digital Euro Package marks a significant advancement in the Euro area's payment system, providing opportunities for innovation and adaptation to the increasingly digital economy. However, it also poses challenges in striking a balance among various interests.

As policymakers deliberate on the proposed regulations for the digital euro, they must thoroughly analyse legal interpretations, namely for the legal tender issues. They should also carefully consider proposed amendments and the ongoing evolution of the project. Establishing a digital euro should focus on developing a suitable technical and business model that factors in public and private interests.

The role of PSPs in distributing the digital euro is a crucial aspect of the proposed regulations. While the involvement of PSPs can encourage innovation and competition, it is essential to ensure a level playing field and maintain the security of the payment system. As the digital euro project advances, it is necessary to consider the broader implications for the European financial system. The proposed Third Payment Services Directive (PSD3) could serve as a foundation for the digital euro, addressing the current lack of anti-fraud, anti-money laundering, and sanctions systems.

The Digital Euro Package raises considerations about the future of EU integration. However, successfully adopting a digital euro may require more integration and collaboration among Member States and a unified approach to regulation and supervision.

Acknowledgements This essay is part of the EU-funded project Next-Generation EU, Mission 4 Component 1 CUP B53D23009710006.

[77] Euro Banking Association (2024).

Authors' Contributions This article is structured to reflect the contributions of each author—Filippo Zatti authors Section One, which focuses on the status of digital euro legal tender. Rosa Giovanna Barresi developed the subsequent sections, covering issues involving payment services providers. The conclusions result from joint work but must be considered attributable to Zatti.

References

Bindseil U, Cipollone P, Schaaf J (2024) The digital euro after the investigation phase: demystifying fears about bank disintermediation. VOXEU. CEPR. https://cepr.org/voxeu/columns/digital-euro-after-investigation-phase-demystifying-fears-about-bank. Accessed 24 May 2024

Coeure B (2012) The euro as a trusted means of payment. BIS. https://www.bis.org/ review/r121116b.pdf. Accessed 18 May 2024

EBA Clearing (2023) EBA CLEARING issues specifications and runs analytical pilot for pan-European fraud pattern and anomaly detection. https://www.ebaclearing.eu/news-and-events/media/press-releases/14-september-2023-eba-clearing-issues-specifications-and-runs-analytical-pilot-for-pan-european-fraud-pattern-and-anomaly-detection/. Accessed 24 May 2024

EBA Clearing (2023a) EBA CLEARING response to the proposed establishment of a Digital Euro. https://www.ebaclearing.eu/media/azure/production/3572/eba-clearing-response-to-proposed-establishment-of-a-digital-euro8-september-2023public.pdf. Accessed 24 May 2024

EBA Clearing (2024) Pan-European verification of payee ready by December. https://www.ebaclearing.eu/news-and-events/media/press-releases/8-april-2024-pan-european-verification-of-payee-ready-by-december/. Accessed 24 May 2024

Euro Banking Association (2024), EBA fraud taxonomy: a pan-European approach to payment fraud categorisation. https://www.abe-eba.eu/market-practices-regulatory-guidance/expert-group-on-payment-fraud-related-topics/. Accessed 14 June 2024

European Banking Authority (2024a) Opinion on new types of payment fraud and possible mitigations. https://www.eba.europa.eu/sites/default/files/2024-04/363649ff-27b4-4210-95a6-0a87c9e21272/Opinion%20on%20new%20types%20of%20payment%20fraud%20and%20possible%20mitigations.pdf. Accessed 24 May 2024

European Banking Authority (2024b) The EBA will start collecting information on natural persons through its AML/CFT database, EuReCA. https://www.eba.europa.eu/publications-and-media/press-releases/eba-will-start-collecting-information-natural-persons-through-its-amlcft-database-eureca. Accessed 24 May 2024

European Banking Authority (2024c) Two sets of Guidelines on internal policies, procedures and controls to ensure the implementation of Union and national restrictive measures. https://www.eba.europa.eu/sites/default/files/2024-11/eaeae49d-81a5-4154-8af9-5014f6ee8881/Final%20Report%20Guidelines%20restrictive%20measures%20.pdf. Accessed 26 November 2024

European Central Bank (2020) The role of cash. https://www.ecb.europa.eu/euro/cash/strategy/cash/role/html/index.en.html. Accessed 19 May 2024

European Central Bank (2021) Benefits of instant payments and recommendations for payment services providers. https://www.ecb.europa.eu/paym/integration/retail/instant/payments/shared/pdf/sept2021/comm.on.instant.pdf. Accessed 24 May 2024

European Central Bank (2022) Core, optional and value-added services for the digital euro – Market Advisory Group. https://www.ecb.europa.eu/euro/digitaleuro/timeline/profuse/shared/pdf//ecb.degov221208item3coreandoptionalservicesmag.en.pdf?. Accessed 24 May 2024

European Central Bank (2023a) A stocktake on the digital euro — Summary report on the investigation phase and outlook on the next phase. https://www.ecb.europa.eu/paym/digital/

euro/investigation/profuse/shared/files/dedocs/ecb.dedocs231018.en.pdf?6fbcce71a4be7bb3b8fabc51fb5c7e2d. Accessed 24 May 2024
European Central Bank (2023b) Progress on the investigation phase of a digital euro – fourth report. https://www.ecb.europa.eu/euro/digital/euro/timeline/profuse/shared/pdf/ecb.degov230713-fourth-progress-report-digital-euro-investigation-phase.en.pdf. Accessed 21 May 2024
European Central Bank (2024a) Update on the work of the digital euro scheme's Rulebook Development Group. https://www.ecb.europa.eu/euro/digital/euro/timeline/profuse/shared/pdf//ecb.degov240103RDGdigitaleuroschemesupdate.en.pdf. Accessed 19 May 2024
European Central Bank (2024b) Opinion of the European Central Bank of 31 October 2023 on the digital euro (CON/2023/34). https://eurlex.europa.eu/legalcontent/EN/TXT/PDF/?uri=CELEX:52023AB0034. Accessed 24 May 2024
European Central Bank (2024c) Opinion of the European Central Bank of 30 April 2024 on a proposed regulation and directive on payment and electronic money services (con/2024/13). https://www.ecb.europa.eu/pub/pdf/legal/ecb.leg.con.2024.13.en.pdf. Accessed 24 May 2024
European Court of Justice (2021) Joined Cases C-422/19 and C-423/19 Johannes Dietrich and Norbert Häring v Hessischer Rundfunk. In: Infocuria Case—Law. https://curia.europa.eu/juris/liste.jsf?num=C-422/19. Accessed 14 June 2024
European Data Protection Board (2024a) Opinion 08/2024 on valid consent in the context of consent or pay models implemented by large online platforms. https://www.edpb.europa.eu/our-work-tools/our-documents/opinion-board-art-64/opinion-082024-valid-consent-context-consent-or-en. Accessed 24 May 2024
European Data Protection Board (2024b) Statement 2/2024 on the financial data access and payments package. https://www.edpb.europa.eu/system/files/2024-05/edpb_statement_20230523_financialdatapaymentpackage_en.pdf. Accessed 25 May 2024
European Data Protection Board -European Data Protection Supervisor (2023) Joint Opinion 02/2023 on the Proposal for a Regulation of the European Parliament and of the Council on the establishment of the digital euro European Data Protection Board. https://edpb.europa.eu/our-work-tools/our-documents/edpbedps-joint-opinion/edpb-edps-joint-opinion-022023-proposal-en. Accessed 24 May 2024
European Parliament (2024) DRAFT REPORT on the proposal for a regulation of the European Parliament and of the Council on the establishment of the digital euro — Committee on Economic and Monetary Affairs (COM(2023)0369 – C9-0219/2023 – 2023/0212(COD)). https://www.europarl.europa.eu/doceo/document/ECON-PR-758954.EN.pdf. Accessed 25 May 2024
European Parliament (2024a) Digital Euro in 'An Economy that Works for People'. https://www.europarl.europa.eu/legislative-train/theme-an-economy-that-works-for-people/file-digital-euro. Accessed 24 May 2024
European Parliament (2024b) European Parliament legislative resolution of 23 April 2024 on the proposal for a regulation of the European Parliament and of the Council on payment services in the internal market and amending Regulation (EU) No 1093/2010 (COM(2023)0367 – C9-0217/2023 – 2023/0210(COD)). https://www.europarl.europa.eu/RegData/seance/pleniere/textes/adoptes/definitif/2024/04-23/0298/P9/TA(2024)0298 EN.pdf. Accessed 25 May 2024
European Parliament (2024c) MEPs want to enhance fraud protection and access to cash in payment services. https://www.europarl.europa.eu/news/en/press-room/20240419IPR20565/meps-want-to-enhance-fraud-protection-and-access-to-cash-in-payment-services. Accessed 25 May 2024
European Parliament (2024d) Vote on payment services: Better access to cash and protection against fraud and hidden charges. https://www.europarl.europa.eu/news/en/press-room/20240212IPR17629/payment-services-fraud-and-hidden-charges-protection-and-better-access-to-cash. Accessed 25 May 2024
European Payments Council (2024) Revised entry-into-force dates for the 2025 EPC Payment Scheme Rulebooks and version 1.0 of the EPC Verification of Payee Scheme Rulebook European Payments Council. https://www.europeanpaymentscouncil.eu/news-insights/news/

revised-entry-force-dates-2025-epc-payment-scheme-rulebooks-and-version-10-epc. Accessed 24 May 2024
Hubbard RG (2005) Money, the financial system, and the economy. Pearson, Boston
Moes A, Ruesing M (2024) A pan-European fraud taxonomy: do you speak fraud? J Payments Strategy Syst 18(1):61–72
Wong P, Maniff JL (2020) Comparing means of payment: what role for a Central Bank Digital Currency? FEDS Notes. https://doi.org/10.17016/2380-7172.2739
Yang BZ (2007) What is (not) money? Medium of exchange = means of payment. Am Econ 51(2): 101–104. https://doi.org/10.1177/056943450705100213

PSD3 and the Regulation on Payment Services in the Context of Crypto Assets as a Means of Payment

Lucía Alvarado Herrera

Abstract The Markets in Crypto-Assets (MiCA) Regulation establishes legal rules for crypto-assets that have a financial use and fall outside the scope of Union legislative acts on financial services. Among these crypto assets, it pays special attention to stablecoins, the so-called MiCA electronic money tokens and asset-referenced tokens, which are characterised by serving as a payment function. It is precisely this function of being a means of payment that raises the question of whether the transactions carried out with these crypto assets, or at least some of them, can be qualified as payment services, to which the legal framework for payment services, contained mainly (but not exclusively) in the Second Payment Services Directive (PSD2), currently under revision, would apply. This paper deals with the relationship between the two sets of rules (MiCA and PSD2). It analyses to what extent the existing and planned rules (PSD3 and Payment Services Regulation) can be applied to or somehow cover electronic money tokens and asset-referenced tokens.

This paper expands and updates the text of a lecture delivered at the III International Congress entitled "Present and future of crypto-assets regulation in the European Union," held at the University of Alicante (Spain) on December 13, 14, and 15, 2023. This work is funded within the framework of: Proyecto CIPROM/2022/26 "Presente y futuro de la regulación de los Criptoactivos en la UE [Legalcripto]". Proyecto Prometeo CIPROM/2022/26, grupos de investigación de excelencia, de la Generalitat Valenciana (P.I. Carmen Pastor).

L. A. Herrera (✉)
Universidad Pablo de Olavide, de Sevilla, Seville, Spain
e-mail: lalvher@upo.es

C. Pastor Sempere (ed.), *Governance and Control of Data and Digital Economy in the European Single Market*, Law, Governance and Technology Series 71,
https://doi.org/10.1007/978-3-031-74889-9_16

1 Introduction

The retail payments market has constantly changed for several years, driven by technological innovation. These innovations have improved the functioning of traditional payment instruments, making them more efficient (instant transfers)[1] and offering more options for initiating payments, such as tokenised payment cards (also known as X-pay solutions, provided by Big Tech, for instance), contactless payments using NFC (Near Field Communication) or QR (Quick Response) codes, mobile payments,[2] etc. Technological advances have also enabled the emergence of new payment services, such as payment initiation services and account information services, which have facilitated the entry and consolidation of new non-bank players (third-party providers). In addition, technical services are becoming increasingly important in the payment chain, and the difference between a purely technical service and a payment service is becoming more subtle. Large technology companies (Big Tech) have become more prominent in the payments sector as technology services providers (offering X-pay solutions) or payment services providers by obtaining a license as a credit institution, payment institution or electronic money institution.[3]

Since the emergence of electronic money (hereafter, e-money), regulated in Directive 2009/110/EC of 16 September 2009, on the taking up, pursuit and prudential supervision of the business of electronic money institutions amending Directives 2005/60/EC and 2006/48/EC and repealing Directive 2000/46/EC (EMD2),[4] all these innovations have not altered the object of payment, i.e. the means of payment (that which serves the debtor to fulfil or satisfy an obligation of a sum of money), which can be cash (banknotes and coins), bank money (also called scriptural money) and e-money. This has been the case until the emergence of distributed ledger technology (DLT), which, together with cryptography, allows the creation of tokens (representations of value and rights), transmissible in electronic form and which, in some of their modalities, can fulfil a payment function; tokens that serve a payment function are called payment tokens. Within the general category of payment tokens are stablecoins, so called because they have mechanisms to stabilise their value, mechanisms that may consist of a backing in assets (official currency, basket of assets, commodities, etc.) or the inclusion of algorithms that

[1] Recently, Regulation 2024/886, of 13 March 2024, amending Regulations (EU) No 260/2012 and (EU) 2021/1230 and Directives 98/26/EC and (EU) 2015/2366 as regards instant credit transfers in euro, has been approved.

[2] Mobile payment refers to a payment in which a mobile device is used at least to initiate the payment order and potentially also to transfer funds.

[3] Another current trend is the significative role of digital platforms in relation to financial services, including payment services [see on this issue, Zunzunegui Pastor 2022. Available at SSRN: https://ssrn.com/abstract=4040930 or https://doi.org/10.2139/ssrn.4040930).

[4] EMD2 contains the rules on authorisation and supervision of Electronic Money Institutions (EMIs), as well as private law rules relating to the issuance and redemption of electronic money.

adjust the supply and demand of the token (algorithmic stablecoins).[5] This distinguishes stablecoins from tokens such as Bitcoin, which are not backed and do not have mechanisms to stabilise their value. This leads to a scenario whereby these tokens, created as an alternative means of payment to "regulated" money, have become primarily an investment product.[6]

The Markets in Crypto-Assets (MiCA)[7] Regulation regulates two types of stablecoins: electronic money tokens (EMTs) and asset-referenced tokens (ARTs). This paper addresses how crypto assets with a payment function (payment tokens) regulated in MiCA fall under the legal regime for payment services, which is contained in Directive 2015/2366 of 25 November on payment services in the internal market, amending Directives 2002/65/EC, 2009/110/EC and 2013/36/EU and Regulation (EU) No 1093/2010, and repealing Directive 2007/64/EC (PSD2)[8] and, in particular, whether certain transactions carried out with these crypto assets can be qualified as payment transactions. The already relevant issue now takes on specific interest due to the ongoing PSD2 revision process. It is indeed an opportunity, not without difficulties, to bring some coherence to two different legal frameworks (MiCA and PSD2), which must be complementary and consistent to protect the holders of crypto assets that perform or may perform a payment function. This is due to the application of the principle of technology neutrality: users of payment services must enjoy the same level of protection when carrying out payment transactions, regardless of the technology supporting the means of payment. We are still at an early stage of the reform proposals. Therefore, the statements made at this stage are provisional, more to raise doubts than to provide certainties about the envisaged regime. However, the answer cannot be delayed; it is necessary to address the question of whether the legal framework for payment services can be applied to payment tokens regulated by MiCA, whether certain adaptations are required, or whether it would be better to provide them with a regime of their own.

Applying PSD2 to payment tokens requires recalling three characteristics of the legal regime governing payment services. The first is the exclusivity of the payment

[5] Algorithmic stablecoins that aim to maintain a stable value relative in relation to an official currency or assets via protocols that provide for the increase or decrease in the supply of such crypto-assets in response to changes in demand will be treated as electronic money tokens or asset-referenced tokens, as appropriate. Where they do not aim to stabilise the value by referencing one or more assets, they should be treated as crypto-assets other than electronic money tokens and asset referenced tokens (see Recital 41 MiCA Regulation).

[6] Madrid Parra (2020), p. 804.

[7] Regulation (EU) 2023/1114 of 31 May 2023 on markets in crypto-assets and amending Regulations (EU) No 1093/2010 and (EU) No 1095/2010 and Directives 2013/36/EU and (EU) 2019/1937.

[8] The Second Payment Services Directive (PSD2) entered into force in 2018, replacing PSD1 which dated from 2007 (Directive 2007/64/EC of the European Parliament and of the Council of 13 November 2007 on payment services in the internal market amending Directives 97/7/EC, 2002/65/EC, 2005/60/EC and 2006/48/EC and repealing Directive 97/5/EC). PSD1 established a harmonised legal framework for the creation of an integrated EU payments market. On the process of elaboration of PSD2 see Peñas Moyano (2020), pp. 43 and ss.

services activity to certain entities, the so-called Payment Service Providers (PSPs). Thus, classifying a given activity as a payment service means that it can only be carried out by those who meet this condition. Currently, there are three main categories of PSPs: credit institutions, payment institutions (PIs) and electronic money institutions (EMIs).

The second characteristic is that, with some exceptions,[9] payment services facilitate or generate movement of funds. This includes services that involve the transfer of funds (credit transfers, direct debits and card payments) and services that do not involve the transfer of funds but are necessary for such a transfer (issuance of payment instruments, payment initiation services). As seen below, applying PSD2 to payment tokens necessarily involves determining whether that which is moved or transferred, the "value" that acts as a means of payment, can qualify as "funds" in terms of PSD2.

The third, related to the characteristics mentioned above, is that PSD2 relies on the intervention of a third party, the PSP providing the payment service, which has a contractual relationship with the customer and executes the payment transaction (provides the payment service). This relationship between the payment service user and the PSP requires and gives meaning to the provisions on transparency, rights, and obligations set out in PSD2. However, this payment services regime appears not to apply to crypto asset transactions, which are designed to be peer-to-peer without the involvement of a third party.

Although full decentralisation does not fit well with the current regime of payment services, where transfers or movements of value require the intervention of a third party, the decentralisation is blurred in MiCA-regulated payment tokens for two reasons: MiCA payment tokens must have a recognised issuer and the so-called "crypto-asset service providers" (CASPs) are entering the crypto asset market, who may act as payment services providers.

2 Review of the Second Payment Services Directive

As mentioned above, the reference standard for payment services is PSD2, which must be complemented with the provisions of EMD2. The latter standard deals with the licensing and supervision of EMIs and the issuance and redemption of e-money. The relationship between the two sets of rules is evidenced by the fact that payments with e-money fall within the scope of PSD2 (indeed, the definition of e-money in EMD2 emphasises that it is issued to make payment transactions).[10]

---

[9]The account information service, for example, does not involve any movement of funds, and it is questionable whether it must be qualified as a payment service. Indeed, it is possible that in the future, after the entry into force of the new Open Finance Regulation, this service will be removed from the payment services regime and included in the aforementioned Regulation.

[10]Electronic money "means electronically, including magnetically, stored monetary value as represented by a claim on the issuer which is issued on receipt of funds for the purpose of making

For several reasons, PSD2's evaluation, originally planned for 2021, did not occur until 2022.[11] Following this evaluation[12] and the Commission's 2020 Communication on a Retail Payments Strategy for the EU,[13] the Commission decided to revise PSD2 by formulating two legislative proposals: a proposal for a regulation on payment services in the internal market and an amending Regulation (EU) No. 1093/2010[14] (henceforth, PSR Proposal) and a proposal for a Directive on payment services and electronic money services in the internal market, amending Directive 98/26/EC and repealing Directives 2015/2366/EU and 2009/110/EC[15] (henceforth, PSD3 Proposal). The Regulation contains the rules governing the provision of payment services, and the Directive relates to access to the profession and the supervision of institutions.

The Commission's initiative, embodied in the abovementioned proposals, has four specific objectives. First, to strengthen user protection and confidence in payments with the following provisions: improvements are introduced in the application of Strong Customer Authentication (SCA), legal bases are established for the exchange of information on fraud and the obligation to educate customers about it; the obligation to verify the IBAN (International Bank Account Number) with the name of the beneficiary is extended to all credit transfers (and not only instant transfers); new protection measures are introduced for users in cases where the authorisation of the payment transaction has been achieved through the use of social engineering techniques (the problem of authorised but fraudulent transactions); PSPs are obliged to improve the accessibility of SCA for users with disabilities, older people and other people facing difficulties regarding the use of SCA; and, measures are also provided to improve the availability of cash, allowing merchants to deliver cash without the need for them to request authorisation as a payment institution.[16]

---

payment transactions as defined in point 5 of Article 4 of Directive 2007/64/EC, and which is accepted by a natural or legal person other than the electronic money issuer" (art. 2°.2 EMD2). Reference to Directive 2007/64 should be read as a reference to Directive 2015/2366.

[11] The review clause of PSD2 (art. 108) required the Commission to report on the implementation and impact of the Directive no later than 13 January 2021. The failure to do so by the deadline was due to the late transposition of the Directive by some Member States and the delay in applying some of its rules, such as those relating to Strong Customer Authentication.

[12] See the evaluation report [European Commission (2023). Commission Staff Working Document Impact Assessment Report Accompanying the documents Proposal for a Regulation on payment services in the internal market and amending Regulation (EU) No 1093/2010 and Proposal for a Directive on payment services and electronic money services in the Internal Market amending Directive 98/26/EC and repealing Directives 2015/2366/EU and 2009/110/EC. Brussels, SWD (2023) 231 final]. https://eur-lex.europa.eu/legal-content/EN/TXT/?uri=SWD:2023:231:FIN.

[13] COM(2020) 592 final, 24.9.2020.

[14] COM(2023) 367 final, 28.6.2023.

[15] COM(2023) 366 final, 28.6.2023.

[16] Recital 10 PSR Proposal: "To further improve access to cash, which is a priority of the Commission, merchants should be allowed to offer, in physical shops, cash provision services even in the absence of a purchase by a customer, without having to obtain a payment service provider authorisation or being an agent of a payment institution. Those cash provision services

Secondly, the PSD2 review aims to improve the competitiveness of open banking services. The regulation of so-called open banking services was one of the key achievements of PSD2,[17] namely the account information service and the payment initiation service. The PSD2 evaluation has highlighted the growth of open banking services and the need to improve their operation. In particular, it requires account servicing payment service providers (ASPSP) to set up a specific interface for data access and implement a so-called "permission dashboard", which allows users to manage the permissions granted for access to data on open banking services. It should be noted that, in addition to the proposals for modification of PSD2, the Commission presented a proposal for a regulation on a framework for access to financial data other than payment account data,[18] which implies an important step in the evolution from open banking to open finance.

The third objective is to improve the enforcement and implementation of PSD2 in Member States. To this end, it will replace most of PSD2 with a directly applicable Regulation clarifying unclear or ambiguous aspects of that Directive and to integrate the licensing regimes for PIs and EMIs into a new Directive, the future PSD3. The PSD3 directive creates a new category of payment institutions, replacing the PI/EMI duality. Within this category, there is, in turn, a subcategory of payment institutions providing electronic money services. Thus, EMIs will disappear and become payment institutions providing electronic money services and a new category of services, "electronic money services", will be created, comprising issuance of electronic money, maintenance of payment accounts storing electronic money units and transfer of electronic money units.[19] As we shall see, the disappearance of EMIs and their consequent qualification as payment institutions providing electronic money services and the introduction of electronic money services are

should, however, be subject to the obligation to disclose fees charged to the customer, if any. These services should be provided by retailers on a voluntary basis and should depend on the availability of cash by the retailer".

[17] Open banking means a framework for allowing payment service users to share their account data with third party providers of payment-related services such as Account Information Services Providers and Payment Initiation Services Providers" [European Commission (2023). Commission Staff Working Document Impact Assessment..., cit., p. 5)].

[18] Proposal for a Regulation on a framework for Financial Data Access and amending Regulations (EU) n° 1093/2010, (EU) No 1094/2010, (EU) No 1095/2010 and (EU) 2022/2554. Brussels, 28.6.2023 COM(2023) 360 final.

[19] Annex I PSR Proposal: "Payment services (as referred to in point 3 of Article 2): 1. Services enabling cash to be placed on and/or withdrawn from a payment account. 2. Execution of payment transactions, including transfers of funds from and to a payment account, including where the funds are covered by a credit line with the user's payment service provider or with another payment service provider. 3. Issuing of payment instruments. 4. Acquiring of payment transactions. 5. Money remittance. 6. Payment initiation services. 7. Account information services". Annex II PSR Proposal: "Electronic money services (as referred to in point 37 of Article 2). Issuance of electronic money, maintenance of payment accounts storing electronic money units and transfer of electronic money units".

particularly relevant to EMTs since they affect both the issuers of these tokens and certain transactions carried out with them.

Finally, the initiative aims to improve access to non-bank PSPs' payment systems and bank accounts. To this end, the rights of payment institutions concerning opening accounts with credit institutions are strengthened. (Art. 32 PSR Proposal) and the possibility for payment institutions to safeguard funds in accounts held at central banks is envisaged (Art. 9 PSD3 Proposal). Regarding payment systems, the rules for accessing payment systems are clarified (Art. 31 PSR Proposal) and, as a novelty, payment institutions are allowed to participate directly in payment systems designated by the Member States following Directive 98/26/EC of 19 May 1998 on settlement finality in payment and securities settlement systems (SFD). To this end, Article 46 of the PSD3 Proposal modifies the definitions of "entity" and "participant" of the SFD (Art. 2). It should be noted that the European legislator has anticipated this change with Article 4 of the Regulation on instant credit transfers, which has already introduced the aforementioned changes to the SFD.[20]

Once the objectives have been set, it is noticeable that there is no mention of how payment tokens regulated under MiCA fit into PSD2 or, more broadly, the relationship between MiCA and PSD2, even though various authorities and organisations have warned of the need to do so. Thus, the European Banking Authority (EBA) pointed out that "a potential future revision of PSD2 should carefully take into account the interaction with MiCA, in particular for ensuring alignment and consistent application of the requirements."[21] The same can be said of MiCA, which, although the final text is more complete than the Commission's proposal, does not address the role of stablecoins as a means of payment with the desired clarity.[22]

3 MiCA Regulated Payment Tokens: Electronic Money Tokens and Asset-Referenced Tokens

Without a legal definition of payment tokens, we must understand that such crypto assets can be a means of payment (i.e., they can perform the functions attributed to money). MiCA Regulation defines a "crypto asset" as "a digital representation of a value or of a right that can be transferred and stored electronically using distributed ledger technology or similar technology" [art. 3.1.5)]. As indicated in Recital

[20]In relation to access to designated payment systems, Regulation on instant transfers also amends the 2015 Directive, in particular Article 35, and adds a new Article 35(a).

[21]European Banking Authority (2022). Opinion of the European Banking Authority on its technical advice on the review of Directive (EU) 2015/2366 on payment services in the internal market (PSD2). EBA/Op/2022/06, p. 111, apartado 472.https://www.eba.europa.eu/sites/default/files/document_library/Publications/Opinions/2022/Opinion%20od%20PSD2%20review%20%28EBA-Op-2022-06%29/1036016/EBA%27s%20response%20to%20the%20Call%20for%20advice%20on%20the%20review%20of%20PSD2.pdf.

[22]Pastor Sempere (2022), pp. 35–36.

16, this broad and technologically neutral definition aims to cover all assets registered in a DLT (or similar) that have a financial use and are not already regulated by any European Union financial services legislation.[23] This explains the exclusions from the scope of application: crypto assets that are already regulated (e.g. financial instruments, deposits, etc.) must be subject to the rules that regulate these types of assets and not to the MiCA Regulation. However, a relevant exception is established for e-money since although it already has its own regime in the EMD2, if the technology used to represent and support it is DLT, it will fall within the scope of MiCA Regulation (and of the EMD2).[24] In effect, Article 2.4.c) MiCA Regulation establishes that the Regulation shall not apply to crypto assets that qualify as funds, except if they qualify as "electronic money tokens".

MiCA Regulation omits any reference to the term "payment tokens"; rather, it refers to crypto assets that aim to stabilise their value by reference to other assets, differentiating, as noted, between EMTs and ARTs. MiCA Regulation defines EMTs as "a type of crypto asset that purports to maintain a stable value by referencing the value of one official currency" (art. 3.1.7 MiCA Regulation).[25] What characterises this payment token is the specific stabilisation mechanism used: its value is referenced to the value of a (single) official currency. The MiCA Regulation included in the definition of EMT an explicit reference to the main purpose of this token: to be used as a medium of exchange,[26] an allusion that has disappeared in the current wording. Without discussing the differences between the function of the medium of exchange and the function of the medium of payment,[27] the configuration that MiCA Regulation has given to EMTs—and their assimilation to e-money—allow us to state that the main function of EMTs is to be a means of payment. Thus,

[23] Recital 16 MiCA Regulation: "The terms 'crypto-assets' and 'distributed ledger technology' should therefore be defined as widely as possible to capture all types of crypto-assets that currently fall outside the scope of Union legislative acts on financial services".

[24] Martínez Nadal (2021), pp. 49 and 56–57.

[25] Digital assets such as Bitcoin are crypto assets under MiCA definition of crypto-assets. However, they are neither EMTs nor ARTs, so the regime provided for these types of payment tokens does not apply to them. One could ask whether it could then be considered a "crypto-asset other than an asset-referenced token or an e-money token", whose legal regime is contained in Title II of MiCA Regulation. The answer must be negative because the regime for these crypto-assets (i.e. those that are not e-money tokens or asset-referenced tokens) is based on the existence of a recognised issuer, which is not the case for Bitcoin. However, to the extent that they are crypto-assets within the meaning of MiCA Regulation, crypto-asset services (and their providers) involving Bitcoins are subject to the MiCA regime, in particular to the provisions of Title V (Authorisation and operating conditions for crypto-asset service providers). [see Ciraolo (2022), pp. 97–98; Palá Laguna and Canalejas Merín (2023), p. 2. https://www.ga-p.com/publicaciones/a-que-criptoactivos-no-se-aplicara-el-reglamento-mica].

[26] Art. 3°.1.4 MiCA proposal Regulation: "electronic money token' or 'e-money token' means a type of crypto-asset, the main purpose of which is to be used as a means of exchange and that purports to maintain a stable value by referring to the value of a fiat currency that is legal tender". It is noted that the expression "fiat currency that is legal tender" has also been replaced by "official currency".

[27] About this issue, see Madrid Parra (2020). Criptoactivos. . ., cit., pp. 812–813.

Recital 18 states that "The function of such crypto assets is very similar to the function of electronic money as defined in Directive 2009/110/EC. Like electronic money, such crypto assets are electronic surrogates for coins and banknotes and are likely to be used for making payments."[28]

Article 48 of the MiCA Regulation provides that the issuer of EMTs must be either a credit institution or an EMI that is otherwise entitled to issue "traditional" electronic money (i.e., e-money that does not fall within the definition of EMT).[29] As mentioned above, the PSD3 Proposal envisages the disappearance of EMIs to be replaced by payment institutions providing electronic money services so that issuers of EMTs will have to apply for authorisation as payment institutions providing electronic money services. Furthermore, the issuance of EMTs is also an electronic money service, as the issuance of electronic money is an "electronic money service". Authorisation as a payment institution providing electronic money services entitles these entities to provide services for transferring electronic money units, which means that issuers of EMTs can offer transfer services on these tokens. In the context of EMTs, it is more difficult to determine what is to be understood by the service of "maintenance payment accounts storing electronic money units". First, it would be necessary to determine the equivalent of the payment account in the scope of the DLT, for which the definition of payment account in PSD2 should be used as a starting point. PSD2 defines a "payment account" as "an account held in the name of one or more payment service users which is used for the execution of payment transactions" (Art. 4°.12). What characterises a payment account, therefore, is their ability to perform payment transactions through them, i.e. to send or receive funds.[30] In the field of crypto assets, such a function could be fulfilled by the distributed ledger address[31] from and to which crypto assets can be transferred, as well as crypto asset accounts if such an account exists and is used to make the transfer.

In turn, ARTs are defined as "a type of crypto asset that is not an electronic money token, and that purports to maintain a stable value by referencing another value or right or a combination thereof, including one or more official currencies" (Art. 3.1.6

[28]The EMTs regime is set out in Title IV of MiCA Regulation, whose provisions set out the requirements to be met by the issuers of EMTs (the reference to the fact that they must be credit institutions or electronic money institutions should be understood after the adoption of PSD3, as referring to credit institutions and payment institutions providing electronic money services); the conditions for issuing and redeeming these tokens (it is expressly stated that the requirements set out in MiCA and not in EMD2 will apply); the specificities regarding the safeguarding of the funds received in exchange for EMTs; and, finally, the special regime for significant EMTs.

[29]Art. 1° EMD2.

[30]The PSR Proposal amends the definition of payment account to clarify that any account used for this purpose shall be considered a payment account (see art. 3.1.15 and Recital 20). For more details on payment accounts, see the comments in note 44.

[31]Article 3°.18 Regulation 2023/1113 of 31 May 2023, on information accompanying transfers of funds and certain crypto-assets and amending Directive (EU) 2015/849 (Travel Rule Regulation): "distributed ledger address means an alphanumeric code that identifies an address on a network using distributed ledger technology (DLT) or similar technology where crypto-assets can be sent or received".

MiCA Regulation). With less emphasis than on EMTs, it is noted that they can be used as a means of exchange,[32] with occasional references to their function as a means of payment.[33]

Supposing EMTs and ARTs can be used to make payments, the question arises as to whether certain transactions made with these crypto assets can be considered payment transactions and, therefore, be subject to the payment services regime contained in PSD2. As a preliminary—and essential—question, it would be necessary to determine whether EMTs and ARTs are "funds" within the meaning of PSD2, as this Directive applies when payment transactions are made with funds. In addition, it would be necessary to analyse whether and to what extent the legislative proposals provide for any novelty or modification in this respect.

Article 4.25 PSD2 defines "funds" as "banknotes and coins, scriptural money or electronic money as defined in point (2) of Article 2 of Directive 2009/110/EC". The PSR Proposal amends the definition of "funds" to expressly include central bank money issued in digital form (Central Bank Digital Currency -CBDC-), i.e. the future digital euro.[34] Thus, funds are defined as "central bank money issued for retail use, scriptural money and electronic money" ("banknotes and coins" are replaced by "central bank money issued for retail use"). Recital 28 PSR Proposal states, "The definition of funds should cover all forms of central bank money issued for retail use, including banknotes and coins, and any possible future central bank digital currency, e-money, and commercial bank money. Central bank money issued for use between the central bank and commercial banks, i.e. for wholesale use, should not be covered". It should be noted that if the digital euro is issued as a crypto asset, it will not fall within the scope of MiCA by the provisions of Article 2.2.c) of MiCA Regulation.[35] The new definition of funds includes EMTs and retail central bank money issued in digital form, although they are not explicitly mentioned in the aforementioned Article. This can be derived from Article 48.2 of MiCA Regulation ("E-money tokens shall be deemed to be electronic money") and Recital 29 PSR Proposal (MiCA "lays down that electronic-money tokens shall be deemed to be

[32] Recital 40 MiCA Regulation.

[33] See Art. 43.1.e) MiCA Regulation establishes as one of the criteria for classifying an ART as significant "the significance of the activities of the issuer of the asset-referenced token on an international scale, including the use of the asset-referenced token for payments and remittances".

[34] For a future digital euro, see Proposal for a Regulation on the establishment of the digital euro, Brussels, 28.6.2023, COM(2023) 369 final. This initiative is accompanied by a proposal for a Regulation on providing digital euro services by payment services providers incorporated in Member States whose currency is not the euro (COM/2023/368 final).

[35] Art. 2°. 2.c): "This Regulation does not apply to [...] the ECB, central banks of the Member States when acting in their capacity as monetary authorities, or other public authorities of the Member States". The exclusion occurs due to the public nature of the issuer [Martínez Nadal (2021). Ámbito de aplicación..., cit., p. 50; Palá Laguna and Canalejas Merín (2023). A qué criptoactivos no se aplicará el Reglamento MiCA, cit., p. 3]. However, such exclusion would also be based on the application of the provisions of Article 2.4(c), which excludes from the scope of MiCA Regulation those crypto assets that are considered "funds" and, as noted above, CBDCs fall within the definition of funds in the PSR Proposal.

electronic money. Electronic money tokens are therefore included, as electronic money, in the definition of funds in this Regulation"). The above shows that EMD2 (PSR in the future) contains the general legal regime for electronic money, and MiCA Regulation contains the specific regime for tokenised electronic money.[36]

As nothing is said about ARTs in the new definition of "funds", nor does the MiCA regulation assimilate them to e-money, their qualification as funds must be excluded. Consequently, they would be outside the PSD2 regime. EBA had recommended in its 2022 Opinion that attention should be paid in the PSD2 review process to ARTs "that are identified as being used widely as a means of exchange, including on whether the tokens should fall under the scope of the definition of funds under Article 4(25) of PSD2, how the payment transactions with these tokens will be treated, and whether it is required to apply SCA to them."[37] The FISMA study went even further, proposing several measures regarding EMTs and ARTs, such as revising the definition of funds in the PSD2 to cover e-money tokens, adding a "quasi-fund" definition to cover asset-referenced tokens, inserting a chapter in the PSD2 title on PSPs covering authorisation and supervision of issuers of asset-referenced token issuers and e-money token issuers; extending the application of the information requirements also to payment transactions using e-money tokens and asset-referenced tokens; excluding the application of Title IV to payment transactions by e-money tokens and asset referenced tokens.[38] As indicated above, ARTs are outside the scope of application of the PDS2 for the time being and always on a provisional basis due to the status of the legislative proposals.

As far as EMTs are concerned, they enter the payment services regime indirectly as they are considered e-money, which is an additional difficulty insofar as the PSD2 revision process has revealed the current uncertainties regarding e-money.[39] Thus, there are difficulties in distinguishing between e-money and scriptural money insofar as both share the same nature of a claim. In addition, the medium that stores the electronic money is sometimes confused with the electronic money itself. In this regard, the Haut Comité Juridique de la Place de Paris[40] recommends the revision of the concept of e-money so that, among other things, it can accommodate crypto

[36]Madrid Parra (2020). Criptoactivos..., cit., pp. 816–817.

[37]European Banking Authority (2023). Opinion..., cit., p. 111, apartado 473.

[38]European Commission, Directorate-General for Financial Stability, Financial Services and Capital Markets Union (FISMA), Bosch Chen et al. (2023), p. 183. https://data.europa.eu/doi/10.2874/996945.

[39]Ciraolo (2022). Paymen tokens..., cit., p. 100.

[40]The Haut Comité Juridique de la Place de Paris set up a working group in May 2022 to consider and examine the changes it wanted to make in PSD2. The document summarising the working group's results is the Report on the revisión of the Payment Services Directive 2 (PSD2), September 2023. https://www.hcjp.fr/banques-et-etablissement-de-credit. Regarding the differences between electronic money and scriptural money, the report points out that in the former case, the holder has a right of claim against the electronic money issuer. In contrast, in the second one the holder does not have a right of claim against the issuer (the European Central Bank) sino against the bank (a claim for a restitution of the deposit) (p. 37).

assets, as well as incorporate in the text regulating e-money the definition of the medium or form in which the electronic money is stored. (Recommendations 2 and 5).[41] Another difficulty highlighted about e-money is that, in many cases, it is impossible to distinguish between a payment account held by a payment institution, in which funds cannot be stored and an account held by an EMI, in which e-money is stored.[42] One of the problems identified in the PSD2 review is that many payment institutions "create" e-money without being aware of it and, therefore, without applying for authorisation as EMI. This is because EMD2 only incidentally refers to the two existing models of e-money: e-money stored in a physical device held by the holder and universally accessible, and e-money stored in electronic money

[41] Recommendation n° 2: "The HCJP recommends the revision of the concept of electronic money, not only because the current definition remains abstruse, but also so that it can be used for the innovations currently underway, in particular concerning crypto-assets, but more broadly the new payment value chains"; Recommendation n° 5: "The HCJP recommends that the future text contain a definition of the electronic money medium, for at least two reasons: (i) electronic money is often confused with the underlying device (payment card, payment account) which stores it, thereby hindering its identification and qualification; and (ii) forward-looking, a definition of the electronic money device suitable for covering the future the future e-money tokens of the MiCA Regulation".

[42] One of the main innovations of PSD1 was the creation of the "payment account" concept, which remained unchanged in PSD2. A payment account is "held in the name of one or more payment service users which is used for the execution of payment transactions" (art. 4°.12 PSD2). Therefore, its purpose characterises the payment account: it is used to execute payment transactions. [payment transaction means "an act, initiated by the payer or on his behalf or by the payee, of placing, transferring or withdrawing funds, irrespective of any underlying obligations between the payer and the payee" (art. 4°.12 PSD2)]. This broad concept covers any account that allows payment transactions (e.g., current or savings accounts). They were created to enable payment institutions to provide payment services. Indeed, since most payment services require an account, payment institutions must be able to maintain them. They could not, however, be current or savings accounts (bank accounts) insofar as these are fed by reimbursable funds from the public and payment institutions are prohibited from carrying out this activity. The payment account thus arises as a broad concept, covering or including bank accounts and other types of accounts, such as those held by payment institutions, which cannot be qualified as bank accounts. Payment accounts also store electronic money and are used to make payments. On this issue, see extensively Haut Comité Juridique de la Place Financière de Paris (2023). Report on the revisión. . ., cit., pp. 85–100.

accounts, also called e-wallets (Recital 8 EMD2),[43] restricted to members; the so-called closed e-money circuits.[44]

However, EMTs may shed some light on the very concept of e-money insofar as they make it possible to "visualise" the difference between the means of payment (a claim) and the support of this means of payment (electronic money account, card or distributed register). In principle, the nature of the means of payment is the same—a claim—. Still, since the medium is different, how the means of payment circulate is different, and the tools that make it possible to initiate the transfer of the means of payment are also different, as are the subjects involved in this transfer. What happens is that, in EMTs, the medium has relevant consequences. It can be said that EMTs are tokenised e-money, which is a new form of e-money whose main characteristic is its registration in a DLT network, which may affect the nature of the claim (claim incorporated in a security[45]—in a similar way to book entries—) and how it circulates. E-money in the form of tokens becomes negotiable because of its special form of representation—DLT—, thus overcoming the shortcomings of the "reusability" of traditional electronic money. On the other hand, the relationship between the issuer of the token and the holder, although of a contractual nature, will not be based on an *ad hoc* contract between the issuer and the holder but on the white paper that each issuer (or whoever applies for the admission to trading of an EMT) will have to draw up.[46]

[43] See also Article 63(3) of PSD2, which states that: "Articles 73 and 74 of this Directive shall apply also to electronic money as defined in point (2) of Article 2 of Directive 2009/110/EC, except where the payer's payment service provider cannot freeze the payment account on which the electronic money is stored or block the payment instrument. Member States may limit that derogation to payment accounts on which the electronic money is stored or to payment instruments of a certain value". "It follows from the definition of electronic money that it can be issued on different media, i.e., either on a physical medium capable of possession (such as a card), or on a software medium (in which computer accounts are created) in which the units of electronic money are recorded (see Haut Comité Juridique de la Place Financière de Paris (2023). Report on the revisión..., cit., pp. 90 and 46-48). It may also happen that once the electronic money account is opened, a card associated with it is issued. In this case, the electronic money is not stored on the card but on the account.

[44] From the latter perspective, e-money is not only a means of payment but also a real payment system consisting of an issuer, a user and a network of merchants [see Lanskoy (2000), p. 2].

[45] In this sense, Madrid Parra (Criptoactivos..., cit., p. 830) states that EMTs "no dejan de ser un título-valor digital referenciado a una moneda".

[46] Madrid Parra (Criptoactivos..., cit., p. 832) points out that in the White Paper "se fijan las cláusulas que han de regir la relación jurídica (de naturaleza contractual) existente entre el emisor y el titular de las fichas de dinero electrónico, sea este el primer adquirente suscriptor o los futuros titulares, que podrán devenir titulares en razón de las operaciones de intercambio (incluido su uso como medio de pago) o mediante la adquisición en una plataforma de negociación de criptoactivos".

4 The Hybrid Nature of Electronic Money Tokens: Problems of Collision Between Payment Services and Crypto Asset Services

What has been said so far shows the hybrid nature of EMTs: they are crypto assets (subject to MiCA Regulation), e-money (in terms of EMD2), and, therefore, funds in the sense of PSD2—and future PSD3 and PSR—. The latter implies that certain transactions carried out with EMTs may be considered "payment services," to which PSD2 must be applied, generating several problems from the outset.

Firstly, PSD2 does not have a concept or definition of "payment service"; it only provides a statement of what payment services are. This makes it difficult to determine whether certain crypto asset transactions may qualify as payment services. With some exceptions, it can be concluded that the activities that PSD2 considers to be payment services are services that facilitate a movement of funds, typically[47] between a payer and a payee (who may be the same person). PSD2 calls these movements of funds "payment transactions", which is defined as "an act, initiated by the payer or on his behalf or by the payee, of placing, transferring or withdrawing funds, irrespective of any underlying obligations between the payer and the payee (art. 4.5 PSD2).[48] Payment transactions, i.e. place, withdrawal or transfer of funds, require the participation of a third party, the PSP, which agrees with its customer the form and procedures necessary to carry out this movement of funds (PSD2 calls this set of procedures a "payment instrument"[49]). After the inclusion of EMD2, the PSR Proposal introduces a new category of services (electronic money services) as services with a certain degree of autonomy regarding payment services. As mentioned above, these are the issuance of electronic money, maintenance of payment accounts, storage of electronic money units, and transfer of electronic money units. The purpose of creating this new category of services is to preserve the autonomy of certain activities related to electronic money, which could be called into question after the unification of the regime for PIs and EMIs. In other words, it would be a matter of regulating what is specific to e-money as an electronic money service.

[47] We say "normally" because there are cases where there is a movement of funds but not between a payer and a payee (e.g., cash deposits and withdrawals) or where there is no such movement of funds (e.g., the payment service consisting of the issuance of a payment instrument and the account information service).

[48] The PSR Proposal amends the definition by emphasising that the payment transaction consists of place, withdrawal, or transfer of funds and that such place, withdrawal or transfer must be based on a "payment order", which may be given by or on behalf of the payer (e.g. in the case of payment initiation services) or by the payee. Art. 3° 5 PSR Proposal: "Payment transaction' means an act of placing, transferring, or withdrawing funds based on a payment order placed by the payer, or on his behalf, or by the payee, or on his behalf, irrespective of any underlying obligations between the payer and the payee".

[49] Art. 4° 14) PSD2, "payment instrument means a personalised device(s) and/or set of procedures agreed between the payment service user and the payment service provider and used in order to initiate a payment order.

Notably, the PSR Proposal elevates two electronic money-related activities to the "electronic money service" category: the maintenance of payment accounts that store electronic money units and the transfer of electronic money units, which were not previously addressed in EMD2, at least explicitly.

Regarding the first one (maintenance of payment accounts storing electronic money units), the PSR Proposal refers to e-money stored remotely on a server and managed by the e-money holder through a dedicated electronic money account.[50] These accounts are characterised by the fact that in addition to allowing the execution of payment transactions—typical of any payment account—they store funds in the form of e-money, i.e. the registration in the payment account represents a claim against the issuer (the payment institution issuing electronic money). They thus differ from payment accounts opened with payment institutions that do not provide electronic money services and do not store funds because the entry in the payment account does not represent a claim against the payment institution. Payment institutions not providing electronic money services shall not acquire ownership of funds the payment service user offers.[51] The relationship between the latter and the payment institution may be qualified as a commission contract, in which the payment institution receives the funds that will apply to making payments as "provision of funds".

Returning to the "storage" of electronic money, it is worth considering whether certain digital wallets can be assimilated into payment accounts that store units of electronic money. Two kinds of digital wallets currently exist: the pass-through wallets, involving the tokenisation of an existing payment instrument (e.g. a payment card),[52] and the staged-wallets, that store electronic money.[53] Regarding the former, the PSR Proposal states that they "are to be considered as technical services

[50]Recital 8 EMD2.

[51]European Commission (2023). Commission Staff Working Document Impact Assessment..., cit., p. 178: "Furthermore, the distinguishing features between e-money and payment services will be spelt out more properly. The difference between funds accepted by a payment institution to be held in a payment account for the purpose of making payment transactions and e-money issued by an e-money institution (then by the payment institution) will be that whilst the funds received for the purpose of issuing e-money remain under the full control of the e-money issuer and are the property of the e-money issuer, funds held in a payment account by a payment institution remain the property of the payment service user. The payment service user can withdraw them or place payment orders for the funds to be transferred (meaning for payment transactions to be executed); these orders do not have to be placed upfront or in a specified period. This will still continue to depend on the business model of the payment institution".

[52]Pass-through wallets can also be linked to a bank account; both (payment card and bank account) would have in common that the value is not stored in the digital wallet.

[53]FISMA, A study..., cit., p. 28: "Digital wallets can also be classified based on the flow of the funds as "staged" and "pass-through" wallets. Staged wallets, such as PayPal and Lydia, divide the payment into two stages to complete the transaction: the funding and payment stages. In the funding stage, the customer makes funds available to the digital wallet. In the payment stage, the wallet moves the funds to the merchant. On the other hand, pass-through digital wallets act as a proxy for physical payment cards for instance, such as Apple Pay and Samsung Pay, and pass the customer's payment credentials to the merchant, which has the transaction processed directly by the acquirer

and should thus be excluded from the definition of payment instrument as, in the Commission's view, a token cannot be regarded as being itself a payment instrument but, rather, a 'payment application' within the meaning of Article 2(21) of Regulation (EU) 2015/751"; the latter, on the contrary, "should be considered a payment instrument and their issuance a payment service". Therefore, digital wallets that store electronic money are considered "payment instruments."[54] Since the issuance of payment instruments is not included among the electronic money services in Annex II of the PSR Proposal, it seems that the issuance of staged-wallets would be a payment service, not an electronic money service. However, the operation of the wallet requires the wallet user to make a provision of funds, which will be "converted" into e-money. There will, therefore, be an issuance of electronic money (electronic money service), which means that the wallet issuer must necessarily be a payment institution that provides electronic money services. Once the digital wallet is created, its operation will be like that of an account that stores electronic money, so its maintenance must be qualified as an electronic money service.

Regarding transfers of electronic money units, no specific provision has been made for these transactions so that, in principle, it is not possible to see the reason for their inclusion as a service other than that provided for in paragraph 2 of Annex I, apart from the fact that the entity executing the transaction must be authorised as a payment institution providing electronic money services. Therefore, electronic money unit transfers must be considered payment transactions without any other provision. In addition, if it is accepted that staged-wallets can be treated as payment accounts storing electronic money units, transfers made through these wallets would qualify as an electronic money service. As EMTs are e-money, transfers of these tokens should be qualified as transfers of electronic money units (electronic money service) and payment transactions subject to PSD2.

Secondly, and as a consequence of the above, a set of rules will be applied to EMTs (the payment services regime) that does not take into account the special features of crypto assets, in particular, the dissociation that may occur between the issuer of the token and the payment service provider. Indeed, in "traditional" e-money, the entity issuing the e-money is usually the same as the entity providing the payment service. There is a direct contractual relationship (i.e. not based on a White Paper, as in the case of EMTs) between the e-money issuer/payment service provider and the e-money holder/payment service user. This makes it easier to identify the entity subject to the transparency obligations imposed by PSD2 and to articulate the rights and obligations of the parties (as well as the liability regime). In EMTs, on the other hand, the payment service provider may be the token issuer, but

bank. Therefore, the pass-through wallet is not involved in the movement of funds and funds are not stored by the wallet operator".

[54] Vid. Recital 24 PSR Proposal.

it may be a third party, the crypto-asset service provider (CASP).[55] The latter must be responsible for compliance with the duties of transparency, the obligations established for executing payment transactions, and the system of liability.

Third, the hybrid nature of EMTs causes some payment services to collide with certain crypto-asset services regulated under MiCA; these services that may collide with payment services regulated in PSD2 are identified in the MiCA Regulation (it should be noted that the MiCA Regulation does not recognise the planned category of electronic money services, and what it has recognised and regulated is the collision with payment services listed in the Annex to PSD2).

Recital 90 of the MiCA Regulation states that "Some crypto-asset services, in particular providing custody and administration of crypto assets on behalf of clients, the placing of crypto assets, and transfer services for crypto assets on behalf of clients, might overlap with payment services as defined in Directive (EU) 2015/2366". Regarding the custody and administration of crypto-assets service,[56] Recital 91 MiCA Regulation notes that "the tools provided by issuers of electronic money to their clients to manage an e-money token might not be distinguishable from the activity of providing custody and administration services as regulated by this Regulation. Electronic money institutions should, therefore, be able to provide custody services, without prior authorisation under this Regulation to provide crypto-asset services, only in relation to the e-money tokens issued by them". It seems that the Recital refers to wallets provided by an issuer of EMTs, and what the MiCA Regulation says is that the entity does not have to seek authorisation as a CASP to provide the custody service in relation to the EMTs it issues. However, it must notify the competent authority of certain information.[57] Under the PSR Proposal, a custodial wallet could qualify as a "payment instrument" to the extent that it allows the initiation of payment transactions, and its issuance would be a payment service. Therefore, the question arises as to whether CASPs other than the EMT issuer providing custodial services to EMTs must apply for authorisation as a payment institution to offer such services.

Another service where PSD2 and MiCA may overlap is the placing of crypto assets.[58] Recital 92 of the MiCA Regulation states that distributing e-money on

[55] As Ciraolo points out (Paymen tokens..., cit., pp. 102–103), it is also possible that the issuer of the token is not the same as the one offering it, a split that would further aggravate the situation.

[56] Art. 3°.1.17 MiCA Regulation: "providing custody and administration of crypto-assets on behalf of clients' means the safekeeping or controlling on behalf of clients, of crypto-assets or of the means of access to such crypto-assets, where applicable in the form of private cryptographic keys".

[57] Artículo 60.4 MiCA Regulation: "An electronic money institution authorised under Directive 2009/110/EC shall only provide custody and administration of crypto-assets on behalf of clients and transfer services for crypto-assets on behalf of clients with regard to the e-money tokens it issues if it notifies the competent authority of the home Member State of the information referred to in paragraph 7 of this Article at least 40 working days before providing those services for the first time".

[58] Art. 3°.1.22 MiCA Regulation: "placing of crypto-assets means the marketing, on behalf of or for the account of the offeror or a party related to the offeror, of crypto-assets to purchasers". The Travel Rule Regulation also offers a definition of crypto-asset transfer, noting that it is "any

behalf of the issuer is equivalent to placing crypto assets under the MiCA Regulation. As a result, it is established that natural or legal persons authorised under PSD2 to distribute e-money may provide the service of placing crypto assets without the need to obtain authorisation as a CAP.[59]

Regarding transfer services for crypto assets, the MiCA Regulation establishes that "providing transfer services for crypto-assets on behalf of clients means providing services of transfer, on behalf of a natural or legal person, of crypto-assets from one distributed ledger address or account to another".[60] The MiCA Regulation considers it a service that can be provided on a stand-alone basis or as part of other crypto-asset services (custody and administration of crypto assets, execution of orders on behalf of clients, exchange of crypto assets for cash or other crypto assets). It also recognises that transfers could be included in the PSD2 definition of payment services if the crypto asset is an EMT.[61] To avoid duplication, the MiCA Regulation

---

transaction with the aim of moving crypto-assets from one distributed ledger address, crypto-asset account or other device allowing the storage of crypto-assets to another, carried out by at least one crypto-asset service provider acting on behalf of either an originator or a beneficiary, irrespective of whether the originator and the beneficiary are the same person and irrespective of whether the crypto-asset service provider of the originator and that of the beneficiary are one and the same".

[59] Recital 92 MiCA Regulation: "The activity of traditional electronic money distributors, namely, that of distributing electronic money on behalf of issuers, would amount to the activity of placing of crypto assets for the purposes of this Regulation. However, natural or legal persons allowed to distribute electronic money under Directive 2009/110/EC should also be able to distribute e-money tokens on behalf of issuers of e-money tokens without being required to obtain prior authorisation under this Regulation to provide crypto-asset services. Such distributors should, therefore, be exempt from the requirement to seek authorisation as a crypto-asset service provider for the activity of the placing of crypto-assets".

[60] Art. 3°.1.26 MiCA Regulation. The Commission's proposal did not include this service among the regulated crypto-asset services, and it was therefore added later. It should also be noted that the transfer requires the intervention of a third party that provides the service so that crypto-asset transfers that do not involve such third party (issuer or CASPs) are excluded from MiCA Regulation. In similar terms, the Travel Rule Regulation defines "transfer of crypto-assets" as "any transaction with the aim of moving crypto-assets from one distributed ledger address, crypto-asset account or other device allowing the storage of crypto-assets to another, carried out by at least one crypto-asset service provider acting on behalf of either an originator or a beneficiary, irrespective of whether the originator and the beneficiary are the same person and irrespective of whether the crypto-asset service provider of the originator and that of the beneficiary are one and the same" (Art. 3°.10).

[61] Recital 93 MiCA Regulation: "A provider of transfer services for crypto-assets should be an entity that provides for the transfer, on behalf of a client, of crypto-assets from one distributed ledger address or account to another. Such transfer service should not include the validators, nodes or miners that might be part of confirming a transaction and updating the state of the underlying distributed ledger. Many crypto-asset service providers also offer some transfer service for crypto-assets as part of, for example, the service of providing custody and administration of crypto-assets on behalf of clients, exchange of crypto-assets for funds or other crypto-assets, or execution of orders for crypto assets on behalf of clients. Depending on the precise features of the services associated to the transfer of e-money tokens, such services could fall under the definition of payment services in Directive (EU) 2015/2366. In such cases, those transfers should be provided by an entity authorised to provide such payment services in accordance with that Directive". The

establishes that if the crypto-asset transfer service provider is the EMT issuer, it does not have to apply for authorisation as a CASP since it is already authorised as an EMI.[62] For the remaining entities (i.e., those offering EMT transfer services but not EMIs), authorisation as a CASP would not be sufficient. Still, they must also apply for authorisation as a PI (payment institution offering electronic money services, in terms of PSD3). Concerning this crypto-asset service, the first paragraph of Article 82 of the MiCA Regulation establishes that the provider must agree with the customer, which must contain at least the following: the identity of the parties to the agreement; a description of the modalities of the transfer service provided; a description of the security systems used by the crypto-asset service provider; the fees applied by the crypto-asset service provider; and the applicable law. The second paragraph of the provision entrusts ESMA, in cooperation with EBA, to develop guidelines on procedures and policies, including customer rights, for this service.

As can be seen, no reference is made here to the transparency and information rules and the mandatory regime contained in PSD2. However, as mentioned above, EMT transfers must be qualified as payment transactions and their execution as payment services (electronic money services, according to PSR Proposal), which, in the absence of an express exclusion by the MiCA Regulation, determines the application of the PSD2 provisions on transparency, information, rights and obligations. It is noteworthy that the agreement referred to in Article 82 of the MiCA Regulation could be qualified as a "framework contract" under the terms of the PSD2 (a payment service contract which governs the future execution of individual and successive payment transactions, and which may contain the obligation and conditions for setting up a payment account). Regardless of the consequences of the statement made (and the subsequent questions, such as the application of the SCA to transfers of EMTs), the application of PSD2 to EMTs places the crypto-asset transfer service provider in a situation that may cause some confusion because if the transferred token is an EMT, it must be subject to the payment services regime. In contrast, if another type of asset is transferred (e.g. an ART), it will only have to apply the provisions of Article 82 MiCA Regulation. At this point, it is necessary to consider whether this solution is the desired one and, if so, whether it makes sense.

Considering the above, while being aware of the difficulties that exist, it is necessary to provide the token (EMT or ART) when it is used as a means of payment, with a special regime to assimilate it to the other means of payment (scriptural money and "traditional" e-money, etc.). Firstly, the holders of these tokens should enjoy the same protection as other payment service users (remember that PSD2 is a standard that focuses on protecting payment service users). Secondly, by applying the "same activity, same rules" principle. It is another matter that the European legislator, neither in the MiCA Regulation nor, for the time being, in the

---

wording of the recital ("depending on the precise features of the services associated to the transfer of e-money tokens") seems to suggest that the transfer of EMTs does not always qualify as a payment service. However, it does not specify what these services consist of.

[62] See Art. 60.4 MiCA Regulation in footnote 59.

PSD2 revision process, has taken up the challenge of providing a coherent legal regime for the provision of payment services by EMTs and ARTs.

5 Conclusions

As a result of the considerations presented thus far, we can draw the following conclusions:

1. EMTs are a new form of representation of e-money using DLT and cryptography. The combination of both features makes them crypto assets. Unlike other crypto assets that have a financial use and are already regulated (e.g. those considered financial instruments), the MiCA Regulation does not exclude tokenised e-money (EMT) from its scope of application. Still, it subjects it to a separate legal regime, although it declares applicable certain provisions of the EMD2 (in particular those relating to the issuers of these EMTs).
2. The qualification of EMTs as e-money determines that they fall within the definition of "funds" in PSD2, with the consequence that certain transactions carried out with EMTs may be considered as payment services (payment services and electronic money services in the PSR Proposal and PSD3 Proposal).
3. Neither PSD2 nor the future PSR and PSD3 would apply to transactions involving ARTs or other crypto-assets that perform payment functions (they are not configured as e-money, and there is currently no rule extending the scope of the above rules to these crypto assets). Transactions involving the movement or transfer of crypto assets other than EMTs, carried out by a CASP, shall be considered as "transfers of crypto assets" within the meaning of Article 82 of the MiCA Regulation and, therefore, subject to its provisions thereof.
4. In the new payment services framework (PSR Proposal and PSD3 Proposal), following the disappearance of EMIs, issuers of EMTs must be credit institutions or payment institutions providing electronic money services. In the same framework, creating the "electronic money services" category means that the issuance of EMTs should be considered an electronic money service.
5. The MiCA Regulation solves the "institutional" problems of payment services involving EMTs but leaves the substantive issues unresolved. It is necessary to adapt the regime for the provision of payment services to the specificities of EMTs, to identify the PSP providing the payment service (issuer or CASP), to whom the transparency obligations and the regime of rights and obligations will apply, and to define, in the context of the EMT, the equivalent of the "payment account storing electronic money units" and the "payment instrument".

References

Ciraolo F (2022) Paymen tokens y legislación europea sobre los servicios de pago. In: Pastor Sempere MC (dir) Dinero digital y gobernanza TIC en la UE. Aranzadi, Pamplona, pp 91–113

European Banking Authority (2022) Opinion of the European Banking Authority on its technical advice on the review of Directive (EU) 2015/2366 on payment services in the internal market (PSD2). EBA/Op/2022/06. https://www.eba.europa.eu/sites/default/files/document_library/Publications/Opinions/2022/Opinion%20od%20PSD2%20review%20%28EBA-Op-2022-06%29/1036016/EBA%27s%20response%20to%20the%20Call%20for%20advice%20on%20the%20review%20of%20PSD2.pdf

European Commission (2023) Commission Staff Working Document Impact Assessment Report Accompanying the documents Proposal for a Regulation on payment services in the internal market and amending Regulation (EU) No 1093/2010 and Proposal for a Directive on payment services and electronic money services in the Internal Market amending Directive 98/26/EC and repealing Directives 2015/2366/EU and 2009/110/EC. Brussels, SWD(2023) 231 final. https://eur-lex.europa.eu/legal-content/EN/TXT/?uri=SWD:2023:231:FIN. Accessed 10 Oct 2023

European Commission, Directorate-General for Financial Stability, Financial Services and Capital Markets Union (FISMA), Bosch Chen I, Fina D, Hausemer P et al (eds) (2023) A study on the application and impact of Directive (EU) 2015/2366 on Payment Services (PSD2). Publications Office of the European Union. https://data.europa.eu/doi/10.2874/996945

Haut Comité Juridique de la Place Financière de Paris (2023). Report on the revisión on the Payment Services Directiva 2 (PSD2). https://www.hcjp.fr/banques-et-etablissement-de-credit. Accessed 12 Sept 2023

Lanskoy S (2000) The legal nature of electronic money. Revista de Análisis del BCB. Banco Central de Bolivia 3(2):2. https://www.bcb.gob.bo/webdocs/publicacionesbcb/revista_analisis/ra_vol0302/articulo_6_v3_2.pdf

Madrid Parra A (2020) Criptoactivos: De nuevo el viejo dinero electrónico. In: Madrid Parra A, Alvarado Herrera L (dirs) Derecho Digital y Nuevas Tecnologías. Aranzadi, Pamplona, pp 801–856

Martínez Nadal A (2021) Ámbito de aplicación y conceptos esenciales de la propuesta de Reglamento relativo a los mercados de criptoactivos: la noción de criptoactivo y sus subcategorías (arts. 2 y 3). In: Madrid Parra A, Pastor Sempere MC (dirs) Guía de criptoactivos MICA. Aranzadi, Pamplona, pp 41–62

Palá Laguna R, Canalejas Merín JF (2023) A qué criptoactivos no se aplicará el Reglamento MiCA. Gómez-Acebo & Pombo. https://www.ga-p.com/publicaciones/a-que-criptoactivos-no-se-aplicara-el-reglamento-mica/. Accessed 30 Sept 2023

Pastor Sempere MC (2022) El nuevo marco legal para los tokens de pago, las criptotransferencias y los servicios de criptopago al por menor. In: Pastor Sempere MC (dir) Dinero digital y gobernanza TIC en la UE. Aranzadi, Pamplona, pp 19–56

Peñas Moyano MJ (2020) Régimen jurídico de los servicios de pago en el Derecho español. Aranzadi, Pamplona

Zunzunegui Pastor F (2022) ¿Cómo regular las plataformas financieras digitales?. Revista de Derecho del Mercado Financiero. WP 1/2022. Available at SSRN: https://ssrn.com/abstract=4040930 or https://doi.org/10.2139/ssrn.4040930

The Non-Financial Crypto-Asset Market: Copyright in Art Non-Fungible Tokens

Fernando Carbajo Cascón

Abstract The market for the sale of art-NFTs is a reality, but due to their diffuse legal nature, there are many doubts about this business model from a legal perspective. This raises uncertainties as to whether it is possible to recognise a property right over the NFT as a digital asset and an online distribution rights model, where the principle of exhaustion is recognised from the intellectual property law perspective.

1 Non-Fungible Tokens: Concept and Regulation

The most specialised doctrine simplifies and condenses the definition of 'non-fungible tokens' (hereinafter NFTs). They can be conceived as crypto assets with a unique digital representation of a certain right or value created and stored using blockchain technology. NFTs are implemented through smart contracts or self-executing, which can be transferred and thus traded autonomously in decentralised

This paper expands and updates the text of a lecture delivered at the III International Congress entitled "Present and future of crypto-assets regulation in the European Union," held at the University of Alicante (Spain) on December 13, 14, and 15, 2023. This work is funded within the framework of: Proyecto CIPROM/2022/26 "Presente y futuro de la regulación de los Criptoactivos en la UE [Legalcripto]". Proyecto Prometeo CIPROM/2022/26, grupos de investigación de excelencia, de la Generalitat Valenciana (P.I. Carmen Pastor).
This work is the result of the research project entitled 'Marco regulador de las plataformas en línea en la economía digital: competencia y responsabilidad en el uso de datos y contenidos (PID2020-119002RB-I00), funded by the Ministry of Science and Innovation within the framework of the state programmes for the generation of knowledge and scientific and technological strengthening of the R&D&I system and R&D&I oriented towards the challenges of society, for the period from 1 September 2021 to 31 August 2024, of which the author is Principal Investigator.

F. Carbajo Cascón (✉)
University of Salamanca, Salamanca, Spain

Multidisciplinary Business Institute of the University of Salamanca (Spain), Salamanca, Spain
e-mail: nano@usal.es

C. Pastor Sempere (ed.), *Governance and Control of Data and Digital Economy in the European Single Market*, Law, Governance and Technology Series 71,
https://doi.org/10.1007/978-3-031-74889-9_17

digital spaces, metaverses, or other disruptive virtual worlds according to the rules pre-established in the smart contract.

In strictly technical terms, an NFT is nothing more than a set of metadata about a digital file containing a non-fungible underlying element as a unit of information that serves as a digital certificate of authenticity and ownership of the file itself and of the underlying element it contains, regardless of its nature, guaranteeing its authenticity and preventing its reproduction, which makes each NFT unique and susceptible to individualised transmission through smart contracts.[1] This makes NFTs an ideal means of generating scarcity in the digital space, singularising the underlying asset in contrast to the abundance of online access, unlimited reproduction and dissemination in the digital market. This highly disruptive and unique circumstance justifies the emergence and development of new, hitherto unknown business models based not on making content available for access and enjoyment online but on recreating a simple sales transaction for a digital asset.[2]

NFTs are created using the 'blockchain' technique, which—as we have already mentioned—guarantees the authenticity of the 'token' and the underlying asset embodied or incorporated in it. This makes the token real and irreproducible, appearing in the creator's crypto wallet. It also allows the token to be tracked or traced in the event of transmission to a third party and registers the NFT's successive holders (or owners).[3]

Once the NFT is created, it can be stored in a computer connected to the network or in decentralised network databases; in either case, the authenticity of the token as a carrier or container and of the asset's underlying element is guaranteed, even though it may be reproduced in a unique or serial form in a single and exclusive NFT or a series of NFTs (NFTs-Replicas).[4]

It is also possible to mint fractional NFTs (F-NFTs), which divide the same original underlying element among several owners who share a percentage of the same tokenised asset, thus facilitating trading those rights to the token in secondary markets.[5]

Regulation (EU) 2023/1114 of the European Parliament and of the Council of 31 May 2023 on Markets in Crypto-assets (MiCA) states in Recital 10: 'This Regulation should not apply to crypto-assets that are unique and non-fungible with other crypto-assets, including digital art and collections. The value of such unique and non-fungible crypto-assets is attributable to the unique characteristics of each crypto-asset and the utility it confers on the token holder (. . .) Although unique and non-fungible crypto-assets could be traded on markets and accumulated for speculative purposes, they are not readily exchangeable, and the relative value of one such

[1] García Vidal (2022), pp. 4–6. Jiménez Serranía (2023), pp. 80–81. Llorente San Segundo (2023), pp. 955–957.

[2] Fairfield (2022), pp. 1268–1269.

[3] García Vidal (2022), pp. 4–5. Jiménez Serranía (2023), pp. 82–84.

[4] García Vidal (2022), pp. 7–8.

[5] Llorente San Segundo (2023), pp. 961–962.

crypto-asset to another, each of which is unique, cannot be determined by comparison with an existing market or equivalent asset. Such characteristics limit the extent to which such crypto assets can be put to financial use, thereby limiting the risks to shareholders and the financial system and justifying their exclusion from the scope of this Regulation'.

MiCA states in Recital 11 that: 'The fractional parts of a single, non-fungible cryptoasset should not be considered unique and non-fungible. The issuance of cryptoassets as non-fungible tokens in a large series or collection should be viewed as an indicator of their fungibility. The mere attribution of a unique identifier to a crypto asset is not sufficient, in and of itself, to classify it as unique and non-fungible. For a crypto asset to be considered unique and non-fungible, its assets or rights must also be unique and non-fungible'.

These are the only two indications that MiCA contains on non-fungible tokens, including—it states—tokens representing underlying digital art. It does so to point out that the legal regime established in the Regulation does not apply to them as they do not have 'a priori' a financial use. However, it does not exclude the existence of a 'non-financial' market for this type of digital asset on the digital market, i.e. a market for the sale or transfer of the NFTs representing a non-financial asset (for example, tokenised digital representations of analogue or digital works of art).

However, it qualifies and suggests—with notable obscurity—that the same underlying element (e.g. a digital representation of an analogue artwork or a work of crypto-art) embodied in a fractional NFT (F-NFT) determines that these fractions of the same NFT will not be considered unique and non-fungible. In other words, F-NFTs will be regarded as fungible and may be traded and marketed separately. For a crypto asset (as a digital object or carrier) to be considered unique and non-fungible, the non-financial asset must also be unique and non-fungible. However, suppose the tokenised underlying asset is broken up or split into several parts, or a series of non-fungible tokens with the same underlying content is issued. In that case, we will be dealing with fungible tokens.

In short, outside these unique scenarios where fractional NFTs of the same asset can be considered fungible assets and be subject to quasi-financial markets, non-fungible tokens remain outside the regulation of crypto-asset markets and, therefore, unregulated. Consequently, it will be necessary to redirect this new asset class and all the problems posed by the emerging market generated around it (especially when they represent assets that are works or performances protected by copyright and related rights) to the familiar institutions of law, in particular intellectual property (IP) law.

2 Art-NFTs

So-called 'Art-NFTs' are digital assets containing a digital representation of a physical or digital work of fine art. In other words, they are an intangible digital medium ('*corpus mechanicum*') containing a digital representation of an analogue or digital art-work in origin ('*corpus mysticum*'). Thus, it constitutes the 'summum' of immateriality, as the content (immaterial good) and the container are intangible and can be stored in decentralised databases, making navigating the network even easier.

These 'Art-NFTs' represent an open door for the art market in the digital environment, as they offer a business model like that of the direct sale or public auction of classic supports of works of plastic art—such as paintings or lithographs—which has not been possible in the digital market until now. A sale of digital assets (NFTs) containing digital copies of analogue (tokenised or minted works of art) or digital (tokenised or minted crypto art) works of art, which has nothing to do with the 'classic' online exploitation model of other content (such as music, audiovisual or publishing products) based on acts of making available by downloading or mere access ('streaming'), 'one act' or on a subscription basis.

This new business model consisting of the minting and sale of 'Art-NFTs' or NFTs with an underlying element of artistic nature can be done in the metaverse, directly on traditional websites or through digital platforms that offer this intermediation service, whether generalist (such as OpenSea, Rarible, Foundation, Olyverse or Telefónica) or specifically focused on tokenised art collections that offer minting and trading services (such as Cryptopunks, CryptoCats or Sotheby's Metaverse).[6]

New business models aim to facilitate the direct or (digital) auction buying and selling of NFTs with underlying art (of analogue, public domain or copyrighted artwork, or crypto-art) for speculation, collecting, virtual museum creation or social purposes (e.g. serial tokenisation of a crypto-art-work to dedicate all or part of the proceeds to social causes). Also, the creation of digital clubs for which membership requires possessing an NFT of a given analogue or digital artwork or even participating in digital games.

One business sub-model consists of tokenising an analogue work of art into a single digital 'copy' or a series of non-fungible tokens (like digital lithographs), destroying the original (which may infringe the moral right to respect the integrity of the work) to increase the value of the digital 'copies' on the market among collectors. Or to perform the same action based on an original copy, without destroying it, owned by a museum or a private individual who decides to capitalise on the ownership of the medium (the canvas or painting) to allow access to high-quality digital 'copies' to collectors who could never acquire the unique or rare copy of that work.

3 Art-NFTs and Property Rights

What is a non-fungible token in legal terms? Is it an asset comparable to a 'digital object' that can be appropriated? Or is it an online service that makes a digital file representing a digital copy of a work of art available to the public? Or can it be

[6] García Vidal (2022), pp. 5–6. Jiménez Serranía (2023), pp. 87–90.

considered a link to a digital file—centralised or decentralised—made available to the public from a computer connected to the network or from a decentralised database?

Suppose it is considered a digital asset comparable to a digital object or medium. Can it recognise an ordinary property right in it, like a physical copy—single or part of a series—of a work protected by copyright or performance protected by related or neighbouring rights?

In the emerging Art-NFTs market, unique or rare NFTs that reproduce a digital copy of an analogue work of art or crypto-art, NFTs-Replicas of the same analogue work or crypto-art issued in a series or collection, or fractions of the same art NFT are being marketed.

So far, the state of the art has not allowed the direct marketing of unique and irreproducible digital files or archives with copies of works in the online marketplace. The business model has consisted from the origins of the Internet to date of interactive (on-demand) acts of communication to the public, allowing access to an online site by wired or wireless means from wherever and whenever desired (cf. Article 3 Directive 2011/29/EC of 22 May 2011 on copyright and related rights in the information society; DSI), followed, where appropriate, by acts of reproduction (durable by download or temporary streaming access) authorised by the rightsholder or his assignee through end-user licence agreements.

However, this is not the way to operate in the case of NFTs, which are not marketed through acts of making them available to the public but through the direct sale of the token with a single digital copy (or part of a series) of the work or related service that it incorporates similar to the classic distribution of copies or tangible media in the physical market, whether they are unique or rare or copies of a series. Moreover, as we have been saying, the same Art-NFT can be split to offer fractions of the same token and the asset it represents for sale. NFTs enable a previously non-existent business model for visual artists or holders of rights in visual works.

The question is whether this business model of 'online distribution' of digital assets with underlying works can be legally accepted without a change in legislation. For this, it is essential to focus on the nature of the NFT as a digital asset and the nature of the legal relationship that one has or can have over it.

To date, experience suggests a logic like ownership over movable tangible objects, but in this case, over a digital asset. It happens, however, that the transmission of NFTs is not based on classical private law rules on obligations and contracts but on the so-called 'lex chryptographica', i.e. the rules of the code that create the token and predisposes the conditions of its use and transmission, using the smart contract.[7]

However, leaving the functioning of the exchange of digital assets and, therefore, of the market that may arise around them exclusively to the will of the creator of the NFT expressed in a code ('Code is Law') could jeopardise legal certainty and the

[7] García Vidal (2022), pp. 8–9. Llorente San Segundo (2023), pp. 962–963. Nassare Aznar (2020), pp. 61–63.

very stability of the market. It is, therefore, appropriate to develop new rules of private law or reinterpret existing ones that shape the legal nature of the NFT and the contract of transfer of the same, providing security to successive acquirers and, therefore, to the market.

So far, there is no regulation on NFTs or digital assets. Still, there are notable examples of 'soft law' dealing with the matter, such as the UNIDROIT Principles on Digital Assets and Private Law of 2023, the Principles of the European Law Institute on the Use of Digital Assets as Security of 2022 (ELI), or the rules proposed by the Final Report of the UK Law Commission Digital Assets in 2023.

The logic of ownership over a digital object is taken up, not without nuances, in the UNIDROIT Principles on Digital Assets and Private Law of October 2023,[8] which define a digital asset as an electronic reproduction susceptible to being subject to control;[9] and the transfer of digital assets as a change in the right of ownership over a digital asset from one subject to another with the consequent acquisition of the right of ownership over the digital asset.[10] In other words, according to the UNIDROIT principles, control over the digital asset is equivalent to a right of ownership, and the transfer or assignment of the asset includes—they say—the granting of a security interest in favour of the creditor or transferee (acquirer).

Thus, a person has control over a digital asset if that control confers on that person the exclusive ability to derive benefits from the digital asset, prevent others from deriving benefits and profits from the digital asset, and transfer control over the digital asset to third parties.[11] Various means may be used to identify the person having control over the digital asset and demonstrate that the person has control over the digital asset.[12] The transferor of the digital asset may transfer control, equivalent to the transfer of ownership of the digital asset.[13] The process of acquiring control will typically involve a third party that effectively controls the digital asset in a decentralised network and provides a custodial service for the digital asset to its owner or successive owners.[14]

Given that the creation of the token and its transfer take place via smart contracts, it is assumed that the contract will normally contain an authorisation from the person initially tokenising or minting the underlying element embedded in the digital asset to allow the transfer or assignment of the digital asset (and the underlying element). This pre-authorisation would facilitate the free transfer of the digital asset and its underlying element (e.g., the irreproducible copy of a digitised analogue or digital art-work at source). The contract may also include authorisations for the private use or exploitation of the underlying element embodied in the digital asset, such as

[8] UNIDROIT (2023) Principles Digital Assets and Private Law. Principle 2(2).

[9] Principle 2(2).

[10] Principle 2(5) (a) y (b).

[11] Principle 6.

[12] Principle 7.

[13] Principle 9.

[14] Principle 10.

making it available to the public from an online site, equivalent to authorising a public exhibition of the work of fine art embodied in a physical object or specimen (painting, sculpture, design, etc.).

But what would happen if the person responsible for the tokenisation or minting of the underlying artistic element prohibits in advance in the smart contract the transfer of the digital asset to which it is incorporated or makes each transfer of the asset subject to his express authorisation? Would this not change the logic of the ownership of the digital asset as well as the dynamics of the business model based on the sale or transfer of ownership to be replaced by a licensing model for the use of the digital asset and its underlying element and how would this licensing or authorisation model influence the dynamics of the Art-NFTs market itself?

The dominant logic recently is the business model based on selling NFTs on the 'normal' Web and in metaverse or virtual worlds. What is the value of acquiring an NFT that incorporates an artistic underlying element (Art-NFT) if it is impossible to transfer it to third parties? Should this business model prioritise ownership and control of the digital asset over the will expressed in a smart contract created by the tokenisation or minting manager? Or, on the contrary, is it necessary to respect the autonomy of will over and above the logic of the sale of digital objects in the market? To put it more directly, if the tokenisers or minters limit the number of transfers of the NFT or make its transfer or sale conditional on prior authorisation, should the autonomy of will expressed in the smart contract by the predisposer be prioritised and respected, or should market dynamics based on ownership be imposed that prioritises the interests and expectations of the purchasers of the NFT over the will of the tokenisers?

The issue of NFT proprietary rights is recognised in the UNIDROIT Principles on Digital Assets and Private Law of October 2023. Moreover, some courts are beginning to validate it.[15] Although the UNIDROIT Principles are no more than mere recommendations, the business model created around the NFTs requires that the logic of ownership/control over the token, which justifies its free transfer, be imposed on contractual dynamics based on the autonomy of the token creator's will. As a result, they would be free to manage the asset without needing the tokeniser's permission.

In short, NFTs can be qualified as encrypted digital assets representing property rights instead of fungible tokens representing securities. Digital assets that contain other underlying assets that provide an advantage or utility, in the form of non-fungible incorporeal objects or real estate, capable of appropriation and transfer in the form of sale or other transfer of ownership (cf. Articles 333, 335 and 337 of the Spanish Civil Code). However, suppose an Art-NFT is split (Art-F-NFT). In that case, each part is fungible, representing a part of the underlying asset embodied in the token, and can be assimilated to a transferable security that can be traded on secondary securities markets.[16]

---

[15] Jiménez Serranía (2023), pp. 93–94.

[16] Llorente San Segundo (2023), pp. 973–975.

Art-NFTs are thus irreproducible single digital carriers (or part of a series) of a work of visual art (or other works of art, such as musical or audiovisual works) that may be sold or the ownership of which may be transferred. This is, of course, perfectly distinct from the intellectual property over the tokenised underlying artistic object. Thus, Art-NFTs will be freely transferable by their successive owners, but this does not imply any transfer of intellectual property over the asset incorporated in it: the use or exploitation of the underlying art will be subject to the relevant authorisation of the legitimate owner(s) of the copyright over it, who may or may not be the same person(s) responsible for the minting or tokenisation.

In short, the logic of the market generated around Art-NFTs would be like that of the sale of works of art. Thus, by analogy with what is envisaged for the physical media of copyrighted art-works, the acquisition of the digital copy ('corpus mechanicum') would not imply the acquisition of intellectual property rights over the work that constitutes the underlying embodied work ('corpus mysticum').[17] In other words, the situation would be comparable to the distinction between the ordinary ownership of the physical copy (single or part of a series) and the intellectual property (copyright) over the work incorporated therein, both rights being distinct, autonomous but compatible (cf. Articles 3 and 56 of the Spanish Intellectual Property Law; LPI).

Therefore, the owner of the Art-NFT as a digital medium would not have any intellectual property right over the work incorporated therein, except for the right of public exhibition if the copyright holder had not reserved it when making or authorising the tokenisation or selling the token with the copy of the work. With the particularity, however, that this right of the public exhibition would have to be carried out physically, i.e. using a screen installed in a physical place of public access, since there is no possible comparison or analogical or extensive interpretation of a purely analogical form of communication to the public, such as the act of public exhibition of works of art or their reproductions (cfr. Article 20.2 h. LPI), with an act of making available online interactively in a digital space (cfr. Article 20.2. i LPI), as this is a different modality of communication to the public subject to the exclusive right, unless '*de lege ferenda*' some legal limit is expressly foreseen, which, in any case, must be perfectly defined in the Law.

Thus, if the acquirer of the NFT with a digital copy of a plastic work wanted to make it available to the public as a digital 'exhibition', they would have to obtain the appropriate authorisation from the author or owner of the rights over the tokenised work to make the Art-NFT available to the public on an online site.

These first considerations on the distinction between ordinary property over container and intellectual property over content, between medium ('corpus mechanicum') and work ('corpus mysticum'), applied to Art-NFTs require more precise explanations on the act of tokenisation or minting of works of art, their sale or transfer and the possibilities of exploitation of the same by successive acquirers.

---

[17] García Vidal (2022), pp. 7–8.

4 Art-NFTs and Intellectual Property

In the process of minting or minting an original work of art (single or part of a series) on an NFT, different situations may arise that require separate examination to appreciate and resolve the emerging issues in each case.

4.1 Art-NFTs of Pre-Existing Works Minted by a Third-Party Owner of the Single Copy or a Serialised Copy Without Authorisation of the Rights-Holder

The author or copyright holder of a work of art may tokenise or mint it to freely dispose of the resulting NFT by selling it or making it available for free or restricted access on an online site.

But if the single or rare copy of the work of art—or the copies that make up a series of the same work of art—has been sold to third parties, can those third parties tokenise or minify that single or serial copy and dispose of it by selling or transferring it to third parties without the authorisation of the copyright owner?

It might be thought, perhaps, that tokenisation or minting carried out by the legitimate owner of the medium containing a work of art should be free by application of the principle or rule of exhaustion of the distribution right with the first sale (cfr. article 4, letter a. Directive 2011/29 and article 19.2 LPI). But this is not the case; tokenisation is not an act of distribution of copies with originals or copies of works protected by copyright, but rather an act of reproduction subject in any case to the authorisation of the holder or holders of the copyright (cfr. article 2 Directive 2001/29 and article 18 LPI).

The doctrine established in the CJEU of 22 January 2015 (Case C-410/13 'Art & All Posters'), according to which the replacement of the medium of a work results in the creation of a new object incorporating the image of the protected work, applies to the case, bearing in mind the distances inherent in the technical process used. This procedure is closer to a new reproduction of that work within the meaning of Article 2(a) of Directive 2001/29/EC on certain aspects of copyright and related rights in the information society (paragraph 43), and therefore subject to the authorisation of the author or rightsholder (cf. Article 18 LPI). What is relevant, then, is whether the object in which a work was marketed with the right holder's consent is materially maintained, modified or replaced (paragraph 45). Consequently, the rightsholder's consent does not relate to the distribution of an object incorporating his work if that object has been modified after its first marketing in such a way that it constitutes a new reproduction of the work. The distribution right is exhausted only after the first sale or transfer of the object with the rightsholder's consent (paragraph 46).

The CJEU concludes that 'Article 4(2) of Directive 2001/29/EC of the European Parliament and of the Council of 22 May 2001 on the harmonisation of certain aspects of copyright and related rights in the information society must be interpreted as meaning that the rule of exhaustion of the distribution right does not apply to a situation in which a reproduction of a protected work, after having been placed on the market in the European Union with the consent of the copyright holder, has been the subject of a replacement of its medium, such as, for example, a transfer onto a canvas of such a reproduction, which appeared on a canvas on which the reproduction was placed on a canvas after having been marketed in the European Union with the consent of the copyright owner, has had its medium replaced, such as, for example, the transfer to canvas of such a reproduction, which appeared on a paper poster, and is now being remarketed in that new form'.[18]

Nor can it be qualified as a transformation if the underlying element is limited to reproducing the pre-existing work in the NFT since this is equivalent to digitisation and, therefore, to a simple change of medium that does not affect the concrete expression of the work. It is a different matter if a prior modification of the form of the work is carried out or if it is combined with other works or elements before undermining, in which case it is an act of transformation that will require the authorisation of the author or rightsholders on the part of the person who carries it out.

Ruling No. 776/2022 of the 9th Commercial Court of Barcelona, dated 11 January 2024, addresses this problem of the incorporation of pre-existing works of art into NFT format by the owner of the original copies without the authorisation of the rights holders. On the opening of a Mango shop on Fifth Avenue in New York, the company that owned the shop hired several crypto artists to create a series of digital pieces in NFT format combining well-known paintings by the artists Miró, Barceló and Tàpies, which the company owns, with some elements from the world of fashion. The paintings in question were exhibited inside the establishment on an easel next to screens showing the digitally modelled versions of these same paintings in NFT format, completing this physical/digital experience with an accompaniment from the virtual world thanks to the exhibition of MANGO's new collection of NFTs within the Museum District of the Decentreland metaverse and on the 'Open Sea' platform.[19]

MANGO was sued by the collecting society VEGAP, the rights holders' representative, seeking damages of €875,000 for non-pecuniary and pecuniary loss. The judgment handed down by Commercial Court No. 9 of Barcelona, rejecting the claim with arguments that are not very rigorous from a technical-legal point of view: it rejects the infringement of moral rights on the grounds that this is exhausted with the first disclosure of the works, which took place in the 1970s; that the digital files in NFT format have never been created in 'blockchain' format ('lazy minted NFTs') and can therefore only be viewed in the metaverse through the 'Open Sea' platform, but cannot be downloaded, reproduced or acquired, so that they have not been the object of commercialisation, but only of public exhibition or viewing by the public

[18] Rubí Puig (2015).

[19] Available https://fashionunited.es/noticias/moda/mango-crece-en-el-metaverso-llevando-a-miro-tapies-y-barcelo-a-formato-nft/2022051038579. Accessed 2 June 2024. Guadamuz (2024).

who went to the MANGO shop and on a platform in the metaverse; that there is no infringement of copyright by the transformation of the works by incorporating new elements in the NFT by crypto-artists; that the owner of the canvases has the right to their public exhibition by virtue of the provisions of article 56. 2 LPI; and in any case that there is no infringement of copyright as it is a transformative use that does not jeopardise the normal exploitation of the works or the legitimate interests of their rightsholders, invoking the USA doctrine of 'fair use'.

The acts in question carried out by MANGO fall squarely within the category of unauthorised transformation of a protected work carried out by crypto-artists hired for that purpose by MANGO. There is also an unauthorised reproduction, although the act of transformation certainly subsumes the act of reproduction of those works in NFT format, as an alteration of the expression of those works is carried out. An act of communication to the public takes place in the form of a public exhibition, which Article 56.2 TRLPI could cover unless it can be proved that the authors excluded that possibility when they sold their canvases. Likewise, the right of communication to the public is infringed in making it available when access to the NFTs that include the modified versions of the protected works is allowed on metaverse platforms exclusively for their visualisation. It is also true that there is an infringement of the moral right to the integrity of the work (article 14,4 LPI), which in no case can be exhausted once the disclosure of the work has been authorised, as the judgement states, since it is an unrenounceable and inalienable right, as stated in article 14 LPI.

The fact that NFTs with the works mentioned above of art have not been marketed does not imply that there is no copyright infringement since profit or commercial end does not determine the existence or not of the infringement but, if applicable, the scope of the compensation. As for the application of the 'Fair Use' doctrine, its direct application in Spain's legal system is inadmissible (Sect. 107 U.-S. Copyright Act), without prejudice to the application of the doctrine known as 'Flexible Copyright' (which is referred to in Spain's Supreme Court judgement, STS of 3 April 2012, in the case of Megakini v. Google). This doctrine is based on the abuse of rights in Article 7 of the Spanish Civil Code and specifically on the principle or Roman right rule of '*ius usus inocui*'.[20] However, it seems difficult for this doctrine—of exceptional application—to apply to the case when it is a question of the principal use of works of art by renowned visual artists for the advertising purposes of a fashion company.

In any case, the act of minting a work in an NFT (whether it is minted with a 'blockchain' system for its subsequent commercialisation) constitutes an act of exploitation '*lato sensu*' that would be subject to the exclusive right of the author or rightsholder provided in general, and as a closing rule to ensure broad protection for rightsholders, in article 17 of the LPI.

If the original, unique, or rare copy of the minting work of art were to be destroyed as a result of the creation of the CLT with the artistic underlay, we would be faced with a clear case of infringement of the moral right to respect the

[20] Carbajo Cascón (2012), pp. 543–547.

integrity of the work (Article 14.4 of the LPI) and a more than possible violation of national rules on historical-artistic heritage.

4.2 Art-NFTs Minted by a Licensee of Intellectual Property Rights

Other possible cases of tokenisation of works of art are those carried out by assignees or licensees 'inter vivos' of copyright (article 43 LPI) or by assignees 'mortis causa' (article 42 LPI).

In the case of 'inter vivos' transferees, the act of minting the work of art over which they have the authorisation to exploit in one or more forms will require a new express authorisation from the rightsholder since the forms of exploitation that did not exist at the time of the transfer are prohibited (cfr. Article 43.5 LPI).

As for the assignees 'mortis causa', be they the heirs or any natural or legal person other than the heirs designated by the last will of the author (cfr. Article 15 LPI), they may authorise the tokenisation or minting of the works of art of their deceased, provided that all of them agree. If one of the transferee heirs does not agree, the rest cannot take that decision (whether it is made for commercial purposes).

4.3 Art-NFTs of Pre-Existing Works Made Available to the Public

In the case where a visual work has been made available to the public by the author or a third-party assignee authorised by the author without incorporating restrictions on access to the online site, it could be a matter of debate whether free access to the work by users would imply an implicit authorisation to make use of it in any form, including for commercial purposes.

This is not the case. The making available to the public on a freely accessible online site and without conditions of use identifying authorised and unauthorised uses is to be conceived as an implicit licence by the author solely for reproduction for the private or personal use of each user who makes up the broad notion of the public. It is not an implied authorisation to engage in other acts of exploitation, including minting that work as NFT to make it available on another website or virtual worlds platform, whether for commercial or other purposes.

This follows from the doctrine laid down by the CJEU in the sentence above of 22 January 2015 (Case C-410/13 'Art & All Posters') for the case of undermining or minting of the work in an NFT, and from that established in the CJEU of 7 August 2018 (Case C-161/17, 'Renckhoff'), according to which 'The concept of communication to the public (. . .) includes placing a photograph previously published online on an internet site without restrictive measures preventing its downloading and with the authorisation of the copyright holder on another internet site. In other words, even if a digital copy of a work is made available to the public for free access and enjoyment, which may include downloading a copy of that work, each user would only be authorised to make a reproduction for personal use, but in no case to perform any act of exploitation or public reuse of the work, which logically includes the reproduction in a different format such as an NFT and the transfer or making available of it to the public.

4.4 Art-NFTs of New (Crypto-Art) or Pre-Existing Works Coined by the Author or Rights-Holders

The tokenisation of analogue works of art or crypto art not tokenised at source is logically part of the powers of the author or assignees 'mortis causa', who may carry out the minting of their works in an NFT or series of NFTs for their commercialisation in the digital market or centralised or decentralised virtual worlds, or for their online availability in the digital space or platforms or any other virtual world spaces.

However, if there are several authors (collaborative work, ex article 7 LPI) or assignees 'mortis causa', the consent of all the co-authors (article 7.2 LPI) or all the co-heirs will be required, and a judge will have to decide in the event of disagreement.

5 The Sale of Art-NFTs

The minting of NFTs usually takes place using blockchain technology, which, in addition to guaranteeing the authenticity and preventing the reproduction of the minted asset, also serves to pre-define the rules for its transfer, both digital objects as well as the conditions of use or exploitation of the underlying asset minted therein. Thus, whoever mints a digital copy of a work of art in an NFT will determine the conditions of its individualised transmission and, normally, the conditions for the use and, where appropriate, exploitation of the underlying artwork contained in the token using a licence of use and exploitation.[21] However, in many cases, smart contracts linked to NFTs do not contain any information regarding the copyright (or related rights) of the artistic assets minted herein, which will therefore depend on possible "ad hoc" external licences or on the general rules provided for in intellectual

[21] Jiménez Serranía (2023), pp. 95–97.

property legislation on the uses authorised to the owners of originals or copies of the work.[22]

The question immediately arises: Is the transfer of the NFT with the underlying asset subject to the free will of the generator of the non-fungible token, or should the transfer of the token and the asset it contains be considered free and unrestricted once the token is minted? In other words, in the case of digital copies of analogue or digital works of art minted on an NFT, is it possible for the smart contract to limit the number of transmissions of the Art-NFT or to set conditions that effectively limit future transmissions of the Art-NFT, or should it be understood, for the sake of legal certainty and free movement in the digital market, that once the token is traded, the power of rightsholder to control future transmissions of the token is exhausted?

Thanks to blockchain technology, by minting an Art-NFT, it would be possible to limit the number of future transmissions of the Art-NFT or subject them, beyond a certain number, to the authorisation of the party responsible for the minting, which could be the rightsholder of the underlying work or a third party licensee authorised by the latter (including a platform in charge of minting and trading NFTs, such as 'Open Sea'). This is because blockchain technology controls the traceability of transmissions, identifies the successive acquirers, and establishes conditions in the smart contract that ultimately restrict or limit the transmission. This affects the legal security of the market created around these NFTs.

Restrictions on the free transmission of non-fungible crypto-assets in the digital market (including markets developed in virtual worlds) would pose significant risks for the consolidation of business models based on the sale or transfer of Art-NFTs, with the consequent loss of incentives for potential buyers and, ultimately, for rightsholders.

At this point, the question arises whether the business model based on the transfer of Art-NFTs in digital markets is in line with the classical distribution of single copies or copies of the work in physical markets (considering the NFT as a digital object or 'copy') to which the exhaustion of the distribution right rule applies, or whether, on the contrary, since an NFT is not a physical copy of a work, the model of successive licences of use applies to tokenised works, each act of transmission or transfer is subject to a new authorisation by the rightsholder of the underlying artistic asset.

The CJEU of 3 July 2012 (Case C-128/11, 'Usedsoft') established that the supply of copies of 'software' using end-user licence contracts not subject to a time limit on use amounts to a transfer of ownership of those computer programs, i.e. an 'online' distribution of digital copies of computer programs. Thus, the first marketing of a copy of a computer program under an open-ended end-user licence agreement leads to the exhaustion of the distribution right, allowing the legitimate user authorised by the agreement to resell that copy freely.

Admittedly, that interpretation is based on the normative basis of Directive 2009/24, a codified version of Council Directive 91/250/EEC of 14 May 1991 on the legal

[22] García Vidal (2022), pp. 8–9. Jiménez Serranía (2023), pp. 97–98.

protection of computer programs; the CJEU makes no distinction according to the material or immaterial form of the copy in question (paragraph 55), Directive 2009/24 being "*lex specialis*" concerning Directive 2001/29 (paragraph 56). This is evidenced in its statement that 'In that regard, it must be held at once that it does not follow from Article 4(2) of Directive 2009/24 that the exhaustion of the right to distribute copies of computer programs, provided for in that provision, is limited to copies of computer programs on a storage medium, It does not follow from Article 4(2) of Directive 2009/24 that the exhaustion of the right to distribute copies of computer programs, provided for in that provision, is limited to copies of computer programs on a tangible medium, such as a CD-ROM or a DVD. On the contrary, it must be held that that provision, by referring without further specification to the 'sale [. . .] of a copy of a program.'

According to Article 1(2) of Directive 2009/24, the protection provided for therein applies to any form of expression of a computer program since that protection covers programs in any form, thus demonstrating the EU legislature's intention to treat material and immaterial copies of a computer program in the same way. In those circumstances, it must be held, according to the CJEU, that the exhaustion of the distribution right provided for in Article 4(2) of Directive 2009/24 relates to both tangible and intangible copies of a computer program and, therefore, also to copies which, at the time of their first sale, were downloaded from the internet onto the computer of the first purchaser (paragraphs 57 to 59). In that regard, the CJEU observes that, even if it were accepted that Directive 2001/29 of 22 May 2001 on copyright and related rights in the information society limits the exhaustion of the distribution right only to tangible objects, this would not affect the interpretation of Article 4(2) of Directive 2009/24, given the different intention expressed by the EU legislature in the precise context of the latter directive (paragraph 60). Thus, after pointing out that, from an economic point of view, the sale of a computer program in CD/CD-ROM format and the sale of the same program using downloads from the internet are similar, the interpretation of Article 4(2) of Directive 2009/24 in the light of the principle of equal treatment confirms that the exhaustion of the distribution right provided for in that provision takes effect after the first sale of a copy of a computer program with or without its consent, irrespective of whether it is a tangible or intangible copy (paragraph 61). The CJEU concludes that the marketing of copies of computer programs on the internet by authorising, even free of charge, the downloading of those copies onto a computer medium, using licence agreements of unlimited duration, is to be regarded as an act of distribution of intangible copies subject to the exhaustion rule, entitling the purchasers to resell them at a later date.

This doctrine, specific to computer programs, is ratified in the CJEU of 16 June 2021 (Case C-410/19, 'The software incubator') where the Court stated that 'The concept of "sale of goods" referred to in Article 1(2) of Council Directive 86/653/EEC of 18 December 1986 on the coordination of the laws of the Member States relating to self-employed commercial agents, must be interpreted as meaning that it may include the supply, against payment of a fee, of computer software to a customer in electronic form, where that supply is accompanied by a licence in perpetuity for the use of that software'.

However, the CJEU's doctrine on online exhaustion differs radically when it comes to marketing digital copies of works other than software, to which the general rules laid down in Directive 2001/29 apply. Thus, the CJEU of 19 December 2019 (Case C-263/18, 'Tom Kabinet') states that the EU legislature did not wish to establish equivalent treatment for tangible and intangible copies in that Directive (paragraph 56), concluding that 'The provision to the public by download of an electronic book for permanent use falls within the concept of "communication to the public" and, more specifically, of "making [the authors"] works available to the public in such a way that members of the public may access them from a place and at a time individually chosen by them'.

Consequently, in the online commercialisation of works and related services protected by intellectual property rights under a licence of use, whether in the form of downloading or streaming, we are not dealing with an act of distribution (not even when the licence of use is perpetual) but with acts of communication to the public in the form of making available which are considered to be services, with Article 3(2) of Directive 2001/29 being applicable, according to which no act of communication to the public or making available to the public may give rise to the exhaustion of intellectual property rights. Thus, each new act of communication or making it available to the public by a user is a service subject to the authorisation of the rightsholders. Consequently, beyond the interpretation made for computer programs (based on an almost 'pre-digital' regulation), there can be no digital exhaustion of content made available to the public utilising end-user licences, even if they are unlimited in time.

Applying this doctrine to Art-NFTs, one would have to conclude that it is not possible to qualify the transfer of NFTs with the underlying artistic asset as an act of distribution, even if it is done in exchange for a price, but as an act of communication to the public subject to the contractual regime of the user licence.

However, the different nature of Art-NFTs compared to common digital files that are communicated or made available online, as well as the also different business models of commercialisation of NFTs (based on the sale of the digital medium with the underlying asset), suggest that a different interpretation, closer to the one followed by the CJEU in the 'UsedSoft' case, would be possible.[23] There would be no normative basis for this, as Art-NFTs would be subject to the general rules of Directive 2001/29 and not the software-specific rules of Directive 2009/24. However, legal certainty might suggest a reinterpretation of the general regulations on distribution and communication to the public of Directive 2001/29 in line with the nature and business models of Art-NFTs, precisely along the lines of the provisions of Article 3.1 of the Spanish Civil Code. This would give a legal status to these new digital objects that is more aligned to the concept of ownership than to that of simple use, as well as to the business model based on their sale, along similar lines to those suggested by the UNIDROIT Principles on Digital Assets and Private Law.

[23] Jiménez Serranía, (2023), pp. 97–99.

Therefore, in order not to distort the business model of marketing Art-NFTs and to provide legal certainty to successive acquirers and the market in general, one could extensively apply Article 4 of Directive 2001/29 (cf. Article 19 LPI) to consider that an Art-NFT - or any NFT containing a digital copy of a copyrighted work - is a digital asset subject to the rules of property law. Moreover, its transfer in digital markets (including those in virtual worlds) amounts to an act of online distribution of the original (in the case of crypto-art) or of artwork digital copies in the form of a sale or any other means of transfer of ownership, with the distribution right being exhausted in the EU once the first sale has taken place, regardless of any limitations that the smart contract may contain.

In other words, the considerations made by the CJEU in the 'UsedSoft' judgment regarding the online marketing of computer programs using end-user licence contracts without a time limit would apply to the logic of the Art-NFTs market.

Consequently, if it is accepted that the acquirer of an Art-NFT acquires ownership of the digital medium and the digital copy of the underlying artistic object incorporated therein through the minting or tokenisation process, they may freely dispose of it regardless of the limitations or conditions, if any, imposed by the rightsholder or a third party authorised by the latter in the smart contract during the minting or tokenisation process. Another thing is that if the smart contract had provided for the payment of a percentage of the price of each sale or transfer to the person responsible for the minting, this must be respected, as it is consistent with the logic of the market unless this percentage is equivalent in practice to a control or limitation of the successive sales of the Art-NFT.

Consequently, the Art-NFT acquirer would own the digital medium or object but would not have any right to exploit the minted work, except for the right to public exhibition of the work on the digital medium. This is conditional on the author not having expressly excluded this right in the act of sale of the original and without prejudice to the author's right to oppose, in any case, the public exhibition through the exercise of injunctions to prevent the harm, honour or professional reputation (cfr. Article 56.2 LPI). However, the right of public display of the digital asset must be carried out under analogue conditions, i.e., by broadcasting on a screen installed in a physical location. There is no analogy between the right of the display and a 'virtual display' on an online site, which constitutes an act of making available to the public, subject to the authorisation of the author or rightsholder (which could be pre-authorised in the smart contract for successive acquirers or obtained 'ad hoc' on a case-by-case basis). The rightsholder of the work minted in the NFT may grant in the smart contract exploitation licences to authorise certain uses to the current owners of the NFT or grant such licences on an "ad hoc" basis at the request of the current owner of the token.

Finally, if the Art-NFT is sold, the author and his successors in title could claim the application of the resale right or 'droit de suite' provided for in the Directive 2001/84/EC of the European Parliament and of the Council of 27 September 2001 on the resale right for the benefit of the author of a work of art (incorporated into Spanish law in Article 24 LPI), when art market professionals participate in the sale as sellers, buyers or intermediaries (such as sales rooms, auction rooms, art galleries, art dealers), and also when they use information society services for the sale (sale on digital platforms).[24] This rule would logically not apply in cases where the author is responsible for the minting, and the payment of a percentage of the resale of the Art-NFT in the smart contract is guaranteed for then.

References

Carbajo Cascón F (2012-2013) Flexibilización del derecho de autor mediante límites externos a la normativa específica. El caso Megakini c. Google. Anotación a la STS de 3 de abril de 2012. Actas de Derecho Industrial, 33: 543-547.

Fairfield J (2022) Tokenized: the law of non fungible tokens and unique digital property. Indiana Law J 97(4):Article 4. Available https://www.repository.law.indiana.edu/ilj/vol97/iss4/4/. Accessed 6 June 2024

García Vidal A (2022) Metaverso, tokens no fungibles y propiedad intellectual. Comunicaciones Gomez-Acebo & Pombo. Available. https://www.ga-p.com/wp-content/uploads/2022/02/Tokens_del_metaverso.pdf. Accessed 6 June 2024

Guadamuz A (2024) Barcelona court rules in favour of defendant in NFT metaverse copyright case. Availabe https://www.technollama.co.uk/barcelona-court-rules-in-favour-of-defendant-in-nft-metaverse-copyright-case. Accessed 2 June 2024

Jiménez Serranía V (2023) Web 3.0, NFTs y propiedad intelectual. In: López-Tarruella Martínez A (ed) Protección y gestión de la propiedad intelectual en el metaverso. Reus, Madrid, pp 73–118

Llorente San Segundo MI (2023) Non fungible token: la réplica en el mundo digital de la originalidad, la autenticidad y la exclusividad de los objetos físicos. In: García-Cruces González JA (ed) De Iure Mercantus. Libro homenaje al Prof. Dr. Dr. h.c. Alberto Bercovitz Rodríguez-Cano. Tiran lo Blanch, Valencia, pp 955–997

Nassare Aznar S (2020) Naturaleza jurídica y régimen civil de los tokens en blockchain. In: García Teruel RM (ed) La tokenización de bienes en blockchain: Cuestiones civiles y tributarias. Thomson Reuters Aranzadi, Cizur Menor, pp 61–92

Rubí Puig A (2015) Agotamiento de derechos de autor, modificación física de ejemplares y principio salva rerum substantia. Indret 4/2015

UNIDROIT (2023) Principles digital assets and private law. Principle 2(2)

[24] Llorente San Segundo (2023), pp. 979–980, note n° 34. Jiménez Serranía (2023), pp. 99–101.

Domestic Tax Regulation in the Face of the Crypto Economy: Challenges Going Forward

Ana Cediel

Abstract Our tax system clings to a traditional economy linked to pre-digital criteria such as territoriality. It tries to update itself by introducing elements that attempt to deal with the new issues without resolving them head-on. The lack of tax regulation produces a sudden injustice barely resolved by soft law derived from binding administrative resolutions, such as the responses offered by the General Directorate of Taxes.

MiCA demonstrates the tax system's obsolescence in a broad and community sense. The lack of provisions for classifying new economic goods for tax purposes fragments their treatment, leads to tax conflicts, and creates legal uncertainty.

This legal uncertainty contrasts with the enormous deployment of mechanisms to control compliance with tax obligations. These include the effective automatic exchange of tax information, joint inspection procedures, and the, at times, unscrupulous application of artificial intelligence to all types of available data, personal and non-personal, without time limitation.

We understand that the rules applicable to the taxation of crypto assets must constantly be updated, and this is our purpose in an economy undergoing absolute digitalisation.

This paper expands and updates the text of a lecture delivered at the III International Congress entitled "Present and future of crypto-assets regulation in the European Union," held at the University of Alicante (Spain) on December 13, 14, and 15, 2023. This work is funded within the framework of: Proyecto CIPROM/2022/26 "Presente y futuro de la regulación de los Criptoactivos en la UE [Legalcripto]". Proyecto Prometeo CIPROM/2022/26, grupos de investigación de excelencia, de la Generalitat Valenciana (P.I. Carmen Pastor).

A. Cediel (✉)
Facultad de Derecho, Economía y Turismo, Universidad de Lérida, Lérida (ESPAÑA), Spain
e-mail: anna.cs@udl.cat

C. Pastor Sempere (ed.), *Governance and Control of Data and Digital Economy in the European Single Market*, Law, Governance and Technology Series 71,
https://doi.org/10.1007/978-3-031-74889-9_18

1 Introduction

The Spanish Constitution establishes in Article 31.1 that everyone must contribute to maintaining public expenses in accordance with their economic capacity in a fair tax system.

As stated in Article 3 of Law 58/2003, of December 17, Spanish General Tax Law (hereinafter LGT), this principle is called upon to be considered in the organisation of the tax system and its application.

It is closely linked to proportionality and equity in distributing the burdens derived from tax obligations, and the principle of non-confiscatoriality is concomitant.

All of this must be observed considering the rights and guarantees of taxpayers and legal certainty. In this sense, the taxable event must constitute a manifestation of wealth that is taxable by a means sufficiently linked to the intended purpose.[1]

In short, the principle of economic capacity must refer to the sufficiency of a natural or legal person to meet a specific tax obligation. This obligation must necessarily be required by an authorised public administration when dealing with operations with international or transnational elements. Therefore, the taxpayer must effectively know which tax administration can demand compliance with the tax obligation when the origin of the taxable act is an operation with crypto assets.

In the same sense, economic capacity must be understood as the manifestation of citizens' duty to contribute to the support of public spending, which requires a fair weighting of their contributory capacity undeniably linked to a manifestation of wealth.[2]

Crypto assets' tax valuation has been established intuitively, producing legal uncertainty in applying taxes that systematically violate the constitutional right for taxpayers to contribute fairly, according to their economic capacity.

To conveniently understand the efficiency of the legislator in alleviating situations of legal uncertainty, we must remember that until April 4, 2023, the valuation

[1]Plenary. STC 194/2000, of July 19, 2000. Appeal for unconstitutionality 1404/89. Promoted by seventy-eight Deputies regarding the fourth additional provision of Law 8/1989, of April 13, on Public Rates and Prices, which regulates the tax treatment of value differences resulting from administrative verification. Alleged violation of the rules of the legislative procedure; violation of the principles of economic capacity, criminal legality, and defence in the administrative sanctioning procedure. Nullity of the challenged provision and its reproduction in the consolidated text of the Tax.

[2]Plenary. FJ 3 of Sentence 59/2017, of May 11, 2017. Question of unconstitutionality 4864-2016. Raised by the Contentious-Administrative Court no. 1 of Jerez de la Frontera, in relation to various precepts of the consolidated text of the Law regulating local taxation, approved by Royal Legislative Decree 2/2004, of March 5. Principle of economic capacity and prohibition of confiscation: nullity of the legal provisions that regulate the tax on the increase in the value of urban land, to the extent that they subject situations of non-existence of increases in value to taxation (SSTC 26/2017 and 37/2017).

rules for crypto assets were not regulated but that these, specifically bitcoin, were launched on the market on January 3, 2009.[3]

Article 3.7 of Royal Decree, 249/2023 of April 4 introduced the aforementioned valuation rules that were established in article 39 bis of Royal Decree 1065/2007 of July 27, which approves the General Regulation of the actions and procedures for tax management and inspection and for the development of common standards for tax application procedures (hereinafter RGAT).[4]

The place and time at which crypto assets must be valued are determined, establishing that the quote will be taken at 11:59 p.m. on December 31, offered by the main trading platforms or price monitoring websites.

Given that the new tokens launched on the market may lack an official website where their value is stated, the legislator establishes a closing rule admitting that if a value cannot be obtained with the previous indications, the valuation established through a reasonable estimate of the virtual currency's market value in euros as of December 31 will be acceptable.[5] Legal uncertainty has improved significantly since the approval of these legal criteria, which should encourage legislators to delve into the legislative needs for taxing crypto assets. This should be a manageable legal action by different national legislators but coordinated action among legislators globally.

The partial regulation of the main sources of insecurity leaves gaps in the norm. It can offer contradictory orders that will always question, for sanctioning purposes, the conduct of those obliged to ensure that what is known as the "right to error" prospers.[6]

Thus, we find another grey area in determining the location of the crypto asset and the origin of the income in the transmissions. The location of crypto assets is linked

[3]Nakamoto (2008). Accessed 16 June 2024.

[4]Royal Decree 249/2023, of April 4, which modifies the General Regulations for the Development of Law 58/2003, of December 17, General Tax Law, regarding administrative review, approved by Royal Decree 520 /2005, May 13; the General Collection Regulations, approved by Royal Decree 939/2005, of July 29; the General Regulation of actions and procedures for tax management and inspection and for the development of common standards for tax application procedures, approved by Royal Decree 1065/2007, of July 27; the Inheritance and Donation Tax Regulations, approved by Royal Decree 1629/1991, of November 8; the Value Added Tax Regulations, approved by Royal Decree 1624/1992, of December 29; the Personal Income Tax Regulations, approved by Royal Decree 439/2007, of March 30, and the Corporate Tax Regulations, approved by Royal Decree 634/2015, of July 10.

[5]Please note that this estimated value must be provided to you by the persons and entities residing in Spain and the permanent establishments in Spanish territory of persons or entities residing abroad, where they have deposited their virtual currencies, in accordance with the data recorded in the form 172 (informative declaration on balances in virtual currencies) that such depositories are required to present.

[6]This right to error is not new and already in 2022 the Council for the Defense of the Taxpayer (Secretary of State for Finance) proposed adopting it through Proposal 3/2022 on the incorporation of the right to error to the Spanish tax system.

to the place of residence of companies that provide deposit or key safeguard services to access crypto assets.[7]

Likewise, determining the origin of crypto assets in lucrative and free transmission operations in international settings, especially in the cases of fungible and non-fungible tokens, is key to fairly determining the obligation corresponding to each tax obligor.

In this sense, European Union Regulation (from now on EU) 2023/1114 of the European Parliament and of the Council, of May 31, 2023, relating to crypto-asset markets and amending Regulations (EU) No. 1093/2010 and (EU) No. 1095/2010 and Directives 2013/36/EU and (EU) 2019/1937 (hereinafter MiCA), clearly demonstrates the obsolescence of the tax system in a broad and community sense. The lack of provisions regarding the classification of new elements of digital value for tax purposes fragments their treatment, leads to taxation conflicts, and creates legal uncertainty.

2 Crypto Assets Within and Outside the Scope of MiCA

2.1 MiCA and the Lack of Tax Regulation

All crypto-economic activity must be interpreted within the framework of the European Union considering MiCA. That is why we base our study on this interpretation. The application of taxes could advance the achievement of constitutional principles by reflecting on the elements regulated in the cited norm.

Crypto assets have an elementary characteristic that links their regulation and fraudulent behaviour: They do not require any centralised entity to keep track of their movements. This fact allows simple and secure transactions between two parties without intermediaries, so the control of these by third parties and authorities may be compromised.

It is easy to conclude that this characteristic also entails substantial risks related to tax fraud and money laundering.[8]

[7] According to article 42 ("quater") of Royal Decree 1065/2007, of July 27, which approves the General Regulation of the actions and procedures of tax management and inspection and the development of the common standards of the procedures for applying the taxes: "Virtual currencies will be understood to be located abroad when the person or entity or permanent establishment that custody them, providing services to safeguard the private cryptographic keys on behalf of third parties, to maintain, store and transfer said currencies, is not required to present the information referred to in section 6 of the thirteenth additional provision of Law 35/2006, of November 28, on Personal Income Tax and partial modification of the Corporate Tax laws, on "Income of non-residents and on assets".

[8] The risks for consumers, companies and markets are also a fact and are the main motivation for the promotion of MiCA. The European Parliament itself recognises that while crypto assets were not regulated in the EU, consumer protection rules did not protect users, who lacked sufficient

The EU promotes the regulation in MiCA of the instruments that a private issuer may have and allows control of their legality, leaving out those already regulated, such as securities, and those with an automatic generation system by mining. The aim is to promote the development and use of these technologies by providing a framework of legal certainty, supporting innovation, protecting consumers and investors, and guaranteeing financial stability.

For example, MiCA addresses the regulation of public crypto asset offerings to provide greater financial stability. But its intention does not stop there since, in addition, it addresses transparency, disclosure, authorisation and supervision of transactions involving the European Securities and Markets Authority (ESMA) and the European Banking Authority (EBA) in supervising the issuance of some of the tokens. It is intended that companies involved in issuing crypto assets or trading in them inform consumers about the risks, costs and fees linked to the operations.

The fees refer to those that EBA must charge issuers of significant asset-referenced and electronic money tokens to cover their costs. For issuers of significant asset-referenced tokens, fees must be proportionate to the size of their asset pool. For issuers of significant electronic money tokens, the fees must be proportionate to the funds they receive in exchange for the tokens.[9]

In our opinion, MiCA should encourage compliance with tax obligations by providing reminders of the fiscal relevance of the operations in the same text since it is an essential part of preventing the use of crypto assets in criminal activities. In April 2023, Parliament endorsed rules allowing crypto-asset transfers to be tracked and identified to avoid their use in money laundering, terrorist financing and other crimes.[10]

The European Parliament's activity focuses on promoting better coordination and efficiency in taxing crypto assets. It states that they should be subject to fair, transparent, and effective taxation but that authorities should consider simplified tax treatment for occasional or small traders and small transactions.

---

information about the risks associated with this type of asset. The possibility of financial instability, market manipulation, and financial fraud entails risks that European legislators must face.

[9]Article 137 of MiCA establishes the supervision fees. For this purpose, it states that (i) EBA will charge fees to issuers of significant asset-referenced tokens and to issuers of significant electronic money tokens. These fees will cover the expenses that EBA must make for the performance of its supervisory functions in relation to the issuers of significant asset-referenced tokens and the issuers of significant electronic money tokens; (ii) the amount of the fee charged to an individual issuer of a significant asset-referenced token shall be proportional to the size of its reserve assets and shall cover all costs incurred by EBA in carrying out its supervisory tasks under this Regulation; (iii) the amount of the fee charged to an individual issuer of a significant electronic money token will be proportional to the volume of the issuance of the electronic money token in exchange for funds and will cover all costs arising from the supervision tasks of ABE in accordance with this Regulation, including the reimbursement of any costs arising from the performance of such tasks.

[10]The new law also allows suspicious transactions to be blocked. The rules cover crypto asset transactions exceeding 1000 euros. The new law was officially approved by the Council in May 2023.

In addition, the possibility of tax collection through the blockchain system was considered to achieve greater efficiency. However, whether the collection could be carried out in the crypto assets regulated in MiCA was not specified.

Tokens with stabilisation mechanisms represent interests or rights over certain assets in the digital world and are usually issued to raise capital for new business projects or emerging companies. They are considered a more reliable payment method as their value is backed by real assets, providing new possibilities for innovation and use on a larger scale. That is why, in our opinion, they could be accepted as payment for tax obligations accrued with operations using crypto assets. This and the MiCA regulation could provide enough information to achieve truly fair taxation on crypto assets.

However, the reality is that the EU's efforts for fair taxation of the digital economy in matters of crypto assets focus mainly on having control tools and avoiding the erosion of tax bases, leaving aside the search for defending the principles of economic capacity previously analysed.

Separately, the EU monitors tax rules to ensure that taxes are fair, effective, and pro-growth while guaranteeing the free movement of goods, services, and capital in the EU single market. In addition, it ensures that companies in one country are not unfairly favoured over their competitors in other countries and that taxes do not discriminate against consumers, workers, or companies in other EU countries.

The lack of regulation aimed at providing tools for the correct taxation of crypto assets is, in our opinion, an impediment to their free market and a violation of their users' right to trade safely. An example of what is meant by fair taxation of the digital economy for the EU is the Directive approved by the Council on October 17, 2023, modifying Directive 2011/16/EU on administrative cooperation in the field of taxation (hereinafter DAC).

This Directive includes a new set of amendments to the DAC rules (known as "DCA 8").[11] The changes mainly relate to (i) the notification and automatic exchange of information on income from operations with crypto assets and (ii) information on previous tax rulings for the richest people (with high net worth).[12]

DAC 8 aims to strengthen administrative cooperation between tax administrations and expand the scope of registration and notification obligations to include crypto assets.

This tool will, therefore, allow tax authorities to automatically exchange the information provided by crypto asset service providers by submitting reports.

This exchange of data, combined with the use of Artificial Intelligence in tax administrations and the new European joint inspection procedures, undoubtedly led to the need to establish a statute for taxpayers that provides them with a guide to defend their rights effectively in the national and European context.

[11] On October 24, 2023, Council Directive 2023/2226 of October 17, 2023, amending Directive 2011/16/EU, relating to administrative cooperation in the field of taxation, was published.

[12] Cediel and Pérez (2023).

So far, it has been difficult for Member States' tax administrations to ensure compliance with tax obligations in this specific area. Since crypto assets are decentralised and easily traded cross-border, strong international administrative cooperation is needed to ensure effective tax collection.

This strong cooperation is not accompanied by express regulation of the taxable event in various crypto assets. Perhaps this fact is part of a larger problem that currently questions the definition of digital goods as services rather than incorporeal assets.

The Court of Justice of the European Union has yet to rule on what should be considered a digital good. A clear example is digital art non-fungible tokens (NFT), defined as incorporeal or unique digital goods.

Currently, the General Directorate of Taxes (hereinafter DGT) does not admit the classification of the sale of NFTs as deliveries of goods; rather, they are considered a provision of services by electronic means (DGT response to binding consultation V1753-23, of June 15, 2023).

The DGT argues that the underlying good is not the illustration or drawing itself as an existing physical good since the possession of the token does not generally give the right to the acquisition of such physical good, but the underlying good is also digital. In short, the object of the transaction seems to consist of the digital certificate of authenticity that represents the NFT without the physical delivery of the image file or the digital file associated with it.[13]

On the contrary, we must understand that if the acquisition of the NFT entails ownership of the digital file (it can be included by smart contract), it could be considered admitted as a delivery of goods. Would it be admissible to classify it as a work of art by applying the reduced VAT rate?[14] If this does not happen, the ambiguity in defining a digital good within the European Union means that if an NFT is accessible to everyone, it will be categorised as providing electronic services.

However, such qualifications will be nuanced when clients request work customising a design.[15] The current regulation, therefore, does not enable action with the necessary legal certainty. The legislator's search to ensure that the tax obligation is not breached is not accompanied by another effort to ensure that it can be fulfilled with sufficient legal certainty.

As we have seen, in the case of art NFTs, some could be classified as works of art as they are unique digital files created using blockchain technology, provided a

---

[13] Harana (2024) https://doi.org/10.47092/ct.24.1.3.

[14] Copyright and professional services of plastic artists, writers, contributors to newspapers and magazines (literary, graphic, and photographers), musical composers, authors of theatrical works, film and audiovisual works, scriptwriters, translators, and adapters are exempt from VAT.

[15] It is DGT itself that, when addressing the qualification of provision of services electronically, states that in this case, what is transmitted is "drawings or illustrations that are the object of sale although, due to the blockchain technology used, they become unique and original digital assets, since there is no other identical digital asset, and the object of transmission is, furthermore, not the digital file of the drawing or illustration itself, but the digital certificate of authenticity that the NFT represents."

certificate of ownership accompanies them. However, it is impossible to apply a reduced VAT rate if they cannot be qualified either as goods or as art due to the lack of definition of the nature of these assets.[16]

In this sense, it is worth reviewing the tokens regulated in MiCA and outside it to determine whether we have enough information as taxpayers to face our tax obligations and comply with them safely.

The MiCA regulation covers (i) EMTs (e-money token), where the value refers to the value of an official currency; (ii) ARTs (asset-referenced token), where the value refers to any other value or right, or a combination of them, including one or more official currencies; and, (iii) Utility tokens of the identified issuer, where access to a good or service is offered by the issuer itself.

Outside MiCA (i) Security tokens: Financial instruments; (ii) Equity token: future profits; (iii) Debt token: participation in the entity's debt; (iv) Cryptocurrencies/virtual currencies: service providers only; (v) NFT: unique asset of the physical world or the virtual world whose units are not interchangeable with each other (Securities); financial services without intermediaries.

3 MiCA-Regulated Tokens and Tax Implications

3.1 E-money Token (EMT): Value Linked to the Value of an Official Currency

Electronic money tokens are considered electronic money. Like electronic money, they are an electronic substitute for coins and banknotes used for payments. From this perspective, they follow the taxation of legal tender.

Issuers of electronic money tokens must ensure that holders can always exercise their right to redeem their tokens for their nominal value in the currency to which they are referenced.

The provisions of Directive 2009/110/EC regarding the possibility of charging a fee in connection with redemption are not relevant in the context of electronic money tokens, so they will not have the relevance they do in the case of legal tender.

The prohibition of interest accrual or netting compensation or discount with interest equivalent effect received by the holder of electronic money tokens directly from the issuer or a third party, in direct relation to the electronic money token or for the remuneration or pricing of other products should be understood to apply to this type of crypto assets.

[16]In this sense, the General Directorate of Taxes establishes that "the object of the sale is not the illustrations themselves, but the NFTs that "grant the buyer rights of use but in no case the underlying rights to the ownership of the work." The Tax criteria would have been different, the expert points out, in the event that the intellectual property rights as a whole were transferred with the sale of the digital files.

3.2 *Asset-referenced Token (ART): Value Linked to Any Other Value, Right, or a Combination of Them, Including One or More Official Currencies*

Significant tokens referenced to assets can be used as a medium of exchange and for conducting large volumes of payment transactions.

To reduce the risk of asset-referenced tokens being used as a store of value, issuers of asset-referenced tokens and providers of crypto asset services must not grant holders of asset-referenced tokens interest based on the time they hold them when providing services related to asset-referenced tokens. The aim is to promote use in debt payment operations and discourage those associated with investment functions and services.

The accrual of interest or any netting compensation or discount with an interest-equivalent effect received by the holder of asset-referenced tokens directly from the issuer or a third party, in direct relation to the asset-referenced token or for the remuneration or pricing of other products, like in the case of e-money tokens, is prohibited.

The issuer of asset-referenced tokens must refund by either paying in funds other than electronic money, an amount equivalent to the market value of the assets referenced by such tokens or by delivering the assets referenced by the tokens. It should be noted that:

(a) The asset-referenced token may lose its value as a whole or in part.
(b) The asset-referenced token may not always be negotiable.
(c) The asset-referenced token may not be liquid.
(d) Investor compensation systems do not cover the asset-referenced token under Directive 97/9/EC.
(e) The asset-referenced token is not covered by deposit guarantee systems under Directive 2014/49/EU.

All this may lead to losses for both individuals and legal entities.

Since these tokens are intended for high-volume payment operations, we may disregard the possibility of analysing their taxation as investment instruments. However, the mere fact that this can happen without being illegal should prompt us to address the situation of those engaging in operations in this regard that may result in financially relevant gains or losses.

3.3 *Identified Issuer Utility Token (UTI): Access to a Good or Service the Issuer Offers*

The so-called "consumption tokens" are a type of crypto asset used solely to access a good or service their issuer provides. In this case, the tokens represent the actual good or future right.

When the public offering refers to a consumption token, it may not be exchangeable for the good or service promised in the crypto-asset white paper, especially in the event of the crypto-asset project's failure or interruption.

This possibility is highly relevant for tax purposes, as the necessary precautions must be established. In principle, the taxation regime of operations with a suspensive or resolutory condition could be followed for the taxation of consumption tokens. We believe the value-added tax on the good or service accessed should accrue when the token is exchanged for the good.

According to Article 4 of MiCA, consumption tokens may or may not be offered free of charge. In the case of a free acquisition, we can affirm that the transmission should not be tax-relevant at the time of the token's delivery in the company's public offer. If, on the other hand, buyers must provide or commit to providing personal data to the issuer in exchange for the crypto-assets or give the offeror any fee, commission, or other monetary or non-monetary benefits in exchange for the mentioned crypto-assets, we must consider that the acquired tokens cannot be classified as "transfer of own capital to third parties" nor as "participation in equity funds." Therefore, they must be valued at market price on the accrual date.[17]

From the above, the issuance of consumption tokens through an Initial Coin Offering or Token Offering (ICO/ITO) will generate taxation under the issuing company's Corporate Income Tax (CIT). Still, such taxation will be deferred until the company effectively delivers the products or provides the underlying services that token holders can access through their exchange.

The income recorded in the financial statements in the years when the services are effectively rendered or the committed products are delivered constitute taxable income for CIT purposes, which, as such, must be included in the tax base of this tax in the relevant fiscal year.

Generally, the transfer of the consumption token will generate accounting income (positive or negative) from the difference between the transfer value, interpreted as the token's market value at the time of its sale or exchange, and its net book value, construed as the acquisition cost.

Similarly, from a tax perspective, and in line with the accounting treatment, a tax income will also be generated from the difference between the transfer value and its tax value, which, if positive, will be included in the taxable base and taxed under the CIT, and if negative, may be deducted for CIT purposes.[18]

---

[17]DGT Consultation V2834-21, of November 16, 2021, issued by the General Subdirectorate of Property Taxes, Rates and Public Prices on IP matters.

[18]Egea (2018), pp. 131–180.

4 Unregulated Tokens in MiCA and Tax Implications

4.1 Security Tokens: Debt and Equity Token (Financial instruments) Directive 2014/65/EU

We must analyse these two types of tokens, considering that the difference is highly relevant for tax purposes. In this regard, we must preliminarily qualify each, understanding that some are part of the company's net worth (equity) or liabilities (debt).

4.1.1 Debt Token

We are dealing with tokens that can be classified as company debt instruments. From a tax perspective, their regime must be followed to comply with the corresponding tax obligation correctly. The operation carried out by the acquirers of the company's debt tokens is essentially a loan in return for a commitment to repay with interest later.

In general, the transfer of this type of token will generate accounting income (positive or negative) for the difference between the transfer value (the market value of the token at the time of its sale or exchange) and its net accounting value (acquisition cost adjusted, when appropriate, by valuation corrections for unreturned impairment), which will be incorporated into the accounting result.

4.1.2 Equity Token

According to the DGT, equity or capital tokens represent a proportional part of a company's ownership, generally a start-up or fintech. Still, unlike traditional securities, their representation is based on blockchain technology.[19]

Based on the above, the DGT concludes that the determining elements to carry out a tax classification of these virtual assets must be sought, regardless of the name given to them, in the powers or rights granted to their holder against their issuer, which, given their IT configuration, will be included in the programming that has been carried out of such assets, without their atypical form of representation, possession and transmission, through distributed ledger technology, known as "blockchain" or "chain of blocks", affecting such classification.[20]

The tax impact of a transfer or exchange is undeniable, as it generates accounting income (positive or negative). If there is no coincidence between the book and tax

---

[19] Binding Consultation Resolution of the General Directorate of Taxes V2834-21, of November 16, 2021.

[20] Binding Consultation Resolution of the General Directorate of Taxes V0766-21, of March 31, 2021.

value, this income must undergo a positive or negative extra-accounting adjustment according to applicable regulations (art. 20 of the LIS). As a consequence of the tax classification, we can infer the application of article 21 of the LIS, understanding that the exemption on dividends and income derived from the transfer of securities representing the own funds of resident and non-resident entities in Spanish territory is applicable.

4.2 Non-Fungible Token (NFT)

According to the DGT in its Binding Consultation V1753-23, dated June 15, 2023, NFTs or non-fungible "tokens" are digital certificates of authenticity that, through blockchain technology, are associated with a unique digital file.

Therefore, NFTs act as unique digital assets that cannot be exchanged for each other since no two are alike. Their underlying asset can be anything digitally represented, such as an image, a graphic, a video, music, or any other digital content, even works of art.

Once the original design is created, it is tokenised, generating NFTs from that creation. Thus, there seem to be two digital assets with their own entity to consider for tax purposes: the underlying digital file and the "non-fungible token" or NFT representing the digital ownership of the underlying digital file.

At this point, two possible scenarios derived from this double entity of assets must be described. It may be that the object of the transfer, through the corresponding online platforms, is only the NFT without incorporating the underlying digital file or that both are transferred in the acquisition of the NFT.[21]

NFTs could be defined as digital assets, but this classification is not legally accepted. The Court of Justice of the EU still needs to address the analysis of the nature of this type of digital asset. For now, we cannot confer the possibility of transferring an NFT in the same way that it is legally permissible to transfer a physical asset.[22]

The two scenarios can impact tax matters, such as whether an NFT is acquired and taxed at a general or reduced rate because it is considered a work of art. The reduced rate applies only if the original file is acquired.

---

[21] A parallel can be established with the engraving technique in which hollow notches are made in the metal, resulting in a plate owned by the artist that will be inked, cleaned and passed through the press, stamping the resulting figures on paper. as many times as reproductions the owner wants to market.

[22] It is defined, for example, in Council Directive 2006/112/EC of 28 November 2006 on the common system of Value Added Tax (OJ L 347 of 11.12.2006), whose article 14.1. configures it as "the transmission of the power of disposal over a tangible asset with the powers attributed to its owner."

Thus, if the transaction object consists of the digital certificate of authenticity representing the NFT without the physical delivery of the image file or the associated digital file, we are dealing with an operation subject to the general rate.

Since it cannot legally be classified as the delivery of goods, VAT must classify NFT operations as electronically provided services that, if considered to be performed within the territory of application of the Tax, must be taxed at the general rate.

4.3 Cryptocurrencies/Virtual Currencies: Service Providers Only

MiCA only regulates activity with virtual currencies, as service providers must comply with this regulation.

Service providers are defined in MiCA (art. 3) as a legal entity whose activity or business consists of professionally providing one or more crypto-asset services to clients, and the legal entity is authorised to deliver crypto-asset services under Article 59. This figure is regulated in Title V of the Regulation, which addresses the "Authorization and conditions of exercise of the activity of crypto-asset service providers."

Article 3 defines crypto assets as a "digital representation of a value or right that can be transferred and stored electronically, using distributed ledger technology or similar technology."

When this crypto-asset functions as a means of payment, it is often called virtual currency in many regulations and follows the tax regime of money. However, delivering virtual currencies is considered a barter under personal income tax regulations.

5 Capital Gains and Losses in Crypto

5.1 Personal Income Tax

5.1.1 Gains

For tax purposes, the exchange of tokens is considered a barter from which capital gains subject to personal income tax may arise.[23]

Utility tokens are the speciality of the exchange we introduced in the preceding lines. If the token's value remains unchanged, the exchange can remain a simple act

[23] Egea (2022), pp. 63–130.

of consumption without further ado. However, the value usually fluctuates positively or negatively.

Thus, if the market value of the product or service and the utility token have increased relative to their acquisition value, we could affirm that a capital gain is generated for personal income tax purposes. Conversely, we must integrate a capital loss if the value is lower.

In the case of crypto assets transfers as payment in the acquisition of security tokens, however, we would obtain a variation in the value of the assets due to their alteration, generating a capital gain concerning the acquirer. Therefore, both the transfer value and the acquisition cost of the transmitted cryptocurrency must be proved with certainty to find their difference since this will be the one that is integrated into the savings tax base.

In the event of debt token transfers, the regulations on income derived from the transfer, reimbursement, amortisation, exchange, or conversion of financial assets will apply, classifying them as income from movable capital (art 25.2.b LIRPF).

Also, in this case, we must appropriately prove the value of the crypto assets individually derived from any of the operations just mentioned and their acquisition or subscription value. The accessory acquisition and disposal costs may be computed after justification. All of this will be integrated into the savings income.

In the case of the capital token, note that the possible transfer will generate a capital gain or loss for the investor holders since, as we have stated, the transfer generates a capital variation.

Again, we must prove the acquisition and sale values following current legislation requirements regarding the gain. In this regard, the legal specifications regarding barter apply if the crypto asset is exchanged for other crypto assets, always considering art. 37.1.h) of the LIRPF. This will require the gain to be determined by the difference between the acquisition value of the delivered token and either the market value of the capital token or the market value of the cryptocurrency received as payment for the price (whichever is higher).

In general, valuations must be made in euros, adding transaction costs and commissions. We must remember that the token exit order applies the FIFO (First in, First Out) rule, meaning that if considered homogeneous values, the tokens acquired by the taxpayer are deemed the first transferred.

5.1.2 Losses

5.1.2.1 Utility Tokens

Suppose the market value of the product or service and the utility token has decreased compared to their acquisition value in the article's application. In that case, a capital loss may occur due to the difference between the market value of the received product or service at the time of exchange and the acquisition cost.[24]

Likewise, capital losses may be obtained from the transfer of the token or its exchange if the token's market value at the time of sale has decreased compared to the acquisition price. A capital loss is generated, and it must be integrated and compensated in the savings tax base.[25]

5.1.2.2 Capital Tokens

As we have pointed out, if the capital token's market value has decreased at the time of sale compared to its acquisition price, a capital loss should be understood to have been generated. This must be integrated and compensated in the savings tax base, provided the corresponding accreditation and justification of the acquisition and transfer values are available.

In this case, as in the previous section, the rules preventing loss generation can operate if a subsequent repurchase occurs. This situation means that recognising such losses is deferred to a later time.

5.2 Corporate Tax

5.2.1 Gains

5.2.1.1 Debt Tokens

The transfer of the debt token generates an income incorporated into the accounting result, which can be positive or negative due to the difference between the transfer value—market value at the time of the operation—and its net accounting value—corrected acquisition cost if applicable—which, once recorded in the accounts, will generally result in a tax consequence. Therefore, the negative value difference will result in a deduction in Corporate Tax (IS), and the positive value difference will be integrated into the taxable base of IS by the necessary extra-accounting adjustments.

---

[24] It could be interpreted by the Tax Administration that the loss is not deductible as long as it is classified as a consumption loss in accordance with article 33.5.b) of the LIRPF.

[25] Since utility tokens do not qualify as securities, we should not apply the loss limitation rules (art. 33.5 of the LIRPF, letter f). We must consider, however, the limitation of the letter "e" of that same article for the repurchase of utility tokens that led to losses within a year.

5.2.1.2 Capital Tokens

If a capital gain is obtained from transferring the capital token, the exemption of Article 21.3 of the LIS can be applied.

5.2.2 Losses

5.2.2.1 Debt Token

The difference between the transfer and tax values generates tax income. If it is negative, it may be deducted for IS purposes.

5.2.2.2 Capital Tokens

Article 21 of the LIS establishes that the taxable base should not include negative income from transferring a stake in an entity. This refusal can be avoided if the transfer occurs in the context of a corporate dissolution.

6 Conclusions

In cases where tax regulations do not apply, the legislator and the tax administration must clarify the classification and quantification of the operations. It is necessary to address regulation by establishing the bases. A clear example is the possibility of assuming, in general, in matters of crypto asset taxation that the base regulation is "ab initio" and governs the crypto assets' underlying assets.

The tax rule by analogy must not be applied because the peculiarities of crypto assets would result in inaccurate taxation scenarios. Streamlining tax policies is necessary for an economy capable of adapting quickly to achieve some tax justice.

In fact, for fair tax application, the EU must not only promote compliance control but also provide European citizens with unified, effective, and enforceable protocols to act before tax administrations of other Member States.

If existing, the regulations on crypto asset taxation should meet a minimum common standard based on the treatment that the tax system grants to operations carried out with analogous assets. The EU rules for financial services must comply with the principles of technological neutrality and "same activity, same risks, same rules," and this structure must also apply to crypto assets.

Therefore, we understand that the tax rules apply to the nature of the "underlying assets" of crypto assets in general terms and should not be understood as using the rule by analogy since the analogy occurs in determining the nature of the asset and not in the tax standard.

In cases where tax regulations do not apply, the legislator and the tax administration must clarify the classification and quantification of the operations. If this does not happen, the doctrine must systematically analyse the application of the tax system to cutting-edge operations in the crypto economy.

Another example of the evolution of the crypto-asset business is its representation through securities such as Bitcoin Exchange Traded Funds (ETF). The mature situation of the crypto-asset markets has led to the decline of some businesses and the renewal of others, resulting in large capital losses and new investments in products such as the aforementioned Bitcoin ETFs approved by the Securities and Exchange Commission (SEC) of the United States Stock Exchange.

The fiscal analysis of this new product allows us to affirm that the Spanish tax legislator's inactivity for 15 years regarding the crypto economy deserves the classification of flagrant negligence since, far from disappearing, the crypto economy is consolidated through its transformation and growth.

Some fundamental questions the legislator did not resolve have received a certain degree of response in MiCA. We are referring, for example, to essential elements for calculating tax liability, such as the way crypto assets are valued. Thus, MiCA establishes the obligation of service providers to publish a fixed price or a method to determine the price of crypto assets (art. 77 MiCA).

Mica does not regulate the granting of financing and loans denominated in crypto assets and, therefore, does not affect the national tax law applicable to this type of operation. However, financing and loan operations outside of MiCA have a financial impact with tax relevance.

The next steps must be to conveniently systematise the existing regulations on the taxation of old and new crypto economy operations to safeguard the convenience and effective declaration of possible losses.

References

Cediel A, Pérez E (2023) Taxation of bitcoin, virtual currencies and tokens. Atelier, Barcelona

Egea I (2018) Tratamiento tributario del "bitcoin" y demás criptomonedas. Dig. Cuadernos de Derecho y Comercio 70:131–180

Egea I (2022) Guía de tratamiento tributario de los NFTs en España. Dig. Cuadernos de Derecho y Comercio 77:63–130

Harana E (2024) Explorando el laberinto fiscal de los activos digitales: el caso de los NFTs. Dig. Crónica Tributaria, https://doi.org/10.47092/ct.24.1.3

Nakamoto S (2008) Bitcoin: a peer-to-peer electronic cash system. Dig. At https://bitcoin.org/bitcoin.pdf. Accessed 16 June 2024

Part IV
New Digital Spaces and Identities

The European Digital Identity Wallet as Defined in the EIDAS 2 Regulation

Julián Inza

Abstract Several legislative developments are taking place in Europe that make some regulations converge with others, and one of the most influential is the one that will govern the new digital identity model that arises from the modification of the European Regulation that defines digital identity and electronic trust services. Regulation 910/2014 is called eIDAS and has been essential in developing European-qualified trust services. Regulation (EU) 2024/1183, called eIDAS 2 because it modifies the eIDAS regulation and increases its scope, has been recently published in the Official Journal of the European Union.

1 SSI, State-Supported Identity

Concerning identity, a term that has become popular is that of SSI, "Self-Sovereign Identity", which defines an identity management model designed to preserve user privacy. The approach to identity management in eIDAS2 does not go in the same direction, but the influence of the SSI concept is visible throughout the regulation; the eIDAS 2 identity management model could stand instead for "State-Supported Identity", which in continental Europe is the general rule.

In fact, States support the management of their citizens' identities, and from there, from the identity within the physical realm, arises the Digital Management of Identity and what we call, therefore, "Digital Identity." One of the aspects

This paper expands and updates the text of a lecture delivered at the III International Congress entitled "Present and future of crypto-assets regulation in the European Union," held at the University of Alicante (Spain) on December 13, 14, and 15, 2023. This work is funded within the framework of: Proyecto CIPROM/2022/26 "Presente y futuro de la regulación de los Criptoactivos en la UE [Legalcripto]". Proyecto Prometeo CIPROM/2022/26, grupos de investigación de excelencia, de la Generalitat Valenciana (P.I. Carmen Pastor).

J. Inza (✉)
EADTRUST, Madrid, Spain
e-mail: julian.inza@eadtrust.eu

C. Pastor Sempere (ed.), *Governance and Control of Data and Digital Economy in the European Single Market*, Law, Governance and Technology Series 71,
https://doi.org/10.1007/978-3-031-74889-9_19

emphasised by the eIDAS2 Regulation is the regulation of the European Union Digital Identity Wallet (EUDI Wallet).

The forecast is that each of the European Union's member states will publish an EUDI wallet in 2026. However, some delays may occur considering the complementary activities that must be developed, such as the publication of Implementing Acts and assessment standards.

It may be the case that a state promotes an EUDI Wallet that it has not developed. In other words, it is not mandatory for the State to develop the EUDI Wallet; it can simply sponsor the implementation of another entity, even a private company. In any case, much progress has been made at present.

The amendment to the eIDAS Regulation started being managed in 2021 after an in-depth reflection on the results achieved by the aforementioned Regulation, particularly concerning identity management in cross-border areas. This aspect had not been as successful as expected. It lacked this capability, among other reasons, because several member countries had not developed systems for managing their citizens' identities, which were necessary for the mutual recognition procedure between countries. Thus, if the country does not have a digital system for managing the identity of citizens, it makes no sense to consider interoperability so another country can enable management with that digital identity.

Several years passed since the Regulation was published in 2014, and the achievements and challenges not met in 2021 were finally evaluated. It was concluded that another model had to be used. The efforts made within the framework of "Self-Sovereign identity" initiatives in pilot projects for the deployment of self-managed identity systems such as Evernym and uPort, or the standardisation progress of W3C in the Working Group on Decentralized Identifiers,[1] were taken into account for the definition of the EUDI Wallet model.

Among the previous initiatives is EBSI (European Blockchain Services Infrastructure). This European Blockchain Service Infrastructure (EBSI) consists of a network of interconnected nodes running a blockchain-based service infrastructure. Each European Blockchain Association (EBP) member—the 27 EU countries, Norway, Liechtenstein, and the European Commission—will manage at least one node. Use cases such as the cross-border interoperability of university degrees and professional certifications or management of Social Security bodies are included among those managed with EBSI.

On 21 May 2024, the Commission adopted the Decision[2] establishing EUROPEUM-EDIC (European Digital Infrastructure Consortium), a new legal entity established by a consortium of 9 Member States. This entity will further deploy and expand the European Blockchain Services Infrastructure (EBSI)

---

[1] World Wide Web Consortium (W3C) (2022) Decentralized Identifiers (DIDs) v1.0 https://www.w3.org/TR/did-core/ Accessed 15 June 2024.

[2] European Commission (2024a) Commission Implementing Decision (EU) 2024/1432 of 21 May 2024 setting up the European Digital Infrastructure Consortium for European Blockchain Partnership and European Blockchain Service Infrastructure (EUROPEUM-EDIC). ELI: http://data.europa.eu/eli/dec_impl/2024/1432/oj.

exploitation to provide cross-border services at the EU level, particularly public services. The aim is to strengthen cyber trust and resilience in compliance with EU regulations, including the eIDAS European Digital Identity framework.

The EUROPEUM-EDIC will support cross-border cooperation between public authorities on Web3 and decentralised technologies, fostering innovation and interoperability of such solutions with other technologies.

Belgium-as host country-Croatia, Cyprus, Greece, Italy, Luxembourg, Portugal, Romania and Slovenia participate in the EUROPEUM EDIC. Poland has also officially applied to join the EUROPEUM DTIS, and other Member States are expected to express their interest. They can participate as members or observers, as can the European Economic Area (EEA) countries.

2 The eIDAS Regulation

Thus, eIDAS had already achieved the consolidation of certain services that included the adjective "qualified": qualified certificate for electronic signature (natural person) and electronic seal (legal person), qualified electronic timestamp, qualified e-delivery service, qualified certificate for website authentication, qualified preservation of electronic signatures and seals and qualified validation of electronic signatures and seals.

Qualified services are presumed to be valid throughout Europe. Lawyers call this a presumption "*iuris tantum.*" It is a type of digital evidence that admits proof to the contrary but in such a way that the one who has the burden of proof is the one who denies it. To date, this presumption has only been held by notaries and registrars.

In other words, qualified digital services have become part of a conglomerate of preventive legal security services. Preventive legal security refers to the steps we take in advance to record facts so as not to have legal problems. So, suppose we find ourselves in a dispute at any given time. In that case, that evidence—the notarial evidence, the registry evidence, and now the proof of qualified trust services—proves that something has happened.

Most of the developments around the eIDAS Regulation have been carried out by technicians. Still, the time is already coming for lawyers to delve into all these issues, and their points of view will be very valuable.

Identity is a right included in the Universal Declaration of Human Rights. Article 6 of the Convention stipulates that "everyone has the right to recognition as a person before the law." In other words, "every person is subject to rights and obligations, under the protection of the law and vis-à-vis other individuals and before any entity."

Legal personality is the element associated with our identity, based on which we exercise our rights. It is very important because we can exercise all those rights when we have a legal personality. All this arises when parents register a newborn in the Civil Registry. So, it is of great importance for identity management to have a registration in the Civil Registry.

When obtaining the identity card, the required document is the birth certificate. A requirement that, together with a photograph, the obtaining of the biometric data of the fingerprint, and the payment of the fee gives rise to the instrument of daily identity management: the identity card itself in which the name, surname, date and place of birth and the names of the parents are recorded.

From identity management in physical relationship models, we can move to digital electronic procedures using digital identity management systems. But identity is what a person is. This is very interesting because the model of reference to identity is completely different from country to country. No one usually has a problem saying their ID number in some countries like Spain. Nor does this number appear on Power of Attorney, driver's license, contracts, or procedures with the public administration.

There is no concern over the potential use for profiling, although this is a concern in Anglo-Saxon or "common law" contexts. It should be said that in these contexts, they do not conceive identity as we conceive it in continental countries, and that is why the "Self-Sovereign Identity" approaches are more relevant in these Anglo-Saxon contexts. In summary, the problem of identity management in the context of physical relationships must be solved, which has led, for example, to the existence of a driver's license for non-drivers in the State of New York. The driving licence for non-drivers would not be necessary if the State granted a Citizen Identity Document with a photo.

Therefore, the fact that this type of product and service exists recognises that this need does not depend on the legal framework in which you operate, even if your legal framework does not expressly provide for the issuance of identity cards for citizens by the state. Another curious case from the point of view of a Spaniard is that in the United Kingdom, when contracting an electricity company or a telephone company, a "Credit Scoring" report of assignment of expectation of payment of debts granted by a private entity such as Dun & Bradstreet, Experian or Equifax, is requested, which measures the risk that the applicant will not be able to repay the money they lend you or meet their payment obligations, which is a way of disguising identity management services. In these countries, the state does not have the power to support the identity of its citizens with a card, and private entities are partially being used to cover this need.

Returning to the eIDAS Regulation, let's examine what services were created. This Regulation defined the services of issuing certificates of natural persons for electronic signatures, of issuing certificates of legal entities for electronic seals, of issuing certificates for website authentication, that are abbreviated as QWAC (Qualified Web Authentication Certificate), of electronic signature and seal validation and preservation, of issuing electronic time stamps, and of registered electronic delivery (such as registered email and sending of electronic invoices) (Fig. 1).

Technically, QWAC certificates are equivalent to those developed for website security (activated when the protocol prefix is HTTPS). The underlying communications protocol was SSL (Secure Sockets Layer) and is currently TLS (Trusted Layer Security). SSL is no longer used because its implementations had vulnerabilities, and with the adoption of TLS, there is no evidence of such kind of vulnerabilities.

Fig. 1 Qualified trust services (European Commission, 2024)

Website certificates for TLS have been issued by certification service providers worldwide for many years. The body that coordinates the development of the regulations for verifying the identity of this type of certificate is the CA/B Forum, an entity without legal personality equivalent to an association. Its partners are entities that create browsers and web page viewing programs and Trust Service Providers (TSP) that issue certificates for website authentication. They collaborate in follow-up meetings to define the security standards against which certification service providers that issue website certificates are evaluated. Then, the browser developers coordinate in that CA/B Forum precisely to say what security measures must be used by the certification authorities and what requirements a Certification Service Provider should meet so that after being audited, they can demonstrate them to the web browser development companies so that they admit that this provider can be included in their "Trusted Service Lists" of trusted providers.

One of the changes included in the eIDAS2 Regulation is that browsers must accept those on the European Union's Trusted Service List as trusted providers. This controversy seems to have been overcome. Browsers continue to have the power to reject certification service providers if they detect a security problem in their management.

Digital trust services end up affecting electronic documents. Electronic documents can be electronically signed or sealed. It is possible to check the validity of a certificate, whether it is revoked, whether it is that of a natural person or that of a legal person. It is possible to check if the certificate is on a trusted list, that is, if the provider that provides these trust services has passed an audit. With the time stamp, the previous existence of an electronic document is recorded concerning the time that appears in the digital file that constitutes the time stamp.

In relation to electronic signatures, there are certificate issuance services, certificate validation services, services for the preservation of signed electronic documents (called electronic archiving services) and remote services for the performance of electronic signatures based on cloud servers with HSM (Hardware Security Module) infrastructure.

This service has turned out to be somewhat striking because server-based signatures were born with the 2014 eIDAS Regulation, but it was not a service that was defined in the articles. Still, it was introduced in recitals 51 and 52 and with a brief mention in the following paragraphs in Annex II:

> 3. The generation or management of the data for creating the electronic signature on behalf of the signatory may only be carried out by a qualified trust service provider.
>
> 4. Without prejudice to point 1(d), qualified trust service providers who manage the electronic signature creation data on behalf of the signatory may duplicate the signature creation data solely for the purpose of backing up the said data, provided that the following requirements are met:
>
> (a) the security of duplicate datasets is of the same level as for the original datasets;
> (b) the number of duplicate datasets does not exceed the minimum necessary to ensure continuity of service.

Thus, despite the service not being explicitly created in the eIDAS regulation, Recitals 51 and 52 were the basis for making the remote electronic signature service. Subsequently, other standards developed at a technical level that complemented the formal structure of the service, which was not considered "per se" a qualified service until it was defined by the eIDAS 2 Regulation in Article 29 b (Requirements applicable to a qualified service for the management of qualified devices for the creation of electronic signatures remotely).

The pandemic suffered from 2020 onwards has undoubtedly contributed to the development of this type of cloud signature service, along with those for remote identification, because certificate holders could not physically travel to the headquarters of the registration authority. A signature holder deployed on the internet receives the electronic documents to be signed, and the signatory uses an App on their mobile phone to demonstrate their exclusive control over the signature functionality implemented with the help of HSM (Hardware Security Module) equipment.

Remote identification was included in one of the identification options of Article 24 (the fourth option), together with face-to-face verification (the first), verification with an existing digital identity management system, such as that provided by a bank or a public administration (the second), or by identification with another certificate (the third option).

Remote identification was subject to audit by a conformity assessment to evaluate whether the system's security and level of assurance for the identity proofing were equivalent in terms of reliability to physical presence.

The timestamp has become one of the great findings of the eIDAS Regulation. It is possible to determine the specific moment in which an event happened. The entity that requires the timestamp transmits to the Time Stamping Authority (TSA) the information of that event translated into a "hash" value.

The TSA creates a "token" with the hash information and the precise moment in which it has a record of it and then signs it electronically. This electronically signed "token" is the timestamp.

Throughout Europe, the timestamp is presumed to be valid unless proven otherwise and gives certainty of the moment in which something happened. A qualified timestamp has an accuracy of 1 second, although the time source used (metrological source of the time standard) can reach accuracies of 50 nanoseconds.

Trust Service Providers have deployed qualified trust services in parallel with the creation of each country's Supervisory and Accreditation Bodies, which endorse the Conformity Assessment Bodies that can operate throughout Europe. The European authorities have built a "Dashboard" where the most important elements of the ecosystem of qualified trust services can be seen.

The Conformity Assessment Bodies audit the Trust Service Providers and issue the Conformity Assessment Report (CAR). TSPs send the CAR to the Supervisory Body of their country, which may request clarifications. Finally, this Supervisory Body determines the publication of the fundamental characteristics of each TSP's qualified trust services in the country's Trusted Service Status List (TSL).

Finally, in the "Dashboard," it is possible to access the "List of National Lists", a single international list that lists all the countries, all the providers in each country, and all the qualified trust services they provide.

The "Dashboard" also lists the entities that audit qualified signature creation devices, which are computer modules where the private key is kept securely (encrypted). Qualified Signature Creation Devices can be a chip card, a cryptographic token, a PCI card, or server with the so-called HSM (Hardware Security Module) configuration. These systems are audited under the "Common Criteria" standard.

3 The eIDAS 2 Regulation

The evaluation report on the former eIDAS Regulation showed that it was unable to respond to new market demands for Identity Management.

Insufficient electronic identification solutions are available in all Member States, and the eIDAS identity management system is not flexible enough to design various use cases. In addition, identity solutions that do not fall within the scope of the eIDAS Regulation, such as those offered by social media providers and financial institutions, raise privacy and data protection issues.

Since the entry into force of the e-identity section of the Regulation in September 2018, only 14 Member States have notified at least one e-identity system. As a result, only 59% of EU residents had access to reliable and secure cross-border e-identity systems. In addition, not all the technical nodes established to guarantee the connection with the interoperability framework contemplated in the eIDAS Regulation were operational, so cross-border functionality was not working. In this sense, the public services deployed at the national level did not contemplate the possibility that people from other countries could access them.

On the other hand, the framework provided for in the eIDAS Regulation did not cover the provision of electronic attributes, such as medical certificates or professional qualifications, which required specific regulations. In addition, there was no provision to control personal information transfer or exercise the right of cancellation.

While the eIDAS Regulation can be considered to have achieved quite satisfactory results in defining and establishing the value of qualified trust services and promoting their adoption, further steps are needed to achieve their full harmonisation and acceptance.

One barrier is that Public Administrations are not aware of all the identity management mechanisms in other countries, starting with how the identity number of citizens of each country and their check digits are encoded. In the case of the Spanish Public Administrations, public bodies only know how to recognise the Spanish DNI (nationals) number and the NIE (foreigners) number.

eIDAS 2 states that the future identity management system must be mandatory for member countries. Perhaps the greatest contribution of the eIDAS2 Regulation is that it creates an identity wallet inspired by the principles of "Self-Sovereign identity" that can be implemented with technologies other than Blockchain.

This wallet will be voluntary and free of charge for individuals. It will keep track of the information that is transferred to third parties (the "attribute attestations") so that at a future time the user may decide to withdraw the information that was transferred at an earlier time, which in practice implies a privacy management system aligned with the General Data Protection Regulation (GDPR) to exercise the right of "Cancellation" or "Erasure".

Qualified and unqualified attribute attestations are fact sheets generated by authentic sources of information, such as a company, a Civil Registry, a Business Registry, a university, etc., who submit data at the request of the citizen holding the EUDI Wallet. The citizen requests this data from the source (or a proxy attribute attestation provider) through the wallet because it is required by an entity that is requested to provide a service using the wallet, to which the entity indicates that to provide the service, it needs certain data, for example, if the citizen is going to enrol on a training course at a university that requires having passed a lower level in another university, or if a new electricity company is to be contracted that requires the CUPS (Universal Supply Point Code) data provided by the previous electricity company.

The fact that the wallet records the "attestations" and has a history of the transfer of information is already valuable. To be able to exercise the right of "Erasure" or "Cancellation" as well. In the end, the EUDI Wallet will be the repository of important electronic documents, similar to the folder in which important paper documents are kept at home. These functionalities of the EUDI Wallet could be considered evolutions of the existing payment wallets on the main mobile phone operating systems: iOS and Android.

A document called ARF (Architecture and Reference Framework) was published in the context of the legal discussion of the articulated text of the eIDAS2 Regulation.[3]

On 3 June 2021, together with the publication of the proposal to amend the eIDAS Regulation, the Commission adopted a Recommendation urging Member States to work on the development of a "Toolbox" including an architectural and reference technical framework, a set of common standards and technical specifications, and a set of common guidelines and best practices. The Recommendation specifies that these results will serve as a basis for the implementation of the European Digital Identity Framework Regulation once adopted, without the process of developing the toolbox interfering with or prejudging the legislative process.

The Toolbox complements the legislative proposal on a trusted and secure digital identity. It is a crucial first step towards creating a robust framework for digital identification and authentication based on common rules across the EU. It aims to ensure a high level of trust in digital transactions in Europe. Member States will continue to work closely with the Commission to update the toolbox continuously.

Based on the Recommendation, the eIDAS Expert Group was created, and it focused on creating the reference document. On 22 February 2022, the eIDAS expert group adopted an outline of a reference framework and architecture for a future European digital identity Wallet and decided to publish it to solicit stakeholder feedback. That document already contained:

- the objectives of the EUDI Wallet,
- the roles of ecosystem actors,
- the functional and non-functional requirements for the EUDI Wallet and
- potential building blocks.

On 10 February 2023, the European Commission published version 1.0 of the "European Union Digital Identity Wallet Architecture and Reference Framework"[4] a document that was delayed, as the expected publication date was October 2022. Other versions were published in the following months, culminating in the reference framework version 1.4, published in May 2024.[5]

The architecture model is extracted from this version and reflected in the following image (Fig. 2).

[3] European Digital Identity Architecture and Reference Framework – Outline. Available at: https://digital-strategy.ec.europa.eu/en/library/european-digital-identity-architecture-and-reference-framework-outline.

[4] Shaping Europe's digital future website, managed by the Directorate-General for Communications Networks, Content and Technology (European Commission). The European Digital Identity Wallet Architecture and Reference Framework. Available at: https://digital-strategy.ec.europa.eu/en/library/european-digital-identity-wallet-architecture-and-reference-framework Accessed 7 June 2024.

[5] European Commission (2024b) European Digital Identity Wallet Architecture and Reference Framework. Available at https://eu-digital-identity-wallet.github.io/eudi-doc-architecture-and-reference-framework/1.4.0/arf/. Accessed 7 June 2024.

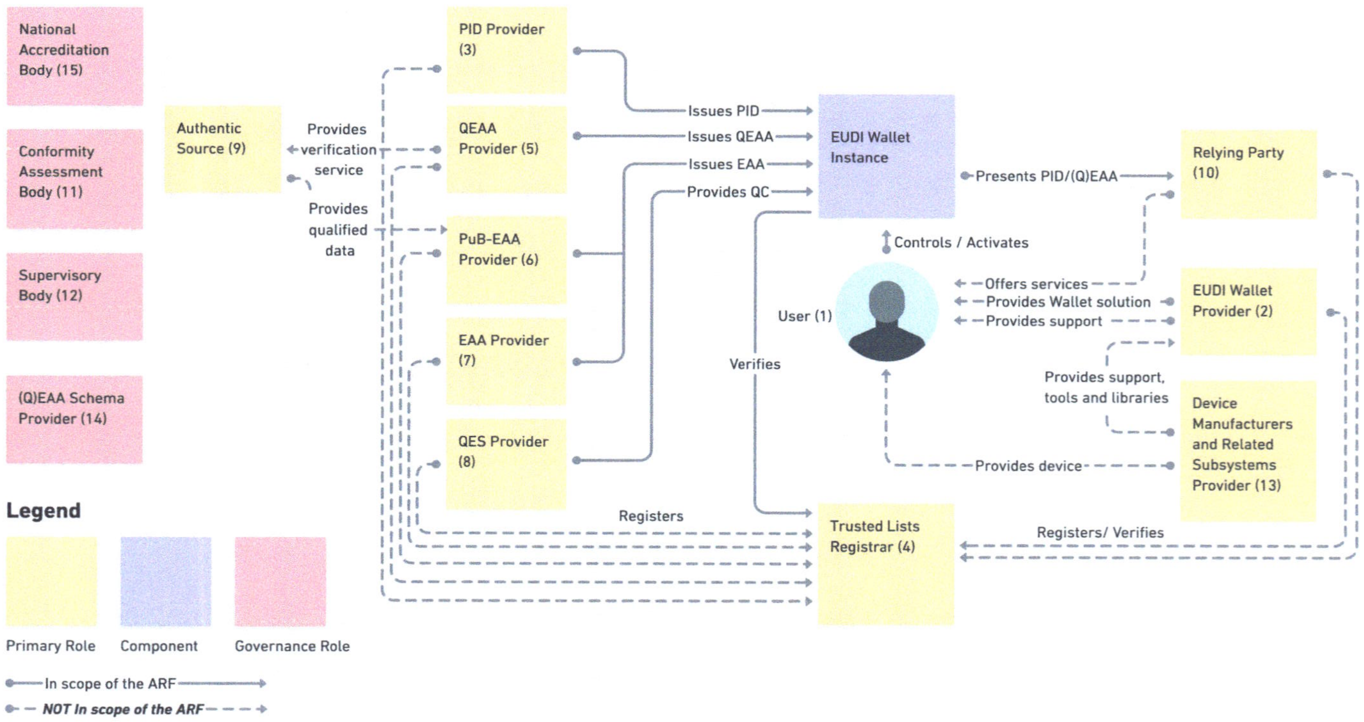

Fig. 2 EUDI Wallet architecture model (EUDI Wallet ARF, 2024)

Further developed by Member States in close cooperation with the Commission, this document can serve as the technical backbone of all future EUDI Wallets, ensuring their security, interoperability and ease of use. Member States, in cooperation with the Commission, intend to agree on the comprehensive toolbox needed to implement the European Digital Identity Framework by September 2024.

The EUDI Wallet will provide a secure and convenient way for European citizens and businesses to share the identity data needed to access digital services, such as airport check-in, renting a car, opening a bank account or logging into their accounts on large online platforms. With the click of a button on your phone, information stored in digital versions of your driver's license, professional or educational diplomas, and prescriptions can be securely shared.

Neither the scheme nor the requirements and specifications set out in the first version of the toolbox are binding until the legislative proposal on the EUDI Wallet has been adopted by the co-legislators. Only the European Union Digital Identity Framework Regulation was finally adopted, and the implementing and delegated acts adopted under that legal basis shall be mandatory. The first batch of 5 implementing acts was adopted on 21 November and 5 additional drafts of the second batch were published on 29 November. These implementing acts have a regulatory character superior to the ARF.

3.1 Tender for the Development of the Reference Source Code of the EUDI Wallet

On December 6, 2022, it was announced that the Swedish company Scytáles AB, together with Netcompany-Intrasoft, had been selected to develop the reference source code for the EUDI Wallet, with the award of a contract covering development, consulting, and support services. The Framework Contract[6] was the conclusion of a bidding process that began on June 3, 2022, and had a deadline for submitting proposals of July 22, 2022.

The tender has been one of the parallel activities undertaken by the European Commission. At the same time, progress was made in the definition of the EUDI Wallet Architecture (by the Toolbox Group of Experts) and in the collection and analysis of proposals for amendments to the articulated text of the Proposal for Regulation.

Developing the EUDI Wallet aims to lay the technical foundation for the secure European electronic identity system available to all EU citizens across the EU and all activities. This will include digital identification, electronic signatures and seals, and electronic testimonies of qualified and unqualified information attributes from reporting parties. It is intended for informed parties who will receive the information from the EUDI Wallet with the citizen's authorisation.

---

[6] EU tenders (2024) https://ted.europa.eu/udl?uri=TED:NOTICE:668669-2022:TEXT:EN:HTML&tabId=1 Accessed 10 June 2024.

Scytáles AB and Netcompany-Intrasoft, the consortium leader, have developed the EUDI Wallet Reference Implementation (https://github.com/eu-digital-identity-wallet/.github/blob/main/profile/reference-implementation.md). It will be offered to Member States and other interested parties to implement the requirements of the Regulation on a framework for European digital identity.

3.2 Large Pilot Projects

Before its implementation in the Member States, the EUDI Wallet was piloted in four large-scale pilot projects, starting on 1 April 2023 and lasting two years. The corresponding consortia are Potential, Nordic-Baltic ID (NOBID), Digital Credential for Europe (DC4EU) Consortium, and EUDI Wallet Consortium (EUWC). The tender began on February 22, 2022, and the proposals were accepted until August 17, 2022. The evaluation of proposals ended on December 16, 2022.

These projects aim to test Digital Identity Wallets in real-world scenarios spanning different sectors. More than 250 private companies and public authorities from 25 Member States, Norway, Iceland, and Ukraine participate.

Specifically, 11 use cases are studied:

1. Mobile Driver's License: Storage and presentation of the mobile driver's license in both online and physical interactions, e.g., a driver handing over their license on the roadside.
2. Access to public services: Secure access to digital public services, such as applying for a passport or driver's license, filing taxes, or accessing social security information.
3. SIM registration: Proof of identity for prepaid and postpaid SIM card contracts (registration and activation), reducing fraud and costs for mobile network operators.
4. Contract Signing: Creating qualified digital signatures to sign contracts online, eliminating the need for paper documents and handwritten signatures.
5. Electronic prescription: Pharmacies can Access prescription data to dispense pharmaceutical products.
6. Bank account opening: Verifying a user's identity when opening a bank account online eliminates the need for the user to provide their personal details repeatedly.
7. Payments: Verifying a user's identity when initiating an online payment.
8. Travel: Submission of travel document information (e.g. user's passport, visa and others), allowing quick and easy access when passing through the airport security area and customs.
9. Diplomas and training certificates: Proof of possession of educational credentials, such as diplomas, degrees, and certificates, making it easier to apply for employment or further study.
10. Access to Social Security benefits: An EUDI Wallet can securely access a user's Social Security information and benefits, such as retirement or disability

benefits. It can also facilitate freedom of movement by storing documents such as the European Health Insurance Card.

11. Support for developing a common EU toolbox: Provide feedback on the technical architecture, standards, and best practice guidelines to the EUDI Wallet developers and the Toolbox Expert Group.

Each pilot project will use components of the reference implementation developed by the European Commission and will contribute to improving its security, usability and interoperability.

3.3 Regulations: Trilogue Phase

After the March 16, 2023, vote, the Trilogues phase was entered, which was reached after taking some steps. The current rules on electronic identification and trust services for electronic transactions in the internal market (i.e. the eIDAS Regulation[7]) dating back to 2014, aim to make national electronic ID systems interoperable across Europe to facilitate access to online services. In the EU Digital Strategy 'Shaping Europe's Digital Future'[8] the Commission announced that it would revise the eIDAS Regulation to improve its effectiveness, extend its application to the private sector and promote it. Article 49 of the eIDAS Regulation already provided for this revision.

The Commission shall review the application of this Regulation and report to the European Parliament and the Council by 1 July 2020. The Commission shall particularly assess whether it is appropriate to amend the scope of this Regulation or its specific provisions, including Articles 6, 7(f), 34, 43, 44, and 45, considering the experience gained in applying this Regulation as well as technological, market, and legal developments.

The report referred to in the first subparagraph shall be accompanied, if necessary, by legislative proposals. The Commission shall also submit a report to the European Parliament and the Council every four years following the report referred to in the first subparagraph on progress towards achieving the objectives of this Regulation.

On 3 June 2021, the Commission published its proposal[9] for amendments to the eIDAS Regulation. With the proposal, the Commission hoped to meet the objectives

[7]European Parliament. Regulation (EU) No 910/2014 of the European Parliament and of the Council of 23 July 2014 on electronic identification and trust services for electronic transactions in the internal market and repealing Directive 1999/93/EC. ELI: http://data.europa.eu/eli/reg/2014/910/oj.

[8]European Commission (2024c) Setting up Europe's digital future. https://commission.europa.eu/strategy-and-policy/priorities-2019-2024/europe-fit-digital-age/shaping-europes-digital-future_es. Accessed 16 June 2024.

[9]European Commission (2021b) Proposal for a Regulation of the European Parliament and of the Council amending Regulation (EU) No 910/2014 as regards establishing a framework for a European Digital Identity https://eur-lex.europa.eu/legal-content/ES/TXT/HTML/?uri=CELEX:52021PC0281&from=EN

of its Digital Compass (Digital Compass 2030: Europe's Approach to the Digital Decade[10]), which says that by 2030, all key public services will be available online, all citizens will have access to their digital health records, and 80% of citizens should use a digital ID.

In addition, the Commission expects that the security and control offered by the updated European Digital Identity Framework will give all citizens the means to control who has access to their digital ID and what data exactly. National digital identity solutions would no longer be promoted, and a new approach to providing e-witness services of valid attributes at the European level would be created.

The dossier was assigned to the European Parliament's Committee on Industry, Research and Energy (ITRE).[11] The rapporteur was Romana Jerković (S&D, Croatia). It published its draft report on 31 May 2022, proposing several changes to the structure, cybersecurity and privacy of the EUDI Wallet. It also proposed a new chapter on governance to facilitate cross-border coordination and the establishment of a harmonised framework for digital identity.

Throughout the process, three reports were presented with proposed amendments to the text given by the committee[12] on 3 June 2021:

Report of 31.05.2022 – 2021/0136(COD) – (PE732.707v01-00) – With Amendments 1 to 139,[13]

- Report of 05.07.2022 – 2021/0136(COD) – (PE732.707v01-00) – With Amendments 140 to 368[14],
- Report of 31.05.2022 – 2021/0136(COD) – (PE732.707v01-00) – With amendments 369 to 653[15].

[10]European Commission (2024d) Shaping Europe's digital future website. Targeted consultation on the 2030 Digital Compass: The European way for the Digital Decade https://digital-strategy.ec.europa.eu/es/library/targeted-consultation-2030-digital-compass-european-way-digital-decade. Accessed 16 June 2024.

[11]Committee on Industry, Research and Energy (European Parliament) (2022) Report of 31.05.2022 – 2021/0136(COD) – (PE732.707v01-00).

[12]European Commission (2021a) Proposal for a Regulation of the European Parliament and of the Council amending Regulation (EU) No 910/2014 as regards establishing a framework for a European Digital Identity https://eur-lex.europa.eu/legal-content/ES/TXT/HTML/?uri=CELEX:52021PC0281&from=EN.

[13]Jerković, R (2022a) DRAFT REPORT on the proposal for a regulation of the European Parliament and of the Council amending Regulation (EU) No 910/2014 as regards establishing a framework for a European Digital Identity (COM(2021)0281 - C9-0200/2021 - 2021/0136 (COD)) https://www.europarl.europa.eu/doceo/document/ITRE-PR-732707_EN.html.

[14]Jerković, R (2022b) AMENDMENTS 140 – 368 Draft report Amending Regulation (EU) No 910/2014 as regards establishing a framework for a European Digital Identity Proposal for a regulation (COM(2021)0281 – C9-0200/2021 – 2021/0136(COD)) https://www.europarl.europa.eu/doceo/document/ITRE-AM-734285_EN.html.

[15]Jerković, R (2022c) AMENDMENTS 369 – 653 Draft report Amending Regulation (EU) No 910/2014 as regards establishing a framework for a European Digital Identity Proposal for a regulation (COM(2021)0281 – C9-0200/2021 – 2021/0136(COD)) https://www.europarl.europa.eu/doceo/document/ITRE-AM-734286_EN.html.

The ITRE Committee adopted its position[16] on 9 February 2023, which was confirmed in the plenary session of 16 March 2023 (with 418 votes in favour, 103 against and 24 abstentions).

The main changes proposed in the report were as follows:

- Structure of the EUDI Wallet: The report would expand the use of the wallet, allowing citizens to prove their identity and, share documents and verify the identities and documents of companies and other citizens. It also stresses that the wallet should remain voluntary and free for individuals and businesses, and users should be able to track all transactions executed through the wallet. Member States would have 18 months (the Commission initially proposed 12 months) after the entry into force of the eIDAS Regulation to issue the Wallet.
- Privacy and security: Both cybersecurity and wallet privacy are strengthened, with the wallet design explicitly calling for ensuring cybersecurity and privacy by design.
- 'One-time principle': citizens and businesses should not have to provide the same data to public authorities more than once.
- Cross-border user identification: Instead of "unique identification" (as proposed by the Commission), the report suggests the term "cross-border user identification" and proposes that Member States with at least one unique identifier issue unique and persistent identifiers for cross-border use only.
- Governance: A new chapter on governance is added to facilitate cross-border coordination and establish a harmonised digital identity framework. The report proposes to set up a European Digital Identity Framework Council (EDIFB), composed of the national competent authorities and the Commission.
- Qualified certificates for website authentication: The report adds that web browsers would not be prevented from taking necessary and proportionate measures to deal with justified risks of breaches of security, user privacy and loss of certificate integrity, thus easing the obligation to accept European QWAC certificates.

At the European Council, the Telecommunications and Information Society Group started examining the dossier in June 2021. On 6 December 2022, the Council adopted its Common Position[17] (general approach) on the dossier.[18] Member States made some changes to the operation of the Wallet to ensure that the person claiming an identity is its holder. It also ensured that the text was in line with other EU laws, such as cybersecurity legislation. According to the European Council's text, member

[16]Committee on Industry, Research and Energy (2023) DRAFT AGENDA Extraordinary meeting 2 Feb 2023. https://www.europarl.europa.eu/doceo/document/ITRE-OJ-2023-02-09-1_EN.html

[17]Council of the EU (2022) European digital identity (eID): Council makes headway towards EU digital wallet, a paradigm shift for digital identity in Europe. Available at https://www.consilium.europa.eu/en/press/press-releases/2022/12/06/european-digital-identity-eid-council-adopts-its-position-on-a-new-regulation-for-a-digital-wallet-at-eu-level/. Accessed 14 June 2024.

[18]Council of the EU (2021) Interinstitutional File: 2021/0136(COD) https://data.consilium.europa.eu/doc/document/ST-9471-2021-INIT/en/pdf.

states would have 24 months after the entry into force of the implementing acts to provide the wallet. Finally, the Council believes that the wallet should not cost anything for individuals, but businesses may incur costs for authentication.

The co-legislators started trilogue negotiations on the dossier on 21 March 2023 (with a basic text[19]), which concluded on 8 November 2023 during the Spanish presidency of the European Union.

The European Parliament's Committee on Industry, Research and Energy (ITRE) approved the text on December 7, 2023, and the Committee of Permanent Representatives of EU Member States (COREPER) on December 6, 2023.

The European Parliament plenary approved it on 29 February 2024 (335 votes in favour, 190 votes against and 31 abstentions).

On 26 March 2024, the Council of the European Union adopted the text amending the eIDAS Regulation, the penultimate step towards the publication of eIDAS2 in the Official Journal.

The Presidents of the European Parliament and the European Council signed the final text of the eIDAS 2 Regulation (Regulation (EU) 2024/1183) on 11 April 2024, which was published in the Official Journal of the European Union on 30 April 2024 (See Table 1).[20]

3.4 Relevant Standards Involved

Table 1 Relevant standards related to EUDI Wallet implementation, components and interfaces

Item Reference	Standard name/details
[2015/1505]	COMMISSION IMPLEMENTING DECISION (EU) 2015/1505 of 8 September 2015 laying down technical specifications and formats relating to trusted lists pursuant to Article 22(5) of Regulation (EU) No 910/2014 of the European Parliament and of the Council on electronic identification and trust services for electronic transactions in the internal market.
[eIDAS 2.0]	Regulation (EU) 2024/1183 of the European Parliament and of the Council of 11 April 2024 amending Regulation (EU) No 910/2014 as regards establishing the European Digital Identity Framework
[ISO/IEC 18013-5]	ISO/IEC 18013-5, Personal identification --- ISO-compliant driving licence - Part 5: Mobile driving licence (mDL) application, First edition, 2021-09.

(continued)

[19]European Parliament (2023) REPORT on the proposal for a regulation of the European Parliament and of the Council amending Regulation (EU) No 910/2014 as regards establishing a framework for a European Digital Identity. https://www.europarl.europa.eu/doceo/document/A-9-2023-0038_EN.html.

[20]European Parliament. Regulation (EU) 2024/1183 of the European Parliament and of the Council of 11 April 2024 amending Regulation (EU) No 910/2014 as regards establishing the European Digital Identity Framework. ELI: http://data.europa.eu/eli/reg/2024/1183/oj.

Table 1 (continued)

Item Reference	Standard name/details
[ISO/IEC 18013-7]	ISO/IEC CD TS 18013-7: Personal identification ISO-compliant driving licence - Part 7: Mobile driving licence (mDL) add-on functions
[ISO/IEC 23220-1]	ISO/IEC 23220-1:2023: Cards and security devices for personal identification - Building blocks for identity management via mobile devices, Part 1: Generic system architectures of mobile eID systems
[ISO/IEC TS 23220-3]	ISO/IEC CD TS 23220-3: Cards and security devices for personal identification - Building blocks for identity management via mobile devices, Part 3: Protocols and services for issuing phase
[ISO/IEC TS 23220-4]	ISO/IEC TS 23220-4: Cards and security devices for personal identification - Building blocks for identity management via mobile devices - Part 4: Protocols and services for the operational phase. Retrievable from: https://www.iso.org/standard/79126.html
[ISO 3166-1]	ISO 3166-1: Codes for the representation of names of countries and their subdivisions -- Part 1: Country codes: alpha-2 country
[ISO 3166-2]	ISO 3166-2:2020: Codes for the representation of names of countries and their subdivisions --- Part 2: Country subdivision code
[ISO/IEC 24760-1]	ISO/IEC 24760-1:2019: IT Security and Privacy - A framework for identity management - Part 1: Terminology and concepts
[ETSI TS 119 612]	Electronic Signatures and Infrastructures (ESI); Trusted Lists
[ETSI EN 319 411-1]	ETSI EN 319 411-1 V1.3.1 (2021-05): Electronic Signatures and Infrastructures (ESI); Policy and security requirements for Trust Service Providers issuing certificates; Part 1: General requirements
[ETSI EN 319 411-2]	ETSI EN 319 411-2 V2.3.3 (2021-08): Electronic Signatures and Infrastructures (ESI); Policy and security requirements for Trust Service Providers issuing certificates; Part 2: Requirements for trust service providers issuing EU qualified certificates
[ETSI TS 119 431-1]	ETSI TS 119 431-1 - Electronic Signatures and Infrastructures (ESI); Policy and security requirements for trust service providers; Part 1: TSP service components operating a remote QSCD / SCDev.
[ETSI TS 119 431-2]	ETSI TS 119 431-2 - Electronic Signatures and Infrastructures (ESI); Policy and security requirements for trust service providers; Part 2: TSP service components supporting AdES digital signature creation
[ETSI TS 119 432]	ETSI TS 119 432 - Electronic Signatures and Infrastructures (ESI); Protocols for remote digital signature creation
[ETSI EN 319 132-1]	ETSI EN 319 132-1 - Electronic Signatures and Infrastructures (ESI); XAdES digital signatures; Part 1: Building blocks and XAdES baseline signatures (XAdES)
[ETSI TS 119 182-1]	ETSI TS 119 182-1 - Electronic Signatures and Infrastructures (ESI); JAdES digital signatures; Part 1: Building blocks and JAdES baseline signatures
[ETSI EN 319 122-1]	ETSI EN 319 122-1 - Electronic Signatures and Infrastructures (ESI); CAdES digital signatures; Part 1: Building blocks and CAdES baseline signatures
[ETSI EN 319 162-1]	ETSI EN 319 162-1 - Electronic Signatures and Infrastructures (ESI); Associated Signature Containers (ASiC); Part 1: Building blocks and ASiC baseline containers

(continued)

Table 1 (continued)

Item Reference	Standard name/details
[ETSI EN 319 142]	ETSI EN 319 142 - Electronic Signatures and Infrastructures (ESI); PAdES digital signatures; Part 1: Building blocks and PAdES baseline signatures
[CEN EN 419 241-1]	CEN EN 419 241-1 -- Trustworthy Systems Supporting Server Signing - Part 1: General System Security Requirements
[SOG-IS]	Agreed Cryptographic Mechanisms v1.2, https://www.sogis.eu/documents/cc/crypto/SOGIS-Agreed-Cryptographic-Mechanisms-1.2.pdf
[SD-JWT]	Selective Disclosure for JWTs (SD-JWT). Retrievable from: https://datatracker.ietf.org/doc/draft-ietf-oauth-selective-disclosure-jwt/
[SD-JWT VC]	SD-JWT-based Verifiable Credentials (SD-JWT VC). Retrievable from: https://datatracker.ietf.org/doc/draft-ietf-oauth-sd-jwt-vc/
[RFC 2119]	RFC 2119 - Keywords for use in RFCs to Indicate Requirement Levels. S. Bradner, March 1997.
[RFC 3339]	RFC 3339 - Date and Time on the Internet: Timestamps, G. Klyne et al., July 2002
[RFC 4122]	RFC 4122 - A Universally Unique Identifier (UUID) URN Namespace, P. Leach et al., July 2005
[RFC 5280]	RFC 5280 - Internet X.509 Public Key Infrastructure Certificate and Certificate Revocation List (CRL) Profile, D. Kooper et al., May 2008
[RFC 3647]	RFC 3647 - Internet X.509 Public Key Infrastructure Certificate Policy and Certification Practices Framework, S. Chokhani et al., November 2003
[RFC 7519]	RFC 7519 - JSON Web Token (JWT): M. Jones, Microsoft; J. Bradley, Ping Identity; N. Sakimura, NRI. May 2015
[RFC 8259]	RFC 8259 - The JavaScript Object Notation (JSON) Data Interchange Format, T. Bray, Ed., December 2017
[RFC 8392]	RFC 8392 - CBOR Web Token (CWT): M. Jones, Microsoft; E. Wahlstroem, S. Erdtman, Spotify AB; H. Tschofenig, ARM Ltd.; May 2018
[RFC 8610]	RFC 8610 - Concise Data Definition Language (CDDL): A Notational Convention to Express Concise Binary Object Representation (CBOR) and JSON Data Structures, H. Birkholz et al., June 2019
[RFC 8943]	RFC 8943 - Concise Binary Object Representation (CBOR) Tags for Date, M. Jones et al., November 2020
[RFC 8949]	RFC 8949 - Concise Binary Object Representation (CBOR), C. Bormann et al., December 2020
[RFC 9396]	RFC 9396 - OAuth 2.0 Rich Authorization Requests, T. Lodderstedt, yes.com; J. Richer, Bespoke Engineering; B. Campbell, Ping Identity. May 2023.
[W3C VCDM v1.1]	Sporny, M., Longley, D. and D. Chadwick, "Verifiable Credentials Data Model 1.1", W3C Recommendation, 03 March 2022
[W3C VCDM v2.0]	Sporny, M. *et al,* "Verifiable Credentials Data Model v2.0", W3C Candidate Recommendations Draft, 16 April 2024
[OpenID4VCI]	Lodderstedt, T. et al., "OpenID for Verifiable Credential Issuance", OpenID Foundation. Available: https://openid.net/specs/openid-4-verifiable-credential-issuance-1_0.html
[OpenID4VP]	TBD, "OpenID Connect for Verifiable Presentations", OpenID Foundation. Available: https://openid.net/specs/openid-4-verifiable-presentations-1_0.html

(continued)

Table 1 (continued)

Item Reference	Standard name/details
[HAIP]	OpenID4VC High Assurance Interoperability Profile with SD-JWT VC -- draft 00, 9 January 2024 [6]
[RPS]	Communication from the Commission to the European Parliament, the Council, the European Economic and Social Committee and the Committee of the Regions on a Retail Payments Strategy for the EU (COM/2020/592 final)
[X.509]	ITU-T X.509 (2019) Cor. 2 (10/2023)
[CSC]	Cloud Signature Consortium (CSC) specification (API v2.0): This specification is in the ETSI standard where the SCA is "defined," namely ETSI TS 119 432.

References

Council of the EU (2021) Interinstitutional File: 2021/0136(COD) https://data.consilium.europa.eu/doc/document/ST-9471-2021-INIT/en/pdf

Council of the EU (2022) European digital identity (eID): Council makes headway towards EU digital wallet, a paradigm shift for digital identity in Europe. Available at https://www.consilium.europa.eu/en/press/press-releases/2022/12/06/european-digital-identity-eid-council-adopts-its-position-on-a-new-regulation-for-a-digital-wallet-at-eu-level/. Accessed 14 June 2024

Committee on Industry, Research and Energy (2023) DRAFT AGENDA Extraordinary meeting 2 Feb 2023. https://www.europarl.europa.eu/doceo/document/ITRE-OJ-2023-02-09-1_EN.html

EU tenders (2024). https://ted.europa.eu/udl?uri=TED:NOTICE:668669-2022:TEXT:EN:HTML&tabId=1 Accessed 10 June 2024

European Commission (2015) Commission Implementing Regulation (EU) 2015/1502 of 8 September 2015 on setting out minimum technical specifications and procedures for assurance levels for electronic identification means pursuant to Article 8(3) of Regulation (EU) No 910/2014 of the European Parliament and the Council on electronic identification and trust services for electronic transactions in the internal market. ELI: http://data.europa.eu/eli/reg_impl/2015/1502/oj

European Commission (2021a) Report from the Commission to the European Parliament and the Council on the evaluation of Regulation (EU) No 910/2014 on electronic identification and trust services for electronic transactions in the internal market (eIDAS). Brussels

European Commission (2021b) Proposal for a Regulation of the European Parliament and of the Council amending Regulation (EU) No 910/2014 as regards establishing a framework for a European Digital Identity https://eur-lex.europa.eu/legal-content/ES/TXT/HTML/?uri=CELEX:52021PC0281&from=EN

European Commission (2024a) Commission Implementing Decision (EU) 2024/1432 of 21 May 2024 setting up the European Digital Infrastructure Consortium for European Blockchain Partnership and European Blockchain Service Infrastructure (EUROPEUM-EDIC) ELI: http://data.europa.eu/eli/dec_impl/2024/1432/oj

European Commission (2024b) European Digital Identity Wallet Architecture and Reference Framework. Available at https://eu-digital-identity-wallet.github.io/eudi-doc-architecture-and-reference-framework/1.4.0/arf/. Accessed 7 June 2024

European Commission (2024c) Shaping Europe's digital future website. https://commission.europa.eu/strategy-and-policy/priorities-2019-2024/europe-fit-digital-age/shaping-europes-digital-future_es. Accessed 16 June 2024

European Commission (2024d) Shaping Europe's digital future website. Targeted consultation on the 2030 Digital Compass: The European way for the Digital Decade https://digital-strategy.ec.europa.eu/es/library/targeted-consultation-2030-digital-compass-european-way-digital-decade. Accessed 16 June 2024

European Commission (2024e) Shaping Europe's digital future website, managed by the Directorate-General for Communications Networks, Content and Technology. The European Digital Identity Wallet Architecture and Reference Framework. Available at: https://digital-strategy.ec.europa.eu/en/library/european-digital-identity-wallet-architecture-and-reference-framework. Accessed 7 June 2024

European Parliament. Regulation (EU) No 1025/2012 of the European Parliament and of the Council of 25 October 2012 on European standardisation, amending Council Directives 89/686/EEC and 93/15/EEC and Directives 94/9/EC, 94/25/EC, 95/16/EC, 97/23/EC, 98/34/EC, 2004/22/EC, 2007/23/EC, 2009/23/EC and 2009/105/EC of the European Parliament and of the Council and repealing Council Decision 87/95/EEC and Decision No 1673/2006/EC of the European Parliament and of the Council. ELI: http://data.europa.eu/eli/reg/2012/1025/oj

European Parliament. Regulation (EU) No 910/2014 of the European Parliament and of the Council of 23 July 2014 on electronic identification and trust services for electronic transactions in the internal market and repealing Directive 1999/93/EC. ELI: http://data.europa.eu/eli/reg/2014/910/oj

European Parliament. Regulation (EU) 2024/1183 of the European Parliament and of the Council of 11 April 2024 amending Regulation (EU) No 910/2014 regarding establishing the European Digital Identity Framework. ELI: http://data.europa.eu/eli/reg/2024/1183/oj

European Parliament (2023) REPORT on the proposal for a regulation of the European Parliament and of the Council amending Regulation (EU) No 910/2014 regarding establishing a framework for a European Digital Identity. https://www.europarl.europa.eu/doceo/document/A-9-2023-0038_EN.html

Jerković R (2022a) Draft Report on the proposal for a regulation of the European Parliament and of the Council amending Regulation (EU) No 910/2014 as regards establishing a framework for a European Digital Identity (COM(2021)0281 - C9-0200/2021 - 2021/0136(COD)) https://www.europarl.europa.eu/doceo/document/ITRE-PR-732707_EN.html

Jerković R (2022b) Amendments 140 – 368 Draft report Amending Regulation (EU) No 910/2014 as regards establishing a framework for a European Digital Identity Proposal for a regulation (COM(2021)0281 – C9-0200/2021 – 2021/0136(COD)) https://www.europarl.europa.eu/doceo/document/ITRE-AM-734285_EN.html

Jerković R (2022c) Amendments 369 – 653 Draft report Amending Regulation (EU) No 910/2014 as regards establishing a framework for a European Digital Identity Proposal for a regulation (COM(2021)0281 – C9-0200/2021 – 2021/0136(COD)) https://www.europarl.europa.eu/doceo/document/ITRE-AM-734286_EN.html

World Wide Web Consortium (W3C) (2022) Decentralized Identifiers (DIDs) v1.0 https://www.w3.org/TR/did-core/. Accessed 15 June 2024

Digital Identity in a European User-Centric Ecosystem and Its Similarities with the Digital Euro Proposal

Ainhoa Inza Blasco

Abstract Digital identity systems have evolved from institutional databases from the sixties through the advent of the Internet and public key infrastructure, social networks, national ID, blockchain implementations and the EUDI Wallet. To ensure the success of implementing and adopting any digital identity system, the critical factor is the digital ecosystem the user can interact with, fostering not only the interactions of the netizens with public services but also between netizens and private entities or even between netizens online. Without habitual use and ease of adoption, resistance to change and increased friction could lead to abandoning the digital identity solution. As the European Digital Identity Wallet is defined in the Regulation and standards are published to complement the requirements laid out, other proposals, like the Digital Euro initiative, share similar broad requirements on usage and acceptance. The results and experience with the EUDI Wallet will be a learning opportunity to ensure the preferred outcome when implementing similar initiatives.

This paper expands and updates the text of a lecture delivered at the III International Congress entitled "Present and future of crypto-assets regulation in the European Union," held at the University of Alicante (Spain) on December 13, 14, and 15, 2023. This work is funded within the framework of: Proyecto CIPROM/2022/26 "Presente y futuro de la regulación de los Criptoactivos en la UE [Legalcripto]". Proyecto Prometeo CIPROM/2022/26, grupos de investigación de excelencia, de la Generalitat Valenciana (P.I. Carmen Pastor).

A. I. Blasco (✉)
Trust Conformity Assessment Body (TCAB), Madrid, Spain
e-mail: ainza@tcab.eu

C. Pastor Sempere (ed.), *Governance and Control of Data and Digital Economy in the European Single Market*, Law, Governance and Technology Series 71,
https://doi.org/10.1007/978-3-031-74889-9_20

1 Digital Identity

1.1 Origins

Historically, identity has been defined as a set of qualities, beliefs, personality traits, appearance, and expressions characterising a person.[1] From a philosophical point of view, identity is considered an emergent characteristic developed during childhood as the self-concept is comprehended.[2]

From the sociological viewpoint, identity is developed through roles. People build their identity by taking different roles within a social group or construct.

From the legal viewpoint, where the focus is on defining an entity with public function in a normative system, there is some consensus that a person is, as such, recognised by a preexisting quality that is natural and inherent to every human being. Over the philosophical concepts of freedom, free will and rationality (developed by Rousseau, Hegel and Windt), the person is defined in the Universal Declaration of Human Rights[3], published in 1948, and recognised by their inherent dignity and equal and inalienable rights.

It is within this declaration that several critical aspects of the legal identity are recognised:

> Article 6
>
> Everyone has the right to recognition everywhere as a person before the law.
>
> [...]
>
> Article 15
>
> Everyone has the right to a nationality.
>
> [...]
>
> Article 18
>
> Everyone has the right to freedom of thought, conscience, and religion; this right includes freedom to change one's religion or belief and freedom, either alone or in community with others and in public or private, to manifest one's religion or belief in teaching, practice, worship, and observance.
>
> [...]
>
> Article 22
>
> Everyone, as a member of society, has the right to social security and is entitled to realisation, through national effort and international cooperation and by the organisation and resources of each State, of the economic, social and cultural rights indispensable for his dignity and the free development of his personality.

---

[1] Schwartz et al. (2011).

[2] Herman (2011), pp. 779–781.

[3] United Nations (1948) Universal Declaration of Human Rights, proclaimed by the United Nations General Assembly in Paris on 10 December 1948 (General Assembly resolution 217 A).

From there, it could be interpreted that the identity is created at birth, originated initially from the parents' identity, and populated by attributes (location of birth, nationality, etc.) available at that time. From then on, it evolves with the person as they interact with society and develop their self-concept.

Therefore, identity proofing[4] was based on face-to-face communication, physical documentation, and verification processes.

In Spain, the Spanish Constitution introduced the definition of a person as a reference to said Universal Declaration:

> Article 10
>
> 1. The dignity of the person, the inviolable rights inherent to him, the free development of personality, respect for the law and the rights of others are the foundation of political order and social peace.
> 2. The rules relating to fundamental rights and freedoms that the Constitution recognises will be interpreted following the Universal Declaration of Human Rights and the international treaties and agreements on the same matters ratified by Spain.

The identification documents were regulated through different acts, and the one currently defining the documents for identification and the factual data is Royal Decree 1553/2005[5] of December 23, which governs the issuance of the national identity document and its electronic signature certificates. In this Royal Decree, it is stated that:

> Organic Law 1/1992, of February 21, on the Protection of Citizen Security, in its article 9, recognises the right of all Spaniards to be issued the National Identity Document, to which sufficient value is attributed to accredit, by itself, the identity of people and grants them the protection that the legal system recognises public and official documents.

Organic Law 4/2015 later superseded this,[6] even though the provision that the National Identity Document had sufficient value to accredit a person's identity was maintained in the superseding regulation.

Any identifiers (traditionally names and factual data originated or allocated at birth) aim to prove a particular individual's uniqueness, ensure accountability, establish some trust between individuals and institutions, and provide reference points for the framework of laws and other social contracts.

Long before computers could effectively communicate with one another, massive databases existed intended to preserve institutional reality. Governments, corporations, and banks owned and operated these databases to better manage and access accumulated data on citizens, companies, employers, employees, customers, and other relevant stakeholders.

---

[4] Identity proofing is the process of proving someone is who they claim to be.

[5] Spanish Royal Decree 1553/2005 of December 23, which regulates the issuance of the national identity document and its electronic signature certificates.

[6] Spanish Organic Law 4/2015, of March 30, on the protection of citizen security.

As technology populated our environment, identity use and development required different interpretations and contexts, and identity protection practices and controls developed through rights and wrongs over time.

The Internet was created without a standard for identifying its users. Online services then began to develop their methods of identifying people and collecting identifying information.

The first means of online identification was a unique username and associated password, introduced by computer scientist Fernando Corbat, who worked at the Massachusetts Institute of Technology (MIT) in the 1960s. The main objective was to help keep individual files secure. Microsoft later popularised this concept to access individual accounts on a shared computer, which later evolved into Microsoft Network (MSN) to access various online services via one login.

In the early days of the Web, described as the Internet of Ideas, in which people were organised in communities worldwide, digital identities were designed ad hoc, focused more on functionality than any other concern.

Cybercommunities have allowed individuals to engage with different groups without a solid structure or institutionalised hierarchy. Every one of these public spheres distributes its roles according to spontaneous negotiation, sometimes performed publicly, rewarding connectivity, reciprocity, and reputation within the specific sphere (Susca 2016).[7]

It is interesting to note that, according to Susca (2016), "the new electronic medium supports a double metamorphosis of the user, dressing and reconfiguring their body, as well as projecting the user to the outside, increasing their identity [...]". This is increasingly relevant as the new user-centric technologies Vossaert et al. (2010) promote the development of culture and connective relationships, easing the creation of the digital persona instead of the previous mass individual belonging to one (or more) cybercommunities.

One of the most accepted definitions of digital identity is the online persona of a subject who can represent themselves online in many ways, Breckenridge (2018). A digital identity is usually needed when accessing a resource online, which is generally considered a service.

Within the service-oriented economy developed on the Internet, the transactions are mainly network-based and automated. As such, they are fundamentally different from the transactions in the physical realm.[8] One of the main differences is the difficulty in maintaining anonymity, as even the slightest interaction with the service online generates potentially identifying information usually transferred digitally across the network.

In this context, identities are data collections about a subject. These data points can represent identifying factual information, attributes, preferences, or traits, even though they are typically grouped as attributes.

---

[7] Susca (2016).

[8] Windley (2005).

This article defines digital identity as *the unique representation of a subject engaged in an online transaction.*[9] A digital identity is always unique in the context of a digital service, but the subject does not necessarily need to be identified uniquely in all contexts. In other words, accessing a digital service may not mean the subject's real identity is known.

When more robust solutions were needed to protect the communication between computers, US researchers Whitfield Diffie and Martin Hellman found a key agreement algorithm that, using asymmetrical cryptography, enabled the unique identification of computers (not yet users) on the Internet.

Trust evolved through parties performing identity proofing and verifying claimed identities, using another application of asymmetrical cryptography and reputation mechanisms within the technical communities to give "trust" to the verified identities. As the communities started to grow, the model was formalised using Certificate Authorities, subject to strict de-facto regulations related to identity verification.

However, even though public key cryptography (asymmetrical) has been at the centre of digital identity systems, their architecture, dependent on certificates and cryptographic devices, is not user-friendly, and their usability interfaces were not a priority until recently.

With the emergence of social networks, digital identity systems based on the identity claimed in the network (using how the subject presented themselves online as a verified persona) were born.

However, privacy concerns started to appear as social network use increased and personal identifying information was transferred to the private entity providing the social network platform.

Social networks are, at last, massive, centrally controlled databases that house and run algorithms over data provided by their users. As delegated login is provided to access other services and resources within the digital ecosystem, interaction, preferences, and other personal data are transferred to the platform's private corporation.

Its user-friendliness and convenience (favouring usability over security) have allowed these platforms to become the most widely used digital identity models.

Nevertheless, this digital identity model does not necessarily have a high level of assurance, and potential attackers impersonating a natural person should not be permitted access to sensitive personal information and resources.

1.2 Digital Identity Authentication

Authentication is the "provision of assurance that a claimed characteristic of an entity is correct".[10] Due to the high impact a successful impersonation can have, the

[9]NIST Special Publication 800-63 Revision 3. Digital Identity Guidelines. 2020.

[10]ISO. ISO/IEC 27000:2018 Information technology — Security techniques — Information security management systems — Overview and vocabulary.

processes related to identity proofing are carefully designed, especially for remote use via a digital service.

Remote identity proofing is crucial in creating trust in a digital environment. The collection and validation of evidence provided by the applicant to complete the verification of their identity could be vulnerable to attacks, and due to the improvement of the attackers' technology and resources, countermeasures must be implemented and improved continuously.

Multiple standards and guidelines relate to identity proofing. In Europe, the recommendations and guidelines published by European Network and Information Security Agency (ENISA) (2022)[11] and the development of standards from ETSI is worth noting.

Authentication typically occurs using one or more authentication factors, such as:

- Knowledge factors: something you know, such as a password or passphrase.
- Possession factors: something you have, such as a token device or smart card.
- Inherence factors: something you are, such as biometric data.
- Location factors: somewhere you are, such as a geolocation.
- Behaviour factors: based on actions undertaken by the user.

Specifying authentication factors will be fundamental when designing a digital identity system, as there are hardware and operational restrictions to consider.

When a subject attempts to access a resource, they should have sole control over one or more valid authenticators associated with that subject's digital identity. For services in which return visits are applicable, successful authentication over time provides reasonable assurance over the validity of their digital identity.

Digital identity presents a technical challenge because identity proofing often involves an open network, and identity authentication is always over an open network.

The STORK[12] framework develops the Quality of Authentication Assurance (QAA) model European Network and Information Security Agency (ENISA) (2011), which describes four levels of assurance mapped to the identity proofing process.

- Level 1: None or minimum assurance. None or minimum trust. The identity credentials are accepted with no verification or identity proofing.
- Level 2: Low level of assurance, which provides a limited degree of confidence in a person's claimed or asserted identity. There is some validation that the claimed identity corresponds to a natural person, and the identification tokens are delivered with some guarantee.
- Level 3: Substantial level of assurance, which provides a substantial degree of confidence in a person's claimed or asserted identity. There is a degree of certainty that the claimed identity corresponds to the natural person, and the electronic credentials are robust.

[11] Remote ID Proofing (2021) and Remote Identity Proofing - Attacks & Countermeasures (2022).

[12] The STORK framework was also outlined in accordance with ISO/IEC 29115:2013.

– Level 4: High level of assurance provides a higher degree of confidence in a person's claimed or asserted identity than electronic identification means with a substantial assurance level. Certainly, the claimed identity corresponds to the natural person, usually with face-to-face identity proofing, and the electronic credentials are delivered with cryptographic hardware.

The principle used to assign a specific level of assurance to an identification mechanism is that factors related to the enrolment, credentials delivery, and electronic authentication process must be considered at a global level.

Other standards, such as NIST-800-63-3,[13] describe similar approaches based on risk assessment of the identity application.

Biometric data is increasingly used as the primary authentication factor, using digital abstractions of physiological and behavioural traits to identify individuals. It is convenient and easy to use when the hardware supports the functionality.

However, caution should be applied when using biometry, as it is not easily changed (sometimes impossible). If a system collecting biometric information does not properly collect and store it and is then breached, it could compromise the consent and privacy of any online transaction performed using the biometric data during the lifetime of its users. Multiple standards and guidelines centre around the secure implementation of biometry-based authentication to avoid that scenario.

2 European Regulation

2.1 Regulation (EU) NO 910/2014: eIDAS

When Regulation (EU) No 910/2014 was published, it was evident in the introductory paragraphs that it was a regulation aimed to promote the development of electronic identification means, but without interfering with the digital identity of the citizens of the different state members:

> (12) One of the objectives of this Regulation is to remove existing barriers to the cross-border use of electronic identification means used in the Member States to authenticate for at least public services. This Regulation does not aim to intervene in electronic identity management systems and related infrastructures established in Member States. It seeks to ensure that secure electronic identification and authentication are possible for access to cross-border online services offered by Member States.

On the one hand, the Regulation aim was to promote the development of electronic identification schemes and digital identity within the Member State through Articles 7 to 9:

> Article 7
>
> Eligibility for notification of electronic identification schemes

[13] NIST Special Publication 800-63 Revision 3. Digital Identity Guidelines. 2020.

> An electronic identification scheme shall be eligible for notification pursuant to Article 9(1), provided that all of the following conditions are met:
>
> [...]
>
> (d) the notifying Member State ensures that the person identification data uniquely representing the person in question is attributed in accordance with the technical specifications, standards and procedures for the relevant assurance level set out in the implementing act referred to in Article 8(3), to the natural or legal person referred to in point 1 of Article 3 at the time the electronic identification means under that scheme is issued;

On the other hand, the Regulation also aimed to foster the growth of the ecosystem through the private sector by providing trust services (which included identity proofing European Network and Information Security Agency (ENISA) (2021) for accessing such services), promoting user digitisation, and facilitating the adoption of digital identity systems by the Member States.

The increasing digitisation of society is accompanied by the digitisation of public administration, which is capable of collecting data directly, processing it, and offering new uses from here on. This double transformation must be accompanied by regulators facilitating transactions and improving general management.

In that sense, the State is considered more of a platform that guarantees the relationships between private individuals and entities, favouring a fluid advancement of society (Sadin 2018).

However, although some Member State developed and notified electronic identification means following the Implementing Regulation (UE) 1502/2015,[14] not all of them did. Their interoperability was also limited, as the eIDAS nodes (a mechanism to interoperate the electronic identification schemes that were also supposed to promote access to public services to citizens in another Member State) had a limited implementation and provided limited or no access to other sector stakeholders.

Therefore, the electronic identification ecosystem relied on private identity providers to cover the gap, as a secure and interoperable digital identity was not available for use, ensuring cross-border and cross-sector interoperability.[15]

2.2 *Regulation (UE) 1183/2024: eIDAS 2*

Ten years after the publication of the eIDAS Regulation, and due to the evolution of the digital identity providers being private foreign companies (covering de facto all

[14]The Implementing Regulation (UE) 1502/2015 mapped and laid out the authentication levels of assurance for the electronic identification systems to be implemented within the European Member States and later notified to interoperate. This Implementing Regulation outlined the same authentication and identity-proofing reliability levels as stated in the STORK framework.

[15]European Commission. Report from the Commission to the European Parliament and the Council on the evaluation of Regulation (EU) No 910/2014 on electronic identification and trust services for electronic transactions in the internal market (eIDAS. 2021). Brussels.

possible use cases but access to public services), the European Parliament was confronted with the emergent need to develop a genuinely interoperable digital identity solution.

Each Member State must develop the implementation to ensure the sovereignty of that digital identity solution in each Member State. Still, the new Regulation is much stricter regarding the interoperability and digitisation of public services. It reflects a holistic approach to digital identity, understanding that identity is formed in context. To accomplish the goal of adoption and usage, a focus on fostering the ecosystem is needed.

Learning from past experiences with digital identity implementations, the Regulation considers the four critical attributes of a good digital identity solution.[16]:

- Verified and authenticated to a high degree of assurance, meeting government and private-sector institutions' initial registration and subsequent acceptance standards.
- Unique: With a unique digital ID, an individual has only one identity within a system, and every system identity corresponds to only one individual. However, this does not mean users must present themselves uniquely in all contexts.
- Established with individual consent: individuals knowingly register for and use the digital ID with knowledge of what personal data will be captured and how it will be used.
- Protects user privacy and ensures control over personal data: built-in safeguards to ensure privacy and security while giving users access to and control over their data, with transparency into who has accessed it.

2.2.1 European Digital Identity Wallet (EUDI Wallet)

The EUDI Wallet, as defined in Regulation (UE) 1183/2024, enables user authentication and provides specific user attributes during an online transaction.

Article 5a of the Regulation defines this means of electronic identification, which focuses on digital identity for accessing public and private services.

To foster trust within the ecosystem, several provisions have been included in Article 5a, paragraphs 2, 3, 6, and 8 defining:

- Governance and supervision by Member States
- Transparency on components installed in users' devices
- Transparency on transactions and identification data,
- Guarantee of sole control of digital identity attributes.
- Disclosure of security breaches.
- Free-of-charge verification to ensure the authenticity and validity of the EUDI Wallet implemented and the authenticity and validity of the identity of registered relying parties.

[16]McKinsey Global Institute (2019) Digital identification. A key to inclusive growth. Brussels.

However, Article 5a, paragraph 3 challenges the transparency goal on components by stating the possibility of components undisclosed to the user. If not handled carefully, any undisclosed characteristic and component could undermine the expected acceptance, as privacy in online transactions is paramount, and there are already cases of government mass surveillance (Snowden, 2013[17]) using the digital environment.

The main characteristics expected of the interface between the EUDI Wallet and its user are defined in Article 5a par 4, 10, 13 and 15:

- Free of charge to natural persons
- Usability
- Information control

  Accountability
  Transactional log
  Storage and selective presentation
  Data deletion request
  GDPR non-compliance reporting
  Suspicious activity reporting
  Data portability
  Data requests

- Secure-by-design
- Verification of the EUDI Wallet (display an EUDI Wallet Trust Mark)
- Pseudonym use
- Qualified electronic signature
- Interoperability between verified Wallets
- Technical request support and technical problems reporting.
- Voluntary issuance and use.

The main characteristics expected of the interface between EUDI Wallets and other participants of the ecosystem are defined in Article 5a par 5 and 12:

- Secure-by-design
- Common protocols and interfaces support (aiming for interoperability) for:

  Identification for access to other trust services.
  Validation of personal identification data and attributes.
  Validation of authenticity of the EUDI Wallet.
  Personal identification and attributes presentation to relying parties.
  Identity proofing in user onboarding processes.
  Interaction between two EUDI Wallet users.
  Relying party identification and authentication.

[17]Greenwald (2013), Accessed June 16th 2024 at https://www.theguardian.com/world/2013/jun/09/edward-snowden-nsa-whistleblower-surveillance.

Data deletion request
GDPR non-compliance reporting

- EUDI Wallet user identification and authentication (level of assurance high).
- Interoperability between verified Wallets
- Anonymity and untraceability of the identification processes (including presentation of electronic attestations).
- Warnings are displayed when using or presenting an electronic attestation of attributes with embedded disclosure policies.
- Free of charge qualified electronic signature means (it may have limited functionality).
- Privacy-preserving techniques which ensure unlikeability

2.2.2 Standards and Conformity Assessment Context

A conformity assessment is a systematic, independent, and documented process that seeks objective evidence to determine the degree of compliance with specific requirements and criteria.[18]

The requirements evaluated during the conformity assessment within the context of eIDAS/eIDAS2 are included in the Regulations and their implementing acts and referenced in the specific standards. As these acts are sometimes published before the standards are finalised, the definition of applicable standards could lie with the National Accreditation Bodies or the certification scheme owner (ENISA).

Within the eIDAS context, the conformity assessment context required several regulatory documents and standards (see Fig. 1).

Article 5a paragraph 23 of Regulation (EU) No. 1183/2024 references implementing acts scheduled for November 2024, where specifications and procedures for establishing the EUDI Wallet will be established. Article 5a par 24 references those who will develop the specifications and procedures for onboarding users to the EUDI Wallet, meeting a high level of assurance.

European standards are documents that have been ratified by one of the three European Standardisation Organisations recognised as competent in the area of voluntary technical standardisation as set out by Regulation (EU) No 1025/2012[19]:

- CEN, the European Committee for Standardization, reflects the economic and social interests of its 34 member countries, channelled through their national

[18] Definition according to ISO 19011:2018, providing guidelines for auditing management systems, including quality management systems.

[19] Regulation (EU) No 1025/2012 of the European Parliament and of the Council of 25 October 2012 on European standardisation, amending Council Directives 89/686/EEC and 93/15/EEC and Directives 94/9/EC, 94/25/EC, 95/16/EC, 97/23/EC, 98/34/EC, 2004/22/EC, 2007/23/EC, 2009/23/EC and 2009/105/EC of the European Parliament and of the Council and repealing Council Decision 87/95/EEC and Decision No 1673/2006/EC of the European Parliament and of the Council (https://eur-lex.europa.eu/legal-content/EN/TXT/?uri=CELEX%3A32012R1025).

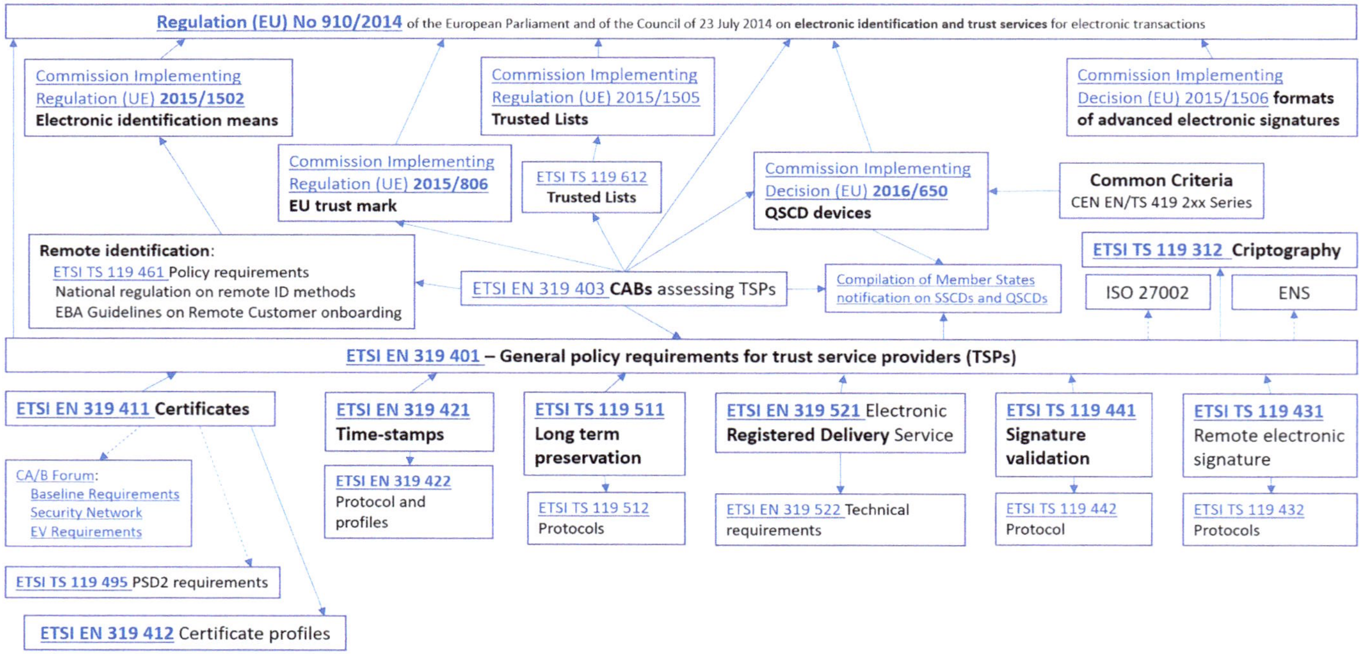

Fig. 1 Conformity assessment context in eIDAS (Source: prepared by the author based on published regulations, assessment frameworks and standards)

standardisation organisations, and provides a platform for the development of European standards and other technical documents;
- CENELEC is the European Committee for Electrotechnical Standardization and is responsible for standardisation in the electrotechnical engineering field;
- ETSI addresses the ICT domain, focusing on communications aspects regarding connected devices and the networks that connect them.

An important aspect is that the industry can be directly involved in the standards development process in ETSI. However, the sector can access CEN and CENELEC only through the national standardisation bodies.

When correctly articulated, requirements laid out in standards and technical should be consistent with the SMART framework.[20]:

- Specific: clear, consistent, not ambiguous and indivisible (it should not be compounded by several sub-requirements[21]).
- Measurable: it is possible to test and verify the compliance.
- Attainable (appropriate, actionable, achievable): feasible regarding state of the art and possible technological constraints.
- Reasonable: it is appropriate considering the risk of noncompliance.
- Traceable: the requirement can be traced to regulatory inputs, dependencies, or risk justifications.

EUDI Wallets certification is described in Article 5c and will be valid for up to five years, provided that it is regularly assessed for vulnerabilities (at least every 2 years).

Considering transparency as a guiding principle in Articles 5a, 5b, and 5c related to EUDI Wallets, the technical community may perform proactive surveillance and vulnerability assessment.

At least one EU certification scheme is expected to cover the certification of the EUDI Wallets (there could be more) (ENISA 2023). This first certification scheme is to be developed by ENISA, per Article 5c par 2 and Article 6, as the reference to Regulation (EU) 2019/881 of the European Parliament and of the Council.[22] National certification schemes may be additional, but the Regulation mandates that these national schemes are transmitted in advance to the European Digital Identity

[20] Although the SMART framework was originally applied to defining specific, measurable, assignable, realistic, and time-bound goals (Doran, 1981)—hence the acronym S.M.A.R.T.- it has evolved and been adapted to different contexts since then.

[21] Regulatory documents generally include several sub-requirements in every legal requirement, as this is considered easier for the human brain to read and interpret. In contrast, standards, especially if expected to be used in conformity assessment, state every requirement as individual items. This approach eases the complexity of managing frameworks and operations impacted by overlapping regulations and standards when requirements are correctly itemised.

[22] REGULATION (EU) 2019/881 OF THE EUROPEAN PARLIAMENT AND OF THE COUNCIL of 17 April 2019 on ENISA (the European Union Agency for Cybersecurity) and on information and communications technology cybersecurity certification and repealing Regulation (EU) No 526/2013 (Cybersecurity Act).

Cooperation Group,[23] which could issue opinions or recommendations before its publication and entry into force.

2.2.3 Impact and Adoption

The impact of this Regulation will not be measurable until several years have passed, and to ensure successful implementation of the digital identity medium of this new user-centric technology, the focus should be not only on the technological core solution of the EUDI Wallet but on the ecosystem around it. If the ecosystem is not sufficiently developed and the integration of the EUDI Wallet within the user habits is not sufficiently ingrained, the usage of the technology will be sporadic; the user will not adopt the solution proposed and migrate organically to other digital identity solutions that permit more integration within their lifestyle.

The solution has been regulated, is being designed and will be implemented by what is traditionally considered elites (Baudrillard 1970), with the main objective of retaining sovereignty over the identity of their citizens on the Internet (where they could be defined as netizens). The distance between the expected acceptance and the actual adoption will depend mainly on integrating existing patterns of use and different user-centric technologies and services. If the proposed solution does not offer sufficient integration within the cyber-ecosystem of the target users, the individuals will reinvent their usage or abandon it altogether.

Learning from the previous experiences with digital identities, the eIDAS 2 Regulation, and understanding the critical aspect of fostering the ecosystem has been included in paragraph 21, introducing the Regulation:

> (21) It is beneficial to facilitate the uptake and use of European Digital Identity Wallets by seamlessly integrating them with the ecosystem of public and private digital services already implemented at the national, local, or regional level.

As Vonnegut said, considering that the users, as creative as they are, usually put chaos in order, a continuous adaptation of the technology will be necessary. This will promote the technology's resilience and flexibility and foment the ecosystem's organic growth, putting order in the chaos. This order in chaos will be the framework to guarantee the rights of the netizens over their own digital identity and how it is projected to the Net.

Regulation (UE) 2024/1183 refers to future Implementation Acts to define several key points within the expected framework for digital identity. Those will be critical for the expected outcome, the adoption of the different stakeholders, and the

[23]Due to previous experience on the fragmentation of the European market on matters related to digital identity and the costing efforts achieving some interoperability (limited) between digital identity national schemes, there has been some consensus for the creation of a consulting group that could issue opinions and recommendations on emergent incompatibilities and interoperability problems.

technology's adaptability to the organic evolution of usage if it is successfully adopted.

However, as Walter Benjamin wrote, Benjamin (2003), "The concept of progress must be grounded in the idea of catastrophe". New accidents accompany every technological progress[24] with a different impact.

Virilio (2005) already stated that interactivity is to information as radioactivity is to energy—a pollution and disintegration factor—and as the EUDI Wallet is used and, hopefully, starts to be a medium of interactions between the user and accessible resources, the system will be put to the test. Scalability and resilience are fundamental aspects to consider when deploying a user-centric identification system, and every component should be developed considering the current capacity and possible future-wide adoption.

Furthermore, if the European digital identity is, as expected, widely adopted (preceded by the early and consistent development of its ecosystem), the implemented system should be flexible and resilient enough to adapt to potential accidents that cannot be predicted.

3 Digital EURO Similarities

Similarly to the EUDI Wallet initiative, the Digital Euro proposal, European Commission (2023b) is based on the European Union's need to retain sovereignty over the euro in a digital context where several countries are issuing central bank digital currency (CBDC).

The Digital Euro is born to provide the same guarantees as the physical euro.[25] As the physical euro is cash, the characteristics the Digital Euro must present in a digital format are similar:[26]

1. Verifiability: Every participant in a monetary transaction must be able to verify the value of the exchanged money and its authenticity, which requires identifying the issuing financial institution.
2. Security: The digital euro cannot be copied or rejected. In a secure system, both parties to the transaction have serious difficulties committing fraud.
3. Anonymity: the identity of the parties must be protected.
4. Untraceability: no one can track or detect the relationship between the parties and the acquired goods.
5. Transferability: The receptor can use the euro exchanged to pay in other transactions, allowing the transference of funds to a bank account.

---

[24] Accident is the revelation of a thing's quality of characteristic that was masked by another of its characteristic, according to Valéry (1894–1914).

[25] European Central Bank (2023).

[26] Carracedo Gallardo (2004).

For the digital money to be considered convenient, it should also support the following:

1. Divisibility: allowing the receptor of funds to transfer to a third party the whole sum or only a part of the funds.
2. Returns: Even if the digital currency allows for the exact transfer of funds (as the physical currency may have limitations a digital one may not have), this characteristic should be present if the currency is issued in indivisible groupings.
3. Off-line payment: Transactions are established without directly connecting to a bank or financial entity.

Even though experts traditionally have considered this last characteristic the least important when defining digital transactions over telecommunication networks, as the Digital Euro is expected to be used in mobile environments, offline scenarios are depicted as critical for wide adoption.

In offline scenarios, the banking authorities may consider different implementations, such as using powered smartcards or mobile environments.[27] Suppose the use of Near Field Communication (NFC) is deemed necessary. In that case, regulatory changes will likely be needed, as some mobile device providers have strict policies that do not allow access to the hardware components supporting secure cryptographic elements and NFC communication. Regulatory development is expected to cover areas such as liability, outsourcing and strong customer authentication, as well as interactions with payment intermediaries and banks, as it will impact several entities in the financial sector.

As the Digital Euro regulation[28] is not expected until 2026, European Commission (2023a), there is still time to change the specifications related to convenience (not the core functionalities) in case the current technology does not support the desired behaviour.

Looking at Article 5a par 4 and 16 of Regulation (EU) No. 1183/2024 (eIDAS 2), which defines the characteristics of the EUDI Wallet, it is clear that they are trying to make privacy inherent to the use of the electronic identification system.

As the personal identification data is to be under the sole control of the user, and it will be under their purview which data to share and present to access resources online (and offline), the EUDI Wallet shall implement controls guaranteeing the anonymity of the user and their identification transactions and the security of the

[27] Payment cards can effectively embed features like crypto-dynamic codes, specific user interfaces, or biometric authentication. Such smartcards aim to significantly reduce bank back-office costs and financial fraud while preserving the privacy and security of the smartcard user's personal data. All these new smartcards must be powered. In many cases, the preferred solutions for powering such smartcards are rechargeable batteries that get recharged regularly through the smartcard chip contact pads or energy harvested through the antenna used for contactless connectivity.

[28] The Digital Euro proposal, published with the Digital euro package on 28 June 2023, has to go through the debate within the European Parliament and Council and approval and implementation by the European Central Bank, so the estimated timeline puts 2026 as the earliest when a Digital euro regulation could be expected.

solution. Offline scenarios where the identification process can be performed would have to be defined, along with the manner and limitations, if any.

Article 5a par 8 mandates that the EUDI Wallet implement free-of-charge controls guaranteeing the wallet's verifiability and the authenticity and validity of relying on parties' identities. They focus on creating a trusted environment with security as a conducting guide.

This requirement mandated that the EUDI Wallet implement controls the guarantee that the identification and authentication interactions are untraceable.

Therefore, some of the technical requirements will be similar. As such, the EUDI Wallet will have the potential to interoperate with the Digital Euro once it is deployed and implemented. Similarly, the architecture and emergent potential accidents of the Member States' digital identity solutions will enable the validation of several models from which to learn and build a trusted solution.

If proved compatible, these similarities may open the door to dual usage, promoting further uses for the EUDI Wallet to initiate payments and integrate with the digital euro if the ecosystem is sufficiently fostered.

4 Conclusions

During the extension of this chapter, a brief description of the evolution of digital identity from a European perspective is provided.

As explained, the European digital identity is currently in flux. Implementation Acts defining specific aspects of Regulation (UE) 2024/1183 are expected to be published at the end of the year, which could significantly change the current interpretation of the Regulation.

The identity formed in the social context is not currently fully translated to digital identity systems, but using a baseline of government-issued identification and focusing on definable attributes as well as interactions and transactions, it is possible to develop a digital identity system capable of supporting the habits and usage of its users.

That is only possible when a digital ecosystem can interact seamlessly with the digital identity solution, and the user sees some advantage to its use to compensate for the increased friction, and fight the inherent change resistance.

"Progress and catastrophe are the opposite sides of the same coin," wrote Hannah Arendt (1965). New accidents with diverse impacts accompany every technological progress. And if the European digital identity is, as expected, widely adopted (preceded by the early and consistent development of its ecosystem), the implemented system should be flexible and resilient enough to adapt to potential accidents that cannot be predicted.

In that manner, the Regulation tries to foster the appropriate resilience, enhancing the transparency needed to maintain social trust in the proposals:

(33) The transparency of European Digital Identity Wallets and the accountability of their providers are key elements to creating social trust and triggering acceptance of the framework.

The Member State should focus on security, resiliency, stability, usability, adaptability, and flexibility through their different implementations of the interoperable digital identity wallets. This double focus will promote ecosystem growth and the adoption of the digital identity solution proposed by European netizens. Hopefully, the solution will guarantee rights to the netizens over their own digital identity, providing control over how said identity is projected on the Net.

References

Baudrillard J (1970) La societé de consommation. Denöel, Paris

Benjamin W (2003). Selected writings, Volume 4, 1938–1940; Eiland H, Jennings MW (eds) Belknap Press of Harvard University Press, Cambridge, p 184

Breckenridge G (2018) What is digital identity? https://medium.com/humanizing-the-singularity/what-is-digital-identity-c77983c03306. Accessed 16 June 2024

Carracedo Gallardo J (2004) Seguridad en redes telemáticas. McGraw-Hill, Madrid

European Central Bank (2023) A stocktake on the digital euro. Summary report on the investigation phase and outlook on the next phase. Frankfurt am Main, Germany

European Commission. Commission Implementing Regulation (EU) 2015/1502 of 8 September 2015 on setting out minimum technical specifications and procedures for assurance levels for electronic identification means pursuant to Article 8(3) of Regulation (EU) No 910/2014 of the European Parliament and the Council on electronic identification and trust services for electronic transactions in the internal market

European Commission (2021) Report from the Commission to the European Parliament and the Council on the evaluation of Regulation (EU) No 910/2014 on electronic identification and trust services for electronic transactions in the internal market (eIDAS). Brussels

European Commission (2023a) Directorate-General for Financial Stability, Financial Services and Capital Markets Union. General Publications. Digital euro package. https://finance.ec.europa.eu/publications/digital-euro-package_en. Accessed 14 June 2024

European Commission (2023b) European Commission, Directorate-General for Financial Stability, Financial Services and Capital Markets Union. Proposal for a Regulation of the European Parliament and of the Council on the establishment of the digital euro. Proceedings 2023/0212/COD

European Network and Information Security Agency (ENISA) (2011) Mapping security services to authentication levels. Reflecting on STORK QAA levels. Heraklion

European Network and Information Security Agency (ENISA) (2021) Remote ID Proofing. Heraklion

European Network and Information Security Agency (ENISA) (2022) Remote Identity Proofing - Attacks & Countermeasures. Heraklion

European Network and Information Security Agency (ENISA) (2023) Digital Identity Standards. Heraklion

European Parliament. Regulation (EU) No 1025/2012 of the European Parliament and of the Council of 25 October 2012 on European standardisation, amending Council Directives 89/686/EEC and 93/15/EEC and Directives 94/9/EC, 94/25/EC, 95/16/EC, 97/23/EC, 98/34/EC, 2004/22/EC, 2007/23/EC, 2009/23/EC and 2009/105/EC of the European Parliament and of the Council and repealing Council Decision 87/95/EEC and Decision No 1673/2006/EC of the European Parliament and of the Council. ELI: http://data.europa.eu/eli/reg/2012/1025/oj

European Parliament. Regulation (EU) No 910/2014 of the European Parliament and of the Council of 23 July 2014 on electronic identification and trust services for electronic transactions in the internal market and repealing Directive 1999/93/EC. ELI: http://data.europa.eu/eli/reg/2014/910/oj
European Parliament. Regulation (EU) 2024/1183 of the European Parliament and of the Council of 11 April 2024 amending Regulation (EU) No 910/2014 as regards establishing the European Digital Identity Framework. ELI: http://data.europa.eu/eli/reg/2024/1183/oj
Greenwald G (2013) Edward Snowden: the whistleblower behind the NSA surveillance revelations, first published June 9 2013 in The Guardian, available at https://www.theguardian.com/world/2013/jun/09/edward-snowden-nsa-whistleblower-surveillance. Accessed 16 June 2024
Herman WE (2011) Identity formation. Encyclopedia of child behavior and development. Springer US, Boston, pp 779–781
ISO. ISO/IEC 27000:2018 Information technology — Security techniques — Information security management systems — Overview and vocabulary. Geneva
ISO. ISO/IEC 29115:2013. Information technology — Security techniques — Entity authentication assurance framework. Geneva
McKinsey Global Institute (2019) Digital identification. A key to inclusive growth. Brussels
Sadin E (2018) L'intelligence artificielle ou l'enjeu du siècle. Anatomie d'un antihumanisme radical. Éditions L'Échappée, Paris
Schwartz SJ, Luyckx K, Vignoles VL (2011) Handbook of identity theory and research. Springer, New York. https://doi.org/10.1007/978-1-4419-7988-9
Susca V (2016) Les Affinités connectives. Sociologie de la culture numérique. Éditions du Cerf, Paris
United Nations (1948) Universal Declaration of Human Rights, proclaimed by the United Nations General Assembly in Paris on 10 December 1948 (General Assembly resolution 217 A). https://www.un.org/en/universal-declaration-human-rights/. Accessed 10 June 2024
USA Department of Commerce. National Institute of Standards and Technology (2020) NIST Special Publication 800-63 Revision 3. Digital Identity Guidelines, Los Altos, CA
Valéry P (1894–1914) Cahiers, vol II. Éditions Gallimard, Paris
Virilio P (2005) L'Accident original. Éditions Galilée, Paris
Vossaert J, Lapon J, De Decker B, Naessens V (2010) User-centric identity management using trusted modules. Paper presented at the 7th European Workshop EuroPKI in Athens (Greece) 23-24 September 2010
Windley PJ (2005) Digital identity. O'Reilly Media, Inc., Sebastopol

‘Human Digital Twins’ and Blockchain: Some Challenges and Solutions for Digital Identity and Privacy

Cristian Javier Vera-Arenas

Abstract This chapter examines the integration of two significant technological developments: the ‘Human Digital Twins’ (HDT) and blockchain technology, focusing on their applications and implications for digital identity and privacy management. HDTs represent an advanced form of digital replicas that encapsulate an individual’s physical, behavioural and psychological characteristics when using multimodal and multisource data. Their implementation promises to revolutionise interaction with the digital world, offering benefits in sectors as varied as personalised medicine and digital identity management.

On the other hand, the blockchain provides a decentralised and secure platform for data management, offering robust solutions to the persistent challenges of privacy and security in a digitally connected world. The convergence of HDT with blockchain technology has the potential to enhance the security and privacy of personal data and radically transform existing methodologies in identity verification, system interoperability and personal data management within regulatory frameworks.

This analysis is further explored by exploring HDT’s architecture, the challenges inherent in its implementation, and the unique opportunities it offers for advanced identity and privacy management. In addition, case studies are discussed, and future trends and emerging challenges in this dynamic field are outlined.

This paper expands and updates the text of a lecture delivered at the III International Congress entitled “Present and future of crypto-assets regulation in the European Union,” held at the University of Alicante (Spain) on December 13, 14, and 15, 2023. This work is funded within the framework of: Proyecto CIPROM/2022/26 “Presente y futuro de la regulación de los Criptoactivos en la UE [Legalcripto]”. Proyecto Prometeo CIPROM/2022/26, grupos de investigación de excelencia, de la Generalitat Valenciana (P.I. Carmen Pastor).

C. J. Vera-Arenas (✉)
Department of Management, University of Alicante, San Vicente del Raspeig, Alicante, Spain
e-mail: cristian.vera@ua.es

C. Pastor Sempere (ed.), *Governance and Control of Data and Digital Economy in the European Single Market*, Law, Governance and Technology Series 71,
https://doi.org/10.1007/978-3-031-74889-9_21

1 Introduction

In today's digital age, effective identity and privacy management has become a central topic of discussion and analysis. The emergence of disruptive technologies such as blockchain offers new avenues to address these challenges. At the same time, the concept of Human Digital Twins (HDT) proposes a holistic digital representation of individuals in cyberspace.[1] This chapter explores the convergence of these two technological developments, analysing the opportunities and challenges they present for digital identity and privacy.

Human Digital Twins refer to digital replicas of people in the physical world, which facilitate detailed modelling of their physical, behavioural, and psychological characteristics using multimodal and multisource data.[2] This digital representation promises to revolutionise how we interact with the digital world, offering new possibilities in fields as diverse as personalised medicine, human performance enhancement and digital identity management.

Furthermore, the blockchain has established itself as a key security and data management technology, providing a decentralised and tamper-resistant mechanism for storing and transferring information. The application of blockchain to the 'Human Digital Twins' has the potential to address critical security concerns, which are fundamental to privacy, ensuring the integrity and confidentiality of personal data in an increasingly connected environment.[3]

This chapter delves into the heart of this technological intersection and is structured in the following sections:

1. HDT Context and State of the Art: This section reviews the evolution of the Digital Twin (DT) concept to today's HDTs.
2. Generic HDT System Architecture: This section explores the structure of HDTs, from data collection to the intelligent interface.
3. Challenges: Identifies the main digital identity and privacy challenges in HDT implementation.
4. Opportunities: The solutions offered by blockchain technology to address these challenges are detailed.
5. In Summary and Conclusion: The main points are synthesised, and future implications are outlined.

This chapter provides a comprehensive overview of the possibilities and challenges at the intersection of HDTs and blockchain by analysing the technological foundations, current applications, and case studies in detail, discussing future trends, and identifying remaining challenges.

[1] Shengli (2021).

[2] Wang et al. (2022).

[3] Raj (2021).

2 Context and State of the Art of HDTs

2.1 *The Digital Twin: Origins of the Digital Twin (DT) Concept*

The digital twin (DT) concept has evolved dynamically since its inception. The idea of building replicas, or what most likely could be called 'twins,' traces its birth to NASA's Apollo program of the 1970s.[4] This was not a DT system like today's HDT, but its origins can be traced back to NASA's work 50 years ago. NASA used two identical space vehicles, one on Earth and one in space,[5] to predict and simulate vehicle conditions in space to develop the concept of DT.

Later, in 2003, Michael Grieves released the term 'Virtual Digital Expression Equivalent to the Physical Product' within his Product Lifecycle Management (PLM) model.[6] Though not originally named a Digital Twin, this idea contained all the essential features of DTs, namely the modelling of physical space in cyberspace and the linkage between the two. This concept was fine-tuned and expanded over the years; it was first named the 'Mirrored Space Model' (MLM) from the years 2003 to 2005,[7] and then it evolved to be called the 'Information Mirroring Model' (IMM) from the years 2006 to 2010.[8] Finally, it was dubbed the Digital Twin. This underlines the transformation of DT from a basic idea of physical replication to complex digital models that facilitate sophisticated interaction of the two worlds.[9]

2.2 *Evolution Towards Human Digital Twins*

Technological intervention through the Internet of Things (IoT), cloud and edge computing, artificial intelligence (AI), etc., has made the concept of Digital Twins transcend its aeronautical basis.[10] Today, the urban governance, transportation, manufacturing, and energy sectors enjoy the benefits of such digital replicas, displaying the ability of DTs to act in an interactive capacity as tools to bridge the physical and digital worlds.

This technological leap ushered in the era of extending the application of DT from its goal to model systems and machinery to model human beings.[11] Therefore,

[4] Piascik et al. (2010).

[5] Piascik et al. (2010).

[6] Grieves (2017).

[7] Grieves (2005).

[8] Githens (2007).

[9] Zhuang et al. (2017).

[10] Lin et al. (2022).

[11] Lin et al. (2022).

Human Digital Twins (HDTs) have become a tool for intelligent interaction platforms, behavioural analysis, and advanced simulations. For example, in the medical field and other industry sectors, the application of HDTs optimises the human-machine interfaces, where performance generally can be enhanced. These scenarios are highly detailed digital twin humans of the physical world, which leverage multimodal data for modelling human attributes at the individual and group levels. This highly complex digital representation encompasses physical, physiological, cognitive, and social aspects, highlighting the intricate design and functional specificity of HDTs in contrast to traditional DTs.[12,13]

However, the evolution from DT to HDT indicates technological innovation and diversification in the application and customisation of digital models. These models are becoming increasingly sophisticated and aim to simulate the complexity of human life and its environmental interactions to the utmost degree.

A milestone in HDT literature was the work of Baskaran et al.,[14] who studied assembly operations at a vehicle factory to develop digital human body models using Siemens Tecnomatix. Physical constraints in the assembly tasks based on gender, weight, and height differences were identified. More importantly, this research integrated DT robots to assist humans in highlighting potential cooperation between human and robotic DTs. That work highlights the possibilities and constraints in modelling human interaction with a DT from the perspective of efficiency and ergonomics. It was also the first time the concept of Human Digital Twin appeared in the literature.[15]

Grieves' conceptualisation of DTs,[16] articulated into three essential building blocks—the physical world, the digital world, and the connection interface—constitutes the underpinning for a clear understanding of HDTs as a natural extension of DTs. These are crucial to developing coherent digital models mimicking the physical object within the digital world. Therefore, the progression towards Human Digital Twin Systems (HDTS) aims to harbour the complexity and dynamism of human attributes within the digital domain.[17]

These new developments underline how digital models are increasingly complex and can be customised to simulate human life with detail and their interactions and devise new collaborations between humans and robotic systems in different contexts, both at an industrial and daily level.

[12] Miller and Spatz (2022).

[13] Shengli (2021).

[14] Baskaran et al. (2019).

[15] Baskaran et al. (2019).

[16] Zhuang et al. (2017).

[17] Miller and Spatz (2022).

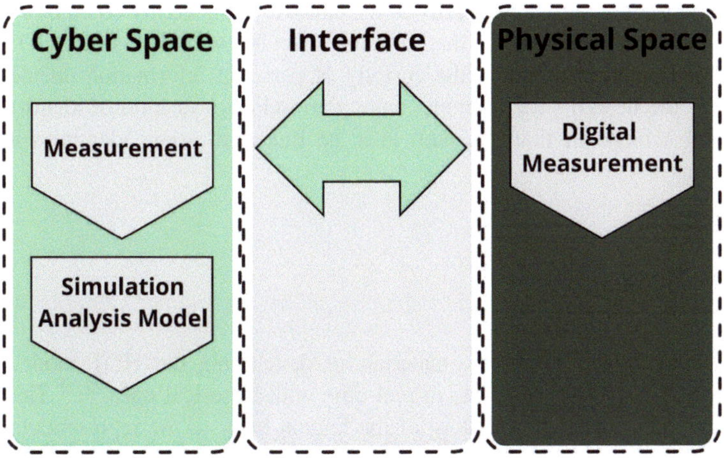

Fig. 1 Digital twin. The three elements

3 Generic System Architecture of Human Digital Twins (HDT)

Human Digital Twins (HDTs) represent an innovative convergence of reality and virtuality in a conceptual framework structured in three interrelated blocks: the physical world, its digital replica, and the interface through which they interrelate.[18] These set elements outlay the grounds for detailed simulation and reliable predictions that capture the nature of a human being (Fig. 1).[19]

3.1 Data Collection and Processing

At its heart, an HDT has at the core a painstakingly detailed data-gathering process, from IoT devices to specialised sensors that could record biometric measurements and environmental and behavioural traits. This full spectrum is crucial for generating life-like HDT modelling. This means a strict data cleaning and storing process as it transitions into its digital form, in which algorithms like the KNN[20] proved quite

[18]Zhuang et al. (2017).

[19]Miller and Spatz (2022).

[20]'KNN, or k-Nearest Neighbors, is a supervised learning algorithm used in artificial intelligence and data mining for classification and regression. It works by identifying the 'k' nearest examples in the training dataset to a new data point and then predicts the label (in classification) or value (in regression) based on the majority of the nearest neighbours. It is known for its simplicity and effectiveness in classification tasks, especially in contexts where the data are well distributed and

effective in maintaining the integrity of the dataset.[21] It is highly crucial for security and data management in HDTS that a unique index be assigned to every HDT within the digital space because it is the custody of personal information deemed to be integral to the design—for example, having an indicator or kind of identity within the digital ecosystem that can then later be linked to some identity within the blockchain.

3.2 HDT Model

The processed data is the raw material for developing the HDT model, which expands by integrating new data in real-time with historical ones.[22,23] This model spans from the physical modelling of the human body to the representation of its behaviour and social relationships, allowing in-depth analyses and adjustments in the HDT to reflect the reality of such individuals[24] accurately.

3.3 Intelligent Interface

The intelligent interface between the human being and their HDT is a key bridge that not only facilitates the transfer of complex data but also, through visualisation technologies such as Virtual Reality (VR) and Augmented Reality (AR), enhances the user's interaction and understanding with their digital counterpart, strengthening trust in the system.[25]

Lin Y et al. proposed the HDTS architecture, which will be the most suitable and adaptive model across different domains and fuse advanced technologies towards a holistic and detailed view of human life.[26] This leads, in fact, to the creation of a multidimensional platform using a multimodal and multi-source data view as a solid base for the personalised and dynamic modelling of the Human Digital Twins.[27,28]

---

the relationships between them are non-linear.' [Cover, T. M., & Hart, P. E. (1967). Nearest neighbor pattern classification. IEEE transactions on information theory, 13(1), 21–27.]

[21] Batista et al. (2002).

[22] Latif et al. (2020).

[23] Tao and Qi (2019).

[24] Miller and Spatz (2022).

[25] Wang et al. (2022).

[26] Lin et al. (2022).

[27] Wang et al. (2022).

[28] Miller and Spatz (2022).

4 Challenges

Including HDTs in all domains, from healthcare and industries to everyday life, represents a remarkable advance towards a connected and digitised future. This progress comprises big digital identity and privacy challenges that need careful attention and respective solutions.

4.1 Challenges of Digital Identity

4.1.1 Strong Authentication and Identity Management

In the digital age, secure authentication and identity management are essential. As HDTs are digital replicas of an individual, the linkage that connects them should be unambiguous with the person, evading any potential identity theft. This challenge is related to data security and the ability of systems to effectively handle the many digital identities an individual may have on different platforms and services. It is critical to implement solutions that will allow for robust authentication but with ease of use.[29]

4.1.2 Interoperability of Identities in Diverse Ecosystems

The different identity management systems across digital services pose interoperability challenges. People will want to move securely between the various services, with uniform recognition and acceptance of their identities. This raises the need to widely adopt open standards and cooperative frameworks across industries to enable fluid and secure identity management.

4.2 Privacy Challenges

4.2.1 Protecting Personal Data in Shared Environments

The complexity of securing personal data from unauthorised access increases as it flows through several entities: health providers, technology companies, and governmental services. It is not a simple technical requirement for privacy protection but also an ethical imperative, given the delicate and sensitive nature of data that will be

[29] Sirigu et al. (2022).

collected by HDTs.[30] Mechanisms guaranteeing that data remains confidential and integral throughout the lifecycle are crucial to implementation.[31]

4.2.2 Dynamic Consent and Preference Management

This means that users must be given control and provided with straightforward, easy ways to grant, adjust, and revoke consent. The critical problem here is the ability to support flexible user interfaces (UIs) in the first place and to have appropriate back-end systems that adapt to changing consent preferences in dynamic ways in the second place.[32] The challenge here lies in balancing user flexibility with the complexity of implementing systems that can handle granular consent on a large scale.

4.2.3 Data Anonymisation and Minimisation

With increased data collection, the challenge of keeping such information anonymous and limited to a minimum of what is needed for the stated purpose has grown commensurately. For example, adequate data anonymisation should guarantee that re-associating information with a given person is impossible. It should be done hand in hand with a data minimisation policy that respects user privacy. This would include developing advanced algorithms for anonymisation and implementing 'privacy by design' policies in developing HDT-related technologies.

4.2.4 Regulatory and Compliance Challenges

The key challenge is compliance with the new global regulatory environment. In Europe, the GDPR sets substantial requirements to treat personal data correctly, comprising demands for transparency, the right to be forgotten,[33] and data portability. For HDTs, this means implementing systems that are compliant with existing regulations and agile and flexible for future legal changes. These challenges highlight the need for digital identity and privacy to be GDPR-compliant from the initial design and implementation of HDTs. While blockchain technology holds much promise for solutions to several of these problems, especially for security, transparency, and control over personal data, a holistic approach considering technical, legal, and ethical aspects is critical.[34] Collaboration between technologists, policymakers,

[30] Bruynseels et al. (2018).
[31] Sirigu et al. (2022).
[32] Sirigu et al. (2022).
[33] ICO (2023).
[34] Bruynseels et al. (2018).

businesses, and civil society will be vital in developing HDTs that are not only innovative but also safe and protective of individual privacy and autonomy.

5 Opportunities

With its intrinsic decentralisation, transparency, and immutability characteristics, Blockchain technology offers robust solutions to the digital identity and privacy challenges associated with Human Digital Twins (HDTs). In the following, we detail how blockchain can technically address these problems.

5.1 Solutions to Digital Identity Challenges

5.1.1 Robust Authentication and Identity Management

Storing digital identities in Human Digital Twins (HDTs) will significantly improve the integration with blockchain technology, which helps issue and verify credentials through decentralised identifiers (DIDs). DIDs offer a means of securing, verifying, and managing digital identities without a centralised authority intervening. Each DID is stored on the blockchain, related to a pair of cryptographic keys (public and private) and other meta information—all operated by its owner. This ensures that only the DID owner possesses the corresponding private key and can authenticate and take action in their name. In addition, DIDs can be used to sign transactions and data digitally, adding an extra layer of security and authenticity.

For instance, in the hypothetical case that Alice is a personal patient using her HDT for health management, Alice can create the DID and will access online medical services securely, share her private health data, and be able to involve these in further transactions. When a service is accessed, an identity based on verification will be conducted using her DID, which will be matched with her public key registered on the blockchain. All this is done without exposing her personal sensitive information. Apart from ensuring her privacy, this approach guarantees the integrity of her digital identity.

5.1.2 Smart Contracts for Access Management

Blockchain smart contracts could further facilitate identity control through the automated verification and authorisation process according to prespecified rules. A self-executing contract would ensure that access to specific data or services can only be gained between legitimate parties to uphold digital identity integrity.

Technically speaking, smart contracts enable rule-based authentication by automatically verifying the user's identity before granting access to the data or services under consideration. Such a verification process includes comparing the given credentials with those stored on the blockchain. In addition, this specification can allow conditional authorisation with specifications about when access is granted exactly.

For example, only doctors holding valid licenses can access a patient's health details. A practical scenario could be one where Alice wishes to share her health data with the doctor. She can provide it through the smart contract, confirming the doctor's DID and then verifying if the doctor's conditions, for example, a valid license, are satisfied. Only then does the intelligent contract allow access to Alice's data.

This whole process is automatic in a way that access to sensitive information is kept strictly within the purview of only those personnel who have been authorised and verified beforehand, thus delivering the twin advantages of both privacy and security. Leveraging DID and smart contracts assures a robust solution for the problems of managing digital identities and access control that protects the security of all participants in the HDT ecosystem.

5.2 Identity Interoperability in Different Ecosystems

In the case of Human Digital Twins, interoperability denotes data sharing and use across all systems and platforms seamlessly and safely, all while rigorously respecting privacy and security. Blockchain increases interoperability by applying open standards for DIDs and processes under smart contracts. These unique combinations allow different entities to establish their access identities in an authorised way.

Essentially, open standards for DIDs and VCs are essential. Such protocols allow different systems to work together. This means that if an entity's identity is verified in one system, it should be automatically recognised and accepted in other systems without further verification. Incorporating trusted networks will enhance the realisation of verified identities across multiple platforms.

To make this more realistic, let's consider a case where Alice uses her DID to access services offered by different health and well-being platforms. Since these platforms have followed open standards and protocols on interoperability, they can identify and accept Alice without subjecting her to other sets of verification procedures used within each platform. This interoperability is not just for an effortless service experience but also to ensure that any data related to her health is dealt with securely and at the level of integration required in services.

5.3 Solutions to Privacy Challenges

5.3.1 Protection of Personal Data in Shared Environments

The most critical privacy challenge associated with deploying HDTs is protecting personal data when they are shared. Blockchain technology is structured through its distributed ledger so that a single point cannot fail, and data security is reinforced from unauthorised access and breaches. Data storage can be encrypted while hashes are recorded within the blockchain, thus attesting to its integrity without revealing the information itself.[35]

Technically, before being stored on the blockchain, personal data is secured by fully sophisticated encryption algorithms. Data hashing on the blockchain further enables one to check if the data was tampered with without seeing it. For instance, Alice maintains her medical records on a distributed network working with blockchain technology. She has encrypted her records and stored their hashes on the blockchain. At any time, anybody wishing to access such records would be subjected to a validation process through the request, and only if each of the access conditions is satisfied will the record be decrypted.

5.3.2 Dynamic Consent and Preference Management[36]

Smart contracts are essential to the dynamic and automated management of user consent for Human Digital Twins. They enable users to define, update, and revoke their consent at any given time, ensuring that access to data is aligned with the latest preferences set. Smart contracts increase data security and privacy by enabling users to have fine-grained control over who should be allowed access to their information and under what conditions.

An advantageous method within this framework is the issuance of dynamic access tokens. These tokens provide fine-grained control over the access of HDT data, indicating the exact access conditions, valid period, type of data access allowed, and even what to do with the data (read, write, modify). The user can revoke or alter tokens anytime, providing greater flexibility and autonomy for managing data.

The essential operation of dynamic access tokens is that users generate the tokens through an intuitive interface, where they can define specific access conditions. For example, Alice could create a token that allows her doctor to access her medical records for some time. Such tokens would be resident on the blockchain, indicating encrypted HDT data, making it tamper-proof and verifiable, with no such data tampering. Smart contracts authenticate and time-reference tokens repeatedly when

[35]Bernal Bernabe et al. (2019).

[36]Zhang et al. (2024).

entities are going to access HDT data under the specific conditions allowed to access or to decline.

Technically speaking, dynamic modification makes it possible to update consent preferences in real time so that smart contracts are automatically updated without further delay in effecting the changes. Moreover, consent changes and access to the data are recorded in such contracts, enabling an immutable, transparent record of any action related to user data to facilitate audit and regulation. A practical example would be Alice changing her consent preferences for her health data. Preferences are updated in a blockchain application and reflected in the respective smart contracts. For example, Alice might create a dynamic access token for sharing data with a researcher for six months. The smart contract on the blockchain will verify that token when the researcher wants to get information, so it is guaranteed that the researcher will meet the conditions set forth by Alice. Concerning this, the process ethically adheres to Alice's privacy while maintaining the data access timeframe she desires.

The advantages of this methodology are many. For instance, the user can modify and change permissions at any given time, therefore removing permissions anytime they wish; that is, data are managed based on present preferences. Secondly, smart contracts are used to manage the encrypted tokens and secure data from any unauthorised access. Lastly, being immutable, blockchain ensures that all data-related actions are recorded and audit-ready, proving compliance with regulations, including GDPR.

At the same time, token transactions at scale can be complex, so scalability is challenging. These involve sharding[37] and two-layer solutions[38] to increase scalability and proficiently manage traffic across the network. In addition, open standards that must be implemented require DIDs and VCs to ensure that a token is recognised and accepted harmoniously and seamlessly by different systems and platforms so that no security is exploited. In other words, smart contracts and the integration of dynamic access tokens in consent management offer a tight and flexible framework to imbibe user privacy and ethical use of data in HDTs. The approach will thus ensure data security and privacy, promote transparency, and be in line with all the regulations that will make the data be used according to the users' expectations and wishes.

[37] Sharding is a technique that divides a blockchain database into smaller parts, called 'shards'. Each shard contains a portion of the blockchain's data and state and can be processed by different nodes in parallel. It improves scalability by allowing multiple transactions to be processed simultaneously in different shards rather than having a single chain that must process all transactions sequentially. It increases the network's capacity to handle a higher volume of transactions per second, reducing congestion and improving overall network efficiency.

[38] Layer 2 solutions work on the main chain of the blockchain (Layer 1) to solve off-chain transactions by supporting the reduction of the load on the main chain. The most outstanding example of a Layer 2 solution might be Bitcoin's Lightning Network, which allows for instant, cheap, off-chain payments at an unbelievable scale. These solutions work by grouping transactions and carrying them off-chain—only the outcome is posted to the main blockchain. This easily increases speed and reduces the costs of transactions while still ensuring security for the main chain.

5.3.3 Data Anonymisation and Minimisation

The data collected should be rendered anonymous and minimised to address privacy concerns adequately. Problems of this type have feasible solutions in blockchain technology, which uses hashing and advanced encryption methods. In this approach, the integrity of personal information is maintained and verifiable at any moment by simply comparing the stored hash of personal data with the newly computed one without storing the information.[39] It uses a technical approach in which this personal data is hashed with another unique hash before entering it into the blockchain. Advanced encryption techniques exist that follow and can anonymise this data so that it can never be linked back to an individual; for example, health data intended for Alice before entering the blockchain. Alice's health data is encrypted using advanced encryption methodologies.

Her data has been hashed and stored on the blockchain. This ensures that any attempt to access Alice's original data illegally would not reveal the original information; it maintains privacy while the integrity of the data is verifiable.

5.3.4 Regulatory and Compliance Challenges

Blockchain technology can also help HDTs avert serious regulatory and compliance issues in their handling. The immutable and transparent record of all actions, from consent management to data access offered by blockchain technology, assures compliance with GDPR, enabling the audit and accurate verification of personal data handling and consent management.[40]

The immutability property of the blockchain ensures that all actions and consents recorded are irreversible in a technical sense. This is to have an accurate and reliable log for auditing. Building in auditability speeds up the verification process of proving that everything is being done within the confines of the law. For example, the data access actions and consents for Alice are immutably logged into the blockchain. These immutable records can allow Alice to audit how her data has been processed in terms of privacy and data protection regulations. This will not only facilitate compliance with the law but also assure trust in the transparency and reliability of the system.

6 In Summary

Several challenges have been identified regarding HDTs' workings thus far, and Table 1 summarises them along with some ideas for potential solutions.

---

[39] Aslam et al. (2021).

[40] Giordano (2021).

Table 1 HDT. Challenges and solutions

Challenges	Possible approaches to resolving the challenge
1. Strong authentication and identity management	Use Decentralised Identifiers (DIDs) and smart contracts to verify and authorise access.
2. Identity interoperability	Implementation of open standards such as DIDs and verifiable credentials (VCs) to facilitate interoperability.
3. Personal data protection	Use of advanced encryption and blockchain hashes to ensure data integrity and confidentiality.
4. Dynamic consent and preference management	Consent management through smart contracts that reflect user preferences in real-time.
5. Data anonymisation and minimisation	Hashing and encryption techniques to ensure that data is unrecognisable and only necessary data is stored.
6. Regulatory and compliance challenges	Immutable recording of actions and consents in blockchain to facilitate auditing and compliance.

Adopting an all-embracing approach should involve secure data collection, sophisticated digital identity management, and access to information for creating and managing Human Digital Twins that assure security and privacy. A detailed framework for the secure process of creating an HDT follows.

The first step in a secure HDT is firmly centred on data collection. Data integrity and authenticity must start at its source. This includes device- and sensor-level securing to ensure that connections between devices and sources are encrypted, updating those devices with the latest security settings and protocols, and, where possible, even new firmware to eliminate vulnerabilities. Once collected, data must be immediately encrypted using solid algorithms, such as AES-256. It is necessary to encrypt this data to maintain its confidentiality and prevent it from being accessed by unauthorised people. Just as important is the safe management of the encryption keys by storing them in critical management systems, to which access is only allowed under solid authentication.

A hash value of the encrypted data is generated to guarantee its integrity over time. This hash is stored in a blockchain to leverage its immutability and provide proof during data integrity verification while not needing to expose the actual content of the data. A trusted hashing algorithm such as SHA-256 will guarantee the uniqueness and security of the obtained hash. Therefore, an encrypted data storage solution must balance accessibility and security. Choosing decentralised storage systems like the InterPlanetary File System (IPFS) ensures resiliencies against attacks and failures. This will also guarantee that the data is secured and available when needed. On the other hand, good strategies need to be implemented along with robust data backup and recovery.

The next step is creating a Decentralized Identity (DID) for each HDT. The identity, account data, public keys, and associated metadata maintained on the blockchain form a good foundation for reliable authentication and identity management. It enables strong authentication without disclosure of personal information and guarantees user privacy at the same time. HDT access management is done through smart contracts operating in the blockchain. Smart contracts ensure authorisation through access tokens corresponding to the DID holder's data and that authorised parties access specific data under well-specified terms. In issuing dynamic access tokens, one can exercise excellent and flexible control over who can access HDT data and under what conditions. The user can change and modify the tokens at any time. That accords with the emphasis on independence when it comes to their data.

Finally, such access tokens are validated against the corresponding intelligent contracts to ensure access can only be given to authenticated and authorised parties; finally, an encryption key is provided, through which the data would be required to decrypt to reach the same. This further completes the process of secure access. A fine-grained framework will emphasise, on the one hand, the security and privacy role during HDT creation and management, and on the other, end-user autonomy with personal data processing transparency. After implementation, this will lay the ground for developing HDT innovations and maintaining user rights and expectations. Hence, it will maintain consistency in security and privacy.

7 Conclusion

Blockchain application in the context of HDTs addresses the technical challenges in digital identity and privacy and sets a new standard for secure, transparent, and autonomous management of personal data. These implementations create the conditions for developing an HDT innovative ecosystem while respecting the rights and privacy of individuals. In summary, blockchain technology offers a beneficial framework for addressing the challenges of digital identity and privacy under an HDT. Blockchain improves security and confidentiality in HDTs, increases trust, and introduces transparency in the digital ecosystem through solutions that will be provided regarding secure authentication, controlled data sharing, anonymisation, data minimisation, and regulatory compliance.

References

Aslam S, Tosic A, Mrissa M (2021) Secure and privacy-aware blockchain design: Requirements, challenges and solutions. J Cybersecur Priv 1(1):164–194. https://doi.org/10.3390/jcp1010009

Baskaran S, Niaki FA, Tomaszewski M, Gill JS, Chen Y, Jia Y, Mears L, Krovi V (2019) Digital human and robot simulation in automotive assembly using siemens process simulate: a feasibility study. Proc Manufact 34:986–994

Batista GE, Monard MC et al (2002) A study of k-nearest neighbour as an imputation method. His 87(251–260):48

Bernal Bernabe J, Canovas JL, Hernandez-Ramos JL, Torres Moreno R, Skarmeta A (2019) Privacy-preserving solutions for blockchain: review and challenges. IEEE Access 7:164908–164940. https://doi.org/10.1109/ACCESS.2019.2950872

Bruynseels K, Sio F, Hoven J (2018) Digital twins in health care: ethical implications of an emerging engineering paradigm. Front Genet 9:31. https://doi.org/10.3389/fgene.2018.00031

Giordano MT (2021) Blockchain and the gdpr: new challenges for privacy and security. In: Cappiello B, Carullo G (eds) Blockchain, law and governance. Springer, Cham, pp 275–286

Githens G (2007) Product lifecycle management: driving the next generation of lean thinking by Michael Grieves. Wiley Online Library

Grieves M (2017) Digital twin: manufacturing excellence through virtual factory replication. White Paper

Grieves MW (2005) Product lifecycle management: the new enterprise paradigm. Int J Prod Dev 2(1-2):71–84

ICO (2023) Overview of the GDPR. https://ico.org.uk/media/for-organisations/data-protection-reform/overview-of-the-gdpr-1-13.pdf

Latif H, Shao G, Starly B (2020) A case study of a digital twin for a manufacturing process involving human interactions. In: 2020 Winter Simulation Conference (WSC). IEEE, pp 2659–2670

Lin Y, Chen L, Ali A, Nugent C, Ian C, Li R, Gao D, Wang H, Wang Y, Ning H (2022) Human digital twin: a survey

Miller ME, Spatz E (2022) A unified view of a human digital twin. Human-Intell Syst Integr 1–11

Piascik R, Vickers J, Lowry D, Scotti S, Stewart J, Calomino A (2010) Technology area 12: materials, structures, mechanical systems, and manufacturing roadmap. Technical report, NASA Office of Chief Technologist

Raj P (2021) Empowering digital twins with blockchain. In: Advances in computers, vol 121. Elsevier, pp 267–283

Shengli W (2021) Is human digital twin possible? Comput Methods Progr Biomed Update 1: 100014

Sirigu G, Carminati B, Ferrari E (2022) Privacy and security issues for human digital twins. In: 2022 IEEE 4th International Conference on Trust, Privacy and Security in Intelligent Systems, and Applications (TPS-ISA). IEEE, pp 1–9. https://doi.org/10.1109/TPS-ISA56441.2022.00011

Tao F, Qi Q (2019) Make more digital twins. Nature Publishing Group

Wang B, Zhou H, Yang G, Li X, Yang H (2022) Human digital twin (hdt) driven human-cyber-physical systems: Key technologies and applications. Chinese J Mech Eng 35(1):1–6

Zhang C, Zhao M, Zhang W, Fan Q, Ni J, Zhu L (2024) Privacy-preserving identity-based data rights governance for blockchain-empowered human-centric metaverse communications. IEEE J Select Areas Commun 42(4):963–977. https://doi.org/10.1109/JSAC.2023.3345392

Zhuang C, Liu J, Xiong H, Ding X, Liu S, Weng G (2017) Connotation, architecture and trends of product digital twin. Comput Integr Manufact Syst 23(4):753–768

The Implementation of U-space: Open Challenges from the Legal-Private Perspective

Yolanda Bustos Moreno

Abstract This paper addresses the main aspects of implementing U-Space in Europe according to its regulatory framework. We analyse the reasons for the delay in its roadmap and the challenges to resolve. In turn, we discuss the importance of addressing data interconnectivity and information exchange and aspects related to cybersecurity and resilience in the field of U-Space, which are not analysed by the doctrine. We also discuss the applicability of the AI Act to U-Space as a critical digital infrastructure and whether some of its services could somehow fit within the "high-risk AI systems" intended to be used as security components in their management and operation, with the important consequences that such qualification entails.

1 Conceptualization and Contextualization of U-Space

U-Space[1] is one of the largest projects initiated by the European Union in terms of technological complexity and operational safety challenges. The system is being developed in a coordinated manner in Europe to manage Unmanned Aircraft Systems (UAS) traffic in airspace, and it is beginning to form what is known as UAS Traffic Management or *Unmanned Traffic Management* (UTM). U-Space is the name the European Union gave to the project that involves creating its own UTM

This paper expands and updates the text of a lecture delivered at the III International Congress entitled "Present and future of crypto-assets regulation in the European Union," held at the University of Alicante (Spain) on December 13, 14, and 15, 2023. This work is funded within the framework of: Proyecto CIPROM/2022/26 "Presente y futuro de la regulación de los Criptoactivos en la UE [Legalcripto]". Proyecto Prometeo CIPROM/2022/26, grupos de investigación de excelencia, de la Generalitat Valenciana (P.I. Carmen Pastor).

[1] "U-Space is not an acronym.

Y. Bustos Moreno (✉)
University of Alicante, San Vicente del Raspeig, Spain
e-mail: bustos@ua.es

C. Pastor Sempere (ed.), *Governance and Control of Data and Digital Economy in the European Single Market*, Law, Governance and Technology Series 71,
https://doi.org/10.1007/978-3-031-74889-9_22

system.[2] U-Space is the ecosystem the European Union is deploying to enable the safe and efficient traffic of drones and their coexistence with manned aircraft. It is constituted as the set of providers, services and procedures that, in a regulated and coordinated manner in Europe, will be responsible for the traffic management of unmanned aircraft systems (UAS) in certain airspaces.[3]

In Europe today, although the number of UAS flights on a typical day is small, the need for the U-Space concept and major projects (*e.g.*, CORUS-XUAM) developed for its deployment is driven by other short—and medium-term forecasts.[4] The forecast increase in drone traffic demonstrates the need for the measures outlined in the following section on the deployment of U-Space and the remaining challenges to be addressed in the last section.

This concept arises to enable a high number of unmanned aircraft operations, especially those of higher complexity, such as beyond visual range (BVLOS), initially at a very low level (VLL),[5] in an orderly, seamless, safe and affordable manner,[6] as well as to reduce foreseeable safety, security, privacy and environmental risks. In certain areas, such as in particular in areas where a large number of simultaneous UAS operations are expected or in areas where UAS operate together with manned aircraft, the safe, secure and efficient integration of UAS in airspace requires the introduction of additional specific rules and procedures for the organisations involved in their operation, as well as a high degree of automation and digitalisation, Recitals 2 and 3 of Regulation (EU) 2021/664.[7] Thus, following this European Standard, U-Space has been defined as the set of specific services and procedures designed to ensure safe and efficient airspace access for many drones incorporating such levels of digitisation and automation.[8]

---

[2]Regarding UTM systems in other countries, such as the United States, see Michaelides-Mateou (2023).

[3]AESA U-Space Service Providers.

[4]The FAA projects the small model UAS fleet to grow from 1.2 million vehicles in 2018 to 1.4 million in 2023, an average annual growth rate of 2.2%. The commercial, small, non-model UAS fleet is forecast to nearly triple from 277,386 in 2018 to 835,211 in 2023, an average annual growth rate of 24.7%, FAA (2019).

[5]Initially, the aim is to coordinate the use of these aircraft in low altitude airspace (up to 120 metres above ground level), for the time being limited to those considered small (up to a maximum take-off weight of 25 kg). However, the greatest complexity of UAS operations occurs beyond visual range (BVLOS), albeit initially at a very low level, https://www.droneuropa.com/U-Space/.

[6]PANDU (2022), p. 6.

[7]Digitalisation is a cornerstone for providing a fully integrated, scalable traffic management system capable of handling growing air traffic, both manned and unmanned, Barrado et al. (2019), p. 10.

Furthermore, to make the digital transformation of the transport sector a reality, the EU must ensure the availability of key digital enablers, such as electronic components for mobility, network infrastructure, cloud/edge resources, data technologies and governance, and artificial intelligence, European Commission (2022), p. 19 ap. 67.

[8]It is an unmanned aircraft traffic management solution that will enable the scaling up of complex drone operations in challenging environments, Michaelides-Mateou (2023), p. 387.

U-Space aims to achieve the safe and automated integration of UAS to enable many simultaneous flight operations, especially in low-altitude airspace and urban environments (UAM), and harmonious coexistence with conventional aviation's existing air traffic management system.[9] This is intended to enable and enhance the development of new markets and realise the sector's expected economic growth potential.[10]

With the right framework, the European drone services market could reach a value of €14.5 billion in 2030, with a compound annual growth rate of 12.3%, and create 145,000 jobs in the EU. Drones are already used as daily tools in an ever-broadening array of data-intensive-demanding economic sectors, such as agriculture, construction, surveillance, filmmaking, healthcare, medical emergency, energy, environment, public safety and security. Drones could also be used in the future, for example, as platforms for communication hubs, weather and pollution monitoring, and maintenance of renewable energy installations, especially for offshore wind.[11]

The ConOps development has been guided by the same set of five high-level principles that inspired U-Space: (1) Safety first: The safety assessment is comprehensively addressed with a newly proposed methodology. (2) Open market: To create an environment where numerous businesses can operate, innovate, compete, and provide cost-efficient services. (3) Socially acceptable: To balance the commercial drive for increased drone use with preserving nature, public health, personal privacy, and European security. Social acceptance has been considered from the outset of the ConOps design. (4) Equitable access: All airspace users must be treated fairly, provided safety requirements are met. Exceptions will apply only to life-saving or other emergency-response flights. (5) Europe-wide: The ConOps is designed to be implemented across all Member States of the European Civil Aviation Conference (ECAC), with minor adaptations.[12]

[9]U-Space should not be considered a defined volume of airspace, segregated for exclusive drone use, but an environment capable of ensuring the proper functioning of drones in all operating environments and types of airspace, in particular, but not limited to airspace, Fernández Vallejo (2020), p. 33.

[10]Retrieved from https://www.seguridadaerea.gob.es/es/ambitos/navegacion-aerea/proveedores-de-servicios-U-Space.

[11]It is stated in the European Commission (2022).

[12]In 2019 the U-Space concept of operations (ConOps) will be presented, produced around three new types of airspace volume, called X, Y, and Z, and the relevant U-Space services that will need to be supplied in each of these, Barrado (2019), p. 3.

2 The Regulation and Implementation Process in Europe

In February 2021, the European Aviation Safety Agency Committee approved the U-Space regulatory package. In April 2021, the European Commission adopted and published the framework governing U-Space in the EU, consisting of three implementing regulations applicable as of 26 January 2023, which regulate the technical and operational requirements for U-Space services and set out the competences and responsibilities for the various actors involved in its implementation.[13] On the one hand, this regulatory package consists of the Commission Implementing Regulation 2021/664 of 22 April 2021 on a U-Space regulatory framework (hereinafter Regulation (EU) 2021/664), which regulates the technical and operational requirements of the U-Space system. On the other hand, two Implementing Regulations are amended to incorporate requirements and obligations for air navigation service providers and manned aviation in U-Space airspaces and to complement the U-Space regulatory regime, namely: (1) Implementing Regulation 2021/665 amending Implementing Regulation (EU) 2017/373 laying down common requirements for air traffic management and air navigation service providers to establish the specific coordination procedures and communication facilities between air traffic systems units, U-Space service providers and unmanned aircraft system operators; and, (2) Implementing Regulation 2021/666 amending Regulation (EU) No 923/2012 [laying down the rules of the air (SERA Regulation)], which establishes common rules for making effectively visible by electronic means the presence of manned aircraft operating in U airspace.[14]

Alongside these Regulations, EASA (European Aviation Safety Agency) has already published two versions of Acceptable Means of Compliance (AMC) and Guidance Material (GM) to clarify the provisions of these Regulations and support the technical implementation of the U-Space regulatory package[15] regarding which gradual implementation is foreseen.

Since 2017, four development phases have been designed for the full and effective implementation of U-Space in European airspace (including cities), depending on the increase in the level of automation and connectivity, as well as the progress of future research and innovation activities. Starting with Foundation Services U1 (2019), Initial Services U2 (2022), U-Space advanced Services U3

[13]The need for solutions related to drones and their integration with manned aviation was quickly identified in Europe. The concept was named U-Space and was announced by the European Commission (EC) at the European Aviation Safety Agency (EASA) High-Level Conference on Drones held in 2016 in Warsaw (Poland), Kotlinski and Calkowska (2022), p. 2; EASA (2016). On the process of drafting the Opinion 01/2020 *High-level regulatory framework for space U* 13 March 2020 (https://www.easa.europa.eu/en/document-library/opinions/opinion-012020), can be consulted Konert and Kasprzyk (2020), p. 306.

[14]Michaelides-Mateou (2023).

[15]EASA Easy Access Rules for U-Space (Regulation (EU) 2021/664) May 2024. Previously, EASA published its first set of AMC and GM of the U-Space regulatory framework (Regulations (EU) 2021/664, (EU) 2021/665 and (EU) 2021/666 on 19 December 2022.

(2027), and finally, phase U4 with Full Services (2035).[16] However, a more realistic implementation schedule is currently envisaged (CORUS XUAM- SESAR).[17] Once the foundations of U-Space have been laid down, the Member States set up registries and define geographic areas under the UAS regulatory framework (2019/947 & 2019/945 and subsequent amendments such as 2020/639, 2020/746, 2020/1058, 2021/1166, 2022/425, etc, together with the corresponding AMC-GM, drones fly without U-Space services. Manual coordination with, and authorisations from, the involved authorities are usually required. ATC procedures make Visual Line of Sight (VLOS) flights possible, although sometimes, they require some effort. Beyond Visual Line of Sight (BVLOS), flights are limited, time-consuming and expensive to set up. From 2023 to 2030, as the U-Space regulatory framework has just entered into force and the corresponding AMC-GMs, only a limited number of services are available, providing digital assistance to the authorities in charge of authorising operations and for operators to plan and declare their operations. Where necessary, temporary or permanent airspace structures are defined to allow drone operations, e.g., corridors for point-to-point transport of goods or passengers.[18]

In Spain, Royal Decree 517/2024 of June 4 *developed the legal regime for the civil use of unmanned aircraft systems (UAS) and amending various regulatory norms concerning import control of certain products concerning applicable safety regulations, civil air demonstrations, firefighting and search and rescue; airworthiness and licensing requirements for other aeronautical activities; registration of civil aircraft; electromagnetic compatibility of electrical and electronic equipment; air regulations and common operational provisions for air navigation services and procedures; and civil aviation incident reporting* (hereinafter Royal Decree 517/2024) has recently been approved, which, among other objectives, provides for the completion of the legal regime of the Implementing Regulation (EU) 2021/664 on a regulatory framework for U-Space in terms of organisation and competences, as set out in art. 1.1.c) and explained in the following section.[19] The

[16]As described in Airbus (Altiscope) 2018 and SESAR JU (2018).

[17]Based on the following elements that should be fulfilled: Availability of the U-Space services; Availability of the required technologies for Communication, Navigation and Surveillance (CNS) and ground infrastructure for drone operations, Availability of the "drones effective enough" to perform specific operations (e.g., carry heavy payload, long haul trip), Evolution of the airspace design and structure, Interactions with crewed aviation in controlled and uncontrolled airspace, Rules of the air, SESAR JU (2023), pp. 13–15.

[18]On the difference between controlled and uncontrolled airspace, see SESAR JU (2023), pp. 13–15.

[19]Previously, in Spain, creating a Plan for implementing U-Space was already anticipated in previous MITMA initiatives. Thus, the Strategic Plan for developing the civil drone sector in Spain 2018-20216 (March 2018) included an initiative to implement the U-Space system within the strategic axis focused on boosting business development and R&D&I in the UAS sector. Furthermore, within the Smart Mobility axis of the Safe, Sustainable and Connected Mobility Strategy 2030 (2020), one of the measures proposed to promote the use of drones is a plan for deploying and operating common infrastructure for implementing U-Space in Spain. The Ministry of Transport, Mobility and Urban Agenda has published the National Action Plan for the Deployment of U-Space

explanatory memorandum states that: "in the application of the provisions of the U-Space Regulation, the competent bodies for the designation of particular UAS geographical areas as U-Space, the certification and supervision of those providing services in these airspaces and the designation of the single common information service provider are established". At the end of August 2021, the Swiss U-Space Implementation (SUSI) partnership started working on implementing the UAS flight authorisation service as described in Article 10 of Regulation (EU) 2021/664.[20]

Also of note are important projects studying the forthcoming implementation in certain Spanish cities,[21] and others involving Eurocontrol in different European States,[22] such as the BURDI project (Belgium-Netherlands U-Space Reference Design Implementation).[23] This is an important initiative in drone integration in European airspace, particularly in Belgium and the Netherlands.

(hereinafter, PANDU) to promote the development and implementation of the U-Space system and services in a coordinated and efficient manner throughout the national territory. The main objective of the Action Plan is to involve all the agents of the sector by defining lines of action that will guide the necessary coordination for the implementation of this new system during the period 2022–2025, preparing the national framework for the adoption of the U-Space regulatory package approved by the European Commission last February 2021, PANDU (2022), p. 9.

[20]On automated UAS flight authorisation testing, see Boekholt (2022).

[21]DALIAH with a high degree of automation. This project, launched with funding from the European Union's Climate, Infrastructure and Environment Executive Agency (CINEA) in cooperation with SESAR 3 Joint Undertaking, has an overall budget of 15 million euros. It is coordinated by the Eurocontrol Innovation Hub and involves seven European countries and 51 partners, including ITG, A López Fidalgo (ITG) (2024).

[22]The main U-Space related research projects in which EUROCONTROL is actively involved are: Single European Sky ATM Research (SESAR) U-Space projects: CORUS-XUAM (Concept of operations for European space services—extension for urban air mobility); BURBUJAS (Building blocks for a U-Space separation management service); DACUS (Demand and capacity optimisation in U-Space); ICARUS (Integrated common altitude reference system for U-Space); INVIRCAT (IFR RPAS control at Airports and TMAs); URCLerED (Unified integrated concept of staying well clear in DG class airspace); AURA (ATM U-Space Interface). Horizon 2020 U-Space related research projects:

5D-AeroSafe (5 Drone Services to increase airport and waterway safety); LABYRINTH (4d unmanned traffic management route planning technologies for drones); Drone4Safety (Inspection Drones for Ensuring Safety in Transport Infrastructure), reported by Khurana (2021).

[23]The BURDI Project was presented at the European U-Space Stakeholders Network meeting in Katowice, Poland, on 22 November 2023. At this meeting, various aspects related to U-Space implementation were discussed, including interoperability with air traffic management (ATM) systems, scalability of drone operations and implementation initiatives in specific cities such as Antwerp, Brussels and Liège, The BURDI project also stands out for its efforts to ensure the social acceptability of drones, addressing concerns related to safety, privacy, noise and sustainability. This integration is essential for more complex, longer-range drone operations, especially in low and densely operated airspaces. In this regard, https://www.eurocontrol.int/sites/default/files/2023-12/2023-11-22-uspace-meeting-katowice-antoon-uspace-in-cities-burdi.pdf.; https://www.eurocontrol.int/event/european-network-U-Space-stakeholders-meeting-katowice.

3 Key elements: Mandatory Services, U-Space Service Providers (USSP) and Common Information Service Providers (CISP)

The first key pillar of this concept is *U-Space airspaces*. These are volumes of airspace in which U-Space services are provided to ensure safe, efficient and interoperable operations, which have been established as minimum and mandatory.[24] Art. 2.1 Regulation (EU) 2021/664 defines *U-Space airspace* as the geographical UAS area designated by Member States, in which UAS operations are only allowed to be conducted with the support of U-Space services.[25] For its part, in Spain, the recently approved Royal Decree 517/2024 states in Art. 62 that the Interministerial Commission for Defence and Transport (CIDETRA) is responsible for designating airspace as U-Space in these cases.[26]

U-Space *services* are the second key element. They are based on a component of digitisation and automation of functions designed to facilitate safe, efficient and secure access to U-Space airspace for many UAS, ex Art. 2.3 Regulation (EU) 2021/664. The U-Space Regulation establishes four mandatory services for flying in any U-Space airspace.[27] Firstly, the *network identification* service, regulated in Art. 8 Regulation (EU) 2021/664, is responsible for providing the identity of UAS operators and the location, trajectory and heading information of drones during operations. It enables continuous processing of the remote identification of the UAS throughout the flight and provides remote identification of the UAS to

---

[24] PANDU (2022), p. 11.

[25] Art. 3 Regulation (EU) 2021/664 states that: "Where Member States designate U-Space airspace for safety, security, privacy or environmental reasons, such designation shall be supported by an airspace *risk assessment*" (emphasis added). Art. 2(3) provides that an *airspace risk assessment* is "an assessment of operational, safety and security risks taking into account the required safety performance levels as defined in the European Aviation Safety Plan and the State Safety Programme referred to in Articles 6 and 7 of Regulation (EU) 2018/1139, the type, complexity and density of traffic, location, altitudes or heights and airspace classification. Regarding the methodology for U-Space safety assessment (MEDUSA), we refer to Barrado et al. (2019), pp. 9–10 to identify and mitigate relevant risks of drone operations supported by U-Space services.

[26] Art. 62 Royal Decree 517/2024: "1. The Interministerial Commission provided for in Article 6 of Law 21/2003 of 7 July 2003 is responsible for designating airspace as U-Space for reasons of safety, security, privacy or environment, in accordance with Article 3 of the U-Space Regulation. A distinction is made between general geographical areas, particular geographical areas for safety, security, privacy or environmental reasons (Art. 45, in accordance with Art. 15.1 Implementing Regulation and Art. 45.4).

[27] As summarised on the website https://www.seguridadaerea.gob.es/es/ambitos/navegacion-aerea/proveedores-de-servicios-U-Space#U-Space. In the U-Space ConOps projected in CORUS (2019), the *Incident/accident reporting* is the service that receives reports describing dangerous situations collected by drone operators and stores them for further analysis, and the *digital logbook* service stores all the essential data of each flight. However, the digital logbook service may not be available in volumes X and Y due to its high provision cost. Barrado et al. (2019), p. 8.

authorised users.[28] The *geo-awareness* service, referred to in Art. 9 Regulation (EU) 2021/664, is responsible for information on operational conditions, airspace limitations or temporary restrictions in the U-Space. It provides information regarding applicable operational conditions and airspace limitations, relevant UAS geographical areas, or applicable temporary limits on the use of airspace within U-Space airspace.[29] In addition, the flight *authorisation* service ensures that operations within the same volume of U-Space airspace are free of conflicts with other UAS and UAS areas that may have restrictions. Finally, the traffic information service informs UAS operators about other unmanned and manned traffic near their aircraft under the terms of Art. 11 Regulation (EU) 2021/664. In addition to these mandatory services, it is foreseen that Member States may require additional services, such as the weather information service[30] and a compliance monitoring service (Recitals 23, 24, 25 and Arts. 3.3, 12 and 13).

These U-Space services are provided by U-Space service providers (USSP). These are legal entities certified to perform the services described (Art. 3, paragraphs. 2 and 3 of Regulation (EU) 2021/664) for UAS operators during all phases of operations in this U-Space airspace. In Spain, the recently approved Royal Decree 517/2024, whose territorial scope is Spanish sovereign airspace, is declared applicable, in addition to air traffic service providers (ATS providers, *Air Traffic Service providers*), to aeronautical information service providers, as well as to these U-Space service providers and the single provider of common information services, as far as they are concerned, Art. 3. b and c Royal Decree 517/2024. Regarding the latter service, Article 2.4 of Regulation (EU) 2021/664 defines the *common information service* as "consisting of the dissemination of static and dynamic data enabling the provision of U-Space services for the management of unmanned aircraft traffic".

The U-Space Regulation leaves the delivery model for such U-Space services to the choice of each State. The service delivery model can be *centralised* or *distributed*. In the so-called *centralised* service provision model, a single provider of common information services is designated for all or some of the U-Space airspaces. This provider is a single focal point for common information and may centralise coordination between USSPs (U-Space Service Providers) and ATS providers.[31] In Spain, Royal Decree 517/2024 determines that the Ministry of Transport and Sustainable Mobility is the body responsible for the designation of the Common

[28] To implement Remote Identification in different countries, see Belwafi et al. (2022). For the Swiss U-Space Implementation (SUSI), members developed NET-RID, which complies with the U-Space Regulation (EU) 2021/664 adopted by the European Commission; in this regard, see Boekholt (2021).

[29] https://www.seguridadaerea.gob.es/es/ambitos/navegacion-aerea/proveedores-de-servicios-U-Space#U-Space.

[30] In this framework, regarding it the Italian Aerospace Research Centre (CIRA, Italy) is implementing the internal EDUS project "Infrastrutture di elaborazione dati locali per U-SPACE", Bucchignani (2023), p. 1684, https://doi.org/10.3390/atmos14111684.

[31] See https://www.seguridadaerea.gob.es/es/ambitos/navegacion-aerea/proveedores-de-servicios-U-Space#U-Space.

Information Service Providers (CISP).[32] Recently, ENAIRE was designated as the sole provider of common information services for U-Space areas in the implementation phase of the single system *for* 10 years, extendable on agreement by the Ministry of Transport and Sustainable Mobility (Additional Provisions 7 and 8 of Royal Decree 517/2024).

To ensure the provision of safe and high-quality U-Space services, this Regulation establishes a common *certification* scheme for certifying U-Space service providers and, where designated by Member States, a single common information service provider, as well as a set of rules for the regular monitoring of compliance with the applicable requirements (Art. 14-15 Regulation (EU) 2021/664). In Spain, AESA is the competent authority for issuing, amending, revoking, suspending or limiting Common Information Service Provider (CISP)[33] and U-Space Service Provider (USSP) certificates, and for the supervision of these providers.[34]

4 Interconnectivity and Data Protection of Exchanged Information

As can be anticipated from the above, one of the main challenges of implementing U-Space and other UTM models (e.g., the United States) is to have various services interconnected. Within the modular architectural design that is U-Space, the different services provided must provide data to each other.[35] The Drones 2.0 Strategy already anticipated that drones, drone operations, and drone traffic management constitute a complex ecosystem of technological components and information exchange platforms, requiring highly optimised, safe, and secure elements such as flight control systems, cyber-secure data links, and connectivity.[36] Given this situation of

[32]In this context, https://www.seguridadaerea.gob.es/es/noticias/nueva-actualizacion-normativa-para-impulsar-el-sector-de-los-drones-en-espana.

[33]Seventh additional provision Royal Decree 517/2024: "*Entity responsible for making available information on UAS geographical areas in a single common digital format.* The public business entity ENAIRE is the entity responsible for making available, in a single common digital format, the information on the geographical areas of UAS identified in Spanish sovereign territory and airspace, in accordance with letter f) of Article 18 of the Implementing Regulation, until the Ministry of Transport and Sustainable Mobility designates another entity or body for this task", in accordance with Article 60, paragraph 5.

[34]The USSP and CISP supplier certification process includes the initial issuance and modification of the certificate. In Spain, in accordance with the PANDU (2022), AESA has enabled the administrative procedures in relation to the certification of USSP and CISP providers in its electronic site once the Acceptable Means of Compliance (AMC) and Guidance Material (GM) of Regulation (EU) 2021/664, which contains the development of the regulatory requirements for certification, have been published by EASA (European Union Aviation Safety Agency): https://sede.seguridadaerea.gob.es/sede-aesa/catalogo-de-procedimientos/certificaci%C3%B3n-de-proveedor-de-servicios-de-U-Space-ussp#descarga_formularios.

[35]Fas-Millán et al. (2024), p. 1.

[36]European Commission (2022), p. 20, par. 78.

interconnectivity, Regulation (EU) 2021/664 already expresses in its Recitals (2 and 5) the concern for compliance with security and privacy requirements, without forgetting the safety of operations in that airspace. In this regard, Recital (1) states that the Regulation should establish requirements for common interoperable and open communication protocols between authorities, service providers and UAS operators, as well as requirements for quality, latency and data protection of the information exchanged, which are necessary for safe and interoperable operations in U-Space airspace.

In those U-Space airspaces where the state has designated them, CIS providers shall disseminate the common information necessary to enable the system's operation, facilitating interconnection with the air traffic control systems of the service providers concerned and between U-Space service providers for the exchange of static and dynamic operational data. In Spain, ENAIRE, as a CIS provider, will be a single and reliable source of all common information.[37]

Specifically, Articles 5.4, 5.5 and 7.4 of Regulation (EU) 2021/664 state that "Providers of common information services shall ensure that the information referred to in paragraphs 1, 2 and 3 is made available following Annex II and complies with the necessary quality, latency, information exchange, interaction, communication and data protection requirements set out in Annex III". And that access to common information services shall be granted to competent authorities, air traffic service providers, U-Space service providers and UAS operators on a non-discriminatory basis, ensuring the same quality, latency, information exchange, interactions, communication and data protection levels. U-Space service providers shall treat air traffic data without discrimination, restriction or interference, regardless of its sender or receiver, content, application or service, or terminal equipment. U-Space service providers shall exchange with each other all information relevant to the secure provision of U-Space services, adhere to a common, secure, interoperable and open communication protocol, and use the latest information made available per Annex II. In addition, they shall ensure that information is exchanged under the quality, latency, and data protection requirements in Annex III and provide access to and the necessary protection for the information exchanged.

For its part, the far-reaching Annex III of Regulation (EU) 2021/664 states that the data quality, latency, information exchange, interactions, communication and data protection requirements in Articles 5(4)(b) and 7(5)(c) require that to meet the data quality requirements, common information service providers and U-Space service providers shall ensure that data quality is maintained, verification and validation techniques are used to ensure that data are received without corruption and that no corruption occurs at any stage of data processing, metadata are collected and preserved, data transfer is subject to an appropriate authentication process that

[37] In the so-called distributed service delivery model, there is no CIS provider, and states are responsible for making common information available to all parties and ensuring that the relevant operational data are made available by the ATS providers. Coordination between the USSPs and the ATS providers occurs directly, without intermediaries, PANDU (2022), pp. 13–14.

allows recipients to confirm that an authorised source has transmitted the data or information, and mechanisms for error reporting, error measurement and corrective action are established and maintained. To protect data, common information service providers and U-Space service providers shall implement security policies that include data encryption and protection of critical data, protect open, secure and interoperable communication protocols against intentional, unauthorised electronic interactions that may result in an unacceptable breakdown of communications, identify, assess and mitigate, if necessary, security risks and vulnerabilities, respect security rules and regulations regarding where data may be stored and ensure that third party providers agree to follow security practices, describe a policy of awareness and training of employees and tools to reduce internal risks and protect data, including intellectual property, and in doing so, monitor user and network activity to provide information on ecosystem vulnerabilities and threats, and deploy solutions that enhance threat detection and intelligence capabilities and ensure the use of technological safeguards.[38]

The interaction and exchange of information between Air Traffic Services (ATS) *providers* and *U-Space service providers are* more complex.[39] As stated above, the integration of services with other UTM systems and platforms can be challenging due to the lack of standardisation in the sector.[40] Art. 7.3 of the Regulation states that "U-Space service providers shall establish arrangements with air traffic service providers to ensure appropriate coordination of activities and the exchange of relevant operational data and information per Annex V.

Under Annex V of Regulation (EU) 2021/664, the information exchange model must possess the following characteristics, which, as stated above, reveal the technological and legal complexity of its implementation: (a) facilitate the management and distribution of information in digital format; (b) detail the characteristics of the information exchanged, including its properties, attributes, data types and associations; (c) incorporate data restrictions and validation rules; (d) employ a standard format for data encoding; (e) provide an extension mechanism that allows user groups to extend the properties of existing features and add new features without adversely affecting standardisation within and between Member States. Annex V sets out two guidelines for U-Space service providers and air traffic service providers on information exchange, already recognised in European legislation in other fields such as geospatial, with corresponding legal and technological challenges for

[38] Regarding data security and privacy concerns in drone operations, see Sindiramutty and Jhanjhi (2024).

[39] A study by Vee Weiland (2021) explored the interconnection between air traffic controllers and Unmanned Aircraft Systems (UAS) to identify potential human factor issues when UAS enter national airspace. By analysing the performance of controllers, UAS operators, commercial pilots, and the equipment, the study found that air traffic controllers lack a full understanding of human factors in UAS integration, which could lead to various human errors during UAS operations in national airspace. Consequently, additional research, education, and training are necessary to reduce these potential errors.

[40] Singh and Pashchapur (2024).

implementation and deployment: 1. use a recognised encryption method; and 2. use a common, secure, interoperable and open communication protocol.[41]

Finally, concerning the authorities' responsibilities in this respect, Art. 18. d) Regulation (EU) 2021/664 establishes, among the tasks of the competent authorities, that they ensure "that exchanges of data between air traffic service providers and U-Space service providers are carried out following Annex V". At the national level, Art. 58 of Royal Decree 517/2024, concerning the processing of personal data, states that the State Secretariat for Security shall keep the Registers of Processing Activities of the personal data contained in the Register of unmanned aircraft. Aircraft data, including related personal data, shall be kept under the instructions of the data controller from their entry in the register until their removal from the register by the data controller and after that for 5 years, except in cases of a legal obligation to keep them. The controller shall transfer aircraft data, including related personal data, to the competent authorities for the prevention, investigation, detection, punishment or prosecution of criminal offences or the enforcement of criminal penalties. Following the applicable data protection legislation, these data may be transferred to the competent administrative authorities in aviation safety. Personal data shall be deleted from the register upon expiry of the time limit, without prejudice to cases where specific personal data have been transferred to the competent authorities. The exercise of the rights of data subjects shall be facilitated under the applicable personal data protection legislation.

5 Cybersecurity Applicable to Aviation, Particularly U-Space

Given the above, security and privacy issues are also of concern in the U-Space domain, as UAMs collect and transmit sensitive data that can be intercepted or hacked if appropriate security measures are not taken.[42] This section specifically addresses these cybersecurity issues, although they are not directly discussed in Regulation (EU) 2021/664, except in some recently amended aspects, as discussed below.

Aviation is one of the classic sectors in terms of security concerns and possible attacks or illicit interference.[43] Aviation is now widely recognised as an attractive

[41] Díaz Díaz (2021), p. 118.

[42] Singh and Pashchapur (2024).

[43] As reflected in the list of Conventions and International Treaties signed by Spain, cybersecurity is mentioned directly and indirectly. The 1970 Hague Convention for the Suppression of Unlawful Seizure of Aircraft can include cyberattacks that control a passenger. The 2010 Beijing Supplementary Protocol explicitly addresses the cyber aspect. The 1971 Montreal Convention and its 1988 Protocol include external cyberattacks and unlawful acts at airports. The 2010 Beijing Convention strengthens protection against cyberattacks on air navigation systems. The 2010 Beijing Supplementary Protocol, which reinforces the Hague Convention, specifies that any technological attack constitutes a crime.

target for cyber-attacks, appealing to various malicious actors. These actors possess different motivations, capabilities, and levels of sophistication, enabling them to successfully exploit vulnerabilities in the aviation ecosystem.[44] Protecting civil aviation assets against interference and attacks seeking to cause significant damage will be a priority in the coming years, both in the airport environment and other critical infrastructures. The Spanish Aviation Safety Agency (AESA) continues to progress in regulating airspace use by airborne vehicles by developing U-Space environments for greater control, as outlined in the Annual Homeland Security Report 2023.[45]

The danger of attacks via the connection to satellite information deserves a separate mention. In recent years, incidents of Global Navigation Satellite System (GNSS) jamming and spoofing have increasingly threatened the integrity of positioning, navigation and timing (PNT) services in Eastern Europe and the Middle East. Similar incidents have been reported elsewhere in the world. GNSS is a service based on constellations of satellites such as the US Global Positioning System (GPS) and the EU's Galileo. 'Jamming' blocks a signal, while 'spoofing' sends false information to the aircraft's receiver. These disruptions pose significant challenges for industries that rely on accurate geolocation services, including aviation. These attacks fall within the scope of cybersecurity, a security threat for which EASA has developed a set of tools in its collaboration with IATA, such as the connection to databases (IATA Flight Data Exchange (FDX) or Eurocontrol EVAIR).[46]

ICAO has had an Aviation Cybersecurity Strategy in place since 2019 and has adopted three resolutions at its Assembly (A39-19 in 2016, replaced in 2019 by A40-10 and, as of today, Resolution A41-19 in 2022). These resolutions address the importance of cybersecurity in civil aviation, highlighting the complexity and interconnectedness of the global aviation system, including systems critical to operational safety and security. It highlights the increasing dependence of aviation on the reliability, integrity and availability of systems and data, as well as the rapid evolution of cyber threats that can affect safety and security. It emphasises the need

---

[44] At its fortieth session, 2019, the ICAO Assembly adopted the amended Resolution A40-10, which addresses cybersecurity in civil aviation. In this resolution, States are urged to implement the Cybersecurity Strategy, stressing the importance of developing a sustainable plan for its implementation and continuing to work on the formulation of a robust framework that provides a basis for States, industry, stakeholders and ICAO to work together to strengthen the capacity to identify, prevent and detect cyber-attacks in civil aviation, , posted by P Martínez Bautista (2024) "Civil aviation: in the age of AI and cybersecurity", https://paisdominicanotematico.com/2024/03/06/aviacion-civil-en-la-era-de-la-ia-y-la-ciberseguridad/.

[45] As can be seen from https://www.newtral.es/wp-content/uploads/2024/03/IASN2023_0.pdf, P. 150.

[46] EASA and IATA also emphasise the importance of immediate long-term measures, including sharing information on incidents and adapting certification requirements for navigation systems. They propose maintaining traditional navigation systems as a backup and underline the need for international cooperation to address these threats, highlighting the increase in attacks and the importance of a coordinated and robust response to ensure safety. https://www.easa.europa.eu/en/domains/cyber-security.

for an international collaborative approach to strengthen cyber resilience and address cyber threats through legal frameworks such as the Beijing Convention and the Beijing Protocol. In turn, the Assembly urges Member States to adopt these instruments and implement measures such as the ICAO Cybersecurity Strategy, designate competent authorities and define clear responsibilities among national bodies and industry stakeholders for effective cybersecurity management in civil aviation.[47]

Similarly, security and cybersecurity are paramount issues in developing Unmanned Aircraft Systems (UAS) operations. However, small drones have been used in various illegal and criminal activities due to their easy availability, affordability, adaptability, and anonymity. These include smuggling and delivering drugs and contraband, gathering intelligence and sensitive data, capturing private information and PIN codes from ATMs, stealing intellectual property, espionage, illegal filming, and being deployed as weapons to carry traditional or improvised explosive devices to or over targets.[48]

Most cybersecurity breaches involve using frequency-transmitting devices to jam or interfere with radio communications. These breaches include GPS jamming and spoofing, video interception, hijacking attacks through communication spoofing of sensors, exploiting vulnerabilities in digital systems, and disrupting or taking control of unmanned aircraft operations. Such actions can be for malicious purposes, such as causing injury to people on the ground, violating privacy, or damaging infrastructure.[49]

Focusing on EU cybersecurity legislation, the starting point is Regulation (EU) 2018/1139, which establishes common rules in civil aviation and creates a European Union Aviation Safety Agency, known as EASA. This Regulation highlights the interdependence between the various facets of safety, including cybersecurity in civil aviation, and promotes cooperation between Member States and the Agency. In this context, EASA plays a crucial role in regulation and oversight to ensure that aviation operators and service providers possess adequate cybersecurity management competencies in a constantly evolving operational environment. Operators and service providers must identify and manage information security risks to information and communications technology systems and data used in civil aviation. These risks must be addressed because of their potential impact on aviation safety and security. In addition, it seeks to strengthen the resilience of the aviation system, which is considered largely interconnected and requires an up-to-date awareness of both direct and indirect cyber threats.

Of particular significance in the field of *security* is[50] Implementing Regulation (EU) 2019/1583, which lays down detailed measures for implementing the common

---

[47] Annex 17 and Aviation Cybersecurity, Lampariello and Boszczowski (2022).

[48] Mateou and Mateou (2021).

[49] Tran et al. (2022).

[50] The two fields of safety and security have traditionally been kept separate in aviation: *safety* and *security*. While the former deals with the risks associated with aviation activities, the latter protects civil aviation against acts of unlawful interference. On the other hand, Regulation (EU) No

basic standards on aviation security regarding cybersecurity measures, amending Implementing Regulation (EU) 2015/1998, effective from 31 December 2021. The requirements of this Regulation apply to airport operators, air carriers, and other entities defined in the National Civil Aviation Security Programme (NSP).

In turn, cybersecurity is covered by Implementing Regulation (EU) 2023/203 (EASA PART-IS Information Security), which implements provisions of Regulation (EU) 2018/1139 regarding the management of *information security risks* that may affect aviation security. *Information security* is defined in Art. 3 as the "preservation of the confidentiality, integrity, authenticity and availability of networks and information systems" and "information security risk" in the sense of risk involving the possibility of an information security event occurring to civil aviation organisational operations, assets, people and other organisations; information security risks are associated with the possibility of threats taking advantage of vulnerabilities in an information asset or group of information assets. A threat is a potential information security breach from when an entity, circumstance, action, or event can cause damage. Concerning the object of study in this paper, it should be noted that Regulation (EU) 2023/203 is declared applicable, among other aeronautical organisations, to "U-Space service providers and single common information service providers subject to Implementing Regulation (EU) 2021/664 art. 2. i)". Consequently, it has amended Art. 15.1. f) and added point l) to Art. 18 of Regulation (EU) 2021/664.[51]

This Regulation 2023/203 has recently been amended by Commission Implementing Regulation (EU) 2024/1109 of 10 April 2024, which lays down rules for implementing Regulation (EU) 2018/1139 of the European Parliament and the Council regarding requirements for competent authorities and administrative procedures for the certification, oversight, and enforcement of the continuing airworthiness of certified unmanned aircraft systems.

Delegated Regulation (EU) 2022/1645, which also addresses information security, amends Regulations (EU) No. 748/2012 and (EU) No. 139/2014, additionally including requirements on the information security management system, with entry into force varying depending on the entity involved, between 16 October 2025 and

376/2014 on occurrence reporting in civil aviation is notable for its provisions on the protection of shared aviation safety information and the criteria it sets for reporting. Regulation (EU) 1035/2011 establishes common requirements for air navigation services, including measures to protect facilities and personnel from unlawful interference. Additionally, it highlights the importance of a functioning safety management system, stating that the air traffic service provider shall implement a software safety assurance system.

[51] Article 15 Regulation (EU) 2023/203: "Amendment of Implementing Regulation (EU) 2021/664 Implementing Regulation (EU) 2021/664 is amended as follows: 1) In Article 15(1), point (f) is replaced by the following: '(f) implement and maintain a security management system in accordance with point ATM/ANS.OR.D.010 of Subpart D of Annex III to Implementing Regulation (EU) 2017/373 and an information security management system in accordance with Annex II (Part IS.I.OR) to Implementing Regulation (EU) 2023/203;'. 2. in Article 18, the following point (l) is added: '(l) establish, implement and maintain an information security management system in accordance with Annex I (Part IS.AR) to Implementing Regulation (EU) 2023/203.

22 February 2026. These regulations underline the importance of addressing cyber risks that may impact operational security.

To ensure an appropriate level of protection for UAS operations within the existing airspace system, legislators and aviation authorities have implemented various measures, including the Specific Operational Risk Assessment (SORA) methodology developed by the Joint Authorities for the Regulation of Unmanned Aircraft Systems (JARUS). The scope of Annex E is limited to areas that directly impact flight safety and the protection of the public, primarily addressed to UAS operators and not to original equipment manufacturers.

To ensure cybersecurity commeasures with the risk in aviation, considering its dependence on interconnectivity between multiple systems and actors, Annex E focuses on aspects that impact flight safety and public security. This annexe introduces fundamental concepts such as cyber security and aviation security, especially aviation cybersecurity, which results from integrating the two, emphasising the need to incorporate cyber threat management into the risk assessment process. It also promotes the application of appropriate and proportionate cybersecurity measures within the SORA method, establishing levels of robustness for cyber requirements associated with proposed operations, including equipment manufacturers, maintainers and service providers.[52]

For its part, Spain has been implementing initiatives to protect against the risks associated with using drones for illicit purposes, both in terms of safety and cybersecurity, as seen in the National Aerospace Security Strategy 2019.[53] Drones generate additional risks and threats by facilitating espionage, attacks and physical risks to citizens and property security. Both state and non-state actors can compromise the aerial environment and continue to be an enabling space for the activities of organised criminal groups, states the Annual National Security Report 2023. The National Council for Aerospace Security (CNSA) has paid particular attention to the risks that drones pose to Homeland Security, pushing for implementing the actions identified in the 2022 study "Drones and Homeland Security".[54] And, among the most recently adopted national measures, Royal Decree 517/2024 provides for the

[52]The document defines essential attributes of aviation cybersecurity that ensure effective systems and data protection. These include *Confidentiality*, which prevents unauthorised access to information; *Integrity*, which ensures the accuracy and completeness of data; *Availability,* which ensures access to information when needed; *Authenticity*, which verifies the veracity of entities or data; and *Authentication* and *Authorisation* functions, which control access. Finally, concepts such as accounting and non-repudiation, which prevent the denial of executed actions or events, are addressed, which is crucial to countering internal threats and post-attack investigations. On the different attacks (Dos/DDoS, Spoofing, Hijacking and Malware), see Annex E (Cyber) Annex E - SORA (Cyber Annex) 17/05/2022 JAR_doc_19 JARUS, http://jarus-rpas.org/wp-content/uploads/2023/06/jar_19_doc_Cyber_Annex.pdfp. 8. More broadly, on the extension of the SORA methodology to cybersecurity and covering the privacy issue, see Tran et al. (2022).

[53]Order PCI/489/2019, of 26 April, publishing the National Aerospace Security Strategy, approved by the National Security Council.

[54]Government of Spain (2023a), pp. 11, 149–150.

creation of the "Registry of unmanned Aircraft of the Ministry of the Interior" so that the Armed Forces can have the appropriate means for the detection, prevention and traceability of these unlawful actions (arts. 53 to 57)[55] and an obligation to report UAS operations in urban environments or over concentrations of people to the Ministry of the Interior (ex art. 40.3.b) Royal Decree 517/2024.[56]

6 Artificial Intelligence and Resilience in the Field of U-Space

Increasingly, integrating artificial intelligence into U-Space could further open new possibilities for improving drone operations' safety and efficiency.[57] AI can process large amounts of data to optimise traffic management, perform predictive analytics to identify safety risks and automate obstacle detection and avoidance. It can also facilitate emergency management by coordinating search and rescue operations and ensuring compliance with airspace regulations and restrictions. The customisation of services according to the specific needs of each operation also benefits from advanced AI capabilities, allowing for greater flexibility and efficiency, all of which are addressed in the study. Let us look at some cases of utilities using AI in

[55] To prevent, investigate or detect the commission of criminal and administrative offences, including the protection and prevention of threats to public safety, the Registry of Unmanned Aircraft of the Ministry of the Interior is established, in which the data of unmanned aircraft shall be linked at all times to their owners.

[56] Art. 40.3 Royal Decree 517/2024: "Within these UAS geographical areas, UAS operations are subject, cumulatively, depending on the circumstances of the operation, to the following limitations:

(a) For reasons of public safety, UAS operators subject to the obligation to register as such who intend to carry out UAS operations in urban environments or over concentrations of people shall give prior notice to the Ministry of the Interior at least five calendar days before the planned date of commencement of the operation. This notification may contain as many operations as are to be carried out in the five calendar days following the date of commencement of the operations foreseen in the said notification, and the operator must indicate the date and the specific time slot with sufficient delimitation of each of the operations to be carried out. The competent public security authorities in the territorial scope of the operation may limit or prohibit its conduct, where it may give rise to serious risks to the protection of persons or property. When non-compliance with the obligation to make such prior notification or with the prohibitions or restrictions that may be imposed on UAS operations may be included in any of the offences relating to public safety set out in Chapter V of Organic Law 4/2015, of 30 March, on Public Safety, the sanctioning regime established in said law shall be applicable".

[57] The deployment will only be possible thanks to a significant component of Artificial Intelligence (AI/ML), further supported by fully digital communications, the use of cloud technologies, and similar methods for scaling services involved in thousands of simultaneous operations, as explained by the EASA, in the Artificial Intelligence Roadmap 2.0 (2023).

U-Space systems and how the recent EU regulation on AI (Artificial Intelligence Act[58]) and resilience could be applicable.

One of the main problems in the U-Space domain is avoiding potential collisions between aircraft, manned or unmanned. To this end, EASA is developing the ACAS Xu system.[59] ACAS[60] stands for Airborne Collision Avoidance System, a universal system-to-system collision avoidance system. It issues horizontal turn advisories to avoid an intruder aircraft. ACAS X stands for NextGeneration Airborne Collision Avoidance System. Airborne collision avoidance system Xu (ACAS Xu) is an air-to-air collision avoidance system designed for unmanned aircraft (drones). In the ACAS Xu system, the drone receives instructions on how to avoid any collision with an intruder. The purpose of an ACAS Xu system is to keep any intruder outside of the desired envelope of the ownship. In this use case, the objective is to produce an ML/DL model that can completely fit the discrete input lookup tables.[61] The ACAS Xu system does not need any communication between vehicles. Collision detection and advisories could be generated only using the ownship sensors. It enables the detection of cooperative traffic (other vehicles also equipped with the system) and noncooperative traffic, such as vehicles without ACAS Xu (small drones), birds, or ground obstacles. However, these tables require 2GB of storage space, which is not insignificant for drones. One way to circumvent this problem is to transform these tables into a neural network of smaller size. Hence, in this use case, the objective is to produce an ML/DL model that can completely fit the discrete input LU tables.

For its part, the AI Regulation (Recital 49) states that: "with regard to *high-risk AI systems* which are *safety components* of products or systems, or which are themselves products or systems falling within the scope of Regulation (EC) No 300/2008" of the European Parliament and of the Council of 11 March 2008 on common rules in the field of civil aviation security and repealing Regulation (EC) No

---

[58]The European Parliament adopted at first reading on 13 March 2024 and with a view to the adoption of Regulation (EU) 2024/1689 of the European Parliament and of the Council laying down harmonised rules on artificial intelligence and amending Regulations (EC) No 300/2008, (EU) No 167/2013, (EU) No 168/2013, (EU) 2018/858, (EU) 2018/1139 and (EU) 2019/2144 and Directives 2014/90/EU, (EU) 2016/797 and (EU) 2020/1828 (Artificial Intelligence Act) P9_TA(2024)0138 (COM(2021)0206 – C9-0146/2021 – 2021/0106(COD)), 19-4-2024, Plenary sitting https://www.europarl.europa.eu/doceo/document/TA-9-2024-0138-FNL-COR01_EN.pdf.

[59]The purpose is to provide a detailed analysis of three different use cases selected to evaluate the different methods and tools used in the scope of the MLEAP project. These use cases address different applications regarding data type, dimensionality, and task complexity. However, they provide an extensive benchmark for approving the applicability related to ML/DL models. Nevertheless, it is not intended to certify these applications but rather to support our conclusions and recommendations for verifications during the development of AI solutions meeting the same criteria (types of data, dimensionality, criticality, etc.). This will feed into the EASA certification process for AI applications, based on the results of this Project, Research Project EASA (2024b), p. 95. Gabreau et al. (2022)

[60]EASA (2024a), p. 41.

[61]This system is based on the data and models provided by the EUROCAE 2020 working group: https://www.eurocae.net/about-us/working-groups/.

2320/2002, as well as with regard to other EU Regulations and Directives, "it is appropriate to amend those acts to ensure that, when the Commission adopts relevant delegated or implementing acts based thereon, it takes into account mandatory requirements for high-risk *AI systems"*. Moreover, it states that "taking into account the technical and regulatory specificities of the different sectors and without interfering with the existing governance, conformity assessment and enforcement mechanisms and authorities established in those acts." In turn, Art. 6.2 and Annex III of the AI Regulation (Recital 55) determine that AI systems intended to be used as security components in the management and operation *of critical digital infrastructures* are high-risk systems.

It remains to be determined whether U-Space can be considered a 'critical digital infrastructure' and whether the operation of any U-Space service fits within the AI systems intended to be used as security components in its management and operation. The answer is to be found in Directive (EU) 2022/2557 of the European Parliament and of the Council, which repeals Council Directive 2008/114/EC and establishes the new Critical Entities Resilience Directive (hereinafter 'CER Directive'), which was enacted on 14 December 2022,[62] to which the AI Regulation refers (recital 55). U-Space integration appears affirmative within the scope of the AI Regulation and the CER Directive, although this is not expressly stated. We can deduce this by including digital infrastructures and air traffic management control in the Annex and Art. 6 of the CER Directive. Art. 6 furthermore states that, regarding identifying critical entities, "by 17 July 2026, Member States shall identify critical entities for the sectors and subsectors listed in the Annex."[63] This conclusion is also drawn from the definition of "critical entity",[64] and "critical infrastructure".[65]

The CER Directive institutes a comprehensive regulatory framework that addresses the *resilience* of *critical entities* to all types of hazards, whether natural

[62] On 16 January 2023, the NIS 2 Directive and the CER Directive entered into force. Member States have until 17 October 2024 to transpose the requirements of the CER Directive into national law.

[63] It is expressly determined in the Annex to the CER Directive that critical entities are air carriers, as defined in point 4 of Article 3 of Regulation (EC) No 300/2008 used for commercial purposes; airport managing bodies as defined in point 2 of Article 2 of Directive 2009/12/EC of the European Parliament and of the Council; airports as defined in point 1 of Article 2 of that Directive, including the core network airports listed in Section 2 of Annex II to Regulation (EU) No. 1315/2013 of the European Parliament and of the Council, and entities operating ancillary facilities within airport premises as defined in Section 2 of Annex II to Regulation (EU) No. 1315/2013 of the European Parliament and of the Council. 1315/2013 of the European Parliament and of the Council and entities operating ancillary installations on the premises of airports.

[64] Art. 2.1. CER Directive: "critical entity" means "a public or private entity identified by a Member State in accordance with Art. 6 as falling within one of the categories set out in the third column of the table in the Annex".

[65] Art. 2(4) CER Directive: "critical infrastructure" means "an item, facility, equipment, network or system, or part of an item, facility, equipment, network or system, which is necessary for the provision of an essential service". Art. 2. 5) "essential service" means a service that is crucial for maintaining vital societal functions, economic activities, public health and safety, or the environment".

or man-made, accidental or intentional.[66] This European regulation addresses a wide range of threats, including natural hazards, terrorist attacks, insider threats or acts of sabotage, covering eleven strategic sectors. Ultimately, implementing this Directive seeks to strengthen the ability of critical entities to anticipate, respond and adapt to various adversities, thus ensuring the stability and security of the European internal market in an environment of increasing risks and threats. Article 2(2) defines *resilience* as "the ability of a critical entity to prevent, protect against, respond to, withstand, mitigate, absorb, adapt to and recover from an incident"; and Article 2(3) defines "incident" as "an event that has the potential to disrupt significantly, or that disrupts, the provision of an essential service, in particular when it affects national systems that safeguard the rule of law".

In the legal field, resilience takes on special importance, particularly in the business context, where it is defined as the ability of an organisation to cope with adverse situations. In cybersecurity, this definition is further refined, described as the ability of an entity to recover after a security incident. Specifically, resilience refers to an organisation's ability to anticipate, withstand, recover from and adapt to significant threats that may compromise the integrity of its data, information, applications and infrastructure. The primary objective is to minimise the exposure time to these threats and the impact on the organisation's services.[67]

As far as high-risk AI systems are concerned, they must be secured and designed to be *resilient* against any attempt to alter their use, behaviour and performance, as well as to compromise their security properties by malicious third parties exploiting vulnerabilities in AI systems. Organisational and technical solutions will be implemented to achieve these objectives. In addition, a cybersecurity risk assessment applicable to high regulatory risk AI systems will be carried out. The AI Act[68] imposes a prior evaluation of the compliance of high-risk AI systems with Regulation 2024/482 (see Recital 78 AI Act). Complying with the standardisation rules is important in this context of alertness to the risks of constant innovation.[69]

Specifically, the AI Act deals with cybersecurity, albeit concisely and mainly in section 15.[70] Recital (76) states, "Cybersecurity is essential to ensure that AI systems are resilient to the actions of malicious third parties", to the extent that they may seek to alter their functionality or compromise their security. It emphasises the importance of vendors of high-risk AI systems adopting appropriate measures, such as security

[66] Critical entities should have a comprehensive understanding of the relevant risks to which they are exposed and a duty to analyse them. To this end, they should conduct risk assessments taking into account their particular circumstances and the evolution of those risks, and in any event, every four years, to assess all relevant risks that may disrupt the provision of their critical services, information obtained from https://www.critical-entities-resilience-directive.com/.

[67] Puente (2023) *Op. cit.*

[68] Published in the EU Official Journal on July 12, 2024, EU Regulation No. 1689/2024 lays down harmonised rules on Artificial Intelligence (AI Act). Enters into force on August 1, 2024.

[69] For more information, see Bustos Moreno (2024a).

[70] For an overview of the aspects regulated by the AI Act, we refer to the recent publication of Muñoz García (2023).

controls.[71] It is described that cyber-attacks against AI systems may target specific AI assets, such as training datasets (e.g. data poisoning) or trained models (e.g. adversarial attacks or membership inference[72]) as well as exploiting vulnerabilities in the AI system's digital assets or underlying ICT infrastructure.[73]

7 Conclusions

The journey towards achieving the levels of service interoperability that the full implementation of U-Space demands is not without complexities.[74] The aim is to ensure technical and legal safety, prevent collisions between drones and other aircraft (with measures such as dynamic airspace reconfiguration, Art. 4 Regulation (EU) 2021/664), and manage the inherent risks of UAS traffic on the ground.[75]

Indeed, once U-Space begins to deploy in its U3 and U4 phases, technical means must be found for the development of services that support more complex situations, such as automatisms for resolving conflicts between aircraft that interfere with each other, as well as functionalities for detecting and avoiding obstacles. Another unresolved issue is *tracking*, which is not specifically mentioned in Regulation

[71] There is a lack of minimum requirements for providers of *foundational* cybersecurity *models*. Thus, it is crucial to strengthen their cybersecurity in the current geopolitical context since the lack of adequate protection may allow malicious actors, whether state or non-state, to exploit vulnerabilities for industrial espionage and military sabotage, Hacker (2024). The recent paper "Generative AI Models" examines Large Language Models (LLM) and their influence on information security. This analysis highlights LLMs' opportunities and risks, proposing essential countermeasures to mitigate potential threats. The report can be found at: https://media.licdn.com/dms/document/media/D4D1FAQHthhZhrZnQ4g/feedshare-document-pdf-analyzed/0/1713053190329?e=1714003200&v=beta&t=sMKce6RXV6LzMBQ39vzU9gZi-PE1KUVppwVd22FdHvI.

[72] In cybersecurity, *membership inference* refers to an attack that aims to predict whether a specific data instance was used as part of the training dataset in a particular model. This attack is especially relevant in training data privacy and has become the most used method to audit the privacy of machine learning models. For more information on this type of attack, see Dickson (2021).

[73] Examples of adversaries and data poisoning are specifically mentioned. Still, it can be assumed that the cyber-attacks mentioned in general could include other specific attacks against AI assets, such as AI backdoors or reverse engineering of models, which also affect data protection and privacy, Soler Garrido et al. (2023).

[74] Some of the main challenges are already mentioned by Singh and Pashchapur (2024) and are summarised below. Among the main challenges of UAV operations are bandwidth limitations for high data rate applications, interference from various communication devices and signal attenuation due to atmospheric conditions. The transmission of sensitive data raises security and privacy concerns, while spectrum allocation and line-of-sight limitations pose additional operational hurdles. Battery life limitations and the high cost of certain communication technologies further complicate the use of UAVs. In addition, the deployment of fully functional UTM services faces challenges such as interoperability, regulatory compliance, limited coverage and user acceptance.

[75] Díaz Díaz (2021).

(EU) 2021/664.[76] This process is crucial in air traffic surveillance and control, improving accuracy and predicting tactical conflicts. In the context of U-Space, tracking is implemented to manage the position and movement data of UAS, which is essential for cooperation between U-Space and drone detection systems. It can be carried out in various ways, either by U-Space service providers, as a shared service, or at the remote pilot station, so it must be determined who will be responsible for these services.[77]

In the final phase of full U-Space service implementation (U4), high levels of process automation and interconnection between aircraft, pilots, authorities, and other stakeholders will need to be included.[78] As discussed, artificial intelligence (AI) is becoming fundamental for transportation automation, and digital technologies play a central role.[79] Likewise, deploying all possible cybersecurity measures is essential to prevent attacks on these interconnected services, an issue to which we have dedicated a specific section above.

Indeed, the regulatory package presented is a starting point for the legislator, but it is not a finished process. Special care must be taken with adaptations of existing regulations. The current air traffic rules are not always valid for this new operational environment that operates with UAS. For example, the flight rules on low-level prohibitions in air traffic, where drones are precisely called to operate, as we have mentioned.[80] A similar legal void exists in civil liability and its insurance within the U-Space environment.[81] To apply for USSP provider certification, you must provide

[76]Tracking is a statistical process that uses observations of where the object has been (the position reports) and builds a model of where it is most likely to be now, how it is most likely to be moving, and hence where it is most likely to be in the near future. There appear to be at least four ways in which tracking can appear in U-Space: it can be a service performed by the U-Space Service Provider receiving the reported positions and movements of the UAS (by the producer), a service 'shared' at some point within the interconnected U-Space service providers as they exchange surveillance data (centrally), a service performed by the U-Space Service Provider using the reported positions and movements of the UAS (by the consumer), or a process applied at the Remote Pilot Station, if applicable (downstream of U-Space), SESAR JU (2023), p. 51.

[77]As stated in SESAR JU (2023), p. 51.

[78]On the difference between automation and autonomy, we refer to Bustos Moreno (2021), pp. 890–893.

[79]The Commission envisions an AI ecosystem of excellence and trust, which will be shaped by research, innovation, and deployment funding through Horizon Europe and Digital Europe programmes. In this context, the Commission will support testing and experimentation facilities on AI for smart mobility under the Digital Europe Programme, stated in European Commission (2020), ap. 69, p. 19. Mestres (2024) recalled that it is important to consider developments such as artificial intelligence that will expand existing applications to achieve the desired levels of interoperability and security.

[80]Konert (2024) believes that the rules should be set ab initio rather than simply revised to apply to UAS flying at very low altitudes.

[81]Previous work has already highlighted the lack of ad hoc regulation on civil liability applied to drones. Other authors, such as Scott and Andritsos (2023), have also highlighted this lack of attention. Specifically in the field of U-Space, Konert and Kasprzyk (2020); Kotlinski and Calkowska (2022).

a general description of your insurance coverage and liabilities. The service provider shall define the authority, duties, and responsibilities of the nominated posts and describe arrangements with the air traffic services providers to ensure adequate coordination of activities, according to Article 15 Regulation (EU) 2021/664.

A more international regulatory approach to U-Space is not just a suggestion but a necessity. We firmly believe that the EU regulatory framework, including U-Space regulations, should be actively promoted among trading partners outside the EU and at the ICAO level. This is the foundation for a future global drone regulatory framework that ensures uniform approaches with other regions and globally. This collaborative effort should also include the revision of ICAO Annex 2 (rules of the air) and the particularities of UAS operations.[82]

Additionally, national and municipal-level development will need to be carried out in the different States, which is gradually coming to light. Indeed, a significant step has just been taken with the publication of Royal Decree 517/2024 in Spain, which has been considered a top priority to address certain pending actions in U-Space matters, such as establishing the regime of competencies at the national level and the designation of the first U-Space airspaces.[83] However, cross-border U-Space has not been fully addressed beyond referring to the designation of such airspaces to future "agreements for the creation of such airspaces, ex Art. 62.2 paragraph Royal Decree 517/2024. For its part, Regulation (EU) 2021/664 only determines that "when Member States decide to establish cross-border U-Space airspace, they shall jointly decide: a) the designation of cross-border U-Space airspace; b) the provision of cross-border U-Space services; c) the provision of common cross-border information services." However, we do not believe this stipulation is sufficient to capture the minimum coordination requirements between Member States, as required by recital (11) of Regulation (EU) 2021/664.

One risk of this regulatory framework is that it may lag behind and not be as proactive as it could, and should be, to keep up with rapid developments, technological advances, the increasing potential use of drones, and the growing drone industry.[84] More research, testing, and training are needed.[85] Ultimately, startups and technology developers need an agile regulatory framework to test and deploy their products. Regulatory sandboxes are proactive tools that allow regulators to keep pace with rapid technological advancements and market changes, fostering

[82] European Commission (2022), ap. 32, p. 8.

[83] Bustos Moreno (2024b).

[84] In a reactive approach, regulators primarily intervene after significant problems arise with new technologies or business models. This can result in the implementation of strict regulations that may be less effective or too late. Additionally, a reactive approach can discourage innovation, as companies may be reluctant to introduce new products or services due to fear of regulatory sanctions or the lack of a clear framework.

[85] Michaelides-Mateou (2023), pp. 391–399. Member States should ensure sufficient training for relevant personnel, including local authorities, to increase their preparedness to identify and respond to non-cooperative drone threats, European Commission (2022) "A Drone Strategy 2.0", pp. 14–15.

innovation while protecting consumers and the public interest.[86] Creating an environment where experimentation and oversight combine can effectively balance innovation and safety. Potential problems can be anticipated, and regulations can be adjusted accordingly. The EU legislator in artificial intelligence has already demonstrated its commitment to facilitating trials and tests and adapting the regulatory framework to innovation to support the deployment of solutions in the market.[87] Similarly, the Spanish Sustainable Mobility Bill (23-02-2024) dedicates chapter I, Tit. V to controlled test spaces in mobility.[88]

Finally, the economic and social cost is another major obstacle to implementing U-Spaces. Regarding the cost of implementing this technology, which is still undefined, it has been stated that U-Space should not be a luxury but a service to the industrial fabric and citizens that allows for leading a booming industry with the potential to generate hundreds of jobs and significant returns to society.[89] An important concern for all traffic management systems and the necessary supporting services is the expense associated with the research, development, creation, testing, and implementation of a safe, secure, sustainable, and effective system to manage unmanned air traffic. Additionally, there is the question of whether this research should be financed by the relevant stakeholders of unmanned aircraft rather than manned aviation. Indeed, ENAIRE has already invested 1.3 million euros to boost U-Space in Spain as established by the eighth additional provision of Royal Decree 517/2024—remuneration for recovering costs for services provided as the sole common information service provider is expected. Furthermore, despite the sector's accelerated growth in recent years, society is still unaware of the benefits and multiple applications that drones could bring to societal improvement. Greater dissemination is necessary to achieve increased social acceptance of drones.[90]

[86]For more information on sandboxes, see Bustos Moreno (2022).

[87]The need to shape future mobility proactively through the development and validation of new technologies and services in order to stay ahead of the curve was identified by the European Commission, European Commission (2020) "Sustainable and Smart Mobility Strategy", ap. 64, p. 18.

[88]https://www.congreso.es/public_oficiales/L15/CONG/BOCG/A/BOCG-15-A-9-1.PDF. Test and experimentation areas are considered essential so that developments, innovations and new applications can be tested and put to the test in controlled and safe environments, prior to their industrialisation. In this sense, Level 3 entities consider that promoting the existence of this type of centres throughout Spain would be very favourable for the sector, in the Report on the results of the 1st general survey coordination survey for the deployment of U-Space in Spain, Government of Spain (2023b), p. 10.

[89]Expression of A López Fidalgo (2024).

[90]Bustos Moreno (2024b); Government of Spain (2023b).

References

Agencia Estatal de Seguridad Aérea - Spanish Aviation Safety Agency (AESA) (n.d.) U-SpaceService Providers. https://www.seguridadaerea.gob.es/es/ambitos/navegacion-aerea/proveedores-de-servicios-U-Space

Airbus (Altiscope) (2018) Blueprint for the Sky. The roadmap for the safe integration of autonomous aircraft. https://www.airbus.com/en/newsroom/stories/2018-09-premiering-a-future-blueprint-for-our-sky

Barrado C et al (2019) U-space concept of operations: a key enabler for opening airspace to emerging low-altitude operations. Aerospace 7:24. https://doi.org/10.3390/aerospace7030024

Belwafi B et al (2022) Unmanned aerial vehicles' remote identification: a tutorial and survey. IEEE Access 10:87577–87601. https://doi.org/10.1109/ACCESS.2022.3199909

Boekholt A (2021) Switzerland launches first nationwide network remote identification service for drones. Swiss U-Space Implementation, Swiss Technol Rep 08, 2021

Boekholt A (2022) UAS flight authorisation automated testing. https://susi.swiss/2022/06/28/uas-flight-authorisation-automated-testing/

Bucchignani E (2023) Methodologies for wind field reconstruction in the U-SPACE: a review. Atmosphere 14(11):1684. https://doi.org/10.3390/atmos14111684

Bustos Moreno Y (2021) La irrupción de los Drones (Sistemas de aeronaves no tripuladas, UAS) y la Responsabilidad civil: El futuro de los UAS autónomos. In Cuestiones clásicas y actuales del Derecho de daños: estudios en homenaje al profesor Dr. Roca Guillamón, coord. J. Ataz/ J.A: Cobacho 1:389–450

Bustos Moreno Y (2022) Civil liability in controlled test spaces (regulatory sandboxes) about urban air mobility and the future sustainable mobility law. Cuadernos de Derecho Privado 2(2):8–49

Bustos Moreno Y (2024a) Aplicaciones de la inteligencia artificial conforme a la Ley de Movilidad Sostenible. Consideraciones en torno al régimen de responsabilidad civil acorde con la innovación. Inteligencia Artificial y Derecho de Daños: Cuestiones actuales acorde al Reglamento (UE) 2024/1689, coord. J.A. Moreno/ P.J: Femenía, Dykinson:119–148

Bustos Moreno Y (2024b) Pending legal issues concerning the implementation of vertiports in Urban areas. In La regolazione del Trasporto Publico Locale, Gaspari, F./ Piazaa, P.S., Dike Giuridica: 361–375

Díaz Díaz E (2021) European regulation of U-Space airspace. Boletín O.J.A. n.4 December 2021: 11–130

Dickson B (2021) Inference attacks: how much information can machine learning models leak?. The Daily Swig. https://portswigger.net/daily-swig/inference-attacks-how-much-information-can-machine-learning-models-leak

EASA (2022) Acceptable Means of Compliance (AMC) and Guidance Material (GM) of the U-Space regulatory framework (Regulations (EU) 2021/664, (EU) 2021/665 and (EU) 2021/666". https://www.easa.europa.eu/en/document-library/acceptable-means-of-compliance-and-guidance-materials/amc-and-gm-implementing

EASA (2023) Artificial Intelligence Roadmap 2.0 A human-centric approach to AI in aviation. https://www.easa.europa.eu/en/document-library/general-publications/easa-artificial-intelligence-roadmap-20

EASA (2024a) Easy Access Rules for U-Space (Regulation (EU) 2021/664). https://www.easa.europa.eu/en/document-library/easy-access-rules/online-publications/easy-access-rules-U-Space

EASA (2024b) MLEAP Final Report Machine Learning Application Approval Research Project EASA.2021.C38. https://www.easa.europa.eu/en/newsroom-and-events/news/artificial-intelligence-easa-publishes-final-report-machine-learning

European Aviation Safety Agency (EASA) (2016) Civil Aviation Authority Warsaw Declaration 24 November 2016: Drones as a leverage for jobs and new business opportunities. https://transport.ec.europa.eu/document/download/04b4e80e-86ee-4c01-870f-25b9acc890e1_en?filename=drones-warsaw-declaration.pdf&prefLang=sk

European Commission (2020) Sustainable and Smart Mobility Strategy – putting European transport on track for the future. Communication from the Commission to the European Parliament, the Council, the European Economic and Social Committee and the Committee of the Regions {SWD(2020) 331 final} COM(2020) 789 final, https://eur-lex.europa.eu/resource.html?uri=cellar:5e601657-3b06-11eb-b27b-01aa75ed71a1.0001.02/DOC_1&format=PDF
European Commission (2022) A Drone Strategy 2.0 for a Smart and Sustainable Unmanned Aircraft Eco-System in Europe. Communication to the European Parliament, the Council, the European Economic and Social Committee and the Committee of the Regions (2022):{SWD (2022) 366 final}, COM_2022_652 final, https://transport.ec.europa.eu/system/files/2022-11/COM_2022_652_drone_strategy_2.0.pdf_drone_strategy_2.0.pdf.
Fas-Millán MA et al (2024) Implementing and testing a U-Space system: lessons learnt. Aerospace 11. https://doi.org/10.3390/aerospace11030178
Federal Aviation Administration (FAA) (2019) FAA Releases Aerospace Forecast. https://www.faa.gov/news/updates/?newsId=93646
Fernández Vallejo AC (2020) La regulación europea de los drones y el U-SPACE. Revista General de Derecho Europeo 52:1–37
Gabreau C et al (2022) Toward the certification of safety-related systems using ML techniques: the ACAS-Xu experience. In: 11th European Congress on Embedded Real Time Software and Systems (ERTS 2022), June 2022, Toulouse, France, https://hal.science/hal-03761946
Government of Spain (2023a) Annual National Security Report https://www.newtral.es/wp-content/uploads/2024/03/IASN2023_0.pdf
Government of Spain (2023b) Report on the results of the 1st general survey coordination survey for the deployment of U-Space in Spain. https://www.transportes.gob.es/recursos_mfom/paginabasica/recursos/informe_1a_encuesta_general_publico_v1.pdf
Hacker P (2024) Comments on the final trilogue version of the AI act. https://www.europeannewschool.eu/images/chairs/hacker/Comments%20on%20the%20AI%20Act.pdf
Khurana M Eurocontrol (2021) Europe is now in the fast lane to implementing UAS traffic management systems. https://www.eurocontrol.int/article/europe-now-fast-lane-implementing-uas-traffic-management-systems
Konert A (2024) Very low level flight rules for manned and unmanned aircraft operations. J Intell Robot Syst 110(2). https://doi.org/10.1007/s10846-024-02084-5
Konert A/ Kasprzyk P (2020) Drones are flying outside of segregated airspace in Poland: new rules for BVLOS UAV operations. J Intell Robot Syst, 100 (2). https://doi.org/10.1007/s10846-019-01145-4
Kotlinski M, Calkowska JK (2022) U-Space and UTM deployment as an opportunity for more complex UAV operations including UAV medical transport. J Intell Robot Syst 106:12. https://doi.org/10.1007/s10846-022-01681-6
Lampariello P, Boszczowski L (2022) AVSEC/FAL ICAO - SAM Regional Officers. Annex 17 and Cybersecurity in Aviation. https://www.icao.int/SAM/Documents/2022-CIBER/PPT%20002-Anexo%2017%20y%20Ciberseguridad.pdf
López Fidalgo A (2024) Tecnología de ITG permitirá el tráfico automatizado de drones en A Coruña y Ferrol a partir de 2026. ITG. https://itg.es/tecnologia-itg-permitira-trafico-automatizado-drones-en-coruna-y-ferrol-en-2026/
Martínez Bautista P (2024) Civil aviation: in the age of AI and cybersecurity. https://paisdominicanotematico.com/2024/03/06/aviacion-civil-en-la-era-de-la-ia-y-la-ciberseguridad/
Mateou S, Mateou A (2021) UASs as an aviation security threat. Aviat Space J 1. http://www.aviationspacejournal.com/wp-content/uploads/2021/04/The-Aviation-Space-Journal-Year-XX-January-March-2021-1.pdf
Mestres M AESA (2024) The new Royal Decree on UAS will allow the development of more flexible operations. https://www.infodron.es/texto-diario/mostrar/4855317/m-mestres-aesa-nuevo-real-decreto-uas-permitira-desarrollo-operaciones-flexibles
Michaelides-Mateou S (2023) Challenges and trends in the aviation industry: integrating UAVs in non-segregated airspace. Unmanned Aerial Veh Appl Chall Trends 377–409

Ministerio de Transportes y Movilidad Sostenible: Plan de Acción Nacional para el Despliegue del U-Space (PANDU) 2022-2025 (2022). https://cdn.mitma.gob.es/portal-web-drupal/aviacion/220208_plan_de_despliegue_U-Space_vfinal_acordada.pdf
Muñoz García C (2023) Regulación de la inteligencia artificial en Europa. Incidencia en los regímenes jurídicos de protección de datos, Tirant lo Blanch
Puente M (2023) Ciberresiliencia: la clave de la continuidad de negocio de la pyme. https://www.redseguridad.com/especialidades-tic/gestion-y-gobierno-ti/ciberresiliencia-la-clave-de-la-continuidad-de-negocio-de-la-pyme_20230817.html
Scott B, Andritsos K (2023) A drone strategy 2.0 for a smart and sustainable unmanned aircraft eco-system in Europe. Air Space Law. https://doi.org/10.54648/AILA2023041
Sindiramutty SR, Jhanjhi NZ (2024) Data security and privacy concerns in drone operations. Cybersecur Iss Chall Drone Ind. https://doi.org/10.4018/979-8-3693-0774-8.ch010
Singh G, Pashchapur RA (2024) Recent trends on UAS-UTM ecosystem and integration challenges. https://doi.org/10.13140/RG.2.2.35346.84166
Single European Sky ATM Research Joint Undertaking (SESAR JU) (2018) European ATM Master Plan Roadmap for the safe integration of drones into all classes of airspace. https://www.sesarju.eu/sites/default/files/documents/reports/European%20ATM%20Master%20Plan%20Drone%20roadmap.pdf
Single European Sky ATM Research Joint Undertaking (SESAR JU) (2023) U-Space CONOPS, 4th edn. https://www.sesarju.eu/node/4544
Soler Garrido J et al (2023) Analysis of the preliminary AI standardisation work plan in support of the AI Act. Publications Office of the European Union, Luxembourg, p 13. https://doi.org/10.2760/5847, JRC132833
Tran TD et al (2022) A cybersecurity risk framework for unmanned aircraft systems under specific category. J Intell Robot Syst 104:4. https://doi.org/10.1007/s10846-021-01512-0.hal-03423248
Weiland LV (2021) Implications between UAV and ATM systems in commercial airspace incorporation. https://commons.erau.edu/publication/1627

MIX
Papier aus verantwortungsvollen Quellen
Paper from responsible sources
FSC® C105338

If you have any concerns about our products,
you can contact us on
ProductSafety@springernature.com

In case Publisher is established outside the EU,
the EU authorized representative is:
Springer Nature Customer Service Center GmbH
Europaplatz 3, 69115 Heidelberg, Germany

Printed by Libri Plureos GmbH
in Hamburg, Germany